THE 50 GREATEST MARATHON RACES OF ALL TIME

THE 50 GREATEST MARATHON
RACES OF ALL TIME

William Cockerell

Book Guild Publishing
Sussex, England

First published in Great Britain in 2006 by
The Book Guild Ltd
25 High Street
Lewes, East Sussex
BN7 2LU

Typesetting in Times by
Acorn Bookwork, Salisbury, Wiltshire

Printed in Great Britain by
Antony Rowe Ltd, Chippenham, Wiltshire

A catalogue record for this book is available from
The British Library.

ISBN 1 84624 009 3

Contents

Foreword   vii

Acknowledgements   viii

Introduction   ix

Top 50 list of Greatest Marathons   xi

Chapter I: *Number 50*   Sure Enough It Was a Girl   1

Chapter II: *Number 49*   Kenya Seeks First Big-City Win   15

Chapter III: *Number 48*   I Said Water – Not Cognac!   21

Chapter IV: *Number 47*   The Last One…Bloody Daft   33

Chapter V: *Number 46*   From Humdrum to Humdinger   43

Chapter VI: *Number 45*   Hunted By the Crazy One   49

Chapter VII: *Number 44*   Flying Doc's Finest Hour   57

Chapter VIII: *Number 43*   Not a Day To Ignore Those 5 Yards   73

Chapter IX: *Number 42*   First To Reach the Holy Grail   79

Chapter X: *Number 41*   Like a Charlie Chaplin Routine   87

Chapter XI: *Number 40*   Herr Hitler as Interested as Ever   97

Chapter XII: *Number 39*   Big Apple Struck By Northern Lightning   107

Chapter XIII: *Number 38*   Wanda-ful Run in a Tokyo Cauldron   115

Chapter XIV: *Number 37*   A Shorter Fuse   123

Chapter XV: *Number 36*   Hunt for Bodies Strewn By the Roadside   135

Chapter XVI: *Number 35*   Old Man Tries his Luck   141

Chapter XVII: *Number 34*   First Shots Fired in the Battle for Sub-2.20 151

Chapter XVIII: *Number 33*   Westminster Bridge Hosts a Threesome   159

Chapter XIX: *Number 32*   A Man Ahead of his Time   167

Chapter XX: *Number 31*   Humiliation Threat to Favourite   173

Chapter XXI: *Number 30*   MicMac Patti Whacked, Give the Roe
                                   a Throne   181

Chapter XXII: *Number 29*   The Threat to World Order   189

Chapter XXIII: *Number 28*   Belgian Strives to Square the Account   199

Chapter XXIV: *Number 27*   South Africa Has Arrived   207

Chapter XXV:	*Number 26*	I Thought I was Going to Die	217
Chapter XXVI:	*Number 25*	Mediocrity takes on a Legend	225
Chapter XXVII:	*Number 24*	For Every Shining Fortune Lurks a Shadow	237
Chapter XXVIII:	*Number 23*	Boston Billy's Biggest Scare	255
Chapter XXIX:	*Number 22*	Japan's Favourite Son	265
Chapter XXX:	*Number 21*	Even Fools had the Power to Wound	275
Chapter XXXI:	*Number 20*	Double Giant Killing by the Fat Kid	287
Chapter XXXII:	*Number 19*	The Image that Flashed Around the World	293
Chapter XXXIII:	*Number 18*	I Like to Make History	301
Chapter XXXIV:	*Number 17*	TV Set a Good Buy for Villagers	309
Chapter XXXV:	*Number 16*	The Little Grey Mouse	319
Chapter XXXVI:	*Number 15*	Tarnished Legend Seeks Redemption	331
Chapter XXXVII:	*Number 14*	World's Top Two Slug It Out	345
Chapter XXXVIII:	*Number 13*	I Couldn't Be Licked	353
Chapter XXXIX:	*Number 12*	The Glorious Sylph	365
Chapter XL:	*Number 11*	Protégé Holds His Nerve	375
Chapter XLI:	*Number 10*	The Ghastly Grin	383
Chapter XLII:	*Number 9*	Hail! Hail! The Gang's All Here	395
Chapter XLIII:	*Number 8*	Eyeballs-out, Gut-wrenching, Lung-buster	409
Chapter XLIV:	*Number 7*	Why is the Sky Blue?	417
Chapter XLV:	*Number 6*	The Great Breed is Not Yet Extinct	429
Chapter XLVI:	*Number 5*	Down-and-out Deek	445
Chapter XLVII :	*Number 4*	I Run Until I Can't Run Anymore	455
Chapter XLVIII:	*Number 3*	Never Such a Dramatic Moment	471
Chapter XLIX:	*Number 2*	The Dried-out, Unsalted Potato Chip	485
Chapter XL:	*Number 1*	Mighty Geb Makes His Debut	497
Bubbling Under			509
Glossary			511
Appendix			515
Snapshot Analysis of Top 50 List			533
Index			535

Foreword by David Bedford

*former 10,000-metres world record holder, and Race Director of
the Flora London Marathon.*

When I first met William to discuss his proposed book I was unsure exactly what would come from his research. It would certainly be an act of love and a book for connoisseurs!

My view has always been that a race is just that with competitions that matter, a tremendous battle between several of the leading runners in the world not just a time trial. When a marvel like Paula Radcliffe comes along and runs times that we have scarcely imagined possible, that is wonderful; but what I *really* crave when I assemble my elite fields is a battle, a saga, and a mystery. Who will win? I strive for there to be at least half a dozen realistic contenders that will contest the result right up until Buckingham Palace. That's what really makes my day.

The London line up in 2002 had all the vital ingredients for a great race: Haile Gebrselassie, the greatest runner ever, running his first marathon, against Paul Tergat who on so many occasions on the track had almost taken Haile's crown, running his second marathon, and Khalid Khannouchi the World Marathon Record Holder. The whole field feared being beaten by Haile. The end result a new World Record by Khannouchi. William rates this the best ever – who would argue?...

What William has done in this remarkable and fascinating book is to comb through the 109 years of marathon races and skilfully select the races that have captured the imagination of the public, provided thrilling entertainment, and yes, sometimes a healthy dose of controversy. I notice that seven *Londons* appear – I remember them all so clearly: very stressful and complex to organise, but then a wonderful feeling of euphoria at the end of the day when a fabulous race has occurred. William brings these races alive and rekindles their magic.

Acknowledgments

I should like to thank all the wonderful runners who spoke to me during the course of this book, and in particular Rob de Castella, Ron Hill, Hugh Jones, Steve Jones, Ingrid Kristiansen, Tegla Loroupe, Antonio Pinto, Bill Rodgers, Kathrine Switzer and Alberto Salazar. David Bedford for his terrific interview and for so generously donating the foreword. The incomparable legend of British sports photography that is Mark Shearman, whose tireless attendance at athletics meets the world over these last 40 plus years have hugely benefited this book. The works of tremendous scholarship of David Martin, Roger Gynn, Tom Derderian, David Wallechinsky, Riël Hauman and Michael Sandrock: although my research has been exhaustive, it is your terrific books that have been of such help to so many chapters. Thanks to Ian Crane for giving up his Christmas holidays to write the index. The staff at the British Library's newspaper library in Colindale who would cower in fear whenever I approached their desk, as I would send them scurrying to seldom visited parts of the building. John Bryant for all his encouragement and interest – and particularly on his advice that Chapter 3 should be included when I had somehow originally contrived to leave it out. How right he was. My fiancée Dorchie for her unswerving loyalty and enthusiasm and for much pernickety but priceless proof-reading. And finally my deepest thanks to the great show of faith, support and patience of Carol, Joanna and everyone at The Book Guild.

Introduction

Although many interesting and informative books have been written about the marathon - several of which I have drawn on in my own research – they have tended to be either works of great scholarship concentrating on the minutiae of a particular event, or very broad overviews giving just the barest details. For instance, in *Boston Marathon* by Tom Derderian, or *Olympic Marathon* by David Martin and Roger Gynn, one can enjoy more than 20 pages of copy on just a single race; while, at the other extreme, the *Century of the Marathon* by Riël Hauman contains just a handful of lines on almost every significant marathon since 1896.

The 50 Greatest Marathon Races Of All Time intends to seek out only the most intriguing and memorable marathon races and carry the reader on a journey through the history of this charismatic, dramatic and heroic event since the first modern marathon at the Athens Olympics 110 years ago.

Not only have the 50 races been extremely carefully selected, but they have also been ranked in order of merit. I have ranked the marathons from number 1 to 50 by a process of 'objective deconstruction'. This means that each race has been broken down into ten different criteria which contribute to a marathon race. Each category – after being marked out of ten – is then weighted according to its importance, i.e. "Weather conditons" are less important than "Profile of event".

The 10 categories are [weighting in square brackets]:

1) Quality of race winner [30]
2) Quality of race field [20]
3) Quality of winner's time [20]
4) Profile of event [25]
5) Drama of event [25]
6) Sacrifice of winner [15]
7) Course difficulty [10]
8) Weather conditions [5]
9) Memorablility of race [20]
10) Overall worldwide news worthiness [20]

For an in-depth description of these categories see GLOSSARY (page 511).

Grading the races in this way means that subjectivity naturally becomes replaced by objectivity. For instance, there is little argument that the Olympics should carry the highest mark for category number 4; or that a world record should score top marks for category 3; or that an undulating course will receive a higher mark than a flat one, etc. After all the categories have been marked out of ten and weighted, the total marks (out of 190) are then translated into a percentage. An Appendix details how all the marks were awarded.

A key decision I have made in the top 50 list is that a race winner may only appear as a race winner once. In other words, all the best races from all the top marathoners from the last 100 plus years have been examined and I have selected what I perceive to be their greatest race/battle/victory (based on the above criteria) for the list. This rule serves a dual purpose. It means the list has terrific variety with 50 different protagonists, and also avoids any essays being too repetitive. For instance both Steve Jones' spectacular back-to-back wins at Chicago in 1984–5 deserve inclusion, but their tales are somewhat similar and would make for slightly repetitive reading if both were included in the list. The same applies for Paula Radcliffe's mighty runs at London and Chicago in 2002, and London again in 2003. However, this doesn't mean that great marathons which do not qualify for the list purely because the winner has already appeared, will be ignored in the book. They shall simply be discussed in the text of the relevant Chapter – piggy-backed on to the main event.

The essays of each marathon won't be solely concerned with racing, but will focus equally on the men and women behind the races. What sort of people were Bill Rodgers/Abebe Bikila/Grete Waitz etc...? What were their backgrounds, their beliefs and ideals? What outside factors contributed to the race being memorable? History and politics, for instance, play a large factor at the Olympic Games.

The point of this book is to entertain and inform, and I do not submit my list as the be all and end all on the subject; but I have attempted to be as objective as possible and I have consulted more than 400 different sources to aid in my research. I have also carried out interviews with many of the leading protagonists of marathon racing over the past 40-plus years.

The Top 50 List of Greatest Marathons

- Percentage grade in final column
- World records underlined
- **Men in bold**; *Women in italics*

	MARATHON	YEAR	WINNER	NATIONALITY	TIME	%
50)	*Boston*	*1967*	*Roberta Gibb*	*USA*	*3:27:17*	*75.4*

'Get the hell out of my race and give me that number!'

49)	**Chicago**	**1983**	**Joseph Nzau**	**Kenya**	**2:09:44**	**76.2**

Who says marathoners don't need a dip finish?

48)	**Olympic**	**1896**	**Spiridon Louis**	**Greece**	**2:58:50**	**77.1**

Colonel M. Papadiamantopoulos fires the gun that still reverberates today

47)	**Commonwealth**	**1954**	**Joseph McGhee**	**Scotland**	**2:39:36**	**77.8**

History's grisliest marathon

46)	**London**	**2003**	**Gezahegne Abera**	**Ethiopia**	**2:07:55**	**78.9**

A bizarre, lethargic race with a truly thrilling finish

45)	*Boston*	*2000*	*Catherine Ndereba*	*Kenya*	*2:26:11*	*79.3*

Cool Catherine outduels hot-favourite Roba to kick-start great career

44)	**Commonwealth**	**1970**	**Ron Hill**	**England**	**2:09:28**	*79.6*

Hill ascends to his highest summit

43)	*London*	*1997*	*Joyce Chepchumba*	*Kenya*	*2:26:51*	*79.9*

McColgan caught napping one step from home

42)	*Berlin*	*2001*	*Naoko Takahashi*	*Japan*	*2:19:47*	*80.0*

Takahashi the first female to crack the magic 2:20 mark

41)	**Fukuoka**	**1975**	**Jerome Drayton**	**Canada**	**2:10:08**	**80.4**

Thrilling win for unruffled – but soon to be very ruffled – Torontonian

40)	**Olympic**	**1936**	**Sohn Kee-chung**	**Korea**	**2:29:19**	**80.5**

Spanning 52 years, perhaps the greatest Olympic tale of them all

39)	*New York*	*1979*	*Grete Waitz*	*Norway*	*2:27:32*	*80.8*

9-times champ smashes the 2:30 barrier, and breaks her own world record by five minutes

38)	*World*	*1991*	*Wanda Panfil*	*Poland*	*2:29:53*	*80.9*

Yamashita captures, then breaks, her host city's heart

37)	**Olympic**	**1972**	**Frank Shorter**	**USA**	**2:12:19**	**81.0**

37) **Olympic** **1972** **Frank Shorter** **USA** **2:12:19** **81.0**
"Running. Somehow it looked…glorious"

36) **London** **1995** **Dionicio Cerón** **Mexico** **2:08:30** **81.1**
Pinto leads by a minute at 22 miles…but that's where the racing *really* starts

35) **Boston** **1922** **Clarence de Mar** **USA** **2:18:10** **81.2**
Media purring over comeback Clarence

34) *London* *1985* *Ingrid Kristiansen* *Norway* *2:21:06* *81.3*
The mistress of the mill shows off her land legs

33) **London** **1989** **Douglas Wakiihuri** **Kenya** **2:09:03** **81.5**
Moneghetti outkicked by three seconds – as he would be six years later

32) **Olympic** **1920** **Johannes Kolehmainen** **Finland** **2:32:35** **81.7**
Father of the flying Finns secures world record on a long course

31) **London** **1997** **Antonio Pinto** **Portugal** **2:07:55** **82.1**
The late, late show from powerful Pinto

30) *Boston* *1981* *Allison Roe* *New Zealand* *2:26:46* *82.2*
Kiwi beauty outshines stellar field

29) *Olympic* *1988* *Rosa Mota* *Portugal* *2:25:40* *82.3*
The changing of the guard

28) **Olympic** **1948** **Delfo Cabrera** **Argentina** **2:34:51** **82.4**
London Olympic marathon repeats heroism and drama from 40 years before

27) **Olympic** **1996** **Josiah Thugwane** **South Africa** **2:12:36** **82.5**
Unknown, illiterate, car-jacked, shot-gun victim comes to the Olympics

26) **Fukuoka** **1967** **Derek Clayton** **Australian** **2:09:36** **82.6**
Stunning world record for brave Aussie

25) **Olympic** **1976** **Waldemer Cierpinski** **Germany** **2:09:55** **82.8**
"The man who invented running" falls prey to his greatest foe: rain

24) *Boston* *1980* *Jacqueline Gareau* *Canada* *2:34:28* *82.9*
Laurel wreath awarded to "Cellulite City" whilst bewildered champion looks on

23) **Boston** **1978** **Bill Rodgers** **USA** **2:10:13** **83.0**
The King of the Roads' most fiendish scrap

22) **Fukuoka** **1983** **Toshihiko Seko** **Japan** **2:08:52** **83.2**
"Inscrutable" Seko wins best ever Fukuoka

21) *Olympic* *2004* *Mizuki Noguchi* *Japan* *2:26:20* *83.3*
Gripping drama as hot favourite runs on empty

20)	**Boston**	**2000**	**Elijah Lagat**	**Kenya**	**2:09:47**	**83.6**

Top two in a photo-finish, with double champ Tanui three seconds back

19)	**New York**	**1983**	**Rod Dixon**	**New Zealand**	**2:08:59**	**83.7**

Brave Smith wins the race to 26 miles; but the prize for the 300 yard dash goes elsewhere

18)	**Boston**	**1988**	**Ibrahim Hussein**	**Kenya**	**2:08:43**	**83.8**

Mercurial Kenyan's lethal, late kick devastates Ikangaa

17)	*Olympic*	*1992*	*Valentina Yegorova*	*Russia*	*2:32:41*	*84.0*

Perennial bridesmaid strikes gold when it matters most

16)	*Olympic*	*1984*	*Joan Benoit*	*USA*	*2:24:52*	*84.1*

Grete, Rosa and Ingrid play disastrous waiting game

15)	*New York*	*2004*	*Paula Radcliffe*	*GBR*	*2:23:41?*	*84.2*

Golden girl finds redemption after Greek tragedy

14)	**World**	**1995**	**Martin Fiz**	**Spain**	**2:11:41**	**84.3**

Nail-biter as Ceron runs out of fiz

13)	**Olympic**	**1932**	**Juan Carlos Zabala**	**Argentina**	**2:31:36**	**84.5**

Absence of milk en route plays havoc with hot favourite Ferris

12)	**Berlin**	**2003**	**Paul Tergat**	**Kenya**	**2:04:55**	**84.6**

Tergat finally breaks marathon duck – and the big two-five

11)	**Olympic**	**1992**	**Hwang Young-cho**	**Korea**	**2:13:23**	**84.7**

Montjuic's gruelling climb the backdrop to tense Asian duel

10)	**Olympic**	**1988**	**Gelindo Bordin**	**Italy**	**2:10:32**	**85.0**

Italy's master tactician paces it perfectly

9)	**Olympic**	**1984**	**Carlos Lopes**	**Portugal**	**2:09:21**	**85.3**

"All cylinders on go" as old man of the field lopes away

8)	**Chicago**	**1984**	**Steve Jones**	**Wales**	**2:08:05**	**85.8**

Unknown Welsh mechanic shocks the World and Olympic champions

7)	*Boston*	*1996*	*Uta Pippig*	*Germany*	*2:27:12*	*86.1*

Frail Fräulein electrifies the crowds at Boston's 100th tea-party

6)	**Olympic**	**1908**	**John Hayes**	**USA**	**2:55:18**	**86.3**

Dorando's collapse becomes sport's most celebrated image

5)	**Commonwealth**	**1982**	**Robert de Castella**	**Australia**	**2:09:18**	**86.4**

Tanzanians terrorize hometown favourite

4)	**Olympic**	**1952**	**Emil Zátopek**	**Czechoslovakia**	**2:23:03**	**86.6**

Czechoslovakian Choo-Choo wins the five, the dime and the Big One

3) **Olympic**   **1960**   **Abebe Bikila**   **Ethiopia**   **2:15:16**   **87.2**
Barefoot Ethiopian soldier comes to Rome to avenge his country's stolen obelisk

2) **Boston**   **1982**   **Alberto Salazar**   **USA**   **2:08:52**   **87.4**
The ultimate duel for duo soothed by Vangelis - but singed by a scorching sun

1) **London**   **2002**   **Khalid Khannouchi**   **USA**   **2:05:38**   **88.4**
The greatest field in history. And the greatest runner too; who came 3rd

I

No. 50 – 1967 Boston Marathon [Women]

Wednesday, April 19th

"...sure enough, it was a girl. We could see the chest development."

Roberta Gibb won the 1967 Boston Marathon in as much as she completed the course. She will never be an official winner of the race because women weren't officially allowed to run until 1972 when Nina Kuscsik from South Huntington, New York, *officially* won in 3:10:26. And indeed it's not even Gibb's performance in '67 which merits its entry into the "50 greatest" list. The reason is for another runner, Kathrine Switzer – the first woman to ever run a major marathon with an official number, even if she was given it by mistake after apparent sharp practice.

To understand the full flavour of what occurred on this famous day, it's important to explore a little of the life and times of Jock Semple, the race director of the Boston Marathon for nearly thirty years from 1953, and in charge of race admissions a long time before that. A controversial, plain-speaking Scot, a case may be made for crediting Semple with crafting the foundation that led to marathon and road-running becoming the fashionable and respected business it is today. A brief defence of this theory is that Semple almost single-handedly built the Boston Marathon up from a few dozen runners in the early 20th Century, to a dozen *thousand* by the time he passed away in 1988. The New York City Marathon owes a lot of its success to the trail-blazed by Boston. Other big-city marathons sprung up like wildflowers off the back of New York's success; of which the biggest, and arguably best was London, founded by Chris Brasher, who had been so inspired by what he had found when he visited the New York race in 1979. So there you have it: Semple made Boston; Boston made New York; New York made London; and the rest caught on very swiftly after that.

Jock Semple was born on October 26th, 1903 in Glasgow into a poor, working-class family. He left school at 14 but found it hard to hold down a job without a trade, so learnt to become a joiner. He worked miserably at a shipyard factory for two years before a strike saw him out of work. "If I were to lend you money for a trip to America, would you go?" his father asked one day. The young Jock jumped at the chance and landed in Philadelphia with a clouded future but caring not one whit.

He had already discovered the joys of running with his club back in Scotland, Clydesdale Harriers. He loved it so much he even trained with a broken arm; but one day, he set out for his run one second before the noon lunch bell and was promptly fired. His knack for getting the sack quickly followed in America. "Get your tools," said one employer, "no job's as complicated as you're making it." Another boss saw that he had changed shoes on shift because his feet were so blistered from a race the day before. Once again he was told to assemble his tools. Semple felt that employers often discriminated against him for his incomprehensible hobby.

After finishing an excellent seventh at the 1930 Boston, Semple decided to move to the city permanently after yet another Philadelphia employer showed him the door. He would remain a New Englander for life. Taking work for desperately poor pay, Semple still trained with great determination only to see a chance to go to the Los Angeles Olympics of 1932 disappear, when his residency papers got caught up in the immigration system's bureaucracy. Semple realised he was good enough to run for Britain too. He wrote to the British selectors saying they wouldn't even have to pay his way to California because he could just hitch there. No thanks, they said, they would send just two runners.[1] Aside from the Games of 1896 and 1904, this is the only Olympics where Britain didn't send a full team.

By the 1936 Games, Semple had his residency, but no longer the ability. He had been pouring his energies into other things though. One of which was becoming a personal trainer, and another, forming a group of athletes to compete for the Boston Athletic Association. The BAA was dying on its feet by now after the glory days of opulence in their splendid clubhouse in Boston's Copley Square, before the Wall Street Crash of 1929 wiped out most of the businessmen running the show.

Semple's recruiting tactics for the BAA are delightful in their unorthodoxy – and their effectiveness. He wouldn't target the runners in a race; he would target their wives and girlfriends. Semple writes:

While the men were out on the course during the race, I'd take the lady aside. "The great advantage to having a man run for the BAA is that my BAA boys come home tired after I'm finished with them," I said. Usually this elicited a polite nod, but little interest. "After men get out of work...you know the diversions that exist for a man," I repeated each weekend all over New England. "Some men don't come home at all. Soon after they get married they discover the gin mills, and the elbow-bending, and soon their wives have to trek down to some dark men's bar in their housecoats. Never my BAA boys. They come home every night, very tired."

And lo, at the very next race about a dozen women would trot up to Semple – their partner's application forms neatly filled out.

The expert and legendary sports promoter Walter Brown set Semple up in the Boston Arena and he became the trainer and masseur of the Boston Celtics, which

1. After the scandal of Paavo Nurmi being barred from the '32 Olympics because of a spat involving expense money, a group of promoters organized another marathon in which Nurmi would compete against the Olympic champion Zabala. But when the race came around, Nurmi's ban still hadn't been lifted and he served as race starter. Semple was there though. He defeated Zabala (and Clarence DeMar), to place second in the race.

Brown owned. The post-war Celtics were a phenomenally bad team for many years, with balance sheets that drowned in red ink. But Brown had a hunch that the New England crowds craved a sport to see them through the gap between the football and baseball seasons, and "bounceball" was what he perceived it to be. In setting up Semple in a tiny clinic at the Arena, and later at the famous Boston Garden after the Arena burnt, Brown gave Semple his greatest break. Semple travelled to the 1948 and 1952 Olympics as a trainer; so in a way he did get his Olympic wish after all.

Brown, who was also president of the BAA had one other great wish, which he told Semple in his office one day, and that was to one day see a BAA runner win *Boston*. Semple never forgot this plea and was always on the lookout for a talented new runner to win the big one. Finally he found it in Johnny Kelley the younger,[2] whom he groomed from a raw seventeen-year-old pup in 1948 to become the finest American distance runner of his era. Kelley went on to win Boston in 1957 against a field stacked with decorated foreigners, amid hugely emotional scenes for both Semple and Brown. Semple wrote of his greatest protégé: "He set a new American record that day, but more important, he made it respectable for college athletes to run on the roads, which some people – mostly college track coaches – formerly had thought were good enough only for us broken down working guys." Kelley's fame mushroomed and he was widely adored, besieged by kids and housewives alike – even if many confused him with his lookalike, the Senator of Massachusetts, one John F. Kennedy. Semple and Brown's dream had come true. Walter Brown died aged 59 in 1964, with the Boston Celtics sitting pretty as one of greatest basketball teams in America.

Will Cloney, a sports journalist who had trained as a lawyer, became director of the Boston Marathon in 1947. Semple soon became his right-hand man and co-director. The two were polar opposites as can be seen 33 years into their partnership in the Rosie Ruiz scandal of 1980 – described in detail in Chapter 27. While Semple spluttered that Ruiz was a "cheat, 'n a fraud 'n a thief!", Cloney "calmly called a hundred witnesses" (Semple et al.).

But it was hard to argue with Semple's passion and commitment to the sport he loved. Amby Burfoot, US editor of *Runner's World* and 1968 Boston winner, says: "In this age of plastic men formed sometimes by Madison Avenue, sometimes by the contradictory forces of life, Jock remains cast in an original and unchanging mould. He will never be packaged. His reactions spring from instinct and are expressed as a splutter and an instant opinion." Semple was in the sport purely for the love of it. One year when Burfoot was picking up his number Semple told him: "Oh Amby, my schedule is terrible. I've got to be here all afternoon, then over to the Garden at five for the Bruins, and then back here tomorrow morning at five to lead everyone onto the buses. I don't know how much longer I can keep this up."

By all accounts Semple became an expert at the rubdown. A plaque in his room

---

2. It most certainly is a remarkable coincidence that America's two greatest marathon runners from the 1930s–1960s were both called Johnny Kelley. A man once said to Kelley the younger when he was seventeen: "If you're going to stay in the running business, you've either got to change your name, or run like greased lightning." To which Kelley replied: "Guess it's too late to change my name..."

read: "To Jock; a guy who has so many friends because he rubs everybody the right way." It was signed Bobby Orr (of the Boston Bruins). And it's not just the great runners like Peters, Hill, Rodgers, Salazar, Shorter and Catalano that he administered to, but the great names from all sports: obviously the hockey players, and other stars like boxer Rocky Marciano or tennis players John Newcombe, Rod Laver and Jimmy Conners. "Connors is my buddy," said Semple. "McEnroe I wouldn't give two cents for."

"Magic fingers" is what hundreds of athletes call the Semple digits. Speaking of Patti Catalano, Semple said: "Patti hurt her hip a couple of years ago. The doctors said she'd never run again. I don't want to go to Mass. State prison for slander, but as far as I'm concerned doctors are 'itis-happy.' Bursitis... arthritis... Anyway, they said Patti would never run again. Well, I started giving her treatments and she's the first American woman to go under 2:30 in a marathon."

* * *

When local girl Roberta Gibb first got the idea of running Boston, after having been thrilled by watching the 1965 edition with her father, she wrote to the BAA but the reply came back that women were not able to run marathons and were certainly not able to enter Boston. "But she wanted to do it," writes Tom Derderian. "She liked to run. She was 23 years old, and she felt good and free when she ran." Gibb, a student at the Boston Museum of Fine Arts school, was more of an artist than a competitor. She didn't want to run the Boston Marathon to be part of a competition, but more to partake in a "stream of consciousness". Not to probe anything political or to beat men at their own game, "but to play".

The disrespectful and disturbing history of women's running before the days of Gibb et al., are documented in Chapter 9, but suffice it to say that things started as they'd go on, in London in 1752. Huge crowds came out to watch a women's 4-mile race, but the presence of the gawping thousands had been captured because the race promoter had advertised that the women would run naked. However, the dames kept their clothes strictly on, and interest quickly waned after that. Women athletes were treated with similar contempt for the next 175 years until the Amsterdam Olympics of 1928, when, although the women ran to a high standard, their exhausted state at the end of the 800-metres so appalled the powers that be that they were banned from running longer than 200 metres up until the Rome Games of 1960.

But a key question is, were men right to ban women from the endurance running? And the answer of course is no – their bias was a disgrace and pure folly. As Tom Derderian points out: "Women were highly regarded as long-distance swimmers. Surely there could be no doubt about a woman's capacity to endure when in 1927 Gertrude Ederle swam the English Channel two hours faster than anyone else, woman or man."

Although Gibb did not train in a scientific way and certainly had no coach or anything like that, she had more than enough talent to defeat most men. After being inspired by the 1965 Boston, Gibb went off to California to live with her new husband in February of 1966, but she told her parents that she'd return to run the Boston two months later. She knew she could do it, even though she had only ever run one distance race. The bad news was that she made it less than two-

4

thirds of the course before her knees gave out. But the good news was that she still covered 65 miles! The race was a two-day, 100-mile equestrian cross-country race. Gibb was ahead of some of the horses when she quit.

After Boston shunned her application, Gibb enjoyed the thought of running as an outlaw. "She was a formidable runner," recalls Charlie Rodgers (brother of Bill) to the author. "Sometimes she'd run over four hours at a time." Gibb states: "My outrage turned to humour as I thought how many preconceived prejudices would crumble when I trotted right along for 26 miles."

After a four-day bus ride from California, Gibb arrived in Boston and carried out her intention of taking part in the marathon. "She was like a little sister wanting nothing more than to play with her brothers and their friends. Fearing that someone would see her and prevent her from running, she hid in the bushes along the Boston course. Like a child listening to adult conversation and fearful of being sent to bed, she tried to call no attention to herself. But she would have to overcome her shyness to make a point."

Tom Derderian describes the reaction of the other runners: "After 5 miles she heard, 'It's a girl. Is that really a girl? Pardon me...' Bobbi turned around laughing. 'Hey, it is a girl...Fantastic. I wish my wife would run. Good for you. Are you going the whole way?' 'I hope so, if they don't throw me out.'"

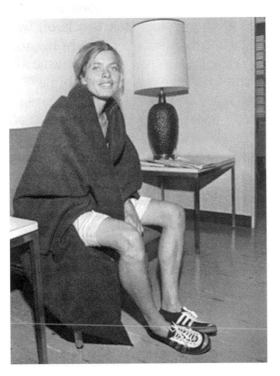

Looking more like a movie-star than a marathoner, Bobbi Gibb takes solace in a hotel after the 1966 Boston. *Boston Herald*

The further Gibb travelled that day, the more the crowds warmed to her, and the press had to rewrite all their well-crafted stories. The excellent Japanese winner, Kenji Kimihara, appeared as an afterthought in the following day's papers. Instead the headlines read: "Hub Bride First Gal to Run Marathon" and "Blond Wife, 23, Runs Marathon." And yet, Derderian reminds us: "She could not join the other runners for their traditional bowl of beef stew in the Prudential cafeteria: Women were not allowed."

What did Jock Semple and Will Cloney think about Bobbi Gibb's running the marathon? Not much. She was not officially in the race. She had not entered. She did not wear a number. Her progress was not monitored at the checkpoints. In their minds she had not participated.

But she *had* run it. And would do so again and again.

* * *

Bobbi Gibb's marriage to her sailor lasted but a few months, but her love of running lasted a lot longer. She returned to Boston in 1967 to have another merry "unofficial" journey through the eight cities and towns that led to Copley Square.

She ran to be free and wanted to be free to run. And that was as far as any statement was going to go.

A young lady from Syracuse, New York, named Kathrine Switzer agreed with almost all of Gibb's ideals, but had a different vision about how she could go about executing them. Switzer had that all-important competitive streak inside her, and any effort she expended in a race, she wanted to be official and recognized. Tom Derderian immaculately describes the contrast between the two women:

> Whereas Bobbi Gibb might sit with a monk on a rock by a reflecting pool and meditate on the wonders of life, Kathrine Switzer might stand on a rooftop with Mario Savio, the Berkeley agitator in the free speech movement who said, "If you can seize the time, you can change the world." It was Switzer's intention to seize the time and shove the world a little further in the direction she thought it should move.

In 1967, the 20-year-old Switzer switched colleges from a liberal arts school called Lynchburg College to Syracuse University, where she double majored in English literature and journalism. She had run races before on the track and cross-country. Now it was time for a little road. When Switzer was at Lynchburg she had run in a one-mile track race that had caused an incredible fuss. Derderian writes: "The campus of her southern religious school was divided between ardent supporters and those who considered her less than honorable." "God will strike you dead," said one piece of hate mail. "I think of you as a freak," said one mindless boyfriend. Switzer never spoke to him again.

The unofficial distance coach at Syracuse was named Arnie Briggs, who didn't believe stories reaching him about Bobbi Gibb. He was also highly sceptical when Switzer came to him and said that she'd like to have a pop at Boston too. Gamely though, he gave Switzer a way into the Syracuse team that would travel to Boston: "If you can show me in practice that you can run that kind of distance, I'll be the first one to take you to Boston." Switzer showed him she could run 15 miles no sweat. Good, but not good enough, thought Briggs. And then she kept up on a 31-miler. Whew, that'll do. There is murkiness as to what happened next. Did Switzer fill out her application form using her full first name, and did Jock Semple – busy as he was – just miss it? Or did she set out to fool him by just writing "K. Switzer". The answer is neither. The author caught up with Switzer at a memorial dinner for the British miler and Olympic gold steeplechaser, Chris Brasher, in October 2003, and several such issues were cleared up.

Switzer signed her application form: "K.V. Switzer", not to con Semple but for three other reasons. She explains:

> I swear to this day, I did not intentionally set out to break the rules.
>
>   I wanted to be a writer. And I thought that was the way a serious writer should sign her name: I wanted to be like my hero, J.D. Salinger. I was also following my parents lead: that was how they signed all their documents and checks: by initials. And I was also sick of everyone always spelling Kathrine wrong. I figured: why give them the chance?

There then followed the small matter of what Switzer would do about the medical in the Hopkinton gymnasium before the race. "You're not gonna want to go anyway *near* that gym, Briggs told her. Lots of naked men dancing about, being told to cough. Not a pretty sight." So Switzer went to her local doctor in Syracuse who, pleasantly amused, signed the document saying she was good to go. The document was mailed in with her entry and Briggs picked up her number before the race with all the other Syracuse numbers. Granted, Switzer hadn't told anyone what gender she was, but then, no one had asked.

Someone nearly did though – although it's not surprising that Switzer slipped through undetected. Jock Semple's most celebrated telephone explosions came after running boomed. As he put it, "the infernal device now rings from morning till night. Every time I get my fingers into a patient's sore muscles, another imbecile calls up with some new bloody stupid questions." Here's an example of a converstion:

"Hi, are you guys gonna have better facilities this year?"

"Just put you gear in a bag, and into the truck in Hopkinton, and you'll get 'em at the end."

"No, I mean *fa-ci-li-ties.*"

"You mean hotels and that?"

"No! I mean will there be toilets at the start?"

"Look for the second tree on the left," Semple would blast before hanging up.

There was a cartoon that hung in his salon of Jock scolding a runner arriving at a bus: "Don't tell me you ran 2:18 last month. You're a goddamn liar...and a bloody fat one too! And make sure you pin that number on the front...and good luck. Now get the hell on the bus."

Semple, who screened all the marathon entries (often between periods while he worked the Bruins and Celtics Games), assumed that "K" was male, and sent her a number. Even so, Tony Nota, another Garden hand who typed the list of entries, nearly caught the oversight. A week before the marathon he rushed over to Jock's clinic brandishing the incomplete application. "Oh blast it, Tony," sighed Semple. "Don't bother me now. I'm trying to get these men into the whirl-pool and the bloody phone hasn't stopped ringing. If I get one more marathon question I'm going to pull the last bloody hairs out of my head. "Then you don't want me to pull this 'K' joker?" "Ah, what the heck, Tony. Leave him in now that I've already sent him a number. We're never going to see the imbecile again anyway." (Semple et al.).

Was ever a man more wrong?

* * *

The day of the 1967 Boston Marathon dawned cold and wet and Col. Will Cloney already had fielded more headaches this year than any previously. His small, elitist, happy-go-lucky, manageable marathon race was *growing*! It was turning into a beast. An untamed, hairy, out-of-control monster. Cloney was getting too old for all of this. But he hated to let the marathon go. He loved it like a child; and besides, who on earth could be found to offer it the same toil, sacrifice, blood, sweat and tears?

"When will it stop?" Cloney asked anyone and no one. "Should I put the lid

7

on?" And he had thought 1962 was bad. There, an unprecedented 285 runners had somehow contrived to enter. Exactly 285 beef stews to be cooked up, and numbers to be made, and runners to be transported. And no one paying a cent for the privilege. But since '62, the numbers had mushroomed: 403 the next year, then 447, and 540 and now 741. "The clerical load alone is staggering," Cloney continued. "In my prayers I'm always sure to mention Tony Nota and Jock Semple." The headaches of beef stews, buses, officials, cops and accommodations were bad enough for Cloney. Then Kathrine Switzer came along to ask some *really* serious questions.

A nervous Switzer pinned on her number and headed to the start line in hooded sweatshirt and sweatpants, like many of the men. The only difference being that the men discarded these garments just before the gun. While the tiny New Zealander Dave McKenzie began to go about seeing off his competitors in the exciting men's race, half a mile or so back down the road Switzer jogged along. She was accompanied by Arnie Briggs and her new boyfriend, conveniently enough a hammer thrower named Tom Miller. This trio made it to around the 4-mile mark before the press bus and photographers' truck caught up with them.

A snapper noticed that not only was a woman running, but that she was wearing an official race number. He and his pals were suddenly all eyes. A sportswriter shouted: "Hey Jock, you've got a broad on your hands today." Semple and Cloney didn't take him too seriously – the year before a similar cry was heard (not referring to Gibb). But then somebody yelled again: "Hey, Jock, this time it is a gal. And holy smokes she's wearing one of your numbers!"

Semple recalls: "You would have thought the bus would tip over with everybody hopping up to see and sure enough, it was a girl. We could see the chest development." Jock ordered the driver to stop immediately once he discovered this "flagrant violation of the rules." Like a shot he was off the bus and bounding down the road after Kathy. Tom Derderian writes: Will Cloney ran up and began to argue that she should not have a number. Briggs argued back. "Arnie, you know better than that," said Cloney.

Jock Semple was in no mood for such polite diplomacy. He ran up behind Switzer and tried to rip the number off her, yelling the now famous refrain: "Get the hell out of my race and give me that number!"[3] But all Semple got was a tiny piece of the corner. He went back for a second go, but grabbed only sweatshirt. Tommy Miller had seen enough and launched a full-scale "blindside" body block on the old man. "Kathy! Run like hell!" Briggs yelled, and the photographers snapped away. So? Did Semple go flying or not? The author thinks he has the official answer – which differs from Semple's version. Semple claims:

Anyway, some big bruiser butted in. He later became Kathy's husband, but that doesn't change the fact that he wasn't much of a football player or that he couldn't knock down an overworked old man. Some newspapermen will tell

---

3. This wasn't the first time Semple had chased an interloper. One year a man jumped over the barricades and ran the last 200 yards with the leader. Semple gave chase and they both beat the leader across the finish line, whereupon they continued running, through the crowd and into the Lennox Hotel. There the chase continued, through the lobby and down into the basement where Semple finally cornered his prey, booted him up the backside, pulled a muscle, and lost a week's pay because he couldn't take the Celtics out for their morning jog.

Kathrine Switzer is knocked off balance in phase one of Jock Semple's mission to expel her from his race... *Bettmann/CORBIS*

...But Semple is the one who's sent flying courtesy of Tom Miller's blind-sided body block. *Bettmann/ CORBIS*

you that I got knocked over the telephone wires. Others will say that Jock Semple went flying across the road into the bushes.

Now I'm asking all you honest people, so we can set the record straight, don't give these liars so much credit. So listen to me. It's true the guy did block me. But this is the God's honest truth, the way it happened: I think I tripped over my shoelace the instant before he hit me.

I asked Switzer the big question: did Semple go down or not? Her reply is instant and certain.

Oh my God, he flew through the air this high [demonstrating with her hand above head high], before landing somewhere in a crumpled ball over there [pointing 10 metres away].

I was genuinely worried, so when he reappeared on the press bus a few miles later, screaming abuse at me, like "You'rrrre in biiiggggg ttrrroubbbbble!" I was actually very relieved to see him!

This sparky interlude would probably have merited little more than a four-line blurb in the papers had it not been captured on camera. As it was, instant infamy for Semple, as Switzer's image was wired to newspapers all over the world. The *Johnny Carson Show* would soon come a-calling. Switzer's race proceeded calmly, albeit at a slower pace than she'd have liked. She finished (don't let the *New York Times* tell you otherwise) in around 4:20, about an hour after the excellent Gibb.

* * *

But it was Switzer who got all the headlines and adulation. In volleyball terms, if it was Gibb who had put up the lob, it was Switzer who had executed the smash. After this famous day, women's running would never look back. Tom Murphy writes: "Semple's shove that day boosted women's running more in two seconds than any thousand editorials written in support of women since."

The editorials in the following day's papers naturally made for entertaining and amusing fare. But one thing should be recognized almost above all else. Cloney and Semple were not misogynists – indeed Cloney had three daughters of his own. Their interest was solely that rules – however archaic and inappropriate – should be followed and obeyed. Carol Liston of the *Boston Globe* was on eloquent form:

Looking for ladies in the Marathon was like a drizzly version of "Alice in Wonderland."

Here they were. There they weren't.

Like most things womanly, you could get several versions of the real fact.

First, there's the official version.

To B.A.A. officials, the girls – no matter who they were or how many they were – didn't exist.

This presented a curious dilemma when Col Will Cloney, Marathon chairman, spotted a nonexistent woman running as he rode along in an official bus.

10

Jerry Nason of the same paper pointed out that:

Cloney blew his cork, but not without justification. His anger was mostly directed at the three boys from Syracuse who smuggled a bird into the official race. "It was an outright subterfuge," said Cloney, "aimed at breaking the rules...from the 'K. Switzer' entry blank to the acquiring of her race number by proxy.

"It disturbs me that so-called 'sportsmen' attempt to do things like this. We're not a business organization. We're just a bunch of guys trying to put on a Marathon as a labor of love and handle a million details on our own time.

"The only thing that burns me up," Cloney sizzled, "is that everybody seems to be protecting the rules breakers and clobbering the people who protect the rules."

Purists pay a terrible price even to inhale deeply these days, Nason mused.

Bob Sales of *The Globe* pointed to the obvious. The whole reason for the shamozzle in the first place is that the all important rule was rotten, senseless and just plain bad:

Gandhi and Thoreau would like Kathy Switzer and Bobby Lou Gibb. They would approve of women running in the Boston Marathon. They would approve of the girls' attempt to change a bad rule through disobedience.

The rule is made by the Amateur Athletic Union, an organization which has never been accused of being progressive.

Arnold Briggs refuted Cloney and Semple's claims that Switzer had cheated: "What rule did she break? There's nothing on the application about sex. She's a bona-fide member of the A.A.U. and she was an official entry in the race."

The last – and arguably best – set of observations go to Erich Siegel, then a 29-year-old assistant professor of Classics at Yale, and soon to become the author of the novel *Love Story*. Siegel had the privilege (in his eyes) of running behind Bobbi Gibb for a mile or so. The experience didn't exactly scar him for life, and goes a long way to describe why women should indeed have been admitted into the world of marathoning: "Beautiful. Beautiful form. For one mile I saw nothing but those beautiful legs. I kept saying to myself, 'I should ask her to dinner...I should ask her to dinner.' But I figured it would be so indelicate at that time." Siegel highly approved of girls running in the marathon – if they were serious about it. "You know why they're throwing her off?" Siegel offered. "Because there's 500 men out there who can't beat her." "[Gibb] adds dignity to the race," he opined, "She comes prepared and she acquits herself well. If we have to preserve male superiority through legislation we are in trouble."

* * *

It wasn't for another five years that women were finally, officially, admitted to run Boston. The cold war between Switzer and Semple simmered. Switzer told the author: "The next day back at home I got a letter from the AAU banning me from competition. Semple must have called them up and told them to ban me that

11

very afternoon. This was a busy guy, post-marathon – but he had made sure to take time out to call them telling them to ban me. That's how cross he was."

Gibb returned in 1968, three other girls showed up in 1969, and the 1970 winner Ron Hill was startled to spot five girls at the start that year. The number dipped to three in 1971 before finally the BAA bowed to ladies in 1972. "The women are permitted to run," Semple announced that spring. "And I wish them good luck." Just like that, Switzer recalls. Like ice. Well Switzer placed third behind Nina Kuscik and was presented with a broken trophy by Semple. He told her he'd have it replaced, but then as she left the stage barked: "I've been mad at you for five years and I'm still mad and you DESERVE a broken trophy!" And all the journalists laughed. It was the first signs of a thaw.

Switzer showed up in 1973 but was still scared to death of Semple. She had written him a long peacemaking letter the previous year about how much she appreciated all the hard work he and Cloney put in, but fielded no response. She dramatically recalls:

When I didn't hear from him after I wrote my long letter in 1972, I assumed he was still mad. Then I saw him. You know how Jock is at the starting line of the Boston Marathon. He literally picks people up if they're out of place and hurls them in the air. Boston 1973 was no different. I was standing at the front of the starting line where they placed all the women and I could hear Jock looking for people with high numbers.

The spat between Semple and Switzer simmered for several years, until finally, at the start of the 1973 race, Semple thawed. They embraced and cuddled for the cameras, and became best of friends until Jock's death in 1988. *Bettmann/CORBIS*

12

I could hear him coming, "AAAAAgggghhh!" and I put my head down. I hear him come closer and then I heard footsteps right behind me. 'AAAAggghh!' he said as he came up behind my shoulder, and I turned. I was scared to death, but he was smiling. He put his face right up beside mine, cheek to cheek, and he said, loudly enough for everyone to hear, "Come on, lass. Let's get ourselves a wee bit of no-tor-EYE-eteeeee!" And he kissed me. Fat on the cheek. The cameras clicked like mad. And Jock and I have been best friends ever since.

* * *

Some running aficionados offer irritation that Switzer became so much more famous than Gibb and that it should be Gibb, not Switzer, who should be credited for opening the door to women marathoners. Gibb got there first they say – and she was the classier runner. Up to a point. Switzer's best at Boston was eventually some half an hour better than Gibb's, and Switzer was the master communicator, the one who was determined to keep the torch burning bright. When she retired from running in 1975 she went on to become a very successful journalist, race promoter and broadcaster. She also founded the world-famous Avon Women's Running Circuit.

These days she looks 20 years younger than her age and doesn't carry a single extra pound on her slim frame. Her running peak came the day she retired: Boston, April 21, 1975, where she ran a fine 2:51:37 to place second out of 52 starters, behind Liane Winter. That's quite a discrepancy I suggest: popping a 2:50 marathon, after that 4:20 back in '67. Why had she been *quite* so slow that day? Switzer's response is priceless: "People are always beating up on me for this, but I just say: how would you feel if a *gorilla* jumped on your back?!"

Race result (unofficial)

Roberta Gibb   3:27:17
Kathrine Switzer   c. 4:20

Sources

Conversations with Kathrine Switzer.
Conversations with Charlie Rodgers.
Derderian, Tom, *Boston Marathon*. Human Kinetics, 1996.
Hauman, Riël, *Century of the Marathon*. Human & Rousseau, 1996.
Lister, Carol, in the *Boston Globe*, April 20th, 1967.
Nason, Jerry, in the *Boston Globe*, April 20th, 1967.
Sales, Bob, in the *Boston Globe*, April 20th, 1967.
Semple, Jock, John J. Kelley and Tom Murphy, *Just Call Me Jock*. Waterford, Publishing Company, 1981.

II

No. 49 – 1983 Chicago Marathon [Men]

Sunday, October 16th

Kenya seeks first big-city win

"One of the most dramatic, magnificent races of all time" is how television summarizer Toni Reavis describes this little-known pearl from Chicago 1983, which has deservedly scraped into the top 50 list: a thrilling battle to the wire between the best of Europe and Africa; with a few old stagers along for the ride.

"Don't write off Bill Rodgers," squealed Linda Kay in the *Chicago Tribune* on the day of the race, as she urged fans not to forget fading star "Boston Billy", quadruple winner of Boston and New York, as well as Fukuoka back in 1977. "The marathon man may be getting older, but he's also getting faster," claimed Kay. "At the ripe age of 35, Rodgers is running faster than he has ever run before and has established personal records for 10 and 20K in the last year."

Rodgers, too, was indicating he might have one last hurrah left in him: "It surprises me that most sports' writers think I'm going downhill. True, I'm no longer one of the best marathoners in the world, but my range is very good." Toni Reavis agreed: "Bill is known as Mr. Consistency. He rarely wins anymore, but he's always in there, placing second or third."

Not this time. Rodgers ran side by side with Greg Meyer, who just six months earlier had dazzled at Boston with his confident 2:09:00 win. But Meyer was unable to repeat such antics as he finished 14th in 2:17. "I feel like going someplace to cry," he said afterwards. "Like computers, you only get what you program into them and I didn't program properly. I didn't have the fitness." As for Rodgers, he was more woeful still, placing 30th. He explained:

> I was very, very tired today.[1] Even at the start, I was a little dizzy. It's disappointing when you end the race after 14, 15 miles. At that point, I was struggling to stay in. But it's hard to drop out when the crowds are so good. They were thick. I kept looking for a side road to turn down. I'll do one more marathon, the Olympic trials, and if I do bad there, that'll be it for me in the marathon. No more.

---

1. Not surprising considering that around this time Rodgers was devoting as much time to business ventures as he was to running. "I'm forever in meetings!" he would wail.

15

Well, Rodgers did do bad there, but three years later he returned to Boston, and electrified the crowds by placing fourth, aged 38. And sixteen years on from Chicago '83, he was still marathoning – shooting for world records in the M50 category.

This 1983 edition of Chicago was also the marathon that marked the debut, albeit an inauspicious one, of the man who would progress to be one the world's greatest: Welshman Steve Jones. However, an easy jog the night before the race, with fellow Brit Hugh Jones, saw him tweak a tendon in his foot. Jones (S) ran with the leaders with nonchalant ease until around halfway before the foot locked up, forcing him to a hobble...and a 'DNF'.

This race, it seemed, was to be a battle of survivors.

* * *

In the closing miles of the 1983 Chicago Marathon, the race had boiled down to a battle of three. They consisted of two American-based Kenyans named Simeon Kigen and Joseph Nzau and the Englishman Hugh Jones. Kigen and Nzau may have been separated in age by over a decade (they were 22 and 33), but they were good friends and becoming responsible for putting Kenya on the road-running map. Linda Kay wrote in the *Chicago Tribune*: "Joseph Nzau (pronounced EN-zow) started running by chasing his father's cattle in Kenya. At the University of Wyoming, where he is a student, Nzau once sprinted after a jack rabbit and caught it."

Jones had been recruited by race director Bob Bright on the strength of his impressive performance in the previous year's London Marathon where he had prevailed over 16,400 others, by no fewer than three minutes in 2:09:24. On that day, in which the warm sun played havoc with the unprepared, Jones shrugged it off, saying how "it never got under my skin."[2] This excellent run had not come out of the blue. Jones, a student at Liverpool University, already had two 2:10 marathons to his name at Tokyo (2nd) and New York (3rd); and had also played a key role in the inaugural World Championship Marathon in Helsinki just ten weeks earlier, where he placed eighth in 2:11:15. The new world champion, Rob de Castella, gratefully paid tribute to Jones for the way he forced the pace in the early stages.

Jones didn't need to do any pace forcing here though. True, he liked an honest pace to compensate for his lack of a finishing kick, but as the race got to the "business end", Jones was merely "hanging on" to the tearaway antics of Kigen. After five runners had still been in the melting pot after 19 miles, there was suddenly a fierce acceleration as mile 20 passed in a stomach-churning 4:46. Kigen had been the man behind the move, and after coasting for a couple of minutes, he surged again. He grabbed a 10-second lead as Jones and Nzau grimly battled for survival. The Kenyan continued to run swiftly and smoothly, zipping off a 4:48 mile, then a 4:52, and then a 4:54 to mile 23.

At this point it looked like Kigen's race, as he had edged his advantage to 100 metres. But such a notion, as Jones reveals to the author, never entered into the

---

2. The London Marathon that year was run at the very late date of May 9th.

Hugh Jones destroyed the rest of the field at the 1982 London Marathon. *Mark Shearman*

Englishman's mind. Displaying the psychology that all top sportsmen possess, Jones dismisses my question: "Did you think you could catch him?" as an irrelevance. "One never thinks 'can I catch this guy?'" Jones explains, "but more '*how* can I catch this guy?'" A defeatist attitude is a non-starter. Indeed, just when it seemed that the novice would romp home to victory, then Kigen began to fade. Spotting the faltering stride, Nzau quickly threw in a surge – Jones at his elbow.

At North Lake Shore Drive, a mile later, the duo of Jones and Nzau drew level with, and pushed past, Kigen. "I had no problem with Kigen out in front," Nzau remarked later. "I let him stay there. A marathon is both mental and physical – there's a long way to go." Nzau and Kigen had met at a track meet earlier that summer, and Nzau has taken Kigen under his wing. "I've been helping him with his running," Nzau said. "He'll do better in his next marathon." Kigen's first effort at the marathon, though, was nothing to be ashamed of.

It was now a battle of two. The bad news for Jones was that he had raced Nzau only a couple of weeks before at a 10K race in Los Angeles. Jones had run an excellent 28:33, but Nzau had thumped him by a *minute*. But, Jones kept telling himself, that was then – this is now. It often doesn't matter whether or not someone has great natural speed – or a lethal kick – toward the end of a marathon, but only how much *you* have left. Jones hoped Nzau would be running low on fuel.

With just 400-metres to go, Jones had managed to inch into a lead of a few metres and Nzau appeared to be suffering. But the Kenyan, using all his strength, whittled away the deficit and with 200-metres to go they were neck and neck again. Thirty-two seconds more of excruciating pain for both men to decide 7,800 seconds' worth of toil. The momentum was now all with Nzau. But then, surprisingly, it was *Jones* who kicked. "Look at Hugh Jones!" yelled the commentator, as the Ranelagh Harrier put in a terrific burst worthy of a much faster athlete.[3]

But the final twist of the race came with less than 50 metres to go as Nzau forced himself into the lead for the final time, and this time Jones had no reply as his legs finally appeared to buckle. Nzau flashed over the line in 2:09:44, a mere half a second ahead of Jones. Despite stiff winds that, top runners said, slowed

---

3. Jones claims to the author never to have broken 60 seconds for the quarter mile. Although he does offer the caveat that his fastest clocking of 61 seconds did come in the last lap of a very slow 10,000-metre race!

times in the first half, all three men broke the course record of 2:10:59 set the previous year by Greg Meyer. The difference between first and second place had been a full $6,000 (the first prize $20,000). They had run the second half of the race in just 64 minutes.

"I wasn't surging at the end," recalled Jones. "There was no real great change of pace. It was just a question of trying to hang on. I was pushing it with three-quarters of a mile to go, but he's a speedier guy than me. When he went with 50 yards left, my legs just gave out. A sprinter has really always got that sprint." "I could see how strong he is, but I could also see by how he was running that I knew I could outkick him," replied Nzau. "I was positive!"

Running along the banks of the River Thames one cold January morning, twenty years later, Jones revealed to the author what he said to Nzau in the press conference afterwards, which reveals much about how wafer-thin the difference is between success and failure at the highest level of sport; in this case, around 100 centimetres: "I said to Joseph that if my lead had been 5 metres with 400 metres to go, I think I would have won. But when I saw it was four, I knew I was in trouble." Jones also spoke of how, although he had "cased out" the closing stages of the Chicago course in the days leading up to the race, perhaps his homework was not as thorough as it could have been. Beginning his final major surge for the tape, Jones had thought that upon turning the final sweeping bend, that the finish line would lie some two or three-hundred-metres ahead. As it was, when he turned, he found the finish close to 500 metres away. A seemingly small error, but perhaps, a very crucial one.[4]

In becoming the first Kenyan to win a major marathon, little did Nzau know what he was starting. *Athletics Weekly* reported:

> Kenya has at last found a world-class marathoner, in the person of Joseph Nzau. One of the most successful competitors of the North American road circuit this year with recent victories over 7.1 miles in 32:20 and half marathon in 62:13 to his credit, Nzau pipped Britain's Hugh Jones to win and break the previous Kenyan record by 1:56.

Nzau went on to feature prominently in the remarkable Los Angeles Olympic Marathon the following year, eventually placing seventh, just two minutes off the winner Carlos Lopes. Jones was a solid twelfth, just ahead of both Alberto Salazar and Toshihiko Seko.

The women's race of this event was significant for Rosa Mota, who won her first big-city marathon, to add to her victory in the European Championships the previous year. The New Zealander Anne Audain had boasted a big lead deep on in the race but spectacularly had her fatigued legs disappear from under her as she collapsed to the ground in a heap. She was able to scramble to her feet and finish

---

4. It is interesting how these minor calculations can come into play. During the latter stages of the 1982 London Marathon, which Jones went on to win by three minutes, he found himself getting very excited towards the end when he realized he had a good chance of running 2:08. But he had forgotten to factor into his calculations the small road that leads on to Parliament Square: Great George Street. It only took him 24 seconds to cover, but his final time was 2:09:24; and he never did manage to run in the two-zero-eights.

the final couple of miles of the race, but not before being passed by Mota (2:31:36), Canada's Jacqueline Gareau and Dorthe Rasmussen of Denmark.

* * *

Over twenty years on from Chicago '83, Jones remained a committed runner and prolific marathoner. In a ten-week spell at the end of 2003, in his late forties, he completed no fewer than three marathons in the unlikely venues of Beirut, Havana and Barbados. The first two were used as a build up to the latter where he placed third in 2:38.[5]

A good example of how the best seem to have a superior work ethic to the masses, long after their top-flight days are over, was illustrated by the time the author bumped into Jones one Sunday morning in North London's Regent's Park. I asked Jones how far he was running.

"Ah, just six," came the reply, "and yourself?"

"It's fourteen today," replied your correspondent, feeling satisfied that I was travelling eight miles further than one of the finest marathoners of the 1980s.

"Fourteen!?" Jones guffawed. "You're doing fourteen laps of the park?!"

"Er, no, I'm doing 14 miles."

"Oh, I'm doing six laps."

At 3½ miles to a lap my smugness was quickly replaced by humility.

Race result:

Joseph Nzau	KEN	2:09:44.3
Hugh Jones	ENG	2:09:44.8
Simeon Kigen	KEN	2:10:52
Agapius Masong	TAN	2:11:57
Christof Herle	FRG	2:12:14
Gianni Poli	ITA	2:12:34

Sources:

Archive race footage.

Conversations with Hugh Jones.

Anonymous in *Athletics Weekly*, October 19th, 1983.

Hauman, Riël, *Century of the Marathon*. Human & Rousseau, 1996.

Kay, Linda, in the *Chicago Tribune*, October 16th & 17th, 1983.

Wightman, Geoff and Dave Bedford, *Funny Running Shorts*. Descartes Publishing Ltd., 2003.

---

5. Jones has now run the Barbados Marathon 13 times – winning on six occasions. He almost added a seventh one year, having built up a lead of several minutes with only a minute left to run. But then suddenly he collapsed through heat exhaustion. Jones refused to be beaten, and since walking or crawling to the finish was not an option – so depleted was his state – he decided to *roll* there! This occurred for a few yards before the medics spotted his predicament, rushed to the strange little scene and carted Jones off to hospital.

III

No. 48 – 1896 Olympic Marathon [Men]

Saturday, April 10th

"Water – I said I wanted water. *Not cognac!"*

The organizers of the first modern Olympic Games in 1896 felt they needed a little more spice to the programme of athletics, but they weren't to know what *beast* they were releasing when they included a "Marathon" race. The race, they decided, would trace the path of the Greek messenger Phidippides, who ran to Athens from Marathon to bring news of the spectacular coup which had occurred there: that the might of the all-conquering Persian army had been brought to its knees – and then ground into the dust – by the inferior and outnumbered Athenian soldiers. "Rejoice, we conquer!" Phidippides exclaimed before dropping down dead. Or so the rather hackneyed old myth goes. If one looks at the story a little closer though, doesn't it strike one as rather odd that Phidippides – a professional long-distance messenger – should have met his match when covering a reasonable but certainly not insurmountable distance?

A referral to the history books tells us that Phidippides was indeed made of sterner stuff. A 40-kilometre trot was but a stretch of the legs to this man; and it is a great injustice to him that he is forever associated with finding the marathon distance fatally beyond his scope. Another reason to pass grave doubt over the "rejoice, we conquer" legend is that the historian Herodotus, who loved to spin tales laced with titbits such as this, makes no mention of such an occurrence in his reports, although he *was* well aware of Phidippides' real capabilities.[1] Whether the legend of Phidippides is corrupt or not doesn't really matter because one thing that certainly did take place is the Battle of Marathon, and if the race of the same name is all about drama and heroism, then so, most certainly, was this remarkable incident, to which it is worth devoting a little time here.

From around 493 BC the Persian army was flexing its muscles in a ubiquitous manner, occasionally with what passed for compassion, but more often, ruthlessly

---

1. The sensationalist side to Herodotus' nature arises in, for instance, his description of a violent gale soon before the battle of Marathon, which he claims accounted for 300 ships and 20,000 men under the command of Mardonius – a fact upon which subsequent historians have place considerable doubt. For one thing Herodotus tended to write in multiples of 300 – so it was almost certainly considerably fewer ships that were actually destroyed; and also this is a historian who also claimed that people died at the hands of monsters as well as shipwrecks...

and cowardly contempt for human life as well as architectural triumphs. By 491 BC, ambassadors were being sent throughout Greece to find out if the communities wanted to voluntarily submit earth and water. Most of the northern territory complied. However, Sparta, ruled by Cleomenes, chose instead to murder the Persian ambassador – something of a breach of convention. It is now clear that, in future, Athens and Sparta would stand against Persia. More destruction followed: Miltetus, one of Greece's cultural centres, was destroyed, after which the Persian fleet assembled in Cilicia and duly arrived at Naxos. The Naxians quickly surrendered but temples were still destroyed – a gambit designed to spread fear. The Persians sailed on, and all the Cycladic islands surrendered. Then, the two comparatively small cities of Carystos and Eretria were attacked, not at the same time, which would have been easily possible such was the Persian dominance, but one by one to ensure maximum brutality and damage. Carystos gave in fairly quickly, but the Eretrians tried to resist. A siege lasted six days before two leading citizens turned traitors and opened the city gates to the Persians, leaving Eretria devastated from rape and pillaging.

The Athenians heard all about this and were understandably tense. A few days later the Persians landed at Marathon, in Attica – Athenian home territory. Marathon presented the Persians with a wide-open flat plain, which suited them since it was the best place for them to use their cavalry. The Persians disembarked. Surely the mother of all defeats was about to be inflicted upon the poor Athenians.

Help from Sparta was urgently required and it is here that Phidippides, an Olympic runner, played his role in the Battle of Marathon. His message to the Spartans was that Athens would perish unless the Spartans help. In his biography of the Athenian general Miltiades, the Roman historian Cornelius Nepos referred to Phidippides as belonging to a "class known as *hēmerodromio*", meaning men who ran for a day, or longer. Phidippides' journey took just a single day, in which he ran about 238 kilometres.[2] (The world record for the 24 hour run in AD 1996 was just 45 kilometres more). Classy stuff indeed from this worthy messenger, who then doubled his spectacular workload by returning to Marathon to deliver the Spartans' reply.

The reply, however, was the worst possible news. The Spartans were celebrating the Carneia, a religious festival, and were thus prevented from fighting for a period of 30 days. The Athenians were therefore alone, and only the faint hope of holding out until the Carneia ended seemed a possible solution. More signs of cowardice from the Persians emerge when Herodotus hints they may have heard from Demaratus, the former king of Sparta, that this would indeed be a good time to attack.

The Athenians commenced work on their delay tactics. They blocked off the road that leads to Athens and protected their left flank by cutting down trees and putting in anti-cavalry stakes. A face-off lasted several days. To aid in their defence the Athenians possessed strong body armour and 9-foot spears. They also

---

2. According to the Roman geographer Gaius Iulius Solinus the distance from Marathon to Sparta was around 1,240 stades, with the length of a *stade* being around 210 yards.

possessed large shields, which left them well defended and hard to kill. Conversely, the Persians were somewhat poorly defended, with just leather tops for their best infantry. The Persians all used the bow and arrow (Darius' coins depict this). They boasted a long knife but did not have strong helmets, only turbans, which were there for display.

Tactics in the Athenian camp conflicted: some generals – including Miltiades – wanted to attack, since the Persians would not be expecting this; others wanted to wait for the Persians to make the first move. Somehow the view prevailed that attack was the best option. The Athenians' formation comprised a deliberately weak centre with strong flanks. They charged at speed so that arrows fired from a distance were useless and the battle turned rapidly into hand-to-hand combat, which meant that the weight of the Greeks was a major advantage over the lightly armed Persians. The Persian flanks quickly fled and whilst pushing forward in the middle, the Athenians turned around and attacked from behind. There was little resistance from the Persian side. Historians have noted that the cavalry were not present during the battle, as it seems that the Athenians had attacked whilst the Persians were watering their horses.

The casualties – probably accurate since the Athenians buried the Persians – were 192 Athenians and 6400 Persians dead. It is seen as the proudest moment in their history.

*   *   *

As noted, the exact details of Phidippides' travails matter little now; the fact is that the *myth* existed, along with the great battle, which in turn led to the creation of the marathon race. But what of modern athletics itself? How did that come into being? After all, the athletics programme at the 1896 Athens Olympics bears a remarkable similarity to that of today. The only events missing from those Games were: the 200-metres, the 5000-metres, the 10,000-metres, the hammer throw and the decathlon.

One of the earliest descriptions of a footrace is in the *Iliad*, when the Greek poet Homer wrote about a footrace between Ajax and Odysseus in around 800 BC. Ancient Greece had many cultural festivals, such as the Nemean and Isthmian games, but the Olympic Games, so called because they were held at Olympia in the north-west Peloponnese, became the most famous. Some historians have traced the origins of the Games to 1222 BC, but the earliest record of any victor seems to be a sprinter called Coroebus, who won the *stade* race in 776 BC. The ancient Olympic Games were halted in AD 393 by the Roman emperor Theodosius, after 1200 years of competition.

The British Isles is where organized sport began to resurface most in the Middle Ages, with some sports that we recognize today becoming common in Britain around the twelfth century. Footracing, jumping and hurling weights could all be found on the programme. These were strictly pastimes for ordinary people though, from which the upper classes would distance themselves at all costs. However, between the sixteenth and nineteenth centuries "pedestrianism" started to flourish in Britain. Massive wagers were placed on the outcome of races even though the actual running was still left to the servants. One of the best-known winners of wagers of this period was when a Scottish landowner, Robert Barclay

Allardice, known as Captain Barclay, walked one mile an hour for 1000 consecutive hours winning a £16,000 bet in the process. It is no surprise that he had to walk the final few hundred miles heavily armed, lest his debtors decide to take pot shots at him in desperation.[3]

By 1850, athletics could be witnessed throughout Britain as at least a dozen purpose-built running tracks existed. And it was around this time that the educated classes began to take an interest. The author Riël Hauman writes: "In 1861 the famous American Indian Deerfoot came to Cambridge to run, and win, a race over 6 miles at Fenner's Ground. Among the spectators was the Prince of Wales, and the future king dined with the flamboyant runner in Trinity College afterwards. This event sparked an immense interest in the sport." Suddenly athletics was an approved middle class activity. Army officers, civil servants, solicitors and bankers were all deciding to run. The modern-day Chase Corporate Challenge 5-kilometre footrace that sees tens of thousands of eager participants each July in London and New York can trace its origins back to these days of the mid-19th century. Civil Service athletics championships are still taken very seriously, and civil servants also compete in matches against such outfits as the army and the RAF.

The first match between Oxford and Cambridge, held at the Christ Church Ground, Oxford, was on March 5th, 1864 and is, according to Riël Hauman, "regarded by many as the foundation meeting of modern athletics". The Oxford–Cambridge "varsity" match still commands enormous importance amongst its participants, both in track and cross-country. The athletes strive for their "blues" (colours) with fierce passion; indeed a captain of the Oxford ladies team relates to the author a pitiful tale of how the Oxford men's captain did not award a single blue at the post-match varsity dinner in 1997. Bitter tears flowed freely around the room. The iconic figure of John Graham Chambers ruled athletics at Cambridge University between 1843 and 1883, and it was he that led the committee of the Amateur Athletic Club, which held its first championship in 1866. The announcement of this meeting stated that the competition would be "open to any gentleman amateur".[4]

The Amateur Athletic Association (AAA) was founded in Oxford in 1880, and the American equivalent of the AAA, the AAU (the "U" standing for Union), was formed in 1888. The earliest world record officially recognized by the IAAF was Alfred Shrubb's 50:40 for 10 miles set on November 5th, 1904 in Glasgow.[5]

Common distances covered by both amateurs and professionals were 15 and 20 miles. But that was pretty much the limit. It was to take the imagination and

---

3. One hundred and ninety-four years later this challenge was reprised when six people attempted it in the lead-up to the 2003 London Marathon. Apart from one withdrawal completely disconnected with the physical or mental side of the event (marital problems), doctors were startled that all five of the other contestants seemed to finish the challenge scarcely any worse for wear – even finishing off the event by running the London Marathon. Six months later though, the challenge winner, Shona Crombie-Hicks, a 2:40 marathoner, did seem to be having complications with her immune system and was also experiencing a succession of 'niggles'. By 2005 she had fully recovered, was racing well again, and lopped two minutes off her "pb".

4. The term "amateur" was defined as "any gentleman who has never competed in an open competition, or for public money, or for admission money, and who has never at any period of his life taught or assisted in the pursuit of athletic exercises as a means of livelihood."

5. Shrubb actually set seven world records in this single race, ranging from 29.59 for 6 miles to 18,742 metres for the hour (Hauman).

foresight of the 1896 Olympic committee to come up with the distance to which we owe this book.

* * *

The first modern Olympic Games had as their centrepiece the reconstructed Panathenaikon Stadium in Athens. And it was obvious that this spectacular venue would be where the marathon would finish. In their study of the Olympic marathon, Martin and Gynn write:

> The original stadium on that site was constructed in ca. 330 B.C. It fell into disrepair but was rebuilt 500 years later by Herodis Atticus. That second version also disintegrated with time and was buried until 1870, when excavations first revealed its dimensions to modern Greece. An estimate of its spectator capacity can be made from the reported sales of 71,800 tickets for the day of the marathon, when the stadium was full.

The rebuilt stadium was modelled after the stadium of Atticus. The straightaways were 100 metres long, and the turns 65 metres long, giving a circumference of 333.33 metres (zur Megede). The impressive marble construction that greets visitors today was not all in place in 1896, and many spectators sat on wooden seats.

It is unknown why the seacoast route that the marathon course followed was selected over a more direct mountainous route. But Martin and Gynn speculate that "40 kilometres is familiar to nations accustomed to the Imperial measurement system." It is also close to 25 miles. Anyone who has run the Athens Marathon will tell you how demanding the course is. It begins 25 metres above sea level, drops down to sea level and then rises 80 metres over the next 10 kilometres, and then a sharp drop before rising by 220 metres between the 15 and 30-kilometre stages. The final quarter of the race is straightforward and mainly consists of descending road, but to any athlete the wrong side of eager, the damage has already been done.

Naturally, Greece craved a winner in the Olympic marathon more than any other race. It seemed not to matter that the host nation hadn't won a single track and field gold (one had come their way in fencing); this was the race that really mattered. Not one but two trial races for the Games were held. In the first just twelve athletes showed up, and the first six across the line were selected. Two weeks later, and a mere fortnight before the Olympic marathon, another trial race was held and this time 38 athletes appeared. They were told, with stunning unfairness, that to qualify for the Games one had to beat the winning time in the previous trial race (that of 3:18 by Kharilaos Vasilakos). Just four men managed this, although two more were selected after all. One was a labourer called Spiridon Louis who ran 3:18:27 and the other Stamatio Masouris (3:19:15). The team selectors had relented because of the rainy, foggy and chilly conditions that existed on the course. For reasons unknown, a 13th athlete was added to the squad, one Sokratis Lagoudakis, but whatever his means of qualification, the race benefited by his colourful command of language.

An unidentified German athlete was intended to partake in the Olympic marathon but he decided to duck out. This meant that 17 runners tackled the inaugural race. The four competing from outside the host nation were: "Teddy" Flack of Australia, Albin Lermusiaux of France, Hungary's Gyula Kellner and Arthur Blake of the United States. Remarkably, Flack had won the 800-metres gold just the day before (in 2:11), and three days before the marathon Flack, Blake and Lermusiaux had come one–two–three in the 1500-metre final, in times over a minute off what are achieved today.

As the runners gathered in the village of Marathon for the big event, a short, patriotic speech, in Greek, was offered. An approximate translation might be: "Men, think of your country; think of your flag on the pole inside the stadium; that flag wants you to do honour for her. Hurrah for your country. Hurrah for the Olympic Games." Martin and Gynn report how Lagoudakis, a medical student, then said this to his comrades: "If you win, we will still think of you as brothers."

The afternoon was cool but sunny, and at 2 p.m. Colonel G. Papadiamanto-poulos fired the pistol to send the runners on their way. An atmosphere of excite-ment mixed with anxiety followed the runners' early path as the crowd of a few hundred local peasant farmers grasped the significance of the occasion. The most complete description of the race, leant upon heavily by subsequent historians and authors, comes from Charalambos Anninos, whose account is in the official report of the Games. Some of his observations must be taken with a pinch of salt, however. It is fairly safe to say, for instance, that the athletes did not pass through 20 kilometres in 52 minutes. Interestingly, at around the halfway mark it was the four foreigners who dominated the fray. Was this to be the ultimate "damp squib" of a day for the host nation? Or were the foreigners having delusions of grandeur way beyond their calling? The Frenchman Lermusiaux led by a massive 3 kilometres at 20K. The first two Greek runners appeared in the form of Lavrentis (one of the trial winners) and Kafetzis, but this was to be token defiance and they dropped out soon thereafter. If they had seen enough, how must the runners up front have been feeling?

Lermusiaux continued to hold the lead at 25 kilometres but his lead had drasti-cally shrunk – to just a minute. Flack followed, with Blake three minutes behind him. The Greek Vasilakos now found himself in fourth, seven minutes off the pace, with Spiridon Louis thirty seconds behind and Hungary's Kellner, hitting all sorts of walls, a further quarter-mile back. Lermusiaux began to crumble just as the villagers of Harvati – at around 26 kilometres – began crowning his head with leaves in a symbolic gesture of potential victory. Martin and Gynn write: "This was clearly premature, for Lermusiaux was paying dearly the price of a fast early start, and the others were catching him. After leaving the village, Lermusiaux had to stop during a noticeable incline to receive an alcohol rubdown from his accom-panist." Flack used this opportunity to take the lead for himself. Did a triple gold beckon in the 1500, 800 and marathon? Now that would be truly something. All the alcohol in Greece wasn't going to revive the spent Lermusiaux, however, and he collapsed at 32 kilometres and was given refuge in a horse-drawn carriage. It was around this time that the gutsy Arthur Blake called it a day as well. For the overeager early pace-setters, the race was exacting intolerable pain.

Five kilometres later and it was time for potential winners to stand up and be counted. Kharilaos Vasilakos now assumed the role of favourite. His name will forever be noted as the man who came first in the first ever recognized marathon race – the Greek Olympic trial on March 10th, 1896 – when he ran 3:18 and won by three minutes. He was born in Pasalamani in 1871, and was a serious athlete – a champion race-walker as well as runner. In later life he became a customs office director. "There, his sportsmanship apparently carried over into his working life, as he had a special reputation for honesty and integrity in a position that often found such virtues difficult to preserve," report Martin and Gynn. The world of exercise obviously suited him well – he lived until 1963, and the age of 92.

But did Vasilakos have what it took to capture Olympic gold, as the race entered its pivotal moments? Although the leader, Flack, was slowing down alarmingly, Vasilakos was experiencing great fatigue of his own. The little known Spiridon Louis caught Vasilakos, ran with him a while, dropped him, and then set off in hot pursuit of leader, Flack. Flack was quickly caught and hung on doggedly as the two descended into the city of Athens. Three kilometres from the finish a crucial moment occurred at the village of Ambelokipi, as Louis spotted his girlfriend. Her enthusiastic cheers and proffered orange slices spurred him on.

It was a surge too much for Flack, who became yet another candidate for the recovery carriages. It was not long before his handler asked a Greek spectator to hold on to him while he went in search of a wrap to protect him from the sun. But Flack was hallucinating by now, and, thinking he was being attacked, struck the hapless fan with his fist! But what a magnificent Olympic Games this 22-year-old accountant from Price, Waterhouse and Company had displayed. Travelling from his London office, he not only had triumphed in the two middle distance events, but had even played in the tennis tournament on the morning of his 800 final, where the record books indicate he won a bronze in the doubles!

So suddenly it was ideally built (tall and thin) Spiridon Louis on whose shoulders a nation's hopes rested. Never have so many known so little about an Olympic contender. "Was he a poor shepherd, a well-to-do farmer, a soldier, or a post office messenger?" asks writer David Wallechinsky. That was all to be revealed, but first there was the small matter of "task completion". The starter Colonel Papadiamantopoulous rode alongside Louis offering support. Louis asked for water. He got cognac – which he promptly spit out. It is well documented that he did down at least a couple of glasses of wine, offered to him by well-meaning villagers en route.

Back in the stadium the 70,000-plus spectators did not know when the finishers were due, or even if the marathon had started on time. Their anxiety and impatience were kept in check by the pole vault final,[6] but finally a German cyclist arrived in the stadium bringing news of the race – even if it was of the worst possible kind. The Australian, Flack, was leading, sending a groan through the crowd. Of course the German's news was extremely dated, and it was left to the starter himself, who had accompanied Louis for much of the latter stages, to bring

---

6. There was never chance of a Greek winner here. Indeed the Greek participants were so outclassed by the Americans that they'd all been eliminated before the Americans started vaulting. In true Olympic spirit, however, the Greeks assisted the Americans in their work by massaging their muscles and giving them drinks.

27

far better news. Covered in dust from his long journey, say Martin and Gynn, "he dashed directly to the royal throne to inform His Majesty King Georgios that in fact Louis was in the lead."

The next day the London *Times* reported:

> The stadion today was a most impressive sight, the vast area being filled by a dense crowd, while the surrounding heights were covered by an immense throng of spectators. At least 70,000 spectators were present when, at half-past 2, the King, accompanied by the King of Serbia, and the Royal Family entered the arena amid loud applause and took their seats on the marble thrones at the end of the semi-circle.
>
> At a quarter to 5 the approach of the competitors in the marathon race was announced. The scene in the stadium when it was discovered that a Greek was leading baffles description.

This was indeed more like it. According to the official report of the Games, the word spread "with the rapidity of lightning". Suddenly a wild and spontaneous atmosphere of euphoria erupted around the stadium as cries of "*Hellene! Hellene!*" (A Greek! A Greek!) were heard, and all attention was focused on the entrance to the stadium. According to Anninos: "a man wearing white, sun-burnt, and covered in perspiration, is seen to enter." It was Louis, wearing number 17.

This painting shows Spiridon Louis of Greece winning the first Olympic marathon in 1896. *IOC/Getty Images*

With just a couple of hundred yards left to run, the leader picked up two enthusiastic sidekicks for his final steps. They were Crown Prince Konstantinos and Prince Georgios, who ran beside him along the stadium straightaway. As Louis broke through a piece of string that had been stretched out at the designated finish line, he stopped in front of the King and bowed, while a band immediately struck up the Greek anthem.

Louis had dipped under the magic three-hour barrier, which today is still seen as the mark of a trained, focused runner, as opposed to just the spirited jogger with a degree of fitness and talent. There was a lengthy pause before the next man – *another Greek* – stepped forward. It was the colourfully named Kharilaos Vasilakos. A reason this marathon doesn't feature somewhat higher in the top 50 list is that, although its importance can't be doubted, it is easily the largest winning margin in Olympic history: 7:13. Bedlam reigned again and it was only heightened when yet another Greek, and another Spiridon – this time Belokas – entered twenty seconds later, hotly pursued by Gyula Kellner of Hungary. No more foreigners would finish. All the remaining six finishers would have got their own hearty welcomes, even the last fellow, Sokratis Lagoudakis, who was estimated to be around an hour down on Louis. As noted above, his fitness was not tested in a trial, but it was certainly tested here, and he came up wanting. Waiting in the wings whilst all this celebration was occurring, however, was a nice, healthy dose of controversy.

As Louis was led away asking for nothing more cooling than a cup of coffee, Queen Olga kissed his forehead and shook his hand. When she remarked how callused it was, she was informed that he was just a common labourer, and immediately – according to his biographer – removed the rings from her fingers and gave them to him, saying: "The honor you have given to Greece is worth far more than these simple rings." But not everyone was happy. Fourth-place finisher Kellner launched a protest. He stipulated that Belokas had completed part of the course in a carriage. Under investigation, the results of which did not make the Official Report, Belokas admitted his deception, was stripped of his rewards and was thoroughly ostracized.[7]

The following day the London *Times* reported: "The result of the marathon race was quickly telegraphed to all the chief towns of Greece, and demonstrations in honour of the victor are reported from many parts of the country. In Athens itself the result has, of course, evoked great enthusiasm. Louis has been presented with a magnificent antique vase."

Whatever became of the cup presented to Louis? The answer is to be found in the text of K. Lennartz' tome *Journal of Olympic History*. The cup never left Amaroussion and is happily stored away in a closet in the home of Eutychia Louis, Spiridon's daughter-in-law. The 25-centimetres-tall trophy is intact, and

---

7. A better-known Olympic incident of such crude sharp practice is the case of Fred Lorz at the St Louis Olympic Marathon of 1904. He rode a car from miles 9 to 19 and won the race easily – accepting the cheers of the crowds. When confronted, Lorz cheerfully admitted his ruse; he was a practical joker and this had been a fine one. Officials didn't share his humour and were enraged. The AAU promptly banned Lorz from competition for life. The hapless clown was shocked: he appealed and the ban was lifted. The following April the *Boston Daily Globe* carried the front-page headline: "Immense Crowds Cheer Splendid Victory of the Game New Yorker" as Lorz won Boston by 85 seconds. "It's a cinch to run 25 miles," he crowed. But, one suspects, it's easier still to drive.

Spiridon Louis receives his gold medal after winning the first Olympic Marathon to the delight of the tens of thousands of partisan supporters.
IOC/Olympic Museum/Getty Images

although oxidation over time has obviously darkened it, the cup is otherwise only slightly damaged.

* * *

"More than any other single event," David Wallechinsky writes, "the victory of Spiridon Louis served as an inspiration to keep the Olympics going through the hard times that the movement faced over the next 12 years." But what happened to Spiridon over the course of the rest of his life, and what were his personal thoughts of the Olympics? The answer is a mixed tale and supports the theory that fame and fortune do not necessarily make a happy man.

Louis was born on January 12th, 1873, which makes him 23 at the time of his victory. He was not possessed with the sophistication required to deal with his new-found standing. He was a humble man, too, and when asked what he'd like as a prize for winning such an important race, he replied that just a new horse and cart would be sufficient to aid him in his work as a water carrier.[8] Louis subsequently married his girlfriend, Eleni, who had given him the crucial cheer at 37 kilometres. Martin and Gynn report that their two boys, Georgios and Nikolaos, went on to do "quite well in life". Spiridon did less well, eventually stumbling into real poverty. He was arrested for forgery in 1925 and jailed, but was found innocent and acquitted in March 1926. The following year he was left a heart-broken man when Eleni died from diabetes.

At the 1936 Berlin Olympics, the German Olympic Committee rediscovered Louis and invited him to the Games, to celebrate the 40th anniversary of his run. The 63-year-old Louis carried his nation's flag and afterwards was escorted to Hitler's viewing box. There, the two men could be compared and contrasted. Hitler in his military uniform, Louis in his humble native Greek costume – no knee-length leather boots for him. Louis presented Hitler with an olive branch from the Sacred Grove of Zeus at Olympia. Many German journalists craved his tale of his Olympic triumph, which he was happy to tell.

In 1895 Louis was finishing his military service in Athens as a groom for the horses belonging to Gen. Mavromichalis. The spot where the Olympic stadium was being constructed was pointed out to Spiridon, and he was sufficiently

---

8. Travelling up to 14 kilometres at a time, trotting beside his horse that carried the load, is one clear reason how Louis became such a competent distance runner.

A contrast in men: at the opening ceremony of the 1936 Berlin Olympics, Louis, a forgotten figure, was reintroduced to the world when Adolf Hitler presented him with a bouquet. *IOC/Olympic Museum/Getty Images*

inspired to try to become a part of the festival. On the night before the Olympic marathon Louis remembers travelling from Amarousion by horse-drawn cart in the rain for five hours until reaching the village of Marathon. Not for him, though, an early night in preparation for the big race. "What did we know about the rules of training and proper diet?" Louis later said. "We sang and ate and laughed until late in the evening." Recalling the moments after his victory, Louis said: "That hour was something unimaginable and it still appears to me in my memory like a dream. People were calling my name. Twigs and flowers were raining down on me. Everybody was calling out my name and throwing their hats in the air...Afterwards it was printed in the papers that I asked for horses and a wagon as a reward and also received them, but it is untrue." Louis reminisced on how his father did buy three barrels of wine and spread their contents freely at an open celebration.

Louis Spiridon died on March 27th, 1940, of an apparent heart attack, whereupon his name entered the Greek language in the expression *"egine Louis"*, which came to mean "ran quickly". His beautiful grave may be found in the local cemetery at Amaroussion. After his marathon triumph, Louis never ran competitively again.

Race result:

Spiridon Louis	GRE	2:58:50
Kharilaos Vasilakos	GRE	3:06:03
Gyula Kellner	HUN	3:06:35
Ioannis Vrettos	GRE	no time
Eleitherios Papasimeon	GRE	no time
Dimitrios Deligiannis	GRE	no time
Evangelos Gerakakis	GRE	no time
Stamatios Masouris	GRE	no time
Sokratis Lagoudakis	GRE	no time

Note: Spiridon Belokas (GRE) finished third (3:06:30) but was later disqualified.

Sources:

Anninos, C. "Description of the Games", in C. Beck, ed., *The Olympic Games 776 BC – AD 1896*, London: H. Grevel & Co., 1896.

Anonymous article in the *The Times*, April 12th, 1896.

Hauman, Riël, *Century of the Marathon*. Human & Rousseau, 1996.

Kitson, J., "The Battle of Marathon", at http://herodotus website.co.uk (April 12th, 2003).

Martin, David and Roger Gynn, *The Olympic Marathon*. Human Kinetics, 2000.

Morites, K. *Spiridon Louis – A Legend in the Olympic Games, 1896–1996*. John Faxdekis, Athens, 1997.

Lennartz, K. "Following the footsteps of Bréal", *Journal of Olympic History* 6 (2): 8–10.

Wallechinsky, David, *The Complete Book of the Olympics*, Aurum Press, 2000.

Zur Megede, E. *The First Olympic Marathon Century 1896/1996*, Deutsche Gesellschaft für Leichtathletik-Dokumentation, Cologne, 1999.

IV

No. 47 – 1954 British Empire and Commonwealth Games Marathon [Men]

Saturday, August 7th

"Don't be a coward...This will be the last one...Bloody daft."

In June 1953 the German distance runner and journalist Willy B. Wange wrote an article about his thoughts of the Polytechnic Marathon in England in which he had recently run, with particular emphasis on whether the course was perhaps a little short, or maybe a little downhill, or if, just conceivably, the astounding times recorded by the Englishman James Peters were merely the result of the athlete's brilliance.

Wange had arrived at Victoria station the night before the marathon, excited by his upcoming adventure in a race that boasted 50 years of history. Just as Wange was wondering what to do next as he stood shivering on the cold, deserted platform, a man appeared carrying a sign: "Marathon Race Poly Harriers". The bearer of this placard was the Dave Bedford of his day: race director and formerly top British distance runner Sam Ferris – eight-times winner of the "Poly". A superb marathoner of his time, like Bedford, Ferris was unable ever to quite master the Olympics (see Chapter 38 for more on one of Britain's finest ever marathoners).

Through streets of merry turmoil the two travelled (they were being decorated for Elizabeth II's coronation), until Wange arrived at his host's house. The hospitality was first-class, but unfortunately for Wange, breakfast the next morning consisted of a tasty British delicacy of fried whale flesh (Britain was experiencing meat shortages at the time). This severely disagreed with the German's stomach and he had no option but to drop out of the marathon at halfway.

"Was my journey to England of no purpose because of this?" asks Wange. "I do not think it was completely so. I saw not only the fastest marathon ever run, but also proved that the standard of the British long-distance runner has reached what to us is an incredibly high level, and that our scepticism of the previous year's performance by Peters, Iden and Cox was without foundation. Peters' time of 2.29.28 in 1951 and his fantastic time of 2.20.42 last year (despite his failure at Helsinki[1]) show what a wonderful runner he is."

---

1. The 1952 Olympic marathon at which Peters had a woeful time (see Chapter 48).

Wange then goes on, importantly, to submit crucial evidence that the Brits weren't producing stellar times on "iffy" courses:

We in Germany explained this amazing time by saying "the course is all downhill," and "the prevailing wind is always from behind." Partly whilst running and partly whilst riding, I have seen the course with my own eyes. The first 10 kilometres is a none too easy up and down stretch such as is not to be found everywhere in Germany. Then the course is flat with occasional downhill sections. It is also admitted that last year there was a slight following wind.

It is all the more remarkable that Peters has now achieved the incredible time 2:18:40 for this year when there was definitely a noticeable head wind. One can accept the accuracy of the timing (for which the British association is recognized) because the AAA, in view of the time, caused the course to be measured again and found the distance to be 196 metres too long.

Thus Germany, and the world in general, slowly came to accept that Jim Peters was truly a star and fully deserved all the accolades going for his splendid feats.

James Audsley of *Athletics Weekly* wrote of the occasion when the 2:20 mark fell in the marathon for the first time: "There is little doubt that, nowadays, the highlight of the Kinnaird athletics meeting is the Polytechic Marathon run in conjunction with it: but it is a highlight that it will be impossible to describe adequately until some genius invents a few new superlatives suitable for the running of J. Peters."

Peters was a leading figure in the *Daily Express*'s "Sports Personality Parade", mixing it with the likes of "mighty" Ben Hogan and "fiery" Fred Trueman.[2] Said the *Express*:

Jim Peters runs the Windsor to Chiswick marathon in the world's fastest time and everyone sits back and gasps. Everyone, that is except Jim Peters. The 34-year-old Mitcham optician just says: "I'm a little stiff" and strides out from his Chadwell Heath, Essex home with son Tobin on a four-mile, Sunday morning walk.

Nine-stone Peters remembers instead that he did not win at Helsinki. And he swears revenge. He trains every lunch hour, every evening. He will be out at midday today, adding another six miles to the 3,200 he has clocked in the 411 runs since September.

The Peters 1956 Olympic plan is the secret he discovered on Saturday: start slowly. "I burned myself out before, trying to smother them all from the start," he says.

Famous last words.

It turned out that the great run at the "Poly" in 1953 was just Peters warming up. In July he won the AAA marathon champs at Cardiff in 2:22 (in torrential rain), and then went to the famous Enschede Marathon in September and ran 2:19:22, a course record that stood for no less than 17 years, before fellow Briton

---

2. The most prominent golfer and cricketer of the early 1950s.

Bernard Allen claimed it. And on October 4th he took five seconds off his world best in Turku, Finland.

In April of 1954 Peters endured a painful defeat at Boston as he charged far too aggressively at its hills at just the point Finland's Veikko Karvonen was experiencing tummy trouble and ran them very defensively. At the top of the hills Karvonen felt better whereas Peters felt "extraordinarily hot and tired" (Derderian) and collapsed over the finish line in 2:22:40, 2:01 behind the Finn. Perhaps he'd learn the lesson to be less brash on hot, hilly courses...

Peters dusted himself down after his Boston reverse and returned to the "Poly" in 1954. He promptly ran a sublime 2:17:39, a world record that stood for over four years before Sergey Popov of the USSR netted a 2:15:17 in Stockholm.

Until Paavo Kotila's 2:18:04 in 1956, the magic 2:20 mark had fallen just four times – all to Peters.

* * *

Peters had been a fine sportsman before the Second World War in both cricket and football, and the junior mile champion of his county, Essex. After he was demobbed in 1945, with a wife and young child and working as a dispensing optician, he still wanted to run again. He made sound progress that took him all the way to the 1948 Olympics whereupon he finished a disappointed ninth in the 10,000-metres final. On the train home from Wembley his coach Johnny Johnston pushed aside any retirement thoughts, saying, "If you want to run in another Olympic games, old boy, it will have to be in the marathon" (*The Times*, January 13th, 1999). And so it was. Jim Peters became a marathoner.

In the February 14th, 1953 edition of *Athletics Weekly,* Peters wrote a fascinating essay on the art of marathoning, and it is remarkable how much of his advice is still sound today. Here are some highlights:

There is no doubt in my mind that this is the most arduous of all the events and requires an enormous amount of preparation over a very long period for any hope of success and a reasonable, comfortable journey when actually competing over the full distance.

What is required of the young athlete with marathon ambitions is an "apprenticeship". The faster you can run 3 and 6 miles, the faster you will run the marathon. Therefore the first target for the marathon man is to acquire the "run a day" habit until 350 runs a year is just bread and butter to him.

In the winter he should help himself and his club by engaging in a full cross-country season. In his early 20s his summer competition season should be plenty of 880 yards and miles. Go for, and master, a 2.02 half and 4.25 mile. If you can even do better, all well and good. Between age 24 and 28 make your presence felt in 2, 3 and 6 miles in the summer. From 28 you will then be ready for all the physical strain that will be necessary to do that 2.30 marathon.

Over 50 years after these words were written, it is hard to quibble with anything. The author only wishes he'd followed the advice more closely.

What was Peters' running style like? Willy Wange writes: "He has a peculiar running style. He continuously moves his body to and fro. He does not appear in any way cramped and, on the contrary, has a wonderful free and easy style. He runs not only with the legs, but forces himself forward with the body." Peters' obituary in *The Times* amusingly explained: "his upper body action was so unwieldy – he hummed Al Jolson to himself to cope with the tedium – that he has been called 'the first rock'n'roll athlete.' " Race photos prove that sometimes his arm action across his body was so pronounced that his thumbnail driving across his chest caused it to bleed through his running vest.

*   *   *

In the build-up to the 1954 British Empire and Commonwealth Games to be held in Vancouver, Peters had two things on his mind, both of which infuriated him. First was that the marathon race had been set for 12 midday, "or perhaps more appropriately High Noon" as one commentator, Derek Young, has written. Problem two, and of even greater frustration, was that when Peters inspected the course with his teammate (the redoubtable Stan Cox) in a car, they found 27 miles clocking up on the odometer time and again. Frank Rostron of the *Daily Express* wrote:

> "Thirty-five-year-old Peters told me the night before the race, when he was a gay spectator at the boxing finals: 'I am still convinced the course is slightly over-long but it doesn't matter because it is so hilly that it will be impossible to put up a good time. In the circumstances I might as well run 27 miles as well as 26 miles and 385 yards.' "

But when your body is programmed to go a certain distance and it suddenly has another five minutes of running to contend with, you could be asking for trouble. When Peters duly submitted a complaint, Alex Frew, chairman of the Games marathon committee measured it, and sure enough 27 miles clocked up, but Frew said, with chilling nonchalance, "well, no car is accurate". Officials were then called upon to officially remeasure, and they claimed the course was just 83 metres too long and reset the finish line. Peters found this outcome almost laughable, but it proved no laughing matter in the week ahead.

On the night before the race, a third "niggle" became apparent to Peters: the superb fitness of teammate Cox who had been starting to show him a clean pair of heels in training and, in particular, had been merrily devouring any undulations they ran. "Such were the weighty thoughts on the mind of the favourite before the race," comments Young. "To coin a phrase, the head on the favourite's pillow rarely sleeps easily."

Saturday morning dawned hot from the outset as Peters' first thought was: "Well, this is the day you've come six thousand miles for." Sun wear could have been a good idea but in practice both Peters and Cox couldn't keep theirs on. Joseph McGhee of Scotland wore his for the first half of the race before "it nearly drove him crazy and he got rid of it" (Young). "No records, today, Jimmie," said the British manager to Peters at the start, "Look at this sun. Just go steady."

The gun, and the early miles, flicked past with Peters and Cox at the helm, with

McGhee joining them to form a British trio. No sign of the more cautious/prudent Australians or capable South Africans Barnard and Mekler, who surely would have been more confident with the heat than the former three. At eight miles the flight lieutenant McGhee had enough of watching his fellow Brits tear chunks out of each other and fell back: "Then ahead of me Peters sprinted up a hill to surprise Cox. He did and went ahead. I didn't see much of them from then on."

Interval running such as this is exhausting at the best of times; but this was surely the worst. By halfway McGhee was running at a pace barely above that of "survival shuffle", a steady pitter-patter which he knew he could just about maintain to the finish. Cox had dropped back as well, but felt that letting Peters get completely away would make it a *very* long run for home, knowing that the race was definitely lost. So he gritted his teeth and tried to keep the gap to around 300 yards. It was a tactic that was key in curtailing one of the greatest running careers of all time.

Three miles later Peters looked around and was astounded to find that the gap between him and Cox remained under a quarter of a mile. "This really disturbed me," he explains, "for I knew that Stan was a world class marathon runner and was much too close for comfort at this stage of the race" (Young). Peters decided to turn the screw even more, which spelt the end for the valiant Cox. But the favourite was dangerously over-heating. He relied heavily on sponges, but when given them at the feeding stations found them almost dry. "On I went – up what felt like a little mountain, I grunted and groaned as I plodded up the slope. I learned later I must have got nearly a mile in front of Stan, but at that time I still pictured him hot on my heels" (Young). As he entered into the last few miles, Peters explains that if he had only known that poor Cox had run into a telephone pole and collapsed from sunstroke, and that his lead was nearly $3\frac{1}{2}$ miles, then he could have stopped at the last feeding station, had a good sponge down, and trotted in slowly.

Another man who didn't have all the facts was McGhee, who went by the Australian Lawrence at about 19 miles, sitting forlorn on the pavement, but able to muster a "keep going, Jock." McGhee goes on to relate: "There's an old wives' tale that I'm supposed to have fallen into a ditch and an old Scotswoman told me the news about Peters. At this point I'm supposed to have jumped up and raced on. It's simply not true. I first knew about Peters when I was about a quarter of a mile from the stadium" (Young).

In Peters' bewildered and boiling mind was the thought: 'You can't give up now. Don't be a coward. This will be the last one. Bloody daft. Get this one over and we'll call it a day." He relates: "I came into the gates of the stadium. In front of me was the very steep ramp we had to climb on the way out. As I approached the top of it I remember wobbling a little again but I wasn't unduly concerned – after all, I was tired, desperately tired. I knew that" (Young). The next three minutes are now the stuff of legend, not only etched on the minds of every one of the 35,000 spectators there that day, but on the millions who saw newsreel of the footage. A little earlier in the afternoon Roger Bannister and John Landy had fought out their magical battle over the mile in which Bannister had just edged out his great rival. The euphoric crowd were ready for more drama. When Peters appeared they rose to pay tribute to another fine British sportsman. But they were quickly silenced.

Heading for the shadows: his mind is fried but instinct tells Jim Peters to hobble towards the comforting shade of the grandstand. *Bettmann/CORBIS*

Usually when Peters entered the stadium at the end of a marathon, he would give a little wave to the crowd to show them he was fine. No wave came. "I was thinking 'Well, Jimmy boy, you know you're really tired this time. Don't bother to wave; don't kid them. Get on and do those last 380 yards.'" But suddenly crash. Peters hit the deck. "I was completely bewildered. Then I made up my mind I was going to finish. I didn't want to disgrace my wife and kiddies. I thought of them and said to myself 'I'm going on; there's a tape you've got to break; you don't stop until you hit that tape.'"

The tape was there, shimmering in the distance for Peters to see – a white ribbon of relief. To Peters it seems like he fell another couple of times trying to reach it. In fact he fell more like a dozen. But each and every time he'd pull himself slowly to his feet, wobbly legs and bleary-eyed. He did not see his friend John Savidge and other teammates thumping the ground on the track beside him, imploring him, *begging* him to reel in the steps to the finish yard by yard. Alarmingly Peters suddenly veered wildly off course – almost at right angles to the finish line he made for the grandstands. He had recalled how when he had run in the 6-mile race the week before that it had been much shadier under the stand. Then hands took hold of him and he passed out.

Eighteen minutes after Peters had reached the stadium, enter Joe McGhee.

38

The British team physician mistakenly thinks Peters has arrived at the finish and beckons him into his arms. But the finish is still 200 yards away. *Bettmann/CORBIS*

"Vividly I can remember seeing the smile on Ewan Douglas's face [a Scot hammer thrower] as I ran in," McGhee recalls. "It could have been disbelief. Then he did a dance which struck me as being extraordinary for such a huge fellow" (Young). McGhee padded along towards the tape that had proved so elusive to Peters, breasted through it, and became the second Scot to take the title.[3] Has there ever been a less recognized, less well-known marathon victor in a major championship? But it is the way of sport that there are times when the man who loses gains more in stature, notoriety and wealth than the man who wins, through no fault of the winner. This was such an occasion.[4]

McGhee had 1:19 to spare over Jack Mekler of South Africa. In third place, the extreme conditions caused Johannes Barnard to run more than 26 minutes slower than the national record time that had won him the South African trial race earlier in the year.

When Peters "came to" in the dressing room, he found a nurse watching over him and he asked anxiously, "Did I win?" She smiled down and, killing him with

3. The first was Duncan McLeod Wright at the inaugural Empire Games of 1930 in Hamilton, Ontario, in a time just four minutes slower than McGhee's.
4. The golfers Jean Van der Velde and Paul Lawrie know all about this from the farcical scenes at the 1999 British Open, when Van der Velde lost his mind – and a three-stroke lead – at the final hole.

kindness, said, "You did very well." Predictably, the media got very squeamish and moral about the whole affair. "I never want to watch such torture again," yelped Frank Rostron on the front page of the *Daily Express*:

> I have seen and personally experienced some sickeningly gory injuries in the boxing ring. I have seen piteously exhausted marathon runners go delirious on the course and qualify for a strait-jacket. But I cannot recall anything quite so shocking as the spectacle poor semi-conscious Jim Peters was allowed to make for 19 minutes of agony in the Empire Games marathon yesterday.
>
> If you think I exaggerate I can only say that more than a score of women fainted at the dreadful sight of the three-parts unconscious Peters staggering and falling, staggering and falling, getting up, crawling, pawing the air, and stumbling blindly like some maimed animal as he tried to reach the tape at the end of the marathon."

The *Express* went on to report how Mrs Sandy Duncan, wife of the England team's manager, had to leave the royal box in which Prince Philip gazed with "fascinated peturbation".

In the *Daily Telegraph* Jack Crump wrote:

> No-one, except the great runner Jim Peters that is, would have given every ounce of energy in an endeavour to bring honour to his country in his poignant failure.
>
> It requires a man of rare physical courage to run himself into a state of utter and complete exhaustion, and it is of little account that in forcing the pace so relentlessly – and taking an unnecessarily long lead – he may have been the victim of an error of judgment.
>
> Peters is unable to run his big races in any other way. He trains hard and conscientiously for a race and, once in it, gives of his all. This attitude towards his sport has brought Peters well-earned fame and the distinction of being the world's fastest-ever marathon runner.
>
> A more genuine sportsman I have never known, certainly no one with finer team spirit and physical and mental courage.
>
> British athletes everywhere will share this sympathetic tribute to him.

*   *   *

Peters, who ran most of his career in simple Dunlop plimsolls reflected in 1996: "We were the good, old-fashioned amateurs, but the modern, well-paid athletes, good luck to them all, still have our old spirit. When the gun sounds you go out there to kill or be killed." This story has a sad ending on top of the sad ending, so to speak, in that Peters never did run another marathon (least of all the European championships he'd been signed up for a mere 18 days later), and did in fact announce his retirement later that year.

But there is a heart-warming postscript to offer. Derrick Young writes:

"In 1967, Peters returned to Vancouver and paid for his wife and family's air

At the 1996 London Marathon, Jim Peters (left) met up with Joe McGhee and they relived their memories from 42 years before. *Chris Cole/EMPICS*

fares to join him as, at nearly 50 years of age and before a crowd of 21,000 at a ball game, he went out on that track and ran that last lap again.

"The cheers were the same, the tears in the eyes of those who watched were the same. Says Peters: 'it was like the ghost came back.'"

But this time the ghost finished.

Race result:

Joseph McGhee	SCO	2:39:36
Jack Mekler	RSA	2:40:57
Johannes Barnard	RSA	2:51:49
Barry Lush	CAN	2:52:47
George Hillier	CAN	2:58:43
Robert Crossen	NI	3:00:12

Sources:

Anonymous, in the *Daily Express*, June 14th, 1953.

Audsley, Jim, in *Athletics Weekly*, June 16th, 1953.

Crump, Jack, in the *Daily Telegraph*, August 9th, 1954.

Derderian, Tom, *Boston Marathon*. Human Kinetics, 1996.

Hauman, Riël, *Century of the Marathon*. Human & Rousseau, 1996.

Obituary, in *The Times*, January 13th, 1999.

Peters, Jim, in *Athletics Weekly*, February 14th 1953.

Rostron, Frank, in the *Daily Express*, August 7th & 9th, 1954.

Wange, Willy, in *Athletics Weekly*, June 23rd, 1953. (Originally published in Germany).

Young, Derrick, *The Ten Greatest Races*. A.C.M. Webb Publishing, 1972.

V

No. 46 – 2003 London Marathon [Men]

Sunday, April 13th

From humdrum to humdinger.

The World Cup soccer final of 1994 at the Rose Bowl in Pasadena, California, was played between the world's two most colourful and superior sides, Italy and Brazil. It was the final the organizers had dreamed about; if this couldn't convert a sceptical, indifferent American public into soccer fans, nothing could. As it turned out, that single game probably drove more nails into the American soccer watcher's coffin than any before or since; the two sides, terrified to attack and risk the consequences, produced a toothless 0–0 bore-draw. "*Now* do you see why we hate this game?" a hundred million Americans asked. However, throughout the tedious 120 minutes of play, one delicious treat shimmered on the horizon. Penalties. "Yee-hah! Way to go! This is more *like* it!" The Americans got their – albeit brief – serving of drama after all.

For 120 minutes, the 2003 London Marathon was as equally defensive, drab and gutless as that World Cup Final nearly a decade before. But one couldn't leave the action. Because one knew that once those two hours were over, then there was a treat to come every bit as exciting as a penalty shoot-out.

* * *

After a glorious three-year spell in which race director Dave Bedford had attracted outstanding fields to run the streets of the capital (including the 'Greatest Marathon Race of All Time', see Chapter 50), the wheels came off slightly for the 2003 edition with the world record holder Khalid Khannouchi withdrawing a few weeks before the race with acute tonsilitis, and then a "gutted" triple champ Antonio Pinto having to pull out with a tweaked hamstring just days before the race.[1]

Shortly before race day Bedford came out with a not totally convincing pep talk, still insisting his would be a marathon to savour: "It is a shame that Khalid has had to pull out, but we still have a strong race with the Olympic and world

---

1. According to one source, Pinto had been going better than ever in training, including one workout of 50 times 400-metres in 64 seconds with 20 second recoveries. Even Emil Zátopek would have been taking a few deep breaths before that.

champion Gezahegne Abera, up against the second-fastest man in history, Paul Tergat." True enough, but it did seem as though this could be a fairly forgettable year with the absence of two such superb and aggressive runners in Pinto and Khannouchi. And forgettable is what it was. Nearly.

Bedford's major ace up his sleeve was the reigning world and Olympic champion. What sort of a man is Gezahegne Abera? And why was he so favoured to win when his best time was only the eleventh best of the race's starters, and when his best of 2:07:54 ranked him a mere 89th fastest of all time? For some answers the *Daily Mail*'s Neil Wilson travelled to Addis Ababa to track down the man known as "Geza".

Wilson painted a very real picture of the backdrop in which Geza underwent his training: "The Sandafa Road above Ethiopia's capital city is a cesspit of squalor. Children in torn, ragged clothes collect animal droppings with bare hands to fuel family fires. Dung beetles feast in shallow pits outside the doors of the mud-walled shacks. Mangy dogs are everywhere." But from out of this haze of filth and decay, Wilson reports, a runner emerged in pristine white running kit and $200 custom-made shoes. Nobody gave him a second glance, just another athlete going about his trade. This particular runner, however, was a dollar millionaire – a far cry indeed from the national average income of £100. But his wealth isn't begrudged. In Geza's young life he has already donated more to famine relief than most of his compatriots will earn in a lifetime. Geza relates: "The people love me because they know I work hard and do a good job. I think they are proud of what I do. So I want to work harder, to do better to show to my people what is possible with hard work."

Abera is a simple country boy made good. He was brought up as one of eight children in the village of Etya in Arsi province, from where almost 90 per cent of the top Ethiopian runners hail. Working on his father's subsistence farm he would listen in wonder of tales of the great Abebe Bikila. He ran 25 kilometres to school and back each day (unlike most of the other pupils who were weekly boarders); and his family and friends soon had to adjust a well-known Ethiopian saying to apply to him. The phrase "He will come when you have made the coffee" were adapted in Geza's case to "He will come when you have finished the third coffee." For even when he returned home after this tough training, Abera would get straight to work ploughing the fields. He soon started testing himself in cross-country races, and his subsequent success attracted the attentions of the national junior coach. His father didn't want to let him go and travel to train and race, since he was such a good worker. But Abera explains: "Later, when I got the good results, he was touched and, I think, very proud."

After winning a hat-trick of marathons at Fukuoka by a combined total of just five seconds, a mere 20-second win at the Sydney 2000 Olympics, and gold at the 2001 World Championships by just one second over Kenya's Simon Biwott, one could be forgiven for feeling that he was either a very lucky runner or the supreme master tactician. But when one considers that Khalid Khannouchi – with a time some two minutes quicker than Abera – dropped out of the 2001 World Marathon, complaining "I can't run slowly", one feels it to be more of the latter. "I run to win the race," Abera explains. "If the race is fast, I can run fast. If it is slow, I can also run slow. If I follow a pace that is slow, I know I will win because

I can sprint faster than anybody. I always follow the pace. I can be flexible. Fast or slow."

And one thing's for sure in all sport: being a flexible tactician is a great attribute to have. If you're a "one-trick pony", it's impossible to make it at the highest level. And for anyone ignorant enough to accuse Abera of being a one-tricker, there is a simple response: he's made it at the highest level time and time again.

* * *

"The 23-year history of London Marathon had never seen a finish like it," wrote Steve Landells in *Athletics Weekly* after the 2003 London Marathon. "Five men entered The Mall shoulder to shoulder racing for victory. Few had ever witnessed such a close finish in the history of the marathon."

The elite men's race could not have contrasted more to Paula Radcliffe's destruction of the field in the women's race. Compared to Radcliffe who was fearless and brave, the men were cautious and circumspect. From the first mile the pace-makers – Kenyans Joseph Kariuki and Eluid Lagat – were restrained, covering the distance in 4:52. Indeed, the first half of the race was a largely featureless affair dominated by the pace-makers, as the bigger names, such as double London champ El Mouaziz, Tergat and Abera, preferred to hang back, spectating a few metres off the pace. A group of 20 athletes went through halfway in a reasonably quick 63:20 – but some 32 seconds slower than the field went through the midway mark 12 months earlier. At 15 miles, Lagat, the last of the pacemakers, dropped out and the race began in earnest, or so one thought. El Mouaziz, the London champ in '99 and '01, tried to stretch the main group only for the bunch to concertina a few hundred metres later.

Abdelkader El Mouaziz, twice a London champion, leads a large group over the cobbles four miles from home. The Olympic champion Gezahegne Abera is number one. Paul Tergat, Joseph Ngolepus and Stefano Baldini give chase.
Mark Shearman

Three miles later and it was the turn of another illustrious name to turn the screw. Lee Bong-ju was the 1996 Olympic silver medallist who fell just 3 seconds short of Josiah Thugwane in Atlanta in that gripping 1996 Olympic Marathon. He was also the 2001 Boston winner who finally put a halt to Kenyan domination of that race – Kenyans had won at Boston for a remarkable ten years in a row. However, Bong-ju, either through lack of confidence or fitness – we know it wasn't lack of ability – was comfortably reeled in after just a few hundred metres, and still the race stagnated – indeed, the split from miles 15 to 20 was the slowest 5-mile split in the race. What was going on? Surely the fireworks should have been going off by now. This was some waiting game.

Three miles from home El Mouaziz put in yet another burst to reduce the

With less than 50 metres to run it appears that Italy's Stefano Baldini has the smoother stride and is set to atone for his disappointment six years earlier when he placed second to Antonio Pinto. *Mark Shearman*

leading group to five – he was joined by Ngolepus, Baldini, Tergat and the wily Abera, who was always content to sit out of trouble at the back of the pack. Five became six as the unheralded 20-year-old Tanzanian Samson Ramadhani joined the lead group with the experience of only one previous marathon on his CV. Two kilometres to go and the pack, incredibly, was still bunched. Baldini, the 31-year-old World bronze medallist, who had so bravely tried to win the classic London of '97 before being outkicked by Pinto, finally became the first athlete to make a serious bid for home, and for the first time in the race, Abera began to take a much closer order. But still no *major* move.

In the final mile the five at the front (Ramadhani had temporarily dropped off the back) almost seemed resigned to the fact the race would be decided by a last-gasp kick. It seemed a clear display that no one had the confidence in attempting the most painful thing a distance runner can do: kick from a long way out. Instead, as Landells writes: "Like a long, drawn-out game of poker, not one of the athletes was prepared to show their hand and spectators and a worldwide TV audience had the exhilarating sight of six[2] athletes shoulder to shoulder rounding into The Mall in a straight shoot-out for victory."

Perversely, the only previous London victor in the quintet, El Mouaziz, was the first to blow, quickly followed by another hot favourite, Tergat, the five-times World Cross-Country champ and double Olympic silver medallist, who had now yet to win a marathon after five attempts, despite possessing the second fastest time in history and several other very fast ones. But his time, of course, would come.

Under the watchful gaze of Buckingham Palace, the 1998 European champion, Baldini, moved into the home-stretch and, for the second time in the day, made a strike for home; this time just 150 metres out. It seemed as though the race was his, as he pulled clear of Ngolepus (whose only previous win was the 2001 Berlin Marathon, after starting the race as pace-maker – much to Paul Tergat's irritation!). With less than 10 seconds left to run it certainly appeared as though Italy was set to celebrate its first London champion, but just as the commentators were starting to call him the winner, Baldini's stride faltered and history repeated itself from six years earlier: he was pipped into second place.[3]

---

2. Ramadhani had by now re-established contact.
3. Interestingly, two heartbreaking, heart-stopping second-place finishes at London, six years apart, is not a stunt Baldini is the first to pull. Australia's Steve Moneghetti did it in 1989 and 1995.

Abera wins the 2003 London marathon by a nod over Baldini, with Ngolepus and Tergat fading in the background. *Mark Shearman*

The master sprinter himself, Abera, had done it yet again, pulling out a devastating kick at the last moment and edging ahead of the brave Italian just a few metres from the line. The top two received the same time. Eternal runner-up Kenyan Paul Tergat trailed home fourth on this day two seconds behind Ngolepus with the fast finishing Ramadhani pipping El Mouaziz for fifth.

Evergreen *Europsport* commentator Tim Hutchings summed up his thoughts: "I've seen many, many marathons in my time, but never a finish like that." Reporter Steve Landells summarized by writing: "It may have lacked the quality and super-quick time of 12 months ago...but nobody will ever forget the epic finish to the men's race at the 2003 Flora London Marathon." As for race director Bedford, all the heartache over losing his leading players was forgotten – he had got his great race. He tells the author:

I don't think you can get anything more exciting than five people turning into The Mall together – having just dropped three people in the previous four hundred! Four other people had a chance as they came around that corner – to win it – and to beat the then current world and Olympic champion. By and large, London races are just that – they are close races. And that fits absolutely in with me – getting the best possible field together so that there is a real competition – a real race; opposed to one person being seen to be the fastest in the world and then making sure that person wins.

* * *

It had been quite a month for the Ethiopian men's distance-running fraternity after Gebrselassie's imperious destruction of the world's best over 3000 metres at the World Indoor Championships in Birmingham the previous month, and Kenenise Bekele's dominance in both long- and short-course races in the World Cross-Country Championships in Lausanne. Speaking through an interpreter at the post-race press conference, Abera said: "I was always confident of my sprint finish, it is my style of running. There were so many in contention but I used my instinct to decide when to time my sprint and it worked to perfection." When quizzed about the threat around him in the closing stages he admitted: "I was aware of them. I knew Tergat could be a threat but I sensed he was a bit tired. The wind from 20 to 25 kilometres was bad, it was causing me problems."

But he looked a little embarrassed when compared with Gebrselassie, adding: "I don't think I've achieved what Haile has; he is a very great athlete." And when asked about whether he regarded himself as the world's best marathon runner he replied: "I'm not the one to say I'm the best in the world, my record will say that."[4]

As for poor Baldini, he was obviously having something of a déjà vu from six years earlier, and seemed to indicate that he was expecting a Geza onslaught: "I knew Abera was the strong guy with the fast finish. The mid-race attacks were hard and I couldn't get away when I wanted with 2 kilometres to go. "With 40 metres to go I thought I had won the race but I'm not too disappointed as it shows after six years I'm at the very top of my game."

Well, perhaps not quite the *very* top – but the Athens Olympics shimmered on the horizon.

Race result:

Gezahegne Abera	ETH	2:07:55
Stefano Baldini	ITA	2:07:55
Joseph Ngolepus	KEN	2:07:56
Paul Tergat	KEN	2:07:58
Samson Ramadhani	TAN	2:08:00
Abdelkador El Mouaziz	MOR	2:08:02
Lee Bong-ju	KOR	2:08:09
Hendrick Ramaala	RSA	2:08:57
Ian Syster	RSA	2:09:17
Javier Corters	ESP	2:10:38

Sources:

Conversations with David Bedford.
Athletics Weekly, October 4th, 2000.
Davies, Gareth, in the *Daily Telegraph*, April 15th, 2003.
Knight, Tom, in the *Daily Telegraph*, April 11th, 2003.
Mackay, Duncan, in the *Guardian*, April 14th, 2003.
Landells, Steve, in *Athletics Weekly*, April 17th, 2003
Wilson, Neil, in the *Daily Mail*, April 8th, 2003.

---

4. Abera's fiancée, Elfenesh Alemu, finished eighth in the women's race. When he later married her, the ceremony took place at the national football stadium to accommodate a crowd of 25,000, so huge was their popularity. Elfenesh's train on her wedding dress was an incredible 300-metres long, and entered the *Guinness Book of Records* as the world's longest ever train (surpassing Princess Diana's). Elfenesh went on to win the Tokyo Marathon – minus, sadly, the train.

VI

No. 45 – 2000 Boston Marathon [Women]

Monday, April 17th

Olympic champion hunted by the crazy one.

Winning the Boston Marathon four times is hard enough – only three men have done it, Clarence DeMar, Gerard Cote, and Bill Rodgers – but winning it four times in a row is something that has thus far proved impossible. And goodness, how the folk who have won it three times on the bounce have tried to add that fourth.

DeMar lost to the quirky antics of Chuck Mellor by just 33 seconds in 1925, the victor chewing tobacco during the run and stuffing a copy of the *Boston Globe* down his front to keep warm. Next to try four wins in a row was Bill Rodgers 56 years later, but as he had predicted after his '79 Boston win, Toshihiko Seko would be nigh soon unbeatable, and he was in 1981, seeing Rodgers off by 68 seconds, with the talented Craig Virgin sandwiched between the two. Next up for trick of four Bostons in a row was the mercurial Cosmas N'deti of Kenya. He won Boston with ease and confidence from 1993 to 1995, and turned up for the 1996 Centennial race telling anyone who would listen that Jesus for one would make sure he won number four. But N'deti went off too fast and two of his cannier fellow Kenyans hauled him in (Moses Tanui was the winner).

What about Uta Pippig on the women's side? Surely she could win four in row. She'd had a bad cold in '94 but won there easily enough, and again in 1995. Her spellbinding antics of 1996 (see Chapter 44) were undertaken in very poor health, so surely with a little luck healthwise, number four was hers for the taking. But Uta endured a strange year since the '96 race. Pulling out of the Atlanta Olympic marathon after being the run-away leader at eight miles, she mysteriously disappeared from both the Olympics and the road-running scene for many months. But she came back to Boston to defend her title but had no answer to the South African duo of Elana Meyer and Colleen de Reuck, and no answer, too, for the winner that day – Olympic champion Fatuma Roba, who won again, then again.

In 2000, Roba was the surest favourite ever to win Boston four times on the trot: "The Boston Marathon will be historical not just to the people of Boston, but also to me and the people in my country. I know that I'm trying to make history," she explained. Mark Murphy wrote in the *Boston Herald*: "By most accounts, surprise will only register today if Roba isn't the first woman running into Copley Square this afternoon. She has developed that kind of hold, and affinity for, this marathon's undulating test."

One of Roba's main challengers for her crown was to come from the Kenyan Catherine Ndereba (pronounced dah-RAY-ba), who had excelled at the half-marathon distance on fast, flat courses where she could use her lethal kick. Perhaps, then, Boston wasn't quite her type of race, and evidence of that came when she only placed sixth the year before, despite being the only woman with Roba at the end of the hills at 21 miles the year before. "I didn't have any experience when I ran this race last year," Ndereba said. "I know I made mistakes, and I had to run with the result of my mistakes. I went too fast and paid the price for it. But I have changed my strategy." Playing down her chances, Ndereba, who had given birth to a baby, Jane, two years earlier, acknowledged: "What I know is that Roba is a wonderful runner. This course is not a problem for her."

Catherine Ndereba is a much-loved runner all over the world. Beneath the inscrutable exterior of those dark glasses and bandana/headband is a striking woman of feline beauty who has dedicated herself to the sport she loves to an extreme. "Crazy Ndereba, Crazy Ndereba, Crazy Ndereba," the children at Ngorano Secondary School used to chant as Catherine would awake early and slip out of her dorm in order to run before class. After class, she would partake in the workout set by her coach with the rest of her group; and then slip off to practise some more. The other girls didn't understand her, so they teased. "Some were runners, and not even *they* were able to understand what I loved," says Ndereba. "Something was in my blood. I could not part with it."

The same compulsion which drove Catherine to fetch water as a young girl in half the time her sisters required, or to finish sessions that would force others (both men and women) to drop out, pronounced itself in the starkest manner in the summer of 1998. Before that, though, in 1995, when she represented Kenya for the first time, and 1996, Catherine had become one of the world's leading road racers.[1] But in 1997 she hardly ran a step as she gave birth to baby Jane. To reach the top again would entail sacrifice and this manifested itself when, in 1998, she left her husband Anthony Maina and Jane back home in Kenya and set off alone to compete on the United States circuit. As journalist Lori Shontz pointed out in an article for the *Pittsburgh Post-Gazette*, there have been many others who have juggled the responsibilities of parenthood with running careers. Ndereba was something else, however:

> No one else has combined such a breath-taking performance with an ability to make casual acquaintances feel like life-long friends and a husband who gladly – and visibly – supports her career and helps raise their daughter.
>
>   This unprecedented combination has turned Catherine Ndereba and her husband into influential role models. They represent the modern Kenyan couple – and a whole new way for men and women to regard each other in Kenyan society.[2]

---

1. Ndereba won 13 of the 18 races she entered in 1996 and was the number two ranked road runner in the world.
2. A similar parallel on the European scene is Ireland's Sonia O'Sullivan, who almost snatched the gold medal at the Sydney Olympics in the 5000 metres, a year after giving birth to baby Ciara. However, it seems although O'Sullivan may not have

Ndereba met Anthony when they were both training to become prison wardens at a college in Nairobi in the summer of 1994. Anthony was soon attempting to charm her, but Catherine refused to be won over easily. While conversing with her in their informal mother tongue of Kikuyu, she would reply in the formal language of Swahili – thus keeping him at arm's length.[3] Slowly but surely Anthony won Catherine over, even resorting to polishing her shoes, according to Lori Shontz. After just missing the Kenyan team for the 1996 Olympics (though she was still named "Road Racer of the Year"), Ndereba and Anthony were married. However, easing down on her running was never an option for Catherine. "He could see what I had done," she explains, "I was double sure he would let me continue what I was doing." For his part Anthony concurs: "I said it in my heart – I should not discourage her. I should let her go until she feels it is enough." Although boasting no running history himself, Anthony started to run too, solely so Catherine would have a training partner.[4] Since giving birth, Catherine's career took off to untouched heights. "The problem with women, the problem is we men," said Mwaniki, Catherine's former coach. But, referring to Anthony, he said: "He is a great man. If it was not for him, she could not be going so far. Some men marry to retain a woman, to have her in her place."

* * *

If not Ndereba, then who else would be with Roba at the top of the hills deep into the Boston Marathon of 2000? A good bet would be South Africa's aforementioned Elana Meyer who knew the course as well as anyone and was runner-up to Pippig way back in 1995. Prior to the past year, marathon workouts had never been the focus of her training, but they were now: "I've made the decision to gear my training more to the marathon itself. I've done well on the Boston course in the past, but the first time I ran this race, it was without any experience. The part I consider encouraging about this is that I know I haven't run my best marathon yet. It's being there when it counts that's the important thing, and that's what I'll try to do today."

Whoever was with Roba come the top of heartbreak hill could count on their opponent gaining a second wind thanks to each year an Ethiopian waving a flag from the homeland. "That has always been a breaking point," said Roba, "Every year, people from Ethiopia are waiting for me there. Last year, I was completely tired, very exhausted by the time I got there, and it gave me a fresh start to see this. Their excitement got me going again." This was the tenth successive year that Kenya's men had prevailed at Boston, but their women had yet to score a single win. And they weren't expected to here, what with Roba on the prowl.

In the early miles Ndereba displayed a confidence that is such a feature of her running. She was seen to be well off the lead pack of Roba, Bogacheva, Meyer,

lost her speed with childbirth, her endurance has been affected. Since Sydney, O'Sullivan had another child, Sophia, and at the World Championships of 2003 she suffered badly in the final (after coping well in her heat), trailing in a distant last. It seems she just didn't have the stamina to cope with two gruelling races in three days. O'Sullivan tried the marathon (NYC in 2002), but her sub par 2:32 also showed that perhaps she just hadn't been able to put in the miles necessary, whilst bringing up two small children. Mere speculation, though, and she did find her way to a 2:29 at London in 2005.
3. Similar to a French speaker using the formal *vous* instead of the familiar *tu*.
4. He even claims he can now beat her in the shorter distances, but cannot touch her in the marathon.

Classic duel: the Olympic champion and three-time Boston winner, Fatuma Roba, left, came to the Millennium race seeking her fourth win in a row, but she knew the inscrutable Catherine Ndereba would keep her busy. *Victah Sailer, Photo Run*

Sun Yingje of China, and Anuta Catuna of Romania, who ran together for the first 16 miles. Unlike some of the "bluffers" in that pack, Ndereba was sure that she could run just as fast for the second half of the race as for the first.

Roba appeared to be on a familiar churning pace when she pulled away from the pack entering the hills in Newton. She was turning the marathon footrace into something it is almost anything but – predictable and routine. By the 18th mile her lead was substantial. But just two miles later Ndereba had appeared and was running tight on Roba's shoulder. For the next several miles the crowd were treated to a riveting duel between Roba and the pretender to her throne. Any betting person would surely have favoured the Olympic champion to secure her fourth Boston on the spin. She looked just as she did in the past three years – cool, calm and assured. But she could not shake her rival. The television race commentary summed up the swelling drama: "Why do people stand in the freezing cold for three hours? Because every now and then you get to see a finish like this!"

There was, however, a chink of light for Ndereba. At the World Championships the previous summer in the crippling heat of Seville, Roba seemed to be on her way to a convincing win as, by 35 kilometres, she had built a convincing lead, which was stretching. But then suddenly and without warning, Roba visibly started to tie up and her lead began to shrink. Feisty Asian pursuers hove into view. By 40 kilometres a capitulating Roba was 30 seconds off the pace and in danger of not even getting a medal. No one had ever seen her display weakness like this before in a major marathon. Korea's Song-Ok Jong eventually won that race in a thrilling battle with Japan's Ari Ichihashi coming in just three seconds down. And Roba, who ended up over a minute off the winner, did indeed miss out on a medal as Romania's Lidia Simon-Slavuteanu comfortably defeated her.

But surely Roba would have been so shaken by that defeat as to not allow it to occur again – especially only some months later. But as 25 miles was approached, slowly, surely and incredibly, Ndereba started to edge ahead, almost imperceptibly at first, but five metres turned into 10, and then into 20. Roba was slowly being asphyxiated out of the race, as "Catherine the Great", as her fans liked to call her, was using her superior finishing speed to great effect. All the way down Boylston Street and the last half-mile of the race, the gap grew metre by metre

52

Ndereba wins a gruelling race, while in the background the startling battle for silver nears its conclusion. *Victah Sailer, Photo Run*

until it was suddenly clear that Roba was a deposed champion. The result had been in doubt until the final 250 metres, until finally Ndereba could relax, safe in the knowledge that she had fulfilled one of her favourite phrases: "If I have nothing to sacrifice, I have nothing to gain." Her splits for the race make interesting reading: 1:13:05 and 1:13:06. People have faded worse than this in marathons...

Mark Murphy wrote in the *Herald*:

Catherine ran the course in strap-on sunglasses which gave her a distinctively mysterious look. By the time this 27-year-old member of the Nairobi Police Deparment removed the shades and took the medal stand in Copley Square for her Boston Marathon coronation, the secret was exposed. Tears started to leak out.

"I was surprised to get No. 1 in Boston," Ndereba said.

It's not something that I expected, but I've worked hard for it. I prayed to God for it, and that's why the tears came out, because I was very happy and overwhelmed. I feel good, and I think each and every one in my country is feeling the same thing.

I ran with a high pace last year, but I faded in the last six miles. So this year I took my own pace, and in the last half of the race I was much stronger. I had the confidence in me that I could do the last half of the race in less than 73 minutes. I've run 69:30 in the half-marathon, so I had confidence in myself for this.

In the process I beat [Roba], something I could not have expected. Even when I came here, I wasn't thinking that I would keep her from that, because she's been winning here for a long time."

There was an extraordinary twist to the end of the race after Ndereba had completed her work. Roba, indefatigable Roba, didn't come second! How is that after one of the greatest female duels in marathon history, with no other runners making their presence felt for many, many miles, did the Olympic champion find herself getting served a dose of bronze? "I'd been leading for a few miles and it's very unfortunate that I finished third," said Roba. "I did not have any problems. The only obstacle was the weather – we do not have weather like this in Ethiopia."

Irina Bogacheva, a 38-year-old resident of Kyrgyzstan, had won seven marathons over the last three years including marathon titles in Los Angeles, Honululu and San Diego last year. But her ability to close on Ndereba and Roba over the last four miles from a distant third appeared to catch the two front runners by surprise. And Bogacheva's ability to pull even with Roba and lean across the line for second place was one of the day's most dramatic results. It was, as the race commentary said, "the most remarkable finish for second ever."

But whose torso really did cross the line first? Was the finish the delightful, canary-yellow and blue paintwork which the BAA lavishly splash onto Boylston street every year,[5] in which case the nod should go to Roba; or is the finish line the one metre further on, where electronic mats are placed to take a reading off the runners' electronic "championchips"? Certainly no one in the supposedly well-informed commentary box consisting of Bill Rodgers, Joan Benoit Samuelson and Marty Liquori had the faintest notion.

According to Steve Vaitones, the managing director of USA Track and Field in New England, the three finish-line timers, as well as Vaitones, all saw Bogacheva as second. "Bogacheva was running faster at that point, and her torso was the first of the two to cross the line." Television footage shows Roba's shoe strike the finishing mat clearly before Bogacheva's, and the runner's chips indicated Roba got second too. But Vaitones was undismayed: "Chip decisions have been reversed in the past. The chip makes no difference in something like this." The drop in prize money from second to third was a cool $17,500 – from $40,000 to $22,500. (Ndereba collected $80,000 for the win.)

As for one of the pre-race favourites, Elana Meyer, her year of training solely for the marathon helped not one bit and she trailed in a dismayed tenth.

* * *

As alluded to earlier, this race propelled Ndereba straight on the road to greatness, and in the years 2002 and 2003 she was the only woman marathoner who could present times that consistently could be spoken of with similar admiration to those of Paula Radcliffe.[6] It is accurate to say that Fatuma Roba, along with Tegla Loroupe, was one of greatest female marathoners of the late 1990s, and that for the first two-three years of the new millennium Catherine Ndereba was the premier exponent of the sport, before being shunted from that position in spectacular fashion by Paula Radcliffe in 2002. But Ndereba, one should note, in the five years between 1999 to 2004 has run over four times as many marathons as Radcliffe and has won nearly four times as many, too.

It's hard to select Ndereba's finest hour as there seem to have been so many. But obviously her electrifying world best of 2:18:47 set at Chicago in 2001 is a stand-out, just six days after Naoko Takahashi had become the first woman to break 2:20. Shontz reports the reaction of Hellen Kimayo, one of Kenya's most enduring female road racers: "I heard, and I was like, 'What?'...I had to take time to listen again and again and again...she was only a mile or so behind the men!"

_____

5. It would be interesting to see the London Marathon organizers try the same approach on The Mall, right under Buckingham Palace's nose.
6. *Athletics Weekly* named Ndereba the eigth greatest female marathoner of all time in July 2003, behind Radcliffe, Waitz, Kristiansen, Mota, Benoit Samuelson, Loroupe and Takahashi (Uta Pippig and Lisa Martin-Ondieki made up the top ten).

For her part, the 29-year-old Ndereba said: "I could not believe my eyes when I saw that I ran under 2:19. For that barrier [2:20] to disappear, made it much easier."

After convincingly winning the 2003 World Championships Marathon, Ndereba came to the New York City 2003 race a hot favourite, but she placed a disappointed second (2:23:01) to countrywoman and key rival, Margaret Okayo (2:22:31), who also defeated her in the 2002 Boston race. Both were pre-selected for Athens Olympics 2004. Ndereba ran superbly in hot weather to win the 2004 Boston, but the Olympic gold medal was sadly just elusive in Athens (Chapter 30).

Nowadays, when Catherine goes to speak to the girls in Kenya's schools, there is a stark change in attitude from her own schooldays. "I see the young girls, and they get more focused," she said. "They would not call me Crazy Ndereba anymore."

Race result:

Catherine Ndereba	KEN	2:26:11
Irina Bogacheva	KYR	2:26:27
Fatuma Roba	ETH	2:26:27
Anuta Catuna	ROM	2:29:46
Lornah Kiplagat	KEN	2:30:12
Ai Dongmei	CHN	2:30:18
Ornella Ferrara	ITA	2:30:20
Sun Yingjie	CHN	2:31:22
Marta Tenono	ECU	2:31:49
Elana Meyer	RSA	2:32:09

Sources:

Archive race footage.
Athletics Weekly, July 9th, 2003.
Downes, Steven, in the *London Marathon News*, April 2003.
Huebner, Barbara, in the *Boston Globe*, April 17th, 2000.
Kimball, George, in the *Boston Herald*, April 18th, 2000.
Murphy, Mark, in the *Boston Herald*, April 17th & 18th, 2000.
Powers, John, in the *Boston Globe*, April 17th, 2000.
Ramsak, Bob, in *Athletics Weekly*, October 10th, 2001.
Shontz, Lori, in the *Pittsburgh Post-Gazette*, May 7th, 2002.

VII

No. 44 – 1970 Commonwealth Marathon [Men]

Thursday, July 23rd

"Take that!" The Flying Doc's finest hour.

"One of the kings of the marathon," is how American "king of the roads" Bill Rodgers describes Ron Hill, the hard-working, hard-drinking, and very, very hard-training textile chemist from Bolton, Lancashire. These days Hill is looked upon as something of a "nutter" by some of Britain's leading distance runners, which is a great shame. Yes, Hill is an offbeat character in many ways, but the fact that this side of his personality overshadows his tremendous achievements, spread over half a century of running, indicates that the British way is often to ridicule first and then ask questions later. But this correspondent knows whose shoes he'd rather be in: those of a man who won several major titles and pinged a 2:09 marathon; or someone sensible, steady and utterly sane who struts around with his head held high and a 2:23 marathon under his belt.

* * *

Hyde, Cheshire, February, 2004. The author greatly anticipated meeting Hill, with whom he was to spend the morning and, of course, share a daily run: an unbroken streak that has lasted over 40 years. I was dismayed to find Hill under the weather with a sore throat. The meeting would be less fun now, Hill probably less entertaining. What bad luck. But then it struck me. For Hill to be nursing a sore throat is like a baby nursing a bottle. Through the 800-plus pages of his autobiography there are probably about 275 sore throats. Hill was forever getting sick because he was forever running himself down: training with ferocious intensity – and frequency – and working like a dog, too, on minimal sleep.
  "How bad *is* the throat, Ron?" I asked.
  "Worst ever."
  I felt truly blessed.

* * *

Ronald Hill was born on September 25th, 1938 in Accrington, just east of Blackburn, Lancashire, and just south of Clayton-le-Moors; headquarters of the harriers club Hill would join as a youth. The first hero in Hill's life came in the fictional character, Alf Tupper, from the comic *Rover*, or "The Tough of the

Track". The hard-running, no-nonsense, straight-talking Tupper captivated Hill with his weekly sagas, and Thursday morning couldn't come soon enough. Hill hatched secret yearnings to be just like his hero. Who cares if he wasn't real? Hill would be the real life version.

Ron Hill had his first competitive athletic in his school cross-country day aged twelve. He found himself getting excited as the end of term approached and upon race day, when another boy bet him nine pence that he wouldn't finish in the top ten, Hill took him on. He placed ninth, was secretly very proud, and the running bug was caught.

Although Hill was an active boy, with a particular interest in trainspotting, he was frequently unwell, with either migraine or crippling stomach ache, which was to trouble him on and off for many years. But despite this, Hill still nursed a secret ambition to become a worthy runner. He writes in *The Long Hard Road*:

> My first positive step towards becoming a runner was in 1953. The desire must somehow have manifested itself to my mother because she told me to go and see Arthur Henderson, the son of a friend of hers, who was in Clayton-le-Moors Harriers. I did, he took me along to one of their Saturday afternoon runs, and I joined the club.

From here Hill raced for the sports club that belonged to the textile company Howard and Bullough. He placed second in his first race for them – a real thrill which focused him for sterner challenges ahead: like racing for Clayton in the boys' division in the East Lancashire Cross Country Championships, and then placing 81st in the Northern Counties event. This was a fair return and of importance to Hill in the latter event was a silver medal: Clayton were the second team.

By the season of 1956/57, Hill was captain of the Accrington Grammar School cross-country team and was training regularly. Hill was already becoming fastidious about keeping a training log: "I had always been a collector – train numbers, stamps, 'fag' packets, cheese labels, match box labels, letters, running race programmes – and now I am sure I was collecting training runs!" All this running didn't hinder his studies, however, and Ron Hill became, as author Tom Derderian would later write, "extraordinarily well-educated". He entered Manchester University on a Textile Finishing Trades Association Scholarship. Shunning university running at first, thinking the other runners would be "toffee-noses", Hill finally accepted an invitation to run for the university's second team. Real potential was quickly spotted as he placed 21st and 4th in his first two races. Promotion to the first team duly followed, as did another top-20 finish and third Manchester counter.

It's nothing new that Hill is seen as something a little removed from the norm. Even back in those days, he writes, "With my broad northern accent, I was something of an oddball, my curly Tony Curtis haircut contrasting with the more traditional parted styles, and my lack of worldly experience was sometimes embarrassing." But his running continued to improve. With a background of just 30 miles per week, Hill placed 14th in the Lancashire Senior Cross-Country Championships and fielded his first ever mention, of several hundred if not thousand to follow, from *Athletics Weekly*: "A stylish runner from Clayton-le-Moors, R. Hill, was third" (in the East Lancashire Junior race).

Hill was becoming ever more inspired and worked diligently at both his studies and his racing. By the summer of 1960 Hill had earned his degree, was dabbling in fell running and preparing to marry his childhood sweetheart, May. Hill and May found digs in Manchester and Hill was funded by the textiles firm Courtaulds to study for a doctorate; albeit for just £300 a year. He slipped into a regular way of life. Four miles at 6.30 a.m. every morning, and 13 training runs per week. The Hill acorn started to grow and grow. A second-place finish at the British Universities Cross-Country Championships was quickly followed by an inspirational anchor leg in the Hyde Park University relays. Taking off with the leader well out of sight, Hill brought his team home to victory by four ticks of the clock.

Although Hill was bossing his competitors at university level, success was coming a little harder in open competition; and in the 1961 National Cross he finished 81st. "How did you get on?" he was asked by the legendary Gordon Pirie. "Bloody awful," Hill replied, who suffered from gut ache for hours after the race. But he was determined to bounce back. One down, 113 to go, is what the date August 12th, 1961 means for Hill. It was his debut marathon. Hill writes: "I loved racing. Apart from exceptional circumstances like holidays, the thought of a weekend without a race was totally alien to me. For August 12th I could find no race in the adverts of *Athletics Weekly*. Only the Liverpool Marathon. I decided on that rather than not race at all."

With a sore right foot and sciatica, Hill hobbled to the start line. No question of him dropping out of the race before it had even begun. What about his morning run? Surely that would be cancelled with a marathon to run at 2 p.m. Not a bit of it; Hill just shaved it from four miles to two. On a hot day, Hill did arduous battle with John Tarrant, the previous year's winner before finally dropping him a little after 20 miles for the long, lonely slog home: "God, let the finish come quickly. I was getting pins and needles around my shoulders. I could see the floodlight gantries of Anfield, Liverpool's Football Ground. That was the finish. Down this street is the finish. No; a turn. Christ, this must be the last street! No; another turn. Where is it? Where is it? At last, no more turns; I was at the ground. My God, at bloody last!"

To a huge roar from Anfield's pre-season capacity crowd, Hill won the race by 2½ minutes in 2:24:22. Everything was tired – even his stomach. Never again, Hill told himself. There was no way he was going to put his legs through such hell again. Hill recalls to the author: "The guy who gave me a lift back to Wythenshawe actually had to prop me up against the bus stop because I was so stiff. I'd never experienced anything like that ever before but like a lot of other people I thought: 'never again!' But then you start to read the favourable press cuttings – and you start thinking, well...it wasn't too bad!"

By 1962, Hill admits that he had become a fanatic for racing. In the first 40 weeks of the year Hill raced an astonishing 64 times... somewhat more than Paula Radcliffe toes the line, one feels! Hill's ever improving form meant that he was always hungry for new challenges, each success making the hard training "easier and easier to accept". The excitement of top-level racing thrilled Hill. First he won a silver medal in the Lancashire Cross-Country Championships, and on the strength of that was picked to run for England in Lille, France: "What a joy it was to be sitting in a first-class compartment of the S.N.C.F. train, rattling across the flat and flooded countryside to the northern part of France. The hotel, "The Royal", was a magnificent old style place and I couldn't believe the luxury. After a run we had a two-hour dinner which was the finest meal I'd had in my life. I couldn't believe it was all on the house."

At the 1962 National Cross-Country, Hill proved he was now one of the leading runners in the country by placing seventh, which meant his first call up to the International Cross-Country Championships (now the World CCCs). A sign of Hill's class and tremendous fighting spirit is that although he struggled terribly in the race he still forced his way through to eventually place eleventh. Eight sherries at the reception before the formal dinner meant that Hill was "well away", and his intoxicated beheviour led to him being removed from the room where the speeches were held. But he didn't mind. England had once again won the International Cross (as they would do for eleven of the next thirteen years), and Hill had played a key part. He was 23 years old and suddenly the Olympics were looking like a pretty safe bet.

In 1962 Hill was selected for the British team to run in the European Championships marathon in Belgrade, on the back of winning the "Polytechnic" marathon earlier in the year. He had suffered badly in the hot conditions that day, just hanging on to win in 2:21, but had no such luck in Yugoslavia where he had a disaster. Suffering with a throat infection and under the scorching heat he dropped out, dejected, two-thirds through. Bursting into tears when he got back to his room, Hill writes: "I was absolutely alone, physically, mentally. I was isolated, a speck of nothing, in the dark." The world of top-level athletics had given him a very sharp jolt.

Hill vowed to come back harder than ever, especially after the unsympathetic British selectors punished his DNF by refusing to take him to compete in the Commonwealth Games the following December. Hill had to stand by and watch as countryman Brian Kilby took the gold. In 1963 his racing frenzy hit fever-pitch as he felt loyalties to both Manchester University and Bolton Harriers. But it all gave him terrific background to defend his "Poly" title. Feeling much better than the previous year, Hill showed marked progress in scoring a 2:18:06. But he couldn't relax at this, since an American teacher named "Buddy" Edelen roared to a 2:14:28 world record. It was the second time in the year that the record had fallen. Things were happening fast in the world of marathoning, and Hill was right there in the mix.

By 1964, Hill broke through and began competing regularly on the world stage, which he'd continue to do for around the next ten years. A disappointing third place at the *National* Cross-Country Championship, still meant another selection to the *International* event (now the "World Cross"). Here, Hill ran the race of his life to place second, and he had the track and road season to look forward to, and in particular a visit, hopefully, to the 1964 Tokyo Olympics. The Polytechnic race was seen as a selection race for the Olympics, and here Hill made another huge breakthrough by clocking 2:14:12. Still, he had reason for disappointment though, as Basil Heatley (who would go on to capture the silver medal in Tokyo, behind

Abebe Bikila) ran to yet another world best on the Chiswick to London course of 2:13:55.

All the while Hill had been studying for his Ph.D., which that summer he earned. Hill writes: "It was now Dr. Hill and I could be labelled, 'The Flying Doctor', which would be a change from 'The Barefoot Bantam from Bolton' ". Hill ran excellently in the trial for the 10,000-metres as well and was selected to double up in Tokyo. But once again top-level international competition treated him cruelly. Horribly nervous, Hill placed just 18th in the 10,000: "Absolute rubbish. I walked off in disgust as quickly as possible, I couldn't stop sweating for ages after the race. I was mad, sick, choked, fed up." Upon careful reflection, Hill reasoned that maybe the high humidity had something to do with his poor run (29:53), but he was still the first British finisher. Maybe the marathon would go better. Hill didn't help his cause by unwinding in somewhat outlandish fashion at a party at the US Tachikawa Air Base. British officials took a dim view of the all-nighter, and Hill felt he needed to run a good race to clear his name. As it was, he started out far too fast in the 85 per cent humidity (15:14 for the first 5K) and endured an agonizing run. His strength and mental fighting spirit still told, though, at the end as he began overtaking people again to place a moderate 19th of 67 runners. But he was gutted:

> I stopped dead over the line...I was crying and, wrapping a towel around my head, I ignored the people shouting to me. I got into a shower, which stung my badly blistered feet, and the tears started again. What a performance. Why did it have to happen to me?

*   *   *

The next few years saw Hill keep up his huge training loads of 100-plus miles week in, week out, with a regular 20-plus-miler on Sundays. He was also working diligently at his job at the research laboratory at the textile firm Courtaulds in Droylsden, just east of Manchester. And he was bringing up two young sons, Steven and Graham.

There were many terrific highlights in these years: smashing the world records for 25 kilometres and 15 miles on the track in 1965, and two victories in the National Cross. The first of the latter, in 1966 was a thrilling win where Hill beat Mike Turner by inches; it was his proudest achievement in running so far. He then repeated the feat, more comfortably, in 1968. But the European Champion-ships marathon of 1966 produced more despair as acute intestinal difficulties saw him plod to twelfth in just 2:26. "Ron Hill plans to retire," screamed one newspaper headline. But it was pure fabrication, as Hill notes: "What the hell was there to retire from? I hadn't done anything yet!"

Over the next year or so though, Hill started achieving major things, and his cross-country record over the winter of 1967/68 makes for stunning reading:

East Lancs: 1st
Lancs: 1st
Northern: 1st
Inter-Counties: 1st

Ron Hill, right, duels with another top British runner Bill Adcocks at the 1966 Polytechnic Marathon. Over the next few years both of these determined young men would record times that would send shock waves throughout the sport. *Mark Shearman*

National: 1st
International (World):   2nd

In the last race, in his quest to be recognized as the best cross-country runner in the world, Hill came down with yet another of his sore throats, but still came within just 12 yards of upsetting the great Mohammed Ghammoudi. Still, however disappointing that defeat may have been, Hill had obviously laid the groundwork for a major stab at the Mexico Olympic marathon; selection for which should have been a certainty. And there was to be no more "messing about", doubling up in both the 10,000-metres and marathon. He warmed up brilliantly by smashing Ron Clarke's world record for the 10-miles (set on the track) by 10 seconds, as he ran 47:02. "Was I pleased! A triple World Record holder!"

And the best was yet to come. As a warm up for the Olympic trial, Hill ran in the "Pembroke 20", running a phenomenal world best of 1:36:28. After it he heard a spectator remarking, "It will be a long time before we see running like that here again, on two legs anyway." For Hill's part, he was convinced the selectors would notice that; regardless of what he did in the trial. "Roll on Mexico!"

To this day, Hill recalls the disaster that awaited him:

For the trial I was going from a rest because I wanted to be at a peak in Mexico, not for the bloody trial. That May I ran 1.36.28 for 20 miles to impress the selectors but I don't think they ever even noticed. I went through 10 in about 46-something. I always say, when they're picking a team, they're looking at hammer throwers, they're looking at everything – they can't be experts in everything, and I didn't have a coach to speak up for me, and you wouldn't speak up for yourself in those days, you were too proud.

But, alas, like clockwork, the monumental fitness that Hill had built up led to an infection and in the Olympic trial for the 10,000-metres, which he ran just in case things went wrong in the marathon, he placed just fourth. The infection still hadn't cleared by the time of the marathon trial a week later, and he placed fourth again. If selected for the Olympics, Hill said he only wanted to be considered for the marathon. Gallingly, the three men who finished ahead of him all said the same. But then even more gallingly, Jim Alder, once out in Mexico City, decided he was more of a track runner after all and said to Hill he'd like to swap, but Arthur Gold, the British team manager, would have none of it.

Alder failed to finish the marathon (collapsing twice), while Hill ran extremely well in the 10,000-metres, hindered only through lack of a finishing kick, and only suffering from the altitude a little. He placed a highly creditable seventh, behind the great Ron Clarke in sixth. Britain's Bill Adcocks and Timothy Johnston performed creditably in the marathon, for fifth and eigth, but if that's where *they* were placing, with times of just 2:25 and 2:28, one reasons that Hill would probably have medalled. Never did so dedicated and classy an athlete have to pay so many dues before finally striking it big.

* * *

But at last, his dues had been paid, and what followed over the next couple of years were marathon performances of brilliance and skill that finally compensated Hill for years of disappointment and heartache in this gruelling event. After setting another world record for ten miles on the track – 46:44 – and winning the trial for the European Championships (where he comfortably saw off the world record holder, Derek Clayton), Hill travelled to Athens in 1969, with family in tow, determined to justify his training and potential. Finally everything clicked into place, although under the hot Greek skies it was anything but easy.

Deep into the race Hill found himself in a relatively safe silver medal spot, but with Belgian legend Gaston Roelants[1] out of sight down the road. Hill was determined not to slow and then with just 3 kilometres to go he caught sight of the Belgian, albeit a tiny pinprick in the distance. But Hill was desperately tired: "For God's sake keep going, Gaston. I don't want a bloody battle now," he thought. But of course in his heart of hearts that's exactly what he wanted. Slowly and thrillingly Roelants came back to him, until suddenly, with just a kilometre to go, Hill sped past. He writes: "My heart was pounding; I was feeling sick; physically sick with the effort. Christ, I was going to win. Pushing, pushing, the wind flying against my face. Cheers – huge cheers – Oh no! I look round – thank God, it's not Roelants – cheers are louder – I look round again for Gaston – still no-one on the track. I've won! I've won!"

Finally Hill was a major-championship winner, and what followed were two prestigious invitations: to the Fukuoka Marathon in December 1969 and the Boston of April 1970. Hill set about training for them with feverish, unrelenting intensity:

But let no one think it was easy. I wasn't a well-oiled machine silkily gliding through all those miles. I was human, and I hated the cold and dark, and the wet weather. And the hammering took its toll on my body – my left knee and hamstring were constantly giving me trouble and as a result of favouring the right leg all the time, I developed soreness in my Achilles tendon and it thickened alarmingly. For 10 days I found I had blood in my urine, which was pretty worrying; but I didn't complain.

---

1. Roelants won the International Cross-Country Championships four times between 1962 and 1972.

Hill delighted himself at Fukuoka with a sub-2:12 clocking, although the Canadian Jerome Drayton managed to defeat him by some 40 seconds. But Hill was inspired. Fukuoka had been on a wet and windy day; what could he do in benign conditions? He wouldn't find out at Boston (where he had an immediate chance of revenge over Drayton) because the conditions there weren't just worse, they were atrocious. But Hill had reached the peak fitness of his career thus far, and nothing like the weather was going to stop him now. No Briton had ever won Boston, despite Jim Peters giving it his all in 1954, and the excellent Fred Norris and Brian Kilby also coming up short.

With weather so cold that Hill was having to blow on his freezing hands to keep them warm – and Drayton having to drop out due to muscle cramp – Hill had a run sent straight from the angels. "Beautiful" was a common refrain he heard from spectators as he whipped along, smashing all the checkpoint records in the process. With five miles to go, Hill got a real shock when informed he was a hunted man – just 26 seconds up on a flying Irishman, Eamon O'Reilly. "Old Mother Riley," Hill's fatigued brain kept chanting over and over. But he wasn't going to give this one up without a fight and forced his tiring muscles to speed up even more. He flashed through the line in an exceptional 2:10:30.

The author reminded Hill that the Kenyans were winning in this time 30 years later.

"I got a medal..." replies Hill (alluding to the fact the winners of 2000 walked away with cheques of $100,000; plus appearance fees...).

"What about the beef stew, Ron?" I asked (which every finisher was traditionally served).

"Oh, yes, I got the beef stew! And I got the laurel wreath, too, but you're not allowed to import that back into the country."

"Do you think that your 2.10 is worth a bit quicker because of the inclement weather?"

"Well, when Bill [Rodgers] broke my record five years later with a tailwind, I was in that race and I remember someone throwing one of these plastic cups away, and it just blew away in front of him, leading him down the road – it was just so windy; so if I'd had those conditions, God knows what I'd 've run."

Hill's major hope now was that he would be selected for the Commonwealth Games without having to run the trial. The British selectors, whom Hill had already fallen foul of twice, just gave him the nod this time, even if their grudging selection letter did arrive in mangled and obtuse English: "...it is very difficult for me not to say 'you are selected', but if I were you, I would be very confident that your time at Boston is good enough."

No one even broke 2:18 in the trial.

* * *

Hill's ten-week build-up for this chapter's featured marathon, the 1970 Commonwealth Games in Edinburgh, was a fastidious, scientific and hugely intricate concoction of all he had learnt in his 15 years of serious running. In particular, he decided to analyse the training of the four finest races of his career – the 1:36 at the Pembroke 20, and the three marathons at the Europeans, Fukuoka and Boston – and average it out: "I virtually had a blueprint for my perfect run-up to

64

the race." Also, although Hill was by no means the first to experiment with a carbo-loading diet (Clarence DeMar, for instance, some sixty years earlier was dabbling with it), he was bringing all his scientific and analytical knowledge to it, and other athletes – such as Jim Alder – were starting to cotton on and follow his example.

But, it seems, there's always something waiting to go wrong. Hill recalls: "I went up to the Games with my family. The car conked out. I took it into the garage, who offered me ten quid for it. What am I doing? A Ph.D. who goes to the Olympics and Europeans driving a car worth ten quid? But the company I worked for saw no value in being a runner." "They did at least give you a welcome reception when you returned from your triumphs, didn't they?" I asked. "A reluctant reception. When I got my MBE my boss called me into the office. 'How did you get that?' he asked. 'We got a guy in the Rotary club – who seemed to get them for selling the most insurance or something.' I thought, that puts me in my place, doesn't it?"

The Friday before the marathon on the Sunday, Hill had a couple of $7\frac{1}{2}$ -milers planned. He got lost on the first and ending up running 12. Would this mean he would trim his evening scamper? No, $7\frac{1}{2}$ it was. Ron Hill never compromised. The competition Hill faced made the race pretty much a world championship. Bill Adcocks was there, who was not only the 1968 Fukuoka champion (2:10:47), but was also the architect of "one of the most spectacular performances of all time" (Hauman), when he won the Athens Marathon in 1969 in 2:11:07, a course record that stood for 35 years until Stefano Baldini beat it at the 2004 Olympic Marathon. World record holder Derek Clayton was in Edinburgh, as was the reigning Fukuoka champion and Hill's big rival, Jerome Drayton. The defending Commonwealth champion, Jim Alder, was representing Scotland, and he was on a mission to prove Clayton, for one, wrong about his pedigree. When quizzed about whether he thought Alder was a threat, Clayton spat. "He's got no class." Alder went on to anyone who would listen about how he would show them.

On the day of the race Hill had yet more shambolic transport problems, as his journey to the stadium could have come straight from the annals of his hero Alf Tupper. Halfway there the penny dropped that it would be useful to Hill if his racing flats were on his person, and not still on his bedroom floor. Panic. He redirected the driver straight through the closed roads of a royal garden party. Suspicious policemen let him through. Dash to get the shoes, dash back to the car, dash back through the party, and Hill arrived at the stadium flustered, and a mere 20-minutes before the gun.

The day had seen rain in the morning, but now it boasted a strong breeze and hot sunshine. Derek Clayton burst into the lead, taking Phillip Ndoo of Kenya and Jerome Drayton with him. Hill hung on grimly: "It was like the start of a 1500-metre race..." A few miles in and Hill noticed that Drayton was pouring sweat. A little out of condition, was he? Maybe. Hill wondered why Clayton was now following, and not forcing the pace as he'd advertised he would. One reason perhaps is that the pace was already fearsome: 23:31 for 5 miles. At eight miles, even though Hill was feeling uncomfortable, he decided that with the pace slackening a shade, it was time to make his effort. He piled on the pressure: "Ten miles was called, 47:45. That wasn't bad. I felt all right. The other two were still within

10 seconds of me here, but I didn't know this. I didn't look back."

The turnaround point came a shade before halfway, but it was still a critical moment of the race. Hill would have to turn and face his would-be executors. However nervous and wobbly he was feeling, Hill made sure not to give his rivals a scrap of encouragement. As Sebastian Coe has said: "Running is like poker, you musn't let your opponents see your hand." Hill writes in *The Long Hard Road*:

> Drayton looked fairly close; I gave him the thumbs up sign as he went past and said, "Keep it going, Jerry." He waved briefly to me. Jim Alder and Bill Adcocks looked uncomfortably close. I just kept my eyes open, looking alert with not quite a smile on my face. Quickly the others were past too, most of them giving me a shout of encouragement, Jack Foster of New Zealand and Cyril Leigh, a fellow Lancastrian, gave me a big shout. Then they were gone. Now I knew the real race was ahead.

It was turning into a glorious – and hot – summer's evening. And it wasn't long before Hill started to suffer, from his own relentless pace. After continuing to "slice away" at the sub-5-minute miles, the gnawing pang of worry began to hammer at his mind, his legs and in the pit of his stomach. The worry seemed to only spur him on, however, as, ignoring the summer flies and midges which he was swallowing (nothing in the rule book against this method of fuel reloading!), and taking the occasional sponge to cool himself, Hill passed 20 miles in 1:37:30. Fortunately, such a magnificent time didn't faze him too much since he had that 1:36 from Pembroke under his belt. Hill heard reports at 18 miles that his pursuers were around 80 seconds back. At 20 miles the gap remained unchanged. A rational mind would think: *Good, 80 seconds is far too much to make up over the course of 6 miles; in fact, I'll probably stretch my lead to over two minutes if I keep on going like this.* But the mind becomes unbearably paranoid when in such a high state of fatigue, and Hill's told him that the slightest falter now would lead to a whole stream of runners flying past.

A woman shouted, "Slow down and wait for Jim Alder." A group of kids, "England – Boooo...!" which Hill disliked. With four miles to go, Hill writes:

> My legs seemed to go dead. Suddenly I felt I had nothing there. I thought, "How the bloody hell am I going to get back?" I seemed to be running oh so slowly. If I got any worse I would stop. May and Steven and Graham, my mother and dad were waiting at the stadium, they had seen the intermediate times, they must think I'm going to win. How disappointed they will be if I fail now. If I fail.
>
> I looked forward to the press bus. How nice it would be just to step on and ride back, then go to a bar and line up a couple of pints of cool bitter beer, and knock them back.

The slightest thing would cheer Hill, or depress him. If his following breeze stopped blowing, he took it personally; if the sun shined in his eyes, he'd think, why me? But then he'd grab a sponge and think that maybe he could finish after all.

A famous quote refers to a simple action he made late in the race: "I kissed my

Hill pings a last lap of 75 seconds to set the Commonwealth record and smash the best of the rest by nearly three minutes. *Mark Shearman*

lucky ring on my left little finger and immediately got cramp in my left elbow through bending it. Christ, I was getting into a hell of a state." But still Hill kept plodding along. Slowing yes, but not nearly as much as he feared. Twinges in his groin alarmed him, but could not fell him. With $1\frac{1}{2}$ miles to go a friend in the crowd yelled at Hill to shoot for the world record. "World's best? No, just let me get home. Just let me win. Time's not important. Just win that medal and do the job." He poured a cup of what he thought was ice cold water over his head and braced himself for the refreshing feeling of the "liquid gold" cooling his body. But all he got was warm, sticky lemonade. Bastards.

Finally, a downhill to the stadium and a lap of the track to cover. Hill remembers the moment well, as, eyes glinting, he tells the author: "I was able to finally relax. Just trot round and wave to my family and friends and enjoy the moment. Yet you know what Mel Whatman clocked me for, for that final lap?" "Eighty?" I replied, "Ninety?" "Seventy-five! I still ran 75. I was sure going well that day," he says wistfully.

Hill raised his fist as he crashed through the tape in 2:09:28; a new championship record by almost twelve minutes. "Take that!" he said to himself. "Take that!"

* * *

Clayton, who Hill was perhaps most afraid of, recorded a DNF, as did the dangerous Drayton. Hill simply flattened them into surrender. After the race Clayton said:

I caught Drayton and we ran together. Just before 18 miles I said, 'There's not much point in carrying on, we're not going to win this one; let's stop and have an orange juice.' Drayton replied, muttering, 'I've got to keep going, I've got to keep going.' Finally we agreed to drop out. Drayton sat on the kerbside and started to cry.

Desmond Hackett of the *Daily Express* wrote:

Dr. Ronald Hill, of Bolton, a specialist in athletic time-and-motion study, almost lounged through the tape to win the Commonwealth Games Marathon in Edinburgh yesterday.

Flying Doctor Hill, wearing the same string vest and mini-shorts he used when winning the European gold medal over the original marathon course in Athens, jogged around and waved to the most enthusiastic audience these Games have ever known.

Alder, the holder, said: "At the turn I saw Ron Hill looking so fresh I said to myself: 'Jim lad, you will have to settle for a silver this time.'" Hill told the media:

Once I got into the stadium and heard that crowd, every ache and pain disappeared. I was tired and uncomfortable after four miles and was wondering why I should be out in front leading. At eight miles I slowed up the race because I felt a bit lonely, and wanted some company. There was nobody inclined to be sociable so I just plodded on. At 17 miles it started to hurt, and at 22 miles it felt like hell.

Over the last mile I looked at the official bus, and was tempted to bum a lift. Then I thought of my wife and kids waiting in the stadium and decided that life would be much more easy if I carried on. You get dazed and anxious and there is no finer sight than plodding into the stadium all alone and seeing that lovely tape and a place to rest your feet.

After the Munich Olympics and the Commonwealth Games in 1974, I might reach for the old rocking chair, because I'll be all of 35. But now I'm going to get sloshed.

* * *

Such performances as Ron Hill's at the 1970 Commonwealths are rare and special, and it's no surprise that he had reached the pinnacle of his career. Granted his running days still had many more fulfilling moments to come, but the decline would now inexorably begin, and crushing disappointments became ever more frequent. What sullied the final years of Hill's career was the blind insistence of the selectors to force him to do the selection races for every major marathon. He had shown what he was capable of in Edinburgh without requiring a selection race: smashing everyone in a world class field into oblivion.

Hill describes a farcical conversation he had with British manager Arthur Gold when he requested exemption from the selection race of the 1971 European Championships: "Gold told me: if you look at your time in the Commonwealths, percentage wise you're not that much better than the guy who was second." The author nearly fell off his chair. What on earth was Gold talking about? Since when did *percentages* come into play? Percentage-wise, someone running 9.85 for the 100-metres isn't much better than someone running 10.15! Or someone running 1:44.2 isn't far ahead of someone running 1:46.8 in the half-mile. When in reality, of course, those comparisons are miles apart. "I just put the phone down," said Hill, "you can't argue against that."

He then (of course) got injured trying to get into the Europeans, yet still qualified. Hill continues: "Getting into the team was hard, and then maintaining fitness was even harder – then I tore a hamstring very badly. With that injury I had, people wouldn't even turn out today." Despite shuffling more than running, Hill still placed a dejected third in the Europeans of 1971, and afterwards pleaded with the selectors to select him without a trial for the Olympics the following year. He laid out a detailed three-page letter stating a tremendously convincing case, but the response was: run the trial. Even when his two greatest challengers, Trevor Wright and Bill Adcocks, pulled up lame before the trial, Hill was still forced to run. He cruised round in a still excellent 2:12:51, 2½ minutes up on the nearest Brit. But he'd had to put his creaking body through *yet* another marathon, and it would take more recovery than he could afford to put it right again.

Ah, the Munich Olympics. A detailed look at Hill's race may be viewed in Chapter 14, but the tale does not make for happy reading. Hill fell into a trap, so often fallen into by top runners: after achieving something momentous, how do they improve on it? They analyse their training and diet and try to do everything *even* more to the extreme. Thus Hill came to Munich over-trained and exhausted. His special carbo-loading diet had been carried out even more brutally. He never felt right the entire race. Hill recalled to the author:

There were two problems with Munich – smashing myself too much at altitude in St. Moritz, and doing "the diet" to destruction – burning too many fats and protein. I was so weak and dizzy that I was doing bizarre stuff like putting sugar on my salad.

My mistake was falling into the old trap of "the harder I drive myself, the better it'll be" – but of course it doesn't work like that. After two laps of the track in Munich I already knew my race was pretty much over. On top of everything else I even had the threat of the Irish threatening to kidnap me in the English Gardens deep into the race.

My one word to sum up how I felt at the finish? Despair. I had spent a year looking underneath every stone and it had all backfired. I had even written "2:07:30" over a map I had of the course in a room at home. My lesson? Stick with what you've always done, and don't try to overcook it – it'll all just backfire.

* * *

With the pain of Munich, Hill's career at the top or thereabouts of world marathoning was over. The phenomenal levels of fitness he had achieved for the Edinburgh Commonwealths would never be reached again. That elusive feeling of just knowing you can run all day. Hill explains: "When I was at my fittest it was a marvellous feeling when you're running along in the lead in a race and you're under no pressure; but even if someone did come up on you, there was the feeling that you could just turn the tap and more power and speed would come pouring out." Hill continued racing all over the world for the next few years, with some pleasing highlights including a 2:13, fifth-place return at Boston, and two fine wins in the Debno and Enschede marathons in 1975 in 2:12 and 2:15. By 1975 Hill had run 38 marathons and won 16 of those. And by the end of 1979 he had broken the 2:20 barrier no fewer than 29 times.

Hill felt he could realistically dream at one final tilt at Olympic glory in 1976. A week before the trial, Hill smoked three cigarettes after a race, and when Ireland's Neil Cusack raised his eyebrows, Hill said, "Don't worry. You'll see. I'll make the Olympic team next Saturday." But it was not to be as, in his saddest race, Hill placed fourth, just as he had in 1968. Still, he was reserve; perhaps someone would twist an ankle. And someone did! – Keith Angus. But an unfit Angus still travelled and competed, and Hill's call as reserve never came. Britain's marathoners in Montreal placed a pitiful 26th, 31st and 45th.

The end had finally come.

* * *

By 1985 Hill had become obsessed with running 100 marathons, and in that year ran six marathons in six consecutive weekends. He finally all but retired from the marathon in 1992 at London when he had his most painful marathon ever, and in

A latter day Ron Hill, although he now wears his hair considerably longer. *Mark Shearman*

running 2:51 he just thought to himself. "Why am I doing this?" In 1996 he came to Boston to join the festivities for their 100th race and recorded a 3:12. It was his 114th and final marathon. In the author's interview with Bill Rodgers, the American commented: "Ron Hill: what a great guy. He's one of the kings of the marathon – and distance racing – because he was good in everything: cross country, track and road racing."

Hill has run around 142,000 miles and hasn't missed a day's running since Sunday, December 20th, 1964. He was certainly still at it on the day the author shared a run with him in spring 2004. Since the autumn of 2001, Hill has battled with a chronic knee injury: one day at an airport on the way to a race his right knee simply buckled away from beneath him. He insisted on doing the race, and it gave way twice during that too. It has never been right since. He warned me that his top speed was very slow. But it wasn't too bad. Close enough to 8-minute miling anyway.

Hill still displays a neat, unfussy cadence on his light frame, with his feet flicking up behind him in a sort of "ten-to-two" effect. When we approached a steepish, narrow gully leading down to Hyde's pretty canal, I let Hill take the lead. This was a part of the course to be taken gently. But instead Hill just let gravity overtake his body, and suddenly he was gone! 30-metres away down the trail while I gingerly negotiated the slope. I suddenly got a vision of what it was like to be competing in a cross-country race with him some forty years earlier. Hanging on for dear life, but then with a lethal, unexpected shimmy he would break the shackles and burst off on his own. Whether 1964 or 2004 it didn't matter: this was a beast made for running.

And long may he continue.

Race result:

Ronald Hill	ENG	2:09:28
James Alder	SCO	2:12:04
Donald Faircloth	ENG	2:12:19
John Foster	NZL	2:14:14
John Stephen	TAN	2:15:05
William Adcocks	ENG	2:15:10

Sources:

Conversations with Ron Hill.

Conversations with Bill Rodgers.

Derderian, Tom, *Boston Marathon*. Human Kinetics, 1996.

Hackett, Desmond, in *The Daily Express*, July 24th, 1970.

Hauman, Riël, *Century of the Marathon*. Human & Rousseau, 1996.

Hill, Ron, *The Long Hard Road. Part I: Nearly to the Top*. Ron Hill Sports, 1981.

Hill, Ron, *The Long Hard Road. Part II: To the Peak and Beyond*. Ron Hill Sports, 1983.

Sandrock, Michael, *Running with the Legends*. Human Kinetics, 1996.

VIII

No. 43 – 1997 London Marathon [Women]

Sunday, April 13th

Not a day to ignore those 385 yards. In fact not a day to ignore those 5 yards...

The defending London Marathon champion from 1996, Liz McColgan came to the streets of the capital a year later in punchy mood. Not only had she endured an extremely disappointing Olympic Games but she was fuming from comments made by her countrywoman Veronique Marot, who had said that McColgan would never break Marot's British record of 2:25:56 because her style was too bouncy. "Crap! That's the only word I can say," shot back McColgan.

> I laughed when I read that in *Athletics Weekly* but I was actually pleased...It was the first time I've ever been described as bouncy in my life. I'll definitely prove her wrong. I've always been an excellent road-runner. I mean I'm the world record holder for 15 kilometre and 8 kilometre and I was the world record holder for the half-marathon so how can she say I'm too bouncy and can't run on the roads?
>
> I think it may need a British best to win on Sunday so I'm not going to blow my chances of winning by going off for the record. But maybe the next marathon or the one after I'll have to just go for it because I'm getting to the stage where I can see my chances slipping away.

McColgan had been held in the highest esteem by the British athletics-watching public over the past several years, mainly due to her mesmerizing performance at the Tokyo World Championships of 1991. In the 10,000 final, just nine months after giving birth, she ground out continuous 74-second laps and by halfway only the Ethiopian Derartu Tulu was able to stay with her. The temperature was 27 degrees, with a humidity of 78 per cent. McColgan's lead was 25 metres with 1 kilometre to go, which she duly covered in 3:04.61 to win by 21 seconds over China's Huandi Zhong. Many observers called it the finest British performance on the track for a generation.

If that was McColgan's highlight, a low point came at the Atlanta Olympics five years later when she entered into the Games as one of the favourites for the marathon, but the freak injury of an insect bite to her foot hampered her running.

She trailed in a dismayed 16th, $8\frac{1}{2}$ minutes behind Fatuma Roba. On the Olympics, McColgan commented:

> If I'd won in Atlanta I'd have retired because how are you ever going to eclipse that? The Olympics is the cream of the crop, so as long as I keep healthy and injury free I'll be going for the Olympics in Sydney 2000. But I won't keep going much longer than that, whether or not I win, because I'd have to go round on my zimmer frame.
>
> OK, I've won London, but I've only run 2:27 and I would hate to retire having not run faster than 2:26; I would be so frustrated. If I haven't run faster than that then something's just not quite clicking so we've changed the training this time.

McColgan came into the 1997 London fit for her defence but, as David Powell noted in *The Times*, "There is a real possibility that she could run faster than last year and not win. This is likely to be the first time that five women break 2.30 on the course. Manuela Machado, the European and world champion, and Anuta Catuna the New York City champion are among the challengers for title." "It is important to think only about winning," McColgan said the day before. "With a field of this calibre, there is a chance to run fast anyway. I am running strong."

There was also at just a shade lesser standard, Xuijuan Ren from China (winner in Beijing 1995), Lidia Simon from Romania, and Joyce Chepchumba from Kenya (London runner-up in 1996). Marion Sutton of Britain also came to race, having surprised by winning in Chicago the previous autumn, and was hunting for a sub-2.30.

The race lived up to all expectations. "This was the day", wrote Powell, "when the London Marathon enjoyed the most spectacular day in its 17-year history. Everywhere you looked, records were falling amid other unprecedented feats of achievement. Never have two marathon races on one city on the same day finished so close." Trevor Frecknall wrote in *Athletics Weekly*:

> But we should have known it was going to be a dramatic sporting day from the moment world champion Manuela Machado was knocked over at an early drinks station. The 33-year-old Portuguese, whose previous unhappy memory of London was to lose to the unrated Pole Malgorzata Sobanska in 1995, jumped up immediately and stayed with the leading pack to halfway but never really mounted a challenge once the real race started.

It wasn't long also before the Chicago champion, Marian Sutton, had problems. At 5 miles she was already 23 seconds off the pace, which became a dismaying 1:17 at 10. She was never a factor thereafter and eventually placed 20th in 2.35.45.

The appointed hare, Lornah Kiplagat, bizarrely went through halfway in 1:13:30, a minute slower than requested. Still, it meant that there remained a lot of interested contenders, deep into the race. Sonja Krolik was the world junior triathlon champ from 1992 to 1994, but was condemned as being too thin to pursue it at the senior level. But the German demonstrated she still had terrific power for running, as she built a lead of 19 seconds by 14 miles, 35 seconds at 15; 39 at 16 and 50 at 18.

With the defending champion, Liz McColgan, having a plethora of mid-race difficulties, Joyce Chepchumba slugs it out with Romania's Lidia Simon [103] and Sonja Krolik of Germany. *Mark Shearman*

Just when it seemed as though the little-known, inexperienced *Fräulein* could be heading for a terrific runaway victory, she committed the oldest sin in the book. She looked behind her. Prudent behaviour at a children's pantomime, but a fatal error in this context. There are no prizes for displaying any weakness or concern in top-level sport. In the course of the next mile Krolik's lead was nearly halved: from 52 seconds to 28. Less than 150 metres of tarmac was all that protected her from her assassins. Renata Kokowska – whose worst position in four previous "Londons" was seventh – led the chasers. Krolik "stumbled through the 22nd and 23rd miles in a painful 5:54 and 5:51, and lost the lead under the tunnel by Lower Thames Street. Chepchumba and Lidia Simon swept into the lead side by side with McColgan a distant third" (Frecknall).

Indeed McColgan had been going through an extremely bad patch and was settling at this stage merely for a position in the top five. Suffering from stomach cramps throughout the race, McColgan had been unable to drink properly and was now feeling weak and dehydrated as the mercury rose. Meanwhile, at 25 miles Chepchumba pulled clear from Simon and commenced what appeared to be a 6 to 7 minute glory run. McColgan continued to battle though, and Simon soon came back to her. The stubborn Scot moved into second. At the final drinks stop, Chepchumba fumbled her drink as McColgan hove into view. Victory was suddenly possible again, and the gritty Scot's energy started to return. A few hundred metres later and McColgan was suddenly, and thrillingly, contesting for the lead. Trevor Frecknall wrote: "There was a vivid memory of Roger Bannister defeating John Landy in the 1954 Empire Games mile, when McColgan swept past Chepchumba's right arm while the Kenyan glanced over her left shoulder."

Suddenly a repeat of the previous year's superbly timed victory seemed likely. It was McColgan, who, with less than four minutes to run, seemed to have a firm grip on the race. The two brave athletes ran up Birdcage Walk towards the finish line, twice Chepchumba hauled herself level with the Scot, and twice McColgan pulled away. As they passed Buckingham Palace, McColgan's lead was around 5-metres. Surely that was enough with just 200 metres left to run.

Fifty metres out, McColgan thought once and for all she had got it. The deafening cheers from the crowd told her so. Well, that was the impression she got anyway. What the crowd were actually trying to tell her was to *get a move on*. With 25 metres to go, Chepchumba, having forced herself to within a couple of steps of her rival, seized the moment and forced herself into the lead. McColgan

As Liz McColgan busies herself with her stopwatch, Joyce Chepchumba has sneaked up on the blindside to snatch victory at the last possible moment. *Mark Shearman*

had been busy finding the stop button on her watch; oblivious to this late, late show of the cruellest kind. Chepchumba won by a couple of yards, to become Kenya's first ever female winner of the event. The last gasp effort won her an extra $25,000, while she had lowered her personal best by 2:47. McColgan had set a 1:40 *pb* (in her eighth marathon), but that was scant reward.

* * *

Seven years on when the author quizzed race director Dave Bedford about his memories of the race, he commented:

The thing about McColgan is she's sprinting for the bloody line and ten metres out she starts messing around with her stopwatch – quite incredible. The press didn't pick it up – I don't think anyone picked it up. It would have been nice for her and nice for the event for a British person to have won – but there we are.

"The whole of London seemed to offer a collective gasp of disappointment as McColgan lost in the last few strides, but she had just been involved in the closest women's marathon there has been," wrote David Powell in *The Times*. "This was one result the spectators didn't want: the first victory in the London Marathon by a Kenyan woman. It is not that Joyce Chepchumba is unpopular, just that Liz McColgan was battling in her typical, unyielding fashion to secure a British victory." With hindsight at her press conference, a distraught McColgan reckoned her overtaking manoeuvre in Parliament Square was when she lost the race. Instead of running alongside Chepchumba and gathering her reserves for a big finish, she pressed on at as hard a pace as she could muster. She said:

I am very, very disappointed. I went through a bad patch, fought my way back, had absolutely fantastic support – yet I feel as if I have let a lot of people down.

From very early on in the race I had stomach problems. It's the first time I've had anything like it. When I was taking in drinks I felt I had to stop and go to the bathroom. I drank only about a third of what I would normally drink. At 18 miles thoughts were going through my head like, 'I'll be lucky if I get in the top five."

At 21 miles the crowd was fantastic. As I was falling apart they pulled me together and I just got my head down. Coming along in the final mile and a half, I was down on Lidia and Joyce, but I worked very hard to catch up. When I passed them I thought "Yeah, I've got a chance. Maybe this was where I made a mistake. I maybe should have sat back and waited a little longer, but I tried to win it in the best time I could. I ran my fastest time... I was just a bit unlucky at the end. Approaching the finish line, I did not realize Joyce was there."

One thing brightened McColgan up though: a little girl who came to see her from the crowd. "I don't know who she was but she just came out of nowhere and said I had run a great race and wanted to give me a medal. She offered me her Daffy Duck medal. She hung it around my neck and I gave her a kiss. So I gave her my medal in return." McColgan's mentor, Grete Waitz, was full of praise for the relentless way in which she and Chepchumba took the event to fresh heights: "It is the first female race in the history of the marathon that has been as close. It really shows how competitive the women's marathon is in the '90s. It's a big step forward for the event. Nobody comes back in a marathon. Certainly Liz did not expect Joyce to."

For Chepchumba, she was overdue a big-city win, having placed fourth in New York in 1995, and third in '96, as well as her second in the '96 London. "We were both going for fast times," Chepchumba said, "I just tried my best." Of her incredible charge for the finish line, she revealed: "I was a little bit confident." Two years later Chepchumba would win London again (in a new course record), and seven years later she came to the capital, seeking to qualify for the 2004 Athens Olympics, for which selectors had controversially left her off the team – all the more bizarre since she'd won the bronze at the Sydney Olympics and had been one the world's most consistent marathoners for nearly a decade.[1] The memories of 1997 were still fresh with Chepchumba: "It was one of my best races ever. I have the pictures and I have the video and I show them to people even now, saying: look what I have done."

For third place: Lidia Simon. She had certainly come a long way since finishing 89th in London in 1991 when she clocked 2:52.

* * *

McColgan never did manage to break 2:26, so in some ways the "crap"-speaking Veronique Marot had the last laugh. McColgan did return to London in 1998, but there she bumped into an extremely fit Catherina McKiernan and left her assault too late to catch the Irish woman. Oddly enough McColgan's stomach was again cited as one of the key factors in her loss, as she explained: "I was thinking about how my stomach was rather than concentrating on the race. With two miles to go I realized I was catching and it was disappointing I left it as late." McKiernan won in 2:26:26 to McColgan's 2:26:54 – two seconds slower than the year before. There's the aging process ruthlessly at work.

By the millennium McColgan had all but retired from competitive athletics but returned from the pastures three years later to add a pleasing postscript to her career by having a successful series of races over the autumn and winter of 2003/04. However, although she managed to win the Scottish cross-country championships and Scottish indoor 3000-metre title, it was all very much *against* doctor's

---

1. Sadly, the selectors were not to be swayed, and ignored her claims for an Olympic spot.

orders. McColgan had already undergone surgery four times, most recently 15 months earlier when the big toe of her left foot was rebuilt, fused and pinned.

McColgan felt the surgery had been so successful that she believed a return to top class action – even marathoning – could be possible; but after winning the National Cross title in Perth, the toe literally "fell apart", and she needed more surgery. McColgan ghoulishly explained: "I've wrecked it. I've shattered the fake toe, burst the screws holding it, everything. It's been spelled out to me that any kind of running at all is now absolutely out of the question."

But it seems the world hasn't heard the last of the McColgan name in British distance running. Liz's daugher Eilish became British Cross-Country champion for the under-13 girls category in the spring of 2004, and Liz spoke of how she derived more pleasure out of watching Eilish triumph than of anything gained from her own experiences.

Race result:

Joyce Chepchumba	KEN	2:26:51
Elizabeth McColgan	GBR	2:26:52
Lidia Simon	ROM	2:27:11
Sonja Krolik	GER	2:28:02
Ramilia Burangulova	RUS	2:28:07
Mausha Machado	POR	2:28:12
Christine McNamara	USA	2:28:18
Renata Kokowska	POL	2:28:21
Elana Mazovka	BLR	2:29:06
Hellen Kimaiyo	KEN	2:30:09

Sources:

Conversations with David Bedford.
Adams, Harry, in *British Runner*, April 2003.
Athletics Weekly, March 3rd, 2004.
Frank, Bob, in *British Runner*, September 2003.
Frecknall, Trevor, in *Athletics Weekly*, April 16th, 1997.
Lewis, Richard, in *British Runner*, September 2002.
Powell, David, in *The Times*, April 12th & 14th, 1997.

IX

No. 42 – 2001 Berlin Marathon [Women]

Sunday, September 30th

Daughter of the Wind first to reach the Holy Grail.

This chapter's essay is significantly the most one-sided of the book, but one of the most important. For it finally broke one of the great bastions of women's distance running which good names and great had been shooting at for around a quarter of a century. This chapter thus presents a good opportunity to investigate just how far women's marathoning had come since a British woman by the name of Violet Piercy set the world's first mark for women in the marathon by returning a 3:40:22 at Chiswick in October 1926.

Before Piercy there is very little news of women marathoners, aside from a Greek woman "Melpomene" who may or may not have run the marathon course from Marathon to Athens as far back as 1896. Her legend is well known and her time widely reported as about $4\frac{1}{2}$ hours. But it wasn't in the actual Olympic marathon that she ran as some suggest – as Olympic organizers were very strict on their men-only policy; far more likely it was in the practice marathon over the Olympic course that occurred a short while earlier. Certainly no official documentation exists regarding this feat; indeed something as simple as Melpomene's surname doesn't appear to be known.

As will be mentioned in Chapter 35, the Amsterdam Olympics of 1928 were a disaster for women's running as blinkered and ignorant officials took umbrage at the poor state in which many of the women finished the 800-metres final. This disregards the fact that the times were very safisfactory (all the medallists were sub-2:19) and that many of the runners in the final were supreme all-round sports-women. Fifth placed finisher Bobbie Rosenfeld also grabbed the 100-metre silver at the Games, and gold in the 4 × 100-metre relay. And the brilliance of Japan's Kinue Hitomi cannot be ignored. Following on from her silver in the 800-metres she travelled to Prague for the third Women's World Games where, according to Wallechinsky, she "delighted the crowd by winning four medals: a gold in the long jump, a silver in the triathlon, and bronzes in the 60-metre dash and the discus." Hardly the form of an incapable athlete. But the men in suits had their disgraceful way, and women were barred from competing in anything longer than the 200-metres until 1960. And women weren't allowed to run an Olympic marathon, of course, until 1984.

Violet Piercy's unofficial world mark stood for nearly 40 years until the feisty and colourfully named American, Merry Lepper, jumped out of the bushes at the start of a marathon in Culver City, got attacked by a marshal, punched him, and subsequently had her time taken by a sympathetic AAU official. Lepper claimed she had every right to run on a public street. The official showed her his watch which read 3:37:03 (Hauman).

At this rate of progress it was going to take well over a thousand years before women would be running the times they are today; but Lepper wasn't the only one who was to stick up for her rights. The women's marathon world mark was about to come in for 40 years of constant attention. Some of the early record-breakers were delightfully offbeat. Nothing remarkable about Scottish woman Dale Greig though, who took 10 minutes off Lepper's mark with a 3:27 clocking in the Isle of Wight. The mark stood for less than two months before New Zealander Mildred Sampson ran 3:19 in Auckland. Only serious runners now needed apply for the world record: Sampson had been New Zealand cross-country champion four times (Hauman).

Three years passed before the Canadian Maureen Wilton aged just 13 ran 3:15 in Toronto. East German Anni Pede-Erdkamp then sliced off 8 more minutes, before on February 28th, 1970, the 3-hour mark came under severe attack from 16-year-old Caroline Walker who ran 3:02:53 in Seaside, Oregon. Hauman writes: "The tiny Caroline, who was 1.53 m tall and weighed 40 kg, had trained by running 70 miles per week."

It is said about Ron Hill that his 2:10:30 at the 1970 Boston Marathon brought times right into the contemporary, and the same could almost be said of the Australian Adrienne Beames at Victoria on August 31st, 1971. Beames not only became the first woman to crack the 3-hour mark in the marathon, she smashed it out of sight, and comfortably took the 2:50 mark with it. Her 2:46:30 took over a quarter of an hour off American Elizabeth Bonner's mark, and now that the way had been shown, the mark was continually altered over the next seven years. In all, it came down eight times, including twice by the American Jacqueline Hansen (including 2:38 at Eugene in 1975), and twice also by Chantal Langlacé of France who ran a best of 2:35. The stage was now set for the icon that is Grete Waitz to continue to tinker with the record books. She didn't so much as tinker as dominate and rewrite. A snapshot of Waitz's 1643 days of world marathon-record-domination (October 22nd, 1978 to April 17th, 1983) is as follows:

New York City, 1978   2:32:29
New York City, 1979[1]   2:27:32
New York City, 1980   2:25:41
London, 1983   2:25:28

It was a truly magnificent spree, but her last record was only satisfying to her for around 27 hours, before word came that it had fallen, 3274 miles away in Boston, courtesy of an irrepressible run from Joan Benoit. Benoit, following a few

----

1. See Chapter 12.

years of underachievement, was a fearless tearaway that day and had the aston-ished men around her warning, "You'd better watch it, lady." Her first mile was a mind-boggling 4:47 (2:05 pace), and her halfway split 68:22. Waitz's grasp on the world record had all but gone. Boston's famous hills wreaked mini havoc with Benoit thereafter, but she still roared home in a stunning 2:22:43, to break Waitz's new mark by approaching three minutes.

Not only had Benoit signalled that she would be *the* woman to beat at the following year's Olympics, but she also set tongues wagging about the possibility of women dipping under 2:20. And so the assault began. Many great athletes would attack the barrier over the next 6735 days but it refused to fall. The most prominent of these was Waitz's successor as the queen of Norwegian – and world – distance running, Ingrid Kristiansen. She attacked 2:20 many times over many years after the '84 Olympics, a mission explored in detail in Chapter 17. Her most potent attempt[2] was the 1985 London Marathon when she roared to a marvellous 2:21:06 – a time that stood up to yet another onslaught by Joan Benoit at Chicago six months later when she clocked 2:21:21.

The greatness of the Portuguese runner, Rosa Mota, lay in her championship pedigree and not in searching for fast times, so she never seriously challenged the 2:20 barrier; but one of Mota's successors, Uta Pippig, most certainly did. In the wind assisted Boston of 1994 Pippig returned a 2:21:45, and she often publicly stated that she had 2:20 in her sights. But it wasn't to be for Pippig as that would be the fastest she would ever travel; instead a leading contender for the "holy grail" passed to the diminutive – and charming – Kenyan Tegla Loroupe of double New York and once London-winning fame (amongst many other achieve-ments). Loroupe came to Berlin in 1999 surrounded by a phalanx of male pace-makers and smashed the world record with her 2:20:43. Some felt that the wall of runners surrounding Loroupe was a little *too* over-protective – that if there was a breath of wind, then it had no chance of finding its way to her, and that the pace-making and thinking that she had to do for herself was nigh on zero. Still, no one could do her actual running for her and the world record was a more than worthy achievement. Berlin it seemed was a truly fast course and became a leading contender (along with Rotterdam) for the 2:20 barrier to eventually fall.

The 2000 Sydney Olympic marathon seemed a good guide to determine who might be the one to step over the seemingly inevitable milestone. And what a terrific marathon it was with the deepest mass finish in women's marathon history: no fewer than 14 runners dipped under the 2:30 mark. The medallists were taken up by three big names. In the bronze was the fine pedigree of Joyce Chepchumba who had been winning major marathons all over the world for several years, and in silver was another old favourite, Lidia Simon of Romania. With two kilometres to go, Simon was 28 seconds down on the leader, but upon glimpsing the Olympic Stadium was filled with adrenalin and desperate energy. She dramatically surged and the lead began to shrink fast. But Simon had left her charge agonizingly late and eventually fell just 8 seconds short of the gold.

---

2. To this day though, Kristiansen is still most riled about her attempt at London 1987 when she pinged through 15 kilometres in 47:23 – that's 2:13:28 pace. And just 6 miles from home was bang in line for a low 2:18. But approaching the Tower a suspect calf locked up and she had to hobble home in a still fine 2:22:48.

Naoko Takahashi soaks up the adulation of the Sydney crowd after winning the 2000 Olympic Marathon. *Mark Shearman*

Securing that gold was a deserved success for the marathon-crazy nation of Japan – after years of near misses at the big championship marathons. The victor, Naoko Takahashi, who was much tipped in the pre-race build-up, came into the race owning the world record for a women's only event. In 1998 she had set a time of 2:21:47 in 32 degrees and 90 per cent humidity at the Asian Games in Bangkok. Earlier on in that year Takahashi had already set a Japanese record of 2:25:48. "Not until the last moment did I think I could win," said Takahashi, on her Olympic triumph. "I have been aiming for this for a very long time and am now a little sad that it is over." "The next thing is to try and break 2:20, and I will try this in the spring." One Japanese reporter was moved to say after Takahashi's success: "Naoko Takahashi will be as big in Japan as Cathy Freeman is in Australia."

Anyone who still has a tinge of sadness – of perhaps unfinished business – after reaching the pinnacle of their sport obviously has a greater thirst for their profession than the normal earthly being. For Takahashi, winning the Olympics was all well and good; but she was a greedy athlete, and thirsty for more success. She had supped from the well reserved only for the greatest of champions and was addicted to its sublime taste. She had heard her national anthem played and the music sounded as sweet as the Sirens singing to Ulysses. She commanded her boat to sail ever closer to the dangerous rocks. If only she could just hear the music a little longer, to sup from the well a little more, before she crashed and burned.

*　*　*

Takahashi became an enormous cult hero back in marathon-obsessed Japan after her Olympic triumph, and in early 2001 she even became the subject of a comic strip called *Kazekko*, or "Daughter of the Wind". All the big marathons fêted the Olympic champion to come and run their race. She wanted a fast course, and instead of the following spring, it was one year and one week after Sydney that Takahashi arrived in Berlin to hunt in earnest for the world record. Takahashi had enjoyed the rewards and acclaim of her Olympic gold (to the tune of around $4 million), but she hadn't let it affect her goal to be the undisputed finest marathon runner in the world – for that she also needed to be the fastest. Tegla Loroupe's world mark of 2:20:43 piqued her interest, but it was the evasive 2:20 barrier that she was really after.

Takahashi had never run in a "mixed" race before the Berlin Marathon of 2001 – all of her marathons giving her solely the help of female competition. With the added bonus of faster, stronger male runners to drag her along, it was seen as a definite chance to go quicker than she ever had before. The organizers renamed the race the "Run for Peace" since it occurred less than three weeks after the suicide attacks on New York, Washington and Pennsylvania. Many of the athletes wore black ribbons. Takahashi seemingly had only one major threat in the race, that of Loroupe, whose world record was set on the same course two years before.

Pat Butcher reported in *Athletics Weekly*:

Takahashi, who bought her own chef, masseur and entourage of a dozen to Berlin, struck out alone from the start. As the runners passed the Brandenburg Gate landmark near the Reichstag after three kilometres, Loroupe was already 50 metres behind.

Takahashi pressed on remorselessly under the grey skies, in cool temperatures of 14/15C and into the slight easterly headwinds. She used every bit of help her five "guards" could give her, as they sheltered the tiny runner from the wind during the first half.

However, the slight hindrance of the wind soon became a priceless benefit when the course veered to the west at 6 kilometres and a slight tailwind began to assist the Olympic champ on her way. A perfectly timed rain shower at halfway eased any concerns about her overheating. At one stage Takahashi was 45 seconds off world record pace, but a magnificent spell from 10 to 25K meant she now enjoyed a 45-second cushion on Loroupe's mark, and a tantalizing finishing time of 2:19:58 was projected.

Now that this remarkably determined runner was on course, it was going to take a major setback to halt her imperious march to the holy grail of a sub-2:20. But other runners had been well on course for it before; most notably Joan Benoit at Boston '83 and Ingrid Kristiansen at London '87; before both runners slowed drastically in the final 10 kilometres. The only question was whether Takahashi had the necessary physical and mental strength.

Had her fate been predicted before her by her own comic strip? Just three days before Berlin, the edition of *Kazekko* showed Naoko passing through the Brandenburg Gate and winning in a world's best time. It made for dramatic reading, but surely life couldn't imitate art so neatly. Besides, Takahashi was starting to tire.

But fatigue was going to have to be at the top end of acute to stop Takahashi in her tracks now, and approaching the final couple of miles, she was 90 seconds ahead of world-record schedule and looking comfortably on for a sub-2:20. The last 2 kilometres were a real struggle as the course and conditions threw all they had at Japan's beloved cult hero. Millions back at home watched and prayed. Finally, the finish line hove into view and the clock spewed seconds into oblivion. Takahashi fixated her stare on it and finally flashed through with a nervy 14 ticks still to spare.

Part two of life dream fulfilled: Takahashi becomes the first female to break 2 hours 20 for the marathon. *Reuters/CORBIS*

The delighted champion said after the race: "Until now I've been happy just to compete against rivals; this was the first time against the clock," as she picked up $100,000 for her morning's work. "I can't compare this to the Olympics. I've always had two aims, to win the Olympic title, and set a world's best, they are both the same for me." Nearly a hundred Japanese media followed Takahashi to Berlin, including the journalist who wrote *Kazekko*. "Next week's comic book sale is likely to run into the millions", commented Pat Butcher in *Athletics Weekly*. "It was a great course," Takahashi added. "Because of the help I got from my pacers and guards it was easy to run. The rain also kept my body from overheating. However, the wind always seemed to be against me."

Takahashi's triumph came as no surprise to her trusty coach, Yoshio Koide, who said later: "Our goal had been to run 2:18:32. However, because of the headwind during the first 5 kilometres, she lost 20 seconds. If she trains for the final 2 kilometres she can cut a further one minute from the record." Pat Butcher, though, laid the first warning signs that Takahashi could be pushing her body to its very limit by continuing the way she was: "It is hard to see how Takahashi can train much harder, though. For she admitted after the race that it is not unusual for her to run 70–80 kilometres (40–45 miles) during a tough day's training."

"I prepared well for today" was how Takahashi interpreted such a breathtaking workload. "I'm not anyone special. I'm just a normal person. I'm a normal athlete. This was a great challenge to run this race today."

* * *

Amazingly this new world record only lasted a week, and one is reminded of Roger Bannister's famous refrain when he first broke the 4-minute mile: "Après moi, le déluge." But Catherine Ndereba, who roared to her 2:18:47 the following week in Chicago, was quick to pay tribute to the importance of Takahashi's run. "For that barrier [2:20] to disappear, made it much easier," she acknowledged.

Takahashi returned to Berlin the following year and won again, this time in a more cirucumspect, but still lethal, 2:21:48, for the 13th fastest time in history. *Athletics Weekly* reported:

> The reason for her slight slowdown was that injury problems had started to affect her, and it was her first race since her world best the previous year: "I had a calf problem at the beginning of September and couldn't train as hard as I wanted, so I didn't even consider the world record, I just wanted to win." It meant she had now won six major marathons in a row: Nagoya and the Asian Games in 1998, Nagoya again in 2000, the Olympics, and Berlin 2001 and 2002.[3]

Obviously the next major aim for Takahashi was the defence of her Olympic title. But first there was the tough prospect of just qualifying for the Japanese squad (of three). Takahashi was starting to suffer from the years of brutal training, and her millions of fans wondered whether she could get in shape to qualify. Heartbreakingly for her she returned just 2:27:21 in the Tokyo Marathon of December 2003, which simply wasn't good enough to persuade the Japanese selectors that she was a risk worth taking. Her major undoing being an awful patch between 35 and 40 kilometres that took her 20:17.

There was a national outcry when Takahashi was formally omitted from the squad, but it's hard to argue with the selectors' decision to take Mizuki Noguchi, Reiko Tosa and Naoko Sakamoto to Athens. They placed first, fifth and seventh respectively. No other nation came remotely close to Japan in the unofficial team race. The world had seen the last of the "Daughter of the Wind", who by the end of 2004 was into her 33rd year, but she then returned to the limelight in November 2005 with a win at Tokyo. Whatever the future holds, Naoko Takahashi will always be able to boast that, "I got there first..."

---

3. Takahashi revealed an intriguing secret after Berlin '02. After training each day she would drink four to five bottles of giant hornets' juice. When will supermarkets start stocking such a supplement, one wonders.

Race result:

N. Takahashi	JPN	2:19:46
T. Loroupe	KEN	2:28:03
K. Weel	GER	2:28:27
G. Mlynarski	POL	2:32:52
S. Terasaki	JPN	2:34:56
A. Sugihara	JPN	2:34:56
Bev Hartigan	GBR	2:36:02
T. Ramos	ESP	2:36:25

Sources:

Athletics Weekly, September 27th, 2000 and October 2nd, 2002.
Butcher, Pat, in *Athletics Weekly*, October 3rd and 10th, 2001.
Derderian, Tom, *Boston Marathon*. Human Kinetics, 1996.
Hauman, Riël, *Century of the Marathon*. Human & Rousseau, 1996.
Martin, David and Roger Gynn, *The Olympic Marathon*. Human Kinetics, 2000.
www.sporting-heroes.net
Wallechinsky, David, *The Complete Book of the Olympics*. Aurum Press, 2000.

X

No. 41 – 1975 Fukuoka Marathon [Men]

Sunday, December 6th

"...it was like a Charlie Chaplin routine. I sort of hopped on by."

To offset the joy and triumph that is liberally sprinkled throughout the pages of this book, there must too be some sadness and heartbreak; because, as we all know, life ain't plain sailing. A far greater proportion of sadness than normal occurs in this chapter, although the story about Canada's greatest ever distance runner is mainly about a survivor. In fact, every pitfall seemed to have been placed against a baby called Peter Buniak entering the world at all.

Kolbermoor, Germany, January 1945. Sonia Buniak was just nineteen and had come to Germany as a girl from a small village in the Ural Mountains of Russia. Sonia had fallen pregnant, and she and her husband worried about the future of their unborn child under the power of the Nazis who were ever alert for conspicuous, foreign-sounding names. And the name Buniak was Ukranian. Friends and family urged the Buniaks to abort, but Sonia insisted on going ahead with the birth even though she did agree "to have the child at home, away from the prying eyes of German authorities," according to author David Blaikie.

A month before her due date, Sonia slipped and fell while boarding a streetcar, inducing early labour. There was no alternative but a hospital delivery. Blaikie dramatically describes the birth of Peter Buniak:

The birth was attended by a disinterested German nurse to whom Sonia Buniak reacted with instinctive distrust. Her fears seemed realized when the nurse held up the newborn infant dispassionately and spoke doubtfully about his chances of survival. Terrified, the new mother snatched her baby away and slapped him on the back until she heard a cry of life. Seizing the first opportunity thereafter, she stole up to the hospital nursery and fled into the night with her infant in her arms.

An adult Peter Buniak takes up the tale: "She had nowhere to go so she just ran, feeding me on potatoes and icicles as she went along."

And thus the baby survived, and would go on to become a great survivor in all the trials and tribulations that lay in his way. The uninvited guest of poverty immediately foisted itself into the life of young Buniak, and that meant a warm home with a loving family were to remain elusive – to be replaced by foster homes. Author Tom Derderian writes:

> To be a Ukrainian boy in a defeated country where the Nazi government had despised all persons non-German and tried largely to exterminate Ukrainians to make living space for Germans, to be poor and slight of stature and unprotected by parents, was to grow up a friendless, scrappy kid who got beaten up frequently. Young Peter Buniak's defence was to retreat to his fortified inner self.

By the time Peter was eleven, his divorced mother had settled in Toronto whereupon she sent for her son. His situation improved. In Germany he had been mercilessly bullied about his strange foreign-sounding name and frequently got into fights, battling back against his tormentors with dark, flashing eyes, intensity and passion. At Toronto's Mimico High School, Buniak paid little attention to what passed for a running track, and instead became a pool hall shark, hustling unsuspecting opponents for a few bucks.

A friend asked Buniak to run in a track meet as a favour. If, the friend reasoned, Buniak could beat the hot favourite in a race, the favourite's girlfriend might lose interest and leave the track star...leaving her available for Buniak's friend. The absurd plan didn't work, even though Buniak did do his bit by winning all three races at the meet he entered. "For the first time in my life I had done something on my own," he recalls.

Buniak was eighteen years old and quickly discovered that running was something he could excel at, aided by his made-to-measure 5-foot 9, 130-pound frame. By 1965 he was one of the leading runners in Canada, and the Mexico City Olympics loomed large. Since his life had been a struggle up until now, it was no surprise that the Canadian selectors made Buniak struggle even more to make their Olympic team. It was a long, bitter stand-off. Special time trials were arranged to convince the selectors that this "foreigner" should have a slot at the expense of a home-grown boy. Buniak promptly broke the Canadian record for 10,000 metres. Still not enough. A marathon was arranged; and he broke that national record too. Finally, his road to Mexico was clear, but his participation was a disaster as he had to drop out at 15 miles in the 1968 Olympic marathon with dysentery.

However, the spectacle and drama of the Olympic Games had hooked Buniak – he wanted an Olympic medal. "The event did not matter," David Blaikie writes. "If it must be the marathon, if that was what physiology dictated, so be it. He would accept the challenge, submit to any discipline to achieve the goal."

To begin his search for that medal, and to press forward with the new identity which being a top athlete gave him, dramatic, bold action was taken. In March 1969 people would no longer ask Buniak constantly to spell his name or belittle him with the words "Peter who?" Because he changed it. "By the stroke of a lawyer's pen he expunged his old name and became Jerome Drayton. Buniak was not a name to which he had ever felt attached. For as long as he could remember, back to the hostile days of the German foster homes, it had been a liability" (Blaikie). Now, as Jerome Drayton, he could begin a new life, as a full and accepted member of society.

*   *   *

Drayton burst into the marathon limelight with an electrifying turn at the Detroit Marathon of 1969. Five months after he had popped a 2:16:11 marathon in Ontario, Drayton took the lead from the start, and in ideal conditions on a flat course, he galloped through 10 miles in 50:30 and 20 in 1:40:38. Six miles later Drayton was suddenly the proud owner of a new North American record of 2:12:00. This got heads turning, particularly at the unofficial world championship marathon run each year in Fukuoka. Drayton fielded an invitation to Fukuoka in December where he would meet the European champion, Ron Hill. It was to be the battle of the continents – the Ryder Cup of marathoning if you like. North America won. Hill describes a little of this "wonderful" event, the 1969 version of which has nearly been this chapter's featured event, only just being edged out by 1975. Hill didn't know much about Drayton; he (Hill) was the race favourite, and besides, the Olympic champion Mamo Wolde was in the field, and that concerned Hill the most. "There was another Canadian due in," Hill writes in *The Long Hard Road*, "Some guy called Drayton who was supposed to have run 2:12, but he hadn't arrived yet." On the morning of the race, Hill writes: "At breakfast Drayton sat opposite me, and said little."

As the runners stood freezing in 1½ inches of water on the Heiwadai track at the start, ready to take on the pancake flat course, Hill was in pole position next to Wolde. Soon after the start Hill found himself back in 20th as Drayton took an early lead. Hill moved through the field but Drayton continued to forge ahead at the front. By halfway Hill was suddenly very worried that this obscure Canadian of whom he knew so little, could be stealing the race away from him. "How's it going, Ron?" asked the charismatic American Kenny Moore. "Not brilliant," Hill replied, "but not too bad." At the 17-mile mark Hill gazed down the road in second place and saw, dejectedly, that Drayton almost certainly could not be caught. Hill then entered into a tremendous battle with Hayami Taninura for the silver and eventually prevailed by nine seconds, with a 2:11:54 clocking. Drayton recorded another North American record of 2:11:12. Sixty-two years after the famous Tom Longboat had won at Boston, Canada had another marathon hero.

Hill was surprised at Drayton's fine run, but ecstatic with his time, and wrote positively about the event: "The whole race is organised by a newspaper, *The Asahi Shimbun*, and what a magnificent job they make of it. It really is a classic race which every good marathon runner wants to get to." Hill and Drayton would meet at another classic race just four months later: Boston. This time, on a freezing, wet day, Hill was ready for the Canadian and got his revenge. In the face of Hill's devastating forcing tactics in the early stages, Drayton duked it out as long as possible before finally having to let go as Hill brought Boston times right into the contemporary with a 2:10:30. Drayton never appeared at the finish. One all between these two dedicated runners, shortly to become two–one to Hill as he destroyed the rest of the field at the Commonwealth Games of the same year, held in Edinburgh (see Chapter 7). But that was to be the highlight for Hill, who was nearing the end of his top-level career. For Drayton, he still had many years to go, and much improving to do.

*   *   *

However, first Drayton had to take a few more of life's hard knocks. Journalist Rick Matsumoto speaks of the next couple of years of Drayton's life: "Since Fukuoka 1969, Drayton has experienced one disappointment after another including financial worries, leg problems and failure to qualify for the Munich Olympics in 1972 because of an error by Canadian track and field officials." Matsumoto alludes to a horrendous blunder by the officials, which makes heart-breaking reading. Drayton's career was littered with injuries, but by the time the trial for the Munich Games came along he was ready to qualify with relative ease. Drayton wanted to be in Munich for two very distinct reasons: for the glory of representing his country at what he saw was the greatest show on earth; and to be reunited with his father with whom he had been estranged since he was eleven. Drayton's father had been alerted to Jerome's running successes and had startled his son by writing to him out of the blue. They started up a tentative correspondence but Drayton had lost most of his command of the German language. The only hope for a satisfactory reunion would have to come face to face at the Olympics.

All Drayton needed was a qualifying time in the trial of 2:17. What a pips. With little competition to worry him Drayton decided to run only fast enough to get the qualifying time. By 30 kilometres Drayton, running a clinical, methodical race, was a comfortable minute inside his schedule. Five kilometres later, he was $1\frac{1}{2}$ minutes *outside* the required pace. How could this be? Drayton had felt he was running strong and fast. But he can't have been. He became discouraged, and then despaired. "I had the feeling at the time that everything was lost," Drayton recalls. "I thought, 'What's the point of pushing any more? Just win the thing.'" So he then reduced his speed to the minimum required to win, which he did in a dejected 2:23.

There was an inquiry as all runners reported inexplicably slow times. The course was remeasured and found to be a *kilometre* too long. The officials argued that Drayton would still have missed the time: an obtuse, self-serving piece of drivel that completely ignores the psychological nightmare he went through on the course, which led to his subsequent deceleration. The officials relented, but only by organizing a second trial, just weeks before Munich. There was no point: Drayton reasoned he'd never recover for the Olympics in time. "You couldn't argue," Drayton says, "It was the fault of whoever organized the marathon and set up that route. You think of quitting. You don't care about the sport any more. But I almost immediately picked up running again."

The next few years, Drayton struggled with odd jobs, his studies and his running. He appeared at Boston in 1974 and ran strongly for third in 2:15. By 1975 Drayton had finally secured steady work at the Ontario government's sports and recreation branch, and with his financial worries easing, and his injuries clearing up, he suddenly found himself in top shape for Fukuoka '75, this chapter's featured race. Man of the moment Bill Rodgers had been invited, fresh from his blinder to win Boston earlier in the year (2:09:55). Others in the field included Australian David Chettle, Giuseppe Cindolo of Italy and Takeshi Soh, one of the dangerous Soh twins.

But just when it seemed as though everything was coming together, Drayton was hit with a classic sucker-punch. Rick Matsumoto reports in the *Toronto Star*:

When he arrived in Fukuoka last week, a pair of track shoes, made by a Japanese manufacturer, was waiting for him. But knowing it takes about two weeks to break in a pair of shoes and find out if they are suitable, Drayton informed representatives of the manufacturer that he had no intention of wearing them in the race. The shoe salesmen, however, weren't going to let him off that easily. On the day before the race, they came to Drayton's room, measured his feet from every angle, and then went away.

"I expected to get a pair in the mail back home about two months later," Drayton said last night on his arrival in Toronto, "but five hours later, they had a pair, made to my specifications, back to me. I felt I had no choice but to wear them. I felt obligated."

That's Japanese ingenuity for you. But still the golden two-week rule gnawed away on the Canadian's mind.

The next morning it was obvious why Drayton acquired the nickname amongst his Fukuoka fans of "Rainy Drayton". It seemed as though every time he came to race in this southern Japanese port the heavens would release a torrent of water. It didn't matter by now to Bill Rodgers, his race chances had already been fatally hindered by a cold.

With the race underway, Drayton's phenomenal fitness was already being severely compromised: his shoes hurt like hell! David Blaikie writes: "The soles felt fine but something in the upper portion of the shoes caused his feet to turn outward, threatening leg injuries. The fact that it was raining, as it had in 1969, did not help. His mind flashed ahead to the 1976 Olympics. Even more than had been the case with Munich he wanted to run well in Montreal. The shoes could threaten his chances if he got injured so he held back, not pushing the pace."

"I became almost paranoid," Drayton later explained to the press. "I have had a lot of problems with my legs in the past and I didn't want to risk injury to them with only six months to go to the Olympics. So I gave up any thought of winning the race, hoping only to come out of it cleanly."

Yet another marathon race seemed to have gone wrong for Drayton as he battled gamely on, refusing to log yet another DNF.[1] However, because of his superb conditioning, Drayton was still not a beaten man as the leaders neared 18 miles, although his leg muscles were certainly beginning to tighten. Suddenly though, the limping, hobbling, wounded Canadian sniffed he was still in with a chance. "I felt I'd come this far, so if something was going to happen, fine, let it," said Drayton. "I took off and I was alone in front."

His glory run to the tape was not to last, however. Five miles later, David Chettle zoomed past. "My heart sank," Drayton recalls. "When the Australian went past me, he did so with authority. It was so close to the end I felt I had no chance of catching him. I was looking for somewhere flat on the roadway on

---

1.Incredibly, Drayton failed to finish 14 of the 33 marathons he entered.

which I could run. Sometimes just inside the white lines on the road, where the cars constantly run over the same spot, it's flat. So I ran there."

It had been a fine, gutsy attempt to regain his Fukuoka crown, after a long six-year break in which fortune had frowned on him often more than not, but surely Drayton's challenge was all over. Then, just as he had all but given up hope, Drayton was startled to notice that with just a mile left in the race, Chettle was still only 80 yards or so in front and not zooming at nearly the same pace as 10 minutes earlier. "I made a desperate rush at him. It was totally agonizing because the shoe made my right leg almost lame. I think he made his mistake by going by me instead of staying with me and then taking off near the end. I caught him with less than a mile to go."

Over a quarter of a century later, the dramatic moment of when he overtook Chettle was still freshly with Drayton. Of his three Fukuoka victories – he would return and win again the following year – this is the one he cherishes the most. Speaking at a Canadian "Hall of Fame" gathering, Drayton said: "The soles gave way in the last five miles and it caused my ankle to stiffen up. When I caught the leader it was like a Charlie Chaplin routine. I sort of hopped on by."

Just before entering the stadium for the final few yards, the runners had to make a sharp right turn. "I was afraid I was going to fall down," Drayton said. "And I didn't want the Australian to think I was in deep trouble because it might have given his adrenalin a final boost." Somehow Drayton managed to keep his feet and made it into the stadium to win a tremendous victory. The leg was stiff that night, but he did not anticipate any lasting problems.

Considering what I went through with the shoes and the strong winds that we were racing into, I'm very satisfied with my performance. If I'm able to stay free of injuries, I'm optimistic about the Olympics next summer.

I'm more relaxed emotionally than ever before. All my problems in the past were related to financial worries. I'm busier now than ever before but because I don't have financial worries, I'm able to handle it.

Rick Matsumoto wrote:

The next time you're out jogging, try running on the outside edge of one of your feet. Chances are you won't last more than a few strides.

Jerome Drayton of Toronto ran 20 miles with his right foot cocked at an agonizing angle last Sunday and still managed to win the International Marathon in Fukuoka, Japan. His time of 2:10:08 was the fifth fastest time ever recorded over the marathon distance.

* * *

Drayton appeared all set to peak for the Montreal Games. He arrived at the Olympics at the top of his game, but disastrously, just five days before the race he was struck down with a head cold. "Canadians watched via television as Waldemar Cierpinski of East Germany ran through the streets of Montreal to victory. Frank Shorter was second and Karel Lismont of Belgium was third. Drayton ran sixth and wept. It was a bitter blow" (Blaikie).

To atone for such a disappointment he returned to Fukuoka where he had conjured up a huge following and won in 2:12, handsomely defeating the Olympic champion. However, it seemed with Drayton as though bad news was never far away. The next day at a post-race gathering, a Japanese man made an impassioned speech about the appalling performance of Japan's runners at both the Olympics and Fukuoka. Drayton didn't like to hear his fellow runners so chastised, and so he made a speech of his own. Whether something got lost in the translation we'll never know, but his words came across as harsh and Drayton had caused offence with his outspokenness. He was not invited back to defend his Fukuoka crown the following year.

If that was a medium-sized gaffe, then a major one was coming right up. An enraged Drayton ran the 1977 Boston Marathon appalled at its haywire organization when compared to the military precision of the Japanese. On a frighteningly hot day – which caused Rodgers to drop out – Drayton ran parched, amazed that there were no official water stops. All this after he had been trampled on at the start after no warning had been given of the gun.

When it dawned on Drayton that the race was his, he reduced his pace to one that was just enough to maintain the lead. If he had spotted an official on the course he would have trotted over and squeezed his neck. He ignored the hysterical, stoned, drunk partying crowds, which author Hal Higdon compared to those he had seen at the Indianapolis 500 auto race: "The race offers a reason to party, and today they cheer, wildly and with sincere enthusiasm, for those funny people in shorts. Tomorrow they may roll down the window of their Plymouth Road-Runner car and hurl abuse and empty beer cans at us, but for now crowd and runner become one."

At the finish Drayton put his burning feet in a puddle of water and yelled to the reporters: "I won't be back to defend my title. You'd figure that after eighty-one tries here they'd set up official watering tables. It's just unfair. What's the point of training for this event when you can get beaten by circumstances beyond your control. Basically, the organizers have to make up their minds if they want quantity or quality."

The Boston media were outraged. How dare he criticize our sacred race, they said. Drayton was slammed mercilessly for being ungracious and devoid of pleasure. A few months later he won the Freedom Trail run near Boston. When he went up to get his prize the crowd booed. Jack Fultz, the '76 Boston winner, was there. He tells the author: "Uh oh, I'm going to have to say something here when I go up. This isn't right. But Jerome beat me to it. He told the crowd he loved their city, he loved the Boston Marathon, but that the race could be so much more than it was. He was just trying to help. Everyone was stunned into silence. You could have heard a pin drop."

From pretty much the next year onwards the improvements in the Boston Marathon were clear for all to see. No one would admit it, but Drayton's comments had been digested and acted upon. The magnificently organized race of the last 25 years or so owes a lot to that one infamous day. Bill Rodgers speaks of Drayton warmly. He told the author: "Drayton was a nice guy. The Boston Marathon was sacred back then – you couldn't say anything bad about it but it needed to be changed. He really was a gentleman about it all, and a good sport."

A rare smile from a serious and sober man: Jerome Drayton celebrates winning Boston in 1977 with the mighty atom that was Michiko Gorman, who won the race in 2:47:11. *Bettmann/CORBIS*

Drayton did return to Boston two years later, and when he saw the human hurricane that was race director Jock Semple, their meeting was humorous. Drayton arrived at the room set aside for the top runners at the start, but since he was wearing his sunglasses – which only added to the mystique of his personality – Semple didn't recognize him. Blaikie records the encounter:

"You can't go in there," Semple barked.
Drayton laughed and pulled up his sweater. Underneath was the same white shirt with the red maple leaf that he had worn in 1977.
"Jock!" he said. "Don't you remember me?"
Semple almost laughed but not quite.
"Oh, you again," he said. "You give me a lot of trouble."

Drayton's numerous biomechanical problems, plus his tremendously severe training, greatly held back his progress throughout his thirties; but there was still time for one last pop at a major title. But it's yet another story of heartbreak. A tightening of the hamstring muscle forced him to withdraw from the 10,000-metres in Edmonton, Canada in 1978, but he decided to give the marathon a try. Canadians tuned in to the television coverage of the race across the nation, rather like the Australians would for their home boy Rob de Castella four years later. At 39 kilometres Drayton burst into the lead and the spectators rejoiced. But his leg was in agony. When an unknown "pencil-thin" Tanzanian named Gidamis Shahanga hove into view with less than a kilometre to run, Drayton was unable

94

to up the tempo, and Shahanga swept past while Drayton reduced his gait to a shuffle. "They say a runner takes twenty-six thousand steps in a marathon," a tearful Drayton said. "If that's the case I must have died thirteen thousand times with my bad leg."

His top-flight career gently wound down after this race, although he continued to appear at the business ends of marathon fields for the next several years, although his last four big marathon results make for grisly reading – Boston 81: 2:28 (250th); Montreal '82: DNF; Toronto '83: DNF; Houston '84: DNF. Finally the strain he had put on his slim frame had caught up with him. But in the long run, despite all the sadness, I submit this is a "feel good" story: Sonia Buniak's premature baby who was born into a hostile, unforgiving, penniless world became a hero to running fans both in the East and the West, and along with Clayton, Hill, Rodgers and Shorter is remembered as one of the biggest marathoning guns of the 1970s.

Race result:

Jerome Drayton	CAN	2:10:08
David Chettle	AUS	2:10:20
Bill Rodgers	USA	2:11:26
Giusepe Cindolo	ITA	2:11:45

Notes: Jerzy Gross set a new Polish record with 2:13:05.
A record 29 runners finished in under 2:20 (Hauman).

Sources:

Conversations with Jack Fultz.
Conversations with Ron Hill.
Conversations with Bill Rodgers.
Blaikie, David, *Boston: The Canadian Story*. Seneca House Books, 1984.
Derderian, Tom, *Boston Marathon*. Human Kinetics, 1996.
Hauman, Riël, *Century of the Marathon*. Human & Rousseau, 1996.
Higdon, Hal, in *Runner's World*, May 1977.
Hill, Ron, *The Long Hard Road. Part II: To the Peak and Beyond.* Ron Hill Sports, 1983.
Matsumoto, Rick, in *The Toronto Star*, 7 December 1975.
Semple, Jock, John J. Kelley, and Tom Murphy, *Just Call Me Jock*. Waterford Publishing Company, 1981.

XI

No. 40 – 1936 Olympic Marathon [Men]

Sunday, August 9th

"The marathon provided a fitting climax, with Herr Hitler as interested as ever..."

Just two cities applied for the right to host the 1936 Olympics: Berlin and Barcelona. The IOC met to decide the outcome in Barcelona in April 1931, but attendance at the meeting was poor so a postal vote amongst delegates was required. Hosting the IOC for a meeting to *decide* the whereabouts of the Olympics, and actually *hosting* the Olympics themselves, are two very different things, and in the vote Berlin trounced Barcelona 43 votes to 16. Despite a worldwide depression, the following year's Olympics at Los Angeles were a magnificent success and the Germans immediately had a crystal-clear task on their hands: to do everything at their Games even better than the high, wide and handsome Americans.

Estimates of the cost of the Games approach $30 million (Constable), a quite enormous amount for those days, but it was clear where the money went. The new Olympic Stadium, for instance, designed by architect Werner March, went up in just two years, and employed up to 2,600 workers per day (Martin & Gynn). Whilst not matching Los Angeles for beauty, the Olympic Village outdid it in most other areas – especially quality of construction. Martin and Gynn report that "Many traditional delights from a variety of cultures were included as village amenities: saunas for the Finns, steam baths for the Japanese, several separate kitchens each specializing in different ethnic cuisines, and even wine at the dinner table for the French athletes." Two hundred buses were always on hand to transport the athletes to and from the stadium. These were the first Olympics to enjoy live radio broadcasts, and the Games were also televised – albeit "restricted to closed circuit broadcasts in special halls throughout Germany" (Martin & Gynn).

What a fantastic stage for the world's best athletes to perform on...but it was no accident. The first meeting of BOOC (the Berlin Olympic Organizing Committee) was held on January 24th, 1933; however, just six days later Adolf Hitler was awarded the Reich Chancellorship and he quickly made sure the BOOC sang to his tune, for sport, as a spectacle, struck Hitler as propaganda of terrific value.

Spending lots of money and having a desire to "dazzle" don't necessarily make for a special Olympics; the much criticized Atlanta Games, 60 years after Berlin showed that. Imagination and original thought are priceless. This is where the general secretary of BOOC, Carl Diem, came to play his great role, with a *great* idea. At the 1928 and 1932 Games, Olympic flames had burnt, but Diem's vision was to link these flames in a personal way, from the original site of Olympia, and the current site. And so, in front of the Temple of Hera at ancient Olympia on July 20th, 1936, a group of Greek women dressed as ancient priestesses initiated a "private and formal ceremony that ever since has started the countdown to each Olympic Games" (Martin & Gynn).

From there, the torch was passed to the first relay runner, Konstantin Koudylis, who ran with it for one kilometre, before passing to the next runner. The process was repeated 3075 times taking in en route the sights of Olympia, Athens, Delphi, Thessaloniki, Sofia, Belgrade, Budapest, Vienna, Prague and Dresden. The torch arrived at the Olympic Stadium at 5:20 p.m. on August 1st, 1936. Martin and Gynn report that: "German middle-distance star Fritz Schilgren was selected as the final torch-bearer to light the Olympic flame because of his unusually smooth running style." Even the type of gas used was a first – propane – giving the flame a beautiful colour and no noticeable odour or smoke. As described in Chapter 3, the occasion became yet more magical by the participation in the traditional parade of none other than Spiridon Louis, the winner of the first Olympic marathon some 40 years before, who carried the flag for Greece.

* * *

Juan Zabala, who had so thrillingly – if not convincingly – won the Olympic marathon in Los Angeles in '32 (see Chapter 38), came to Berlin to defend his crown. He had trained unmercifully, but who was to test him? Great Britain, South Africa, Finland, Japan and United States – all nations with fine records in the Olympic Marathon – sent complete three-man teams. Zabala's preparation for the upcoming battle sounds almost modern day in its thoroughness. Splitting from his coach, Alexander Stirling, who had served him so well during his journey to the top, Zabala had arranged his training and racing to take place for several months in Germany to "ensure optimal time zone adaptation and competitive opportunities" (Martin & Gynn). Sounds more like 1996 than 1936. It was all paying off, however: Zabala came to the Games as the South American record holder for 10,000 metres on the track, plus world record holder for 20 kilometres of 64:00 – a time which takes some getting even today.

Of the above competing nations, the United States sent a wonderfully charismatic team. Alongside the redoubtable Billy McMahon, they served up Ellison 'Tarzan' Brown and Johnny Kelley "the Elder".[1] Brown, nicknamed Tarzan, because of a penchant for swinging through trees in his younger days, was born into poverty as a Narraganset Native American. Nothing would sway him from his talent and love of distance running though. Born in Rhode Island on September 22nd, 1914, Brown grew up playing in the woods, but occasionally joining in with swift adult runners on their 15-mile workouts. As an eleven-year-old kid he would appear, gallop alongside one of his heroes for ten miles, then disappear again to play in the trees. Jack Barnwell of the *Boston Post* gave this

---

1. As opposed to Johnny Kelley "the Younger" who was such a dogged force on the American scene in the '50s and '60s.

colourful description of Brown as he arrived at the 1936 Boston Marathon to try to qualify for the team for Berlin: "a penniless, mahogany-hued and full-blooded Indian...dark-skinned warrior." The author Tom Derderian writes: "Brown was regarded as a freak – undisciplined, uncontrollable, unintelligent, a child of nature, an awesome natural talent..."

Johnny Kelley, sen. caught Brown who had seemingly gone out too fast on the second of the four hills in the '36 Boston Marathon. He patted him on the backside in a gesture to imply: "nice one, kiddo, now let the real men take over." Two hills later and on the final ascent it was Kelley turning a shade of pea green as Brown roared straight back past. To this day the hill is named "Heartbreak Hill" because of this dramatic moment. Kelley shuffled to a walk – which he'd do six times in the closing miles. He placed fifth, his Olympic dreams all but extinguished. Brown roared to a convincing win: "I guess you white people can't say after this that the only good Indian is a dead Indian," he memorably suggested afterward. Kelley had one last chance – six weeks later in Washington. He placed second and the selectors decided to take him to Berlin over the perhaps more deserving Mel Porter.

Brown and Kelley would both go on to win Boston twice: Brown in '36 and '39; Kelley in '35 and '45. But the paths their lives took could not have contrasted more greatly. Brown, forever prejudiced by the colour of his skin, never settled in life or found people willing to hire him. His indomitable spirit could not save him. Not for ever anyway. It did save him in a Berlin bar before the Olympic marathon, when several Nazi Brown Shirts accosted him. He fought back – and so perhaps became the first American to take on the Nazis. But his luck finally gave out in 1975, after another fight, outside another bar room. Tarzan Brown died unimportantly, penniless and unknown (outside the running community).

As for Johnny Kelley – he thrived. He would go on to compete in the Boston Marathon a staggering 61 times (where he'd place second *seven* times), and compete again at the Olympics in 1948. He spoke wittily and clearly at the graduation ceremony at Boston University in 1996 where he was awarded an honorary degree in Humane Letters. After 37 years with *Boston Edison*, he pursued a second career as a painter. He died peacefully in 2004, aged 97.

With the US marathon team arriving at the 1936 Olympics with high hopes, the British selectors sent a useful team of Bert Norris, who defended his "Poly" title to earn selection, Donald McNab Robertson and Ernie Harper. Harper, similarly to Johnny Kelley, could have been left at home since he had finished second in the AAA championships in a furious finish, to Robertson, and he had also been defeated by Duncan McLeod Wright in the "Poly". To Wright's chagrin, for he had placed a super fourth at Los Angeles in '32, Harper was given the nod. Would the selectors be proved right for this courageous piece of intuition?

Perhaps of most interest of all, however, were the up-and-coming Japanese. At the previous two Olympics the diminutive, determined, focused fellows of the Land of the Rising Sun had turned many a head with their brave forward running. At Amsterdam in 1928, Kanematsu Yamada missed out on a bronze by under 30 seconds and his team-mate Seiichiro Tsuda placed sixth. Four years later, the consistent Tsuda improved to fifth, while Onbai Kin placed sixth. All very impressive, but no medals. Something, surely, had to give. The team they sent, in common with America and Britain, had two straightforward picks and one wildcard: Tamao Shiaku earning his place over the hapless Fusashige Suzuki who had defeated him in the trial. The other two on the team were Kitei Son and Shoryu Nan. To illustrate just how dangerous the marathon runners of Japan were becoming, a glance at the list for the top-ten marathon performances of all time as at January 1st, 1936, shows that four of the top-five spots and *seven* of the top ten belonged to Japanese runners. And at the very top of the list, in a world record that would stand for twelve years, was a 2:26:42 clocking by Kitei Son at Tokyo in November 1935.

There was, however, a dark shadow hanging over both Son and Nan. These were not their real names, but only translations, from South Korean into Japanese. The conflict of interest between the Russians and the Japanese in Manchuria resulted in the Russo-Japanese War (1904–5), and consequent defeat for the Russians. As a result of this triumph, Japan came to occupy the Korean peninsula, formally annexing it as a colony in 1910. Thus the name Sohn Kee-chung became Kitei Son, and Nam Sung-yong became Shoryu Nan. Born in Sinuiju, North Korea, Son grew up in poverty in one of the most primitive regions of Asia. Although the locals were scarcely aware of what the Olympic Games were, it was on these steep hills in what was a wooded mountainous region, that Son toughened himself into a fearsome competitor. These two extraordinarily fast runners would therefore be running for a country that they didn't belong to, like, or care for. But there was racing to be done, and if these two men couldn't control history and politics, they *could* control how they ran.

* * *

The out-and-back course designed by the Olympic organizers was a relatively simple affair: a couple of quite stiff climbs, which were compensated by plenty of downhill running. The first and last 12 kilometres occurred through the pleasant, well-forested Grunewald, running alongside Lave Havel. The middle 17K were a banal, monotonous test of who perhaps could concentrate the longest on a perfectly straight section of hard concrete road known as the *Avusrennstrecke* ("Avus raceway") – used for automobile racing. "So a rather monotonous, perhaps, but not very difficult journey," is how the *Times* described it.

It is estimated each year that around one million spectators line the route of the Boston Marathon. The *New York Times* estimated that the same number lined the route for this marathon. If a few previous Olympic marathons had tested the runners with chilly, rainy weather, this one was to be run in sunny and dry conditions, with the shelter from the forest making conditions nigh on perfect. Fifty-six runners from eighteen nations started, and the exciting figure of Juan Zabala was one of them. It could have been Los Angeles all over again. There he was, the white kerchief covering his head, the same even, chiselled features; the same look of focused determination from the dark, handsome eyes; the same outstanding running.

Zabala had got away with the positive tactics of "forcing, forcing, forcing" the issue in Los Angeles by the skin of his teeth. The race had hurt him tremendously, and the canny but ultimately bashful Sam Ferris had almost run him down. Why

100

put himself through the same agonies again? Why not take solace in the comfort of the pack? It seems nerves and an overdose of passion were running through Zabala's Latin blood as he was seduced into striking out on his own, into the terrifying loneliness of command.

Zabala led by a full 30 seconds at the 4-kilometre checkpoint; enough to either have his supporters shaking their fists in triumph or their heads in dismay, depending on whether they believed in realism or magic. Portugal's Manuel Dias followed. Tarzan Brown hunkered in fourth. Perhaps Zabala would realize his folly and cool it. This was, after all, a significantly stronger field than Los Angeles. But no: a sizeable hill came along between the fifth and eighth kilometres, and the Argentine tore into it. After cresting, his lead over Dias had risen to 43 seconds. Was Zabala just getting better and better? Not exactly. A closer inspection shows that although Zabala's lead had increased, his rate of progress had dwindled by over 50 per cent (30 seconds for the first 4K, 13 seconds for the next 4K). This was not the way to run a marathon.

Did Zabala sense he was not extending his lead at the same rate? We shall never know. But what we do know is that between 8 and 15 kilometres he hit the hammer hard. Dias fell a minute behind, then a minute-and-a-half, then a full 100 seconds. Still he hung on grimly to second place. Such bravery must always be applauded, but the grisly facts speak for themselves: from this moment on, poor Dias would haemorrhage nearly *a minute per kilometre* to the eventual winner of the race. One can always fool oneself into thinking that second place in the Olympic marathon is where one should be, but one can never fool nature.

Behind Dias things were happening fast: it was time for those who wanted to be in the final shake-up eighty minutes hence to start gearing themselves up for the showdown. Kitei Son was only 30 seconds down on the Portuguese, and running alongside him was the English coal miner Ernie Harper – over twelve years Son's senior (photographs of the pair running together imply an even greater age gap than that). Experience, though, counted for nothing regarding Harper's footwear...one *mean* blister was developing.

With the absence of any local talent, the Germans had taken Zabala to their hearts since he had come to train in their country and had almost adopted him as one of their own. Now the crowds cheered him on his way, delighted that all his hard work on the trails of their homeland was paying off so well. Halfway approached, Zabala's grimace showing that if he did defend his title he was going to have to put himself through the wringer once again. Dias started to visibly falter, and by the turnaround Son and Harper had taken him out. Now they set their eyes on the champion: boring their eyes into his back, watching intently for any sign of weakness. They did not have to bore for long.

At 25 kilometres, a totally spent Zabala refused to slow down; but that was the good news. The bad news was that he fell down instead, and in a moment, Son was upon him and straight past. Two seconds later Harper flew by too. It had been a valiant defence, if, one might argue, a tactically poor one. Zabala got up, brushed himself off and trotted onwards – there was still one more medal to fight for. He fought for four more kilometres before bowing to the inevitable and removing his wrecked body from the field of play. Around this time another high profile casualty bit the dust: Tarzan Brown had to bow out as well. As for Johnny

Sohn Kee-chung and the immaculately coiffured Ernest Harper of Great Britain do battle at the 1936 Berlin Olympic Marathon. *Bettmann/CORBIS*

Kelley, he was hanging on doggedly, but would never feature with the leaders, and eventually finished in 18th place.

Son and Harper had paced their race with expert precision. The Japanese was racing with the same brilliance that he had used to become the world-record holder, while Harper was drawing upon all his reserves of experience and fitness – he had been the English cross country champion a full ten years earlier. The pain from his blister made him wince, but it was nothing he couldn't handle. Terrible blisters were part and parcel of foot racing: squelch, squelch, squelch went Harper's shoes, as they filled up with blood.

Harper may have been slowed by his problem, by there's no denying that Son was a mighty opponent. By 33 kilometres the indefatigable Son was 25 seconds up on Harper, and it seemed the battle for the top two medals was secure. Behind them, a couple of "flying Finns" – Erkki Tamila and Väinö Muinonen battled it out for the bronze, alongside Johannes Coleman of South Africa and Don McNab Robertson, another Brit. But as they fought amongst themselves for the medal ware, another expertly judged piece of Japanese pace-making caught them unprepared. It was the man who defeated Son in the Japanese trial: Shoryu Nan. On this day, Nan would have to acknowledge that his teammate was the better runner, as he had around half a mile to make up – and that, most certainly, was never going to happen. But Nan never gave up, and his race tactics had been thoughtful and clinical enough to have him surging onwards for a place on the podium.

102

In front of a packed Olympic Stadium Kee-chung breasts the tape looking as though he's just won the 400-yards dash. *Bettmann/CORBIS*

By 40 kilometres, Son's motoring had him leading the 1936 Olympic marathon by 87 seconds. He proceeded deftly through the twisty small streets to the stadium, where 100,000 were crammed in waiting to greet him. They had already enjoyed a feast of entertainment, for a little time earlier the remarkable Jesse Owens had led off for the United States in the 4×100-metre relay as they had set a new world record of 39.8 seconds.[2] Then, to the sound of bugles, Son's arrival was announced. A huge roar went up. Newsreel footage shows him looking inconceivably fresh – as good as any runner at the end of a marathon today – as the little marvel put his head down and produced an electrifying kick. He covered the last 100 metres in a mere 13.3 seconds, and became the first Olympian to break 2 hours 30 for the marathon. Harper was some 600 metres down the road. Nan, closing fast on the Englishman, was 19 seconds further back.

Humiliating. That's the only way to describe what Son and Nan had to go through next. Whereas the medal ceremony is usually the most satisfying, delightful moment of any athlete's career (apart from actually finishing their competition), here it was enough to make both men want to hang their heads in shame and sorrow. Up went the Japanese flag, to the tune of the Japanese anthem. David Wallechinsky writes: "Interviewed by the press afterwards, Sohn used the opportunity to educate the world about the plight of his nation. Few reporters were interested, and most seemed relieved when he turned to the race itself. "The human body can do so much," he said. "Then the heart and spirit must take over." Son also went on to pay tribute to Harper's steady nerve and tactical nous. The *New York Times* reported how Son commented: "Much credit for my victory must go to Harper of England. From the time we started he kept telling me not to worry about Zabala, but to let him run himself out."

The London *Times* were full of pride at Harper's terrific return:

2. This race was sullied by unsavoury activity behind the scenes. On the day of the final, two Americans were dropped from the team: Marty Glickman and Sam Stoller. The US coach, Lawson Robertson, claimed the change was made because he feared the speed of the Dutch and Germans. But nothing could hide the fact that Glickman and Stoller were Jewish. Fifty years later Glickman returned to the Olympic stadium, stood on the stretch of track where he should have run, and screamed abuse and obscenities at the royal box where Hitler and US Olympic Committee president Avery Brundage had sat. Ever since Glickman had been 18, the injustice had gnawed away at his soul. Finally he had found a chance to release his emotions (*New York Times*).

Great Britain has at last emerged with full credit from a day in the stadium,[3] and none too soon, for today saw the last of the athletic events. A magnificent victory in the 1600 metres relay race – a first success on the track – was followed by the no less magnificent effort of E. Harper to win the marathon.

He ran so well on a hot afternoon that he beat the existing Olympic record, and yet failed by a couple of minutes to outstrip an amazingly fit little Japanese called Son, who finished as if he could have gone on for ever. Furthermore in this most heroic of races, Great Britain and her dominions between them provided four of the first eight men home.

The marathon race provides a fitting climax, and, needless to say, its start and finish lost nothing in dramatic effect in the Berlin stadium, with Herr Hitler there, apparently as keen and interested as ever,[4] and the huge arena more packed than ever.

Harper's mighty run couldn't however deflect that these had been a very poor games for Britain. And in an editorial *The Times* tackled the issue:

As the Olympic records show, the whole world has taken to sport with a zest and precision which Great Britain, the originator and teacher, finds it hard to rival.

British successes in this festival, as in others, have been few and far between. It is possible of course to take our poor showing in the Games as a whole too seriously. Many people are doing so. But it is also possible to take it too lightly. There is no need to lament the decadence of the race or to make sport into one of the more solemn of life's occupations; but there is every need to inquire into the decided progress which so many other countries have been making.

* * *

The following day there was big trouble. The Korean daily newspaper *Dong-a Ilbo* produced a photograph of Son on the medal podium, but a picture editor had airbrushed out the Japanese flag from his sweatshirt. Japanese authorities in Korea were enraged and threw eight of the newspapers employers into jail. Production at *Dong-a Ilbo* was suspended for nine months.

Happily, this tawdry tale has a sublime ending. After the Olympics, Son retired from marathon running with an immaculate record of Run 13, Won 10, never appearing outside the top three. Redemption for the pain and heartache that he was put through in Berlin came in triplicate, with each occasion sweeter than the last. Korea regained her independence after World War II and twelve years after

---

3. This, after the previous days had seen crushing defeats for British athletes in the 400-metres and 5000-metres and "deplorably", the mother of all defeats on the polo field when Argentina crucified Britain 11–0. One can still almost feel the *The Times'* special correspondent's pain as he wrote: "Argentina were known to have a well-mounted and excellent team, but few would have prophesied a victory over the British four by such an overwhelming score."

4. It wasn't just the athletics that Hitler was interested in, as Helen Stephens of the USA found out. Upon winning the 100-metres final, Stephens was taken to meet Hitler in his private box. "Hitler comes in and gives me the Nazi salute," the 6-foot farmgirl later explained. "I gave him a good old Missouri handshake. Immediately Hitler goes for the jugular vein. He gets a hold of my fanny, and he begins to squeeze and pinch and hug me up, and he said, 'You're a true Aryan type. You should be running for Germany.' So after he gave the once-over and a full massage, he asked me if I'd like to spend the weekend in Berchtesgaden" (Wallechinsky). For some reason, Stephens passed.

his Olympic success, the renamed Sohn Kee-chung carried his nation's flag at the procession of athletes at the London Olympics' opening ceremony in 1948. He had by now settled in Korea where he was training the country's marathoners.

Forty years later, at the opening ceremony of the Seoul Olympics, a magical moment occurred. David Miller of *The Times* was there:

At 76, and the oldest torch-bearer of the 1988 Seoul Olympics, Sohn Kee-chung poses before receiving the Olympic torch, and trotting into the Stadium to startle and delight the 85,000 people inside. *S&G.*

Opening ceremonies so often disclose the soul of the nation, and so it was in South Korea. As they opened their arms to 159 other nationalities, and five billion TV viewers, we saw them for what they are: tranquil yet with an inner strength, graceful yet energetic, moulded by ancient dynasties yet ambitiously modern.

The people are determined yet poetic; their pageant was a picture of history, colour and elegance. Into the stadium came the flame, and the climax of a journey through South Korea that had brought emotional involvement for hundreds of thousands in countless villages, now carried by a national hero; Sohn Kee-chung, aged 76, the winner of the marathon as an enforced, reluctant Japanese in 1936.

The benign old champion skipped like a five-year-old through the crowd of athletes pressing on to the track around him and passed the torch to Lim Chun-ae, unheralded winner of three gold medals at the Asian Games in 1986.

If ever justice was served; then that that was it.

David Wallechinsky writes how it was a moment that "brought tears to an entire nation" as Sohn bounded around the track "leaping for joy and bursting with pride for himself and for his country."[5] And if all that wasn't enough, four years later, at the 1992 Barcelona Olympics, the icing on the cake was adorned with the juiciest of cherries. Sohn's protégé, Hwang Young-cho, finally won an Olympic marathon for Korea, defeating a Japanese, Koichi Morishita, into second place, whilst wearing Japanese shoes! (see Chapter 40). Weeping more tears of joy, Sohn Kee-chung sat watching intently in the stands.

---

5. The author has studied back-to-back footage of Sohn emerging from the tunnel in 1936 on the way to his win, and emerging from the tunnel again in 1988 at Seoul. Sohn's jubilant and excitable mannerisms of childlike joy on the latter occasion belong to a far younger man. Sohn had been forced to grow old way before his time...but in his latter years was forever young. He could still run pretty fast too.

Race result:

Kitei Son (Sohn Kee-chung)	JPN	2:29:19
Ernest Harper	GBR	2:31:23
Shoryu Nan (Nam Sung-yong)	JPN	2:31:42
Erkki Tamila	FIN	2:32:45
Väinö Muinonen	FIN	2:33:46
Johannes Coleman	SOA	2:36:17
Donald McNab Robertson	GBR	2:37:06
Henry Gibson	SOA	2:38:04
Mauno Tarkiainen	FIN	2:39:33
Thore Enochsson	SWE	2:43:12

Sources:

Archive race footage, *The Olympic Series: Golden Moments, 1920–2002*. Paramount Pictures.

Anonymous, in the *New York Times*, August 10th, 1936.

Anonymous, in *The Times*, August 10th, 1936.

Barnwell, John, in the *Boston Post*, April 19th, 1936.

Constable, G., *The XI, XII, and XIII Olympiads*. World Sport Research & Publications, Inc., Los Angeles, 1996.

Derderian, Tom, *Boston Marathon*. Human Kinetics, 1996.

Hauman, Riël, *Century of the Marathon*. Human & Rousseau, 1996.

Martin, David and Roger Gynn, *The Olympic Marathon*. Human Kinetics, 2000.

Miller, David, in *The Times*, September 17th, 1988.

Wallechinsky, David, *The Complete Book of the Olympics*. Aurum Press, 2000.

XII

No. 39 – 1979 New York City Marathon [Women]

Sunday, October 21st

Big Apple struck by Northern Lightning.

A lot can change in nine years, and a statement Riël Hauman makes in his 1996 book *Century of the Marathon* now appears a little dated: "There can be little doubt that Grete Waitz is the greatest female distance runner ever." Whether the likes of Kristiansen, Tulu, Wami, Ndereba, and most especially Radcliffe agree with that statement is a moot point; but what one can certainly claim is that Waitz is the greatest female *trail-blazer* of all time, picking up the torch from Gibb, Switzer, Kuscsik and Gorman, and lowering the marathon world record on four separate occasions over a five-year period by a margin of over nine minutes. Waitz first reduced the record in October 1978 (from Christa Vahlensieck of Germany's 2:34:47), all the way down to 2:25:28 at London in 1983. Just 24 hours later, Joan Benoit decided – in spectacular fashion – that it was finally time someone else did the work.

Waitz was born Grete Andersen on October 1st, 1953 in Oslo. Her father was a manufacturing pharmacist and her mother worked in a grocery shop. In Norway's "sports heaven" Grete's two brothers Jan and Arild, let her join in with the games they'd play with the other boys, which as author Michael Sandrock notes, "helped her develop the toughness that would come in handy once she started racing". Waitz explains in her book *World Class*: "As children, we used to play cops and robbers, and it was from this game that I sensed for the first time that I had some running ability. When I was a robber, no one wanted to be the cop to chase me, as I simply wore them down by continuing to run for such a long time."

Waitz joined Oslo's Vidar Sports Club when she was twelve and found that the longer the distance she raced the better she did. It was not long before she started training seriously for the 1500-metres, despite a lack of support from her parents who preferred her to stay home doing chores or playing the piano. After winning the Norwegian open 800- and 1500-metre titles in 1971, Waitz set the European junior record with 4:17 in the 1500. Failure to qualify from her heat in Grete's first major championships, the Europeans of 1971, left her crying for two hours in the stadium bathroom as the team coaches "kept their distance". Waitz writes: "I was disappointed, perplexed, angry, and only 17 years old...My bitterness fed my desire to excel. Just as with my parents, this denial of support strengthened my determination."

But Grete soon found out what *real* suffering was all about the following year, when her childhood sweetheart passed away, as she performed a helpless vigil by his bedside for several weeks. The year 1972 brought another "failure", even though she ran a personal best at the Munich Olympics. Grete was frustrated by the fact that she only rarely got to run the 3000-metres, and when she did, the reception from the "hacks" could have been more sensitive: "Oh, save us from these women running seven laps around the track" was a common attitude.

For the next four years up to the Montreal Olympics, Waitz led an incredibly disciplined lifestyle of getting up at 5:30 a.m. to train before her teaching job at elementary school. This work ethic paid off with bronze at the European Championships of 1974 with bronze in the 1500, but her training of roughly 100 miles a week would have been much more suited to the 3000 in Montreal, which wasn't included in the programme. In a strong semi-final heat she was eliminated. The Norwegian press blasted her for her failure, ignoring the fact she was teaching full-time plus commuting two hours a day. She writes: "This added to the already enormous pressure, creating a weight that threatened to crush me. Despite my warnings, the Norwegian people were led to simply assume I would win. I became a victim of the Norwegian expression 'a silver medal is a defeat' – if you don't win, you lose."

After the 1978 Europeans, in which Waitz took another bronze in the 3000, and fifth in the 1500-metres, she strongly considered retiring. The heartless Norwegian press was losing none of its venom, and Waitz believed she'd never find the kick to outmanoeuvre the East Europeans.[1] Grete was not looking at the big picture though, which is that women's running was obviously more competitive by now, and that her 8:34.33 was a very fine time. But the Norwegian sportswriters did not agree and devastated Waitz with their blinkered, vitriolic outbursts. Waitz recalls: "They wrote about me as if I had more or less come last. That, plus the fact that some of the girls were proven to have been using drugs, made me feel that it was just no fun any more. Another factor was that the 1980 Olympics wouldn't have a 3000. So I made up my mind that now was the time to call it a day."

Something needed to happen quickly for Waitz not to walk away from the sport she loved. And it did, in the form of a letter from a man named Fred Lebow in New York City. The now legendary Lebow was inviting Waitz to run in the marathon he directed that November in New York. "No! No, *absolutely*, no!" wailed Waitz to her husband, Jack (Sandrock). After all, Grete had never travelled further than 12 miles in training. She wasn't about to go twice as far and then some, in a race. But after much cajoling, and a "see how it goes" attitude, Waitz relented. At least she'd get a long weekend in the Big Apple.

Through 16 miles of her debut marathon, Waitz remained with the other leading women, before taking off on her own. At 18 miles the race became very hard, her legs began cramping as the never-ending streets of Harlem refused to

---

1. She was probably right, many of them tested positive for anabolic steroids in 1979.

meet Central Park. (And then, even when they did, three excruciating hilly miles remained.) But blow up she did not, and Christa Vahlensieck's world record of 2:34:47 from the previous year had been lowered to 2:32:30. Grete's prize? Twenty bucks, for a cab ride to the airport. (These days Paula Radcliffe scoops the same reward in her marathons once every 1.2 metres).

Grete was, however, besieged by the media who loved the story of an unknown, lean, blonde Norwegian coming to America, running her first marathon, defeating the field by nine minutes and breaking the world record. Her life would never be the same again, something that such a private person was somewhat uncomfortable with. "I lost my anonymity forever," she concedes.

The next year was a great success for Waitz as she repeated as World Cross-Country champion, and set a world best for 10 miles of 53:05. And then she was back at New York for this chapter's featured marathon. If she had startled the watching punters the previous year, then Grete had a real treat in store for them in 1979.

Glenn Fowler in the *New York Times* wrote: "It was the biggest marathon in history, and it drew a record crowd. And as it has increasingly each year, yesterday's New York City Marathon turned the five boroughs into a cheering section for what Mayor Koch labels 'the best happening in the world'." Just as man breaking the 4-minute mile is commonplace now, so is woman breaking the 2:30 marathon; but it's still an extremely elusive goal for many top runners, and still the benchmark for determining whether or not an athlete is national and world-class.

Waitz reached halfway in 1979 in 1:14:51, four minutes faster that she had the previous year. Off Queensboro Bridge at 16 miles, Grete's husband yelled to her that she was on a record pace, but Grete – as ever – was in pessimistic mood. "I complained as I usually do when I see him," she said. "I said 'my legs are stiff and sore.' But he knows me, and he knows I'm always complaining."

Complain she could – and would – do all she liked, but slow down? Never. However frisky her halfway split may have been, Waitz showed the hallmark of all great marathoners by speeding up over the second half of the race, in this case by two minutes and nine seconds, to clock 2:27:33. She was aided by a male runner over the last six to seven miles who pulled her along just when her body was starting to fail. He finished ahead of her and she never did manage to find him and give thanks. Second-placed runner Gillian Adams of Britain was almost 11 minutes adrift. The women's world record time was suddenly closing fast on the men – they were now just 19 minutes off Derek Clayton's record set all the way back in 1969, at which time the female record was Anni Pede-Erdkamp's 3:07:26!

The *New York Times*' Al Harvin penned a character sketch entitled: "A Wonder of the Race" and pointed out: "Mrs Waitz's record run represented another major advance in women's distance running. In 1970, the first year the New York City Marathon was run through Central Park, no women finished the race. Yesterday, 27 finished in less than three hours, and the time posted by Waitz would have beaten all of the men who competed in 1970 including Gary Muhrcke, who won in 2:31:28." Out of the 19 previous Olympic marathons, Waitz's time would have won 12, and she would have asked serious questions of both Emil Zátopek at

Helsinki in 1952, and even more so, Alain Mimoun in 1956.

Neil Amdur, also in the *New York Times*, was equally impressed with what he witnessed:

> Bill Rodgers and Grete Waitz again gave New Yorkers something to cheer about yesterday with spectacular victories in the 10th NYC Marathon. Mrs Waitz, a 26-year-old teacher from Norway, became the first woman to run a marathon in under 2 hours 30 minutes.
>
> The significance of her effort was extraordinary: in a field of 11,533 starters, including 1,800 women, she finished in 69th place. Her time would have been good enough for second place over all in the Chicago Marathon, which also was held yesterday with 7,500 runners.

Waitz explained how the experience of running through the streets of New York had evolved on her return visit: "When I came here last year, I had never been to New York City before, and I was just running along watching the sights. For me the people play a big role in the race. They cheered me all the way, the men especially. They kept saying I was looking good and I could break the record."

Rival women were as awed by Waitz's showing as the spectators who lined the route. Gillian Adams admitted:

> The last time I saw her was at the starting gate. She's just really, really fit. I've watched her a lot in races in Europe. She's well built for running – long legs, slim – and she's very determined. I'm not surprised she's run that fast. A lot of men aren't going to be able to sleep tonight when they hear her time. They're not going to believe that they can run 2:30 and then finish behind a woman!

Bill Rodgers, champion for the fourth year in a row, said he had thought Waitz would run 2:29: "She's always a step ahead of me. She's outrageous."

Unfortunately, despite all this fabulous progress for women's distance running, the Olympic organizers were disgracefully behind the times, with the longest women's event for the following year's games advertised at just 1500-metres. A clearly unimpressed Waitz noted: "I haven't made any plans to participate in the Olympics because they don't have my distance in the Olympics. The longest distance women are allowed to run in the Olympics is 1500-metres. That's a middle distance. I'm a long-distance runner."

* * *

Waitz went on to win New York another seven times and would come back the following year to lower her world record by almost two more minutes. After she won the inaugural World Championships marathon in 1983 (in 2:28:08 – by three minutes over Marianne Dickerson), her Olympic record is a little frustrating. By far her best chance of striking gold came in 1984, but she was out manoeuvred into silver by an inspired Joan Benoit (see Chapter 35). It was one of just two defeats in fifteen completed marathons (Martin & Gynn). In the 1988 Olympics she was one of the favourites in a terrific field, but ended up as one of just five DNFs in the race as arthroscopic knee surgery just a month before had left her

Grete Waitz wasn't just a big hit in New York. The London crowds came to know and admire her imperious ways where she was a double winner. Here she kicks off the first of those triumphs in April 1983. *Mark Shearman*

short of fitness. How ironic. Her tormentor at Los Angeles, herself underwent arthroscopic knee surgery before the Olympics, but it seems that Waitz recovered far less well from hers.[2]

Throughout these Olympic disappointments, however, one factor remained a constant: Waitz's success at New York. In 1985 she won New York for the seventh time and, improving as she got older, won London by nearly six minutes in 1986 in a personal best of 2:24:54. That fall she returned to New York and won yet again before recording her ninth and final victory at the 1987 edition. The years 1988 and 1989 saw her have to sit out the race with injury problems before making a creditable swansong appearance in 1990 with a fourth placed 2:34:34. It was her last competitive race and it was appropriate that she bow out on the Manhattan stage where she made her name.

Perhaps the most memorable and emotional of all Waitz's marathons was her 5:32:34 clocking at the 1992 race, where she participated alongside her great friend Fred Lebow. Lebow was dying of cancer and Waitz finished this marathon in tears as she knew it would be the last time she and her friend ran together. Lebow died shortly before the 1994 race where emotional tributes were paid to the president of the New York Road Runners club and NYC Marathon race founder.

---

2. Timing is everything, of course, and Benoit had her surgery around five months before the Olympics, compared to Waitz's one.

Waitz calmly and clinically won the inaugural World Championship Marathon at Helsinki in 1983. *Getty Images/Tony Duffy*

Waitz still shows up at the New York Marathon where she gives interesting seminars about all aspects of running and fitness, but she no longer has any desire to compete.

Deservedly, a statue of Waitz has been erected outside Oslo's Bislett Stadium, and every year over 40,000 women run in the Grete Waitz 5K run in Oslo. Journalist Katy Williams summed up her appreciation for Waitz in *Running with the Legends* by writing: "Grete is the one people adore. She is just a warm person. There was so much written about her and she is so much in the public eye, yet she's so charming and so genuine. I had read about her for years, and thought it was just a gimmick. But it isn't."

For her part, Waitz is keen to dispel the impression she has oft given over of being a less than merry person. She pointedly denies this and once described herself in an interview as such: "Sometimes people look at me and because I am not always smiling and laughing they think I am sad. I'm not sad. I'm not. I'm maybe a little cool. Not impulsive, but controlled. That's the word. Controlled (Hauman)."

In April 2005 blood tests revealed that Waitz had cancer, which she is now battling with her typical resilience and courage. Waitz states: "I walk uphill on my treadmill, six miles every day, and it is boring like hell. I am going to beat this cancer s***. No matter what, I am going to."

Race result:

Grete Waitz	NOR	2:27:33
Gillian Adams	GBR	2:38:31
Jacqueline Gareau	CAN	2:39:04
Patti Lyons	BOS	2:40:17
Carol Gould	GBR	2:42:19
Vreni Forster	SUI	2:43:12

Sources:

Conversations with Ingrid Kristiansen.
Conversations with Bill Rodgers.
Amdur, Neil, in the *New York Times*, October 22nd, 1979.
Fowler, Glen, in the *New York Times*, October 22nd, 1979.
Harvin, Al, in the *New York Times*, October 22nd, 1979.
Hauman, Riël, *Century of the Marathon*. Human & Rousseau, 1996.
Lewis, Richard, in *Athletics Weekly*, November 23rd, 2005.
Martin, David and Roger Gynn, *The Olympic Marathon*. Human Kinetics, 2000.
Sandrock, Michael, *Running with the Legends*. Human Kinetics, 1996.

XIII

No. 38 – 1991 World Championships [Women]

Sunday, August 25th

Wanda-ful run in a Tokyo cauldron.

The 1991 Tokyo World Athletics Championships were expertly organized and boasted some hugely dramatic moments, most notably the 100-metres final that many regard as the most splendid 100-metre race of all time. Six dipped under 10 seconds in the final, in which the pecking order ran: Lewis 9.86, Burrell 9.88, Mitchell 9.91, Christie 9.92, Fredericks 9.95 and Stewart 9.96. Christie was so overwhelmed by the perfection of the race that he promptly retired from the sport, happy in the knowledge that he had fulfilled his potential. What a pity. Who knows, he could have won an Olympic medal the following year if he had only stayed in the sport. Oh, that's right, he did.

If Lewis was ecstatic at winning the hundred, he was denied gold in the long jump, another event regarded by many as the best drama that particular competition has ever produced. Both Lewis and his American rival, Mike Powell, traded world records during the thrilling final, before Powell finally edged the day, leaping to 8.95 metres, just 4 centimetres further than Lewis. There were two highly memorable turns for British fans to savour. To close the championships with a spectacular flourish was the sight of the British 400-metre-relay squad pipping the Americans by four-hundredths of a second to secure the gold medal, thanks to Kris Akabusi's final lunge.

And before that, came the sight of Scotswoman Liz McColgan grinding her opponents into the dust as she claimed an unlikely triumph. Onlookers had felt that African runners would rule the day in the oppressive conditions, but they struggled almost worse than anyone. Ethiopia's Derartu Tulu was the leading African in 8th, with the Kenyan runners Delilah Asiago and Jane Ngotho finishing 12th and 21st (last). McColgan also faced great challenges in the face of Lynn Jennings, Ingrid Kristiansen and Uta Pippig, but those three could only place 5th, 6th and 7th.

What could be said for sure is that McColgan coped with the stifling conditions far better than many of the marathoners a few days earlier, and she had certainly marked her card as someone who had a promising blend of both mental and physical resolve should she decide to move up in distance.[1]

What many of the spectators remember from the Tokyo World Championships is the fierce and sapping heat. Friends of the author, Alan and Pat Mead, travelled to Tokyo to celebrate their 25th wedding anniversary and watch the championships. Both clearly recall the discomfort that went with viewing the action. Pat often had to leave the stadium to save herself from almost passing out, so fierce was the temperature. Alan recalls the runners before the women's 10,000-metres being drenched with sweat at the start of the race, with McColgan having pulled back her flowing locks so tight it seemed to stretch her face.

It is no surprise, therefore, that whilst not quite qualifying as the most gruelling marathon featured in the book, the 1991 Women's World Championship Marathon at Tokyo took its toll on the competitors in a major way. Only 38 felt able to start,[2] and of those, 14 failed to finish. Such a statistic immediately had the author reaching for the record books because women are significantly feistier, more stubborn marathoners than their male counterparts. One of the reasons women are such unbreakable marathoners, the author submits, is because it took men, in their wisdom, 88 years before they allowed women to compete in the Olympic marathon. The girls felt they had a point to prove. Thus, in the first few Olympic marathons in which women were allowed to compete, the drop-out rate was far lower than the men. In the 1984 Olympics, 27 per cent of the men returned a DNF, compared to 14 per cent of the women. For 1988, men DNFs were 17 per cent, women DNFs just 8 per cent. In 1992 the percentages were: men: 22 per cent and women 19 per cent.

So with a 37-per-cent drop-out rate, this chapter's featured race is indeed an anomaly, and leads it to qualify as the marathon with the third most casualties in the book: 51 per cent failed to finish at the 1908 Olympics – including, of course, Dorando Pietri – and 47 per cent scored a DNF at the inaugural Olympic marathon of 1896.[3] It would thus take a competitor of renowned toughness to win the 1991 World Championships, and since they were to take place in Japan, it was an odds-on bet – with the help of partisan home support – that an Asian competitor would triumph.

Although the final leaderboard is not exactly littered with them, the 1991 World Championships had some heavy hitters. Undeniably the biggest star was the diminutive 45-kilogram Rosa Mota who had won most of the important races that had come her way over the past half-dozen or so years. A year earlier, in

---

1. Which, of course, she did, winning major marathons in New York (a world-best for a debutante), Tokyo (where she beat the Olympic champ by four minutes) and London. But her marathoning is best remembered by some for a spectacular failure – see Chapter 8.
2. Fifty started the Los Angeles Olympic marathon seven years earlier, and 69 started at Seoul in 1988. An impressive 88 runners set out at Atlanta in 1996, but, oddly, just 46 began at Barcelona in '92 – another very hot day. The question of why there is such a wide variance between runners beginning the Olympics at 1988, '92 and '96 puzzles the author, since the men follow a strict pattern of steadily increasing numbers as the chronology of the Olympics progresses. As for why so few women started at Tokyo is something of a mystery – could so many really have been scared off by the heat? Surely it is as oppressive for all and one. One guesses that the World Championships is attractive to fewer contenders than the Olympics, even though the qualifying criteria are less severe.
3. The prize for the highest marathon drop-out rate of all time goes to the Intercalated Games at Athens in 1906, when an absurd 71 per cent had to call it a day. It is no surprise that the brutal Olympic marathons of 1900 and 1904 saw their share of mayhem, as in each race 56 per cent failed to trouble the scorers.

Split, Mota had executed a remarkable treble by winning three consecutive European Championship marathons; on this occasion it was a squeaker though – by just 5 seconds over the formidable Valentina Yegorova – who was also present in Tokyo, and would go on to win the Olympic Games the following year. However, for once, at Tokyo, Mota arrived nursing a niggle. Although she had won the London Marathon convincingly four months earlier in 2:26 (held in conjunction with the World Cup), Mota had since had surgery to remove an abdominal cyst, and some wondered whether she would have recovered in time.

But if the queen of European marathon running was perhaps just off her best, there was a very real new danger for the favoured Asians to consider, and her name was Wanda Panfil. Panfil was born in Poland but now lived in Mexico, where she was coached by her husband, Mauricio Gonzales, himself an Olympian. She came to the World Championships having won, earlier in the year, a quite scintillating marathon at Boston, which was a hair's-breadth from qualifying for this book's top-50 list. Before that she had won thrice in the year of 1990 – at Nagoya, London (where she beat one of the strongest fields for years) and New York, where Kim Jones chased her very hard, but Panfil managed to survive by 5 seconds. A resurgent Benoit Samuelson was at the Boston of '91, with the thought of one day dipping under 2:20 still forever gentle on her mind. An on-the-wane, but still threatening, Ingrid Kristiansen came to race, as did the excellent Pole Kamila Gradus. America's Kim Jones was improving every time out, as was the new darling of the crowds with her cover-girl looks, East German Uta Pippig.

Author Tom Derderian speaks of the dedication that Panfil brought to her sport: "Running with a potent stride, her face hawkish, Panfil moved at the peak of preparation for her fierce vocation. She had rearranged her life to run, changing continents, cuisines, and languages." At the halfway mark in the Boston of '91 Panfil broke free of the attention of her iconic chasers, Benoit Samuelson and Kristiansen, being bothered by the roars of the crowd for Samuelson: "The noise was a bit of a distraction, and played a role in my decision to move early," she explained. Whilst five talented racers scrapped fiercely in a constantly evolving top order, one factor had always remained a constant, the leader. Panfil "crossed the finish line wearing a relaxed, satisfied smile" (Derderian). It was, wrote Derderian, "the tightest, most exciting finish in women's marathoning history. These sprinting women had to find a plumb line through the tangle of racing men. A man could, in his fatigue, inadvertently influence the fortunes of a female marathoner by thousands of dollars. Fortunately every woman manoeuvred through these dodge 'ems with skill and grace."

Pippig just passed the Olympic champion of seven years earlier, by 2 seconds. Gradus failed to catch Benoit Samuelson by one second. The three women were within a 3-second span, with Jones 12 seconds ahead of them in second. Never before had five women run under 2:27 in the same marathon. "It looked like the finish of a 1500-metre race rather than a marathon" (Derderian). But none of these hugely talented runners had an answer to the power of Panfil.

* * *

As the runners lined up to start the World Championship marathon at 7 a.m. on August 25th, 1991, other runners who might perhaps pose a threat to Panfil were

117

Wanda Panfil 580 allows Rosa Mota to edge into the lead during the early stages of the 1991 World Championship marathon. The key threat of Germany's Katrin Dörre is number 331, while over to the right Sachiko Yamashita [481] settles in, and to her right is Yuko Arimuri, who would feature both here and at '92 Olympics. *Mark Shearman*

Katrin Dörre of Germany, who had won 15 of the 21 marathons in which she'd run, Kristiansen, the two other Poles, Kokowska and Gradus, and, of course, the Japanese themselves, on whose shoulders rested the hopes of an entire nation. It was already warm and humid. Author Riël Hauman writes: "The 38 competitors did not relish the uncomfortable conditions, but Mota nevertheless immediately took the lead. A group of fifteen formed around her and they went through 5 kilometres in a slow 17:53."

The pace over the next 10 kilometres continued to be understandably sluggish, and 15 kilometres passed in 53:04 with Panfil looking dangerous, accompanied by Dörre, Norwegian runner Sissel Grottenberg and German Iris Biba. But meanwhile the heroic Mota was starting to realize that this was not to be her race as her breathing difficulties started to cause acute abdominal pain. She would jump ship soon after.

When the Portuguese runner Manuela Machado had to drop back between 30 and 35 kilometres, Yuko Arimori broke Japanese hearts everywhere as she found she could no longer keep up either. Arimori had been seen by many to be Japan's best hope for a gold medal. However, there was one last joker in the pack which the adoring Japanese fans had to play, and it belonged to a little known 27-year-old called Sachiko Yamashita, who boasted a modest personal best coming into the championships of 2:31:02 at Nagoya, the previous March.

Dörre, Panfil and Yamashita, locked together in battle, charged the final few kilometres through the streets to almost hysterical support – even though conventional wisdom had it that the Japanese would be the one to crack first. But no, it was Dörre. "The second half of the race was very difficult," she said later. "I tried

Panfil wins, just a few steps ahead of Yamashita.
Mark Shearman

to sprint with Wanda at 39 kilometres, but I just couldn't keep up with her."

Not only was Yamashita somehow keeping up, she amazingly started dictating the pace. Receiving "vociferous support" with every staccato step, Yamashita used the crowd's energy to help her to surge in an attempt to get away. But however hard she pushed, the nagging shadow of Panfil wouldn't go away. During the 42nd kilometre Panfil made her own break. A gap of 10 metres soon appeared and grew inch by agonizing inch. Yamashita clung on desperately. Emerging from the darkness to the bright-orange track of the Olympic Stadium, Panfil had a 20-metre lead over Yamashita, who was leading Dörre by double that. The roars of the crowd would do no good. Panfil was just too strong and won by four ticks of the clock. She and Yamashita were the only athletes to break 2:30. For Yamashita, to break her personal best by over a minute in such oppressive conditions was some going.

Oddly enough, one national record was broken in the race – by Gina Coello of Honduras – but try as she might she couldn't get her beloved nation's mark down below the three-hour mark, as she ran 3:00:03 for 23rd.

Ken Mays in the *Daily Telegraph* reported on some British pluck when he revealed:

Britain's Sally Ellis worked her way past 15 runners to finish tenth in 2:35:09, and then announced that she planned to climb 12,000ft up Mount Fuji on Wednesday.

Ellis, 33, said, "Obviously it takes a long time to recover from a marathon, but when you come so far across the world it would be daft not to see the country's great sight. I think it would be wonderful to climb up Mount Fuji overnight and see the sun rising."

Tom Knight in *Athletics Weekly* was quick to point out:

We thought it might have been the end of an era when reigning champion Rosa Mota retired from the fray at 26 kilometres. But it wasn't. After the race, her coach, Jose Pedrosa, was quick to quell rumours that she had run against her will, under pressure from the Portuguese federation: "We would never accept pressure from any quarter to compete," he said. "Rosa was in good shape and came to run in Tokyo confident of winning."

However, unbeknown to Mota at the time, the London event of four months earlier was to be her last completed marathon at the age of just 31.

*   *   *

What the marathon giveth it soon taketh away. Just when it seemed as though Panfil was unbeatable and would be on top for a few years to come yet, she became yesterday's hero. She came to the Boston Marathon in 1992 in search of all sorts of good things, her appetite for being the finest female marathoner in the world almost insatiable. Tom Derderian summed up her philosophy at this time: "For some people winning is not enough. Such was the case for Wanda Panfil. Panfil dedicated herself completely to running. After her win in 1991, Panfil this year wanted to set a personal record (2:24:18), break the course record (2:22:43), and break the world record (2:21:06). Running a cagey race, winning, and picking up $60,000 was not what she was about." Panfil passed five miles in an almost crazy 26:02. Her challengers dropped away. She was on her own running into no-man's-land. On the long hill before the firehouse at mile 17 – where the real hills starts – Panfil found fatigue beginning to snuff out her dreams. Olga Markova of Russia came up on her, but Panfil had no race left. Markova had masses and would go on to win by nearly three minutes. "All Panfil could do was finish on legs that had become painful posts" (Derderian). Her bravery was commended on air as she finally finished sixth in 2:29:29.

At the following year's Olympics, Panfil ran a dismal 2:47 for 22nd and failed to finish the next year's Boston. It seems that her intense dedication had finally exhausted her willing but unable body. She would never figure on a significant leaderboard again. But for a couple of years in the early 1990s, Wanda Panfil's flame burned brighter than anyone else in the marathoning world.

Race result:

Wanda Panfil	POL	2:29:53
Sachiko Yamashita	JPN	2:29:57
Katrin Dörre-Heinig	GER	2:30:10
Yuko Arimori	JPN	2:31:08
Maria Rebelo-Lelut	FRA	2:32:05
Kamila Gradus	POL	2:32:09
Manuela Machado	POR	2:32:33
Ramilya Burangulova	USSR	2:33:00
Iris Biba	GER	2:33:48
Sally Ellis	GBR	2:35:09

Sources:

Derderian, Tom, *Boston Marathon*. Human Kinetics, 1996.

Hauman, Riël, in *Century of the Marathon*. Human & Rousseau, 1996.

Knight, Tom, in *Athletics Weekly*, August 28th, 1991.

Martin, David and Roger Gynn, *The Olympic Marathon*. Human Kinetics, 2000.

Mays, Ken, in the *Daily Telegraph*, August 26th, 1991.

XIV

No. 37 – 1972 Olympic Marathon [Men]

Sunday, September 10th

Having a Shorter fuse works wonders.

After the spectacular, tender closing ceremony of the Rome Olympics, with thousands setting light to their rolled up newspapers to form flares, and the electric scoreboard reading "*Arriverderci Roma*", the Tokyo Games followed suit and said "*sayonara*" in another memorable closing. And then, as Arthur Daley wrote in the *New York Times*:

> Mexico City had the most exuberant of all finales, and this fiesta carried on almost until dawn as revellers in the downtown streets tooted their auto horns and screamed a joyous '*May-Hee-Co*.' The happy-go-lucky Mexicans had exceeded all expectations and produced a magnificent set of Olympic Games. Munich also will be remembered by Olympic historians but for all the wrong reasons.
>
> It was raining when closing day dawned and the day was to remain damp, dark and dolorous. It is difficult to envision a more appropriate setting for these unhappiest of Olympic Games than the grey, funereal backdrop that the weatherman provided.

The cover of *Newsweek* magazine in autumn 1972 asked, "The Haywire Olympics – What went wrong?", after the Games had been forever marred by the grotesque outrage of eight Palestinian terrorists – and a woefully botched salvage operation by the West German special forces – which led to the murder of eleven Israeli athletes.

Except for Mark Spitz and the other swimmers, the United States had its least productive Olympics. American athletes were sub par, while American officials displayed incompetence and arrogance. These traits were not confined to the US however. The Games were riddled by both – especially in events where judgement is involved – because prejudice too often flavours judgement.

In what Wallechinsky calls "one of the greatest controversies in the history of international sports", the Soviet Union defeated the United States by a single point in the basketball final. They somewhat deserved it after US coach Hank Iba abandoned his team's favoured style of pacey play for a more deliberate approach. But it was the manner of defeat that really riled the Americans, reached after three seconds had been dubiously added on after the United States had already celebrated a win. Soviet basket-hanger, Aleksandr Belov, knocked down an American defender in front of the Bulgarian referee and dropped in the winning basket with less than a second remaining on the clock. Final score, 51–50 to the Soviets. The Americans had previously won all 62 games of basketball they had played at the Olympics since it was introduced in 1936. Disgusted by the unjust way their winning streak was halted, the Americans voted unanimously to refuse the silver medal. While signing the official protest form at 2 a.m., Hank Iba had reason to feel robbed again as $370 was picked from his pocket.

Some of the US players were haunted by the loss for years to come and refused to refer to it again. Others were more sanguine, putting the loss into perspective next to the far graver issues at the Games. Kenny Davis told *Sports Illustrated* in 1992:

I went back to my room and cried alone that night. But every time I get to feeling sorry for myself, I think of the Israeli kids who were killed at those Games...think of being in a helicopter with your hands tied behind your back and a hand grenade rolling toward you...and compare that to not getting a gold medal. If that final game is the worst injustice that ever happens to the guys on that team, we'll all come out of this life pretty good.

Neil Amdur of the *New York Times* wrote:

Long after the memories of who won and lost have been absorbed, analysed and forgotten, the Games of the XX Olympiad will be remembered for their chaos, confusion and tragedy. Power politics, nationalism, death, drug abuse and even cheating overshadowed the lofty proclamations of brotherhood and goodwill that had brought thousands of athletes and officials from 124 nations to this charming Bavarian capital.

It was a Games that began as one country's dream to show the world a new face. It ended in a series of nightmares.

The Games began and finished in farce for 84-year-old Avery Brundage, the outgoing president who had served the IOC for 20 years. A bloc of black African nations led by Kenya and Ethiopia threatened to withdraw from the competition if Rhodesia were allowed to compete. Under pressure, the IOC withdrew its invitation to Rhodesia after long deliberations and a close vote. It was the darkest administrative defeat ever for Brundage. Appropriately even the closing full stop of the Games were crowned with a toe-curling gaffe as the XX Olympiad bade farewell to Brundage on the electronic scoreboard in massive gold letters with the message: "Thank you Avery Brandage."

Basketball aside, the States had another legend coming to grief in Munich, as miler Jim Ryun was tripped in his 1500-metre heat, which had lads from Pakistan and Ghana making up the numbers, and, bizarrely, the defending Olympic champion Kip Keino. The reason Keino was in the same heat as his biggest rival is a classic in bureaucratic incompetence: the US had submitted Ryun's personal best time to the organizers as a ludicrously slow 3:52 – his time for the mile of course, and thus his seeding was as one of the worst of all competitors.

Brash, cocksure but sublimely gifted Steve Prefontaine was seen as a shoe-in for at least a medal in the 5000-metre run. But his warnings of running the last mile in 4 minutes did not concern the gazelle-like swiftness of Finn Lasse Viren who snatched the gold. The ever-ready Tunisian Mohammed Ghammoudi, who picked up no less than four medals in the 5000/10,000-metres between 1964 and 1972, was just too experienced and shrewd; and then, just to add vinegar to the floundering "Pre"'s wounds in the home-stretch, he was pipped by fast-finishing Ian Stewart of Britain.

American Bob Seagren came to the Games as world record holder in the pole vault, but was forced to use a fibreglass pole, after officials, in a deeply unedifying affair, banned him from using his normal one. That saw off his challenge as Wolfgang Nordwig of Germany took the gold in an event that the US had won at every Olympics since 1906.

All the while this jumbled mess was limping along, there was, mercifully for America, one man waiting patiently in the wings who was to go a long way to right these wrongs. He wasn't going to be put off by his event being put back a day, or by the fact that an impostor would jump into his race in the closing moments attempting to steal his glory. No, only an extraordinarily fit human being could deny one American his destiny.

* * *

Anyone who "invents" something which becomes common usage the world over has done a very special thing; and whilst *Outside* magazine might have been getting a little carried away when they said that Frank Shorter had "invented" running in 1972, they were right to highlight the significance of his achievements. Shorter had taken a subculture sport and made it capture the imagination of the general public, and in turn, had inspired those folks to take that imagination and transform it into action. In other words, to leave their couches and TV sets, and head outside to partake in something called exercise, or if you like (and whisper this very gently), something called jogging.

There's no question that Frank Shorter was the right man, for the right job, in the right place. To change people's perception of something that is uncool and turn it into cool, something that's tiresome and turn it into fun, something that's painful and turn it into pleasurable, needs a certain kind of man and leadership. Someone who can say: "Follow me, this is the way, you *might* enjoy it." That man was Shorter. Feisty, outspoken and confident, Shorter was never afraid to speak his mind, to defy convention and reject the herd instinct. Independence was his watchword and short of suffering fools gladly, he wouldn't suffer them at all.

Perhaps a reason why Shorter's great rival a few years later, Bill Rodgers, was so universally and openly adored, is that Rodgers was completely unthreatening. People knew that he'd be friendly and polite. Journalists knew he'd return their calls. Shorter carried far more menace. Criticize me if you like; I couldn't give a damn, he'd say. I'm on a mission, and that mission is to be the best runner in the world. Shorter explained to the *New York Times*:

The people who get upset about my image, I don't care about them. They need to be shook up a little anyway. A lot of people I've met have the "if only" blues. "If only I could have trained harder, if only I could have trained more." That's what they say. I had to zero in on one thing. I knew maybe I wouldn't make it, but then I wouldn't be saying to myself, "if only".

Born in Munich on October 31st, 1947, Shorter grew up in Middletown, New York. One of six boys and five girls, Frank was the second youngest and grew up passionate about reading, singing and skiing, with a fondness for football, swimming and baseball. But one day, after a game of flag football which degenerated into a particularly rough game, Shorter asked his gym teacher if he could run *around* the football fields instead of playing football *on* them. The teacher, as author Michael Sandrock records, "not knowing what force he was unleashing upon the world, agreed, and thus the first steps toward an Olympic gold medal were taken."

Shorter enjoyed running so much that he even took to travelling that way to and from school. "I liked the feeling the first time I ran, and I enjoyed the idea of being a bit unusual." It was an Olympic skier and not runner that he really dreamed of being, however, with his heroes the likes of Jean-Claude Killy and Guy Perillat. "I wanted to be a ski racer, and I had read that skiers trained by running in the off-season, so I thought I'd do it, too." In the fall of 1964 more seeds were sown as Shorter was glued to the Tokyo Olympics: "I was inspired by Mills and Schul in '64. The 53-second last lap Schul ran, with mud flying everywhere on the cinder track, stood out in my mind" (Sandrock).

After being accepted to Yale, Shorter kept up his training but prudently kept below 50 miles per week until midway through his senior year. Without any visible means of support, promising young American runners have often drawn their careers to a close post college, and besides, with a degree from Yale, one had the blueprint to the American dream. But Shorter refused to stop running until he'd found how far his potential could take him. First of all Shorter tried medical school, but the stifling atmosphere and emphasis on memorization disagreed with his creative mind and he chucked it in after just three months. Shorter moved to Taos, New Mexico, to pursue his running and work construction jobs. It wasn't long before he was hitting 140 miles a week.

Breakthroughs come suddenly in running, and the one that showed Shorter just how good he could be was when he was featured on the cover of *Sports Illustrated* in the summer of 1970 for winning the 10,000 metres in a USSR–US meet. A few months later he defeated the great Ron Clark in the Australian star's last race, in a fine 28:33. Law school was the next avenue of potential vocation for Shorter to try as he continued to search for ways to keep his athletics going. At Florida Law School he was soon banging out workouts such as 15×400-metres in 62-3 seconds with just a 50-yard jog recovery. In 1971 he qualified for the Pan-American Games with a 2:17 debut marathon – the encouragement he needed to pursue the marathon as his prime event. The Pan-American Games, run in extremely hot weather, suited Shorter who always ran well in heat. (It was rain that was his arch enemy.) Winning in 2:22 over Kenny Moore and a couple of fast Colombians felt easy, and the Shorter reputation was growing. Come December he was suddenly one of the world's foremost marathoners as he won Fukuoka – the unofficial world championship of the time – in 2:12:51 on a windy day.

In early 1972 Shorter went to Vail with his sidekicks, Jack Bacheler and Jeff Galloway, putting in up to 170 miles a week for six weeks. "Vail was our laboratory, and we were the experiment," Shorter explains. He came into the summer of 1972 in supreme shape and won the US Olympic trials in both the 10,000-metres (28:18) and the marathon (2:16:51).

* * *

Shorter carried through that top shape into the September 1972 Olympics, feeling a confidence which was fuelled by an Italian miler Francesco Arese telling Shorter after a meet in Oslo "*Tu gagnera le marathon*". Shorter ran extremely well to hang on like he did in the 10,000-metres final in history's fastest ever race of that length up till then, with such greats as Viren, Puttemans and Gammoudi. He broke his American record by finishing fifth in 27:51. Far from thinking this could mean he'd be fatigued for the marathon, Shorter went into it with the belief that he was much faster than anyone else on paper.

After the Israeli terrorist massacre on September 5th, which Shorter describes as "an incredible day, a sad day", the IOC debated whether to cancel the Olympics entirely, but instead delayed them by 24 hours. The marathon's 24-hour delay played havoc with the tactics of one of the pre-race favourites, Briton Ron Hill, who felt it skewed all his careful preparations. At dinner the night before the race, Shorter recalls: "He was ranting and raving about how he needed to run on the day planned for. I said, 'Ron, you've been training for four years. One more day isn't going to make a difference.' And I said to myself right then that he was not going to be a factor" (Sandrock).

In his detailed autobiography, *The Long Hard Road*, Hill gives insight to how he viewed his main competitors:

Usami, Akio, Japan: A good and tough runner, carrying the hopes of Japan, but he has run a lot of marathons in the last eighteen months and his times have got slower and slower.

Philipp, Lutz, West Germany: He beat me in the British Trial, but I think that was his run of the year. I don't think he will be a danger.

Lismont, Karel, Belgium: The winner of the European Marathon championship in Helsinki last year, where I was third. That was a bloody lucky race for him; I was injured, the standard of the field was not that great and his winning time was nothing special under those cool conditions. I don't expect to see him anywhere near at the end.

Moore, Kenneth, USA: Kenny was joint first in the USA trial in a time of 2:15-odd but ran in the lead with Frank Shorter and therefore was obviously not fully extended. Even so, their trial only being nine weeks ago should make him still tired from that race.

Hill, Ronald, GBR: That's me! The 2:09:28 looks good in the list, the second fastest time ever.

Clayton, Derek, Australia: the world's fastest marathon runner with 2:08:33. Now he could be a danger. Although he has had a lot of injury problems in the last four years he still managed the world's best time of 1971 with me third on that list and he has been lying pretty low this year, reportedly conserving his energies for the Olympic Marathon. He will have to be watched.

***Foster, Jack, NZL**: another great runner for his age – must be 40 by now, but I don't think he will be in the medals; but I hope he is well up there as he is a pal of mine.*

***Shorter, Frank, USA**: Frank has a very good record although he has never broken 2:12 yet and he should be fairly tired after running the heat and the final of the 10,000-metres. Clayton does not think he is a natural marathon runner as his leg action is too high.*

What only two runners in the field knew about, however, was Shorter's ability to shock with a powerful mid-race surge. Only Usami and Moore had seen this first hand. The other leading contenders would see it soon enough, though.

Soon after the runners left the stadium, Ron Hill writes: "Just after the bridge we have a short right turn up a dirt hill and the electric van [filled with photographers] has difficulty making it; it forms an obstruction and throws up clouds of

Frank Shorter 1014, lays down the gauntlet almost from the gun of the 1972 Olympic Marathon. One of the favourites, Ron Hill 289, already appears to be out of the comfort zone. Directly to the right of Hill is another big name, the world record holder Derek Clayton. *Mark Shearman*

128

dust. Shorter, right up its backside, gives a vigorous, hysterical V sign into the telephoto lenses of the cameramen riding it. I think, 'What a cock-up.'"

Hill was having an inexplicably woeful time. Five-minute miling in the early stages should have felt easy, but the 3-mile split of 15:21 had him running almost flat out. Clayton and Usami begin to draw away. Then Jack Foster eased past, then:

> ...the three Americans pass me, Shorter, Moore and Bachelor in echelon, all tall, white vests and navy shorts. Oh hell! This can't be true. The nightmare intensifies as two Ethiopians pass me, one is Mamo Wolde, now Lismont, now Roelants, now two Finns. They spread right out across the narrow road and I try to hang onto them but I feel awful. I realize that I am nowhere near in control of the race as I ought to be. I'm just following, hanging on and hoping.

That hoping paid off as the leader, Clayton, slowed up and the pack concertinaed. Hill went into a lead as his lethargy momentarily left him. At around 10 kilometres the course entered Nymphenberg Park, and just the slightest of ascents was enough for all of Hill's weariness to return.

Ten kilometres passed in 31:15 as Hill became needlessly concerned about the terrain they were travelling on: "the surface in the park is bloody awful to say the least. It's like a yellow brown sandy gravel and they claim to have bound it together with resin or something but in fact it's smooth in some parts and loose in others." In a similar development to the 1984 Los Angeles Olympics, where Rob de Castella dawdled at a drinks station and found the leaders steal a march on him, the same happened to Hill as he almost collided with an equally floundering Shorter. "Some bitch pinched my soda!" squealed the American as his loped off to rejoin the pack. Hill gave himself a "sponge shower" that, far from energizing him, made him feel even more heavy.

This aura of feistiness that Shorter was displaying with the hand signals and name-calling showed that he was in aggressive mood – a priceless state of mind to be in when looking for an effective race performance. It seems that Shorter raced best when in this state of high nervous anxiety. An illustration as to the type of mood he was in at Munich is given the following year at the Mainichi Marathon in Japan, when he was caught, quite literally, with his pants down. When a giggling course marshal snapped a picture of Shorter during the race as he was relieving himself behind a building, Shorter became so incensed that he gave chase, caught the marshal, wrestled with him, got hold of the camera, smashed it to the ground, and then rejoined the race – winning in 2:12.

By the 15-kilometre checkpoint Hill had watched the race slip away for a second time. He writes: "I look up far ahead and there is a lone figure in a white vest and dark shorts, well in the lead. I can't see who it is but I guess that it is Shorter; he must not have been able to hang around any longer at that pace. It suddenly hits me: *I'm not going to win this race.*"

Shorter had meanwhile felt the lead pack's pace just slacken a little; but instead of slackening with them, he just maintained his pace, and suddenly he found he had a lead that had begun to grow and grow. Shorter's splits for the first three sets of 5 kilometres of 15:51, 15:33 and 14:57, showed how by starting steady and gradually applying more and more pressure, he would find himself in a 5-second lead by the 15-kilometre mark (Martin & Gynn). Shorter recalled: "I got goose bumps all over my body and said to myself: 'They are making a big mistake, I may actually win this thing'" (*British Runner*, March 2002).

Here, instead of taking stock (perhaps feeling it was too early to be "going solo"), Shorter decided to push on and increase the pressure. His next 5-kilometre split, a tangy 15:09, meant he increased his lead to 29 seconds over Belgium's Karel Lismont. Martin and Gynn write: "At 25 kilometres (1:17:05), Shorter's stride seemed easy as he sped down the main street of Munich at Stiglmaierplatz. His lead was now 57 seconds." After just 60 per cent of the race it was seemingly game over. "I ran in the 4:30s for the next several miles and by mile 17 it was essentially all over," Shorter recalls. "From there on, I simply tried to not slow down. Their mistake, really, was not finding out how I ran. I read magazines and knew everything about those guys" (Sandrock).

It was around this time that Shorter kicked off a trendy craze amongst distance runners for the next generation or so. As he grabbed for his water bottle, reporters wondered what the dark liquid was inside. Simple. Flat Coca-Cola. Shorter had filled it the evening before and allowed it to stand and de-fizz overnight. In the days before all the newfangled energy drinks which currently saturate the market, this was a simple, much cheaper form of fluid and energy replacement.

At 30 kilometres, as Shorter ran through the picturesque 8-kilometre stretch of the English Garden, he had exactly a 1 minute lead over teammate Kenny Moore and defending champion Mamo Wolde. The next 5 kilometres were a painful time for Moore as he leaked a minute to Shorter and slipped down to fourth and out of the medal reckoning. It was pretty painful for Wolde, too, who had lost another 38 seconds to Shorter and had the added alarm of Lismont bearing down on him.

Thus the momentum was now set for the remainder of the race with Shorter forever building on his lead, and Lismont taking a significant upper hand on Wolde. Shorter entered to a packed Olympic stadium with its splashy $61 million acrylic glass roof, to a crowd that had been eagerly anticipating the arrival of the first marathoner. The final track events were over – including the 4×400-metre relay – and the spectators had had the chance to convalesce before welcoming the marathoners. They had been told by the announcer that Shorter was leading and were expecting him. When Shorter entered the stadium, however, he was greeted only by loud jeers and boos. He was baffled. "I know I'm American," he thought, "but this is ridiculous."

The crowd were actually booing an imposter, 22-year-old West German student Norbert Südhaus, who decided to add a dash of humour to the Games, which he felt were getting too uptight. He had entered the stadium a minute before Shorter, and complete with a running kit and number had been mistaken by the crowd for the real thing.[1] ABC commentator Erich Segal (author of *Love Story*, Shorter's professor at Yale and a marathon runner himself), screeched out: "That's not

---

1. Keen athletic observers would have not been foxed however. Although Südhaus was young and fit, his build was stocky, like that of a football player, rather than skinny and lithe.

Frank! It's an impostor! Get that guy off the track! How can this happen in the Olympic Games? It's bush league, get rid of that guy; there is Frank Shorter; come on Frank, you won it." The German police however had been strictly instructed not to interfere with the athletes under any circumstances, so even when the crowd realized they had been duped and began booing, Norbert continued merrily trotting along; not turning the second time into the finish straight however, but heading back out of the tunnel and into oblivion.

The United States were therefore in a remarkable rut – of sorts: none of their three Olympic marathon champions of 1904, 1908 and 1972 had entered the stadium first! The year 1908 belonged to Dorando Pietri (Chapter 45), and in the 1904 Games at St. Louis, Fred Lorz hitched a ride between between miles 9 and 19 and came in over 10 minutes ahead of Tom Hicks. Lorz was immediately confronted about his ruse and he cheerfully admitted it (see Chapter 3).

Soon after finishing, Shorter was told of the reason behind the booing as the cheers and tributes rose for the true victor. He had run a personal best, when it mattered most, seen off the best in the world by over 2 minutes, and was just 8 seconds off Abebe Bikila's Tokyo Olympic record. As Martin and Gynn note, Shorter was just the third American to win a medal in a distance-running event after Bob Schul (Tokyo 500-metres), and Billy Mills (Tokyo 10,000-metres). "I thought if I could finish the race, I would finish in the top three," Shorter explained to the press afterwards. "Running the marathon can be a very difficult

An exhausted Kenny Moore, right, who placed fourth, congratulates his pal Frank Shorter at the race's end. *Mark Shearman*

psychological experience. I felt pretty good when I took the lead today and I wanted to make sure I stayed that way."

He then gave an interesting insight into what role a solid training background and confidence play in the make up of a marathoner: "a distance runner always knows how good he is because he knows the distances he runs, the strength he has. He can't hide anything from himself." And never is one's fitness queried more than when you are out on your own leading a quality field. What was Shorter thinking, and was he handling the pressure on the inside as coolly as he appeared on the outside? Not entirely, as he concedes: "You just say to yourself, 'Oh God, how much further? Please let me finish.'"

In second place came the remarkable Karel Lismont. The Belgian is one of the greatest "championship" marathoners of all time with a breathtaking sequence of seven top-ten finishes in eight championship races between 1971 and 1984. Born in March 1949 in Burgoon, he won the

Belgium national title just four years after he started running in 1970 aged 21. He worked as a tax collector, and brought the discipline and attention to detail one might require in a job such as that, to his running. His international championship career, flawed by just the one win and one DNF, saw him take to the podium no fewer than five times, and is worth summarizing here:

1971 European Championships	2:13:09	1st
1972 Olympic Games	2:14:31	2nd
1974 European Championships	DNF	
1976 Olympic Games	2:11:12	3rd
1978 European Championships	2:12:07	3rd
1980 Olympic Games	2:13:27	9th
1982 European Championships	2:16:04	3rd
1983 World Championships	2:11:24	9th
1984 Olympic Games	2:17:09	24th

Ron Hill finished a dejected sixth, just managing to outkick his teammate Donald Macgregor. "Congratulations, Don, Commiserations, Ron," summed up their straight-shooting team manager. Hill writes: "I ached in my stomach, my guts, my legs, my hopes. There are no tears. Just an intense and sickening disappointment."

Shorter had done it his way, said the *New York Times*. "Wearing his Elliott Gould moustache and drinking beer and sleeping late and ignoring those who have questioned his independent lifestyle, his long hair or his leave-me-alone training methods." Author John Jerome paid a memorable tribute to Shorter's run, and the influence it had on the sport: "There was something about that silken, light-footed stride and flying hair that lodged forever in our consciousness, something about all those minutes through the streets of Munich. Running, somehow it looked glorious...

The seeds had been sown, and just a few short years later, 10,000 Americans would be running the New York City Marathon.

*   *   *

Shorter's first TV guest appearance came the following February, when he appeared on Johnny Carson's *Tonight Show*, the most popular show of its kind in the land. That was the first indication that the repercussions of the gold medal were to be far-reaching, and of the big role TV would have in spreading the gospel of running. "People had started to come up to me and say that they'd seen the telecast of the Olympic marathon and that they, too, were now running," Shorter explained to Sandrock. Sandrock goes on to write in *Running with the Legends*:

Before Shorter, when the media portrayed marathoners they appeared to be gaunt, emaciated people with strange names who ran millions of miles in foreign countries. The perception of runners in America was that they turned to running because they could not make it in any of the "manly" sports like

132

football or baseball. Shorter showed the world that not only were marathoners athletes – they were very good ones at that.

Shorter's successes for 1972 weren't over yet. He recorded a personal best of 2:10:30 for a second win at Fukuoka later on in the year – a race he eventually won four times in a row. The Japanese finally stopped inviting out of fear he was ruining their event as a spectacle. His bittersweet return to the Olympics is documented in Chapter 26. One mind-boggling statistic is that even allowing time off for injury, illness and rest, Shorter still managed to average 17 miles a day *for every single day of the 1970s* (Sandrock) – that's 62,000 miles right there. But such a brutal assault on his body led to a sudden decline in his performances from his late 20s onwards. He was still capable of sublime days once in a while, and some of his duels with his successor, Bill Rodgers, linger in the memory, but generally Shorter's is a story of success coming very big, very early.

However, Shorter still keeps incredibly fit, running regularly and also cycles to a high standard. His competitive instinct fires as great as ever; which comes in useful for his role as chairman of the United States Anti-Doping Agency. The job requires "a distance runner's mentality," says Shorter. "What you want to be to cheaters is to be the person running on their shoulder, and you're still there and you're smiling at him. You're not going away. The time of the clean athlete worrying about the guy next to him being on something has become reversed. Now the concern is with the person on something."

Race result:

Frank Shorter	USA	2:12:19
Karel Lismont	BEL	2:14:31
Mamo Wolde	ETH	2:15:08
Kenny Moore	USA	2:15:39
Kenji Kimihara	JPN	2:16:27
Ron Hill	GBR	2:16:30
Don Macgregor	GBR	2:16:34
John Foster	NZL	2:16:56
Jack Bacheler	USA	2:17:38
Bedane Lengisse	ETH	2:18:36

Sources:

Conversations with John Bryant.
Conversations with Ron Hill.
Amdur, Neil, in the *New York Times*, September 11th, 1972.
Anonymous, "Profile of Frank Shorter", in the *New York Times*, September 11th, 1972.
British Runner, March 2002.
Daley, Arthur, in the *New York Times*, September 11th, 1972.

Derderian, Tom, *Boston Marathon*. Human Kinetics, 1996.

Hauman, Riël, *Century of the Marathon*. Human & Rousseau, 1996.

Hill, Ron, *The Long Hard Road. Part II: To the Peak and Beyond*. Ron Hill Sports, 1983.

Martin, David and Roger Gynn, *The Olympic Marathon*. Human Kinetics, 2000.

Sandrock, Michael, *Running with the Legends*. Human Kinetics, 1996.

Sports Illustrated, August 1970.

Wallechinsky, David, *The Complete Book of the Olympics*. Aurum Press, 2000.

XV

No. 36 – 1995 London Marathon [Men]

Sunday, April 2nd

Sack-wielding Pinto hunts for bodies strewn by the roadside.

By 1995, the London Marathon needed pepping up. Steven Downes wrote in the *Daily Telegraph*:

> Of five big marathons in April with combined race budgets of $15 million, the notorious breeze that London often gives us may mean its marathon fails to match the razzmatazz of Boston's 99th running in a fortnight or the times produced in Rotterdam a week later. Even the London founder Chris Brasher was grimly forced to admit this week: "We could do with a world record for the prestige of the event."
>
> The prevailing wind is one of the few problems which Brasher has failed to resolve in the 16 years since he had a brainwave after running the original big city race in New York and wondered in his newspaper column: "Whether London could stage such a festival?"

In March 1981, Brasher proved that such an event *could* be staged in London. The race soon catapulted above New York as the world's biggest marathon, spawning 115 other marathons in Britain in 1982. Yes, that's *one hundred and fifteen*. In 1983 Grete Waitz produced the capital's first world-best. Two years later her countrywoman Ingrid Kristiansen popped her jaw-dropping 2:21:06, a mark that would stand for over a decade.

Although such boom years had passed, London still attracted more than 70,000 applicants each year, although only the small minority of these were what might be called serious athletes. It did indeed seem that the London Marathon was going through a difficult period. "Under siege from rival races," Downes wrote, "even 26,000 runners pounding around the capital's streets, raising millions for charity, no longer guarantees the rapt attention of the nation..." What London needed was a real cracker of a race, and in 1995 it got just that. The capital hasn't looked back since.

* * *

The 1995 London Marathon had plenty of bravado and banter in its preceding days. That's understandable. When one has trained several thousand miles for a single race, there's a feeling of great anticipation that the big day has finally arrived. And for top-class athletes at least, they only turn up if completely fit and ready. And completely fit and ready tends to mean confident. The only problem is that for every person that has a good race in a marathon, about another three or four will have a bad race.

The former British Prime Minister John Major once contrasted his two great loves, cricket and politics, by noting: "Whereas cricket tends to be about dreams, politics is mainly about nightmares." The author submits the same can be said about training for the marathon, and then the marathon itself: one dreams of great things during the training, but the race itself often turns into a nightmare. And yet we keep coming back for more. Convinced that the marathon is something that can be cracked, providing everything goes to plan on the day; which about one time in five it will. But such a theory meant not a thing to the leading contenders for the '95 London. Whether they intended to run aggressively or passively, it seemed they were feeling confident.

In his preview of the race, the *Daily Telegraph*'s Ian Macleod wrote:

Last year, Dionicio Cerón, the Mexican, produced probably the finest display seen in London to win in 2:08:53, and is rightly adjudged the favourite in a field which 1993 winner Eamonn Martin says was no better nor worse than last year.

Cerón's confidence knows no bounds. Earlier this week he spoke of how, given the forecast of mild weather, he believes the streets of the capital could yield the world record which stands at 2:06:50 and is held by Belayneh Densimo, of Ethiopia. "If it is fine I think a 2:06 is possible," said Cerón.

Cerón said he expected Abebe Mekkonen of Ethiopia [who won a scintillating Boston Marathon in 1989] to be a threat, while Antonio Pinto of Portugal and Willie Mtolo of South Africa cannot be underestimated, any less than Australia's Commonwealth champion Steve Moneghetti.

When Pinto was informed of Cerón and others' intention to go hunting for a time in the 2:06s, he uttered one of running's great lines: "If they do, I'll follow along in a sack and put them in as I go past." Hopes of a blazing fast time were dulled further by the fact that temperatures on the outset of the race were already threatening to creep into the 70s. Gary Staines, with a searing 46:11 personal best for 10 miles, did an excellent job as pace-maker, with Poland's Jan Huruk (second at London in '92) as an able sidekick. The tempo was brisk and honest from the outset. After passing 5 miles in 24:07 and 10 miles in 48:21, halfway was sped through in 63:31. This was more or less world record pace, but then Staines and Huruk stepped off the course, their job done, and the pace slackened.

Also the wind started to get up, but Antonio Pinto only noticed that the leading group weren't running as fast as they once had. Pinto, the race winner in '92, perhaps didn't want a repeat of that occasion when, in an exciting finish, he prevailed by just five seconds. Here, he went searching for more a comfortable triumph. The stocky, powerfully built Pinto poured it on. He blitzed the 15th mile in an lung-busting 4:37 and scarcely let up the following mile. Soon he had the comfort of a 200-metre lead. The Portuguese had blown the race wide open, and ran inside the world-best pace of 2:06:50; now all he had to do was keep it going for 10 more long, lonely miles...For a good while it seemed he had the situation well in hand. At 20 miles Pinto's lead had grown to 300 metres, the chasing pack mere pinpricks in the background. By 22 miles his lead was an even minute and he was out of sight. However, the expert summarizers noted a stubborn fact: Pinto no longer ran at world-record pace – he was instead in line for 2:07:30 marathon. Still a magnificent time, but it indicated a wobble. Was his "stock" in the race, just possibly, going south?

Pinto it seems had forgotten all about his "sack-wielding" utterance of the day before, but his two main pursuers, Dionicio Cerón and Steve Moneghetti of Australia, were starting to think about getting sacks ready. They tasted blood in the water; well, one of them did at least. Moneghetti had abandoned all thoughts of winning, Pinto was just too far ahead. Cerón, however, urged his co-hunter to hang in there, that Pinto could still be caught. Together they set off in pursuit of the leader. "Off the cobblestones we were smoking," Moneghetti explained later, recalling the 23rd mile, past the Tower of London. For almost three more miles, the brave Pinto clung onto his lead, but Cerón and Moneghetti drew ever closer. Finally, as late as the 26th mile, they were upon him. And then they went by.

Pinto valiantly tucked in behind the new leaders, but it was a token gesture, lasting no more than a quarter of a mile. As they approached the turn into The Mall for the final furlong, Pinto had been dropped, and the Australian and the Mexican fought a gruelling duel to the death. Passing Buckingham Palace, Cerón was two strides ahead, and try as he might, there was nothing Moneghetti could do to close the gap – he simply lacked that killer finish. In fact, the gap grew a little. Incredibly, history was shaping up to repeat itself, since poor Moneghetti had also finished second by three ticks of the clock at the 1989 London. Cerón duly became the first man to win the London Marathon twice, with a time second only to Steve Jones' course record of 2:08:16. Pinto finished just 18 seconds behind in the end, and it was the first occasion that three had beaten 2:09 in London.

Oh not again: Steve Moneghetti experiences a sickening déjà-vu as for the second time in six years he places second at the London Marathon by just three seconds. Dionicio Cerón meanwhile defends his title. *Mark Shearman*

Ian Macleod wrote: "Dionicio Cerón did not get the world record he had spoken of earlier in the week but the Mexican demonstrated, particularly in the closing stages of the race, that he was an athlete of steady nerve, iron dsposi-tion and rare talent."

Moneghetti spoke of how he was impressed by the way in which Cerón refused to accept defeat, adding that without the Mexican, "I would have got to a stage where I thought we were running for second. It was Dionicio who kept it going".

David Powell of *The Times* described Pinto's sanguine attitude to departing so dramatically from his pre-race tactics:

Antonio Pinto sat back in his chair and smiled, seeing the funny side. "It happens," he said. What else could he say? He had failed to heed his own advice and paid dearly in the most absorbing race in the 15-year history of the London Marathon.

Cerón said that he had always been confident that Pinto would come back. The Mexican's performance demonstated why Nutrasweet, the race sponsor, parted with some $200,000 to ensure his participation. In all, with prize money and bonuses, Cerón collected some $280,000 – the biggest payday for one athlete competing in Britain.

Cerón, it was noted, was a businessman first, and enthusiast second. None of his

Cerón celebrates a bumper payday with Poland's Malgorzata Sobanska. *Mark Shearman*

138

family came to support, while Moneghetti, a consultant for the Victoria State education department, had with him his wife, daughter and parents. "Why would you take your wife to work?" asked an incredulous Cerón. "I have a job at home and this is just a hobby," Moneghetti jabbed back.

It certainly wasn't to be the last the world would see of Moneghetti as his long and illustrious career seemed to stretch on and on. Indeed, nine years after this race he would come out of retirement to place a gutsy 30th in the World Cross Country Championships to send a strong message of rebuke to the Australian selectors who had opted not to send a team to the World Cross the year before, because they believed they didn't have enough talent to offer. After the London race of '95 he signalled his intent to keep fighting on for big city marathon honours: "When you get beaten by the number 1, you want to come back, even if Antonio thinks I'm an old-timer." The following year he would place a fine seventh in the Atlanta Olympic Marathon, handsomely beating Cerón and Pinto in the process.

This was Cerón's fifth victory in six marathons, and he had also become the first man to run 2:09 for four years in succession. (Hauman). But there was another man who was also making a habit of winning marathons with great regularity, and he and Cerón would soon be colliding. London was one thing: the World was next (see Chapter 37).

* * *

In the women's race David Powell demonstrated how infuriatingly quick journalists can be to write off top sports stars, only to purr at their brilliance a short while later. Of British runner Liz McColgan, he wrote: "McColgan's performance fuels the doubt over whether she can make her mark at world level again – yesterday she was out of the running at half-way. After her winning debut in New York in 2:27:32, each of three marathons has been slower than the last. Yesterday she slipped to 2:31:14." A year later, Powell would perform a turnaround as McColgan won an enthralling marathon, which Powell ranked it as "among her finest victories", paying tribute to the new "wise and patient" McColgan.

Cerón returned to London in 1996 and, scored a terrific "threepeat". Once again Cerón sat back and watched as an athlete said one thing in the pre-race press conference, and completely ignored his own advice. Belgian star Vincent Rousseau, the runner-up, was to be haunted by his own words, just like Pinto the previous year: "I do not want to lead and get a knife in my back," said Rousseau, the only athlete up till then in marathon history to have broken 2.08 twice. However, when the pace-maker dropped out at halfway, the Belgian was the one pushing it along for most of the way until Cerón appeared with his blade. Cerón had run it the way Rousseau had advised, concealed in the group, rather than taking the reins. "Every victory has a special place in my heart," Cerón said, "but I won for the third time. I feel very excited about that."

Cerón's celebrations down The Mall cost him $5,000 for failing to break 2:10, but he could afford it. Cerón owned five houses, a sports club and a clothing business and now he had another winner's cheque for $55,000.

Rousseau was the notorious athlete who had it written in his contract that he was allowed to withdraw from any marathon if the thermometer exceeded 16 °C.

On this occasion at London in 1996 he had not bothered with the clause, and could only watch at the start as the thermometer read 18C and was rising. "I did not expect these warm conditions," he said afterwards. "When I saw the weather at the beginning, I was like that," indicating that he had crossed his fingers for luck. "I stayed out of the way in case he was looking for me," cracked elite race director Dave Bedford.

Race result:

Dionicio Cerón	MEX	2:08:30
Steve Moneghetti	AUS	2:08:33
Antonio Pinto	POR	2:08:48
Xohile Yawa	RSA	2:10:22
Paul Evans	GBR	2:10:31
Joaquim Pinheiro	POR	2:10:34
Willie Mtolo	RSA	2:11:35

Sources:

Conversations with David Bedford.
Conversations with Antonio Pinto.
Athletics Weekly, April 5th, 1995.
Downes, Steven, in the *Daily Telegraph*, April 1st, 1995.
Hauman, Riël, *Century of the Marathon*. Human & Rousseau, 1996.
Macleod, Ian, in the *Daily Telegraph*, April 1st & 3rd, 1995.
Powell, David, in *The Times*, April 3rd, 1995.

XVI

No. 35 – 1922 Boston Marathon [Men]

Wednesday, April 19th

Old man DeMar tries his luck against the new batch.

Clarence DeMar didn't have too much going for him if the two subtitles in the *New York Times*' obituary of him – "Had a Weak Heart" and "Used Shuffling Gait" – are to be believed. Of course these sweeping statements paint a misleading picture and when his heart was examined in his autopsy it was found to be in perfect condition. It was cancer that killed him, and nothing heart – or gait – related.

Since I never saw DeMar run, I shall reserve judgement on just how aesthetically pleasing and effective his running style was, but I would suggest that the *New York Times*' description of his style is surely misleading and exercises a little journalistic licence: "A wispy looking athlete, Mr. DeMar ran with a shuffling gait as if the next stride would be his last. His face was screwed into wrinkles, his knees were stiff in action, and he threw his arms out like no other runner." After all, a style that works is a good style. It carried DeMar to victory in the Boston Marathon in 1911, after which followed an eleven-year hiatus while he – by and large – obeyed doctors orders, who warned that he had a dodgy ticker, not to run. He returned to his great passion and won the big race in 1922, 1923, 1924, 1927, 1928 and finally 1930, at the age of 41.[1]

Of these seven Boston marathon wins, it is DeMar's great comeback win of 1922 that is the focus in this chapter, as there is nothing more pleasing in sport that the return to the limelight of a once great hero.

* * *

DeMar's charming autobiography, published in 1936, opens with three short sentences which instantly show this is to be a story of an underdog, and a humble one at that. The words go: "An article in a Cincinnati paper once stated that I could run down a jack-rabbit when I was a boy on Indian Hill, near that city. This was hardly a fact. As a boy I was about the slowest moving youngster in school."

---

1. This latter victory reminds the author of golfer Jack Nicklaus' swansong win at the US Masters, aged 46 (his sixth triumph).

DeMar was born on June 7th, 1888, and found early on in life that he simply preferred running – or "dog-trotting" as he refers to it – to walking; choosing this modus operandi to travel the mile or so to school each day and back in Madison-ville, Ohio. People rarely feel awkward running these days, but back then young Clarence was often ashamed when fielding comments such as "Say, sonny, don't you ever walk?"

DeMar had it tough from an early age, and upon the death of his father he immediately took it upon himself to be the chief bread winner of the family in order to support his mother and five smaller brothers and sisters. "So I sold things like pins, needles, thread, and soap around the neighbouring towns and country. Usually I walked ten or twenty miles when on one of these trips." DeMar doesn't pass comment on how effective his sales techniques were except that they weren't good enough to keep the family together. Young Clarence was placed in a home called the Farm School, on Thompson's Island in Boston Harbour.[2]

Although DeMar is often portrayed as aloof, or stern, or private, or brooding, or difficult to get to know, there was a cunning, playful wit to his repertoire, and a sense of humour was essential to many of the hardships he endured in his life. Referring to Thompson's Island, DeMar writes: "I became known as a good student, but very poor at anything else. The only running I did was once when several of us tried to run away. Our 'running' was done by swimming and by pushing a boat." He and his chums were of course caught, and Clarence was placed in the "deepest disgrace" for several months. "I especially recall," he continues, "the Superintendent mentioned my swimming with a peculiar kick which he called a 'twin screw propeller on a Chinese junk.'" A venomous insult indeed, but Clarence wittily comments: "Later in life I was to have my foot and leg motion again ridiculed, but this swim was the only time it failed to get me there eventually."

At the age of sixteen DeMar was released to go and work on a farm at South Hero, Vermont. He feels this is where he picked up a lot of his endurance, writing: "I am sure that it was much more fatiguing to pitch hay or cut corn all day than to run a marathon for a quarter of a day." It is not a new phenomenon for a young boy to dream of being a famous sporting hero, and young Clarence was no different. But a graceful, natural talent for sports he had not. He dreamed of becoming world boxing champion but the two or three times he pulled on the gloves led to pitiful displays. What about a major league baseball player then? Sure. Except every time out was a swing and a miss.

Still, upon entry to the University of Vermont he loved to hang out with the sports stars, and "if one of the athletic heroes even spoke to me I was thrilled." During the winter of 1908–9 Clarence was given the errand of ferrying milk samples the mile or so to the State Hygiene Laboratory for analysis. In order to keep warm and save time, he ran. Suddenly, one morning the thought dropped, plop, into the centre of his mind that he could run a marathon. DeMar had never

---

2. Thompson's Island was the scene of the most bizarre "road race" of the author's career and still takes place today. It consists of sandy paths and, distressingly, pebbled beaches. Pretty though.

had time to read newspapers and so he only had the vaguest notion of what marathoning was, but he still felt it was something that he could do.

All the best teachers and professors have the ability to inspire. DeMar tells of a Professor Sterson of the German department, who related a simple but powerful theory that there were lots of kinds of men and lots of sports. If each one would look around he could find something in which to become a champion. But which sport to try for such an unnatural talent? DeMar decided to try cross-country. After a couple of weeks' practice, in a meet with Union College he came in fourth – almost winning a coveted "V" awarded to the first three. The next night a fraternity brother summed up DeMar's high spirits by observing: "He has talked a blue streak all night." And DeMar agrees that the feeling he got after athletics meets was often "very much waked up and exhilarated".

He didn't see out his time at university but instead went to live with his mother and siblings in Melrose, Massachusetts, deciding whatever else he'd do with his life that he would become a marathoner. Upon buying a little Spaulding book about distance running for ten cents and absorbing its information, DeMar "felt a serene confidence that I could eventually do as well as any of [the stars in the book] in a full marathon. And I had never run over eight or ten miles in my life!"

Christmas 1909 saw the great man's first marathon, albeit in practice. He trotted to a sign in Andover, Massachusetts, where he found a sign that said "Boston 20 miles". Upon running to Boston he then continued on to home (Melrose) – a further 7 miles. DeMar writes: "I did the 26 miles in about three hours without much exertion and so felt very confident." Keeping up his mileage all through the winter of 1910, Clarence ran in a 10-mile handicap race in which he received a 5:15 start over the scratch runner. This was far too much and he won by a long way, with the day's second fastest overall time. His handicap was immediately cut to 2:15 for 10-mile races, and remained at that same level for the next *25 years*! Now that's called durability.

April 19th, 1910 was the day that one of the all-time great marathon careers kicked off, and it did so with a bang. Immediately what became clear was that DeMar was a patient racer and brilliant tactician. If the day was hot, then he in turn would start out slow and watch his opponents burn themselves out. The art of pacing – elusive to a vast majority of otherwise capable marathoners – is perfectly explained in this extract: "After we got started I kept a vision of the distance before me and was continually gauging my strength accordingly. This is a sort of subconscious process that takes concentration but always works, barring accidents like the loss of confidence, a gambling spirit, or mild sunstroke."

At halfway Clarence was a whopping seven minutes down on the leaders. He finished in second place, one minute down on the winner, with a cushion of 5 minutes over third and 9 minutes on fourth. Not bad for a debut at age just 21. "I feel that I have lots of time in which to develop as a runner, he commented. Everyone back at work remarked on how well Clarence had run and pointed out that while all the "crack" racers were surrounded by handlers with sponges, "you just ran right past them without ceremony". DeMar indicated that he thought such frills were actually a handicap. But for every positive comment came a stark warning. A man could only do one or two of these things in a lifetime.

143

*   *   *

Amongst much "publicity and ballyhoo" (which was very stimulating for a while), DeMar returned to Boston the following year and won in the terrific time of 2:21 (for a 24.5-mile course) by nearly three minutes. He had been running the astounding level (at the time) of regular 100-mile weeks with lots of 20-mile runs. This compares to Jonny Kelley, snr, who won Boston in 1935 and 1945 but often ran only at weekends, when working for Boston Edison.

Along with the ballyhoo, DeMar received numerous postcards and letters of congratulation from young ladies. However, this was the only marathon at which it happened. "Perhaps my face acquired too many wrinkles with the years. A man's face looks worse than usual after he finishes a marathon, anyhow." However, before the race in the medical check-up which all runners had to undertake, Clarence reports that the doctors "listened quite a while at my chest and gave the verdict that this should be my last race and I should drop out of it if I got tired. They said that I had heart murmurs."

It wouldn't be long before DeMar took this ill-informed advice seriously, but first he longed to win the Olympics. Since the Olympics have always been the primary exponents of amateurism, let us digress for a moment and examine DeMar's thoughts on the subject, since he was quickly being offered sops to compete in races after Boston 1911. Once, when asked to compete in a race, the organizer offered to pay DeMar's taxi fare there and back – even if he walked. He conscientiously declined. But looking back on his long career he admits that later on in his career he may well have accepted: "Such is the evolution of a conscientious amateur. At twenty-three he refuses money; at thirty-eight he accepts and uses for boys' organizations,[3] at forty-eight he accepts and uses for his family with the mental excuse that the game owes it to him; at seventy I may accept and use the money to keep myself out of the poor house, but we shall see.[4]

The 1912 Olympics were an unsavoury affair for DeMar and he did not enjoy many aspects, least of all being told what to do. (If he didn't enjoy it on Thompson's Island, he certainly wasn't going to take to it now he was a fully grown man representing his country.) Interestingly, one of the men bossing him about was none other that Johnny Hayes, he of 1908 Olympic gold who was now a pro and "special trainer of the marathon team". When he saw fit to tell DeMar to run more on his toes during a practice run, he might as well as told him to breathe less through his mouth or stop blinking so much. "I've always stated that when I get through with amateur running at least I'll get out of the way and stay there and not hamper the future champions by trying to tell them something which they don't want me to." DeMar found that the Canadian runners were experiencing just the same problems and goes on to write: "I have never checked on the many other nations, but wouldn't it be a paradox if we found that in coaching at the Olympic Games 'the democracies were tyrannical and the tyrannies democratic?'"

---

3. DeMar dedicated years, if not decades, of his life to looking after and training Boy Scouts.
4. He never really gave the 'poor house' a chance, since DeMar died just four days after turning 70.

144

DeMar found that trying to make good every day in training purely to appease the coaches made him stale, and he ruptured a blood vessel with all the effort. He was "hopelessly outclassed" in the Stockholm Olympic marathon, coming into it "lame", even at one stage breaking his stride...He only twice did that in 65 marathons. Kenneth McArthur of South Africa won the race in 2:36:54. One thing was for sure: DeMar would never be ruled over to such an extent again, and he was true to his word some twelve years later when he had a far more successful stab at the Olympics.

In late 1912 DeMar started resenting losing a day's pay here and there to run and began skipping races. He also decided to take a rest from marathoning, mainly because of the frequent warnings from doctors and fans. Also, taking religion seriously, he began to suspect "that the whole game of running was a selfish vain-glorious search for praise and honor".[5] Finally, what with working as compositor and taking evening classes at Harvard and Boston University, DeMar found he simply didn't have the time to give marathoning the time it required.

This self-imposed exile lasted six years until, with war clouds looming America's way in 1917, DeMar decided, since he may well get killed in service, to have a little fun at marathoning first. This he did in a hard fought scrap with "brick-layer" Bill Kennedy and Sydney Hatch, coming off the worst of the three, but defeating the great Olympic champion of 1920 Hannes Kolehmainen, and the able Chuck Mellor who would pip DeMar in the 1925 race, thus denying him four wins on the trot. A few days later the top-three finishers all went off to serve in France.

Service in France in the First World War left little time for running but DeMar did run in the occasional inter-Allied relays and suchlike. His printing shop was glad to have him back on his return to America, but it wasn't long before he was fired for joining the Typographical Union's strike action, even though he was very happy with the deal he was getting. After spending much of 1921 unemployed, DeMar finally found a job in a country shop in Medford – but which paid Boston wages. DeMar began running the 4–5 miles to work, since the "trolley" would have taken ages. It felt fine. He read in the papers about his friend Frank Zuna from the army winning Boston. Also, his boss Joe Miller was a sports fan who encouraged DeMar's running. His five-year self-imposed exile from the marathon was about to come to an end. According to Derderian, he was just six pounds heavier than in 1911. Before New Year's Day 1922, DeMar decided he would make a return visit to the big race.

DeMar it seemed had two key rivals for his comeback race: a fine, local runner called "Smilin'" Jimmy Henigan who was a dab hand at the 5 to 10-milers all over the area. "Henigan Has Great Hopes" declared the *Boston Globe*. Chuck Mellor was DeMar's hottest tip, a mad-keen racer who had won the past three Detroit Auto City marathons. He'd also been second the year before. But not this year – he would be one of several high profile DNFs in the race, with the 1920 champ, Peter Trivoulidas, also bowing out.

---

5. When the Olympics came to Amsterdam in 1928, some of the Protestant church leaders opposed it as a "carnival of the flesh" and advised their constituents to stay away (DeMar).

The old-timers maintained that just the one good marathon was all that was possible – that it uses a man up. "Jack Caffery, with his wins in 1900 and 1901, had been an exception," says Derderian. The press doubted whether the interest in DeMar's return was really worth any bother. The *Globe* asked: "Whether DeMar can cope with the present day marathoners after a gap of eleven years is something to be doubted." But whatever the outcome, the writer admitted: "He was a great runner in his prime and today will tell whether he can show anything like his old time speed. No matter what he does, his running will offer an interesting lesson for the students of athletics."

An Indian runner called Albert Smoke, who did indeed smoke big black cigars, appeared from Canada to race. He was a trapper and fisherman of the Missausuggi people from Petersboro, Ontario, but nobody knew much about him. Nonetheless he was to prove to be an important ally to DeMar.

Lining up on the start line, DeMar felt the defending champ Zuna looked well. Bad for Zuna, good for DeMar. Extremely fit marathoners shouldn't look too well, or, as DeMar thought, "content". There shouldn't be the lining of fat around the belly (which Zuna had), and there should be the hollow cheeks (which Zuna hadn't). He had obviously not been training with the same vengeance, and DeMar wrote him off there and then. Lined up as well was a future icon of Finnish distance running who would become nearly as great as his countrymen Hannes Kolehmainen and Paavo Nurmi. His name was Willie Ritola and he would go on to win three Olympic golds at three different events, plus a silver during the course of the following two Olympics.[6] For now, though, Ritola was just an unknown 26-year-old, blond, Finnish immigrant who worked as a carpenter.

The marathon pace felt easy to Jimmy Henigan as he ran comfortably in the lead in the early stages. He of the puppy fat, Frank Zuna, felt the pressure of defending his crown and was compelled to follow. Ritola ran in third while Henigan's brother Tommy followed on behind the Finn. By the 10-mile mark in Natick, Henigan ran a suicidal 80 seconds in the lead. Zuna ran equally boldly, still in record pace behind. But by halfway and the girls of Wellesley College, Henigan's lead was down to a minute and Zuna had faded dramatically and was no longer a factor. DeMar ran steadily, picking off runner after runner until after a gritty duel with the Indian Smoke, it was down to battle with the two Henigan brothers. Tommy couldn't hold DeMar for long but Jimmy stayed with DeMar for a while longer.

When DeMar surged, his pace caused few alarms for Henigan who had so much natural speed in his legs. But suddenly – and the brutal thing about capitulation in marathoning is how sudden it can be – Henigan's legs ceased to obey orders. He stopped and a helper struck his calves with a yardstick to make them unclench. But his calves had had quite enough fun for one day, and no amount of beating was going to rouse them into action. The race had, however, captured Henigan's imagination and he was now obsessed. Nine years later, after plenty more pain

---

6. Ritola won gold at the Paris '24 Games in the 10,000-metres and steeplechase, and silver in the 5000-metres behind Nurmi. Four years later at Amsterdam he turned that 5000 silver to gold.

and humiliation (and several drop-outs), he would finally triumph at Boston by over two minutes.

With DeMar running on course-record schedule only a handful of miles from the finish, he had broken all of his rivals, except one. Ritola. But unfortunately for the Finn he had "consulted the wrong schedule and missed the train" (Derderian), or in other words, decided on a pace, stuck to it brilliantly, only to arrive at the finish in second place, some three and a half minutes behind the winner, with the valiant Smoke a minute behind in third.[7]

The public and press were astounded as to what they saw. It's difficult to get the staid and formal *New York Times* worked up into a frenzy, but DeMar succeeded near as any. "The greatest 'comeback' performance ever registered," yelped the paper:

> This afternoon DeMar, who raced wonderfully over hard roads and in a chilly wind, covered the twenty-five miles ahead of one of the greatest fields of distance runners that ever has entered the event. [Boston became the full marathon distance two years later.]
>
> DeMar's victory stood as the "comeback" victory of all time. Eleven years ago the same runner led the field of nearly 100 runners across the finish line, although then a record, being slower by nearly twenty-one minutes than the great mark he established today.

Do not adjust your set: This speckled image is due to the 1925 Boston Marathon taking place in snow flurries. Clarence de Mar #1 battles with Chuck Mellor #68, who'd stuffed the morning paper down his front to keep warm. It worked – Mellor won. *UPI/Bettmann*

---

7. Ritola's 30:23 at the Olympics two years hence showed him putting together more sub-5-minute miles than DeMar did in a lifetime. Indeed it is fairly certain that DeMar never ran a single mile in under five minutes.

Lawrence Sweeney of the *Boston Globe* wrote, "The superman of marathon runners is Clarence H. DeMar of Melrose," in an article entitled: "*Defying Father Time*".

Amusingly, there was still room in the press for criticism. Mike Ryan of the *Boston Herald* observed: "He carries his chin high and did not have sufficient swing in his leg action to give him a smooth working appearance. He insisted on running down the hills instead of loosening out and letting his stride carry him down." In a first-person article for the *Boston Post* DeMar wrote: "I must confess that I expected to win the race. I do not say this with any conceitedness...I do not know whether or not I will ever do any more marathons. If I find time I certainly will, but it is business for me first, and marathon running afterwards."

Find time for more marathoning DeMar certainly did, as he would continue to run in the BAA for another 32 years, until 1954, when at the age of 65, he placed 78th out of 113 entrants and still broke four hours.

*   *   *

The following year, after his great 1922 comeback, was in many ways just as spectacular an achievement. Out for a training run shortly before the race, DeMar was attacked by a dog. He kicked out and immediately its owner appeared and punched DeMar in the mouth. The profuse bleeding led to erysipelas and infection spread over his entire face. He was confined to bed for ten days with a systemic fever. On April 19th he crawled out of bed to compete in the marathon. When a bicycle ran over his foot, the heel came off DeMar's shoe and folded underneath his foot. It hurt but did not slow him down. He couldn't stop to correct the problem because he was worried about the tireless Frank Zuna[8] chasing him down. But Zuna would finish nearly two minutes off his target. According to Derderian, "The biggest crowd ever yet on hand to watch a Boston Marathon gave DeMar universal applause, but the press had used up all its superlatives the year before." Tom McCabe of the *Boston Herald* said, "Last year we were dumbfounded; now we are lost in amazement."

DeMar was equally spellbinding in 1924 for his "threepeat" as he had perhaps his finest ever day. Wrenching his back that winter he had visited an osteopath, who had poked at his back and realigned his bones far better than they'd ever been before. He had had a "shuffle-ectomy" so to speak and now ran with an uplifting, smooth style. Says Derderian: "DeMar squeezed every second from the road. His body seemed electric. He had never felt like this before. His physiology sang down the streets." He smashed Kolehmainen's time from the 1920 Olympics by three minutes and the press had to start resorting to puns, since their thesauruses had run out of superlatives: "Mister DeMarvelous", "Mister DeMarathon" they crooned.

DeMar made the Olympic team of course, whereupon he looked to atone for his poor showing of twelve years earlier. On an extremely hot day in which just 30

---

8. Tom Derderian tells a delightful tale of this winner of the 1921 race. When Zuna was a boy, a policeman caught him shooting illegal craps with his pals. He grabbed Zuna by the collar but he slipped out of his coat and ran off. The police gave chase but were only allowed to travel at 6 mph in their cars. After four miles of chasing Zuna, expecting him to tire and surrender – which he never did – the police gave up on their prey.

Four great Boston champions pose in 1926: left to right, Jimmy Henigan, Clarence DeMar, Albin Stenroos, and Johnny Miles. *Boston Herald*

of the 58 competitors managed to finish, DeMar was his typical, clinical self, finishing a fine third, under a minute off silver. The wholly unpredictable Albin Stenroos won in 2:41:22 in the only marathon win of his career.[9] Compare this to DeMar who had run 40 marathons (17 wins) after Boston 1930. Four years later, aged 40, DeMar was still of Olympic standard, this time finishing 27th in Amsterdam, and two years later, shortly before he turned 42, he won Boston for the seventh and final time in 2:34:48.

---

9. Between 1907 and 1928 Stenroos ran twelve marathons, failed to finish five, placed second in five others and third in one, plus of course, his Olympic win. A curious set of numbers indeed.

Upon DeMar's death his autopsy (reported in an article in the *New England Journal of Medicine*), in June 1958 found that his heart arteries had been so large so as to be protected from any aging effects, and "the coronary arteries were estimated to be two or three times normal size". In a *Boston Globe* eulogy it was written, "occasionally a career like his comes as a reminder of what human nature can achieve when great ability is united with strong character and single-minded devotion to essential values."

DeMar summed up the reasons for his success in distance running with this quote, which gives clues as to why so many the world over are drawn to the mystique of the marathon: "After all, do most of us want life on the same calm level as a geometrical problem? Certainly we want our pleasures more varied, with mountains and valleys of emotional joy, and marathoning furnishes just that."

Race result (24.5 miles):

Clarence DeMar	Massachusetts	2:18:10
Willie Ritola	New York	2:21:44
Albert Smoke	Ontario	2:22:49
Victor MacAuley	District of Columbia	2:24:02
Willie Kyronen	New York	2:24:42
Otto Laakso	New York	2:24:45
Carl Linder	Massachusetts	2:25:29
Frank Zuna	New York	2:26:26

Sources:

Boston Globe, Eulogy, June 12th, 1958.
Boston Globe, Race preview, April 19th, 1922.
Currens/White, article in the *New England Journal of Medicine* 265: 988–993. June 1958.
DeMar, Clarence, in the *Boston Post*, April 20th, 1922.
DeMar, Clarence, *The Clarence DeMar Story*. Cedarwinds Publishing Co., 1937.
Derderian, Tom, *Boston Marathon*. Human Kinetics, 1996.
McCabe, Tom, in the *Boston Herald*, April 20th, 1923.
Martin, David and Roger Gynn, *The Olympic Marathon*. Human Kinetics, 2000.
New York Times, Obituary, June 12th, 1958.
New York Times, Race report, April 20th, 1922.
Ryan, Mike, in the *Boston Herald*, April 20th, 1922.
Sweeney, Lawrence, in the *Boston Globe*, April 20th, 1922.

XVII

No. 34 – 1985 London Marathon [Women]

Sunday, April 21st

First shots fired in the battle for sub-2.20.

When listing the achievements of Ingrid Kristiansen, one question might be: "Where to start?" For many years a "lady-in-waiting" to her arch rival and countrywoman, Grete Waitz, when Kristiansen did finally assume the mantle of the finest female distance runner in the world, she grabbed it with both hands and took standards to a whole new level. For where Waitz had gained deserved acclaim for bringing the women's marathon record down to below 2:30, Kristiansen had another target in her sights: 2:20. And she almost succeeded in her quest.

Outside the world of gymnastics and swimming, few can say they represented their country at just 15 years of age, but Kristiansen did, at the 1500-metres in the 1971 European Championships. "I was a little girl, the other runners were big, and after two and a half laps I fell over," she recalls. So much for that. After all, why run when you can ski? Especially as that was where the *real* adulation of the Norwegian sporting public lay. Kristiansen explains: "In Norway, skiing is the big sport. Skiers are much better known than runners" (Hauman). In the 1978 World Cross-country Skiing Championships she had finished 21st, and had appeared in the Norwegian team at the 1976 Olympic Games.

By the turn of the decade, however, Kristiansen was back running extremely well, starting out, as author Riël Hauman describes, "on the trail blazed by compatriot Grete Waitz – a journey that would bring her Zátopek-like success as the most versatile female distance runner the world has ever seen." In 1981 Kristiansen set her first world best: 15:28.43 for 5000-metres and three years later she became the first woman under 15 minutes when she clocked 14:58.89. By 1986 she had scorched to 14:37.33, which today has even the likes of Gaby Szabo, Paula Radcliffe and Edith Massai struggling to match. Exactly a month before this run, Ingrid had also run a world record for 10,000-metres – 30:13.74 – having the previous year been the first woman to dip under 31 minutes. All this was achieved while holding down a demanding job as a medical engineer analysing cancer cells. Kristiansen explains: "the only place I was tired was in the head, in the concentration. I think too many runners today are too serious about their running. Of course you have to be serious, but you can do other things, too" (Sandrock).

Kristiansen's marathon career began in 1977, when she ran in the Trondeim Marathon (from whence she hails) and returned a promising 2:45:15 – exactly 10 minutes off Chantal Langlacé's world record. Over the next half a dozen years she was improving at a rate of two minutes a year, until by 1983 she was clocking 2:33 – a useful time but not up with "the rate of inflation", since Joan Benoit's world record was now eleven minutes away. But by now, after years of paying her dues, Kristiansen was ready to step up her game, especially since she was even more battle-hardened after the challenges of giving birth: "I'd rather run two marathons back-to-back than give birth again," she explained. Just five months after son Gaute was born, Ingrid won the Houston Marathon in 2:27:51. She was now undeniably world-class, and that was proven still further with a European record 2:24:26 win at the London Marathon in 1984.

Next stop the Olympic Games, where surely a medal could be hers. Chapter 35 has an in-depth description of this race, but it was not quite Ingrid's day to shine – however praiseworthy fourth place might be. "In that race I didn't use my head. I do another person's race and I lose the whole thing..." she said. Twenty years after the race she still feels somewhat peeved. She tells the author: "My coach told me I had to do what Grete did, don't go off ahead of her. Grete also kept telling me to hold back, that Benoit would come back to us. If only I had just run my own race!"

It was also around this time that Ingrid confronted what was seemingly a mental block about being unable to defeat Grete Waitz. She sought out psychological help. According to Sandrock, a doctor in Oslo told Ingrid: "You have one problem: You don't *think* you can beat Grete." Kristiansen started to reflect: "Maybe that's right." And that was that; Ingrid never lost a race of substance to Waitz ever again. Although, as with Coe and Ovett, their paths barely, if ever, crossed. Kristiansen, perhaps speaking with hidden meaning, commented: "We are almost never in the same place. It is strange that we never meet."[1]

* * *

The featured event for this chapter, the London Marathon of 1985, was the day Kristiansen finally burst out of Waitz's shadow. The implication was clear: *Grete's time in the limelight is over, now it's time to see what I can do.* If one of Waitz's greatest achievements was to smash through the 2:30 barrier for the first time with her superb run at New York in 1979 (see Chapter 12), Kristiansen now began a long, painful pilgrimage to run below the 2:20 mark.

A recent influenza epidemic took nearly 15 per cent of runners out of play for the 1985 London Marathon, with only 15,500 of the 18,000 entrants toeing the start line. But Kristiansen was there, and she was in good health. "The hype surrounding the race in the days leading up had been incredible," recalled the *Guardian's* Duncan Mackay, "because there was not only Kristiansen's world

---

1. Kristiansen has since explained to the author that for some reason New York Marathon race director Fred Lebow never invited her to his race when he had Waitz as well. Lebow seemingly believed that having Waitz win year after year added to the mystique of the New York Marathon. Kristiansen explains: "I could have gone on my own accord of course, but other marathons were offering me $100,000 to attend!"

record attempt but also Wales' Steves Jones taking on England's Charlie Spedding in their first races since setting the world best and winning the Olympic bronze medal respectively."

Ingrid also had a significant bonus for this year's race. *The Times* noted: "Unlike last year, when Mrs Kristiansen ran 32 of the 42 kilometres alone, the women are starting with the men tomorrow, and the Norwegian thinks that that is just the impetus she needs to bridge the 1:43 gap between last year's time and the world record." And that is exactly how it panned out. With people to run hard with, especially in the early going, Kristiansen blasted through 10 miles in 53:29 and halfway in 1:10:10, despite experiencing stomach pains. She then reeled off several even faster miles – almost 5:20 miling to place her comfortably under

Shielded by a couple of Norwegians throughout most of the race, Ingrid Kristiansen heads to her world record that would stand for well over a decade. *Mark Shearman*

world-record pace. Her three 10-kilometre splits to 30 kilometres were 32:52, 33:38 and a scorching 32:48, giving her a projected finish time of 2:19:40. (Hauman). Duncan Mackay recalls to *British Runner* magazine: "On the couple of occasions I did manage to squeeze through a gap to see Ingrid I was struck by how uneconomic her action appeared. Her legs were like metronomes but from her waist up, she always seemed to be struggling and her shoulders appeared particularly tense."

Ingrid lost very little time to 35 kilometres although the enormity of her actions finally impeded her for the home stretch. "Over the last 7 kilometres I slowed down and lost more than a minute," she said afterwards. But her 2:21:06 had still smashed the world record by a massive 1 minute and 37 seconds, with Britain's Sarah Rowell finishing a full 7 minutes behind. "The atmosphere around the course was fantastic," recalls Ingrid. "I felt strong and inspired, everything was going well and I had mostly positive thoughts." To illustrate just how special the run was, the world record stood for 13½ years until Kenya's Tegla Loroupe finally claimed it with a 2:20:47 run at Rotterdam in October, 1998.[2] Pat Butcher of *The Times* wrote:

> Mrs Kristiansen was far and away the heroine of the day, even if there may be some qualms about the transparent way that she was paced by a former Norwegian male club colleague, who was wearing a women's number. She failed in her towering ambition to become the first woman under 2:20, but that is now a distinct probability. Her winning time would still have won her the Olympic men's marathon up to [and including] 1956.

It was an excellent day for British female marathoning as well, with Sarah Rowell and Sally Ann Hales both dipping under Priscilla Welch's British record set at the previous year's Olympics. Ann Ford, the 1978 Commonwealth Games 1500-metres champion produced an outstanding 2:31:9 for fourth, in her first attempt at the distance.

Despite clearing around $100,000 in prize money on the day, Kristiansen was keen to remark: "I don't run for the money. I run for the fun of it. But that's not to say, I'm not glad about the money. I was a bit slow at halfway, but I managed to make it up with the help of some good athletes in front of me, and with some Norwegian colleagues running alongside."

Race director Chris Brasher was delighted with how the fifth London Marathon turned out: "Despite all our fears, it turned out to be the best London Marathon ever. When so few came through the registration point earlier in the week, we began to worry, but it all turned out fine in the end. The conditions were superb, and the athletes responded, and so too did the public, who made it a magnificent occasion."

---

2. The marathon world record has fallen around 70 times (for both genders), and Kristiansen's is significantly the longest-standing marathon world record ever. Other marathon world records which are notable for their durability include Albert Michelsen of the USA who held the mark of 2:29 between 1925 and 1935; Japan's legendary Kitei Son who held 2:26:42 between 1935 and 1947; Derek Clayton's 2:08:33 stood throughout the entire decade of the 1970s (1969 to 1981); and Belayneh Dinsamo's 2:06:50 stood between 1988-1998. Up to Kristiansen, the women's record fell at regular two to three-year intervals from 1963 to 1985. There is, however, Britain's Violet Percy to consider, who ran 3:40:22 in October 1926 at Chiswick; but that was believed to be an informal time trial (Hauman).

Steve Jones (right) is no longer the world record holder as over in Rotterdam, Carlos Lopes has bettered Jones' time. But no one is now within two minutes of Ingrid Kristiansen's new world best. *Mark Shearman*

The weekend of April 20th–21st, 1985, had indeed been a memorable one for the sport, and sponsors Nike proudly took out nearly a whole page advert in *The Times* with the massive caption: "TWO DAYS RUNNING". And then in smaller letters at the bottom:

Saturday	**Rotterdam**	**Carlos Lopes**	**2:07:12**	**WORLD BEST**
Sunday	**London**	**Ingrid Kristiansen**	**2:21:06**	**WORLD BEST**

And to cap a great weekend for records, there is one more that will surely never fall: five Norwegian brothers managed to record a total time of under 15 hours, to break the world record for a family of that size.

* * *

Her magnificent London effort meant Kristiansen was now the first athlete, man or woman, to hold the world records for the 5000-metres, 10,000-metres and marathon simultaneously. Zátopek tried, so did Gebrselassie, and Radcliffe will continue to try and try, but at present nobody can match Ingrid's astonishing range.

One thing London '85 could not claim was that it was an epic duel, but Ingrid got that in Chicago the following October in a hypnotic tussle with Joan Benoit Samuelson. As was her terrifying habit, Benoit set off like a startled hare, running

155

the first two miles in 5:09 and 5:07, but Kristiansen refused to be intimidated and stayed right with her. Rosa Mota wasn't having any of it and stayed back. Fifteen kilometres was reached in 49:00, a full 50 seconds faster than Kristiansen had achieved in London. At 19 miles, Samuelson surged, but Kristiansen clawed back the deficit; then again at 20 miles, and again the brave Norwegian matched her. Finally, after her third surge Kristiansen had to let go. As Ingrid's world record was preserved by fifteen seconds, Samuelson noted after the race: "It's a completely different ballgame, running with someone right on your tail. I didn't feel as in control in this race as in some others. This was a very tough race mentally because Ingrid always was right there. We are all eyeing 2:20; me and Ingrid and Rosa Mota. When you talk about 2:20, you really are talking about 2:18-2:19. And that's a darn fast time for anybody." The final podium results read: Samuelson, 2:21:21; Kristiansen, 2:23:05; Mota, 2:23:29.

July 5th, 1986, marked Ingrid's finest track race, at the Bislett Stadium, when she tried for a new world mark for 10K. Running "negative splits" for 25 laps (speeding up over the second half of the race) is tremendously difficult – but even more so when one considers that Ingrid passed that halfway mark in 15:11. However, speed up she did, by nine seconds to finish in another world record – of 30:13.74 – that would stand for many years, until Wang Junxia, erased it in 1993. Ingrid's 5000-metre track world record lasted even longer, from August 1986 to July 1995, when she scorched to her 14:37.33 in Stockholm.

When the author asked Kristiansen to name the top three greatest races of her career it is no surprise she fondly opted for Bislett, and of course London '85. On Bislett she wistfully recollects: "There had been sections of the media that said that the 10,000 for women was far too boring but they were proved wrong in this race. The crowd were completely captivated and made an electric atmosphere. They even started doing Mexican waves!" Her third choice is lesser known: the 1987 Rome World Championships 10,000, which she won by three ticks of the clock over Russia's Yelena Vyazova. Ingrid recalls: "I had been injured and wasn't confident at all. I went off way too fast and I remember Liz McColgan asking afterwards why I had gone out so fast when I was short on fitness. At about half-way I began to get very tired and my lead came down and down. I was convinced I would be caught. It was tremendously satisfying to go on and win."

The holy grail of a sub-2:20 for the marathon was something that Kristiansen chased for several years to come. "Every year I go for 2:20," she said in an interview in *Track and Field News*. "You have to train and train some more. You have to keep on going if you want to be on top." If we take London 1985 as the first time a woman realistically shot for sub-2:20,[3] there follows Chicago 1985, when both Benoit and Kristiansen shot for it. Ingrid's list of attempts then goes something like this: London 1987, Ingrid passed halfway in 69:27, but slowed to a still fine 2:22:48. She returned to London in 1988 and passed halfway in 69:45 but this time tied up badly for a 2:25:41 win. At Boston in 1989 halfway came in 69:31, but with the hills and the heat saw yet another win but in "only" 2:24:33.

---

3. Joan Benoit could disagree with that since her first half of Boston 1983 was 68:22, but that was more a tactic designed to demoralize her rival Allison Roe, and she slowed dramatically in the second half. Her tactics worked perfectly, with a dejected Roe walking off the course at 17 miles because she couldn't see her rival and saw no point in continuing.

We'll never know what would have happened if Ingrid had instead opted to run London six days later where the conditions were much kinder. One hundred men ran under 2:20 that year, compared to just eleven in Boston (in marathons of comparable quality). Kristiansen's sixth and final assault on the 2:20 mark came when she was probably past her best, at New York in 1989, a breathtaking 18 years since she first appeared for Norway. But Ingrid, never one to shirk a challenge, was almost right on schedule at the half – 1:10:20 – before stomach problems slowed her to a 2:25:30. She did, of course, win the race in a time that was only bettered once at New York in the next six years.

She is philosophical when I ask her if she has regrets about not breaking 2:20. "It just wasn't meant to be. London 1987 was my best chance and the one where I felt the easiest, but with just a few miles to go my hamstring went, and I sort of hobbled home." It is well known that Kristiansen trained a great deal on a tread-mill.[4] One way to describe treadmill running is by a word that Frank Shorter favours: *monomania*. But when compared to the harsh Norwegian winters, almost anything was preferable to being outside. Kristiansen logically explains: "Outside it may be cold and dark, dangerous with snow and cars. But I run here, with no wind, and my husband sitting nearby reading the paper and my little boy playing alongside" (Hauman).

Ingrid opted for the 10,000-metres instead of the marathon at the 1988 Seoul Olympics but had to drop out due to a fractured bone in her foot. Thus one of the greatest runners of all time never did manage to win an elusive Olympic medal. But Kristiansen went out at the very top. She won New York and Boston in 1989 and ran the two fastest times in the world. Her five fastest marathon times averaged 2:23:11.

US coach Catrina Campbell still felt in 1995 that Ingrid was "probably the greatest women's distance runner ever. She will always be unique for what she did. And what makes her even more amazing is that she did it while leading a balanced life. She wasn't a one-dimensional person" (Sandrock).

* * *

These days Kristiansen barely runs at all, but pursues with great enthusiasm the sport of Nordic walking: power walking – often in the mountains – with ski poles. Three times a week, sometimes twice a day, Ingrid takes classes that are enthusiastically and well attended. To some, Nordic walking may appear a rather esoteric pursuit (much like distance running before 1972), something which isn't quite running, walking or cross-country skiing. But the author much enjoyed the class he took with Ingrid. It's a good cardiovascular session in which both the upper and lower body are given equal workout, but with none of the pounding of running. In a session of 10 × 1 minute hill reps up a steep ascent, Ingrid strictly admonished me for bending the rules. Trying to get up with the leaders, I threw in a little shimmy. "*WAAAALLLK*"!! screamed Ingrid. Running, it seems, is truly behind her.

---

4. Ingrid would have a picture of Joan Benoit, her greatest rival breaking the world record in 1983 taped to the wall in front of her. "I shall break that record," vowed Ingrid in the year before London '85, as she ran mile after mile on the spot.

I ask her if she sees much of Grete. "We lead very different lives now. Grete still travels the world speaking about her glory days. But you must remember that the last global race she won [the 1983 World Championships] was over 20 years ago. I prefer to let go and find new things to do."

Ingrid's house is gorgeously put together with a real personal touch and littered with clues as to another of her great passions: embroidery and quilt-making. Judging by the curtains, sofa covers and tablecloths, she obviously has a real skill for it. The treadmill, where she trained for so many of her great races is still there in what is now her children's den. It is an enormous, menacing, white monster of a thing; and it is easy to picture Ingrid in her heyday, galloping away on it with a grimace of determination, eyes fixed on newspaper and magazine clippings of her rivals on the walls – in particular Joan Benoit, who she was setting out to conquer.

As we walk through her house she taps a computer. "After you leave," she says, "I must email Paula about her marathon..." (It is the day after Radcliffe's nadir in Athens). Ingrid may not be a runner anymore – but her passion and knowledge for it remain.

Race result:

I. Kristiansen	NOR	2:21:06
S. Rowell	GBR	2:28:06
S. Hales	GBR	2:28:38
A. Ford	GBR	2:31:19
M. O'Connor	NZL	2:32:35
K. Schilly	USA	2:33:20
L. Bain	GBR	2:33:38
S. McDiarmid	GBR	2:34:58
V. Marot	GBR	2:35:12

Note: Eighteen years later Marot was still going strong – the champion in 1989, she recorded a 2:55:01 at the 2003 London, to easily win the W45 category.

Sources:

Conversations with Ingrid Kristiansen.
Butcher, Pat, in *The Times*, April 20th & 22nd, 1985.
Derderian, Tom, *Boston Marathon*. Human Kinetics, 1996.
Hauman, Riël, *Century of the Marathon*. Human & Rousseau, 1996.
Mackay, Duncan, in the *Guardian*, April 20th, 1985.
Mackay, Duncan, in *British Runner*, April 2002.
Sandrock, Michael, *Running with the Legends*. Human Kinetics, 1996.

XVIII

No. 33 – 1989 London Marathon [Men]

Sunday, April 23rd

Westminster Bridge plays host to a threesome.

The 1989 London Marathon was the first battle of the real heavyweights over the streets of the capital and has stuck in the minds of many who follow the sport. There was, of course, the classic duel between Jones and Spedding in 1985, but that was a domestic battle with relatively little international interest. Marathon legend Toshihiko Seko came to London in 1986, but it was a weak field and he had the race to himself. The year 1989, however, was bursting with international talent, and no one would ever be alone for very long.

The race had a whiff of controversy in the preceding days, as the world of officialdom came under fierce attack for their archaic ways. Ken Mays wrote in a *Daily Telegraph* preview:

> England's top competitors made a blistering attack on the English Amateur Athletic Association two days before the ADT London Marathon, for their failure to include tomorrow's race as a selection point for the Commonwealth Games in Auckland next January.
>
> Charlie Spedding, England's premier marathoner, condemned the AAA for their actions despite the race being the best line-up since it began.

The problem was that the AAA had agreed that the Merseyside Marathon in Liverpool on September 3rd was to be the designated race for the men – with the first two across the line to be selected for New Zealand – while the women were to race in Birmingham three weeks later.

Both Spedding, the London winner in 1984, but out of the 1989 race, and Kevin Forster, who was likely to be the leading Briton, said they would stay away from Liverpool, while Veronique Marot, of Leeds, who had the fastest time in the women's line-up would also boycott the Birmingham race. "The AAA have not appreciated that the trial is totally different from other races," Spedding wailed:

> We are not in this sport for the money but with only two good races a year, it does help some of the athletes to pay the mortgage. The London race would have given some athletes the chance to qualify and earn a living at the same

time. Their idea of picking the Merseyside Marathon is proof that they are not living in the real world and do not have the athletes at the front of their consideration.

This was not a new problem. It had been around for decades. Ron Hill maintains to this day that he would have performed much better in major championships, especially in his devastating turns at the 1971 Europeans and 1972 Olympics, had the selectors dealt with the issue of the trial race more sympathetically. He writes in *The Long Hard Road*:

I tried to avoid the trial for the European Championships by writing to the B.A.A.B. asking to be excused on the grounds that the European Games were only nine weeks after the trials and a hard marathon such a short time before the Championships would surely take the edge off my performance.
Arthur Gold rang me with his answer. Everyone must run the trial. After all, I wasn't that much better than anyone else.
Bloody hell! Not that much better? Only 2½ minutes if you looked at the Commonwealth Games result.

Hill went on to win the trial comfortably in 2:12:39 but wrote: "Selectors take note. I need inspiration to run great marathons and you have just stolen some of that inspiration for the European Games by making me prove myself in the trial!"
Hill trained as hard as he was able over the next nine weeks but felt constantly stiff and often in severe pain due to the stress of having to run two hard marathons within such a short period, with almost no chance to rest. His left leg seized up at just 11 miles in the European Championships marathon and he limped home a dejected third, even though he was clearly the best man in the field. Karel Lismont of Belgium won the gold in perfect conditions in a time of 2:13:09 – slower than Hill ran the trial in. Hill ran 2:14:34. He explains:

I really blamed the selectors for losing me that gold medal. If I hadn't run that trial I wouldn't have got that injured leg, and I would have been full of inspiration for the European Championships. No – not selectors – how could they be selectors? They didn't select anything. All they did was bloody well rubber stamp the first three in the trial. But I blamed "Them", whoever they were. I blamed the system; I blamed British running. British running had had me.

Nearly twenty years later and the most promising British runners were still having the same old battles with the powers that be.

* * *

The man who stood as favourite in the eyes of many to cross Westminster Bridge in front was an enigmatic 25-year-old, Tokyo-based Kenyan named Douglas Wakiihuri. He had won the 1987 World Championships and followed this up by earning an Olympic silver in 1988.
Born in Mombasa, Douglas Wakiihuri actually grew up at an altitude of 2000 metres. He lived just a mile or so away from school, but he ran the distance four

times a day because he used to go home for lunch since his family were so poor they couldn't afford the school meals. A key development in Wakiihuri's life came at the age of 19 when he met Kiyoshi Nakamura,[1] the legendary coach of Toshihiko Seko. Under Nakamura's influence, Wakiihuri moved to Japan. "You absorb the culture," he later said. "I was very happy with how I was brought up. Not by books, but by learning with my eyes and ears and head. I am a Kenyan, but think and feel Japanese" (Hauman). In other words his body-mind connection formed the most lethal distance running cocktail known to man. He spoke three languages: English, Swahili and Japanese. Although, tragically, Nakamura wasn't in Wakiihuri's life for long before his death in May 1985, he had imparted into the young Kenyan enough philosophy and wisdom to prepare him well for the challenges ahead.

Wakiihuri was almost a complete unknown when he burst on to the world scene in 1987. Coming into the World Championships marathon in Rome he boasted a personal best of just 2:13:34, with a second-best time of 2:16:26. In a field which had included the defending champion from Helsinki, Rob de Castella, plus Juma Ikangaa, Geoff Smith, Abebe Mekonnen and Orlandon Pizzolato, the Kenyan was still in a group of seven at the 35-kilometres mark. With him were other formidable runners such as Ahmed Salah of Djibouti, who had won the World Cup the previous April, Steve Moneghetti of Australia, Englishman Hugh Jones and Gelindo Bordin of Italy. Against all the odds it was the inexperienced near newcomer, Wakiihuri, who burst into the lead at 38 kilometres and built up a 42-second advantage by the finish.

One year later Wakiihuri and Salah were at it again – right at the forefront of world marathoning at the Seoul Olympics. This time there were just 15 seconds separating them, but they both had to bow to the winner, Gelindo Bordin, who, in a brilliantly judged race, was another 15 seconds up the road (see Chapter 41). A friend of both Wakiihuri and Tanzanian top man Juma Ikangaa highlighted how the two athletes contrasted: "Ikangaa is a diplomat. When he's not running, he's watching CNN for hours. He understands *you* much better. Douglas understands *himself*" (Hauman). Wakiihuri certainly had a self-confident approach and an attitude which at times could have been said to be superior to the masses; especially those who wrote about his sport without ever having participated: "There is the truth about the marathon and very few of you have written the truth," Wakiihuri once exclaimed to the press. "Even if I explain it to you, you'll never understand it, you're outside of it."

In the *Nairobi Daily Nation's* preview of the race, the paper said: "World champion Douglas Wakiihuri, takes a unique blend of Kenyan talent and Japanese science into Sunday's ninth London marathon. He renews his rivalry with Djibouti's Ahmed Salah, the double World Cup champion who finished one place behind him in both the 1987 Rome World Championships and the Seoul Olympics." "I am still Kenyan but I think like a Japanese," Wakiihuri told a news conference. "Japan is more serious. I still have a lot to learn and the training is more scientific, we are planning three years ahead."

---

1. For more information about this remarkable man, see Chapter 29.

The London organizers had made sure, however, that Wakiihuri would have to sing for his supper. Included in the line up was the ubiquitous and highly talented Salah, who, as mentioned above was a World Cup winner in both 1985 and 1987. Other world-class talent included Wodajo Bulti of Ethiopia and Denmark's Henrik Jorgensen – the previous year's winner. Also toeing the line were Australia's Steve Moneghetti and Tanzania's Suleiman Nyambui. Rob de Castella, the double Commonwealth Games winner, had been troubled by a knee injury and wasn't certain to be among the starters.

Salah was delighted to be renewing this old rivalry; indeed it was the key reason for his presence. "I'm very happy that Wakiihuri is running – that's the reason I've come," he said. "I didn't do myself justice in Rome or Seoul and I've come here to get my revenge."

* * *

The race lived up to all hype and expectation and, as Riël Hauman wrote in *Century of the Marathon*, "London was a battle royal." In excellent conditions, the three main men of Salah, Moneghetti and Wakiihuri went through halfway in a conservative 64:42. But the pace then picked up although the leaders refused to separate. There were still a dozen runners in contention at the 19-mile mark before two fell off the back. The most dramatic break came two miles later when Salah, Wakiihuri and Moneghetti finally extricated themselves from the rest and began a 5-mile, shoulder-to-shoulder battle.

At around this time near disaster struck when there was a mix up at a watering station which left Wakiihuri and Moneghetti with 30 yards of daylight between them and the sole leader Salah. However, they reeled him back in dogged fashion over the next couple of miles. The streets of London were packed with tens of thousands of cheering spectators who roared their approval. Salah and Moneghetti constantly exchanged the lead over the last two kilometres, with the Kenyan tucked in just behind. Great suspense mounted as the trio stayed together until the 26th-mile marker.

Suddenly there were just three hundred metres to go, with all three protagonists still locked together. Riël Hauman writes: "Who would kick first? It was Wakiihuri. But the other two went with him. The finish line was looming ahead when the Kenyan found that little bit extra, accelerated again and drew away to win in a PB. Moneghetti's time was also his best." It all resulted in the best race and finish in the nine-year history of the London Marathon and while Wakiihuri smiled as

With just half a mile to go, Douglas Wakiihuri puts on a mean snarl and attempts to break the shackles which Steve Moneghetti and Ahmed Salah have had on him all race. *Mark Shearman*

When the clock strikes 11:40... kick!: Big Ben looks on with polite interest as Wakiihuri sprints away from Moneghetti and Salah to the finish on Westminster bridge. *Mark Shearman*

he crossed the line, Veronique Marot, the women's winner, collapsed in the arms of officials.

The quality of the race was clear to see. It was only the second time that a marathon had produced six runners under 2:10. In seventh, Pat Petersen, who had been fourth in New York in 1987, clocked 2:10:04 – the fastest time by an American since Alberto Salazar ran 2:09:21 in the 1983 Fukuoka race (Hauman). Race director Dave Bedford still purrs about the drama and quality of the race to this day: "1989? Stunning. Absolutely stunning race – all three on the bridge at the same time..."

British hopefuls Kevin Forster and Mike Mcleod fared poorly, recording a 19th and a DNF respectively. It was left to the 30-year-old Tony Milovsorov, a Wolverhampton teacher, to cheer the host nation, finishing sixth and taking over four minutes off his previous best with 2:09:54. Dedication to the cause was illustrated by the fact that Milovsorov's four children had been struck down with chickenpox and his wife Sharon with shingles, but his £7,000 share of the prize money compensated nicely.

Anthony Denton in the *Nairobi Daily Nation* was ebullient: "Kenya's World Champion long distance runner, Douglas Wakiihuri, has become the first Kenyan to win the London Marathon after a thrilling battle with his old rival, Ahmed Salah of Djibouti, and a relatively unknown Australian Steve Moneghetti." "It all went to plan," said Wakiihuri, "it was my tactics not to take the lead at any time until near the end and it worked perfectly. I felt fine when I finished but I won't be running too many marathons this year. This time I was ready for Salah. He always is really tough."

The big blazing front-page headline in the *Daily Telegraph* the following day read:

22,406th Finisher Sets a Record:

A teenager dressed as a French maid finished in 22,406th place in the London Marathon yesterday – and established the marathon as the world's biggest.

As Melanie Jones of Teddington, West London strode imperiously across the finishing line she beat the record for number of participants from the previous year. She had returned a 6:20 clocking.

The following day the chairman of the Kenyan Amateur Athletics Association announced they were to reward their "World Marathon Champion". "That a

Kenyan can win the London Marathon is something every Kenyan should be proud of," the delighted KAAA proclaimed. "This proves once again the prowess of the Kenyan athletes wherever they take part in world championships. Wakiihuri's victory has also underlined Kenya's great talent in athletics and the KAAA will do everything possible to tap the talent to the maximum."

The world had been warned.

* * *

The following year's Commonwealth Games saw another superb battle between Wakiihuri and Moneghetti in an extremely competitive Commonwealth Games marathon that also featured Steve Jones (4th) and Ibrahim Hussein (5th). On a humid day over a flat point-to-point course in Auckland, Wakiihuri battled it out with Moneghetti and Simpon Robert Naali of Tanzania, taking the lead just 600 metres from home, with the top three finishers having just 11 seconds between them. It was the fourth time that the Kenyan had beaten Moneghetti in a major marathon. Moneghetti would however finally win the Commonwealths in 1994 by a margin of over 3 minutes. Thus his progress in an eight-year period had amounted to a remarkably consistent bronze–silver–gold streak. Now that's resilience.

Wakiihuri's great dream though, was to turn his Seoul Olympic silver into Barcelona gold, but his winning streak was over. He placed just 36th at Barcelona, one place ahead of another great Kenyan runner of the late 1980s, Ibrahim Hussein. Steve Moneghetti toiled to 48th. If the Barcelona Olympics signalled the beginning of the end for Wakiihuri, it should be noted that even with his career in decline he still managed to grab one more major victory: the 1995 World Cup.

Race result:

D. Wakiihuri	KEN	2:09:03
S. Moneghetti	AUS	2:09:06
A. Salah	DJI	2:09:09
M. Matthias	POR	2:09:43
S. Nyambui	TAN	2:09:52
T. Milovsorov	GBR	2:09:54
P. Petersen	USA	2:10:04
W. Bulti	ETH	2:10:32
T. Nakamura	JPN	2:11:51
Z. Guowei	CHN	2:12:03

Sources:

Conversations with David Bedford.
Conversations with Ron Hill.
Daily Telegraph, race report, April 24th, 1989.
Denton, Anthony, in the *Nairobi Daily Nation,* April 24th, 1989.

Hauman, Riël, *Century of the Marathon*. Human & Rousseau, 1996.
Hill, Ron, *The Long Hard Road. Part II: To the Peak and Beyond*. Ron Hill Sports, 1983.
Martin, David and Roger Gynn, *The Olympic Marathon*. Human Kinetics, 2000.
Mays, Ken, in the *Daily Telegraph*, April 22nd, 1989.
Nairobi Daily Nation, race preview, April 22nd, 1989.
Wallechinsky, David, *The Complete Book of the Olympics*. Aurum Press, 2000.

XIX

No. 32 – 1920 Olympic Marathon [Men]

Sunday, August 22nd

A man ahead of his time.

There were no Games of the 6th Olympiad (1916) because of the First World War, just as there were no Games of the 12th and 13th Olympiad either (which were due to be held in 1940 and 1944). If the Games are not held, it doesn't alter their four-year cycle and the Olympiad is thus still numbered sequentially. The final choice for the 7th Olympiad was between Antwerp and Lyon. Martin and Gynn write: "In terms of worldwide linkage via rail and ship, Antwerp meant superior travel ease for far-away delegations. Politics probably played a role in the final decision, as only five years before, Belgium had been the victim of invasion by Germany, and Belgium's selection could be seen as a gesture of recognition for its regained independence."

While Germany and Hungary did not receive invitations to compete, 29 other nations sent athletes comprising 2591 men and a somewhat paltry 78 women – albeit a stuttering rise from the 57 at Stockholm 1912.[1] These Olympics have two significant footnotes. They were the first to include the Olympic oath that the goal for all athletes is to abide by fair play (Wendl), and they were also the first Olympics to display the iconic emblem of the five intertwined Olympic rings. Pierre de Coubertin had actually developed it in 1913, but a seven-year wait then took place before it was formally used at the Games.[2]

The Olympic Stadium from the Antwerp Games still stands – complete with cinder track – and goes by the name of the soccer club it houses, Beerschot. There is a key difference between major championship marathons of say 40, 50, 80 years ago, in that instead of showcasing the host city to the max – as for instance the mayor of Barcelona unashamedly (and quite rightly) did at the 1992 Olympics – these early Games tended to lead the athletes off on roads and trails directly out of the city and into rural surroundings, where most of the marathon would occur.

---

1. The men's participation rose by 101, just a 3.8 per cent rise, so the women's rise of 26.9 per cent showed progress was at least being made, however small.
2. The flag symbolizes the five continents linked in unity, and the colours of blue, yellow, black, green and red were chosen because at that time at least one of those colours appeared in the flag of every participating geopolitical entity (Martin & Gynn).

Chances on there being respectable times at the Antwerp marathon were increased twofold: the course was fairly flat and the weather was likely to prove to be far cooler than the cauldron that had greeted the runners for most of the previous Games. Indeed, race day dawned bleak and cloudy – a marathoner's favourite habitat! But the racers had one remarkable factor working against their favour: an extremely long course...By 1920 the marathon course had still yet to be standardized and the distance for marathons was left largely to race organizers. However, this oversight was soon to be corrected. On May 27th, 1921 the Fifth IAAF Congress met in Geneva and standardization of the marathon length was high on the agenda. The distance settled upon – 26 miles and 385 yards – happens, of course, to be the length of the 1908 London Olympic marathon. There are two fairly clear reasons for this decision: strong British influence amongst the IAAF, and the fact that the 1908 race had already become, in less than 13 years, a race of epic proportion and publicity. But this decision helped the Olympic marathoners of a year earlier not one bit, and they ended up running nearly half a mile longer than today's standard distance – 26 miles, 992 yards.

The gun sounded for the 1920 Olympic Marathon at twelve minutes past four on Sunday, August 22nd. Forty-eight competitors (down twenty from Stockholm 1912) from eighteen nations set off on the daunting trek. The most notable presence was that of distance running's first real star, the triple Olympic gold-medal winner from the Stockholm Games, Johannes Petter Kolehmainen (known as Hannes). His talented brother Taavetti (known as Tatu) was present also. American Chuck Mellor – who would go on to win Boston in 1925 – was also there. He had recently won in Detroit in 2:30:04 (over 25 miles). All three top men from Boston the year before were also competing: the Greek Peter Trivoulidas who had defeated the two fancied Americans Arthur Roth and Carl Linder. In the annual "Polytechnic" Marathon in England an inexperienced British farmer named Bobby Mills scored an excellent win in his debut marathon with a time of 2:37:40 and become the new British record holder. Mills defeated the Italian champion, Valerio Arri, by over seven minutes and both would go to the Olympics. There, although they would run well, experience would count for rather more.

But it was Kolehmainen who grabbed the spotlight and media interest. He was born in Kuopio, Finland, on December 9th, 1889, and ran his first marathon when just 17½ years old. In 1909, he ran three marathons within 18 days during September, "showing not only incredible injury resistance but also competitive drive" (Martin & Gynn). Only the very few have dominated the distance events at an Olympic Games quite like Kolehmainen did at Stockholm in 1912. Their names spring easily to mind: Nurmi, Zátopek, Viren, Yifter and El Gerrouj. On this occasion he conquered all in the 5000-metres, the 10,000-metres and then the – now defunct – 12-kilometre cross-country race. When one considers that each of the track races had a heat, Kolehmainen's total distance covered was a marathon in itself. At one stage after the Stockholm Games, Kolehmainen held world records at 2000, 3000 and 5000-metres.

Kolehmainen became a naturalized US citizen when he moved to New York, but he was obliged to compete for Finland in Antwerp because of the tried and trusted Olympic rule that once an athlete has competed for a country at an

Hannes Kolehmainen (809) tours the track at the 1912 Stockholm Olympics on his way to winning gold in the 10,000-metres from Lewis Tewanima (USA) in second. *EMPICS*

Olympics, he could compete for that country only at any subsequent Games.

The London *Times* described the start: "The marathon race, of course, was the great event of today. The 47 marathon runners were started at 12 minutes past four. The rain then descended heavily, rather spoiling the effect of the various exhibitions of Swedish exercises which were going on in the stadium." Two Brits Mills and Piper were on prominent display just behind the leader, Henri Teyssedou of France, as the runners departed from the Olympic Stadium. Memories were revived of early British prominence/dominance in the London Olympics of 1908. On that occasion such premature exuberance had proved disastrous as the British team performed dismally in the final shake-up. Behind these "rabbits", the daunting figure of Kolehmainen and his aggressively receding hairline could be sighted, looking every day his 30 years. In fact this correspondent puts him looking closer to 50.

Just back a handful of metres was another impressive figure, that of Jüri Lossman, he of the slick, Brylcreem hairdo. Born in the Köo district of Estonia in February 1891, Lossman was a far less frequent racer than his rival Kolehmainen but a still successful figure when he did "toe the line". His effectiveness could be put down to a diligent training regime of 120 to 130 kilometres per week: a large amount for those days, and Martin and Gynn observe that he'd undertake his workouts "sometimes wearing lead weights on his training shoes". His marathon record before the Olympics was run four, won four. Photographs of him show a man looking around forty, as opposed to his 29 years. The theory that the Great War aged men well before their time appears credible in the cases of Kolehmainen and Lossman.

After the leading British runners had been displaced, the race up until 10 kilometres featured an assortment of runners with one position a constant: first. This belonged to a fine South African runner called Chris Gitsham who was well known to the knowledgeable as a key player in the 1912 Stockholm Olympics. On that occasion he had pushed countryman Kennedy (Ken) McArthur hard, before landing the silver medal, 58 seconds adrift. It seemed as if Gitsham had spent a lot of time brooding. People react in different ways to a silver medal. For many it is more than enough – an outstanding achievement over which they can retire happy. For others it is mere incentive to work harder, much harder, to atone for such a failure.

By 15 kilometres Gitsham found for the first time that he had company, from the man he feared most – Hannes Kolehmainen. Other respected runners up with the leaders included Auguste Broos of Belgium, Tatu Kolehmainen (brother of Hannes, who had incidentally done his fair share of leading eight years earlier), Juho Tuomikoski (another "flying Finn"), Italy's Valerio Arri, enjoying an even feistier run than at the Polytechnic Marathon, and, of course, Lossman.

An acceleration occurred as Gitsham and (Hannes) Kolehmainen passed halfway in a dazzling 1:13:10; outstripping the world record pace by some 10 minutes! They were 48 seconds clear of their nearest rivals, Broos and Blasi, who themselves were travelling at suicidal pace. Something had to give. Indeed two of the top four would fail to finish. By 27 kilometres – passed in just an hour and a half – Gitsham had begun to falter due to one of his shoes tearing open. Broos and Blasi were dramatically slowing down as well. But not the great Hannes. Lossman stalked not far behind, accounting for Broos and Blasi and moving into the bronze position.

Ten kilometres later Kolehmainen had ruthlessly and clinically extended his lead over Gitsham to around half a kilometre and was stretching it all the while. Soon after fading into fifth position, Gitsham faded from the race altogether for a DNF. The British were feeling the effects after their early forward running, but *The Times* remained upbeat and portrayed the British as heroes: "At intervals through the megaphone, announcements were made of the position of the competitors. The whole population of every village turned out to cheer the runners, the little Union Jacks on the breasts of the British competitors being frequently singled out for a special cheer."[3]

Lossman however refused to accept defeat and was launching a furious assault on the leader, whittling down Kolehmainen's lead to only a minute or so. Theirs was a battle of the diehards, who had run at an alarmingly quick pace all day. Meanwhile, three-quarters of a mile further back the battle for bronze hotted up

---

3. Those cheers must have evolved to sympathetic grunts of encouragement as the race wore on. The early British pace-making once again proved costly, with the runners trailing in 14th (Mills) and then 7th from last (Piper) and 5th from last (Housden). The last two ran well outside 3 hours.

Kolehmainen enters the Olympic stadium to head for the world record and Olympic gold number four. *EMPICS*

as the conservative Valerio Arri, who had hunkered just inside the top ten all day, suddenly deduced he had a surplus of energy and nicked one man, then another, then another...six in total. Finally, he found himself in no-man's land: the bronze medal secure, the leaders too far up to catch.

Meanwhile, Hannes Kolehmainen and Lossman slugged out their duel, separated by 200 to 300 yards of macadam, a distance that was shrinking all the while. As they approached the stadium it appeared that Lossman may even have a chance to catch his prey. Martin and Gynn write: "In fact, it took a world record to prevent Lossman from winning.

Hannes crossed the line in an amazing 2:32:35 – faster than any previous performance, even those on a shorter 42.2 kilometre course! Lossman was less than 13 seconds behind, however, and the drama of these two men racing nearly together around the track was unforgettable." It was significantly the closest Olympic Marathon finish ever, and would stand as such until Josiah Thugwane's win 76 years later (see Chapter 24). There are varied reports about how third-placed finisher Arri celebrated as he crossed the line. Did he, as one scribe would have us believe, perform three "somewhat ungainly somersaults"? Or did he, according to another report, perform a more pleasing feat of "three cartwheels"? Or did he, as yet another scribe submits, perform three "cartwheel somersaults" (whatever they are)? We may never know for sure.

Kolehmainen's lap of honour, adorned with a laurel wreath and draped in a Finnish flag, brought enthusiastic cheers from the crowd who were further buoyed by a spectacular rainbow appearing as the day's drizzle finally passed. No longer were Americans and Canadians dominating Olympic marathons. The first six places all belonged to Europeans as it seemed the tide of superiority in the marathon had turned.

To emphasize further just how remarkable these runs by Kolehmainen and Lossman were, it's worth recalling that four years later, at Paris, the time was nearly 10 minutes slower, on a course 555 metres shorter. At Amsterdam in 1928, winner Boughèra El Ouafi was also slower, and although Juan Carlos Zabala's great run at Los Angeles 1932 was quicker, it would not have been had he run the same distance. Then came Sohn Kee-chung in 1936, who would have defeated Kolehmainen by only a minute and a half. Finally, and most notably, at the London Olympics *28 years after* the Finn, Delfo Cabrera would have trailed in some four minutes off the pace. It wasn't until the human piston himself – Emil Zátopek – came along, 32 years later, that Kolehmainen would have finally had to let the leaders go. He was truly a man ahead of his time.

Kolehmainen's world record was to stand for over five years until America's Albert Michelsen captured it at Port Chester in 1925 with the world's first ever sub-2:30 clocking. It seemed Kolehmainen's career would go on to still greater achievements in the marathon. But it wasn't to be. Although he went on to set world-best marks for the 25 and 30-kilometre runs he would never finish another marathon. Automatically selected for Paris in 1924, he returned a DNF, and then four years later he tried to qualify for the Amsterdam Olympics in the Finnish trial at Kauhava, but failed to finish that one either.

As for Jüri Lossman, he finished the 1920 Olympic marathon in something of a rage. On the day of his great race, other members of the Estonian team had chosen to undergo an excursion and missed the marathon. Lossman believed that with their support he may well have gone on to win. The Estonian was a man who often held authority to account. Athletes who criticize the way officials run the sport often catch a lot of flak for being rude and ungrateful, but Lossman was never slow to show displeasure if he thought organization was poor. In one race, two years after Antwerp, he ran an excellent 2:18 for a course he thought to be 40 kilometres long, but was then informed it was actually only 38.5. He made his frustration quite clear. Characters like Lossman are important to keep the powers that be on their toes, but they are unfortunately often labelled the "bad guy" at the time of their outbursts. An example of a latter-day Lossman is the Canadian Jerome Drayton (Chapter 10), who covered himself in enormous negative publicity after criticizing the shabby organization of the 1977 Boston Marathon (which he won). Drayton's comments were eventually absorbed, however, and that marathon was soon a far less chaotic affair.

Race result (42.75 kilometres):

Johannes Kolehmainen	FIN	2:32:35
Jüri Lossman	EST	2:32:48
Valerio Arri	ITA	2:36:32
Auguste Broos	BEL	2:39:25
Juho Tuomikoski	FIN	2:40:10
Sofus Rose	DEN	2:41:18
Joseph Organ	USA	2:41:30
Rudolph Hansen	DEN	2:41:39
Urho Tallgren	FIN	2:42:40
Taavetti Kolehmainen	FIN	2:44:03

Sources:

Anonymous, in *The Times*, August 23rd, 1920.
Derderian, Tom, *Boston Marathon*. Human Kinetics, 1996.
Hauman, Riël, *Century of the Marathon*. Human & Rousseau, 1996.
Martin, David and Roger Gynn, *The Olympic Marathon*. Human Kinetics, 2000.
Wallechinsky, David, *The Complete Book of the Olympics*. Aurum Press, 2000.
Wendl, K., "The Olympic Oath: A Brief History", *Citius, Altius, Fortius* – The ISOH Journal 3 (1): 4–5, 1995.

XX

No. 31 – 1997 London Marathon [Men]

Sunday, April 13th

Humiliated favourite shoots for mediocrity...and then just keeps on shooting.

On a perfect, dry, cool day – ideal for marathon running – the buzz before the 1997 London race was that the deep field could produce terrific times and a thrilling finish. The race favourites may have boiled down to a choice of two, but there were many extremely capable athletes on hand to pounce should either of them falter.

The 1996 Olympic champion, Josiah Thugwane, came to race. Just eight months after his stunning, emotional win in Atlanta, people wondered whether this diminutive South African was going to turn out to be a one-trick pony or a truly world-class player. For as Sebastian Coe has, somewhat pompously, pointed out: "The Games are littered with people who had one good day and were never heard of or seen again."[1] Life had been by no means straightforward for Thugwane since his Olympic win. Indeed, he positively lived in fear of his own survival. The *Daily Telegraph*'s sports writer, Sue Mott, interviewed Thugwane on his arrival in London, and the extended highlights of their meeting may be referred to in Chapter 24. To summarize, Thugwane commented to Mott:

> It's true I should be happy; I won but on the other hand I have this fear for my life. Fear for the life of my family. But what can I do? Soon after the Olympics I went back home and there were people who were looking for me. They wanted me to pay something to them. They were after my blood. I changed houses. So now I'm sitting here and there's nobody looking after my family. I don't know whether they'll eventually drag out my family, do something with them.

The other men's favourite was the mercurial 31-year-old Portuguese runner Antonio Pinto, who had triumphed at London in 1992 in a thrilling race where the final leaderboard read: Pinto 2:10:02, Huruk 2:10:07, Naali 2:10:08 and

---

1. Oddly enough, Coe uttered this comment in 1979, before he himself had even been to an Olympics.

The 1996 Olympic Champion Josiah Thugwane came to the streets of the capital in 1997 to prove he was no one-trick pony. *Mark Shearman*

Negere 2:10:10. Showing shrewd tactics that day, Pinto then encountered greater problems in 1995 when he came in third, having led by a minute at 22 miles. "Pinto can excel in land of elite," claimed the headline in the *Telegraph* the morning before the race. The paper's Iain Macleod indicated a home-grown challenge, too:

The London Marathon is becoming a byword for the quality of its choice competitors. The 1997 edition through the streets of the capital tomorrow is high on talent and expectation and, rarely, since the race began in 1981, has there been such anticipation surrounding the potential performances of the elite.

Richard Nerurkar, who has temporarily eschewed the virtues of championship racing for his first big-city marathon, acknowledges the quality of the field and the test it will provide, but believes that in an "unpredictable event", the "form book is not always the best guide for a marathon".

This third contender, a school-teacher from Marlborough, Richard Nerurkar, who had two major victories to his name in the Hamburg Marathon and World Cup (both 1993) writes in his book *Marathon Running* about whom he saw as the main contenders:

Thugwane would be running, but there was some doubt as to whether he could reproduce his Atlanta form. Antonio Pinto was coming back to one of his favourite race venues. He had already run four 2:08 marathons, although in my favour was the fact that I had beaten him in all three championship marathons that we had contested.

Likewise Steve Moneghetti, the 1994 Commonwealth champion, had four 2:08 clockings to his credit, but I had beaten him in our two most recent encounters. Stefano Baldini, the 1996 World Half-Marathon champion, was also in the field, but he was still a relative novice, with a personal best of 2:11:01. This was a race I felt I could definitely win – if I could produce my best on the day.

Eamonn Martin, the 1993 winner, surveyed a list of contenders and had no

174

doubts about London's commitment to excellence. "The depth of quality suggests it will be the best for a long time – if not the best ever." "This is a particularly intriguing race," Mcleod continued.

Indeed, the race is so open that few are willing to venture an opinion on the outcome. There is no shortage of character; Thugwane's chin, for example, displays a bullet scar, and, due to local jealousies, he has been assaulted twice, and constantly lives in fear of his life.

Pinto is perhaps marginally the favourite, for what it is worth in such illustrious company. Winner in 1992, and third two years ago, Pinto has generally excelled over the distance."

The Australian Steve Moneghetti said that when he first competed in London, in 1989, he had thought the field "awesome"; eight years on and the man who had twice been second on London's streets said: "I think we've now got an equivalent depth."

Another British contender was Paul Evans, who had impressively won the Chicago Marathon the previous October, after the great disappointment of missing out on the Olympic marathon due to questionable selection by the British selectors.[2] Evans was feeling more than a little bullish:

Winning Chicago finally made me realise that, over the marathon, on my day, I am as good as anyone in the world. This time I have planned how to win London. I have never done that before. The pacemaker is going to go through the half in sub-64, which is what I want. I honestly think that this could be the greatest London ever and somebody is going to have to run very fast to win it.

* * *

In ideal temperatures of 11 °C, with hardly a breath of wind, the runners set off – knowing that if ever there was a chance to run fast, this was it. The tempo which the pace-makers were to set was an interesting bone of contention, as the race got under way. Nerurkar, whom so many placed their hopes on, requested 63:45–64:00 for halfway. Antonio Pinto requested 63:15-30. Only a small difference, but it is often wafer-thin details like this that matter a whole lot in top-level sport. It was Pinto who got his wish; which is somewhat odd given that the organizers were so pinning their hopes on the British boy. But Nerurkar writes: "The appointed pace-makers were two Portuguese runners, Carlos Patricio and Paul Catarino. They had the same manager as Pinto, so not surprisingly, Pinto's preference won out since it would be 'his' pace-makers who would be doing the running."

By nine miles the leading group consisted of ten runners, with all the key names

---

2. Evans was the leading Briton in the 1996 London race, placing third overall, but the selectors opted for Steve Brace who had placed at the Houston Marathon in January in 2:10:35 (a meagre 5 seconds quicker than Evans at London). Peter Whitehead was also selected ahead of Evans due to his fourth place at the previous year's World Championships. However, sending athletes who had shown form such a considerable time before the Olympics backfired on the selectors as Whitehead and Brace placed a miserable 55th and 60th in Atlanta.

– minus Baldini, who was conservatively hanging back – in the mix. There were the two South Africans, Thugwane and Peu; the two Brits; Nerurkar and Evans; Pinto, Moneghetti, the German Stephane Franke and the Spaniard José Garcia. By ten miles, the split read 48:19, which put the group 6 seconds up on Belayneh Densimo's world record set nine years earlier. Richard Nerurkar recalls in *Marathon Running*:

As we crossed Tower Bridge at 12½ miles, it felt as if we were hit by a blast of exuberant cheering from spectators on both sides of the road. We were still trying to keep our nervous energy under wraps – though the same could not be said of the crowds. They were going wild with excitement, and for a stretch of about 400 metres before we came off the far side of the bridge, we were swept along by a wave of encouragement. This was more powerful than anything I had encountered in previous marathons, even including my recent Olympic experience.

Executing a clinical job, the pace-makers reached halfway in 1:03:28, and Catarino stepped off the course. Two miles later his compatriot followed suit. It was down to a race of eight, and everyone looked good. Nerurkar, feeling energized and positive, then committed what he now rues as a major blunder: he employed a new pace-maker. Himself. It wasn't for long that he used up this unnecessary nervous energy, but it was enough. Not only did Nerurkar cast a lonely vigil at the head of the field, he even turned up the heat, running 4:51 for mile 16, a 5-second acceleration on the mile before, and over a stretch of tarmac that was also uphill in parts. The pack happily accepted Nerurkar's pacing like thirsty bloodsuckers. He reflects: "This strategy was playing into the hands of my opponents, many of whom – like me – still felt full of running. By front-running I was simply acting as a pace-maker for the other runners, who were still keeping something in reserve for the latter stages. By contrast, I was using up unnecessary energy too early in the race."

After 10 minutes Nerurkar realized his folly and settled back in the pack. But the irretrievable damage to himself was done. At around the 20-mile mark, two noticeable developments occurred. The Italian Stefano Baldini, who had passed halfway in a more circumspect 1:04:15 (over 45 seconds slower than the pack), arrived to join the lead group, and then soon after, threw in a surge to test out his comrades. The response was mixed. "Thugwane and Kimaiyo went after him," writes Nerurkar, "Evans and I followed – though now we were both operating at close to our limit." Nerurkar doesn't mention Pinto, who noticeably dropped off the back and was seemingly out of contention at this stage. Baldini's surge had seemingly killed off one of the race's key danger men.

After Evans and Nerurkar had managed to claw back the deficit, the five leaders ran together between 32 and 35 kilometres. Cruelly, Baldini then surged again. Nerurkar writes:

This was a critical moment in the race. I knew that if I didn't keep up with the leaders now, my hopes of winning the race would be over. I dug deeper into my reserves and over the next kilometres clawed my way back to the leaders as we

Catch me if you can: a dumbfounded Stefano Baldini, right, can do nothing about the human train that hurtles past in the latter stages of the '97 London Marathon. *Mark Shearman*

approached the cobbled stretch through the Tower of London. By this stage I was doing all I could just to stay up with them. As they maintained their pace over the cobbles, I again fell off the lead.

Baldini's surging had now shaken off the two fancied British contenders, as well as Pinto. Nerurkar entered what he refers to as the marathon runner's equivalent of the "Death Zone". He became less aware of his competitors and of the thousands of spectators screaming with excitement. Raw determination propelled him to the finish line. "I survived those last few miles simply because I owed it to myself to survive them."

At the 25-mile mark, Pinto, from out of the blue, drew level with Nerurkar, and then passed him at terrific speed. Whatever problems the Portuguese had suffered half an hour earlier were over. All cylinders were not just on "go", but also on overdrive. Nerurkar helplessly watched him disappear off down the road. Soon Pinto was up with Thugwane and Kimaiyo, who offered scant resistance as he tore after Baldini, a few metres further down the road. David Powell of the *The Times* wrote: "Pinto took up the running without hesitation. Thugwane and Kimaiyo fell back. Coming into the Mall, it was like a re-run of the women's race: two athletes raising their pace together in sight of the finish." Drawing level with Baldini, a magnificent tustle developed as the athletes rounded in front of Buckingham Palace and hammered their way down The Mall. Baldini fought valiantly but it was Pinto, the former racing cyclist, with a 3:39 clocking for the 1500-metres, who just had the edge. Steve Jones' course record of 2:08:16 from 1985 was finally being surpassed – by 21 seconds. Baldini dashed over the line just two seconds later, and Thugwane showed what a fine competitor he was by securing third, nine seconds further down.

The combination of the best weather in the history of the London Marathon and the strong fields assembled by Dave Bedford had brought the records tumbling and pushed the time bonus payouts to an all-time high. "Dave promised me he would be under budget, but I cannot quite see it happening," Nick Bitel, the London Marathon chief executive, said. "The treasurer is looking very pale."

Afterwards, an amazed Pinto declared:

It was the most astonishing marathon I've ever run. I ran it differently to 1995 when I went very fast in the first half and suffered for it. I didn't have enough respect for my rivals on that occasion.

With a *'can-you-believe-it?'* look on his face': Antonio Pinto has run an astounding last couple of miles to steal the race away from his rivals. *Mark Shearman*

After 36 kilometres I was just thinking about finishing in the top three, but from 40 kilometres I began to think I could win. When Thugwane faded I was confident because I'm more experienced at the marathon than Baldini. I don't know where I got the energy to catch the leaders but the more the race went on, the more I thought I could win it.

Runner-up Baldini was delighted with his run, even though he had just fallen short: "I haven't got much experience at the distance. I was surprised when Pinto suddenly came through and the last 5 kilometres was hard, but I am very happy to have recorded such a fast time. I was expecting a sprint finish with Thugwane, then Pinto came from nowhere." It wasn't the last time that Baldini would finish second by just two ticks of the clock. He'd do so again six years later (see Chapter 5). But all such disappointment would be atoned for by his triumph at the 2004 Olympic marathon. Josiah Thugwane was satisfied he'd laid some doubters to rest: "I thought I had a chance of winning but Pinto was very strong when he caught me. Although I didn't win, I'm very pleased to have run so fast and proved a point to some people."

When Paul Evans crossed the line in eighth place he thought they'd got it wrong when the volunteers told him that Pinto had won: "He didn't pass me until nearly 24 miles. But then he just went *bang, bang, bang.* He's a pretty cool customer to leave it that late. I thought we would break up more than we did. Even at 21 miles there were about ten of us – it was a phenomenal race."

* * *

Pinto would return to London several more times and after 2001 had never finished outside the top three – in seven appearances. In 2000, he was on scintillating form as he smashed the European record with a 2:06:36, running one of the later miles in 4:34 – that's a 1:59:49 marathon pace. He also won the European 10,000-metres title in 1998, and set a short-lived world record for the half-marathon of 59:43, also in '98.

London Marathon race director Dave Bedford speaks fondly of a man who, for over a decade, greatly enriched the spectacle of the London Marathon: "In 1997 he came through, he pulled everyone up, he ran them down, went by them, and destroyed them. Until that stage it looked as though Thugwane was going to follow up on his Olympic success." Bedford also went on to pour scorn on those who cast doubt as to whether Pinto's amazing sequence has ever been aided by artificial stimulants:

The people who whisper about Pinto, must *de facto* whisper about Paula Radcliffe. Steve Jones ran 2.07.13 in 1985, right? So here we are, 15 years later and Pinto runs 40 seconds faster, and people immediately say: "he must be cheating". Then people are saying Takahashi's a cheat, Ndereba's a cheat; all of a sudden Paula runs 2:15 and she's not a cheat – it's illogical.

Pinto is a dream for any race director for the way he forces it all the time in his races, and he's a nice guy as well. He won three times and was top three another four. He'll come back to our 25th anniversary next year [2005] and we'll welcome him back as a great champion.

A somewhat porky Pinto competed at the 2004 London Marathon, hoping to secure a qualifying time for a fourth consecutive Olympic Games. His previous three had been an underachieving DNF (Barcelona), 14th (Atlanta) and 11th (Sydney).

Cornering Pinto in the hotel lobby I told him about this book and his inclusion in it. He beamed and nodded. I told him we had met before – indeed competed against each other in Lisbon at the catchily titled European Club Champions Half Marathon Championships.[3] Pinto beamed some more. I asked him a couple of questions about the 1997 London; and he beamed yet more. He hadn't actually spoken yet. Finally after I had babbled away to him for a few minutes he rested his hand on my arm and said:

"I speak only *tiny* Ingleesh."

Fortunately he had his translator with him.

"With three miles to go, had you all but given up winning the '97 London?" I asked.

"Oh, that race was totally lost," Pinto replied. "I had given up all hope. But then I suddenly became very embarrassed. The organizers had paid me a lot to be here, and I was not running with the leaders. What would happen to my cheque? Would I be paid? I thought I would have to give the money back! I thought I would never get invited back here again."

"So what did you do?"

"I decided to try my best to finish in the top four or five. To make it look respectable. To avoid disgrace. Then I found myself coming into the top three and I thought hold it there and you have done OK! Then I am second and I realize I have a chance to win. Amazing!"

"So the organizers paid you after all..."

"Oh yes, a great amount, it was the course record after all!"

"Still on a bottle of wine a day?"[4]

"Of course!" he said, licking his lips.

---

3. An alarmingly overweight Pinto defeated the author that day by just 3:01 (which had more to do with his wild fluctuations in form than any genius on my part).

4. Pinto lives on a vineyard, and when his training is going through an easy spell, he has claimed to drink a bottle of wine a day.

Wine or no wine, Pinto failed to finish the London '04 race, in which he sought to qualify for the Athens Olympics. It seemed that a long and terrific career at the top was finally at an end.

Race result:

Antonio Pinto	POR	2:07:55
Stefano Baldini	ITA	2:07:57
Josiah Thugwane	RSA	2:08:06
Eric Kimaiyo	KEN	2:08:08
Richard Nerurkar	GBR	2:08:36
Steve Moneghetti	AUS	2:08:45
Lawrence Peu	RSA	2:09:10
Paul Evans	GBR	2:09:18
José Garcia	ESP	2:09:30
Stephane Franke	GER	2:11:26

Note: Eamonn Martin the British winner from 1993, was 13th in 2:12:29.

Sources:

Conversations with Antonio Pinto.
Conversations with David Bedford.
Athletics Weekly, preview and race report, April 9th & 16th, 1997.
Macleod, Iain, in the *Daily Telegraph*, April 12th, 1997.
Mott, Sue, in the *Daily Telegraph*, April 11th, 1997.
Nerurkar, Richard, *Marathon Running*. A & C Black, 2000.
Powell, David, in *The Times*, April 14th, 1997.
Will-Weber, Mark, ed. *The Quotable Runner*. Breakaway Books, 1996.

XXI

No. 30 – 1981 Boston Marathon [Women]

Monday, April 20th

MicMac Patti Whacked, Give the Roe a Throne.

The 1981 BAA Boston Marathon proved to be a moving and memorable race in which a battle royal was fought between the "beauty" and the "beast". The term "beast" is used in the loosest sense of the word because American Patti Catalano (née Lyons), to whom the word refers, was a woman of striking looks thanks to a mother who had been a Micmac Native American. But Patti was a strong-willed girl, immensely determined, driven, hot-tempered, and erratic of mood, of diet, of tactics. She broke American records for every distance from five miles to the marathon. She was the first American woman to break 2:30 in the marathon. And all this from someone who never came across a doughnut she didn't like. At one stage, before she turned her considerable wrath on the world to running, she packed 152 pounds onto her 5 foot 2 inch frame. But then, in order to lose weight, she started running 140 miles a week. So, yes, a beast of sorts.

Catalano's dream was to follow in the footsteps of two other native Americans who had won the Boston Marathon: Tom Longboat in 1907 and the great Ellison "Tarzan" Brown who won in 1936 and 1939. Could Catalano continue the tradition after a 42-year hiatus? Native Americans weren't just well known for winning Boston, however, but also for heartbreaking second-place finishes, like the Mohawk Bill Davis, in 1901, or hapless Andrew Sockalexis who returned two excruciating runner-up spots in 1912 and 1913. Which category would Catalano fall into? The ecstatic winner or the sorry second? The two previous Bostons had seen a tearful Catalano finish second both times – in races she was heavily backed to win. A painful bursitis in her foot had been her undoing in 1979, and her adventures in 1980 may be viewed in Chapter 27. But in 1981 she was fitter than ever. No way was she going to finish second again.[1]

A few years earlier, working as a nurse at New Hampshire's Quincy Hospital, Lyons was stuck living at home and caring for her eight younger siblings. Happiness eluded her. She hated college, she hated work and was in constant conflict with her mother. Patti was the biggest in the fatherless house, and her sisters

---

1. With a quarter mile of the 1975 Boston to go, a debilitated Tom Fleming realized he was about to finish second for the third year running. So abhorrent was the notion that he waved Steve Hoag on through and took third.

Patti Catalano: intense, passionate and vulnerable.
Boston Athletic Association

looked to her for guidance – not their mother. Until her mother threw her out. Patti moved to Cape Cod, got a job as a nurse's aide, then quit and moved back to Quincy. Author Tom Derderian writes in *Boston Marathon*: "She ate donuts by the dozen, smoked Parliament by the box, and drank beer by the six-pack. She was in and out of school and work, fat, poor, and unhappy, so she decided she had to do something about her life. She decided to take some time out for herself – to, as she called it, be nice to Patti."

* * *

The word "beauty" is used in the strictest sense of the word: one Boston writer once referred to New Zealander Allison Roe as the "Renaissance woman of running", and she quickly charmed all who saw her with her lithe frame, smooth stride and porcelain features.

The *New Zealand Herald* gave a little background on Roe over Boston Marathon weekend. Although she had never run more than 18 miles, Roe (née Deed) entered into the Choysa Marathon in Auckland in February 1980 and told her parents, Dr Alan and Mrs Deed: "Don't bother to come and watch – I'll probably 'bomb out' at about halfway." Her parents stayed away, but Roe surprised herself by becoming the first New Zealand woman to finish. The winner was Joan Benoit, who popped a 2:31 to Roe's 2:51. There was something for her to aspire to.

Roe found the joy of running in company with her father at Takapuna Beach, and while still a secondary schoolgirl she won the New Zealand women's cross-country title. She did not lack able teachers like the great British runner Gordon "Puff-Puff" Pirie and Max Golder. The *New Zealand Herald* went on to report: "Yet amid a career of records, New Zealand representation and titles galore, there have been times of stress. She won her first national title after a bout of glandular fever. And there was a setback from a hairline fracture to her hip and the struggle to overcome a nagging foot injury."

However, just seven months after her marathon debut, Roe ran a 2:34 at the Oregon Marathon, and when she returned to Auckland the following year she scored a 2:36. Roe stood 5 foot 8 inches tall and weighed a healthy 129 pounds. And she certainly loved the world of sport: you name it, there was a fair chance she'd had a go: the high jump, tennis, swimming, waterskiing had all been skilfully attempted. Roe's one possible Achilles heel was that she descended from a wealthy family. What's wrong with that, one might ask. Only that a theory often found in distance running circles is that the privileged will never have sufficient fire in their bellies to truly make it as distance runners. It remained to be seen how much fire Roe possessed.

The above duel, however, wasn't supposed to happen at all. Because there was a third party who was supposed to win the 1981 Boston with ease, so exceptional was her level of fitness. And her name was Joan Benoit. Tom Derderian writes of how in the run-up to the 1981 Boston Marathon he was in 31-minute shape for 10K. That was superior to what any woman in the world could manage, and yet his friend "Joanie" was leaving him for dead in workouts. There was, therefore, in Derderian's mind no one who could touch Benoit.

Benoit, who would go on to capture the inaugural Olympic crown in 1984, was rapidly becoming the most feared female marathoner in the world. She had sprung into the public eye with her Boston debut of 1979, and she was now a far superior athlete. But had Benoit reckoned on Catalano? The only woman to beat Catalano in her last 33 races had been Grete Waitz, and Waitz was not in Boston.

* * *

Julie Shea took the early lead in the 1981 Boston Marathon. An excellent collegiate track runner, this was her first serious marathon after a cursory attempt at Bermuda in 1979 where she frolicked in the 2:50s. No one could boast such an immaculate pedigree: she was the current women's collegiate champion at 3K, 5K, 10K and cross-country. She had gangly style, or as Derderian once colourfully wrote; "she ran splay-legged, like a colt saddled too soon." Shea didn't like that one bit and forcefully told Derderian so out running one day. However unconventional someone's running style is, they almost always dislike having it pointed out.

Julie Shea's questionable style and unquestionable class carried her to the hills and the final third of the marathon in first place. And then it was time for the college star to take a bow and make way for the stars. Feeling feisty, with a real sense of destiny, Patti Catalano burst into the lead. Tom Derderian, who ran in the race alongside the leading female athletes, recalls the atmosphere and the leader's impeccable technique: "Catalano had perfect running style. Her straight blue-black hair blew straight out behind her. She ran concentrated and relaxed. Catalano seemed to have a million fans. At times she acknowledged friends, but mostly she concentrated on her race. The pace seemed easy for her, but I expected Benoit to soon come up and make a race of it, eventually leaving Catalano to finish second again."

And then a plot development. While the college star, Shea, had refused to alter her rock-steady pace up the challenging hills, Catalano starting tossing in a series of crazy surges. She had held her emotions in check for 20 miles but here she was becoming intoxicated by her own exuberance. Alarm bells started among her support team – particularly her long-suffering coach and husband Joe Catalano. Patti, however, still managed to crest the hills looking peaceful and at ease; if she had trashed herself over the past couple of miles, she wasn't showing it yet – and now it was all downhill to the finish. Where was Benoit? She'd better get her skates on (so to speak).[2]

---

2. During these years in the late '70s and early '80s when roller-skating was such a popular sport, a group of skaters would start the race just ahead of the pack and have their own little Boston "Roller Marathon". There was one rule: don't get caught by the runners! Or else the race marshals were liable to grab the skater by the scruff off the neck and toss him/her into the gutter.

As the leader started making inroads into the final 6 miles, the crowds became ever more dense, their screams ever more deafening. They encroached ever further onto the road, ever closer to the runners. Just as Derderian expected, he soon heard a second set of roars for another female runner coming closer and closer up behind. He writes: "Just as I expected – here comes Joan, or maybe Julie. But I turned to see a tall, blond woman runner, wearing black, approaching us, a woman a head taller than Joan." New Zealand had come to play, having already played a lethally cunning waiting game. Top on Roe's list of priorities had been to settle in behind Benoit, and do whatever she did. However, at around 10 miles she realized that Benoit was not running quickly enough and that it was actually Catalano who needed chasing. Roe had stalked Catalano for a distance of over 10 miles until, "on Roe's way down the hills, she watched Catalano and realized that she coud 'have her' right there..." (Derderian).

Roe started whittling away the distance. This was the first time the Boston crowds had a *real* women's contest to enjoy at the Boston Marathon, and they screamed hysterically "in a rapture of sisterhood". Bill Squires eloquently wrote later: "Roe bears down at 20 miles...She floats extravagantly high over the road, her track muscles taking the pace in stride. Catalano clings low to the tarmac, knowing only the roads, only that this is HER Boston Marathon, seething with dark passion. Her eyes, normally coals, compress into black diamonds of rage and pain." A mounted policeman, trying to control the fans, suddenly lost control of his horse. The beast sidestepped straight in front of Catalano, who in turn ran straight into the horse's buttocks. As she was falling, another male runner instinctively caught her, and the leader escaped injury. But Catalano was now starting to lose her nerve and confidence – the collision had unsettled her.

Finally, during the 24th mile Roe pulled even, as hesitation interfered with Catalano's stride. Derderian recalls: "Neither spoke to each other. The skin on Catalano's face tightened over her high cheekbones. She looked gaunt, hollow. She seemed to be digging down as deep as she could go. Roe's face, by contrast looked peaceful, in control. She looked like an actress coming onstage to take the leading role." Roe decided to surge, not by very much, but the move still served as a deal-clincher. The look of frozen blankness on Catalano's face said it all. There was no coming back from this – she was about to finish second for the third year in a row. Roe allowed herself the smallest of grins, and a quarter of an hour later broke the course record by a cool 7:42. Catalano never gave up and came home 65 seconds later, in an excellent time. As for Benoit, she placed a damp squib and troubled third. She later told Derderian: "I really can't explain my disappointing finish at Boston. I had hopes of winning for a second time, but they were quickly dampened when I found myself as far back as eleventh in the first half of the race...I didn't expect so many other runners to show me their backsides in the early stages...my biggest asset, my fluid stride, abandoned me." Tom Derderian, her training partner, called her a "head case" after the race, and predicted that she'd never truly make the grade. Famous last words.

A photograph of Catalano weeping uncontrollably after the race, with her two sobbing, lookalike sisters, overlooked by a bemused husband and coach, Joe Catalano, is one of the Boston Marathon's most powerful images. "I don't know what to do with you, Patti," Joe said. "You ran an American record. I just don't

An ecstatic Allison Roe wins the 1981 Boston Marathon. Number 305 is Tom Derderian author of *Boston Marathon* to which this chapter – and book – owe much. *Jeff Johnson*

know what to do. Please stop crying." Catalano's view of the race was stark and simple: "When Roe passed me she kept hammering, hammering, hammering. She ran exactly the way I wanted to...only she ran faster."

As for Roe, she stated:

"I don't even really believe this is happening. I liked the course very, very much. I liked the undulating nature of it. I much prefer it to a flat course. I gauged myself by looking at Joan Benoit and Jackie Gareau. It's very easy on a course like this to run fast on the downhills, and I had to really try and control it because I'm inclined to run away too quickly. I can't believe I ran that fast."

Both the Boston and New Zealand newspapers were ecstatic at this hot, new find in women's marathoning. The *New Zealand Herald* remarked:

"It was a remarkable performance for a runner, who was only competing in her fifth marathon in just over a year. Roe had no fear of Boston's hills, for on many a Sunday morning trains over the famous Waiatarua Ranges course in

185

Allison Roe beams with delight on the podium.
Boston Athletic Association

Auckland. Many famous athletics figures – Snell, Halberg, Baillie, Magee, Ryan and Quax – are familiar with the testing 22 mile stretch. One more name can be added to that eminent list – Allison Roe."

"Boston got its first pleasant look at Allison Roe yesterday," reported Steve Marantz in the *Boston Globe*. "The marathon field got a look at her back, and the tall, blonde whippet from New Zealand glimpsed into a dazzling racing future. Roe's time was the second fastest in history."

The *Boston Herald* splashed their Monday morning front page with a none too subtle headline "The race was a beauty", as they displayed a large photo of Roe on the winner's rostrum, caught in a pose that accentuated her curves. George Kimball of the *Herald* noted why he had picked Roe to win in his preview column: "because she's been training over the hills with Kevin Ryan. Nobody else could do that unless they were really serious about winning the race." "Why didn't anybody else pick her, then?" wondered his sport's editor. "Because nobody else had seen her," leered Kimball. "Allison Roe," he added, "happens to be about a 9.5."

* * *

What happened to Roe after Boston? The truth is, not a lot in top-level marathons, save for one more masterful run, this time at New York six months later. Grete Waitz had to withdraw from the race with shin splints and Roe lowered her best to 2:25:28 – and with it the world best which had belonged to Waitz of 2:25:41. Roe beat the second-placed athlete that day by nearly 5 minutes, one Ingrid Christensen, soon to become better known as Kristiansen. Unfortunately in December 1984, Roe's New York course was found to be short (by 148 metres) so her time in the record books was erased. Still, for one and a half years Roe was seen as world-record holder, before Joan Benoit's mighty run at Boston in '83.[3]

However, all Roe's brilliant tactics and pace judgement in her great year of 1981 seemed to desert her thereafter and she often fell victim to her own excitement. Her friend Lorraine Moller – a superb tactician, who placed fifth in the 1984 Olympic marathon and third at the Barcelona Games of 1992 (aged 37) – almost managed to curb Roe's enthusiasm back in 1980 at the Oregon Marathon: "I

---

3. A remarkable coincidence occurred the day before Benoit's race though: in London Grete Waitz shot for Roe's world record of 2:25:28.7 and ran 2:25:28.7! So for a 24-hour period the pair shared the record to within a tenth of a second. Well...every step counts in a marathon.

know how to pace, you don't; if you pass me I'll hit you." Roe listened, obeyed, and both ran excellent times. But she couldn't adopt the discipline full-time. This weakness, along with a brittle body and a temperament shy on steel, all hindered her progress.

At the 1983 Boston, Roe became so dismayed on the hills when the leader Joan Benoit was nowhere in sight that she quit the race, got "picked-up" by another quitting (and opportunist) runner, and went to a house party along the course instead. As one does. In 1984, with her friend Moller's advice on the morning of the race ringing in her ears, she still insisted on going out far too fast, then faded and faded some more. Moller passed her in the 20th mile and went on to win by over four minutes. Roe dropped out with just two miles to go. That seems to say it all. If you don't have tactical nous, at least have *stickability*. Still, the 1981 Boston Marathon will live long in the memory. Allison Roe was an unforgettable runner.

Race result:

Allison Roe	New Zealand	2:26:46
Patti Catalano	Boston, MA	2:27:51 (American record)
Joan Benoit	Exeter, NH	2:30:16
Julie Shea	Raleigh, NC	2:30:54
Jacqueline Gareau	Canada	2:31:26
Sissel Grottenberg	Norway	2:33:02

Sources:

Anonymous, in the *New Zealand Herald*, April 20th & 21st, 1981.
Derderian, Tom, *Boston Marathon*. Human Kinetics, 1996.
Harris, Steve, in the *Boston Herald American*, April 21st, 1981.
Hauman, Riël, *Century of the Marathon*. Human & Rousseau, 1996.
Kimball, George, in the *Boston Globe*, April 21st, 1981.
Marantz, Steve, in the *Boston Globe*, April 21st, 1981.
Semple, Jock, John J. Kelley and Tom Murphy, *Just Call Me Jock*. Waterford
    Publishing Company, 1981.

XXII

No. 29 – 1988 Olympic Marathon [Women]

Friday, September 23rd

Down Under's finest tries to turn world order upside down.

At the outset of the women's Seoul Olympic marathon of 1988, there appeared to be one overwhelming favourite, Portugal's Rosa Mota, who was not only winning every major marathon that she started but destroying her opponents by huge margins. At just 5 feet 1¾ inches and a mere 97 pounds (45 kg), Mota was winning marathons with nearly a *mile* to spare. In the 1983 inaugural World Championships Mota had finished a disappointed fourth while Grete Waitz won in serene fashion. But four years on, Waitz was injured and Mota went on to win by a jaw-dropping 7:21. Exhibiting the strong camaraderie and friendship that exists between top marathoners, Mota said after the race: "I want to dedicate this race to Grete. Even though I don't know her too well, the comradeship that exists among marathoners has brought us close together" (Hauman).

Mota was born in Foz do Douro on June 29th, 1958. Although competition for girls was sparse in Portugal as Rosa was growing up, she excelled at whatever she did and came to love the thrill of winning races. Along with her sister, Paula, Rosa would jog through the streets of her hometown. But their activities would be met with derision by the locals of the city of Porto: "Women at that time were not going out," recalls Paula. "They stayed at home. When we ran through the streets, they would say, 'Go home! Go home and help your mother wash the dishes.' Things like that" (Sandrock).

After 1975 Mota competed in races sponsored by the Portuguese Track Federation and typically ran 800 and 1500-metre races. By 1978 she was able to handle the endurance required to run 3000 metres. Both in winning and losing, Mota was enjoying her sport. Mota's inspiration and coach in her championship years was José Pedrosa, a medical doctor, who hit it off with Mota right from the time they met. Mota was having difficulties with her running at the time (1980), constantly feeling heavy-legged in races. Doctors lazily diagnosed Mota's problem as all being in her head, but Pedrosa took a more scientific view and eventually concluded that Rosa suffered from exercise-induced asthma. After an arduous road to recovery, Mota finally began to pick up her training workload again. Pedrosa says: "It took so long for Rosa to get to that bad spot, and so long for her to recover from it. The first part of the recovery was psychological, helping

189

her believe that it was possible to recover. What I noticed about Rosa is that definitely, she enjoys running very much." By the end of 1981 Mota was winning road races again, and in the spring of 1982 the Portuguese authorities selected her to run in that summer's European Championships. The 3000-metres is what we'd like you to do, they said. Mota replied that she'd prefer to try the marathon. After an impasse, it was agreed that Mota *could* do the marathon, providing she do the 3000-metres first. And so began one of the greatest, most successful marathon careers of all time.

Her heart not in the 3000-metres, Mota padded around the $7\frac{1}{2}$ tracks near the back of the field. With this meaningless training run out the way, and her blinkered, stubborn superiors pacified, Mota could now dedicate herself to her mission for the Games: to run and finish a championship marathon. The 1982 European Championships at Athens was the first major meet where women were allowed to compete in the marathon. The following year they'd also be allowed to compete in the marathon at the inaugural World Championships, and then of course – most famously of all – at the Olympic Games in Los Angeles. But it all started here, and Mota was delighted to be a part of it. Until she viewed the course that is. "Forget it, Zé, [Pedrosa's nickname]," Mota whimpered. "It's too far and too hilly." But then, just as she was about to back out, she rationalized, "The important thing for me is to finish. That's all. If I don't save myself as much as possible, I might get into big trouble and die like Lazaro[1] or Pheidippides."

Holding back in the early part of the race served Mota well. Temperatures were close to 90 degrees and humidity over 90 per cent. After halfway she started picking her way through runners and by 30 kilometres found herself running with the white-hot favourite Ingrid Kristiansen and Italian Laura Fogli. "I was running, but not to win," Mota recalls. "Then at 30 kilometres I said, 'Let's try to go,' and it felt easy." Five kilometres later, Mota had pulled ahead of her two rivals and then gone past the brave but wiltering leader [Carla Beurskens of Holland], so it was now a three-way duel. Amazingly, Mota won. Wanting to avoid the dangerous Kristiansen kick, she forced the pace in the few miles before the stadium, and neither the Norwegian nor the Italian could respond. "When I crossed the finish line, I smiled, and I could see José taking pictures and crying," Mota said. Author Michael Sandrock writes: "He had good reason to cry. Mota's victory over the extremely challenging course was vindication for Pedrosa, who had gone out on a limb with the Portuguese Federation by advising Mota to run the marathon." Suddenly Mota's life had changed: back home she became a national hero. "It was a win for all Portuguese, something that made the fishermen, the farmers, and the grape pickers proud. The phone never stopped ringing at Mota's home, and she was fêted and honored with champagne and parties."

It was just the encouragement Mota needed to boost her training and believe

---

1. The hapless Francisco Lazaro (born January 8th, 1891) was a Portuguese marathon runner who competed at the 1912 Stockholm Olympics. Hard-working and ahead of his time in his dedication to succeed, poor Lazaro was way behind his time in his grasp of science. He felt that sweating in races was a bad thing as one lost too much fluid. So, under Sweden's stifling skies, he coated himself in a thick cream waterproofing material, and consequently died after the race from overheating. To this day, someone down on their luck in Portugal is said to be "just like Lazaro".

that she could indeed compete with the very best in the world. For the next four years Mota proved that she was here to stay as a marathoner of the highest calibre. She triumphed in Rotterdam in a solid 2:32 seven months later, won back-to-back Chicagos in '83 and '84, placed fourth in the inaugural World Championships of 1983, just 41 seconds off the silver, and also returned an impressive bronze medal at the 1984 Los Angeles Olympics, once again getting the better of Kristiansen.

After a quiet 1985, Mota returned to the European Championships seeking to defend her crown. There would be no stunning the world this time. With Kristiansen out of the running (four days later she'd win the first major championship women's 10,000-metres ever contested), Mota arrived in Stuttgart as hot favourite, although she was expected to receive stiff competition from the redoubtable Katrin Dörre who had won her last ten marathons on the spin. Dörre had, however, dropped out of the last European Championship marathon, and would do so again here. Mota's nearest challenger was once again Laura Fogli. But times had changed. This time, instead of being right on her Portuguese heels for most of the race, Fogli finished over four minutes adrift.

This win launched Mota on a quite magnificent spree of victories, leading right up to this chapter's featured race. After Stuttgart, Rosa won by $4\frac{1}{2}$ minute margins in both Tokyo and Boston. Tom Derderian writes in *Boston Marathon*: "She ran; she smiled; she blew kisses. The people smiled back. Americans of Portuguese descent waved red-and-green Portuguese flags. Rosa Mota liked that. Even her ever-distant competitors liked her. None of them could say anything bad about her."

Were her victories conclusive enough? Not in Mota's book. At the Rome World Championships of 1987 Rosa took her incredible superiority to new heights. With Waitz out through injury and Kristiansen concentrating on the 10,000-metres (successfully too), Mota could have been forgiven for taking the race steadily, knowing that just a sound and circumspect piece of running should be enough. But that wasn't her style. By the time the 41 starters had even exited the stadium, Mota had *already* asserted a notable lead. In severe heat Mota still blasted to a time of 2:25:17, which was the second fastest ever for a women-only race (Hauman). Silver medallist Soviet Zoya Ivanova clocked 2:32:38.

Amazingly, despite all her stunning successes, Mota and Pedrosa were constantly at loggerheads with the Portuguese federation, which disliked the way Mota trained in the clear air of Colorado rather than the polluted, traffic-choked streets of Lisbon. This was where the powerful Portuguese federation operated from, and they didn't like that Mota lived in Porto, and spent so much time training in Boulder. Mota refused to join one of the three power clubs in Lisbon, and would never ditch her coach, who the federation felt so threatened by. Pedrosa explains: "They didn't like me...They said Rosa's only problem was José. The federation wanted her to move to Lisbon. They didn't like her to live in Porto or in Boulder. They didn't like me to coach her. I had friends who were important people, but the guys in the federation and Olympic Committee were too old, and they didn't understand world-class athletes. For them, the most important thing was to have their pictures taken at the airport."

But the pair were stronger than anything the federation could throw at them,

THE 50 GREATEST MARATHON RACES OF ALL TIME

and returned to Boston in 1988, for Mota to win by almost 5 minutes. Runner and playwright Israel Horovitz wrote about the 1988 Boston Marathon for *New England Runner* magazine: "But Mota's lonely run in Boston gets the imagination wandering across the waters to Seoul, South Korea. What a good shot she will have, really! Ingrid, like Grete, may well be a bit beyond it, now. So, it is entirely possible that in South Korea, Rosa Mota will be the one to beat."

* * *

Mota averaged 110 miles per week for the entire year before the Seoul Olympics of 1988 and came to South Korea looking to win the unprecedented triple crown of the European, World and Olympic marathon golds. The field was to be extremely deep, with nearly a score of contenders boasting personal best times of sub-2:30. Ingrid Kristiansen was a high-profile absentee, as she decided to once again concentrate on the 10,000-metres. But the great Grete Waitz of Norway would start, and having clocked an impressive 68:49 in Newcastle's Great North Run two months earlier, she had shown that her dazzling career still had some way to go. Anthroscopic knee surgery since the Great North had raised questions as to her basic fitness, however.

The most controversial *non*-selection of the Games involved the inspirational figure of Priscilla Welch of Great Britain, who had a proven championship pedigree (sixth at Los Angeles '84). Welch had also won the 1987 New York Marathon in what was described as one of the most remarkable performances in running, as she triumphed aged 42. The previous year in London, Welch had run a magnificent 2:26:51 to smash the 'Masters' world record. But despite proving her fitness with a fourth-place run at Boston (2:30) in 1988, the British selectors punished Welch for shunning the London race and kept one place open for Veronique Marot instead, pending a good performance. Welch's coach and husband, Dave, furiously told the selectors that Cilla would not be available.[2]

Marot never did prove her fitness, and Britain sent a worthy, but hardly world-beating team. *Athletics Weekly* reported:

Sadly Britain is in a shambles. And the way things have been going Joyce Smith [aged 50] might have expected a call! If selectoral confusion did not rule them out, injuries and four-year-old kids certainly did. After a well-documented saga, we are lucky to have Susan Tooby who will not let Britain down but has only a remote chance of a medal. Late additions, Angela Pain and Sue Crehan do not. But what do you expect from sixth and seventh choice runners?

"Australia's Lisa Martin could be a serious contender," continued *Athletics Weekly*, "although there is a question mark about her in the major championships after 'bombing' in Rome." What *Athletics Weekly* fails to mention though is Martin's excellent win in the 1986 Commonwealth Games, where she won by over two minutes over Lorraine Moller in 2:26:07. Earlier on in 1988 she had scored a

---

2. Priscilla Welch commented on her age by saying: "I think old age is a social disease that people think they cannot overcome." She started running when she was 34, and had been smoking a pack of cigarettes a day. "For those who really want to go for it, I hope this [her NYC win] will be an inspiration."

women-only course-best performance of 2:23:51 in Osaka. Mota would indeed have to tread carefully.

Another key contender to Mota's bid came from East Germany's Katrin Dörre. Dörre had the remarkable record of starting seven marathons in Japan and winning six. She showed how dangerous she was by setting a national record of 2:25:24, in winning Tokyo in November 1987. She also went on to win the European Cup Marathon on April 30th, 1988, in Huy, Belgium in 2:28:28. Four American women broke 2:30 in the run-up to the Games, but unfortunately the 1984 Olympic champion, Joan Benoit, was not one of them. An injury earlier in the year meant that she was unable to defend her title in Seoul.

* * *

Beginning at 9:30 a.m., the 1988 women's Olympic marathon saw the athletes trying to secure the first track and field medals of the Games. The humidity was a high 92 per cent and the temperature a warm but manageable 67 °F. The field comprised 69 athletes from 39 nations.[3] Martin and Gynn remark: "It was anyone's guess regarding the outcome."

A magnificent field deep in concentration: Wanda Panfil, Grete Waitz (438), Rosa Mota (460), Lisa Martin (17) and Katrin Dorre (260) all fancy their chances at Seoul '88. *Mark Shearman*

---

3. Los Angeles four years earlier boasted 50 competitors.

Mota explains in Michael Sandrock's *Running with the Legends* what it is that occupies her mind during a championship race: "First off, I think about myself, and the pace I'm running. I don't want to run too fast during the first part and then [drawing a finger across her throat] hit the wall. And I try to look at the runners, to see what they are doing. This one might be running too fast, and not be good enough to keep up at that pace. And I try to enjoy it, and wait for the finish." A large pack of runners clocked metronomic splits for the first 15 kilometres of 17:10, 17:03 and 17:17. The race's "big-four" of Mota, Waitz, Martin and Dörre were amongst the leaders, although, unlike the previous year, Mota was yet to show signs of wanting to be alone, content here to bide her time.

A pack of 13 passed halfway in a respectable 1:12:45. Waitz was grimly hanging on, but the recent surgery had indeed taken the edge off her fitness, and slowly but surely her dream of securing an Olympic gold medal disappeared. The brave Norwegian, nicknamed "Northern Lightning" who had been winning marathons for two months shy of ten years, faded off the back of the pack, and then dejectedly stepped off the course.[4]

By 25 kilometres the pack had dwindled as one by one the contenders had gone the way of Waitz. The temperatures rose, and Mota, an exceptional warm-weather runner, still appeared the favourite. But her dominance from the World Championships was missing. She struggled to shake off her challengers. By 30 kilometres three runners still doggedly hung to Mota. Martin and Dörre being the two in particular that Mota would have most wished away. There was also a relatively unknown Soviet named Tatyana Polovinskaya, who had impressively won the Soviet championships in 2:28:02. Eventually, going up an incline before 35 kilometres, Polovinskaya was forced to let go of her brave challenge for a medal.

Mota recalls: "We were only four: me, Lisa [Martin], Katrin [Dörre], and the girl from Russia [Polovinskaya]. And then Tatyana stayed behind after 30K, and we three stayed together. And I said to myself, 'Well, I'm going to get a medal. I don't know what kind, but one medal is for sure' "(Sandrock). "At that stage," wrote *Athletics Weekly*, "Mota began to look a little frayed. Wherever Mota went, Martin followed in her shadow. It looked as if Mota, who normally runs away from her rivals, may succumb to the pressure."

As all great coaches do, José Pedrosa had thought long and hard about how he could have maximum impact on the race from the sidelines. He analysed whereabouts on the course that his presence would help Rosa the most. He settled on 38 kilometres. If Rosa was still in a group at that point of the race Pedrosa would be sure to let her have a piece of his mind. He hoped she wouldn't need guidance by the time 38 kilometres came along. He hoped it would be all sewn up. That was her way: to crush her opponents way before the finish. But this time it was not to be.

Pedrosa saw Mota hove into view at 38 kilometres with Dörre and Martin for company. "Now Rosa!" he screamed. "Go now!" But would she be able to? The

---

4. But it was by no means the end for Waitz. Six weeks later she would win her ninth New York crown, by the comfortable margin of nearly 3½ minutes, in 2:28:07.

A delighted Rosa Mota crosses the line just 80 yards up on Australia's Lisa Martin. *Mark Shearman*

pressure of the occasion and her opponents' terrific fitness had for once made Mota uncertain. She had been unsure of quite how to play it. Pedrosa's shout gave her the information she needed. Mota said to herself, "Let's go," and she did.

Mota ran those final 2½ miles to the stadium in a cold fear that someone would come back to her. If ever she looked back, a figure clad in green and yellow could be spied chasing her down. She was never certain of victory until the moment she crossed the line, whereupon she beamed and waved to the crowd. Lisa Martin finished just 13 seconds adrift, with Dörre another 28 seconds further back. Mota reflected:

Anything can happen in the marathon. We were so close until 38K. When I finished, it was almost a dream, because I had wanted to win three titles in a row: European, World and the Olympics. I'll always remember the race; I always remember the stadium, going into the tunnel, then showing up in front of all those people. And you think...All the people in my country, they are watching and they are happy. And I think people I know in other countries are happy also. I think all my friends live my races.

Martin had shown that her flunking at the World Championships the year before was just an aberration, and that she was a true championship contender: adding an Olympic silver to her Commonwealth gold. After marrying Kenyan distance runner Yobes Ondieki in February 1990, Martin went on to defend her Commonwealth title in an excellent 2:25:28. Thereafter her career, interrupted by having a daughter, spluttered somewhat. There were two good races at New York – third in 1991 and first in 1992 (2:24:40) – but she failed to finish at either the 1992 or 1996 Olympics, the latter due to an Achilles tendon, whereupon she retired from top-level racing.

As the packed stadium witnessed the first track and field medals of the Games, the joyous nation of Portugal saw their first female athlete win an Olympic track and field medal of any colour. Katrin Dörre paid tribute to Mota, saying later: "Rosa is easily the cleverest and most popular runner of the moment. She has not been beaten recently, but that doesn't mean she can't be." Dörre, like Lisa Martin, still had many years of racing ahead of her. Martin and Gynn write:

Starting in 1982, Dörre has amassed a record of unsurpassed excellence in the women's marathon. In the Olympic Games, she was third at Seoul, and she then went on to place fifth at Barcelona in 1992, and fourth at Atlanta in 1996. In the IAAF Marathon World Cup, she was the inaugural winner in 1985, third at Seoul in 1987 and fourth in London in 1989. In the World Championships, she placed third at Tokyo in 1991 and sixth at Stuttgart in 1993. As of late 1999, out of 43 marathons, she has finished 41 and won 24.

The first Briton home was Leeds City's Angie Pain who had only been drafted into the team a few weeks before Seoul. Her finishing time 2:30:50 sliced nearly four minutes off her best and underlined her ability in major championships: she was 11th at the World Championships, and 6th in the Commonwealth Games. An ecstatic Pain said: "I am so pleased and without a doubt that is the highlight of my whole life. I just felt so good all the way round. I was aiming for around 2.30 but I thought that was optimistic. I have never felt so good before and I was thinking 'I'm going to have a flyer', and had to stop myself getting too excited and try and keep the lid on."

* * *

In an interview the author carried out with Hugh Jones, one of the top British marathoners of the day, Jones eulogized about what a brilliant runner Mota was, noting:

> What was so fantastic about Rosa was that she could win a marathon in three different ways. In Rome in 1987, wisdom said not to go out hard early; that the heat would get you. By employing these tactics, she was laying herself open to the only way she could lose. Yet she just ran serenely and won by a massive seven minutes.
>
> At the Olympics she had the very real threat of Lisa Martin stalking her, but refused to let her close her down; and then at the 1990 Europeans it was a gripping head-to-head. She could win from the front, being chased, or doing the chasing.

This latter example at Stuttgart in 1990, was a notable feat in many ways, as Mota's usual ally, the heat, worked against her and she started to weaken having built up a considerable lead. Yegorova drew level with her at 35K, and it seemed as though winning the Europeans for a stunning third time in a row was not to be. But, as Riël Hauman writes: "The two exchanged a few words and then Mota pulled away. It was not easy, though, and over the last 500-metres in the stadium she continued to glance over her shoulder to check the distance between her and the Soviet. She won her third gold medal by a tiny margin – 5 seconds."

This third Euro triumph in a row, cemented Mota's iconic status in Portugal. Dr. Robert Rinaldi, who hosted Mota when she first came to train in the United States, recalls how much loved she was by her people: "Once we stopped in a poor section of town, a ghetto. There was a little boy there, who took Rosa by the hand and led her to his house. It was a shack, literally made out of cardboard. And on the door of the shack were two pictures: one of Queen Elizabeth, the other of Rosa."

In May 1991, Mota had an operation to remove an ovarian cyst the size of a grapefruit, and she sadly wasn't fit enough to defend her world title, recording a DNF in Tokyo. It made Mota all the more determined to be fit for Olympic year in 1992, but she picked up a hip injury just ten days before the Barcelona Olympic marathon. Mota was hugely disappointed – feeling she had let her country down. New Zealander Lorrain Moller, a good friend of Mota's who went on to claim the bronze, agrees that it would have been a totally different race with Mota involved (Sandrock).

In the fall of 1995, Mota was elected to the Portuguese Parliament, and she began to divide her time between her beloved Porto and less beloved Lisbon. At the end of her competitive career she had won 14 of her 21 marathons – a magnificent winning percentage of 66.6 per cent. Joan Benoit, for instance, won 9 of her 24 marathons (37.5 per cent), and Gelindo Bordin, who won in Seoul nine days after Mota, won 8 out of 18 (44 per cent). Mota may never have run as fast as many of her rivals (her personal best was "only" 2:23:29), but she was victorious more than almost any. She explains: "For me the marathon always is a fight against my opponents, not the clock. The courses and weather are so different that nothing really is comparable. It's impossible to judge the value of a performance so for me all that matters is winning."

Race result:

Rosa Mota	POR	2:25:40
Lisa Martin	AUS	2:25:53
Katrin Dörre	GDR	2:26:21
Tatyana Polovinskaya	URS	2:27:05
Zhao Youfeng	CHN	2:27:06
Laura Fogli	ITA	2:27:49
Daniele Kaber	LUX	2:29:23
Maria Curatolo	ITA	2:30:14
Zoya Ivanova	URS	2:30:25
Angela Pain	GBR	2:30:51

Sources:

Conversations with Hugh Jones.
Anonymous, in the *Athletics Weekly*, September 14th & 28th, 1988.
Derderian, Tom, *Boston Marathon*. Human Kinetics, 1996.
Hauman, Riël, *Century of the Marathon*. Human & Rousseau, 1996.
Horovitz, Israel, in the *New England Runner Magazine*, November 1988.
Martin, David and Roger Gynn, *The Olympic Marathon*. Human Kinetics, 2000.
Sandrock, Michael, *Running with the Legends*. Human Kinetics, 1996.
Wallechinsky, David, *The Complete Book of the Olympics*. Aurum Press, 2000.

XXIII

No. 28 – 1948 Olympic Marathon [Men]

Saturday, August 7th

Brave Belgian strives to "square the account".

If ever there was a race with a twist in the tail...or two...or three, this was one. The city of London has hosted two Olympic marathons, and they have both kept all and sundry guessing right to the bitter end. These were, of course, the first Olympics to be held since 1936, which leads the author George Gretton to deduce: "This shows that we are more businesslike about war these days: in Ancient Greece the Olympics were celebrated for some 1,200 years, and when there was a conflict of interest between war-lords and Olympic organisers, it was the war that was called off." The Games of 1948 defied the sceptics who said that a post-war, impoverished, rain-soaked London could never host a plausible Olympics. But typical British resilience kicked in, existing facilities were given a facelift, and the athletes were housed in army barracks.

The marathon wrapped up a week of drama on the track, including the great Fanny Blankers-Koen – at the ripe old age of 30 – winning the 100-metre dash, the 80-metre hurdles, 200-metres and 4 × 100-metres relay. And then came the thrashing, churning, agonizing, grimacing human piston 'Emil the Great', who decimated the field in the 10,000-metres, and then, three days later, wowed a spell-bound Wembley in the 5000-metres. This latter race was a rare defeat for Emil Zátopek, but his daredevil exploits instantly won him millions of fans as he took nearly 50 metres out of an unsuspecting Gaston Reiff over the last lap, but ended up a meter and a half shy of the Belgian.

The field of athletes in the marathon was similar to that of the Berlin Olympics of 1936: 24 Europeans from 13 nations, and 17 more from 4 other continents. There were three redoubtable survivors from the Berlin race: South Africa's Johannes Coleman, and two famous Boston winners from 1945 and 1946, Johnny Kelley, sen. and Greece's Stylianos Kyriakides. The 12-year aging process had remarkably little effect on these hardy souls, with Kelley and Kyriakides[1] stepping

---

1. Kyriakides' triumph at the Boston of 1946 is a moving and inspirational tale. He asked his superiors back in starving, war-ravaged Greece to send him to Boston so that if he triumphed there he could spread the word of his country's plight and raise funds from the Americans. Having taken on extra food from his underfed people, George Demeter, his employer, told him: win or die. Kyriakides would return home like an ancient Greek warrior – "either victorious with his shield or carried upon it, dead" (Derderian). He won by two minutes.

just three and seven steps down the leaderboard, while Coleman improved on his sixth of twelve years earlier to play an important role in the thrilling shake-up of the 1948 Olympic marathon. The Germans, Soviets and Japanese were not invited to send teams.

The British hopes lay mainly with Jack Holden who had emerged as their post-war marathoning star by winning the Polytechnic Marathon trial race in 2:36. Seventy-seven seconds further back that day came the experienced 38-year-old Welshman Tom Richards, with Stan Jones grabbing the third spot by just ten seconds over Northern Ireland's John Henning. It was hoped that these three would do rather better than the farcically poor show of their countrymen 40 years earlier when the Olympics were last in London.

Holden aside, this seemed an open race and relatively little was known of the rest of the field. A new star it seemed would surely emerge. August 7th dawned hot (73 °F), humid and windy, after the previous thunderstorms that had soaked much of the Games. Instead of running a point-to-point course as at the 1908 Olympics, the athletes of 1948 were presented with a loop course, starting and finishing in the world-famous Wembley Stadium. The course around the London suburbs of Stanmore, Elstree, Boreham Wood and Mill Hill had several rolling hills, but none were too exacting in nature.

After the Argentinian Eusebio Guinez had enjoyed an early lead, a previously unheralded 25-year-old Belgian parachutist called Etienne Gailly surged to the front, passing 10 kilometres in a more than frisky 34:34 – a shade off world-record pace. He was 12 seconds ahead of an unknown from China, Lou Weng-au (Martin & Gynn). Gailly – known as "Steve" to his English friends, of whom there were many – seemed to be handling Olympic pressure with a cool head. This was perhaps because his life thus far has not been for the faint of heart. When his native country was occupied by German forces in 1943, 20-year-old Etienne left home with the intention of travelling through France and making it to Britain. Alan Mead writes in *The Belgravian*: "...But upon crossing the Pyrenees he was arrested and spent six months incarcerated in a Spanish gaol. Upon his release Gailly was ordered to return home, but instead his travels took him to Portugal, Gibraltar and finally England." Gailly made two decisions quickly: one to join the Brigade Belge and undertake tough paratroopers' training, and the other was to join the famous South London running club, Belgrave Harriers, in April 1944. It wasn't long however before plans were being laid for the liberation of Europe, and, returning home to his family, Gailly's athletics progressed. By 1948 he was the Belgian marathon champion.

Before the Olympic marathon, Gailly and his coach concluded that his fitness should allow him to follow a schedule that would bring him home in 2:30 – and that he'd just ignore what the other runners did. The grave flaw in this strategy was that Gailly and his coach had based their calculations on a level course, which it was anything but.

Gailly pressed on and by 20 kilometres he had extended his lead over the determined Lou by 24 seconds. Jack Holden hunkered just inside the top ten but did not appear to be travelling smoothly. By 25 kilometres, Lou was slowing dramatically and would go on to record a dreaded DNF. The Mexican Guinez took up the chase of Gailly, as the Belgian had now extended his lead up to 41 seconds.

200

Just as the crowd were beginning to wonder whether Gailly was to proceed without incident to the finish and the gold medal, two critical things occurred: a Korean runner called Choi Yoon-chil had a spectacular burst of energy to scythe through the field and take himself from eighth to the bronze medal position. And he didn't intend to leave it there. The other development happened, not surprisingly to Gailly. He began to tire.

Gailly recalls his thoughts around the 32K mark, where his 40-plus second lead from the 25 kilometre mark was about to disappear:

I was surprised when I saw that I was ahead of the entire field at such an early stage and was convinced the others would soon re-establish contact with me. In fact I was often glancing back, expecting Heino and Holden to appear at my side. I considered them my most dangerous rivals and it was baffling not to see them coming to the fore. When after about 32 kilometres, the Korean, Choi, passed me and I could not respond, I asked myself: "Is he travelling so fast or am I fading?" I had to admit to myself that my strength had left me temporarily. I could only watch how fast Choi was running.

Although I hated this tiredness, I was not unduly alarmed. I had been alone in the lead for 27 kilometres: things looked not quite so good now but, after all, I felt nothing more than a normal tiredness which I hoped to overcome soon. Next the Argentinian Cabrera passed me. This, however, did not discourage me, not even when he gained some 60 yards on me, because just at this time I felt my rhythm coming back. I had got my second – or was it my third? – wind [Mead].

It was now that another major twist of the race occurred as the Korean, who had run an amazing middle part of the race and was beginning to look a likely winner, began to limp, and before long was forced to drop out of the contest. British entrant Tommy Richards of Wales was looking stronger and stronger as the race progressed and with just 2 kilometres remaining it was impossible to predict the winner as just 80 yards covered separated the Argentinian, Cabrera, the Belgian and the Welshman.

Gailly takes up the story of how he reacted to Cabrera passing him:

I joined issue again...and closed quickly...No sooner had I got into the Argentinian's slipstream than I decided to spurt without delay. I no longer felt powerless: on the contrary, I thought that now was the time to square the account...I passed Cabrera, and having regained the lead, seemed to be travelling well. Certainly I was tired, but quite convinced that I would last the distance.

It was then that I committed my biggest blunder...To rejoin Cabrera I had to make good some 70 yards. Having achieved this I drew away from him too quickly because after about 1 kilometre I had left him 60 yards or so behind.

This works out at over 100 metres of ground made up in only 2 kilometres. The damage was done. Gailly was terribly exhausted – far more than he realized. He still led as the stadium was approached but was mercilessly exposed to the two men doggedly trailing him. Michael Sheridan writes in *100 Years of Olympic*

201

Make way for Etienne! With a huge crowd looking on, horses are panicking, photographers are jostling and a Belgian's stride is crumbling. The ominous figure of Delfo Cabrera may be spotted just to the right of the first car. *Bettmann/CORBIS*

Marathon Races: "...with only a few hundred yards remaining it became apparent that all was not well...Etienne Gailly was in obvious distress. Ashen faced with eyes bulging, he lost his sureness of stride and was almost staggering. Was he to undergo the same fate as had befallen Dorando Pietri forty years earlier?"

The next day the London *Times* reported:

...a figure fully as tragic as Dorando's emerged from the tunnel. It was the Belgian, Gailly, so sore of foot and weary of leg and soul that he could hardly make any progress at all. Suddenly, quite close behind him, appeared another figure, that of the strongly built Cabrera, whom doubtless was tired too, but looking a fresh and lively sprinter by comparison. The Argentinean passed him in a few strides and set off to complete a lap that must have seemed like 5 miles or more to the poor tottering Belgian. No more than 20 seconds later came the loudly and justly cheered arrival of Richards – a pleasant surprise indeed for most people.

Richards had little pace, but he easily passed poor Gailly in the back-stretch and lessened by a little the original 100 yards between himself and Cabrera. Richards finished only 16 seconds behind the winner. A lifetime of training and racing had paid off for Richards, but how tantalizing to lose the race by so little. After having trailed the favourite Jack Holden for the first 15 miles, Richards went on by and had started ruthlessly to pick off runners. At the 15-mile mark he had been a full 3 minutes down on Gailly. With about eight miles left to run Richards looked down the road and counted the runners ahead of him: "One, two, three...five, six." Encouraging, but then a British official shouted to him that he was eighth. "The leader must be long gone," Richards thought.

At the next drinks station, someone handed him a cup and Richards drunk mightily...and then heaved and wretched. He had been given cold, stewed tea. "It wasn't what I needed at all. I'm sure if the Olympics hadn't been held in Britain, I could have done better – that cup of tea was bloody awful! The worst I ever had." As Richards ran the last mile up Wembley Way, unbeknownst to him he had moved into third, quickly coming up on the fading Gailly, whom he passed inside the stadium. Gailly once almost pulled up dazed and hopeless with the appalling distance of 60 yards still between him and the tape (Hauman). Already "other gallant runners were appearing, and it was in no grudging spirit that one breathed again when Gailly at long last staggered into third place." He then collapsed and was carried off on a stretcher.

Describing the longest two minutes of his life, Gailly dramatically recalls: "I cannot deny that this last lap was hard for me. It was like the progress of a martyr. I was horribly weak, indeed, I almost fainted...first Cabrera and then Richards passed me, as behind a veil. I was no longer fighting them but that awful engulfing weakness, wanting more than anything to get to that unbelievably distant finishing line. I got there...somehow" (Mead). Wembley stadium was packed to the rafters, but although their delight at seeing Richards snatch the silver was great, the most extreme emotions were those of relief to see Gailly finally totter over the finish line, some 33 seconds ahead of the evergreen Johannes Coleman, and book himself a place on the medal podium.

In searching for someone who was in the stadium on that famous day, the author found a member of Britain's 5000-metre squad, Bill Lucas, who recalls his thoughts on the champion:

I can add little more to your report than to say that with only 5 kilometres to go, only 16 seconds covered the first three and the finish with the first three in the stadium raised some real excitement. It was a great effort by Gailly, and I was much impressed with the fitness of Cabrera who finished in fine fettle and obviously judged his race to perfection.

You must remember we were used to seeing runners struggling with dehydration in the final stages of a marathon. Witness Jim Peters, whom I knew very well, and now Paula – who I hope will recover to show her true capabilities.

Gailly returned home where he was awarded the Grand Prix d'Honneur as the outstanding athlete of the year and the Trophie National du Mérite Sportif for his performance in London. Still a young man, Gailly had at least two or three Olympics left in him to try and improve on his bronze-medal return. But it was not to be. Lieutenant Gailly was, after all, a soldier first, athlete second, and his adventures continued. In November 1951 while with his regiment of paratroopers in Korea, he was wounded by an exploding mine that shattered seven bones in his left foot. Etienne was expected to have a permanent limp for the rest of his life, and it is thought he never competed again. Tragically, he was killed by a car on the outskirts of Brussels in October 1971, aged 48.

As for Cabrera, he did compete again. Born in Cordoba, Argentina, and boasting natural track speed, London had felt easy to Cabrera. He had finished many times a bronze medallist at South African track championships between 1945 and 1947, before he finally won the national 10,000-metres championship. All this five-minute miling stood him in excellent stead for the marathon where he was only required to run at 5:52 per mile in London. After the London Games, Cabrera won the inaugural Pan-American Games marathon in 1951 (where one Frank Shorter would burst on to the world scene 20 years later) by 10 minutes. Cabrera returned to the Olympics at Helsinki and placed an excellent sixth. Upon his retirement from racing in 1957 Cabrera became a physical education teacher and was eventually elected president of the Argentine Olympic Association. With

Two Olympic champions: at the 1952 Helsinki Olympics, the 1936 Olympic marathon winner Sohn Kee-chung meets and greets the defending champion, from London four years earlier, Delfo Cabrera. *S&G*

macabre coincidence, Cabrera, like Gailly, was also taken well before his time in a car accident on August 2nd, 1981, aged 61.

Tom Richards had come into the Olympics seen by most as a lesser runner than the great Jack Holden who had won the famous 1947 and 1948 Chiswick Polytechnic or "Poly" races. But where Holden returned a disappointing Olympic DNF, Richards chose London to record a personal best when it counted most. His career best came at the 1954 "Poly" – aged 44 – where he placed sixth in a neat 2:29:59 behind Jim Peters' astounding 2:17:39. Between 1950 and 1956, Richards won five Welsh marathon titles.

Regarding the 1948 Olympic marathon, Richards commented, shortly before he died in 1985: "I'm not saying I would have won the race, but no one told me my position in the last few miles. It would have been nice to have known." He went on to race well into his 50s and scored a world-best for 50 miles en route to winning the London to Brighton race in 1955 (Downes). He also became a regular marshal at South London cross-country races, often shouting runners' positions to them as they passed. "After all," he poignantly explained, "it's always nice to know."

Race result:

Delfo Cabrera	ARG	2:34:51
Thomas Richards	GBR	2:35:07
Etienne Gailly	BEL	2:35:33
Johannes Coleman	SOA	2:36:06
Eusebio Guinez	ARG	2:36:36
Sydney Luyt	SOA	2:38:11
Gustav Ostling	SWE	2:38:40
John Systad	NOR	2:38:41
Armando Sensini	ARG	2:39:30
Henning Larsen	DEN	2:41:22

Sources:

Conversations with Bill Lucas

Athletics, 1948.

Athletics Weekly, October 30th, 1971.

The Belgravian, 1948 & 1949.

Derderian, Tom, *Boston Marathon*. Human Kinetics, 1996.

Downes, Steven, in *British Runner*, April 2002.

Gretton, George, *Out In Front*. Pelham Books, 1968.

Hauman, Riël, *Century of the Marathon*. Human & Rousseau, 1996.

McNab, Tom, *Olympic Games*. Knight Books, 1971.

Martin, David and Roger Gynn, *The Olympic Marathon*. Human Kinetics, 2000.

Mead, Alan, "So Close to Olympic Glory", *The Belgravian*, March 1999.

Nankeville, Bill, *The Miracle of the Mile*. Stanley Paul, 1956.

Sheridan, Michael, *Good Reasons: 100 Years of Olympic Marathon Races*. Published by the author, 1996.

The Times, August 9th, 1948.

Wallechinsky, David, *The Complete Book of the Olympics*. Aurum Press, 2000.

World Sports Magazine, 1948 & 1952.

XXIV

No. 27 – 1996 Olympic Marathon [Men]

Sunday, August 4th

"The learning curve is over – South Africa has arrived."

Not all Olympics will pass by smoothly, and after three hugely successful chapters in the journey of the Olympiad, Atlanta 1996 drew a shorter straw. Athens seemed a logical choice for the Centennial Olympics, one hundred years after that city had revived the Olympic movement, and when they didn't win, due to some very fancy footwork by two men in particular, people were ready to criticize, and, boy did they. The two men who constructed Atlanta's successful bid were Revd Andrew Young, the ex-mayor of Atlanta and a former United States ambassador to the United Nations. His sidekick was an expert in real-estate law and great lover of sport, "Billy" Porter Payne. Together, the two conjured a vision that the Centennial Olympics should be held in *their* city and not Athens. Authors Martin and Gynn write: "In the beginning [Young and Payne] scarcely knew any of the voting IOC committee members, let alone understood the complex political machinations of international sports federations. But they had superb business acumen, and they were wonderfully friendly people." The basic message on offer was: "We are your friends, we want to join with you to help the world have a wonderful sporting legacy for the next millennium, and if you will entrust us with the Olympic Games, they will be successful."

The representatives of six nations with hopeful Olympic bids convened at the New Takanawa Prince Hotel in Tokyo on September 18th, 1990. The competing nations were Belgrade (no chance), Manchester (no chance), Melbourne (hosted the Games just 34 years earlier), Toronto (slim chance), Atlanta (fair chance) and Athens (hot favourite). Voting required all five possible rounds. Athens dominated the first two rounds, before flutters were sent through Greek hearts as they tied with Atlanta in round three as Melbourne bowed out. Pangs of fear occurred in round four as Atlanta took a slim lead in the vote as Toronto bit the dust. The final round was a head-to-head duel between Athens and Atlanta. Where would the allegiance of the 22 Torontonian voters lie: anti or pro American? Well, remarkably or otherwise, 17 were pro, and in the final round, Atlanta won by 51 votes to 35. "Thus launched a 2,129-days building and planning frenzy that created the largest sports spectacular in history," write Martin & Gynn.

Just shy of six years later and Atlanta fielded a brutal blacklash from the sports' media, the Olympians and the public alike. It has gone down as a haywire, haphazardly organized Games. Most technology worked very well: BellSouth, Swatch, ChampionChip all take a bow. But in the first few days of the Games, IBM's computer results system inconsistently routed results to world news agencies. Although this bug was eventually corrected, newspaper editors were irritated enough to replace space that should have been dedicated to hard sports news with negative copy about the organization of the Games. Problems with transportation were another moan to be constantly heard. And even IOC president Juan Antonio Samaranch complained about "rampant commercialism" during the Olympics. Which does seem a bit hypocritical, as Martin and Gynn point out: "If it were not for a well-funded coterie of megasponsors each anteing up $40 million or more as major sponsors, the Games as a spectacle would have been severely diminished." Samaranch had the last laugh at the closing ceremony declaring the Games "most exceptional" but not "the best ever", as was the normal, expected refrain.

But what the Games did boast was a fantastically exciting atmosphere, that not even a crude pipe bomb, exploding on Saturday, July 27th, killing one and injuring 110, could deflate for long. Lingering memories include Michael Johnson's 200-metre world record, Carl Lewis's fourth consecutive long jump title, all the thrills and spills from the Georgia Tech Aquatic Centre, and the superb, if somewhat melodramatic, performance of the winning US gymnastics team, who were roared on by 32,000 partisan spectators who seemed unaware other nations were competing.[1] And at the end of the fortnight's festival came a stellar men's marathon race.

* * *

Gary Lemke wrote in the *Durban Sunday Tribune*, on the morning of the 1996 Centennial Olympic marathon, that it was "arguably the most open to have ever graced the Games". Lemke continued:

> [Dionicio] Cerón, the first back-to-back winner of the London Marathon in 1994/5, won four consecutive marathons from '92 to '94 and has gone on record as saying he will yet run a 2:05:30. One's not quite sure whether that statement was made after a few tequilas went straight down the hatch of the 30-year-old Mexican. However, he must be rated a possible winner – though the demanding roads of Atlanta will surely mean the race won't be run under 2:10.
>
> Much will depend on today's weather. The heat is what the South Africans have been training for at between 6000 and 10,000 feet in Albuquerque the last few months. Privately there are those who readily concede that should the sun blaze away, it's Josiah Thugwane and not Gert Thys who represents our best

---

1. The key drama in this event came in the form of the inimitable 4 foot 9, 87-pound Kerri Strug, who injured her ankle on her first vault in the team competition, scoring a poor 9.2 into the bargain. With Russian athletes in tears all around her, knowing they'd surely lost the battle for overall team gold, Strug was still coerced by her teammates and coach to have another vault, since the States "needed a 9.6". Strug replied that she couldn't feel her leg. But in front of a riveted TV audience, who were not informed by commentary that America were going to win anyway, Strug scampered down the runway, leaped over the vault, stuck the landing, and collapsed in agony. Score 9.712. She immediately became a household name and national hero. Three years later she ran a marathon, although she admitted to *Runner's World* that the ankle had yet to heal.

A dark horse at Atlanta was South African Josiah Thugwane who had shown he ran well in oppressive conditions by winning the Honolulu Marathon the year before. Colleen de Reuck (South Africa) is the women's winner. *Mark Shearman*

chance at upsetting the likes of Cerón, along with world champion Martin Fiz, Kenjire Jitsui, Alberto Juzdado, Lee Bong-ju and Antonio Pinto. Last year he triumphed in the most uncomfortable conditions when capturing the Honolulu marathon in 2.16.[2]

For me, Fiz is the one to beat. A former five and 10,000m track runner as well as five-time world cross entrant, the 33-yr-old Spaniard has the tactical brain of Garry Kasparov. He has won five of six marathons entered, including last year's world champs in Gothenburg (see Chapter 37).

It would be unfair to suggest which of the South African trio stand the best chance but probably a safe punt would be once dawn breaks today. If it's hot, stick something on Thugwane. If it's cool, try Thys. If you're still totally confused opt for Peu. It's that type of Olympic Marathon.

Another contender came in the form of Korea's Lee Bong-ju. One of Asia's finest ever competitors, he had a host of titles and classy performances to his name. He first entered the international marathon scene with a seventh-placed 2:19:18 effort at the December 1992 Honolulu Marathon. He then recorded his first marathon win: a 2:10:58 in March 1993 at Kyongju. Interestingly, like Thugwane, Lee was also a Honolulu champion – in 1993 – displaying the ability to manage heat and humidity well that was to prove so crucial to both athletes at Atlanta. He improved again at the exceptional 1994 Boston where his 2:09:57 placed him just eleventh, even though he had returned a Korean national record. In March 1996 he placed second in the Korean Olympic trials at Kyongju with a 2:08:26. Improving pretty much every time out, he was indeed an athlete to be feared.

It was all set to be the most open and fiercely contested Olympic marathon in history. Britain sent a strong team, feeling able, remarkably, to omit Paul Evans from the line-up even though he had placed third in the London Marathon in 2:10:40. But the British selectors preferred Peter Whitehead and Richard Nerurkar, who had placed fourth and seventh in the World Championships the previous year, and Steve Brace who ran just 5 seconds quicker than Evans in Houston in January.[3] The Mexicans were also exceedingly strong. Not only did they boast the

---

2. In conditions, Thugwane said, that were "not fit for a lizard".
3. Evans bounced back from his disappointment to win the Chicago Marathon the following autumn.

aforementioned Cerón but also the exciting duo of German Silva and Benjamin Parades who had featured in a stunning duel at New York in November 1994 – Silva winning by two seconds.[4] Finally, of course, came the ever-growing Kenyan threat, even though the team came without Moses Tanui (running the 10,000-metres) and the enigmatic Cosmas N'deti, who had qualified in the Kenyan trials. His absence was a mystery. Kenya did bring Ezequiel Bitok and Lameck Aguta (future 1997 Boston champion). Of most danger however, appeared to be Erick Wainaina, who followed in the footsteps of his successful countryman Douglas Wakiihuri by living and training in Japan. He boasted two impressive marathon victories on his CV in Tokyo in 1995 and Otsu in '96 – both in 2:10.

* * *

The race began in typically nervy and pedestrian fashion at 7.05 a.m. to avoid Atlanta's stifling mid-summer heat. The runners emerged from a near-deserted stadium in foggy but already humid conditions. Nothing of note had happened by the time the halfway mark came about; indeed the lead pack still consisted of 48 hopefuls. Either this really was the deepest field in history or else the pace was straightforward. It was, of course, the latter, as due respect was being paid to the second, and far harder, half of the race. The mid-race leader was the interesting figure of Ethiopia's Belayneh Dinsamo, the world-record holder, who had been relatively quiet since his exploits of eight years earlier in Rotterdam. The leader's halfway split was given as the snail's pace of 1:07:36. Somebody was going to have the energy to run some very quick miles, very soon.

At 25 kilometres, with the hordes thinning out a little behind them, 13 runners ran abreast. Among this group it was noticed that all three South Africans ran: the little known Thugwane to whom few paid any attention, and the two bigger guns, Peu and Thys. Other athletes of note included the Mexicans Silva and Parades, Nerurkar, Australia's ubiquitous Commonwealth champion Steve Moneghetti, Antonio Pinto and experienced Brazilian star Luiz dos Santos (the current Fukuoka champion).

It was a great sight for all South Africans when, during the 27th kilometre, the three confident Springboks decided to strike out for home on their own as one, close-knit, remarkably talented unit. But just as some began to wonder whether South Africa really could hit the Olympics with not just their first champion in the marathon since Kennedy McArthur's heroics at Stockholm in 1912, but a *triple whammy*, then the merry little one-nation show was over, with two of its participants about to descend into freefall down the leaderboard. Surprisingly, it was Thugwane who remained in command. By 30 kilometres, no fewer that 18 athletes still ran within a second of the leader.

The tempo picked up between kilometres 30–35, largely due to the energetic Thugwane who started throwing in a series of spirited surges. The distance was

---

4. This race became particularly memorable when Silva followed what he thought was the lead motorcycle in Central Park as it made a right turn, half a mile from the end, but it was actually just a cameraman nipping off to take a short cut to the finish! Horrified spectators yelled at Silva and he corrected his error after around 20 steps. Hastily retracing those steps, he found he had nearly 50 metres to make up on his countryman. That's where a kick comes in handy, and Parades could not defend his lead.

covered in a torrid 15:11. Eric Wainaina of Kenya grimly stayed with him. By 35 kilometres the two had prised a 3-second opening over Korea's Lee, and just a second more over the excellent duo of Silva and world champion Fiz.

Of great interest to British fans at around 30K was the presence 6 seconds further back of ex-Oxford University student and schoolteacher from Marlborough College in Wiltshire, Richard Nerurkar: a runner of impeccable pedigree with a blazing 46:02 for 10 miles as one of his impressive personal bests. Nerurkar was also the World Cup Marathon winner and three-time National Cross-country champion. Just when it seemed he could be a real danger in this race, the dreaded stomach trouble hit. Referring to a break the leaders made that he could not cover, he writes in his book *Marathon Running*: "I tried to respond but was still bothered by the need to empty my system." His troubles eventually passed and Nerurkar overtook all the runners who had gone by in his time of distress, eventually working his way up to an impressive final position of fifth. Who knows what would have happened if he hadn't, as he puts it "overloaded his system" with energy drinks before the race. He now lives in Ethiopia, with wife Gail and small children. One of his duties is organizing the new and fantastically successful Great Ethiopian Run.

A riveting 5-kilometre section along the famous Peachtree Road up to around 40 kilometres saw Thugwane, Wainaina and Lee all locked together in a grim struggle for supremacy. Just 2 seconds separated the trio as they approached the stadium, Thugwane, forever the aggressor, throwing surge after surge at his

Thugwane struggles to break Korea's Lee Bong-ju, and when the stadium arrived there was still almost nothing to separate them. *Mark Shearman*

211

contenders. Sadly, just 8000 were in the stadium to welcome the runners as it was being prepared for the evening's closing ceremonies. Most locals were at home, resting up for the celebrations and watching the event on television. The final lap was a hypnotic, seemingly never-ending affair as Korea's brave Lee seemed to be travelling so much faster than Thugwane, yet unable to reel him in. The tiny South African eventually prevailed by just 3 seconds. It was by far the closest Olympic finish of all time,[5] and to add to the fun Wainaina came home just 5 seconds later, to become just the second Kenyan Olympic marathon medallist in history. In only his second loss in five starts, Martin Fiz settled for fourth.

In last place, came Abdul Baser Wasigi, a 21-year-old from Kabul, Afghanistan, who boasted a personal best of 2:33. He was nearly two hours off his personal best on this occasion as, running with a bad hamstring, he captured the imagination of the crowds by refusing to drop out and hobbling along, over an hour after the next last man. Some spectators even ran (or power-walked) alongside, offering encouragement and water bottles. Officials were about to wave him to a finish line other than the stadium when they had a change of heart. Abdul was allowed to enter the stadium. The preparations for the closing ceremony were put on hold. Even a new finishing tape was created for him to reach, which, to the band's welcoming fanfare, he broke.

* * *

Josiah Thugwane had arrived at the Olympics ranked 41st in the world at the time. At 5 feet 2 inches tall he was the smallest in a field of 123 runners and a featherweight 99 pounds. He was 25 years old and could not read or write. He had a humble cleaning job in one of the mines close to his hometown of Bethal, 120 miles east of Johannesburg. The *Durban Daily News* devoted an editorial to Thugwane's exploits, an extract of which reads:

> There have been several occasions in the past couple of years when South Africans, so long divided by apartheid, have had to almost pinch themselves as triumphs in sport continued to lift and unite the spirit of the nation. Memorable moments have come and gone but it would be true to say that the most thrilling – because it was so unexpected – occurred yesterday when Josiah Thugwane became the first black South African to win an Olympic gold medal.

Thugwane, a father of four daughters, aged eight, five, three, and five months, dedicated his remarkable victory to president Mandela:

> It's important that I won. This medal is for a very special man, President Mandela. I was running for the president. I was running for my country. I was very confident during the race. I was testing them out with a few fartleks from the 37-kilometre mark. At home I train with the telephone pole method,[6]

---

5. For the previous closest, see Chapter 19.
6. A simple, enjoyable method of fartlek training, brought into the public eye by Zátopek; it entails the athlete quite simply surging for a set of telephone poles, say ten, then resting for four or six or eight, and repeating the process – often tinkering with the length of surges or rests.

and I put that into practice in the marathon. The Korean was very tough.

Now I just want to go home. I'm homesick. I want to see my family and friends. Two months is a long time, but now it's worth all the sacrifices.

At the closing ceremony in front of 83,000 and billions more worldwide, *Nkosi Sikeleli i'Afrika* was played for the first time in Olympic track and field history in what must rank as one of the most emotional sporting moments for South Africa. The odds were heavily stacked against Thugwane's chances of even making it to Atlanta, let alone pulling off his stunning victory. The gutsy, self-trained athlete's running career suffered a serious setback in 1993 when he underwent his rite of passage as a Ndebele male with near-tragic results. The ritual circumcision went horribly wrong, putting Josiah, who was national Marathon champion at the time, out of running for three months. And then, shortly before he left for his training camp having qualified for the Olympics, Thugwane picked up some local hitch-hikers who attempted to rob him. Shots were fired and the bullet passed through his chin where it left only a grazing scar.[7]

His teammates paid tribute to him. Gert Thys enthused: "He's a real toughie. When we were in the pack with Cerón and Fiz I could see they weren't responding to Thugwane's surges. I knew from the 30-kilometre mark that he would win." "I couldn't bear to watch the last few hundred metres," said Banele Sindan, manager of the South African athletics squad and the person who handed Thugwane the country's flag after finishing the race. "We screamed to him because those last 400 metres seemed to take as long as the whole race itself with those other two guys on the track."

Julian Drew in the *Johannesburg Mail and Guardian* wrote:

In just over two hours and twelve minutes on Sunday, a simple and largely unheralded young man from the Eastern Transvaal changed the face of athletics forever. Josiah Thugwane's victory vindicated everything that has ever been said about the Mathews Temanes, Mathews Motshwarateus, Zithulele Sinques and all the other great South African runners.

These athletes never had the chance to show the world what they were capable of, but on Sunday, Thugwane proved that we too can do what the Kenyans have done. Although they didn't stay there long, that image of three supremely confident Olympians in the green and gold was beamed around the globe. The message was clear: the learning curve is over, South Africa has arrived.

Bobby McGee, widely regarded as one of South Africa's foremost coaches said: "Josiah is actually uncoachable and everything he has done is absolute credit to himself. Josiah is very much a feel runner and he takes what works for him and basically designs his own training programme."

---

7. The author learns from a comrade of Thugwane's, the *Daily Telegraph* editor John Bryant, that the issue here was actually to do with a beer stall which Thugwane had set up by his home. Local competitors did not like this, and a turf war developed.

* * *

The story of how Thugwane's life went after the Olympics is a mixed and troubled affair that casts the human race in a poor light. David Wallechinsky injects his rough summary of Thugwane's upcoming tribulations with a dash of dry humour, but in general, they were no laughing matter: "Thugwane celebrated his victory by buying a CD player and thirty CDs. But, as the first black South African gold medal winner, Thugwane's days of innocence were numbered. Before he had time to prepare himself, Thugwane was inundated by journalists, sponsors, agents, politicians, beggars and criminals." Celebrated sports journalist of the London *Daily Telegraph*, Sue Mott, interviewed Thugwane as he came to the capital to compete in a star-studded field for the 1997 London Marathon. Mott observed:

> When the first question to Josiah Thugwane takes 43 seconds to translate into the tongue of the Ndebeli tribesman, with its clicks and plosives and glottal detonations like the working of a gentle popcorn machine, you realise this is no ordinary Olympic Marathon champion.
>
> And when that same question is all about the fear that infects his life, as opposed to the joy or wealth or pride of satisfaction you might expect from a man who became the first black South African to win an Olympic gold, it becomes clear this is no ordinary story. England's capital may be fraught with overpriced coffee and the occasional mugger but it would be fair to imagine that Thugwane's two and a bit hours racing would constitute less adventure than his preceding 25 years.

On his Olympic title, Thugwane commented: "It's true I should be happy I won but on the other hand I have this fear for my life. Fear for the life of my family. But what can I do? Soon after the Olympics I went back home and there were people who were looking for me. They wanted me to pay something to them. They were after my blood. I changed houses. So now I'm sitting here and there's nobody looking after my family. I don't know whether they'll eventually drag out my family, do something with them." As he relates the story, about the carjacking incident, his friend Lawrence Peu and coach Jacques Malan are laughing. "I had a similar case, like Josiah," giggled Peu, "I have been through the same situation. My girlfriend was shot through the shoulder." Mott observes: "What strikes you, apart from what rotten shots these carjackers must be, is the victims' common joviality. Then you remember it may be their only defence mechanism when lawlessness is rife."

On top of everything else, there was Thugwane's father, a demanding tractor mechanic. "My father is asking for a truck," Josiah explains, "but I don't help nothing. Not even small. I don't think so. The reason I cannot talk to you directly, the reason I have to talk to you via an interpreter or speak in broken English is because my father decided to abandon me at an early age. If it wasn't for that, if he'd looked after me, I'd have had an education." But, perhaps, not an Olympic medal. Mott summarizes: "His complete lack of sophisticated coaching, indeed any coaching may have been a factor in his free running in Atlanta that changed his world. He'd arrived with dreadlocks and bed blocks to keep away the evil spirits on the ground. He left with a gold medal and a CD player, a hero with a price – in every sense – on his head."

Thugwane went on to prove that he was indeed a world-class marathoner at London when he ran 2:08:06 to place just behind Antonio Pinto and Stefano Baldini in that year's superb race. The following December he hammered home his class with a more than impressive 2:07:28 to win at Fukuoka. Since then there has been very little except for a whole collection of DNFs (two at London, one at New York and the 2003 World Championships). He now lives in a middle-class home on a paved street adjacent to the Koornfontein Mines premises (Martin & Gynn). But even if he never runs another step, Josiah Thugwane's story will forever be one of the most inspirational Olympic tales of all.

Race result:

Josiah Thugwane	RSA	2:12:36
Lee Bong-ju	KOR	2:12:39
Erick Wainaina	KEN	2:12:44
Martin Fiz	ESP	2:13:20
Richard Nerurkar	GBR	2:13:39
German Silva	MEX	2:14:29
Stephen Moneghetti	AUS	2:14:35
Benjamin Paredes	MEX	2:14:55
Danilo Goffi	ITA	2:15:08
Luiz Antonio dos Santos	BRA	2:15:55

Sources:

Conversations with John Bryant.
Durban Daily News, editorial, August 5th, 1996.
Drew, Julian, in the *Johannesburg Mail and Guardian*, August 5th, 1996.
Lemke, Gary, in the *Durban Sunday Tribune*, August 4th, 1996.
Martin, David and Roger Gynn, *The Olympic Marathon*. Human Kinetics, 2000.
Mott, Sue, in the *Daily Telegraph*, April 17th, 1997.
Nerurkar, Richard, *Marathon Running*. A & C Black, 2000.
Wallechinsky, David, *The Complete Book of the Olympics*. Aurum Press, 2000.

XXV

No. 26 – 1967 Fukuoka Marathon [Men]

Sunday, December 3rd

"I thought I was going to die – the pace was so fast."

The April 2003 edition of *GQ* [*Gentleman's Quarterly*] magazine had this to say about the marathon runner Derek Clayton, in a feature article about determination: "Derek Clayton, the lone-wolf Australian, treated pre-race warm-ups like boxing weigh-ins, psyching out his rivals with a silent glower. Clayton broke the world record in 1969 and promptly vomited black gunk. He pissed blood for a week." Charming. On the web site anecdotage.com devoted to "famous people, funny stories", they speak of other brave athletes who appear in this book:

In the 1960s Ethiopia's Abebe Bikila braved the baking-hot cobblestones of Rome in his bare feet to win the Olympic Marathon; Moses Tanui once won a 10,000-metre silver medal, despite having one of his shoes fall off; Alberto Salazar ran with such recklessness that he received last rites after one race; and Emil Zátopek galvanized his nerve by playing suicide catch with a javelin, hurling it back and forth to his wife from 50 yards away.

Feisty fellows all; but none can quite match the bravery and bloody-mindedness of Clayton, born November 17th, 1942, in Lancashire, England, before living a while in Belfast, Northern Ireland and finally emigrating to Australia in 1963. Alluding to Clayton's mission to run for – first and foremost – himself, Time-to-run.com writes: "Clayton was Lancashire born, Northern Irish raised and Australian finished. He was considered to combine all the bad qualities of all those particular cultures. And throughout his career he never did anything to dispel what people thought of him." Clayton for his part agrees that he was never much of a "people" person: "I don't run to be regarded as anything by anybody. I don't care whether people think I'm the greatest runner ever or the greatest bum ever. I don't run for other people; I don't run for my country. I'm not very nationalistic. Derek Clayton comes first in my book."

Clayton, who was too slow for the mile, opted for a career in the marathon instead. He may never go down in history as one of the *greatest* runners because his career was cut short by injury, and he never won a championship medal; but he did do one of the greatest of things one can do in their chosen sport: to set a standard so high, so astounding, so trail-blazing, that their impact will remain for the many generations that follow in their footsteps. Long jumper Bob Beamon is such an example with his leap at Mexico '68. Then there are the ultimate "clutch" performers, such as discus thrower Al Oerter and rower Steve Redgrave, who won four and five consecutive Olympic golds respectively. Pole vaulter Sergey Bubka may have had a somewhat more chequered Olympic career (winning just once in 1988), but he set no fewer than 30 world records between 1984 and 1992. If Clayton doesn't *quite* fit into the same pantheon as these icons of their sport, then he certainly runs them close. Only three men have broken their own world record in the marathon: Jim Peters, Clayton and Khalid Khannouchi. And to those who accuse Clayton of running his on short courses,[1] the rebuke must surely be: once perhaps, but twice shows that he was doing *something* right.

One thing can't be denied: Clayton was a ferocious trainer. Completely self-trained, he averaged a brutal 140–170 miles per week, occasionally peering over the dangerous ravine of 200 miles, and then taking the plunge. He turned up to the Fukuoka Marathon of 1967 – this chapter's featured race – and the unofficial world championship at the time – with a personal best of only 2:18:28. His intentions in Japan were to lower that time significantly, but that was about it. He had no delusions of grandeur of actually winning the race.

Derek Clayton: the meanest, hungriest, and two-time deadliest marathoner of them all. *Mark Shearman* [See Chapter 14 for an image of Clayton in action at the 1972 Olympics].

The previous year, the legendary New Zealand runner Mike Ryan, who would go on to grab a deserved Olympic bronze at Mexico City '68, had won in a national and course record of 2:14:04, thrillingly edging out Hidekuni Hiroshima by just 0.6 of a second. Ryan was just one of several runners at Fukuoka '67 who boasted personal best times several minutes quicker than Clayton. Another "Kiwi", David McKenzie, who had won Boston earlier in the year in 2:15, came to race. Commonwealth champion Jim Alder was in the field searching for a fast time, as were several highly trained Japanese, including the dangerous Sei-ichiro Sasaki who had run one of the world's fastest ever times, 2:13:38, back in February at Beppu. It was only Clayton's fifth marathon and the first he had run out of Australia: to the casual, and even not so casual, onlooker, he could easily be dismissed as a contender.

Under ideal conditions for mara-

---

1. To this day for instance, Charlie Rodgers, brother of Bill, claims "Clayton was a 2:11 marathoner!"

thoning – 13 °C and cloudy – the runners set off and immediately it became clear that this was going to be a memorable day. Michael Ryan was seemingly shooting for a 2:06! And incredibly, he had company. This came in the unlikely form of the big-boned, 6 foot 2 inch, 160-pound frame of Clayton, who was running way faster than he ever had before. Surely this was a one-way ticket to disaster and a DNF. If the first 5-kilometre split time of 15:06[2] didn't have the enthusiastic Japanese fans gasping, a second 5 kilometres of just 14:51 most certainly did. Ten-kilometre split: 29:57. World marathon running had suddenly leapt forward by about a generation in just one day. American Frank Shorter is often credited with turning the marathon into a straight-up, tempo footrace right from the gun, but even he would have struggled to live with this.[3]

Ryan and Clayton soon had just one solitary figure to worry about: the brave little figure of Sasaki who refused to let the two leaders have it all their own way and decided to break from the comfort of the pack and give chase. But however much Sasaki poured on the pressure, the more Clayton and Ryan moved away. Kilometres 10–15 showed no let-up as the distance was covered in an immaculate 15:00; Sasaki, battling gamely, 39 seconds off the pace. He was comfortably ahead of the chasing pack who were now nearly a minute down. A mere 15 minutes and 2 seconds later a special moment occurred as for the first time in history the one hour mark for 20 kilometres was broken in the marathon, as Clayton flashed by in 59:59. Ryan, meanwhile, was finally starting to toil and Clayton found himself leading on his own. The Australian had a 100-metre cushion over Ryan, who in turn had a mere 80 metres on Sasaki (who had covered kilometres 15–20 in 14:57). The gap between him and Clayton had ceased to grow, and instead had begun to shrink. Not only was this scintillatingly fast running that the vociferous Japanese crowds were witnessing, but it was also turning into a thrilling duel, with the home-boy favourite refusing to yield to this blistering foreign attack.

Passing halfway in 63:22, Clayton forged on alone, although the little white speck behind him was looming larger and larger. By 25 kilometres (75:11), Clayton boasted a lead of a mere 20 seconds, and still Sasaki closed. Clayton began to slow, but not by much; meanwhile Sasaki put in a burst of acceleration to finally, to the crowd's delirium, draw level at 30 kilometres.

For the next 4 kilometres the two runners ran grimly side by side at breath-taking trail-blazing pace. There is an old motto in the marathon that once you are caught, then there's no coming back. But there are a select few who do respond: the runners who are so overwhelmingly tough that, although their minds and bodies are screaming fatigue, they are able to register that their superiority in the race is being questioned and that acceleration is the apt response. Clayton saw that however fast he was travelling, he still had a race to win, and so he refused to slow down. It helped that his rival, having chased so hard, was now surviving on whatever scraps of energy could be found in his reserve tank. Unfortunately, the

---

2. Interestingly this was the identical split Ron Clarke ran when leading the 1964 Olympic Marathon, before crashing to a 2:20.
3. Indeed the fastest Shorter would ever run was 2:10:30, nearly a quarter of a mile off the pace of this race.

scraps could not save Sasaki, and a side-stitch slowed him down and forced him out of contention for the lead.[4]

The two 5-kilometre splits for Clayton between 30 and 40, show him running a more reasonable, though still excellent, 15:39 and 16:05; and his lead over the heroic Sasaki grew to 54 seconds. Dave McKenzie, running supremely well, overtook his countryman Ryan and forged into third place. It mattered not that Clayton took 19 seconds longer than Abebe Bikila in Tokyo over the race's final 2.2 kilometres: he was so far ahead of world-record schedule that this small stumble barely registers. It wasn't actually Bikila's time that Clayton had been unknowingly shooting for, since that record had fallen to Morio Shigematusu of Japan, who had scored a world best at the Polytechnic Marathon in Chiswick in 1965: the third year in a row that the world record had fallen at that event. The time: 2:12:00. Clayton arrived at the finish in 2:09:36. The elusive 2:12 barrier had finally fallen, and for good measure, the 2:11 and 2:10 marks had gone too.

The web site www.iaaf.org reports:

Clayton did not realise the significance of his performance immediately after the race. He did not even realise that he had just broken the world best for the marathon until he was handed a piece of paper with 2:09:36.4 written on it. After the race, he said, "I was hoping to improve my personal best, but I never thought of a possibility of setting the world marathon best. In fact, I did not even think about a possibility of winning until after half-way."

The first three runners in this extraordinary race were now first, second and fifth on the all-time list (Hauman). After the race, Clayton remarked: "I was always planning to run with such a pace. It may have been fast compared to the conventional marathon pace, but I didn't think it was fast. I was confident that I was able to continue with the pace. Jim Alder, who placed fifth, wholly disagreed: "It was so fast, I thought I was going to die. I wanted to stay with the leader, but it was impossible because the pace was so fast."

Recalling the day many years later, Clayton said:

The Fukuoka International Marathon was the most memorable event of my life. Breaking the world record is something you dream of. I never dreamed I was running a world best time. I was just thinking of winning, of crossing the line first. This fact most probably will remain true for the rest of my life. It was a very special day for me, and the emotional high I experienced on the day cannot be described in words.

The *Sydney Morning Herald* wrote:

Outside athletics, Derek Clayton is virtually unknown. But yesterday in Japan the Victorian ran a tremendous marathon that will make him an athlete of world repute.

---

4. Sasaki is now a highly respected coach in Japan. One of his female protégées, Eri Yamaguchi, ran 2:22 in Tokyo in 1999.

Clayton, bitterly disappointed when passed over last year for a trip to the Jamaican Commonwealth Games, now has assured his ticket to next year's Olympic Games in Mexico City. His great victory in Japan is even more meritorious because he was out of action the whole of last season with an Achilles tendon injury.

The Japanese press ran headlines praising Clayton. The *Tokyo Shimbun* said: "The marathon has now entered an era of 'super-express.' Clayton is now the target of the world's marathon runners. It was as if the marathon world had all of a sudden entered the 21st century." The *Asahi Shimbun* purred: "Clayton, like a phoenix, kept up his astonishingly high pace with his will power." Mr Susum Takahashi, marathon coach of the Japan Athletic Association said that Clayton had "made an ideal run, keeping a high pace from the beginning to the end. A marathon runner starting out at a slow pace and accelerating his pace in the last half of a race is now outdated."

Finally the *Melbourne Age* was of course ecstatic about its home-town hero:

The 25-year-old Melbourne marathoner outpaced a crack field today in the fastest ever time recorded for the traditional marathon distance.

Clayton, who migrated to Australia from Northern Ireland four years ago, had an operation in January and it was feared he might never run again. But the operation was a success and since resuming training in May he has gone from strength to strength as evidenced by his performance here today.

Clayton, a design draftsman of Elm Grove, Armadale, a Melbourne suburb, was by far the tallest man in the field.

* * *

Clayton naturally became the clear favourite for the Mexico Olympic Games but he had the problem of a cyst on the cartilage of his right knee. Before the race, doctors had told him that he needed an operation. "Sure I needed an operation, but that would have meant giving the Games away. I told them I'd run even if it meant losing the leg."

He gamely ran with the leaders as long as he could, before eventually placing a creditable seventh. Many, however, doubted whether he'd compete at the highest level again. But by 1969 he had put together a solid spell of uninterrupted training. His Sunday long run usually constituted a marathon, or else 22 miles through the woods and over hills with anyone who could keep up. Clayton most certainly didn't believe in LSD (long slow distance): "I never ran slowly; really bombed it every time." At his peak, before Antwerp, Clayton followed a ten-week training cycle in which he ran seven weeks of 160 miles, "resting with three 100-mile weeks" (Hauman).

Upon arriving in Antwerp, Clayton knew that "everything had peaked at the perfect time. I knew I was facing a once-in-a-lifetime chance." He explained his return to form after the injuries of Mexico by noting: "I've got a damn good surgeon, and that's the only reason I'm still running."

He was certainly in more than a feisty mood. He found amongst his competitors the European champion James Hogan and the Commonwealth champion James

Alder, who had pipped Bill Adcocks by just six seconds in Kingston, despite being misdirected as he'd approached the stadium. Clayton laid down the gauntlet with a sharp diatribe: "I'm glad you guys are here because I'm going to smash you into the ground. I think I can run a world record. I've just come from Ankara in Turkey where I ran 2:17 and it was a breeze and I think I can go under 2:10." Alder was underwhelmed, spewing back: "I don't give a damn about world records. I would rather win the Olympic gold even if I ran 2:30. I reckon that nobody remembers who holds world records. Everybody forgets them almost as soon as they're made." That really got Clayton going: "Well I'm going to run the world record anyway and I bet you're wrong. People will remember my world record. You won the Commonwealth Games but they won't remember you. They'll remember my world record."

No disrespect to the excellence of Alder, but it was Clayton who was proved right on this occasion. Without really understanding the splits he was being given (because they were all in kilometres), Clayton ran Antwerp like a man possessed, feeling "like a well-oiled machine". Over the last 7 kilometres, "running with a string of motorcars and cyclists in attendance, doubts set in as the exhaustion crept into his legs" (Hauman). Clayton recalls: "I began to speed up, to push through this wall of exhaustion. Those last six miles blended together in a nightmare of horns, shouts, bicycles, exhaustion, pain, and fear." Upon losing his rhythm, he said, "Then I panicked even more. And the more I panicked, the more effort I put into it. It became one excruciating effort..."

Clayton finished in a magnificent 2:08:33; a world record that stood for 12½ years until countryman Rob de Castella finally beat it in 1981 at Fukuoka.[5] If there are the select few who claim that the course at Fukuoka '67 was short, there are many more who submit that Antwerp was short, with one highly unscientific argument being that Belgian courses are notoriously short. There is, however, remarkably little hard evidence to back up the rumour-mongers. And the evidence that Clayton had indeed travelled the full distance far outweighs the theory that he didn't.

In an interview with *Track and Field News*, Clayton told how he had specifically warned the Belgians that he would be going for a record, and that they'd taken extra special care to measure the course. The Belgians then indicated "that the course had been measured by a calibrated wheel attached to a car, both before and after the race" (Hauman). And in an interview with *New Zealand Runner*, Clayton stated: "Both times there was 6 metres difference in the damn thing – we're not going to worry about 6 metres – so they assured me it was checked out." Author and statistician Riël Hauman notes:

It is unfair to single out this performance as being on a short course. According to Martin and Gynn "the evidence brought forward by the rumour-mongers has not been sufficient to cause the measured distance to be seriously questioned. Race conditions were such that performance recorded by most of

---

5. Alberto Salazar ran 2:08:12 in New York a few weeks earlier than de Castella, but his course was later found to be 148 metres short.

the top athletes were comparable to what they had achieved or would achieve during the coming months."[6]

Some final evidence comes in the comparison of Clayton's Fukuoka and Antwerp splits. They are remarkably similar although it should be noted that Clayton is actually *behind* schedule at Antwerp until after 35 kilometres. He then ran 15:41 for the stretch to 40 kilometres, compared to 16:05 in Fukuoka: both perfectly believable times. Clayton's coup de grâce was his final 2.2 kilometres in Antwerp: 6:38.6. Perhaps there's a shortfall in distance there – because that really is some going. But compare for instance this split with the author's final 2.2K at the 2004 London Marathon: 7:39. With tight hamstrings, in driving rain and a stiff breeze, this is a respectable time: but I'm running merely to *hang on* and get to the finish, I'm *not* trying to produce the greatest piece of distance running of all time. Oh, and I'm just a club runner on 90 miles per week – around *half* of Clayton's recipe. Finally, what did Paul Tergat score for his final 2.2 kilometres in his world-record 2:04:55? Answer: 6:19. Message to the sceptics: these numbers are fitting perfectly.

* * *

Championship gongs continued to elude Clayton though, as he placed a moderate 13th, barely dipping under 2:20 at the Munich Olympics of 1972; and he failed to finish at both the 1970 and 1974 Commonwealth Games. His exhausted body finally called time on him thereafter, at the age of just 31, a time when most marathoners believe their best times lie ahead. He had no fewer than nine major operations behind him.[7] Reflecting on his career, Clayton said: "If I had my competitive career to run over again, I would change some of my attitudes to injuries. I would show them more respect. Because, after all, injuries weren't some unknown barrier I was trying to break through. Injuries were simply my body telling me that something wrong was happening" (www.time-to-run.com).

Clayton's profile in Australia isn't nearly as high as perhaps it should be, as leading distance runner and Melbourne Marathon champion Phill Sly comments:

Comparing him to de Castella, Herb Elliott, John Landy or Ron Clarke, Clayton's profile in Australia is incredibly low. But the stories of his training are still told: running three times a day; running a 2:25 marathon on a Saturday morning for training, followed by a hard ten that night. Most of it would be in the beautiful Red Hill area just outside of Melbourne, and he'd just pound the miles in his crappy Dunlop shoes.

To those who say Antwerp was short, remember that Clayton feels that he could've done a *2:04* had he turned up with fresh legs, but the Turks had put their top man against him at Ankara a few days earlier when he ran a 2:17 and that dulled his edge.

---

6. An excellent case in point being Commonwealth champ Alder. In high temps on the brutal Athens course a few months later he would slow by just 2½ minutes from his Antwerp time; and the following year he would run 4½ minutes quicker when defending his Commonwealth crown in Edinburgh.
7. Four to his Achilles tendons, two to each knee, and one on the heel.

The stories of him and Ron Clarke smashing each other to pieces on 20-mile training runs at nearly world record pace are legendary. I've heard that the key thing he'd change about his career is that he'd get more than six hours sleep a night.

It seems though that Clayton couldn't remain uncompetitive for long and took up cycling with a vengeance. Stories abound that even into his 50s he was annoying Australia's lead club cyclists by refusing to be dropped from the *peloton* (lead pack). His running career may only include two truly outstanding moments, but these were so exceptional that Derek Clayton's achievements deservedly remain as two of the most notable in running's history. He certainly showed what could be done through sheer dedication and maniacal hard work.

Race result:

Derek Clayton	AUS	2:09:36
Sei-ichiro Sasaki	JPN	2:11:17
Dave McKenzie	NZL	2:12:25
Masatsugu Futsuhara	JPN	2:14:40
James Alder	SCO	2:14:44
Yoshiaki Unetani	JPN	2:14:49
Hidekuni Hiroshima	JPN	2:15:16
Kazao Ito	JPN	2:15:19
Mike Ryan	NZL	2:15:41
Kazuo Matsubara	JPN	2:15:42

Sources:

Conversations with Phill Sly.
Anecdotage.com, "famous people, funny stories".
Asahi Shimbun, December 4th, 1967.
Gentleman's Quarterly, April 2003.
Hauman, Riël, *Century of the Marathon*. Human & Rousseau, 1996.
Iaaf.com.
The Melbourne Age, December 5th, 1967.
Sydney Morning Herald, December 5th, 1967.
Time-to-run.com, "hall of fame" section.
Tokyo Shimbun, December 4th, 1967.

XXVI

No. 25 – 1976 Olympic Marathon [Men]

Saturday, July 31st

A "living example of mediocrity" takes on a legend.

It was inevitable that after Munich's "haywire Games" of 1972, with the terrorist outrage of eleven slain Israeli athletes, that the Olympic movement was going to struggle to bounce back as a happy-go-lucky, peaceful, harmonious festival. Indeed, before the huge damage at Munich could be fully repaired, a few more wrinkles would have to be ironed out first. Montreal of 1976 did its level best, but the Games, notwithstanding some sublime athletic feats, were not a resounding success. Too many nations squabbled bitterly with each other, which led to many sad boycotts. As for the financial side of the Games, that really was a shambles. The cost of putting the Games on, not only nearly brought the city of Montreal to its knees, but the entire Olympic movement too.

On the day before the closing ceremony of the Games, Red Smith of the *New York Times*, wrote:

The Games of the XXI Olympiad end tomorrow, and not a moment too soon. Another day or so of camaraderie and good will on the fields of friendly strife and somebody could wind up with a knife between his ribs. Up to now, this sweaty carnival has run as smooth as the course of true love, if you don't count the angry withdrawal of 30 nations, cheating, disqualifications, rumours of attempted bribery, political and ideological clashes, threats, bluffs, defections, charges of kidnapping and the use of forbidden steroids. It won't be easy to wait four long years to see them do it all over again in Moscow.

A couple of days before the start of the Games, Smith wrote: "With occasional exceptions, the world's finest athletes who meet in these Games like and respect one another; it is their leaders who stir up trouble. For the first time since the ancient Olympic Games were revived 80 years ago to encourage brotherhood among nations, country after country quit the global carnival in anger today." The leaders to whom Smith refers are in particular those of the uninvited or boycotting nations. The first problem involved Taiwan. They wanted to participate independent of China who did not have an IOC affiliation until 1979. Beijing – who were opposed to Taiwan's inclusion, and who purchased large quantities of

Canada's wheat – exerted pressure on the Canadians to withdraw Taiwan's invitation to the Games. Eventually Canada buckled, and although other nations who threatened to quit in this case because of the Taiwan saga did not follow through, 24 other nations *did* boycott the Games. This was due to the inclusion of the small, friendly nation of New Zealand, who had sent a rugby team to South Africa, which supported apartheid. Many African nations took severe umbrage at this even though rugby isn't even an Olympic sport and other nations at the Games had also sent sporting outfits to South Africa. But after a bitter stalemate in which time the IOC ignored the problem, naively hoping it would go away, just three days before the Games started, word went through the Olympic village that no fewer than 24 nations were calling their athletes home.[1]

Whilst the athletes of places such as Upper Volta (now Burkina) might not have been troubling the scorers too frequently, the Montreal Games were still denied some classic battles, not least Filbert Bayi of Tanzania duelling with John Walker in the 1500-metres – the world's fastest milers that they were. Kenya had a troupe of potential medal winners in boxing and track, headed by Mike Boit, a stand-out at 800 metres. Uganda's departure deprived the track meet of the presence of the defending champion in the 400-metre hurdles, John Akii-Bua. Although quite how he would have handled the challenge of a 20-year-old senior studying at Morehouse College in Atlanta named Edwin Moses is open to debate.[2]

Then there was Don Quarrie, the Jamaican sprinter, and a strong choice for gold medals in the 100 and 200-metre dashes. "They're going to have to literally pull me out of here," he wailed. Track and field coach for Jamaica, Heb Mckenley, said: "mentally and physically Quarrie's at the best he's ever been. It would be a tragedy if he could not compete." Philip Ndoo, a 30-year-old Kenyan marathon runner noted that his government's decision to withdraw was announced only five hours before the opening ceremony:

> Africans would not get up at the team meeting and make a statement like "I'm staying". But that does not keep us from being disappointed. This time it is particularly hard because there is no logic in the decision. There is never any logic in politics. I'm disgusted, but I go along with our government's decision. I suppose you could say the government and the people of Kenya sent me here, and I could never have come myself. But my sacrifice and sweat were not enough. I'm an individual, not the majority. But it was an individual who was going to beat Frank Shorter.

* * *

If the politics were liberally sprinkled with doom and gloom, the financial side of the Games were just as troublesome. Eight years later, the city of Los Angeles would ruthlessly show how to finance the Games by announcing at their conclu-

---

1. They were Nigeria, Tanzania, Ghambia, Iraq, Sri Lanka, Algeria, Chad, Central African Republic, Congo Republic, Egypt, Ethiopia, Gabon, Ghana, Kenya, Libya, Madagascar, Malawi, Niger, Sudan, Togo, Uganda, Upper Volta, Zambia and Zaire.

2. Moses went on to beat Akii-Bua's 1972 Olympic and World record (47.82) in the final with a 47.63 clocking. A true all-rounder, Moses attended Moorhouse on an academic rather than athletic scholarship, and commented after the Olympics his major regret was that his training had interfered with his studies – even though he was still an honours student.

sion a stunning profit of £222 million. Montreal suffered from almost the complete opposite. When the Games were awarded to Montreal on May 12th, 1970 in Amsterdam, it seemed like such a perfect choice. Martin and Gynn write: "Already a beautiful city on an island at the confluence of the St. Lawrence and Prairie Rivers more than 1,000 kilometres inland from the Atlantic Ocean, the plan was to enhance it with dramatic sports architecture. It was a bilingual city whose residents spoke the Olympic movement's own languages. The world economy was booming, Québec's even more."

But alas, the dreams and aspirations of the Montreal organizing committee for such futuristic and flashy architecture meant that costs rocketed and schedules fell alarmingly behind, leading to crippling overtime payments and more rocketing costs. A vicious circle indeed. Between May and October of 1975 the workers' union decided to go on strike, spelling the death knell for the completion of the project on time. Matters weren't helped by unfortunate contributory factors like the bitterly cold winters (even by notorious Canadian standards) and a sixfold increase in the price of steel between the start and finish of construction. The final cost of construction was U.S. $795.4 million (Martin & Gynn), somewhat over the initial $132.5 million predicted. The Olympics finally took place in an unfinished stadium, which would be used for athletics only for the Games, before being transferred into an arena for the Montreal Expos baseball team.[3]

* * *

As alluded to by Philip Ndoo, Frank Shorter, the defending champion, was seen by many as the man to beat in the 1976 Olympic marathon. And he came to the Games in good form, cruising round the Olympic trial with the new star of the American distance-running scene, Bill Rodgers, in 2:11:51, 7 seconds up on Rodgers. In third place, 2 minutes back and the third American qualifier, was a Stanford graduate named Don Kardong.

There was an interesting array of talent on offer from other countries looking to stop Shorter from completing his double, even though the event was weakened by the absence of athletes from seven boycotting African nations who had sent marathoners. Perhaps most intriguing was the presence of the Finn Lasse Viren, who, earlier on in the Games, had converted an exceptional "double-double". At Munich 1972, Viren had won both the 5000 and 10,000-metre finals, and he repeated the feat in Montreal, defeating first Carlos Lopes in the "ten" in a relatively straightforward race, and then having to overcome far more complex obstacles, both on and off the track for the final of the "five". Viren found himself facing a grilling from both the press and the IOC before the 5000 final. The press wanted to know all about the mysterious new Scandinavian practice of blood-doping, and in particular whether Viren indulged in it himself. David Wallechinsky describes the process:

---

3. The stadium's signature reclining tower wasn't finished until February 3rd, 1987. Stadium officials fight hard to this day to recoup as much of the debts as possible. Retractable stands have been fitted into the stadium, which allow 12,900 metres of extra floor space; and when the Expos aren't playing, the stadium is used for anything from rock concerts to stunt car shows to large rallies and trade shows.

This unnatural, but, at that time, not illegal, procedure involves the extraction of a quart or more of blood from a runner before a major competition. This blood is frozen, while the runner's body rebuilds its blood to a normal level. Then, just before the race, the extracted blood in unfrozen and reinjected into the runner, increasing the body's haemoglobin level and oxygen-carrying capability, and thus providing the runner with greater endurance.

Viren denied indulging in the practice, explaining the reason he performed so well at the Olympics is that his training schedule was organized so that he would peak at just the right time, and that the Olympics were his overwhelming priority in his running. The "man in the street" and newspaper scribes (looking for sensational stories) tend to be much more convinced of Viren's guilt in this area than the historians, statisticians and athletics authors. Viren never was found officially to be a blood-doper and this observer, like many authors, gives him the benefit of the doubt that his marvellous athletic feats were due to supreme ability and dedicated, highly intelligent, training. As he himself has pointedly remarked: "Some do well in other races, but they cannot do well in the ultimate, the Olympics...The question is not why I run this way, but why so many others cannot."

Viren's other spot of bother before the 5000 final involved the IOC quizzing him about why he had jogged around the track after his 10,000 triumph having taken off his spikes and seemingly waving them to the crowd. Was Viren indulging in a little commercialism? No, he replied. He removed his shoes because he was suffering from a blister, and was simply waving to the crowd with his spikes an extension of his hands. The IOC were satisfied with his explanation. Viren had the battle of his life in the final of the "five". With one lap to go, he memorably describes his agonies as Dick Quax of New Zealand pushed him all the way to the tape:

At the bell, I gave just one quick glance behind me and took in the situation in all its ghastliness. The wall at my heels was thick...I had put in a couple of sixty-second laps and almost everybody was still chasing me, damn it! I was the fugitive now, and I realized I had to flee as if my life depended on it...In the far turn I had the most frightening experience of my career. Some guy in black was forcing himself past me. It was Quax, whom I really hadn't reckoned very seriously...I found my last gear, and it was just enough.

Viren's presence in the marathon – *just the day after the 5000-metres final* – drew immediate and obvious comparisons with the remarkable "triple crown" secured by Emil Zátopek at the Helsinki Games of 1952. Could Viren repeat Emil's whitewash of the Games' three distance races (62,195 metres of toil). He was going to try (although *his* final quota would be 72,195 metres of racing). Viren's coach gave him simple instructions: just do whatever Shorter does. The ultimate game of cat and mouse was in store.

There was sadness for the British running at their Olympic trial that one of their greatest ever marathoners, Ron Hill, would not be back for his fourth consecutive Olympics. He had dedicated himself to one last hurrah, and flew to Dusseldorf for the week before the trial for a race sharpener. At the post-race reception Hill writes in *The Long Hard Road*: "I had a few beers and foolishly smoked three cigarettes. Neil [Cusack] raised his eyebrows, but I said, 'Don't worry. You'll see. I'll make the Olympic team next Saturday.' Christ, what a time for bravado! And the fags made me feel bad the next day." At the halfway stage in the trial race at Rotherham, Hill ran in third, feeling awful but hoping that he might still do it. However, by 17 miles, two other runners had taken off after the leaders. "Go on, Ron, you can do it," the spectators shouted, but Hill writes: "I just shook my head. I was feeling desperately tired, and my left thigh was painful and stiffening. I was alone, in limbo, knowing that I would have to suffer all the way home with no reward." Hill eventually finished a dejected fourth and a great international career, spanning back to the mid-1960s, was over. The team of relative newcomers Britain sent to the Games of Barry Watson, Jeff Norman and Keith Angus performed poorly at Montreal, with none breaking 2:20.

Other key contenders for the crown of Shorter included "Mr. Consistent" Karel Lismont of Belgium. Lismont came to Montreal with a silver medal from Munich and a gold from the European Championships. The tax collector was showing himself to be a superb performer when it mattered most, and would continue to prove this over the next eight years. He came to Montreal in even better shape than he had been in Munich.

Canadian sports-lovers, rarely for them, had a runner of true pedigree in Jerome Drayton to cheer. Despite a career littered with injuries, Drayton arrived at the Games seemingly at the top of his game. This was a man who knew how to win the big ones as a double win at the prestigious Fukuoka Marathon testified. A nation tuned in their TVs not just to cheer for the Olympic Marathon, but more specifically, for one of theirs.

* * *

One thing became very clear at the outset of this race: however little one sweated, one wasn't going to finish the race dry. Indeed this became the first – and so far only – Olympic marathon to be run entirely in the rain. Good news for the umbrella vendors, bad news for Frank Shorter, who hated rain. Shorter boasted so little body fat that his muscles tended to tighten up in the cold rain. "Uh oh," he said to himself, when he looked up at the start and saw the grey heavens start to open. He would never let the other runners know about the troubles he felt he was going to have; indeed his experience and professionalism enabled him to blank the weather from his mind, but deep down he knew he was in trouble.

More problems came for Shorter when warming up for the marathon. The soles of his custom-made shoes became unglued and began flapping about. Fortunately, he had a back-up pair, but had to send a volunteer to collect them. The minutes ticked by, and the other athletes waited for Shorter on the track. Was he going to miss the start? Shorter refused to panic: these things have a habit of sorting themselves out. Finally the new shoes arrived just in time and Shorter dashed out on to the track.

The temperature was a warm 25 °C. After encircling nearly three laps of the track, the athletes made for their tour of Montreal. Not a tour so much of the city centre, but more of a rectangular journey around the outskirts of the city. It was not a complex journey undulation-wise, with the only significant ascent occurring between 25 and 28K. Otherwise the runners were generally on the flat or the downhill.

Bill Rodgers towed the field through the early stages, quickly too – the 5K checkpoint registered a time 31 seconds quicker than that of four years earlier: 15:19. This was a brave move from "Boston Billy", since he had been nursing a foot injury since the Olympic trial and came into the Games not fully fit. The lead pack consisted of a quirky surprise in India's Shivnath Singh, the hunted Shorter, the iconic Viren, the local hero Drayton, the South American hope of Rodolpho Gomez, and the ever-game 44-year-old Jack Foster from New Zealand.

Two years earlier in the greatest moment of his career, Foster had received the Commonwealth Games silver medal from Queen Elizabeth II, having set a world record for a veteran of 2:11:18. By the age of 49 he was still managing 2:22. Described by his son as like "a white Kenyan", and "an oxygen processing unit on legs"; Foster said of his trail-blazing veteran's career: "What I've achieved as a runner may have inspired other 35-year-plus men to get up and have a go. I'd like to think so." In Munich, aged 40, he had placed a terrific eighth and here he was duking it out with the leaders again. He may not have nursed realistic hopes of a medal (he would go on to finish 17th), but his mere presence was an inspiring sight. Jack Foster was tragically killed on June 5th, 2004, in a motor accident when indulging in his second great love – cycling – in his home town of Rotorua.

With 10 kilometres passing in a more conservative 30:48, Martin and Gynn write: "Behind Rodgers in a huge pack of eleven, one notable athlete not visible was Italy's Giuseppe Cindolo, who had the fastest time for 1976 (2:11:50). Unknown to most, he was injured, and he dropped out before 15 kilometres." But it seemed that most of the other leading players were still very much in contention. The pace continued to be excellent, with Shorter starting to do some leading. He had not been resting on his laurels since his Olympic triumph, and indeed had won Fukuoka three times in the interim, to make it four times in a row. He was only denied a chance to shoot for a fifth consecutive win because the Japanese officials decided not to invite him back to their city out of fear that his dominance of the race was robbing it of some glamour and suspense. Lasse Viren watched Shorter like a hawk. Shorter would sometimes go and take solace in the comfort of the pack and shield behind other runners. He enjoyed watching the way Viren would look about wildly for him in concern. Another runner appeared to be watching Shorter very closely too. He was an East German by the name of Waldemar Cierpinski.

Cierpinski may have been a new face in running, but running certainly wasn't new to him; he had been doing distance runs since the age of *seven*. In 1972, aged 21, Cierpinski won the German Democratic Republic's national steeplechase championships, but the choosy Olympic selectors deemed him not worthy of an Olympic experience. Cierpinski quit the steeplechase there and then, and was attending these Olympics due to an impressive turn at the East German trial race in Wittenburg where he ran 2:12:21. There were also fine runs from the athletes in second and third that day; but the secretive, highly competitive GDR sports system only entered athletes for international competition whom they felt had a real chance of competing for a medal; and Cierpinski's basket was where they decided to place all their eggs. No pressure there then. The trial race had come just two months before the Olympics, but Cierpinski seemed to have recovered well. He had already proved that he was a good recoverer since he had run a 2:13 just six weeks before his 2:12. Shorter wasn't fazed that Cierpinski was watching him so closely. In fact, he didn't even know who he was.

At 25 kilometres Bill Rodgers' lack of background finally started to scream at him and he faltered,[4] while Shorter meantime was thinking the time had come to start *winning* his title back rather than merely *defending* it. He began to toss a few surges into the mix – and the field didn't like it one bit. Shorter was so focused that he barely noticed the rain, although that "silken, light-footed stride" was noticeably tighter. Soon Shorter was on his own, and seemingly it was Munich (see Chapter 14) all over again: this superb, highly-tuned machine, running for his second consecutive gold – doing a Bikila, if you will. And then, after a mile or so of this lead stretching ever more, something unexpected happened. Another figure hove into view. It was an almost ghostly figure, clad all in white, and it wasn't Lismont, or Drayton, or Kardong or Viren – it was Cierpinski. The figure drew level with Shorter, who looked over and did not recognize his challenger. "I thought it was Carlos Lopes," admitted Shorter.

As for Cierpinski, the momentum was all with him now. He recalls: "It was a wonderful feeling when I came alongside. I glanced at Shorter as I did so, and looked right into the eyes of the man who was my idol as a marathon runner. I knew all about him. And yet I could tell by the return glance that he didn't know much, if anything, about me. The psychological advantage was mine" (Walle-

Who's he? – the man who Shorter couldn't quite place, Waldemar Cierpinski. *Mark Shearman*

chinsky). Cierpinski burst into the lead and it was now a two-man, eyeballs-out, lung-buster for the gold. By 35 kilometres, the 5 foot 7 inches, 130-pound Cierpinski had forced himself into a 13-second lead, and during the subsequent 5 kilometres Shorter refused to let go, bringing the gap down to as little as 20 yards at one point. But just as Shorter had reached his limit, Cierpinski chose to slip into yet another gear. "This time around, I thought I would win," said Shorter, referring to the fact that he hadn't believed he was favourite at Munich. "But with three miles left, I knew I had had it." It was not to be his day after all. His normally efficient stride pattern simply refused to function as normal in the rain.

It turned out later that Shorter was

4. The closing miles of the race were "agony" for Rodgers, and he faded to 40th.

also running the race on a *broken ankle*. Notoriously tough, Shorter was able to train for several months through the slight pain. Making light of the "rain" issue, he notes: "I think it was really more a factor that my foot was broken. I think my conditioning was a little off. Between the Olympic Trials and the Games I was not really able to train that well because of my ankle" (Sandrock).

Meanwhile a great duel had also developed between Kardong and Lismont, as they fiendishly scrapped for the bronze. Kardong held a slight lead in the closing kilometres, but later wrote in *Runner's World*:

> Lismont caught me, and I pushed as hard as I could, matching him stride for stride. On our right, the Olympic stadium, heartless megalith, loomed into view. It was a duel to the death, and we both angled for the lethal kick. I reached deep and found...cement. My quads beaten over 25 miles, were lifeless. Merciless, the Belgian outpaced me on the downward slope and burst into the stadium in third place.

Cierpinski entered the Olympic stadium full of running, toured it, and when he arrived at the finish line, to his confusion, he found the lap counter still reading "1", so he toured it again. But it was actually reading "1" for Shorter and subsequent finishers, and when Cierpinski arrived the second time, Shorter was waiting to congratulate him at the finish. Cierpinski's time was the fourth fastest marathon in history (after Clayton in 1969, Thompson in 1974 and Hill in 1970), and the top four finishers all dipped under Bikila's old Olympic record of 1964. Although this record was well overdue to take a fall, the fact that it stood for so long illustrates just what a special runner Bikila was.

Cierpinski, looking and feeling fresh, arrives at the finish – only to then run another lap of the track in error. *Mark Shearman*

Upon shaking hands with Shorter, Cierpinski asked: "*Sprechen Sie Deutsch?*" Shorter thought, "That's a funny thing for a Portuguese to say." He later reflected: "I knew Cierpinski was a good steeplechaser, and I knew he had run a 2:12, but to tell you the truth I just never thought of him before as a marathon contender. I could do no more than I did...I will just have to accept the fact that I was second best."

Jack Foster watched a film of the race the next day and highlighted the unpredictability of the marathon: "I still think Shorter's the greatest marathon runner in the world. If he and Cierpinski were to race against each other over and over, I think Frank would beat him nine times out of ten" (Hauman). "It was very difficult," the East German said, "because Shorter always changed the tempo. Shorter tried to go off after 20 kilometres, and he was very fast so this group exploded. After 25–26 kilometres, I tried to know what Shorter could do. That's when I went off the first time."

Lasse Viren came in a valiant fifth and Dave Anderson in the *New York Times* wrote about the "the blood scandal":

> When asked about the charges of "blood doping," Lasse Viren played dumb.
> "I don't know what it is. I never heard of it."
> "It's supposed to raise the haemoglobin," he was told.
> "How do you raise the haemoglobin? I don't know. Do you know?"
> That's a non-denial denial, a Watergate denial. Under the Olympic medical rules, blood doping is not illegal. But it is unethical. Other runners call it "cheating" and it is. The problem is proof.
> "It's so new, nobody knows yet what the after-effects might be," one world-class runner says. "I'm not going to mess myself up for the sake of sport."
> But tonight Lasse Viren finished fifth in the Olympic Marathon – with or without the extra pint of blood.

David Wallechinsky tells a great anecdote about the East German soccer team who watched the marathon on television while waiting for their gold medal match against Poland. Goalie Jürgen Croy later recalled, "We just sat there staring at each other, thinking that if this living example of mediocrity can lift himself up and win the marathon, and we don't beat Poland, we are never going to hear the end of it." They won.

Shorter admitted he was "a little disappointed" with silver instead of gold, and the hurt showed on the victory stand. Shorter stood with hands on hips, almost eager to complete the proceedings as quickly as possible. When a reporter asked Shorter if he would continue running, Shorter replied, "Yeah, if I find some good doctors." This referred to his rising number of "niggles". But at the age of just 28, and with 15 years of hard running behind him, Shorter's days at the very top were over. He would go on to race a few more reasonable marathons, and some woeful ones, and placed just 85th at the 1980 Olympic trials.

As for Waldemar Cierpinski, his long and terrific career was less than one-fifth complete. He would prove the doubters, who said he lacked pedigree, wrong by winning no fewer than eight more marathons in his career, and would go on to defend his Olympic title in an exciting race (with a winning margin of 17 seconds) over a moderately weak field at Moscow four years hence. And seven years later, Cierpinski would place an excellent third at the inaugural World Championships, just 34 seconds down on Rob de Castella. And in 1982 he placed a creditable sixth in the European Championships. GDR's boycott of the Los Angeles Games deprived Cierpinski of shooting for an unprecedented triple, and he intended to go out with a bang at the 1985 World Cup. Sadly, however, the GDR selectors had other ideas and refused to pick him, deeming him to be out of touch. In 1995, aged 45, Cierpinski was still running – he clocked a 2:45 marathon in Sydney (Hauman). He was born in Neugattersleben on August, 3rd, 1950.

* * *

The British press wailed over the atrocious performances of their athletes at the

233

Cierpinski celebrates defending his Olympic title in 1980 with Gerard Nijboer (left) and Satymkul Dzhumana-zarov. *Mark Shearman*

Montreal Olympics, and they weren't the only ones. The *Dimanche Matin* in Canada carried an article about "the incredible weakness of our Canadian athletes", while the Australian and US governments called at the top of their political voices for a post-mortem. Just six golds for the US out of 37 events represented a very poor return, while Australia failed to pick up a single athletic medal at all – and just five (one silver and four gold) in the entire Games. What remarkable strides that sport-obsessed nation made in 24 years. At the Sydney Olympics, Australia won 58 medals (16 gold).

Red Smith's closing article in the *New York Times* summed up the fortnight. Had it all really been worth it? He seemed to think so. Just.

> It has been a crowded fortnight, loud with dispute, cluttered with untoward incidents like the dismissal of a Soviet fencer who was caught with a sword illegally wired, the disqualification of three athletes for using anabolic steroids and reports of death threats to the United States high jumper, Dwight Stones, and the Soviet sprinter, Valery Borzov.
>
> At the same time there were spectacular performances by athletes who set scores of world records and hundreds of Olympic standards. Capacity crowds paid scalper prices for tickets and gave every indication of loving it.
> On the TV screens appeared the words: "Adieu Montreal, à bientôt Moscow."

The party was over.

234

Race result:

Waldemar Cierpinski	GDR	2:09:55
Frank Shorter	USA	2:10:45
Karel Lismont	BEL	2:11:12
Donald Kardong	USA	2:11:15
Lasse Viren	FIN	2:13:10
Jerome Drayton	CAN	2:13:30
Leonid Moiseyev	URS	2:13:33
Franco Fava	ITA	2:14:24
Aleksandr Gozki	URS	2:15:34
Hendrik Schoofs	BEL	2:15:52

Sources:

Conversations with Bill Rodgers.

Anderson, Dave, in the *New York Times*, August 1st, 1976.

Hauman, Riël, *Century of the Marathon*. Human & Rousseau, 1996.

Hill, Ron, *The Long Hard Road. Part II: To The Peak And Beyond*. Ron Hill Sports Ltd., 1983.

Kardong, Don, in *Runner's World*, September 1976.

Martin, David and Roger Gynn, *The Olympic Marathon*. Human Kinetics, 2000.

Sandrock, Michael, *Running with the Legends*. Human Kinetics, 1996.

Smith, Red, in the *New York Times*, July 15th & 31st and August 2nd, 1976.

Wallechinsky, David, *The Complete Book of the Olympics*. Aurum Press, 2000.

XXVII

No. 24 – 1980 Boston Marathon [Women]

Monday, April 21st

"For every shining fortune lurks the shadow of a lie." – Orson Welles,
Citizen Kane

The saga of the women's Boston Marathon of 1980 is not a pretty one; but after seven days and 23 hours of confusion, dismay, dishonesty, tears, tantrums and exhaustive investigation, a French Canadian named Jacqueline Gareau was crowned Boston champion. Come across a Canadian runner today – a quarter of a century on – and ask him or her what the name Jackie Gareau means to them, and you will hear stories about a distinguished survivor, someone as straight as the proverbial arrow with an instinctive understanding of what is right and proper, and how to behave on any occasion. How ironic then, that on Monday, April 21st, 1980, Gareau crossed swords with someone as crooked as the San Andreas Fault.

But before we speak of the *non-genuine*, what of the genuine protagonists for the 1980 Boston Marathon? To be sure it was another excellent field, with 37 women dipping under the 3-hour mark. To illustrate just how quickly women's marathoning had progressed, five years earlier just seven women broke 3 hours, and 24 years later, at the 2004 Boston, a pitiful 22 broke 3 hours. There were two outstanding candidates for the gold medal: the quiet, humble Gareau, and the brash, streetwise, ex junk-food addict Patti Lyons, who one day would become the first American woman to break 2:30. Lyons' Boston record makes for garish reading: second in 1979. Sniff. Second in 1980. Gulp. Second in 1981. Snivel. This may have been a woman who loved to win, but more often than not she found herself having a good cry.

The life and times of Jacqueline Gareau, a quiet, mousy, diminutive 5 foot 2 inch, 100-pound nurse, weren't so far removed. After college, Gareau moved to the swinging city of Montreal where a keep-fit, stay-healthy attitude to life ranks low on the inhabitants' priorities. Gareau studied respiratory technology, kept irregular hours, attended late-night parties and smoked half a pack a day. Like Bill Rodgers she quit the cigarettes when she saw their effect on hospital patients.

With defending champion Joan Benoit absent from the field, recovering from an appendectomy, along with that untouchable streak of "Northern Lightning"

Grete Waitz, Gareau was wistful, almost dreamy at the start: "I suppose the laurel wreath would look good on me."

Gareau's race day started as it would continue: in complicated chaos. Making one last nervous dash into the bushes for a final pit stop before the noonday gun, she arrived at the start line just a minute or so early. An official bunged her in with the 2:50 brigade. "They don't have my time here," Gareau protested. "They're slower." Annoyed, the official threatened to bar her from the race if she tried to move forward.

"OK," she conceded, "OK." As the gun blasted Bill Rodgers off for his fourth Boston victory, Gareau stood still, her watch spewing priceless seconds out into oblivion. Finally the crowd of runners started moving and Gareau started a manic 5-mile slalom, desperately seeking to catch a glimpse of her female competitors among this annoying throng of incompetent, inferior male wannabes.

Rule number one in marathoning is not to start too fast, *especially* if it is hot. It was decidedly warm, the mercury rising into the 70s. But Gareau had no choice. She wove and bobbed and weaved. After two miles she overtook Gilles Lapierre, a Montreal banker who was Gareau's confidant and manager. "Whuh??!" he exclaimed. What the heck was Jackie doing so far back? He vociferously urged her on. Finally, between the fifth and sixth miles, Gareau caught sight of her prey and overtook home-town favourite Patti Lyons and Ellison Goodall, a fine American collegiate runner, but not expected to be a contender here.

Kathrine Switzer watched proceedings from the press bus. She held up her index finger and flashed a grin at Gareau. "You're number one", she shouted.

Lyons fixated her stare on Gareau, her overwhelming determination convincing herself that Gareau was "catchable, definitely catchable". But the miles passed and Lyons could not get the stubborn 150-yard gap to lessen. The two ran, to terrific applause and cheers, in lock step. They ran a hard, honest, absorbing race. And then something funny happened.

At 25½ miles, just when the frenzy should have been at its most extreme, where crowd control was at its most precarious and the booze-fuelled holiday crowds at their most raucous, they quieted. The two leaders dashed by, but only to polite, sympathetic applause. "You're second," a man called to Gareau. But she knew she was first.

A few minutes earlier an impatient woman named Rosie Ruiz from New York City, whose company was expecting great things of her because she had fibbed she was a good marathoner, had stood in Kenmore Square, a mile from the finish. The nuances of marathoning were foreign to Ruiz as she watched 25 runners go by, then 125, then 175. All were men. But Ruiz didn't notice this, and she didn't want her company to think she'd had a bad run. So she slipped in amongst the athletes and started trotting. A few metres down the road, the leaning crowds, eager for the first lady started cheering. "The first cheers legitimized the others" (Derderian).

After around six minutes of this phoney charade, with deafening roars in her ears, Ruiz blundered straight over the finish line and into a policeman's arms. The only official television camera on the women's race was at the finish, and the sight of Ruiz bumbling down the straight would be almost comical were it not for the fact that she was disgracefully robbing another highly trained and dedicated

No sweat: wearing a heavy t-shirt, displaying irregular sweat patterns and having just 'smashed' the American record, Rosie Ruiz, the 50th seeded runner in the race, is given a police escort to the victory podium. *Bettmann/CORBIS*

athlete of the greatest moment of her life. Granted Ruiz looks exhausted and lacking in rhythm on the footage, as a marathoner might; but this was because i) six minutes was a long time for her to run and she was thus tired; and ii) she wasn't a naturally gifted runner: an awkward, heavy-legged action was her style. It wasn't up to the policeman into whose arms Ruiz collapsed to ask questions. His role was to hoist her into the arms of BAA officials, who in turn hoisted her – no questions asked – straight up on to the victory platform, such is Boston tradition.

Three minutes later and a highly perplexed Gareau arrived...to no welcome party. She looked up to the victory platform and saw men's champ Bill Rodgers standing on the victory podium, and close by a woman she'd never seen in her life – in a heavy yellow T-shirt with irregular sweat patterns for someone who'd just smashed the course record on a very hot day. It wasn't just Gareau who was bemused. Bill Rodgers was a careful student of his sport and he knew not this 130 pound, 5 foot 8 inch woman, who shared his platform.

The television shots later of Rodgers sitting at a press conference are a delight. There he sits, when Ruiz comes and joins him. At the best of times, Rodgers has a wide-eyed, vacant, staring expression, with more than a hint of surprise and confusion. But now he was dumbfounded for real. "What time did you run?" he asked Ruiz. "2:31" came the reply. Rodgers double-takes, blinks, shakes his head in shock, and says "whew!" under his breath. Either he's sitting next to a miracle, or else someone's having him on. Ruiz' time would have broken Joan Benoit's

239

course record by more than three minutes and would rank as the world's third fastest ever.

Gareau meanwhile felt frustrated, fatigued and stupid. No one would talk to her. All the reporters buzzed around Ruiz. Gareau just wanted to board a plane and head back home. She hadn't been racing long and had no idea how to launch a protest. She thought in fast, furious French, but articulate English was evasive. She would later comment:

> It was around 18 miles that I realized I'd win. At the 18th mile I put my finger up in the air as a sign to the spectators: 'Am I first?' They said yes. By that time, I knew Lyons was behind me but I didn't know exactly where. At the finish I was a little surprised. I was curious about who the other girl was. But then I just said to myself I was proud about my own timing. I was a little disappointed, since, after all I thought I was first.
>
> I was much more disappointed later, when it became clear that it might all be a big joke. I felt I'd at least like the honour, the recognition. I felt I deserved it. If she'd run fairly it wouldn't have bothered me; I'd still have been proud of my own achievement. But if she is not the winner, then that really makes me a little angry. It is after all moving to win; it would have been moving for me. I would have liked it.

Tom Derderian explains how reporters could be duped into thinking Ruiz was kosher:

> It was *possible*, if unexpected, that someone with a number like W50 could win. To win the 1926 race Johnny Miles had come out of nowhere, but he had been the last unknown to do so, 50-some years ago. In the fairly new sport of women's marathon racing, though, a new star could fall from out of nowhere. Someone with an accomplished track or cross-country background could be new to the marathon but have run an easy qualifying race and then go all-out in Boston.

Race reporter and pioneer of women's running Kathrine Switzer asked Ruiz how many miles she ran per week. "Sixty-five," came the reply. Somewhat less than Rodgers' 140. "Are you doing a lot of intervals," Switzer quizzed. "What's an interval?" In a famous refrain Charlie Rodgers, brother of Bill, needed no persuading this was a fraud: "The first thing I did was look at her legs, and I said to myself, 'Uh, oh, we have a problem here.' I mean it was cellulite city." Meanwhile third place Patti Lyons stood off to the side and shook her head. "Another Oscar Miranda," she muttered.[1]

It was down to race director Will Cloney, who had been involved with the Boston Marathon gratis since 1931, and director since 1947, to investigate the matter with a cool, objective head while all around him were losing theirs. "She's

---

1. Oscar Miranda was a disgraced 53-year-old runner from the year before who won the Masters' division in 2:16:53, a time that officials realized he couldn't possibly have run and so disqualified him.

a thief, 'n' a cheat, 'n' a fraud," spluttered old Jock Semple, in charge of race admissions since 1955; while Cloney, meanwhile, just quietly went about interviewing a hundred witnesses. Attorney and BAA Governor William B. Tyler warned Cloney to tread with extreme care since Ruiz was both a woman and a minority. The lawsuits could fly. Author David Blaikie writes:

> Will Cloney reeled in the disaster that the eighty-fourth Boston Marathon had become. In the half century he had been part of the marathon, years that included Les Pawson and Tarzan Brown, and John Kelley "the Elder" and "John the Younger", years of foreign domination when even a starving Greek runner, Stylianos Kyriakides, outran the best America could muster, and the years of the modern boom which had swamped the marathon with unmanageable numbers and given rise to a carping new class of elite runners critical of the old way of doing things, through all this and more Cloney had encountered nothing to prepare him for the havoc wreaked by Rosie Ruiz.

Before Gareau could return to the airport the reporters swarmed her for a statement. "I supposed I was first, then I arrived at the finish line," she said with plausible restraint. Cloney's own statement was a "masterpiece of spontaneous diplomacy":

> There is an obvious problem with the determination of the women's winner. At this moment we have no proof one way or the other that would cause us to reverse the decision immediately. But we will try to do everything possible within the next week to check whether there was a discrepancy. If this proves to be the case we will invalidate the final results and adjust the places accordingly. If the medal had not already been awarded it would have been held up. I have not talked to the young lady in question. I have no reason to accuse her of anything. We do have grave doubts.

* * *

The media coverage of the fiasco was of course exhaustive, with the saga hitting the headlines all over America and beyond. The next day the *Boston Herald* published a photo of the start of the race with the headline: "Win $1,000: Find Rosie in this photo." The jokes started flying. Have you seen the Rosie Ruiz panty hose? Guaranteed not to run. Why did Ruiz do so much better in Boston than New York? Better transit system there.

Tuesday, April 22nd's *Boston Globe* carried the headline:

> Rodgers leaves no doubt – he is King of the road...but the Queen
> gets sceptical looks.

John Powers wrote:

> Her name is Rosie Ruiz, and she came out of nowhere. Thousands of spectators including the Governor of the Commonwealth saw her cross the finish line at 2.31.56 yesterday afternoon. But nobody seems to have seen her at any of the

official checkpoints...not Montreal's Jacqueline Gareau, who thought she had won the women's race, and not West Roxbury's Patti Lyons, who thought she had come in second.

"I really didn't expect to win," Ruiz admitted. "I came across in 2.31, that's all I have to say. I know I ran the course. I did the best I can. What else can I say? How would you feel? To be sincere this is a dream."

Patti Lyons certainly had her doubts: "I never saw her, her name isn't familiar, never heard of her," insisted Lyons. "I heard I was second. It wasn't until I came in here that I found out I wasn't. Do I doubt that she was the winner? I doubt it now. I doubt it very much." Serge Arsenault, the director of the Montreal marathon and a close friend of Gareau, who was at her side during the run, explained:

> Jackie said, "OK I won it and what can I do?" She felt alone. "I just won the Boston Marathon, at least I think I did, and I am completely alone." She's so naïve, and she loves the sport so much. She said, "all I wanted to do was to get to meet Bill Rodgers, to shake hands with him and give him a kiss, then sit next to him and talk to the newspaper men."
>
> She was lost and afraid. I asked her whether she wanted me to file a formal protest with race officials and she said, do whatever you want, I'm completely lost. I don't know what to do. She was sorry and ashamed a bit...for her sport that something like this could happen. She felt stupid, standing there alone in a cold garage, listening to the sportscasters asking their questions and listening to the girl's stupid answers. She said, 'For two years I have dreamed of this moment, and now all I get to do is go back to the *Sheridan* for a beer, just like all the other 5,000 runners."

The *Globe* headline dealing specifically with the women's race read:

> Ruiz wins no sweat – and that's what raises the question.

Powers continued:

> If it was a fraud, Ruiz pulled it off with a nonchalance that would have done justice to Redford and Newman in *The Sting*. She accepted the laurel wreath and champion's medal from Governor Edward King at the outdoor victory stand, then proceeded to the underground garage, where she posed with Bill Rodgers and answered reporters' questions for nearly half an hour. Although the temperature had been in the 70s, she was barely perspiring.

"No salt stains?" wondered New York Marathon director Fred Lebow. "Her hair in place? Her sides? Dry?"

The *Globe* reported even the unflappable Will Cloney somewhat losing his cool:

> I am thoroughly disgusted that for the second year in a row there is a doubt about a race involving sportsmen and sportswomen. If this is the state of

amateur athletics, it's pretty deplorable. "If it's true that she didn't win, it not only disturbs me, it distresses me. Why are we knocking ourselves out to put on this race? So many people have worked so hard for so long to put on a good race. That's hard enough without something like this. If it's true, the person I feel sorriest for is Jackie Gareau.

Race "spotters" for the TV station WGBH Toni Reavis, Gayle Barron and Kathy Switzer never saw Ruiz at any time. Reavis, who had a radio show devoted to running and was positioned at the 13-mile mark with Barron, was explicit: "We didn't miss any 'W's' and we saw the first 15 women go by. We never saw her. Kathy Switzer was with the women the whole way. She drove six or seven minutes in front to make sure she was following the lead woman. She kept asking spectators and they kept saying no, no, the first woman isn't here."

Newshounds tracked down many runners who were astonished by the news that Ruiz won. "I went out in 54 mins for the first 10 miles," said Jeff Clark of Costa Mesa, California. "I faded and ran 2:36. The only two girls who passed me were Jacqueline and Patti. When Jacqueline went past me between 22 and 23 miles, the crowd was yelling that she was the first woman." And then there was crucial testimony from Robert Rozesky of New Waterford, Ohio: "I started in the sixth row of runners and heard a 70.15 split at halfway," he said, before finishing four seconds behind Ruiz (and was next in line). "The only woman I saw was in a wheelchair and she was getting big applause. I didn't hear any applause up ahead. No woman passed me. I know that."

Friday's *Boston Globe* reported on the previous day's "trial by media" that Ruiz attended. Did she remember a single landmark in the first 20 miles of the race? "I remember houses and churches," she said, fingering the Boston Marathon gold medal around her neck, "and some twisting roads. "No one waved to me that I was first. Maybe they thought I was a boy. I wish now I had taken the names of those around me." Ruiz said she trained only 15 weeks for her "remarkable" run, "around Central Park during my lunch hour and sometime in the mornings, but that running is not my profession." "I think just because I am not a well-known runner no one was looking for me," she continued. "I know I ran the whole Boston race. I don't have to prove myself innocent."

Malcolm Robinson, a marathoner and a writer for *New York Running News* was certain that Ruiz was not telling the truth. At the press conference he held up a photocopy of the notes he took during the marathon. Robinson charted the first 13 women to pass him at the 22-mile mark. The notes were initialled by BAA official Jock Semple.

"You aren't on this list, and I know every woman runner around."

"Maybe you and others didn't see the 'W' before my number. It moved up and down you know," Ruiz countered.

Paul Fletcher, a veteran of 100 marathons ran in his tenth Boston in 1980. He said Ruiz came over to him a little beyond the finish: "It was obvious she hadn't run a marathon. Her face was not even flushed. Her eyes were white and clear." Nina Kuscsik, head of the New York runners rules committee and the very first official Boston winner said: "Women runners' especially have laboured long to win acceptance, and along comes something that gives women less credit than

On with the waterworks: Ruiz faces a sceptical press the day after the race. "I'm as confused as you," she said. *Bettmann/CORBIS*

they deserve. I think a real runner knows that finishing the whole race is the truly important thing, not what order you finish."

* * *

Ruiz met with Cloney on the Monday a week later and commented:

I can't blame people for saying that I didn't finish the race. The facts are stacked against me. I've been trying to duck people all week long. There are so much more important things going in the world than this thing happening to me, such as the danger of World War III. I've spent one whole damn week of running from one place to another because of this. I feel it's something I've earned.

I feel Mr Cloney will do everything he can to get to the truth. I feel positive after our meeting. He's a very kind and compassionate person. He invited me to return for next year's BAA marathon even if I don't have the necessary qualifying time. And I will come back to Boston.

Asked if she would return her winner's medal if her victory was invalidated, Ruiz emphatically replied, "No, I told Mr Cloney I wouldn't give back the medal."

Cloney countered that he was convinced that Ruiz, "sincerely believes in her own mind that she won the race. Ours was a very friendly and helpful discussion. I wanted her to understand what the situation was, but I didn't want to put her through an inquisition." The main evidence Cloney came up with involved the fact that there wasn't any: nowhere in the entire marathon distance did any official checkpoint register the passage of W50. No journalist showed her on film until the finish. She did not appear in any one of the 10,000 frames taken by the official race photographers. After a week's exhaustive investigation Cloney eventually disqualified Ruiz from his race. But she never did confess, and the $300 medal encrusted with a diamond stud remains hers to this day.

On the day that Hollywood's master of suspense and artist of anxiety, Alfred Hitchcock, died peacefully aged 80, Gareau was in turn relieved of her suspense and anxiety and finally crowned with the laurel wreath. "I would rather hail Miss Gareau," said Cloney, "and do as much as possible to let Rosie fade into the background." "Is Rosie Ruiz a liar, a fraud, a cheat?" Cloney was asked. He replied:

I would never use those words for another human being. People want me to say that she came up with the intention of doing this. I don't believe that. If she did do anything wrong it was on the spur of the moment. I'm not a doc, a psychiatrist, or a psychologist. I wouldn't presume to figure it out. I'm convinced that Rosie thinks she ran the race and won the race. She is equally convinced, and this is a little bit strange, that our information is overwhelming. She is as baffled as we are.

Ruiz' final statement went as follows:

I'm afraid this thing will be with me for a long time, at least until my next race. I can truthfully and honestly say without hesitation that today has been the second saddest day of my life, only to be surpassed by the day I had to leave my father in my native country 18 years ago. I want to thank Mr. Cloney and all of the officials of the BAA from the bottom of my heart. I know they have deliberated for the past nine days and that they have taken every possible evidence for and against me and given it all careful consideration.

Jacqueline Gareau had to commute from Montreal to Boston no fewer than four times in all before finally being crowned champion. Cloney was congratulated on his fairness and tact and for safeguarding the prestige of the Boston Marathon. "It was worth it," said Gareau. "I visited with the Governor, Edward King, and he read a proclamation. Then we went to the Eliot Lounge and there was champagne and flowers and we sang, 'Oh Canada.' Tommy Leonard had always been so nice – like all the people in Boston. I can't really regret what happened, because Boston, the people are so nice there."

* * *

Rosie Ruiz is the classic example of someone caught up in the tenacious tentacles of their own lie. Ruiz' lie began five months before Boston at the 1979 New York City Marathon. Ruiz wanted to run at New York but the application deadline had passed. No problem: Ruiz pretended to have a brain tumour and claimed she might not live till next year. Sympathetic officials granted her entry. Ruiz used her fine finishing time in New York to gain the qualifying standard for Boston. Except she never ran the race.

The following day Ruiz' co-workers saw her high finish at New York and congratulated her. She did not deny finishing, even though she hadn't; of which more later. Her company then offered to pay her way to the Boston Marathon; perhaps she could really fly down Beantown's hills and bring yet more credit on the firm. Her boss told her he looked forward to seeing her name in the papers again, except this time, perhaps, even further up the leaderboard.

Born Maria Rosales in Havana, Cuba, Ruiz first came to the US in 1961. In 1973 and again in 1978 she underwent brain surgery for the removal of benign tumours. Her employers were a firm called Metal Traders, Inc., and she wore the letters MTI on the front of her give-away yellow shirt as she spoke to the press. There are so many overwhelming pieces of evidence of Ruiz' double-cross that it's not possible to go into them all in detail. But there are some witnesses who must be examined. Four in particular deserve close inspection: Jack Faulkner, a Harvard senior; Susan Morrow, a Manhattan knitwear designer; John Emptage, Ruiz' MTI boss; and, most damning of all, Steve Marek, a marriage counsellor from Lexington, Kentucky.

Faulkner

Jack Faulkner was standing on Commonwealth Avenue at around twenty past two on race day with a classmate, Sola Mahoney, around a mile and half from the finish line. Mahoney competed for the Harvard track team. David Blaikie writes:

> From where they stood it was less than a mile to the marathon finish line – a good vantage point and a good day to watch the runners go past. Bill Rodgers, the hometown hero, had just sailed by en route to his fourth Boston victory and Faulkner and Mahoney were waiting for a glimpse of the Canadian runner that radio announcers kept saying had taken a commanding lead in the women's division. Then a moment of commotion occurred that both would recall later.

"I saw something right across the street that was sort of strange," Faulkner said. "I saw a woman stumble out of the crowd. She looked like she wasn't a runner. Her arms were flying around. She was wearing a number. I didn't take her very seriously. I watched her stumble along the right side of the street. When the Canadian girl came by everybody thought she was the winner."

Mahoney remembered the woman, too.

> She was running in a very awkward manner, almost out of control. My feeling was that nobody was taking any notice. Nobody was applauding. She did, in fact, have a number. I said to my friend, "Is this for real?"
>
> When the Canadian girl came by everybody thought she was the winner. I went home knowing a Canadian girl had won. I picked up the *New York Times* and the *Globe* this morning and saw the picture of the girl that came out of the crowd. I can't believe she was still recognized as the winner. What happened was so obvious, that's what prompted my call to the *Globe*.

Morrow

In television interviews Susan Morrow comes across as articulate, intelligent and eminently believable. Her story is of meeting Ruiz on the New York subway the previous November. A Manhattan knitwear designer and freelance photographer, Morrow was startled when she saw Ruiz had won Boston on the evening of the race. Impossible, thought Morrow. After all, this was the woman whom Morrow remembered meeting on the subway the day of the New York Marathon, while the race was still in progress. "She was wearing, you know, just a number," recalled Morrow to journalist Kevin Paul Dupont sixteen years later. "She looked like a marathon runner. Turns out, she was a psycho."

246

Morrow met Ruiz when they got on the subway at West Fourth Street in Greenwich Village. Ruiz, said Morrow, told her that she had withdrawn from the race after about 10 miles, hindered by a twisted ankle. They then got off the subway at Columbus Circle and walked together toward the Central Park finish line, Ruiz in pursuit of medical attention and Morrow "thrilled by the sights and sounds that surrounded the first marathon she ever had attended" (Dupont).

"By a fluke, a miracle, whatever, I ended up a foot from where the runners came in – it ended up one of the peak experience days of my life. I've gone to many marathons since then and I've never gotten anywhere near the finish line like that." The key to Morrow's passport to this behind-the-scenes vantage point was, of course, Ruiz. Repeatedly coming up against police barricades, Ruiz would identify herself and her companions as runners and the women would be allowed to pass. A volunteer then ripped the bar code off Ruiz and placed it on the finishers' spindle.

It was on the grounds of Morrow's testimony that New York race director Fred Lebow reviewed all his finish-line footage from around that time of the race (2:56:31) and found no sign of Ruiz. He disqualified her, giving Boston race director Will Cloney an easy way out, since Ruiz' very entry into Boston was fraudulent. Cloney chose not to take it.

Morrow and Ruiz had made tentative plans to meet up for lunch after the marathon. One day Morrow got a telephone message from a Rosie. Thinking it was another friend, Morrow returned the call and was surprised to get Ruiz. "Oh Rosie, it's you...I was expecting someone else." "Huh! Forgotten me already have you?!" Ruiz snapped back. Whoa, thought Morrow, this isn't something I want to get into. And the two never did meet up for lunch. Morrow wishes she'd had her camera on her that day of the NYC Marathon. "I could have made thousands and thousands of dollars selling her picture," she sighs.

Emptage

Ruiz' boss at the time was John Emptage, the president and CEO of Metal Traders, Inc. The *Boston Sunday Globe* tracked him down to Amagansett, New York, in 1996, where he was the owner of several businesses. As one might expect, there was tremendous excitement in the office on the day of Ruiz' win.[2] "We're all in there, with the radios blaring," said Emptage, who at the time oversaw an office of some 40 employees. "And then we hear the winner: 'Rosie Ruiz from New York City.' It was crazy. Everyone was jumping up and down. All was wonderful. Rosie comes back, wearing her crown into the office, and everyone was really thrilled for her. "All of a sudden, though, the phones start ringing...the questions."

Emptage decided to give Ruiz paid leave to redeem herself. There would soon be another marathon in upstate New York. Go and train, he said. And prove you can run. "I felt I was going above and beyond, for her to get back to a competitive

---

2. Patriot's Day is only a holiday in Massachusetts, the rest of the country is at work.

level. I said, 'Look, you go run the race, and whatever it takes to do the job here in the office, we'll cover for you. But, Rosie, you run that race...and I don't care what your time is, but *finish* the race.' She said she would and, well, exit stage left."

Shortly thereafter, said Emptage, Ruiz came back and said she couldn't run, she had a bad ankle. Her biggest mistake was telling Emptage that she had been training on the roads of Montauk, the same route that Emptage frequently ran. But he had never seen her when he was out pounding the tarmac, and he was a keen runner. "The thing about being a marathon runner is, you're running five or six days a week. People see you everywhere. They think you're nuts, out of your mind, because that's all you do, run. So when she said Montauk, I said, 'Gee, Rosie, tell me where you're running out there.' And she couldn't. Right there I knew this isn't going the way it ought to go."

His trust gone, Emptage fired Ruiz. He simply couldn't have someone like her in the back office making large cash movements. Emptage talks movingly about what it might've been that drove Ruiz to her folly:

> As I saw it, she wanted to be part of the "in" group at the office, and running was her attempt of being accepted. It was a fun, spirited group we had, everyone young and everyone running. There were corporate running challenges the whole summer; close to 100 companies had people running. It was a girl trying to break through – the wrong way, obviously. The sad part was, the company was very accepting – we had people who didn't run well. So what? That was OK. They found their fun with it.
>
> But Rosie got caught up with all this crazy-ass lying and then she couldn't get out of it. I expect it changed her whole life.

Marek

The most damning evidence of all comes from the offbeat world of Steve Marek, a rival race promoter to Fred Lebow, who originally stepped into the fray as Ruiz' only supporter. Marek, who used to attend races dressed up as Superman, claims he waved to Ruiz at the start of the Boston Marathon and saw her again at the finish.

> I can't say what she did in between because I didn't see her. Maybe she ran it, maybe she ran it in her head. If she ran New York in 2:56, I tend to think it is possible she finished Boston in 2:31. I think she is innocent until proven guilty. But I realize there is strong evidence that she did not run the whole race. Maybe she didn't run, maybe she is a cheat, but people have not treated her like a human being. We don't plan a lawsuit at this time, but we haven't ruled it out.

Marek had himself been the subject of controversy. On his 1978 entry form for the New York Marathon, Marek estimated that his best time for a marathon was 2:58:10. But when asked again at Boston he said 5:58. Then why put 2.58 in New York? "I meant to put 5.58."

Halfway through the 1978 New York Marathon, Marek dropped out and got in a car with a colleague, Rosalie Princeball. According to Princeball, he drove with her to the finish then said he wanted to get out and check on some members of his road running club. "He was wearing that superman outfit," said Patricia Owens, an organizer of the New York Marathon, and he crossed the finish line. "We subsequently banned him from any of our races."

A marriage counsellor in Lexington, Kentucky since 1983, Marek told the *Globe* in 1996 that Ruiz eventually revealed to him some six to nine months after the race, that she had indeed sneaked into the Marathon in its final stages. According to Marek, Ruiz doused herself with water to make it look as if she were perspiring, then entered the race between Kenmore Square and the finish line. "She jumped out of the crowd, not knowing that the first woman hadn't gone by yet," said Marek. "Believe me, she was as shocked as anyone when she come in first. But at that point they had put the crown on her, gave her the medal and told her she's the winner. How could she say, 'No I'm not'?"

Marek remembers saying to Ruiz months later, " 'Obviously, you didn't run it.' And she looked at me and said, 'I'm embarrassed to say it – why do I have to tell you?' It was something much like that, to paraphrase, 'I don't have to tell you, Steve; I think you know.' " It is believed that Marek is the only person in 25 years to say publicly that Ruiz admitted taking the infamous short cut. Marek goes on to defend Ruiz to some degree:

Let's face it, the BAA did a poor job of monitoring the female side of the race up till Rosie ran. Really, they didn't give a poop what the ladies did. I have to say, though, that Will Cloney was a wonderful man through it all. I was there when he wanted the medal back, but Rosie was adamant – she really believed at that point, I think, that she had run it. And Will said to her, 'Go ahead, keep it honey, that's OK.' He looked at me and winked, as if to say, 'Look she's had enough trouble, let her go.'

* * *

Stealing the medal is a bad enough misdemeanour in itself, but far worse is what Ruiz stole from Gareau, who so dedicated herself to her sport. This was Gareau's first Boston run, and her eighth marathon overall in a progression that has seen her run a 2.57 in Buffalo in 1978, a 2:47 in Ottawa, a 2:40 to win Montreal the previous August, and a 2:39 for third in NYC in October 1979. She would in the future go on to run as fast as 2:29. On the feeling of crossing the line in first, Joan Benoit – winner from the previous year – commented: "It's all in one minute, or one second or a couple of seconds. You say 'I did it.' It's all captured in an instant. The thrill of a lifetime. Now Jackie Gareau will never know that feeling, unless she wins it again. Although I'm sure Billy Rodgers will tell you it's the first one you savour most."

One thing Gareau was in sport was a true fighter. A cross-country skier, Gareau once decided to enter the daunting 100-mile Canadian Ski Marathon from Lachute, Quebec, to Ottawa. On her first attempt, the wrong kind of wax on her skis slowed her, and unsympathetic officials forced her to stop just 10 miles from the finish because she missed a checkpoint deadline by a matter of minutes. The second year Gareau did finish, in horrendous conditions at that. David Blaikie writes:

> The thermometer plunged to thirty-five below Fahrenheit and the wind chill pushed the effective reading dangerously below that. Gareau was the only woman to finish and it took all her strength. Trouble occurred late in the race when the phenomenon known as honking – fatigue, dizziness, the sense of impending collapse – overcame her. Instinct told her to eat and she dug a handful of nuts, dates and chocolate from her pocket.

"My strength came back instantly. I just couldn't believe the change. I thought to myself, I just saved my own life."

For a woman this dedicated, tough, hard-working and modest to have the thrill of a lifetime stolen from her by a dishonest scam-artist is indeed a gross miscarriage of justice. What explanations are there for Ruiz' refusal to come clean? A Dr Daniel Goleman suggests Ruiz slipped into a lacuna, "a black hole of the mind, diverting attention from select bits of subjective reality – specifically, certain bits of anxiety-evoking information." Ruiz apparently repressed the memory of not running. She "forgot she didn't run the race, and then forgot she forgot" (Derderian).

Writers Sam Merrill and Marc Bloom of *The Runner* magazine visited Ruiz at her apartment that summer and found her intelligent and charming. They decided Ruiz was a sociopath. They wrote: "She intended to do exactly what she did in both the New York and Boston marathon and had even told her mother before Boston that she had to win it. She had acted rationally, with no commonly accepted symptoms of psychosis – no neurotic anxiety or unease in situations that would unsettle the average person, no sense of responsibility, guilt, regret, or shame." Merrill and Bloom saw a woman with poor judgement, who failed to learn from experience of punishment. "Not only did Rosie Ruiz not follow the rules, she could not even see them" (Derderian).

In the following years, Ruiz was charged with writing bad cheques totalling $1000 to New York department stores. In 1982 she was arrested on charges of grand larceny and forgery for stealing $15,000 in cash and $45,000 in cheques from her employer. In 1983 she was caught dealing high-grade cocaine worth $52,000.

* * *

Twenty-three years later, Bill Rodgers spoke to the author about what he remembered from the dramatic day of the 1980 Boston. His memories were still vivid:

> She was heavy, there was not enough sweat, and you wouldn't wear a shirt that long – you'd wear a singlet – it was a very hot day. But a lot of people and a lot of the BAA officials of the time were not runners – they did not really know what to look for and would not have been able to detect this – except for the runners in the room who started asking questions.
>
> My brother Charlie was in the room, and Fred Lebow said, "Something's

wrong". I thought it wasn't my job to say...I mean they found out – it was a whirlwind – an absolute whirlwind. You guys in the media – you smell blood!

But the thing was you know, a lot of the public believed that she won! Most people don't understand that someone could come in and cheat like that, they tend to say: "Well, she won, how do you know?" Because the story of how she cheated was kind of in the fine print months later.

I tried to talk to her and make her admit, and I could tell she was weakening, but I felt sorry for her – she was crying and all that. I said to her: "All the runners will respect you if you just say: 'I'm sorry I made a mistake.'"

As it is she must have had to change her name and suchlike – move to Florida. I mean this sort of thing ruins your *life*!

But what I always say, William, is that she's the most famous marathoner of all time!

Upon returning to the Centennial Boston of 1996, Gareau indicated that she bumped into Ruiz once more:

I saw her in Miami two or three years later, when I ran in a 10-kilometre race.

25 years to the day after the fiasco, the BAA invited a youthful-looking Jackie Gareau to re-enact the finishing moment that she had been denied. *BRIAN SNYDER/Reuters/Corbis*

She came up to me and said, 'Hi, I'm Rosie Ruiz.' She was there but she hadn't run the race. 'And I said, 'Why did you do that in Boston?' And she said, 'Oh, I did run it.' So hey, there's no way you're going to have a conversation with her, you know? Later I heard she got in trouble with drugs. I don't think she was on the right road.

*   *   *

In April 1998, with the Boston Marathon just two years from entering into its third century, Ruiz spoke to reporters. But it was the same old wan tale. Claiming she'd be back to Boston to run again in 2000, she told the *Palm Beach Post*: "I'm going to do it by the book." Not that she feels she didn't do it by the book before. She claimed she had collected photographs and other evidence from supporters to prove she ran the entire race on April 21st, 1980. Her "victory", she still insisted, was a "triumph" for women in sports. And her medal is tucked safely somewhere in South Florida, though she won't say where. "It hurts me to know I did something so good but got so many problems."

Unsurprisingly she was reluctant to go public with the evidence she claimed could clear her. Ruiz, then 44, went by the name of Rosie M. Vivas, the name she kept since August 1986 when her 2½-year marriage ended in divorce. She said she was a client representative for a medical lab company and was living in Tequesta, Florida. Ruiz claimed the short hairstyle she wore in 1980 may have caused officials to miss her when scanning the videotapes of the route – believing she was just another male runner. She blames being stripped of a medal on politics – saying people wanted the favourites to win, not an amateur.

"What I can promise myself and the American public who believes in me is to run again," Ruiz said in a written statement to the newspaper. "I may not win this time, but I will be there and I'll run again, the entire course just as before, except this time I'll be more prepared...I'll look just like any other runner. I'm sure they won't mistake me this time." Of course Ruiz never did run in the 2000 Boston, and as far as anyone knows, never did run another race after her 1980 ruse.

Bill Rodgers sums up with bittersweet irony: "Great for our sport, isn't it? Think of the two most famous marathoners – Phidippides and Rosie Ruiz. One dropped dead and the other was crazy..."

Race result:

J. Gareau	Quebec	2:34.28
P. Lyons	Boston, MA	2:35.08
G. Adams	Bromley, England	2:39.17
L. Binder	San Diego, CA	2:39.22
K. Samet	Albuquerque, NM	2:41.50
E. Goodall	Wellesley, MA	2:42:23

Sources:

Conversations with Bill Rodgers.

Blaikie, David, *Boston: the Canadian Story*. Seneca House Books, 1984.

Boston Herald, April 22nd, 1980.

Derderian, Tom, *Boston Marathon*. Human Kinetics, 1996.

Dupont, Kevin Paul. *Boston Sunday Globe*, April 14th, 1996.

Hauman, Riël, *Century of the Marathon*. Human & Rousseau, 1996.

Merrill, Sam and Marc Bloom, in *Runner Magazine*, July 1980.

Powers, John, in the *Boston Globe*, April 22nd, 1980.

Ruiz, Rosie, letter to *Palm Beach Post*, April 1998.

Semple, Jock, John J. Kelley, and Tom Murphy, *Just Call Me Jock*. Waterford
    Publishing Company, 1981.

XXVIII

No. 23 – 1978 Boston Marathon [Men]

Monday, April 17th

Boston Billy suffers his biggest scare.

There is a quick and simple test one can apply to find out how dedicated a runner is. Watch him at an airport while he passes the time before his flight. Does he follow the herd by relaxing in the terminal lounge, eating a danish and reading the funnies? Or does he lace on his running shoes and head outside for a quick scamper?

The bad news for Bill Rodgers as he sought to repeat his electrifying victory from the 1975 Boston Marathon in the closing moments of the 1978 race was that the man cutting into his lead with every stride was a fiercely religious Texan named Jeff Wells. "Oh, God," Rodgers thought. "He's going to beat me. He's a fanatic. He trains at *airports*." What Rodgers was omitting to tell himself was that Wells had only run at an airport (on the way back from the World Cross Country Championships in Edinburgh) because he had taken Rodgers' lead – as it was he who had initiated the run. It was Rodgers who was the fanatic; Wells just wanted to be with a runner he greatly admired – so he'd tagged along.

The character of Bill Rodgers is a paradox. How is it that this mild-mannered former schoolteacher with the surprised, distracted demeanour, the thatch of scruffy, overlong blond hair, and the limp handshake belonging to a man twice his age and half his strength, could turn into such a ferocious competitor on a race course?

Two anecdotes illustrate this point well, the first from Benji Durden, an American 2:09.59 marathoner who made the 1980 Olympic team. Durden explains: "Billy was a nice guy, except when he was racing. In a race, he became an animal and would do anything to beat you." Midway through the Wheeling 20K in 1979, Durden made a break on Rodgers and got a 100-metre lead. Durden recalls: "It was a nasty day, raining hard and windy. Billy caught up to me, looked over, and surged. I responded, then Billy surged again and I responded again. This went on for three miles. Finally, he looked over at me and growled. Just growled, 'Arrghhh!' and put on another surge, getting away from me with a mile to go. It had just pissed him off that I made him work so hard. Billy just never gave up."

When President Jimmy Carter boycotted US involvement in the 1980 Moscow Olympics, Rodgers for one was angry and spoke out against the decision. His views did not go unnoticed. One day in his running shop, a telephone call came through; the caller said that Bill Rodgers would not make it alive past Coolidge Corner in that year's marathon. The crowds were so large at Boston that they pressed right up against the runners. It would be easy for someone to conceal a gun. The State police decided they would form a phalanx of motorcycles around Rodgers the entire race – which made it impossible to gain access to water on a 70-degree day. Rodgers had to contend with both the distance and his own disintegrating body. Tom Derderian sums up Rodgers' suffering, but also what a supreme competitor he was:

> On the brink of collapse he felt oddly invincible. As is true for many in this state of extremity, a little craziness possessed him. After hours of pushing at the ragged edge of oxygen debt, he detached from the real world to live in one of pulse, push, and rhythm. In his imagination he taunted the assassin: Come on, you son of a bitch. Like many runners before him Rodgers would have socked anyone who interfered with his running, even someone with a gun.

*　*　*

Bill Rodgers was born on December 23rd, 1947, and became a fine runner in high school at Newington, Connecticut. He was recruited by other talented runners to attend Wesleyan College near by, where his room-mate was a dedicated junior called Amby Burfoot. While Burfoot put together dozens of 25-milers in his dedicated build-up to the 1968 Boston Marathon, Rodgers would tag along for just the final few miles. When Burfoot returned to college after weekend visits home, he looked for evidence of room-mate Billy perhaps having done some training. But the main evidence he'd find would be merely of drinking and smoking. It would frustrate Burfoot, therefore, that when Rodgers did tag along for the Sunday run he'd do so effortlessly, floating along, looking around him absent-mindedly, while Burfoot, with furrowed brow, had to concentrate on every step. Burfoot went on to score an emotional win at Boston 1968, while still in college, and went on to become a leading running author and US editor of *Runner's World*.

No one describes the inimitable Rodgers style better than Jim Fixx in his iconic book, *The Complete Book of Running*, an enormous seller in the late 1970s when the running boom was in its heyday. Fixx once shared a run with Rodgers after he had become world-class, and asked him to demonstrate what race pace was like. As Rodgers accelerated, Fixx writes:

> His arms rock back and forth effortlessly, his gloved hands as loose as laundry on a clothesline. With each step his legs cover so much pavement that I take three steps for every two of his. Now, for the first time, his shoes make a faint sound, a feathery *whooshwhoosh*.
>
>   I notice that he is not breathing hard, and it occurs to me that I am running a foot or so from one of the most perfect cardiovascular systems on earth. If you were to ask a particularly cunning engineer to invent a two-legged machine expressly for running, he would no doubt come up with something very much like Rodgers.

256

The world, however, came very close to never seeing this superb engine in action. After college, Rodgers became an unhappy, aimless drifter. Securing himself conscientious-objector status from the Vietnam War, he got a job shifting dead bodies around a hospital. He soon got fired though for organizing a demonstration. Tom Derderian writes: "Rodgers smoked Winstons. He borrowed money to buy a used 650-cc Triumph motorcycle. He would buy half a pint of gin, a mixer, and some cashew nuts and ride around. Bill spent a long time unemployed; he was in turn aimless, happy, confused, angry and frustrated. He wandered between rebellion and destitution, like many from the graduating classes of 1970."

Quitting running after Wesleyan was seen as no big deal, explains brother Charlie: "There wasn't much logic to continuing running. Even in high school you were some kind of fruitcake if you ran, like you were naked in the wind. Nobody else did it; there were no cheerleaders or anything like that. So to drop out of it was no problem" (Sandrock). Rodgers describes the "shazam!" moment in 1971 when it occurred to him how much he missed running: "I can recall being down in Provincetown, Mass., sitting there smoking and thinking, 'This can't be it. This just can't be it. There has to be something more to life than drinking and smoking.' That's what drove me out of it."

Rodgers enjoyed watching old friends he knew like Olympian Jeff Galloway place highly at the 1971 Boston, and two years later he was at the start line himself, with a raw hunger to see how high he himself could place in the famous race. He promptly bombed out, told himself he'd never be a really top-level runner and quit for two months. But then he tentatively returned. Fifty-mile weeks became 70s, which became 90s which became 110s. He raced bravely with the leaders in 1974 at Boston, and found himself in fourth quite deep into the race, before losing his grip and finishing fourteenth.

Rodgers, though, was an out-and-out runner now, with a respectable teaching job to match. Far behind him were his loafing days. He trained tremendously hard over the next year, forever working on his strength and speed. His breakthrough race came after he qualified for the International Cross-Country Championships in 1975, where Rodgers pulled the mother of all blinders and "flew through the 12K in one of the best races of his career" (Sandrock). He placed third – only getting out-kicked in the final 100-metres. Rodgers' warmdown that day was an amazing 7-miles – after he'd just proved himself to be one of the finest runners in the world.

Although close observers of the sport knew Rodgers to be a class apart going into the 1975 Boston, most just saw him as a talented local runner. In his customary floppy gardening gloves and a hand-lettered T-shirt with "BOSTON GBTC" (Greater Boston Track Club) written on it in huge letters and his race number stuck on wonky, Rodgers took on a handful of more established stars like Ron Hill, Jerome Drayton and Tom Fleming...and left them for dust. Rodgers cruised along in his carefree daze, aided by a beauty of a breeze from the southwest. Running sub-5-minute miles so smoothly "looked like a lark" to brother Charlie watching from the press van. And after yelling "Billy, slow down, are you nuts?" in the race's early stages, Charlie was soon vowing never to question his younger brother again. As Rodgers relieved Frank Shorter of his American record that day (2:09:55), his life changed for ever.

257

* * *

The big news before the 1978 Boston was that Frank Shorter – Olympic gold and silver medallist from the '72 and '76 Games – was to make his first appearance in the race. Shorter had previously complained about Boston's policy of not paying runners' expenses to run in their race. Boston maintained they didn't have to. They were the world's most prestigious footrace outside of the Olympics; athletes should be more than happy to pay their way. Shorter disagreed with that, but deep down this was a man who liked to win races, and Boston was the only big race he hadn't won.

Things had not gone completely Rodgers' way since his 1975 humdinger. He'd endured an excruciating Olympic marathon, where from towing the field through the early stages he had stumbled home in 40th place with foot problems. He had then bounced back to crucify Shorter by three minutes in New York; but then had to drop out of the '77 Boston race, falling foul of his greatest enemy – heat.

But if there was one thing that inspired Rodgers to race well, it was a bad race. As Amby Burfoot said: "Bill was particularly devastating after a bad race; you didn't want to run against him then." Indeed, Rodgers then went on to startle the road racing scene by winning New York again (by almost 2½ minutes), and just six weeks later would toe the line at Fukuoka and triumph by 62 seconds in a fine 2:10.55.

But Boston was the one he wanted most. And for the 1978 race, Derderian writes: "He had resolved after the previous year's race never to run a marathon unprepared, and for this one he had prepared unmercifully." Questioned about his readiness, Rodgers replied chillingly: "No, not as ready as I could be. I'm a little leery of the distance because I've only averaged 133 miles a week over the last ten weeks." (His average mileage for the ten weeks before Boston '75 was 122).

The first major development of the race came from Canada's Drayton who bowed out at 3½ miles due to a leg niggle. Quickly following this, Shorter, tested his fitness with a surge at 5 miles, which Rodgers covered. Shorter, less of a world-class marathoner by now – and somewhat more of an entrepreneur businessman – died from the front. The lead pack came down to a battle of three: New Zealander Kevin Ryan, "Flying Finn" Esa Tikkanen and Rodgers. Then came the hunters, chasing them down. These included Jeff Wells, who had great track speed and had defeated Rodgers at the International Cross-Country Championships the month before. At 17 miles Rodgers made one of his famous mid-late race bursts and dropped Ryan and Tikkanen. He was where he wanted to be – in the lead. But his path home was to be far less comfortable than three years earlier.

A feature of big-city marathons in the late 1970s was appalling crowd control. Some 18 years after this race, as I shared an early-morning workout with the fourth-placer, Jack Fultz, at Harvard University's running track, the memories were still fresh in the mind of 1976 Boston champion, of the 1978 edition. Fultz's eyes became wide with animation as he recalled the obstacles he faced as he desperately chased down the leaders:

At around 22 miles there was a large press truck in front of me but the thickness of the crowds meant it was only going very slowly. I, meanwhile, was full of running – in the best shape of my life – up for a massive 10-minute PB. But I couldn't get round the truck! There was just room for me to squeeze alongside it, but I was pretty much running sidestep.

I invented a rhythm where I'd run three steps and then whack my hand into the side of the truck: "Step, step, step, BAM! Step, step, step, BAM!" Eventually after around a quarter of a mile of this, just enough room materialized for me to squeeze by. Then, however, a small way down the road, a police car presented the same problem! I decided right there to place one foot on the bumper, the next on the trunk and the next on the roof – and quite literally steeplechase over the darn thing. Just as I was about to pull it off, a space again opened up.

So with the crowds so close that if Rodgers ran with his arms outstretched he could touch people with both hands, he ran just 40 yards ahead of his club mate, Randy Thomas. But as Thomas, having charged through the field, found himself staring at the Promised Land, the marathon turned around and bit him. Derderian writes:

As if a spell had been cast, the fine muscles in his legs did not work the way they were supposed to. He began to lose ground, as well as balance and a sense of proportion. Jeff Wells, the man studying to be a reverend, came up on him.
"Randy, how far to go?"
"Two and a half miles. You'd better get going."

And that's exactly what Wells did. A 4:06 miler and a 28.27 10K runner meant Wells possessed superior basic speed than Rodgers. But would there be enough time left to depose the "King of the Roads"?

Rodgers turned around and thought he saw Thomas, and worried that he'd never hear the end of a defeat dealt to him by his club mate. Rodgers wanted just to cruise in and soak up the adulation of the crowds. But marathon running is almost never that simple. One of the greatest marathoners ever, Italy's Gelindo Bordin, once said that only one marathon he ever did was easy. His first. Twenty-five years later, Rodgers reminisced to the author: "So I'm going up the hills, up the hills, up the hills, often looking back, not afraid to look back – *glad* to look back, I wanna win – you know!"

Rodgers had run the second half of the course faster than any winner in history, and yet here was someone coming up on him. He had run at a tremendous pace and thought his rivals should be outta sight, outta mind. Suddenly he saw his pursuer was not Thomas but Wells, and he worried even more. "That airport training fanatic!" as Rodgers thought of the man whose finishing speed he greatly feared. Rodgers recalls:

I knew with about a mile to go that I had problems and that I was a hunted man. A motorcycle cop told me: "Bill, someone's moving up on you *fast!*" And I said "What!" And I looked behind, and in those days there was no crowd control. So I was a little bit freaked out because I'd looked back earlier many times because I'd broken away at about 17 miles.

I don't know what Wells' last couples of miles were but they must've been very fast – the problem was that he was running the race like the end of a 10K and not a marathon. He had me in his sights big time!

Wells' second-half split for the Boston Marathon of 1978 was an astounding 1:04:22; but such a dazzling piece of footracing brought him no pleasure as the finish line hove into view. Wells was ebullient that the race was almost over – yet all he could think to himself was: "I wish I had more time to chase Rodgers." Such is the fickle nature of marathoning.

After 26 miles and 285 yards it all came down to a 100-yard dash. Both runners kicked furiously. There was, appropriately, chaos on the roads even for this heart-stopping segment, as first a police motorcycle, then a protester with a big sign proclaiming Israel to be an outlaw state, got in between the runners. People later said the buffoon foiled Wells' kick, but he did not. Rodgers squeaked home because the finish line engulfed him just in time.

Rodgers tells me: "As I came around the last corner there was a commotion with some sort of political protest going on. All these motorcycles going around –

Mad finish: A protestor fails to foil the furious kick of Jeff Wells, while Bill Rodgers maintains just enough speed to arrive at the finish line in front at the 1978 Boston. *Jeff Johnson*

and sirens screaming...'' "Do you think the protestor interfered with Wells' kick?'' I ask.

No, I don't – people say he did, but I don't think so. *Nothing* was slowing Jeff down – or me! I was running as hard as I could, but he had a better finish than me – another fifty yards and he would have beaten me. I went across that line scared to death. In the photo you can see me running fairly normally, but he was running in a crazed state – he was *sprinting*! I didn't feel it physically as much as I felt it psychologically – a kind of anguish – which is just as bad as fatigue.

It was my advantage in that it was my fifth Boston and I think his first. So I knew the course and the crowds knew me. So it really was my advantage from that point of view. I had them on my side, which is a huge plus for anybody.

But I know Jeff as a person, and if I was going to lose to anyone I should like to lose to Jeff – but at the time I didn't know who the hell it was!

What this race does do is throw into question just what is the best way to run a marathon. We all know that going out fast and trying to hang on is the wrong way; but what about Rodgers and Wells? Had Rodgers' tactics been correct – to hit rivals with a mid-race burst, then hang on? Or had Wells been prudent to hold back and then treat the race like a 10K? Rodgers defends his strategy: "I did it right – I thought I made my move right and yet here was someone coming up on me. Actually Jeff should've stayed with me, 'coz if he'd have stayed with me, he would've probably won. I guess he took it too conservatively for the first 10 miles – but he ran a hell of a last half though that's for sure."

A relieved Rodgers waves to the crowd from the podium. *Jeff Johnson*

Wells admitted his strategy had been too bashful: "My biggest disappointment is that I didn't get into the race soon enough. My goof was in letting Rodgers get a big lead early."

What followed was a deluge of runners with the fastest mass finish in the history of the marathon. Perfect weather conditions helped an unprecedented six men run under 2:12. Thirty-two men broke 2.20; and an incredible 160 dipped under 2:30. Modern-day big-city marathons see less than 60 athletes finish in under 2:30.

* * *

Bill Rodgers would keep on winning major marathons for many years to come and would even place a dazzling fourth in the 1986 Boston race, aged 38. In all Rodgers ran 56 marathons, winning 21 of those, and 35 times – more than anyone in history – he would break 2:15. He won Boston and New York four times each.

Has the marathon seen the last of Rodgers? His last foray was in 1999 as I ran alongside him as he attempted to break the world record for a 50-year-old. On

261

Autumn 2003: the author interviewed Rodgers for this chapter only to find him with the first serious injury of his 35-year career. The hirsute fellow is brother Charlie, who manages Bill's famous store in Boston's Quincy market. *Will Cockerell*

pace until around 20 miles he started hallucinating and ended up in a hospital bed with a DNF. "I can still run these things," he explained, "I just can't duke it out anymore." But he still runs over 20 races a year and keeps on churning out 75-mile weeks, as he's been doing, and then some, for the last 30-plus years.

Top 1970s runner Gary Bjorklund once had this to say about the man nicknamed "Feathershoes": "In his day, you could throw a brick wall at Billy and he'd come through it, and wouldn't even have dust on him." He did, however, have his leg in plaster in the autumn of 2003, as the author found a sight as rare as a dodo – an injured Bill Rodgers. Some 140,000 miles of running will do that to you! But he wasn't going to stay down for long. As soon as his stress fracture was healed, Rodgers was looking to hit the roads again. No chance of "Boston Billy" slowing down and taking it easy then. "Us runners – we're not practical people, are we?" I asked.

"Oh no!" Rodgers laughed, "we're totally impractical people – we're *really* bad! But everyone gets something out of running, that's what makes it such a wonderful sport. The slowest person with biomechanical problems – it's a wonderful thing just to finish."

Race result:

Bill Rodgers	USA	2:10.13
Jeff Wells	USA	2:10:15
Esa Tikkanen	FIN	2:11.15
Jack Fultz	USA	2:11.17
Randy Thomas	USA	2:11.25
Kevin Ryan	NZL	2:11:43
Don Kardong	USA	2:14:07
John Lodwick	USA	2:14:12
Yutaka Taketomi	JPN	2:14:34
Tom Fleming	USA	2:14:44

Sources:

Conversations with Bill Rodgers.

Conversations with Jack Fultz.

Derderian, Tom, *Boston Marathon*. Human Kinetics, 1996.

Fixx, James, F., *The Complete Book of Running*. Random House, 1977.

Hauman, Riël, *Century of the Marathon*. Human & Rousseau, 1996.

Rodgers, Bill and Joe Concannon, *Marathoning*. New York: Simon and Schuster, 1980.

Sandrock, Michael, *Running with the Legends*. Human Kinetics, 1996.

XXIX

No. 22 – 1983 Fukuoka Marathon [Men]

Sunday, December 4th

Japan's favourite son faces stomach-churning test of nerve.

The road Toshihiko Seko took to become the world's most dangerous marathoner, if not quite the most successful, was never smooth, heavily undulating and littered with potholes. A feature of all great sportsmen is how, as soon as they start to perform under par, the public and media immediately write them off as a spent force. But, as the old saying goes, only the mediocre are always at their best. Seko was certainly written off many times in a long and terrific career. He was even written off, it could be argued, before he had even started out.

Seko, born on July 15th, 1956, grew up on the island of Kyushu, and at school adopted baseball as his first love, as was the Japanese craze in the 1960s. However, author Michael Sandrock writes: "Seko slowly discovered that, like many others, he was drawn to running. Whenever he had to run, he simply enjoyed it. Soon, Seko was displaying not only a real talent for running but a spirit of *makenki*, or hating to lose."

At Kuwana Technical High School near Nagoya, Seko trained with the school track team and in just his second year won the inter-high school championships in both the 800 and 1500-metres. In his third year of high school he set the Japanese high-school 1500-metre record of 3:53.3 (Sandrock). Already he had earned the nickname of "Kaibutsu" or "Monster". Toshihiko Seko it seemed, was destined to become a middle-distance star. But then the wheels came off.

If education in Britain and America is competitive, try Japan. The torrid training Seko was undertaking played havoc with his schoolwork, and when it came to take the entrance exam to Tokyo's prestigious Waseda University, Seko flunked – the ultimate social stigma. His parents sent him packing to the University of Southern California (USC), where at least he'd get some good running done. But as it turned out, he did anything but. Toshihiko became pals with two other Japanese, and they took to lazing around all day, eating. The USC gave Seko his marching orders and when he returned home, his horrified parents found him significantly overweight and in no shape to run. His friends teased him, calling him by the names of not the best sumo wrestlers famed not for their skill but for their size. Seko was all burnt out; surely he'd never run again.

But his parents decided to play the very last card in the pack – and it was an ace. Living in a humble house on the grounds of Waseda University was the legendary figure of Kiyoshi Nakamura, the university's track coach. Nakamura, a great runner in his day, had made millions in Japanese business after the Second World War, and had been able to retire and return to his great passion – distance running. Nakamura had around 90 athletes in his stable and his life was now dedicated to moulding them into the best possible runners – and people – that they could be. Nakamura not only agreed to take on Seko, but he made a promise to his startled parents: that within five years he would be a world-class marathoner. Neither Seko nor his parents had any confidence in this plan since Seko was a middle-distance man. But Nakamura had a belief, and that formed the structure and backbone to all he taught: "*Tensai wa yugen da go, doryoku wa mugen da.*" Or, if you prefer, "Talent is limited, but effort is unlimited."

Some coaches talk endlessly to their athletes; others even run with them; few move in with them. Nakamura did, feeling that this total immersion in the athlete's way of life was the way to learn about their soul and what made them tick. Under Nakamura's guidance, Seko's running not only improved but he also scraped his retake exams into Waseda. To illustrate the enormous pressure there is to enter one of these universities, Seko describes his pass as "the greatest thrill of my life, even greater than winning Fukuoka."

Nakamura's key belief in training, above all others, was a simple one. Log the miles. Thousands and thousands and thousands a year. The Japanese believe that because they are not built as big and strong as runners from other nations, then their workloads must be increased to compensate. They needed to be capable of "unlimited effort". Nakamura had devised a system in which his athletes took whatever he said to be the gospel truth. Michael Sandrock writes: "If Mr. Nakamura pointed to a piece of white paper and said, 'This is black,' then his runners would say, 'Yes, that is black.'"

It took the tubby, unfit Seko a while to adapt to this Spartan, somewhat hostile approach, and it wasn't long before he ran away. But turning up on his parents' doorstep was a wrong move as they simply transported him back to Nakamura's cabin telling coach to do with Seko what he must: "He's yours." Tough love maybe, but soon the dividends were starting to pay. Under almost 24-hour attention, Seko was placed on a riveting diet of a piece of lettuce and toast a day to shed the extra USC pounds, and slowly but surely he worked up to 120 miles per week. Nakamura made it almost his life's mission to fulfil Seko's potential. As he told journalist Hans Maler years later: "God gave Seko to me, and I want to thank God by making Seko the best."

The relationship between Nakamura and Seko was closer than that of a father and son. It was more like a priest and a disciple. No one under Nakamura was allowed a girlfriend, to go out at night, or to drink beer. All athletes sported the same haircut. It used to be that Nakamura beat his students in order to get the best of out them, earning him the nickname of "Satan". But he soon realized that words were a much more powerful tool, and his athletes would listen in rapt attention as he would quote to them his particular brand of philosophy which he called "Zensoho" or "running with Zen" – a form of Buddhism, concentrating on the enlightenment of the student. According to Michael Sandrock, Nakamura

266

explained to Maler: "The idea is to clear your mind of everything and to let your body function naturally, undisturbed by thought".

Every night the great coach's runners would gather round as he preached his "Nakamuraism" to them. This was a mixture of great stories and exploits of wise men from the past – from passages in the Bible to Japanese poets. According to Sandrock, one of Nakamura's favourite sayings was this powerful aphorism from Daruma-taishi, a Buddhist monk: "Welcome the hardships when they come. Be patient and work through the burdens. Only then can you overcome them and grow stronger."

Sandrock goes on to give more insight into the training Nakamura had his pupils doing: "The asphalt loop around Meiju Jingu National Garden next to the Olympic Stadium is a perfect oval and is exactly 1,325 meters long. Here Seko ran lap after lap, sometimes as many as 50 in a row. Once each lap he passed Nakamura, who carefully timed each lap in an attempt to mold Seko's raw talent and develop it until Seko was renowned throughout the world for his marathoning prowess." Of even greater brutality were the training camps Nakamura would take his pupils to, often in New Zealand, known as *gasshuku*. On one occasion, so the story goes, Seko ran 1200 kilometres in a mere eight days. "My body was a little confused after that, but I did it," he explained.

Seko began his marathon career by doing the sensible thing – which so many marathoners find so difficult – getting round in one shape and feeling good: a tenth-place effort of 2:26 in Kyoto in February 1977. Nine months later, he took a cool 11 minutes off that with a 2:15:01 at Fukuoka, in the first of several memorable scraps with American "King of the Roads" Bill Rodgers, who won that race, after winning at New York just the month before.

After the 1978 Japanese track and field championships, where Seko blasted to a fine 27:51 in the 10,000-metres, Nakamura had Seko train for the marathon full time. Bill Rodgers came to the 1978 Fukuoka Marathon with an air of invincibility about him. He had been undefeated in his last three marathons (New York, Fukuoka and Boston – the triple crown of marathoning) and came to defend his title. But slowed by a cold, Rodgers could only watch as Japanese men stormed to a one – two – three finish, with Seko winning his first major marathon in 2:10:21 over Hideki Kita and Shigeru Soh (one of the two great Soh twins).

Next up was the Boston Marathon, the following April of 1979. This time Rodgers was ready, and a famous duel ensued. Rodgers had been humiliated by a kick Seko had unleashed on him at a 10,000-metre race in Stockholm and had resolved not to let the race be close enough for there to be a repeat of that. Rodgers searched for a hat-trick of Boston wins. He treated the race as a dress rehearsal for the Olympics, which he and Seko anticipated with such relish in the upcoming year. With six miles of the race to go, a leading Rodgers glanced behind him to see an "inscrutable" Seko following silently in his wake.[1] Rodgers, roared on by the partisan crowds, hammered away at the tarmac, before finally he dared look back in the last mile. He glimpsed his rival 200 metres back. Phew, no kick in the world would be able to rescue Seko now. But Rodgers was in no doubt as

---

1. "Inscrutable" was the term Rodgers used to describe Seko's impenetrable racing expression. "I wonder how he's feeling," Rodgers would think to himself. But he would never find out because the expression would never change.

to where the future lay. "I better move out the way soon," he joked, "or else I'll get run over."

Twenty-five years after the race the author caught up with Rodgers and asked him if Seko was the most demanding opponent he had ever faced. He replied:

Well, he was most certainly a higher level opponent. At that time he prepared better than anyone in the world – he was very professional: professional coach, professional life. He had a lot of belief and studied the Bible and Zen and believed in himself – which is a lot of what the marathon is about: *believing* you can reach that higher level.

And also, lethally, he had all these fast twitch muscles – Like Abera today, he could shift gears at the end of a race. Shorter could do that, too – he was a 4.02-miler. So you have some of these marathoners who can kick – most of them can't. I can't – I'm not a kicker. I never trained for a kick in my life – What? What's a kick? No one ever told me about kicking!

I trained hard for Boston of '79 having just beaten the world record for 25K on the track. Fortunately for me that year I don't think Seko quite realized how hilly Boston was. But he would be back.

If only, Rodgers thought, I could just keep my strength for one more year, and win the Olympics. But tragically, for all the heroes of the gripping Boston of '79 – Gary Bjorklund, Don Kardong, Tom Fleming, Seko and Rodgers – "within a year, politics a world away would steal the dreams of these men" (Derderian). Japan joined America in the boycott of the Moscow Olympics in protest of Russia's invasion of Afghanistan, and Seko's shot at Olympic glory was destroyed. He had returned to Fukuoka in 1979 and won for the second time, and was becoming fitter and more dangerous by the week. "Without the boycott, I believe the marathon would have been won by Seko," said Yoichi Furukawa, a well-known race promoter in Japan. "We all believed there was absolutely no way anybody could have beaten him." Seko concurred: "I was disappointed in not being able to run in the Olympics. My country put faith in me, and I was not going to let them down. I trained especially hard because I was representing all of Japan."

It would just have to be Los Angeles then, four long years away. But in those years Seko would run the gauntlet of all the mind-spinning highs and lows which top-level international sport can throw up.

* * *

This chapter's featured marathon, Fukuoka 1983, shows the classic marathon that is Fukuoka at its best. It was, perhaps, its glorious swansong, before its place as the unofficial world championship was overtaken by, well, the *official* World Championship which had made its debut some four months before. Make no mistake, Fukuoka is still run, attracts terrific fields and boasts great champions. However, because of the worldwide boom in big-city marathons over the past 25 years, Fukuoka doesn't command quite the mystique and awe from the West as it used to have in the 1970s. If the current-day leading Fukuoka contenders these days are lesser-known, more obscure names, there was nothing obscure about the field lined up for the 1983 race. It was crammed with quality, talent and some of the biggest names in distance running. But the name of most importance to the Japanese public was that of Seko.

Since the 1980 Olympic boycott, the intended destiny of Seko's life had followed a rockier than intended path. There had been undoubted highlights including the spectacular Fukuoka race of 1980 when Seko came searching for his hat-trick. He got it, but only just. A sprint finish was required over Takeshi Soh as eight men broke 2:11 and two broke 2:10 for the first time in one race. Seko then returned to have another crack at Boston where an aging but still hungry Rodgers awaited. Also there was an even bigger threat in the form of cross-country and track expert Craig Virgin. Seko's mysterious and secretive aura perplexed Rodgers. Seko and his entourage drove to Rodgers' store before the race to find out the location of a nearby track. Rodgers gave directions while spotting Seko waiting in the car outside. Why not come in and say hello? Tom Derderian writes: "Rodgers's experiences in Japan had taught him that politeness and formalities ruled there. Wouldn't it be the polite Japanese thing to do to come into the store for a greeting? It would be all formal and distant, with bowing on both sides. Seko would call him Will-san, they would smile and say the ritual nice things. But Seko stayed in the car."

A couple of days later Seko stayed in the lead, too, all the way to the finish line. Virgin and Rodgers battled valiantly but Seko prevailed by an even minute. The great champion from the East had finally won in the West, too. What a titanic Olympic battle it would have been one year earlier. And what an exciting next few years Seko seemed to have lined up. But that's not quite how it worked out.

A knee injury was the first gremlin to rear its ugly head, and Nakamura took decisive action. If his training programmes followed a no-holds-barred approach, then so did his timetables for rest. "We're gearing up for LA," Nakamura explained. "Toward that end, I plan to have Seko rest for one whole year." Seko didn't run a single marathon between Boston in April 1981 and Tokyo, February 1983. Did all the rest and acupuncture do him good? It most certainly seems that way. Up against strong opposition in Tokyo, Seko powered away from the field to a superb 2:08:38, the fourth fastest time ever run and just 20 seconds off Rob de Castella's world record.

The inaugural World Championships approached. It wasn't clear whether Seko would be there as he went off with Nakamura to one of their brutal training camps in New Zealand. Sometimes Seko would train so hard that the only thing he had an appetite for at the end of a day was beer. Lots of it; sometimes as much as ten pints in a night! Perhaps owing to this curious trait, Seko contracted hepatitis, and he had to swap running for walking. Everywhere. Journalist Dan Schlesinger wrote: "Outsiders said he could be seen walking everywhere with feverish intensity, his face and neck swollen by either the effect of hepatitis or medications." Had Seko, some wondered, really overcooked it this time? Was this the end of the great fighter after four or five terrific years at the top? It seemed as though it could be, but instead "this great Japanese warrior rose up again to do battle. Reports began filtering out of Japan that he was running as much as *six hours at a time*, because his rivals, Takeshi and Shigeru Soh, had been doing very long runs" (Sandrock).

269

To the consternation of many, and the relief of Rob de Castella, Seko opted out of the inaugural World Championships. Instead he focused all his physical and mental might on regaining a fourth Fukuoka crown, to match Frank Shorter's record. He had many doubters to appease, and many questions to answer. Aside from his stellar Tokyo performance nine months before, Seko had done precious little to satisfy his fans' appetites in nearly three years.

The field that came to battle against Seko was unquestionably a fine one – one of the deepest in marathon history. Not only were great runners from around the world attracted, but the race also doubled as the Japanese Olympic trial for Los Angeles Games – arguably the most pressure-charged, competitive trial of any nation at that time. Hideki Kita, who had pushed Seko hard in the '78 Fukuoka to place second, came to race. As did another Fukuoka favourite Kunimitsu Itoh,[2] who had placed third in the dramatic 1980 event. The dangerous Soh twins turned out – intent on at least one, or preferably two, of the Soh family performing at the Olympics. Double Olympic champion Waldemer Cierpinski showed up, as did American marathon icon Alberto Salazar, triple New York champion and Boston '82 winner (see Chapter 49). To round off with a flourish, and to ensure that this would be a fast race, as well as an exciting one, Juma Ikangaa was present – the superb new Tanzanian talent who had given Rob de Castella such a scare at the previous year's Commonwealth Games.

Ikangaa dressed all in white as was his custom, and Seko wore white shorts and a red vest, with the letters "SB" written in large on his front (the company S & B were the major food processor whom Seko represented). Ikangaa's tactics in the Commonwealth Games, and as it turned out, throughout most of the 1980s, involved bursting into the lead in marathons, dictating the pace, and ensuring that the races were always fast, honest...and painful. Ikangaa seemed to be from the Steve Jones school of thought, who wanted to make sure that if anyone did defeat him in a race they had at least been put through the wringer first. It was a tactic that lost Ikangaa more races than he won, including no fewer than three second-place finishes *in a row* at Boston. But such an approach won Ikangaa something perhaps more priceless than mere races: adoration and respect from running fans the world over, and particularly, of course, in Tanzania. "Everyone wanted to be like Juma after that," said one Tanzanian, after the epic de Castella tussle (Sandrock).

Seko and the pack settled in behind the bold, front-running Ikangaa. The solid but light, 5 foot 6 inch Seko actually looked fairly tall when compared to the tiny 5 foot 3 inch, 117-pound African. Alberto Salazar towered above them both. The sweat poured off the athletes in the sultry, humid conditions, tension evident on their faces. All top runners may like to convey an appearance of total relaxation, but when the pace is fierce and the stakes high, it's hard not to betray some emotion.

---

2. Itoh found real notoriety three years later by his participation in the 1986 Beijing Marathon. After some 20 marathons, Itoh suddenly improved on his pb by a whopping 1:38 to record 2:07:57 the fifth fastest time ever. The winner of that race, Taisuke Kodama, ran 2:07:35, the third fastest ever. The times were never erased from the record books even though they were greeted with incredulity by the athletics' world. Subsequent unofficial investigations found the course to be 400m short (Hauman).

Ikangaa whizzed through 20 kilometres in 61:30, and took just 30:23 over his next 10 kilometres to clock 91:53 for the 30-kilometres checkpoint. The group behind hadn't thinned much. Seko had sustained a leg injury three weeks earlier, but seemed to be coping well. Four kilometres later it seemed as though Ikangaa had been swallowed up by the pack, as Salazar, the two Sohs, Itoh, Kita and Seko engulfed him. But far from skulking off quietly, Ikangaa simply stepped on the accelerator again in a bid to shake off his captors.

The field began to string out. Salazar, after winning a whole posse of marathons between 1980 and 1982, was suddenly vulnerable and seemed to have lost his magic touch. He had placed an intolerable workload on his young body and it was already showing major signs of wear. He was the big American hope for the Los Angeles Olympics, but he somehow needed to find that elusive winning touch again. On this occasion, he became detached from Ikangaa and Seko at around 38 kilometres, and would eventually place fifth.

Ikangaa and Seko presented very different running styles, Ikangaa's looking wild and scrappy in front of the rhythmic, metronomic Japanese on his shoulder. "Look how smooth he runs," Nakamura once commented. "Did you see his relaxed expression? That's the key to his strength." Ikangaa poured on the effort, his hands flapping above shoulder height at times. By contrast, Seko's just made a easy pendulum movement between waist and chest – no wasted energy here.

The tension built – less than 2 kilometres to go – a straight battle between the brave little African and the inscrutable Asian. Seko had sacrificed so much for this: the appalling 6-hour training loads, the injuries, the illnesses, the World Championships. The hopes of a nation rested on his shoulders – what a catastrophic failure it would be judged, if he failed to win.

One kept waiting, thinking, *expecting* Seko to pass Ikangaa and take the lead. Seasoned observers knew of Seko's great finish. As Frank Shorter reminds us: "He was the man you least wanted to see when you turned around to look with one kilometre left in the race." The stadium approached and was suddenly upon them. Just one lap of the track remained. Thousands crammed inside, thrilled yet deeply anxious that their hero only owned second spot. Ikangaa refused to relinquish the lead. Three-hundred metres to go...then only two hundred. Ikangaa running strongly, boldly and fast. Seko ice-cool as ever, following two steps behind. Just 100 metres to go – the final straightaway. Go Toshihiko! Go! It was now or never.

And suddenly it happens. After 2 hours 8 minutes and 40 seconds, the moment has arrived and Seko bursts into gear *six* with an astonishing change of pace. Ikangaa has not slowed and yet he appears to have come almost to a standstill as Seko powers by, arms and legs pumping furiously, focus fixed on oblivion. Seko takes a stunning 3 seconds out of Ikangaa in the last 80 metres. That's over 20 metres – pretty good work for a mile, let alone a 10-second dash.

It was Seko's fifth major marathon in a row, and at the finish line instead of celebrating he bowed to the master, his guiding light, his prophet and his teacher: he bowed to Kiyoshi Nakamura. Twice in one year Seko had broken 2:09 for the marathon and for the first time ever six runners had broken 2:10 in a single marathon (Hauman). If de Castella was the official world champion, there were many now who saw Seko, and not the Australian, as Olympic champion in waiting.

*   *   *

The 1984 Olympic Marathon will be explored in detail in Chapter 42, but the name of Toshihiko Seko receives little copy. If Fukuoka had been warm, Seko found he just could not cope with the heat and smog of Los Angeles and trailed in a dejected 14th – a result viewed as a national disaster in Japan. (Takeshi Soh finished 4th, and twin brother Shigeru 17th). "I tried my best," Seko explained, "I feel sorry I couldn't do my best. Now I need rest, I'll try again in four years." If this "catastrophic" failure wasn't bad enough, much worse was to follow. In May of 1985, Nakamura died. He was found floating face down in a stream where he had gone trout fishing. Although his death was officially ruled an accidental drowning, rumours persist that he committed *jissatsu* (suicide).

An exhausted Seko didn't race another marathon until the streets of London were lucky enough to boast him in an otherwise weak field in 1986. Wanting to make up for his Olympic disappointment, Seko advertised plans for a 2:07. But the streets of the capital are often very windy and that was the case here. A 2:10:02 gave him his seventh win in eleven starts. He went world-record hunting in Chicago that autumn and powered through halfway in 1:03:42, before slowing a shade to record a personal best – 2:08:27.

Toshihiko Seko is seen here running to victory at the 1986 London Marathon to go with his other major big city races from all over the world. *Steve Powell/Allsport*

Boston fielded Seko and a large entourage in 1987, and this time Seko did go to hang out at Bill Rodgers' store. Charlie Rodgers, Bill's brother, remarked of the visit: "That is the fittest human being I've ever seen. Just sitting there, you could see that this guy was really ready to rock." Double Boston champ Geoff Smith of Liverpool came searching for a third crown. Rob de Castella came back to defend, and Steve Jones searched for an elusive first Boston crown. But they just were no match for Seko's strength and passion. Tom Derderian writes: "Seko finished with a clenched fist in the air and gruesome concentration on his face. When he saw Mrs. Nakamura the gruesomeness drained from his face; he bowed."

Thus came 1988 and a final shot at Olympic glory. For ten long years Seko had been duking it out with the very best and time's winged chariot was fast catching up. Yet more injuries felled him as the Olympic trials approached, and he missed the two official Japanese Olympic

Toshihiko celebrates with Grete Waitz after the 1986 London. *Mark Shearman*

trials. However, the selectors shirked at the notion at sending a team to Seoul minus the master. He was given one final chance to prove himself. In very hot weather at the Lake Biwa Marathon, Seko pulled out a beauty and defeated two other Japanese hopefuls who were favoured by many to defeat him. He was selected for his second Games. A little past his best in Seoul, Seko was delighted with his ninth place, calling it his best race, because of all the struggles he had overcome to simply get there. Of course people in Japan took a dim view of his clenched fist of celebration at the end, since he hadn't won; but perhaps it would have helped had they looked at the whole picture.

"Seko's last race was moving, an event of national importance," Michael Sandrock writes. Some 10,000 people came to pay their respects to Seko at the International Chiba Ekiden on December 18th, 1988. The result was just a footnote. For a decade Seko "had come to symbolize Japanese running". Nowadays, one of his roles is to fill the shoes of coach Nakamura and stand in the same spot as his mentor did outside the Jingu Garden by the National Stadium. His competitive days over, the race face vanished. No longer was Seko "inscrutable". Instead he became friendly, approachable and talkative. His training sessions are much more light-hearted than Nakamura's. Athlete Brian Sheriff notes: "Toshihiko is very down to earth, and a great guy. He's a family man, the complete opposite of his image" (Sandrock). Japan have had many successes at the Olympic and World Championships since Seko's day, but his place in Japanese running folklore is secure; and his legendary dedication – and racing – will be discussed for many decades to come.

Race result:

Toshihiko Seko	JPN	2:08:52
Juma Ikangaa	TAN	2:08:55
Shigeru Soh	JPN	2:09:11
Takeshi Soh	JPN	2:09:16
Alberto Salazar	USA	2:09:21

Sources:

Archive race footage, Japanese television.
Conversations with Bill Rodgers.
Derderian, Tom, *Boston Marathon*. Human Kinetics, 1996.
Hauman, Riël, *Century of the Marathon*. Human & Rousseau, 1996.
Kiyoshi Nakamura, interview with journalist Hans Maler.
Sandrock, Michael, *Running with the Legends*. Human Kinetics, 1996.

XXX

No. 21 – 2004 Olympic Marathon [Women]

Sunday, August 22nd

"As her descent gathered pace, even fools had the power to wound."

And so, 108 years after the "greatest show on earth" kicked off, the modern Olympics returned to their birthplace. There was great disappointment and dismay among Athenians when the city failed to win the Centennial Games (which were awarded to Atlanta), and for that matter the Millennium Games, which went to Sydney. But finally the IOC voted for a return to the Greek capital. The four-year build-up to the Games was a tense and difficult period for the host nation. Almost since the giant electronic scoreboard in Sydney flashed up "See you in Athens" at the closing ceremony, the Athenians came under fire for not being ready, or at least, not appearing to be ready.

The media's part in this story, or perhaps that should read non-story, was disgraceful. Athens was of course ready for the Games – and they put on a magnificent show, but not before countless media reports were filed, warning: "these Games are going to be a disaster, they'll never be ready, the whole thing is a nightmare." Whatever happened to giving a man – or city – a chance? One newspaper printed a story which said: "Look! We got one of our reporters in to the Olympic stadium and no one asked him any questions. These Games are going to be a sitting duck for terrorists." And the Athenians' response? They knew perfectly well of the hack's presence, but they were still trying to *build* their stadium, and their security wasn't in place yet.

Tragically, the main victim of the media scare stories were the Games themselves, as spectators were turned off attending. "Have you seen all the empty seats? Why isn't anyone here?" was the media's next line of attack. Little wonder – since for the last four years we'd been told the Games were going to be the biggest disaster since Chernobyl. But of course, for the people that did attend, there was a wonderful atmosphere to greet them, friendly and helpful volunteers, and terrific action to enjoy.

* * *

It's sad when the cheque-book wins out over common sense and majority opinion, but that was a key factor for what happened when the marathon returned to the course that created the whole saga with Spiridon Louis' win of 1896. The women's

275

Olympic marathon of 2004 was always going to be a brutal test of strength and heat resistance, and the organizers, with television schedules at the forefront of their thinking, decided they'd start the runners off – not at some sensible hour such as 6.30 in the morning – but at 6 p.m. when the sun would be nearly at its hottest. The marathon indeed began with the temperature at a scorching 35 °C. But what did the TV fat cats care about creating a race that could become more of a freak show than one that was pure and fair? The lure of the filthy lucre held sway.

If ever a race seemed to be all about one woman – then this would appear to be it. Paula Radcliffe, the golden girl of British athletics, came to Athens as nothing short as the overwhelming favourite. After all, no one in the field boasted a time within 3 minutes of her world best. For extensive discussion of the progress of Radcliffe up to this point in her career, see Chapter 36, but suffice it to say that, in the marathon, she had finally found her perfect match. A reminder of her three attempts at the distance reads: London '02, first, 2:18:56; Chicago '02, first, 2:17:18; London '03, first, 2:15:25.

This was all very spellbinding, but did Radcliffe have yet another gem to offer – or was the beast that is the marathon ready to bite back? "Some day the marathon will humble you," warns one of the all-time greats, American Bill Rodgers, about the event, and there isn't a top star that hasn't been humbled by it. Grete Waitz? Boston '82. Steve Jones? Stuttgart '86. Toshihiko Seko? Los Angeles '84. Jim Peters? Vancouver '54. Frank Shorter? Boston '78 and '79. Ron Hill? Too many to mention. Even Paul Tergat: Athens '04. Ah yes, the list is endless.

Radcliffe also had one or two other things to think about: she hadn't actually raced a marathon for 16 months; she had only run good marathons in cool–cold weather; she had lost a couple of recent races; and she had never experienced a Championship marathon, let alone the uncommon pressure of being overwhelming favourite at the Olympics. Exactly two weeks before the Olympic marathon, Radcliffe's worst fear, a debilitating injury called crepitus had come back to haunt her. Her teams of physios dealt with it with a strong programme of anti-inflammatories, which would themselves cause her problems. The outside world was ignorant of these wrinkles, however. To them, it was very hard to see Radcliffe losing.

Who else though to medal? The most obvious contender seemed to be Catherine Ndereba. Not only did the Kenyan boast the second fastest time in history of 2:18:47, but she was also reigning world champion, and had won Boston earlier in the year in one of its hottest races ever. Elsewhere in the field the first thing to look for in any Championship marathon these days is the quality of the Japanese presence. And it was clear they had sent a crack team. The clue? Their current Olympic champion, the great Naoko Takahashi – the first woman to break the magic 2:20 barrier and the heroine of a comic strip (*The Daughter of the Wind*) – was ruthlessly and controversially left off the Japanese team because the selectors deemed they had found three more able runners. They were Naoko Sakamoto (personal best 2:21:51 and winner of Osaka '04), Reiko Tosa (winner at Nagoya '04 in 2:23), and Mizuki Noguchi (personal best 2:21:18, runner-up in the 2003 World Championships).

Other threats came from one of the world's leading lights of the past few years, the Kenyan Margaret Okayo – the reigning New York and London champion with a 2:20:43 personal best; and from Deena Kastor (née Drossin), the brilliant 31-year-old American who had won World Cross-Country silver in 2003, the same year that she had finished third on her debut in London, in a more than promising 2:21:16. The Ethiopian contingent was led by another world-record holder, the wife of the men's Olympic champion Gezahegne Abera, Elfenesh Alemu. It is questionable whether Alemu's world-record was strictly connected with athletics though: she held it for boasting the world's longest ever train on a wedding dress (some 300 metres long), booting Princess Diana into second place. But Alemu had shown herself to be a consistent performer on the world stage for several years. Twice she had placed in the top six of the World Championships, had won at Tokyo, and had been runner-up in Boston earlier in the year.

Liz Yelling, who had managed a 2:30 at Berlin the previous year, and the colourful character of Tracey Morris, an optician from Leeds, completed the British line-up. Morris was sweepingly portrayed by the press as a "fun" runner who came out of nowhere to suddenly find herself qualifying for the Olympics by dint of her 2:33 clocking at London. Morris, with a classic touch of British inverse snobbery, milked this image to the full, securing herself a newspaper column, with a "Wow! What am I doing here?" theme. Of course, Morris was in truth an extremely talented runner who trained bloody hard.

* * *

Paula Radcliffe wore an ice vest for half an hour before the race as the mercury flirted with 100 °F (with 31 degrees humidity). She has since revealed that even at the start of the race she was in turmoil. Upon taking an ice bath she had shaken so violently that she immediately had to get out, when usually she could easily handle the water's temperature. Her last meal, five hours before the race, also presented grave problems. Radcliffe writes: "Subconsciously I know something is wrong. The food that I have eaten feels like it is too much for my digestive system. All the visits to the bathroom at our apartment have signalled a problem: is it the anti-inflammatories that I have been taking to keep the inflammation down in my leg and give me a chance of running? Have they upset my stomach?"

The grimly anticipated hour of 6 p.m. arrived and the runners set off on their long journey from the village of Marathon. After half a mile, Radcliffe was right where she wanted to be: leading the Olympic marathon. What were her tactics to be this day? Of course this was a closely guarded secret and sightings of Radcliffe in the weeks building up to the big race were rare or non-existent. Surrounded by only her closest family, her physio Gerard Hartmann, her husband and training partner, Gary Lough, and coach Alex Stanton, she had locked herself away at an undisclosed location, which later turned out to be Seville (a city nicknamed the "frying-pan of Europe"). Little was known about her state of mind, fitness or confidence. She hadn't even fraternized with the other British athletes until a couple of days before the race. After the excruciating hurt of the Sydney 10,000-metres final four years earlier she had dedicated her entire being to this race.

The kilometres passed by relatively peacefully and quite slowly – around 17 minutes for the first and second 5-kilometre splits. As reported in the *Daily*

Burn, baby, burn: Paula Radcliffe leads the 2004 Olympic Marathon from the gun. *Yiorgos Karahalis/Reuters/ Corbis*

Telegraph, "The sun was so pitiless that you could feel it burning the skin beneath your shirt." At 3.1 miles the Moroccan Kenza Wahbi moved into the lead but Radcliffe and the rest of the field quickly closed her down. The lead pack started to slowly but surely dwindle. By 4.4 miles it was reduced to 13; two miles later to 10. Radcliffe refused to let anyone else lead. Bobbing on her chest was the necklace with the five Olympic rings given to her by her mother. She insisted on keeping herself half-a-body's length in front. It soon became clear that Radcliffe had a complex tactical conundrum on her hands. Surely it was an ultra-risky tactic to try and burn off the field quickly and brutally like she had in London twice and Chicago. But if she wasn't going to burn them off in a quick coup *à la* Joan Benoit at Los Angeles, then was it *entirely* necessary to do *all* leading. But that wasn't the way Radcliffe worked. To not lead a marathon? Eh?

Meanwhile, ahead at the beautiful old marble Panathinaiko Stadium in Athens, being used for the finish of the marathon, just like in Spiridon's day, a carnival atmosphere developed amongst the gathered British spectators. This was what they had come to see. The golden girl of British athletics taking on all before her and leading the Olympic marathon. When would she break away, they asked one another. At 15 kilometres? Halfway? At 30 kilometres? Or would she leave it until close to the finish? It wasn't a question of "if" but "when"?

At 9.3 miles another leader tried her luck, this time in the form of the Japanese girl Mizuki Noguchi. Radcliffe's head was starting to nod freely now and she was seemingly gasping for air. Just 4 foot 11, the tiny, 91-pound Noguchi (whose 2:21:18 had her ninth on the all-time list) ran along displaying the long, bouncy strides for which she was so well-known back home: "She runs like a rubber ball," said Akemi Masuda, a Japanese commentator in *Athletics Weekly*. "She can do it because of her strong muscle power." Noguchi, notable for her striking looks, with a well-placed beauty spot below left of her mouth, ran wearing a Japanese good-luck charm – an *omamori* – on her shorts, which resembled a parachute pouch. Paula Radliffe, Margaret Okayo, Catherine Ndereba and Elfenesh Alemu were beginning to wish it really was a parachute and that they could pull the little cord that dangled down. There was no doubt about it: Noguchi was displaying remarkable and dangerous levels of fitness.

Had this been a track race, Radcliffe needn't surely have worried. Her personal bests in comparison to Noguchi were overwhelmingly superior. Noguchi boasted just 15:34 for the 5000-metres (over a minute slower than the British girl), and 31:51 for the 10,000-metres – nearly 2 minutes slower than Radcliffe's best. But here, a different story was unfolding – against all expectation, it was Radcliffe who seemed to be holding on.

A critical moment came at 25 kilometres when Noguchi passed her coach Nobuyuki Fujita, who indicated that the time would soon come for her to surge. This audacious strategy had been exhaustively calculated by the Noguchi team. Their meticulous preparation had already taken them to Athens twice to analyse the minutiae of the course, and their thinking focused on Noguchi's running technique. Journalist Ken Nakamura explains:

Although Noguchi had worked on her weakness, the downhill running skill, at her training camp in St. Moritz in Switzerland, she still was not totally comfortable with it. So Fujita decided on a strategy that involved Noguchi surging early and gaining a substantial lead by the top of the hill at 32 kilometres. The strategy was geared to take full advantage of Noguchi's strength, the uphill running.

Noguchi steeled herself, gathered up her reserves, and prepared to test her opponents. The pace quickened and then, almost to the disbelief of the watching public, Noguchi not only forced herself into the lead but started to draw away from Radcliffe – at precisely the time the course entered into a devastating 5 miles of uphill road. For a mile or so the runners ran lock step about 10 metres apart. Not exactly the plan one thought; one would prefer Radcliffe to be tucked in; but well, what's 10 metres? But then suddenly it was 20. Alemu looked ice-cool and in control; Radcliffe inscrutable behind her dark glasses and cap. But she was rolling her head much more than she had in her previous marathons. The effort was unmistakable.

Noguchi began to slowly stretch away from Alemu, with Radcliffe, experiencing terrible stomach cramps, valiantly hanging on. But by 18.6 miles Noguchi led the Olympic marathon by some 23 seconds over Alemu, with Radcliffe a further 8 seconds down. The time had come to strike back, and briefly and thrillingly it seemed that a magnificent rally was on the cards: "My mind stayed strong. *Don't panic here. Stay relaxed. You know you can run the closing ten kilometres of a marathon faster than most people*" (Radcliffe). Alemu fell to Radcliffe's stride and the Bedford girl fixed her sights on the indefatigable "rubber ball". But the ball was not coming back and instead disaster struck for Radcliffe as a previously down-and-out Ndereba soared back into the race, caught up with Radcliffe, and then went straight past. Still, a bronze medal was worth fighting for – especially if you've never won an Olympic medal before.

For around two miles this was how things came to pass, until the ultimate plot twist broke Radcliffe's heart. Alemu, just like Ndereba, had a surge of energy, which took her up to and past a distraught Radcliffe. Having fallen 10 metres behind, Radcliffe abruptly stopped running at the 36-kilometre marker. Her bewildered body language said it all. Radcliffe looked clueless and afraid arriving at this strange and surreal place in her life – similar one presumes to how Dorothy felt when landing in Munchkinland.

Radcliffe tossed a frightened glance over her shoulder, and, after resting briefly with her hands on her knees, had a think, and decided to recommence the pitiless battle. Thousands of British spectators ahead at the stadium roared their approval. Could she possibly launch one final assault on the leaders? No. After just a minute or so more of running, Radcliffe stopped for a second time, promptly burst into floods of tears, and slumped down on the kerbside, head in hands.[1] Her mind told her: *You're not going to be able to get anywhere near the next drinks station, let alone to the finish. You can't do this, you have nothing left. Your legs are just too sore and dead, too exhausted.* James Lawton later wrote in the *Independent*: "Her fortune is estimated at £5m after her world records and marathon wins. But there was an overwhelming sense that she would have given much of this booty in exchange for an easier passage through the wall of heat that awaited her in the home of the classic foot race."

While the favourite haplessly waited for medical attention, a lift home and a good psychologist, a magnificent race developed without her. Noguchi ploughed on ahead but Ndereba's second wind was causing concern to anyone partial to a Japanese win. Alemu hung

We are not amused: Radcliffe weeps by the roadside, six million millimetres short of intended target. *Nick Laham/Getty Images*

1. The similarities here with the Olympic marathon of 1952 are remarkable. On that day the overwhelming favourite was British and a multiple world-record holder who insisted on leading the Olympic marathon from the outset. It was, of course, Jim Peters, who finally bit the dust at around 35 kilometres. "Peters was feeling the pace and though still third, falling back when he was finally seized with cramp. He made several attempts to resume running, but it was no good." (*The Times*, July 29th, 1952). History had indeed repeated itself in an uncanny – almost spooky – manner.

gamely onto third, but further down the field, one of its classiest runners, Deena Kastor, was producing a run of immaculate pace-judgement, and she could be seen ruthlessly picking off runners until soon she had Alemu and a medal in her sight.

Ndereba stalked Noguchi on the long, dark road to the magical marble stadium. It was pretty much all downhill now after the brutal 10 kilometres of uphill that had recently passed. The seconds separating the two dwindled, until eventually they were less than 20, then 15, then 10. Noguchi entered the stadium to rapturous cheers from the near-capacity crowd – but could she hold on to her slender lead and handle the pressure of the world champion bearing down on her? The answer came quickly. Not only could the Japanese handle it, but she accelerated, powering through her last 300 metres. She waved to the 50,000 crowd and shot them one of her dazzling smiles. While this observer thought she still had a race to win, Noguchi knew it was all wrapped up and that the time had come to savour her – and Japan's – marvellous achievement.

The finishing ribbon almost swallows up the diminutive Mizuki Noguchi. *Mark Shearman*

Noguchi explained later: "I was so excited when I came into the stadium. I heard everybody screaming for me." Noguchi bounded through the line 12 seconds up on Ndereba ("the conditions were tough, but God was with me"), and a full 10:55 behind the world record. Heat and hills there may have been, but such a time should have been comfortably within Radcliffe's range. Japanese women had now won at least one medal at the marathon (four of them gold) in every global championships contested since 1991, with the exception of Göteborg '95. A remarkable haul.

Exactly a minute behind the winner came a highly emotional Kastor, whose conservative approach was never going to result in gold – you have to take the risk of going with the lead pack in Championship marathons – but such a tactic will often result in a high forward placing, and Kastor's astute judgement of the conditions led to a fully deserved bronze medal.

* * *

The overwhelming story of this marathon, though, is of Radcliffe's demise, and her failure has been the talking point in wine bars, pubs, restaurants, schools, colleges, offices and running clubs the world over. Two questions: What happened? And should she have finished? Radcliffe was in no fit state to talk about her disaster with any lucidness in the couple of days following the marathon. "I just don't understand it," was her most common refrain. Three weeks or so after the race she came out with a lengthy and detailed explanation of her problems, which we shall visit shortly. But let us first visit the sticky issue of whether or not she should have finished.

The author has listened, investigated, consulted and researched this issue in great detail, but of course there is no simple answer. There are two strong arguments – basically yes and no. Among "Joe Public" the overwhelming impression is: "Yes, she jolly well should have finished." Hundreds of thousands, if not millions, of people all over the world run marathons: there isn't a weekend of the year where you couldn't attend one. And for those millions, over 99 per cent of them are in it just to finish. And if these novice runners finish marathons after hitting the wall and stumbling along for five or six hours – why couldn't Radcliffe – on her feet for just a couple of hours? The author has run 14 marathons, hit the wall in about eight of them, but not finishing has never crossed his mind.

The perception seems to be that Radcliffe, after watching her medal chances disappear said to herself: *That's it, I'm in it to win it, I'm gonna end up about seventh here...to hell with that...*After all: she wasn't injured, and would she have quit if Alemu hadn't come along? There were only 6 kilometres to go – just 20 minutes of pain. Many feel that Radcliffe had no time for the Olympic ideal. After all, the days of amateurism were long gone.

The British media, it is no surprise, were united in their disagreement. Robert Philip of the *Daily Telegraph* wrote: "Call me a cynic, but the way I see it is that unless the medics in Athens can come up with a physical reason why she quit just over three miles from the finish, Radcliffe stopped running and started blubbing for the simple reason that she had just seen gold, silver and bronze disappear into the distance." Philip's post bag (according to him) was 90 per cent in approval of his views. Another decorated writer, Jeff Powell in the *Daily Mail*, wrote: "The truth often hurts even more than the punishment, and the closest she came to it was when she admitted that being left trailing by two rivals and then overtaken by a third applied 'an emotional kick in the guts'. If our Paula couldn't win, then our Paula no longer had the will to struggle on." But on the other hand, Martin Samuel in *The Times* wrote: "Radcliffe didn't choke or lack courage on Sunday. Who dares level that accusation, anyway? What do any of us risk compared to the dance with death that is marathon running? In every aspect of her life, Radcliffe has shown courage."

I put these three views to an American friend, Jack Fultz, a serious runner for some 40 years, who himself won the hottest Boston Marathon on record, in the 100 degrees heat of 1976. Fultz revealingly responds: "Martin Samuel is by far the closest to the reality of the situation. She was in an existential hell when it all finally came crashing down on her. She was there to win or die trying – came closer to the second after being very close to the first for quite a while. She made the race in the early miles. The weight of favourite in the Olympics is heavy indeed!"

* * *

The *Daily Telegraph*'s Sue Mott wrote a themed piece about the fact that "Favourites lose", and Ingrid Kristiansen backs this up. "Look at me at London

'87!" she told the author the day after Radcliffe's DNF. "Six miles to go and I'm in line for a low 2:18 – but my calf seizes up and I have to hobble home. This is sport – there will always be problems." Kristiansen also feels that Radcliffe has some sort of mental block about *having* to lead a race – whatever the conditions or circumstances.[2] A sportsman who is inflexible in their tactics may often be found wanting.

Radcliffe's initial response in her tearful, somewhat ill-advised press conferences to questions about what happened out there on the road, was: "I don't know." The heat? "I should have been able to cope. It was tough, but I didn't feel dehydrated. I was in no distress from the heat. I was in shock last night. I was numb. I was unable to cry. I felt I had let everybody down. But no one was hurting inside like I was." Simon Barnes responded to these words in *The Times*: "That was the bit that unlocked the floodgates for her: the thought of her own distress. What she needed was someone to give her a damn good hug and say: 'Lighten up, old girl, it's only a bloody game.'" Regarding the battery of tests Radcliffe was to undergo to find out what was wrong with her, Barnes continued: "It won't tell her why she gave up, but that seems quite clear. She gave up because she wasn't going to win. She was utterly unable to accept that reality. And so the knowledge utterly destroyed her. Yesterday, she faced her press conference with courage and honesty. But oh, that face, those tears, those gently cooing voices all around her: tell me, dear one, who died?"

The chief sports writer of the *Daily Mail*, Patrick Collins was far more sensitive, however:

> When at last she stopped, bewildered and hopelessly distressed there were those who expected something more. They expected her to crawl the four remaining miles into Athens so that national honour might be satisfied.
>
> They spoke of surrender, of betrayal. Of course, it was as cruel as it was ignorant and in normal times Paula Radcliffe would have treated the charges with the derision they deserved. But as her descent into wretchedness gathered pace, even fools had the power to wound.

*   *   *

A few weeks after the race, Radcliffe revealed the full extent of the pressures and injuries that led to her Olympic misery. An injury to her quad muscle had been the major setback. "The injury would clear but then return each time I tried to run," she told the *Daily Telegraph*.

> I was unable to sleep with worry some nights and suffered an upset stomach from the doses of anti-inflammatories. My quad felt a little tight during a run in Spain and afterwards went into total spasm. I was determined to get to the start line and we took a very aggressive line of treatment but the period was very stressful.

---

2. Kristiansen knows all about these "blocks" – she had two of her own in her long, distinguished career: the first was never believing she could beat Grete Waitz; and the second was her own agonizing mission to break 2:20 – which she never did quite manage.

I was very nervous on race day but when I warmed up, I felt that the leg would hold out and I relaxed. However, after just 10 kilometres my stomach problems started and my legs were also feeling very weak. Eventually I had to concede that there was no way I could push my body any further.

I was in shock and disbelief that it could end like that and even tried running again but my legs could not carry me. The night of the marathon was the worst of my life. My body hurt all over but my heart was totally broken.

Despite her marathon agony, Radcliffe decided to compete in the Athens 10,000-metres five days later, but dropped out with eight laps remaining. On whether she should have done the "ten", commentator Brendan Foster sums up the thoughts of most when he said that although she was quite wrong to take the risk, he acknowledged: "I'd have given it a bloody crack! 'Course I would." Radcliffe explained: "I don't have any regrets about trying the 10,000 metres. At least I won't always be wondering if I could have raced it. My legs were just unable to recover from the trauma."

*   *   *

One factor that hasn't been called in to question is that Mizuki Noguchi is a worthy Olympic champion; indeed the pedigree of all three medallists is beyond doubt. A detailed analysis of the terrific career of Catherine Ndereba, can be found in Chapter 6. Noguchi had proved her pedigree with a fine second place in the previous year's World Championships and a previous best of 2:21:18. She was known better in Japan as "Queen of the Half-marathons" since part of her Athens build-up entailed racing a "half" once a month. (*Athletics Weekly*).

Ken Nakamura, an expert in Japanese distance running told the IAAF: "After Paris, Noguchi realized that in order to win the major championships marathon, she had to learn to surge at the late stage of the race. In Miyaki [where she ran 67:47], she showed she is gaining such an ability" (reported in *Athletics Weekly*, August 25th, 2004). It should also be noted that Noguchi has claimed that her primary goal in the Paris World Championships was not to win but merely to qualify for the Japanese Olympic team; but it had been the perfect dress rehearsal. According to Nakamura, Noguchi proved she could handle the enormous workload required for top-level marathoning when she ran 1720 kilometre in 50 days at high altitude before her marathon debut in Nagoya in 2002. That's 21 miles, day in, day out. Her lifetime best in Osaka duly followed.

Noguchi, born on July 3rd, 1978, comments on that gruelling training stint in Kunming, China: "The long interval workouts (like 15×1 kilometres, 6×2 kilometres) in the windy conditions were tough, but because I had done five 40 kilometre-long runs, I had no fear of distance." As mentioned above, Noguchi's track times are relatively poor. But the track isn't her forte. What she excels in is gruelling marathons in hot weather, preferably over undulating courses. Prior to Athens she focused her training on hills, which she thought was her weakness. On the eve of the Games, Noguchi ominously stated: "I like running hills." This utterance became painfully obvious for her rivals when she made her race-winning surge on the most devastating section of the course. The awesome shape Noguchi was rounding into approaching the Olympics was illustrated by the 40-kilometre training runs at her camp in St Moritz being five minutes quicker than those of 2003. A year after her Olympic triumph, Noguchi won the Berlin Marathon in 2:19:12.

Bronze medallist Deena Kastor, who ran an astonishing *4-minute* negative split[3] pointed to three errors she perceived Radcliffe to have made: The way that Radcliffe isolated herself in her training, the way she insisted on "warming up" before the race, and then by starting out too quickly. Kastor had taken the advice of two physiologists, who armed her with "hundreds of pages" of documentation. "I surrounded myself with people I believe in." Not only did the physiologists' reports convince Kastor to start cautiously and work through, she took friends and training partners to her preparation camp, while Radcliffe cut herself off from the outside world. Kastor explains: "One of the greatest things I did was to have these guys training with me. We laughed and it was playful, which took the pressure off."

* * *

Whatever one may feel about Paula Radcliffe's adventure at Athens '04, pretty much all agree that her overwhelming self-pity was somewhat overcooked. There were howls of derision at the way a hapless Steve Cram handled his interview with her the day after the marathon, and that a "professional" journalist should have been given the task. But why was Cram's mission perceived to have been so delicate in the first place? The poor girl had set her standards so high, had sacrificed so much, and locked herself away from the world for so long, that everyday, normal, emotional behaviour was no longer coming naturally. Compare Radcliffe's reaction to that of the American hurdler Allen Johnson, the Atlanta '96 champion. He came to Athens hoping to repeat his gold but made a horrendous botch of his heat, smashing into any hurdle that got in his way – except his final one – which he proceeded to execute a very elegant swallow dive *underneath*. The wry smile on his face as he lay on the track with his Olympic dream in ruins, said it all: *Well, I sure messed that up...but hey? Whaddayagonnado?!*

We all know Radcliffe is a bubbly, intelligent and charismatic person. But during Athens 2004 it all seemed to have become a deadly serious matter of life or death. Perhaps injecting a little more nonchalance into her running would have helped. Granted, she hadn't got to the top by being nonchalant, but one of the most laid-back runners in history is a fellow named Rob de Castella – and he was no mug. When "Deek" had a bad day he would just say with that carefree charm: "No worries – I'll just be out banging away again tomorrow."

Whatever happens, Paula will be remembered as one of the all-time greats of marathoning, comfortably rubbing shoulders with "the big four": Waitz, Benoit Samuelson, Mota and Kristiansen. The time had come to start enjoying her running again. She deserved it.

---

3. That is, the second half of the race, was faster than the first half.

Race result:

Mizuki Noguchi	JPN	2:26:20
Catherine Ndereba	KEN	2:26:32
Deena Kastor	USA	2:27:20
Elfenesh Alemu	ETH	2:28:15
Reiko Tosa	JPN	2:28:44
Olivera Jevtic	SCG	2:31:15
Naoko Sakamoto	JPN	2:31:43
Lyndmila Petrova	RUS	2:31:56
Svetlana Zakharova	RUS	2:32:04
Bruna Gerovese	ITA	2:32:50

Sources:

Conversations with Ingrid Kristiansen.
Conversations with Jack Fultz.
Barnes, Simon, in *The Times*, August 24th, 2004.
Collins, Patrick, in the *Mail on Sunday*, August 29th, 2004.
Hayward, Paul, in the *Daily Telegraph*, August 23rd, 2004.
Mott, Sue, in the *Daily Telegraph*, August 24th, 2004.
Nakamura, Ken, in *Athletics Weekly*, October 20th, 2004.
Phillip, Robert, in the *Daily Telegraph*, August 25th, 2004.
Powell, Jeff, in the *Daily Mail*, August 24th, 2004.
Samuel, Martin, in *The Times*, August 25th, 2004.
Radcliffe, Paula, *Paula – My Story So Far*. Simon & Schuster, 2004.

XXXI

No. 20 – 2000 Boston Marathon [Men]

Monday, April 17th

Double giant killing by late-starting, self-confessed "fat kid".

As the Boston Marathon entered into its third century on April 17th, 2000, the *Boston Globe*'s Dan Shaughnessy summed up what Boston meant for the masses:

> How would we explain this event to someone who has never been to Boston on Patriot's Day? It's a Massachusetts-only holiday – a no-school day with mail delivery, stock trading, 11am Major League Baseball, and open liquor stores. But it is also a holy day of obligation for those who worship at the feet of the Greek Warrior, Pheidippides. There are mega-marathons in New York, Fukuoka, and every four years at the Summer Olympic Games, but ours is the biggest, best 26.2 of them all.

Shaughnessy may well be indulging in a little "Beantown" hyperbole, but it is worth exploring his remarks further since they give a quick potted history as to why the lore of Boston remains so powerful: "Boston is about 92-year-old Johnny Kelley throwing out the first pitch at Fenway on Sunday, then serving as race marshal Monday. It's about Jock Semple, Tarzan Brown, Clarence DeMar, the Wellesley College "tunnel of sound," Bill Rodgers, Rosie Ruiz, Alberto Salazar, Uta Pippig, Joan Benoit Samuelson, Kathy Switzer, carbo-loading, beef stew and laurel wreaths."

All of the above names, minus Brown (the winner in 1936 and '39) and Kelley (1935 and '45 – plus seven runner-up spots), have chapters dedicated to their exploits in this book. By the year 2000, however, Boston was faced with a problem. Not an insurmountable one, and in many ways it wasn't a problem at all, more that the race was a "victim of its own success". It had almost become *too* competitive. The Kenyan runners who came to Boston in 2000 were vying for *10 straight wins on the spin*. Was the race becoming too predictable?[1] Journalist Michael Gee offered these views in the *Boston Herald* after the 2000 race:

---

1. Be careful what you wish for – you might get it. In 1985 Boston was in grave danger of becoming 'just another local road race', so poor in quality had its field been for two straight years (on both occasions the race was won by the only world-class performer on show, Englishman Geoff Smith). The top runners had stopped coming to Boston because it didn't pay

The 2000 race gave the marathon what it needed most – a reason to remember what happened at the head of the pack. The thrilling duel regenerated the excitement that's been leaking from the men's race for the better part of a decade. Marathon watchers can respect and admire the Kenyan champions, but it's difficult to bond with athletes who spend one week a year here, then go back and live on the other side of the world.

So although a Kenyan once again donned the laurel wreath at Boston in 2000, the race's drama and charisma had returned with a vengeance (and the women's race wasn't bad either – see Chapter 6). The men's race *was* a "thrilling duel" as Gee suggests, but it was also more than that. It was the first time in history that the top two returned the same time, and also the first time that third place was right in the frame too.

* * *

Defending champ and 1998 runner-up Joseph Chebet returned to Boston to defend his crown. By all accounts he was going to take some beating. Master tactician Moses Tanui returned, winner for the Centennial race of 1996, and again in a breathtaking finish over Chebet in '98.[2] Up-and-coming 22-year-old Ethiopian Gezahegne Abera turned up, fresh from proving that he was a force to be reckoned with, after a whippy 2:07:54 win at Fukuoka the previous December, defeating France's Mohamed Ousadi by just one second. Another Kenyan Elijah Lagat was in the mix too – a former schoolteacher who now worked for his government at the ministry of education.

Lagat was the *Herald*'s dark-horse favourite to win. A late starter in athletics, he had never seriously run until at age 26 his doctor told him to start exercising to lose weight or die early. Since there are no gyms in Eldoret, Lagat did what is the in thing there. Run. He recalls: "I was too fat [only 155 pounds!]. The doctor said I needed to take exercise, so I began to run, not to be an athlete, but to be fit." He managed to shed 15 kilograms in 1992. To keep to this weight Lagat sustained his running. It didn't take long for him to start winning marathons. His first victory came in 1997 at Berlin where he returned a career best of 2:07:41. The following year he also won at Prague in 2:08:52. In his previous marathon before Boston 2000, he had stuttered slightly, finishing sixth at New York five months earlier.

* * *

Morning-glory Makoto Sasaki of Japan led the field by 27 seconds after four miles. The give-away that he was out of his depth and had no confidence in the folly of his actions was that he continually looked at his watch. As the athletes raced into a freezing, biting headwind, this was not a day for leading. Sasaki

---

expenses or prize money. Then, in 1986 under the wing of John Hancock Financial Services, Boston decided to break with tradition and start paying up; so much in fact that many of the greatest distance runners in the world were flocking to the Hopkinton start – and a healthy number of them were Kenyan.

2. Tanui ran 2:07:34 in this race, and three broke 2:08 in a marathon for the first time.

Double Boston champion Moses Tanui seeks a hat-trick at the Millennium race, closely tracked by Gezahegne Abera, fours months shy of a triumph at the Sydney Olympics. Elijah Lagat (7), grimly hangs on. *Victah Sailer, Photo Run*

eventually finished a wrecked 95th. As John Powers[3] of the *Globe* wrote: "Thus was boldness punished all afternoon. Anybody who ventured forward as the race grinded on through Natick and Wellesley and into Newton ended up swirled away like Dorothy Gale soaring off to Oz."

There were still nearly 20 men in a loose scrum when they turned onto Commonwealth Avenue at the Firehouse and headed up into the Newton Hills. Once the hills were over, there were still eight running stride for stride. Four miles out from Copley and, amazingly, there were still eight. Too many for double champ Tanui as he threw in a dangerous surge and nailed a wicked 4:37 mile. "I wanted to test them," he explained. This he did, as everyone fell off the back of the van, except for Lagat and Abera.

Charging down Beacon Street's gentle descent, almost nothing could separate them; indeed if one looked closely a little jostling could be spotted. The inexperienced Lagat tended to do most of the leading, with Abera – sandwiched in between the two Kenyans – and Tanui drafting off him.

In a real slow burner of a race, the last mile made for quite electrifying viewing. It was completed in 4 minutes and 42 seconds. With a third mile to go, Moses Tanui decided it was time to go hunting for Boston title number three, and he quickly built up what looked to be a decisive lead. His pursuers certainly thought so. "In the last kilometre, I thought my friend Moses would win," explained Lagat later.

But drafting behind other athletes into a strong wind is a sensible tactic, and out on his own Tanui's legs quickly filled with lactic. Abera, annoyed from all the jostling, soon realized he had enough nervous energy left to launch an assault of his own. He went after Tanui, slowly dragged him back, and then went past. With 150 metres to go the race now looked his and it seemed Kenya's stranglehold on Boston was finally broken. But in the final dozen or so seconds of the race, it was Lagat, the final man to start his kick, who had timed his race to perfection and sped past the rapidly crumbling Tanui and the fading Abera. "I realized Moses was not also moving fast, so I started to sprint," Lagat said. "I found I was

---

3. To indicate just how much tradition means at the Boston Marathon, it is interesting to note that Powers is just the third journalist to write the *Boston Globe*'s lead story on the event since 1932! He follows in the footsteps of the indefatigable Jerry Nason (1933–82), and Joe Concannon (1983–1999).

When three heads make up one giant head at the conclusion of a marathon, chances are it has been a close finish. Lagat wins from Abera, with Tanui three seconds back. *Victah Sailer, Photo Run*

moving closer and closer to him, so I sprinted to the maximum." It was to be Kenya after all, as Lagat blasted down the final home stretch of Boylston Street, raised his hands in victory and broke into a broad smile. "I thought I was winning for a third time," Tanui shrugged, "but the best man wins. Everyone makes mistakes, starting my kick too soon was my mistake."

The following day John Powers wrote in the *Globe*:

> This was the year the Boston Marathon ended up a drag race, when three men turned onto Boylston Street with a chance to win – and the least likely of them did. After the Boston Marathon was in real danger of losing the drama and theatre that had produced so many wonderful moments over the past hundred plus years, then here finally was not one, but two races that proved that this was still a sports event that commanded attention.

Television race commentator Bill Rodgers summed up the general mood by saying: "I think that was the greatest Boston Marathon finish I've ever seen in my life!"

However, although Lagat's victory was tremendously satisfying for him, not all of his co-competitors were as satisfied. There was a case of sour grapes among one of the athletes that earned a fair amount of media attention. Michael Holley, also writing in the *Globe* reported: "There was a great ending, with three seconds separating the top three finishers. There was also a great case of whining." The whining came from the young Abera, who felt that the two Kenyan athletes had conspired to gang up on him in the closing stages. Abera stated through an interpreter: "I was running between two Kenyans, and had a hard time dealing with some pushing and kicking. I can't say if the pushing and kicking was intentional, but with one Kenyan in front and one behind, that was a strain on my muscles, and resulted in me not finishing first."

All rather tiresome and unsavoury, and, one feels, a situation that Abera could easily have extricated himself from. Michael Holley wrote:

> In this scenario, let's hope that something *was* lost in the translation. Abera doesn't really believe that does he? It is true that the Kenyans dominate Boston. At the beginning of races, they run as a collective. Trying to get by them is like trying to pass a fleet of 18-wheelers; you don't pass unless they let you.

This, understandably can lead to some road rage. Especially if it happens for the better part of 26.2 miles. But, according to Tanui, that didn't happen yesterday. He said he was kicked and stepped on as well, but that's part of being in the lead. He also said at one point he stepped aside so Abera could get by, but the runner chose to follow him instead.

"He is accusing Kenyans," an angry Tanui said when told of Abera's remarks. "These are his problems. Abera did it to me also, two or three times. This is not correct that he accuse the Kenyans because he is the one who kicked several times. Also, when he was in front, he kicked me several times. He was the big problem."[4] As for Lagat, he explained: "I told him I could step aside, but he never went ahead, he wanted to follow me." What was clear, continued Michael Holley was that: "As the Kenyans continue to dominate, more accusations will come. That always happens to extraordinary performers. There will be more Aberas, saying that a Kenyan conspiracy led to a loss. There will also be increasing jealousy and contempt."

* * *

It had, all in all, been an exceptional weekend for Kenyan marathoning where the nation also triumphed at London and Rotterdam, with Tegla Loroupe winning in London and Kenneth Cheruiyot in The Netherlands. An editorial in the *Nairobi Daily Nation* paid tribute to the performances but pointed out a very important gong missing from Kenyan athletic achievement – the Olympic marathon.

These achievements are important for two good reasons. At a time when Kenyans have very little to feel good about, the likes of Loroupe and Lagat make us proud to be Kenyans. Secondly, they keep Kenya firmly on the world map of sport and are thus the best ambassadors the country could ask for.

It is unfortunate to note that despite this depth of talent, no Kenyan has ever won the Olympic marathon gold medal, something they can easily achieve if their hearts are in it. In fact, it is most unfortunate that the athletes are no longer interested in those sports that do not offer them immediate rewards. The attitude should change.

They now have enough time to train before the Sydney Olympics; this is a rare opportunity for them to forget the pay-packet and go for the gold.

However, victory in Sydney was not to be, as Kenya sent a weaker team to the Olympics than necessary due to petty internal disputes. Most significantly, Tanui was dropped from the team. Lagat and Cheruiyot returned pitiful DNFs, while it was left to Eric Wainaina to fly the flag as he lost a close duel but won silver. Ethiopia, of course, had the last laugh with the "whining" Gezahegne Abera winning gold and Tesfaye Tola the bronze. One thing though was for sure. A wrinkle at the Olympics aside, the Kenyan domination of the marathon looked set

4. More evidence that Abera was indeed "whingeing" rather than making valid points comes from the fact that he is the best *kicker* in the business. If you are going to point-blank refuse to lead any race in which you participate until the very death, then surely a little bodily contact should be expected.

to continue. Michael Gee wrote in the *Boston Herald*: "Lagat's story says it all about that nation and long-distance running. Even inside Kenya's fat people, there are marathon champions struggling to get out."

Race result:

Elijah Lagat	KEN	2:09:47
Gezahegne Abera	ETH	2:09:47
Moses Tanui	KEN	2:09:50
Ondoro Osoro	KEN	2:10:29
David Busienel	KEN	2:11:26
John Kagwe	KEN	2:12:26
Laban Nkete,	RSA	2:12:30
Joseph Chebet	KEN	2:12:39

Sources:

Archive race footage.
Gee, Michael, in the *Boston Herald*, April 18th, 2000.
Hollins, Michael, in the *Boston Globe*, April 18th, 2000.
Nairobi Daily Nation, editorial, April 19th, 2000.
Powers, John, in the *Boston Globe*, April 18th, 2000.
Shaughnessy, Dan, in the *Boston Globe*, April 17th & 18th, 2000.

XXXII

No. 19 – 1983 New York City Marathon [Men]

Sunday, October 23rd

The image that flashed around the world.

There are only a handful of sporting events in a given year that command "front-page" attention from everywhere from Miami to Moscow, Trinidad to Toronto, London to La Paz. The World Cup Soccer final is one such event, or a particularly memorable Olympic final another. For a lesser sporting event to command the attention of picture editors the world over, something spectacular, controversial, memorable or unusual is required – or preferably all four. Jean Van de Velde debating whether to play from the canal in front of the 18th at the Carnoustie British Open perhaps; or maybe John McEnroe having a tantrum at Wimbledon; or Greg Louganis splitting his head open on a diving board with a mistimed reverse two-and-a-half pike somersault. Or yes, an image of Geoff Smith and Rod Dixon at the conclusion of the 1983 New York City Marathon would do quite nicely, thank you.

Neither New Zealander Rod Dixon nor Liverpudlian Geoff Smith were household names at the start of the '83 New York, but most everyone knew what they looked like the following Monday morning as the drama they had played out seemed to tap straight into what people understood about sacrifice, toil, pain and despair. It was a true "water-cooler" moment:

"See that race in New York yesterday?"

"Yeah, poor guy – all that hard work."

"Cruel to have it snatched away like that."

"He seemed to think so."

* * *

In some ways the field for the 1983 NYC Marathon appeared disappointing. This was chiefly because the triple winner from 1980–82, Alberto Salazar had not come to race.

The reigning champion claimed that it didn't fit in with his plans, but rumour had it that he rested after the Helsinki World Championships, then went straight up to 140 miles per week and landed himself with serious hamstring problems. Rodolfo Gomez, Salazar's most troublesome opponent at previous New Yorks, had sciatica. Carlos Lopes who had pushed Rob de Castella to the limit in

Rotterdam the previous spring was reported injured. So the big three from 1982 were absent. However, main contenders included the still worthy lights of Ron Tabb, Tony Sandoval and Kirk Pfeffer – all of the US and all with times under 2:10:30. The Brits had John Graham (2:09.28), Jim Dingwall (2:11) and Dave Long (2:12), with the former miler Geoff Smith making his debut.

Of Smith, Mel Watman of *Athletics Weekly* wrote:

Smith had an unusual running background in that he was 22 before he started to take the sport seriously. A fireman at the time, he recalls: "it was advertised at work in November 1975 that the first six in the National Fire Brigade CCCs would be selected for an international race in France in March 1976. As I had raced a few times before I decided to have a go. I trained every day up to the race, which I won, and went on and won in France. Since then I haven't looked back."

After four years of solid progress, Smith won his first title of real significance when he captured the UK title in the 10,000m in 1980 in 28:20, to book his ticket to the Moscow Olympics.

However, a fireman he may've been, but the stifling conditions were just too much in Moscow ("I just couldn't move, it was so hot!"). Later that year Smith enrolled as a Business Management and Marketing student at Providence College, Rhode Island – noted for John Treacy's attendance. Smith hit peak form in the summer of 1981 when he ran in a GDR v GB meet and was the star of the match. A magnificent burst of speed over the final two laps was a revelation as he shot away from Werner Schildhauer, and moved to sixth on the British all-time list with 27:43. His second 5000 took just 13:41 and in covering the last lap in 58 he had shown he was certainly ready to take on the world. Smith then won the famous Emsley Carr mile at Cwmbran in August, astonishing everyone by winning in 3:55.8 to become the eleventh fastest British miler in history. Smith was displaying a truly impressive range, but as for his chances in the marathon, he suggested: "Timewise, I'm capable of going close to the world record. But I'm not going to be concerned with time. I'm going to be concerned about winning."

Geoff Smith, pictured in his days as a track star.
Mark Shearman

New Zealand sent a dangerous trio to New York in 1983 in Dick Quax (2.10), Rod Dixon (2.11) and Kevin Ryan (2.11). On top of all this, just to ensure a fast race, there was the late entry of Gidamis Shahanga, the 1978 Commonwealth champion (where he'd defeated hot home-town favourite Jerome Drayton). In attempting to defend his title four years later, Shahanga had gone out at a pace that could be described as terrifying. He was consequently reeled in, but had shown he still had pace to be feared. All applicants were asked to predict a time on their application form. Rod Dixon, who had a mile best (3:53.62) two seconds quicker than Smith, predicted 2:07:38. The Kiwi had won his last 19 road races – plus the Auckland Marathon in 2:11:21 in May '82, and had won an Olympic bronze in the 1500 way back at the 1972 Games.[1] Neil Amdur of the *New York Times* observed: "Sitting on the floor of the gymnasium at the Fort Wandsworth staging area on Staten Island before the start and scanning other seeded runners among the record field, Dixon said: "It's a whole new bloody world. They look hungry, they look mean. I wonder if I've got that look.""

The New York Marathon was now cementing itself as perhaps the world's leading marathon. Amdur advertised: "There will be more of almost everything for today's 14th running, including a record number of competitors, medical units at every mile and the possible choices of an eventual men's champ. In an event which has come to symbolize a coming together of the city's five boroughs, even no-parking signs along the course will be posted in three languages (English, Spanish and Hebrew) for the first time."

It seemed that it could be a race to savour after all.

* * *

The weather forecast called for cloudy skies, south-easterly winds and 50-degree temps with the possibility of showers by noon. As it turned out, those showers arrived early, and conditions were wet throughout the race. But they didn't dampen the spectacle, in fact they enhanced it, as calves and hamstrings going into spasm because of the cold and wet only added to the drama.

As many had predicted, Gidamis Shahanga led off at suicidal pace. It wasn't the sensible way to run marathons, but it was the only way he knew. By nine miles Shahanga was away and ripping through in 43:26. He went on to pass halfway in 63:12, with Smith now having left the comfort of the pack and doggedly stalking him nine seconds back. This all compared with the 64:10, which had been scored in the record year of 1981. Either the world record was going to fall very heavily, or else mother nature was going to exact some serious revenge over the second half.

Shahanga passed 15 miles in 1.12.33, but with less than 60 per cent of the race complete he was now starting to tie up. Smith pounced. After catching and passing him, the Tanzanian tucked into the Englishman's slipstream. Chris White of *Athletics Weekly* reports: "Geoff was working hard but Gidamis looked good. Geoff had stated before the race that he was going to win but nobody had listened. The next mile, on the Queensborough Bridge took 4.59, but on the fast next mile, the 17th off the bridge and down 1st Avenue, Geoff threw in a 4:28 and

---

1. An emotional man, Dixon began sobbing at Munich when he realized his dream of an Olympic medal had come true, even if a German official in doping control tried to cut him down to size. David Wallechinsky writes: "Still weeping, [Dixon] was ushered backstage for the urine test. After producing a meagre sample, Dixon sheepishly asked the official if it was enough. "For the gold medal, no. But for the bronze medal, it will do.""

Shahanga was gone." 4:28 miling...The world of marathoning had found a new star, and it was clear that the classic race was evolving. Fast. Evolving into a race where tremendous leg speed over the shorter distances would soon become a requisite for leading performances on the world stage.

Rod Dixon was still in the race but his thoughts were negative. He later recalled: "When I came off the bridge and looked up First Avenue I saw Geoff and Shahanga a half mile away and said 'oh my God, it's not enough time'. Then I looked at the pace car, and it had 47 minutes left, so I said to myself 'stay within your pace, stay within your race.' Slowly they started to come back to me, but it's a helluva way to run a race."

Dixon was running in third, Tabb fourth, Sandoval fifth and Graham sixth. At 20 miles Smith clocked 1:36:51, still on schedule for a monumental sub-2:07, but perhaps now looking somewhat drained. Dixon, meanwhile, had passed the brave but ailing Shahanga and closed to within 35 seconds. Just as it looked as though Dixon could be coming right back into contention, he ran into trouble, clutching his right hamstring. He had slipped on the wet surface at 5 miles and hurt it, and the cold water splashing up was not helping. "Both men were in trouble," reports Chris White: "If anyone was in range and going well, he could have picked them off. But at that pace, there was no-one. The miles were coming slower now – 5:02, 5:08, 5:12 – and Rod was 18 seconds back at 23. The courage of both men was visible on their faces as they fought to keep it going..."

Two more painful, scratchy miles came in 5:16 and 5:21 and the 25-mile split arrived at 2:02:53. However much Smith was dying on his feet, he was valiantly keeping a hold of his precious lead. Dixon was still 14 seconds adrift. At this rate, with less than 2 kilometres to go he just wasn't going to make it. "A miler's kick does the trick, a miler's kick does the trick," Dixon chanted to himself, believing that his superior track speed would win the day. He wasn't aware that, coincidentally, he was racing a man with a mile time nearly equal to his own. White continues: "Half a mile later, Geoff rounded a corner, stumbled and almost fell. Rod hadn't seen. The ghosts of 1908, 1948 and 1954 were hovering. Rod stopped clutching his hamstring which he had been doing every few yards, and dug deep to try to find something left. Geoff knew there was someone there. He didn't know who it was and didn't care." It's usually good news for an athlete when they can taste "blood in the water". Smith could taste it all right, but sadly for him it was his own. There was only one thing for it – *hang on*. Easy to say, but near impossible to do when in his state of near collapse. Smith passed the 26-mile marker at 2:07:54 and a moment later Dixon drew alongside. Smith looked over and knew. The game was up.

Dixon pushed on over the final 300 yards, and, suddenly refreshed, crossed the finish in 2:08:59, sunk to his knees, with arms outstretched with the joy of victory – and the relief of winning. After breaking the tape, he raised his arms high, and then knelt as if in prayer and bowed. Soon he was up, thrusting his right arm in the air and wobbling slightly. "Thank God," he could be heard mumbling, "Thank God."

A devastated Smith crossed the line nine seconds later. Victory had been snatched from his grasp. He too dramatically hit the deck, poleaxed on his back, not an ounce of energy left in his spent body. Three stewards immediately

The pole-axed figure of Geoff Smith gasps for breath like a fish out of water, while Rod Dixon basks in the glory of winning New York '83. *Keith Meyers*/The New York Times

swooped upon him and dragged the seemingly lifeless sack of potatoes away from the finishing area and to, one presumes, medical aid.

Neil Amdur wrote: "In an ebullient display of emotion after surging across the line, the lanky, moustachioed Dixon dropped to his knees, lifted his arms, kissed the wet pavement, again raised his arms and put his hands to his head. "I did want it very much," he said after extending his string of road-racing victories to 20 over the last 14 months. "And somehow you just express how you feel. I had tears." He had been the favourite and it wasn't supposed to have been as hard as that, or as fast as that. But it was. It was his second marathon, his second victory. He had become the eighth runner in history to break 2.09. Unlike some shorter-distance stars who race marathons unprepared and pay the penalty, Dixon had done a specific 3-month preparation in the States with two long runs weekly, and was spending $300 a week on phone calls to New Zealand to his coach, brother John.

At his first attempt at the marathon, Smith had deprived Ian Thompson of his longstanding British mark of 2:09:12 set when winning the 1974 Commonwealth Games. Ron Tabb placed third in 2.10.46, and in fourth the Canadian John Tuttle improved from his best from 2:12:32 to 2.10.51. John Graham ran well for fifth in 2.10.57. Gidamas Shahanga hung on for sixth, coincidentally the same position as he landed in when he'd employed similar tactics against de Castella in the '82 Commonwealths. This men's race had 11 men under 2.12 and 34 under 2.16.[2] Today's marathons may have faster times at the very top, but none can approach such incredible depth. The world's marathon boom was truly at its peak.

* * *

"I was pushing as hard as I could, short of falling over," Dixon told the *New Zealand Herald.* "I guess he was pushing himself to the point where he fell over. I think we both ran our tails off pretty well. That was a long, lonely haul to pick up the other guys," Dixon said. Dixon remained surprisingly humble after his victory. "The marathon is a discipline all its own," he said. "It takes a very special type of person. When you look at Salazar, de Castella, Grete, they all have special

---

2. Skiing legend Jean-Claude Killy found going slower in running shoes, but managed to break four hours in 3:58:08.

qualities. I have yet to earn that quality, and I'm not sure I have the time and patience to pursue it.

"That's the only way you win races today," he said.

That's what makes it so tough for everybody else: unless you're in shape you're not going to do anything.

I feel good, I've been out and had a few champagnes...things are going all right. Tomorrow I appear on "Good Morning America", and a few other things...then I'll take a break. I'll certainly keep jogging.

On his age Dixon, who was 33, commented: "I don't think there's any set time really. You've got to be resilient; you've got to be versatile and yet you've got to have that maturity. People like de Castella and Salazar are the perfect mould, because they're young enough, and yet they've been on the international circuit a good six or seven years." Ragarding the future, Dixon philosophized:

I don't know. I've put the icing on my cake now, and now it's on my terms. I'm going to run when and how I like. I think I've proved with this race now that I'm very much to the fore and I'll continue my road racing of course, because that's my forte over here. The sport is my business over here, and that is my interest and my first love, and it's what I enjoy doing and get recognised and respected for.

Dixon celebrates at the post-race party with women's winner Grete Waitz, who had won her 5th New York title in 2:27 dead. Four more to go. *Bettmann/CORBIS*

Several years later Dixon concluded: "That win was the topping off my whole career. New York is the one you have to win."

Geoff Smith attempted to put into the words the awful dual feeling of being a hunted man and pure exhaustion. The marathon for him had indeed been a baptism of fire: "I never felt as bad as I did over those last two miles. It was like running with a hangover – like having gone out and partied yourself to death and trying to get up the next morning. I really thought I was going to win, but my legs were shot."

* * *

It rounded off a fantastic year for Antipodean sport: Australia won the America's cup yacht race; Rob de Castella won the marathon at the first World Championships. Chris Lewis of New Zealand reached the Wimbledon final, Australia had reached the final of the tennis Davis Cup, and their cricketers had defeated England in the Ashes Test series.

Both Dixon and Smith went to the Los Angeles Olympics. Dixon placed a not unworthy tenth, while Smith failed to finish. Smith, however, would go on to play an important part in marathon history, in particular with the evolution of the Boston Marathon. He recorded back-to-back wins in Boston in 1984–5, but the fields were very substandard. Boston, even in this new age of professionalism, was still refusing to pay appearance or prize money to its leading runners, and consequently saw them staying away.

In 1984 Smith won by four minutes in 2:10:34 (to earn his Olympic selection), and the following year he won by *five* minutes, but only in 2:14 having hobbled, limped and walked the final miles after a spectacular "crash and burn" in a bold world-record bid (he passed halfway in 1:02:51). But where were all the runners? Something had to be done, and it was. Boston rejuvenated itself, signed a huge deal with John Hancock Financial Services, and in 1986 returned as one of the premier world marathons – having faced the uncomfortable prospect of becoming just another local road race.

Race result:

Rod Dixon	NZL	2:08:59
Geoff Smith	GBR	2:09:08
Ron Tabb	USA	2:10:46
John Tuttle	USA	2:10:51
John Graham	GBR	2:10:57
Gidamis Shahanga	TAN	2:11:05

Sources:

Amdur, Neil, in the *New York Times*, October 23rd, 1983.
Amdur, Neil, in the *New York Times*, October 24th, 1983.
Derderian, Tom, *Boston Marathon*. Human Kinetics, 1996.
Dixon, Rod, interview with the *New Zealand Herald*, October 24th, 1983.
Watman, Mel, in *Athletics Weekly*, October 26th, 1983.
White, Chris, in *Athletics Weekly*, October 26th, 1983.

XXXIII

No. 18 – 1988 Boston Marathon [Men]

Monday, April 18th

"I like to make history."

"Possibly the best of all Bostons" is how Joe Concannon of the *Boston Globe* described the 1988 edition in a reflective article at the Centennial race of 1996. "It turned out to be a race for the history books and in terms of raw drama, 1988 has to go down as number 1." Fred Lebow, race director of the New York City Marathon, gave this colourful prediction before the race: "If it's rainy, the Brits will win. If it's hot, the Kenyans will win. If it's snow, the Finns will win. And if the Italians drink a lot of wine tonight, they will win it." Lebow's logic was based on the fact that he'd seen Italians romp home with three of the last four New York races. But, whatever one made of Lebow's whimsical comments, one thing was for sure: the runners who came to Boston weren't just shooting for forward positions to impress their national selectors ahead of the Seoul Olympics; they were shooting for fast times too, because the day before the world record had finally fallen in Rotterdam.

"This will motivate the other athletes," said the ever-game Juma Ikangaa of Tanzania, as he studied the superb exploits of Belayneh Dinsamo (2:06:50) and Ahmed Salah. The world record had been stagnant for quite a while: three days short of three years in fact and was due to fall,[1] agreed Allan Warner, the coach of former record holder Steve Jones: "The event had stood still. It needed something like that."

For his part, Ikangaa hatched immediate plans that a course record was possible at Boston, even if his course debut the previous year had led to "thigh-smash" and a painful 2:16. The tremendously popular, front-running Tanzanian, who had placed second at both the 1982 Commonwealth Games and the thrilling 1983 Fukuoka, said: "I feel comfortable. If de Castella can run 2:07 here, then other people can do under 2:07. I'm not saying me but some athlete. It depends upon the weather." Ikagnaa had broken 2:09 a startling six times, and 2:10 eight times. He owned three major crowns from Tokyo (1984), Fukuoka (1986) and Beijing (1987). His Beijing run the previous autumn showed him to be in good

---

1. It would now stand at this mark for 10½ years.

form, and on Valentine's Day 1988, Ikangaa had placed second to Ethiopian Abebe Mekonnen at Tokyo in 2:08:42. He was ranked the number-one marathoner in the world in 1986, and felt that his best was yet to come.

Despite the absence of the Ethiopians – who had ducked out late in the day and opted for the faster course at Rotterdam – a large African contingent of some 36 runners came to Boston seeking Olympic qualification. The Kenyan Ibrahim Hussein came to test himself over the hills for the first time. Hussein's childhood idol had been Kip Keino. A nine-year-old Hussein had watched in awe as Keino had returned triumphantly from the Mexico Olympics of 1968 as a hero to great acclaim from the crowds at Nairobi airport. Hussein dreamt he too might one day be Olympic champion. He started running everywhere: the 3 miles to school, the 2 miles to his grandmother's; and while he ran, he pretended he was Kip Keino.

Before turning his attentions to the marathon, Hussein developed a lethal kick by competing in the 800 and 1500-metres and the steeplechase. He scored a 1:47 in college. He loved running long distances, though, and felt his kick would be best utilized in the marathon. He wasn't wrong. The 29-year-old Hussein's credentials coming into the Boston on 1988 included three wins at Honolulu. And perhaps more significantly, he had proved himself to be a trail-blazer: finally, after 18 years of the race's existence, an African runner had won the New York Marathon. It was Hussein, in 1987, six months before the 1988 Boston. Could he now repeat the feat at Boston, where no African had won either? Hussein weighed 120 pounds and stood 5 feet 8 inches. Tom Derderian writes in *Boston Marathon*: "Hussein looked pleasant and moved with the demeanour of a relaxed and hospitable tour guide. Strangers felt instantly at ease with him. Teammates followed his example. Polished, bright, articulate in English and Nandi, passable in Arabic and Swahili, Hussein earned a degree in economics from the University of New Mexico in 1984. Everyone who met him liked him – a nice guy."

Africans had come to try their luck at Boston before, most notably in the form of Abebe Bikila and Mamo Wolde in 1963 (they toiled somewhat to finish fifth and twelfth), and Commonwealth bronze medallist Richard Mabuza of Swaziland in 1975 and '76 (right up with the leaders in both years before crawling home in 39th and 36th). But now three dozen Africans rolled up to the start line in Hopkinton in 1988: they had finally arrived en masse. Tom Derderian continues:

The idea of Africans coming to Boston would have astounded the original founders of the BAA,[2] men who grew up acclimated to segregation.

At the end of the 19th Century wealthy members of the BAA, in imitation of the colonial British, went on safari to Africa, then returned to their clubhouse to mount their rhino and wildebeest trophies.

Nearly a century later events had turned full circle: Africans safaried to Boston to take a different kind of trophy – money and a Mercedes-Benz – back to Africa.

There were many other highly decorated runners in this race, as Olympic team

---

2. Boston Athletic Association.

selectors from Kenya, Tanzania, Italy, Finland, England, Ireland and Mexico all thought the Boston race would be an accurate guide to the form of their leading men. Two other ex-New York champions came in the form of Orlando Pizzolato (NYC 1984, '85) and Gianni Poli (1986). Brits Steve Jones and Geoff Smith were in town, hoping to impress their country's oh-so-fickle Olympic selectors. They had placed second and third the year before, and Smith of course had won twice (in 1984 and '85). As for Jones, he had once, not so long ago, owned the world record himself. But now he was seen as a tactically flawed runner owing to an excruciating turn at the 1986 European Championships, when he whipped through the first 15 kilometres in 45:02, far too fast for the hot weather Stuttgart was enjoying. He eventually finished a painful 20th in 2:22.

The winner in that race was the rapidly up-and-coming Italian Gelindo Bordin, who finally won a marathon after nine attempts at the distance. And he certainly suggested there was a lot more to come, as along with great strength and strategy, he had fired off the last 2.2K in 6:55 to sprint away for a narrow win over Pizzo- lato. Bordin said he was only in Boston as a warm-up for the Olympics, but he could not be discounted.

Another person who couldn't be written off was the mercurial talent of John Treacy from Ireland. A double winner of the World Cross Country Champion- ships, Treacy only signed up to run Boston a few days before. He was certainly the most dangerous dark horse in the field, as his nightmare run a year earlier (where he hobbled home in barely under 2:18) could be counterbalanced by an Olympic silver medal from Los Angeles '84. Treacy had not intended to run a spring marathon, and only decided on it three days before, after an encouraging 15-kilometre time in the famous Ekiden road relay. "I asked my wife on Thursday night what she thought about me running," he explained. "She thought I was joking."

* * *

The weather, unlike the prevous year's humid conditions turned out perfect: cool and damp. The race unfolded slowly with 22 runners still in the mix at 5 miles (23:41). Hussein hunkered in the pack – he was in no hurry. Why be in a hurry when you have the leg speed of a top-class 400-metre runner? A capability of running the quarter-mile in 47 seconds meant Hussein would relish any last- minute burn-up with which he became party. Meanwhile, he sat in and watched, as 10 miles passed by with barely any trimming of the pack. The split: 47:57. "They all looked good," writes Derderian. "The almost perfect running weather made a fast second half seem likely. There would be no sun-baked suffering in this race, only the high drama of barely restrained speed."

Only the very naive runner or observer thought to double the halfway split of 63:12 and imagine the breaking of Densimo's one-day-old world record. "The Boston course has a seductively easy first half – and a heartless second" (Derderian). One by one runners fell off the back and heading up Brae Burn hill, the first of the dreaded Newton Hills at around the 17-mile mark, the race seemed to be between Hussein, Ikangaa, Treacy, Steve Jones, Gianni Poli, Morocco's Nechadi El-Mustapha, and José Gomez of Mexico. The latter two were little-known runners and their resilience to stick it out this far was brave but foolhardy. El-Mustapha would go on to place 36th, and Gomez an equally painful DNF.

The 20-mile split read 1:37:36 – an extremely fast time, which indicated that not only was the race fascinating to watch, it was one of the highest quality too. It had come down, finally, to a race of three. The evening before Steve Jones and Treacy had struck up a plan. They feared that the leading Africans would work as a team to see off any threat that Jones and Treacy posed. So why not form a European team of their own. A good idea in theory...if you are able to hang on. Jones couldn't. He said later, "We were together half the way, but it didn't work because they ran so aggressive. There was nothing we could do about it." Treacy's grand plan – now that he was working alone – was to somehow stay within striking range till around 25 miles, and then let his superior speed do the work. The two Africans kept dropping the brave Irishman, but he kept clawing himself back to parity. Finally, at Cleveland Circle, around 2½ miles from the finish, Ikangaa and Hussein forced themselves to prise open a gap over Treacy that would prove to be insurmountable. It was down to a two-man race – between a couple of the finest marathoners Africa had ever produced.

The contrast in their styles was marked. Ikangaa, as ever, ran with a manic and fierce passion to keep hammering on and on, never letting up, never allowing the pace to slacken. This all played into the hands of Hussein, as it had famously played into the hands of other great marathoners like de Castella and Seko. But just because Ikangaa had fallen into this trap before – of letting others follow his lead, before hitting him with a lethal sting – it didn't make the spectacle any less absorbing. After all, although Ikangaa lost more than he won, he was no stranger to crossing the line first, and he was a far better-known runner than Hussein, whose personal best was only 2:11:01. Derderian writes: "Regardless of Ikangaa's hammering, Hussein ran blithely, with a childlike joy to his stride. Treacy agonized while Bordin followed dispassionately. But between Hussein and Ikangaa the drama swelled."

One mile to go and nothing can separate the Tanzanian Juma Ikangaa, and the Kenyan Ibrahim Hussein (right). But it's a kicker's world... *Fay Foto*

The runners ran almost step for step down Commonwealth Avenue, sweeping right on to Hereford Street, forced themselves up its slight incline, and swung left onto Boylston. They had 90 seconds to run. The 26-mile marker came and went, and still no clue as to who would flash through the line first. The television director switched to his camera perched high above the finish line, looking straight down on the approaching stars. It was a wonderful image as the two dark figures, like sleek racehorses, homed in on the huge, garish blue-and-yellow awning that advertised the promised land. At one stage they ran in Indian file, and it appeared there

304

With Juma Ikangaa in his wake, Ibrahim Hussein becomes the first African to win the Boston Marathon. But as Roger Bannister once said: 'Après moi, le deluge.' *Fay Foto*

was just the one of them; that's how close it was. Ikangaa refused to let Hussein pass.

The runners' two coaches stood beyond the finish, Robert Ouko with the Kenyan flag and Samuel Tupa, the Tanzanian coach. They basked in the African tone of the race – their rivalry forgotten. "One of our boys is coming," said Ouko. "Our boys are coming," corrected Tupa. Hussein dropped three steps behind Ikangaa, and Ouko fretted. He said later: "I was a bit scared and I told the people with me, 'I'm worried,' I thought we had lost it." Finally though, Hussein's plan – and dream – came true. "Hussein lifted his knees and flickered his elbows," wrote Derderian, and Hussein achieved what almost no one can do: running at a pace of sub-50-seconds per 400-metres, when muscles are screaming and 26.18 miles have been run. Because of the soft patter of rain, Ikangaa couldn't hear Hussein's shoes. Maybe he wasn't there. Maybe he had dropped back. No. With less than 100 metres to go, Hussein finally edged into the lead and triumphed by 1 second and 3 yards. Hussein had won $45,000 and a $35,000 Mercedes-Benz 190E automobile. That lethal kick therefore was worth $58,000 to him, as Ikangaa picked up $22,000 – $19,300 a yard some might say.

* * *

Pretty much all scribes were in agreement. It had been the most exciting and dramatic of all the 92 Bostons. Joe Concannon wrote in the *Boston Globe*: "Their names and images transported out of a drizzly springtime afternoon will be forever linked in the history of this race. They became a significant part of its folklore, personally transforming yesterday's marathon into a showcase that belongs to posterity." Robert Ouko crashed through security ("The security, they have guns, but it was most important that I get through with our flag") and greeted a hugely relieved Hussein at the finish line. Ouko told his runner, "Congratulations, we are proud of you," and the runner told Ouko, "I did not expect to win." Michael Madden of the *Globe* then wrote: "Ouko protected Hussein from the cold dampness of a Boston April day with a most appropriate blanket. He warmed Hussein with the red and white and black and green flag of his country. It was a sight and a race and a finish, indeed."

Hussein explained his win to the waiting media:

When I came here, I was confident I could win the race. I had heard about Boston, how it was a tough course, with downhills and then uphills. I had run New York, but they told me Boston was real tough, and if you're not ready and if you haven't trained well, you'll pay the price.

I felt 'just let Juma lead by one step.' I'll just be there, but I'm not going to provoke him or spook him to make him mad. Whenever we'd reach a water station, I'd take the water and I'd give it to him. I wanted him to take me towards the end. At one point, it thought, 'OK, well go with 1 mile to go.' I could see the response from him. He wasn't pulling away. He didn't make a move, so I said, 'OK let's keep on going.'

I like to make history. I was the first African to win New York and I was the first African runner to win at Boston."

Ikangaa philosophically explained: "I wanted it to be a sprint, but with one mile left, I discovered it was too far away. I was a bit upset to be dropped with 100 metres to go. I just knew he was behind me. I didn't even hear his shoes."

John Treacy had held on for all his might, and imposed great uncertainty into the minds of the Africans. He explained:

I was right there. I remember a big group of us made the turn at the Newton fire station and headed into the hills. Slowly but surely, it just happened. I remember running with Juma and Ibrahim. I tried to stay with them. I got the distinct impression they were running as a team to make sure they beat me.

The few times I got close, they pulled away, and in the last mile, they went farther away. I had to settle for third, because on the couple of times when I was close, they went away. I think it's easier to run with someone and not have to run alone. If you're alone, it's easier to be caught from behind.

If you told me last week that I would finish third in the Boston Marathon, I would have told you that you were out of your mind.

* * *

The future for Hussein was a mixture of more stellar triumphs and crushing disappointment. He was given the high honour of carrying his nation's flag in to the Olympic Stadium at Seoul five months later, but then went on to record a DNF. Then, after not racing for an entire year, no one considered Hussein a threat when he turned up to the 1991 Boston. An Achilles tendon injury had forced him to drop out of the 1990 race, and insiders asked whether a short but very sharp career had come to a close. Hussein was pitted that year against Douglas Wakii-huri, who "appeared to American runners and the American press as an invincible hybrid. In him the mysteries of Africa and the Orient combined" (Derderian). But while all the other runners keyed off Wakiihuri, Hussein stole away from the pack, and then stole the entire race, defeating Abebe Mekonnen by 16 seconds.

In 1992 he playfully acknowledged the crowds in the early stages by putting his fingers in his ears, before casually tossing away his gloves and forging into the lead with 6 miles to go. Then he was all business, his face grimacing with the effort. Tom Derderian writes: "He drove himself to his best ever time, and Boston's second best ever, of 2:08:14, and promptly burst into tears upon crossing the line. Just two years earlier it appeared that his career was over, but here he was crushing the rest of the field by nearly 2½ minutes. He had reached his physical and emotional peak."

Such effort and achievement took its toll however and Hussein had indeed reached a peak, as he ran to just 37th in the Barcelona Olympics and failed to finish the '93 Boston. But his victories, kindness, carefree spirit and joyful running style will long be recalled, and in particular the mesmerizing duel with Ikangaa at Boston '88. No one is better qualified to judge the greatness of that race than Fred Lebow: "This is the 100th marathon I've seen in every part of the world. I've seen them in Fukuoka, Tokyo, Rotterdam, Chicago, New York, Boston and the Olympics, and this is the most exciting finish I've ever seen. I remembered what Hussein told me last week: 'If I'm in sight of the finish line, I'm going to win it.'"

Race result:

Ibrahim Hussein	Kenya	2:08:43
Juma Ikangaa	Tanzania	2:08:44
John Treacy	Ireland	2:09:15
Gelindo Bordin	Italy	2:09:27
Gianni Poli	Italy	2:09:33
John Campbell	New Zealand	2:11:08
Orlando Pizzolato	Italy	2:12:32
J. Makanya	Tanzania	2:14:04
Steve Jones	Wales	2:14:07
T. Taniguchi	Japan	2:14:18

Note: Bill Rodgers was the first American finisher in 28th place, aged 40, in 2:18:17.

307

Sources:

Archive race footage.
Concannon, Joe, in the *Boston Globe*, April 19th, 1988.
Concannon, Joe, in the *Boston Globe*, April 13th, 1996.
Connolly, John, in the *Boston Herald*, April 18th, 1988.
Derderian, Tom, *Boston Marathon*. Human Kinetics, 1996.
MacMullen, Jackie, in the *Boston Globe*, April 19th, 1988.
Madden, Michael, in the *Boston Globe*, April 19th, 1988.

XXXIV

No. 17 – 1992 Olympic Marathon [Women]

Saturday, August 1st

*The villagers of Iziderkino raise money for a television set,
to cheer on their girl.*

To win the Olympics, you gotta get there first...and for the world's leading women shooting for the Barcelona 1992 Olympic marathon, that was easier said than done. The hard luck stories of highly talented, world-class runners being ignored by their national selectors were aplenty. The problem with having just one selection race for the Olympics as some nations chose is that there are often classy marathoners who are not ready for the selection race, but *more* than ready for the Olympics. Like those running for the unified team of the Commonwealth of Independent States (CIS), or as was mainly the case, the Russians. The CIS selectors chose the Los Angeles Marathon on March 1st, 1992, as their trial race for the Barcelona Olympics, and Belorussian Madina Biktagirova (2:26:23) was selected, along with Russians Ramilya Burangulove (2:28:12) and Valentina Yegorova (2:29:41).

The controversy came six weeks later when Russia's Olga Markova, who had forever been trying to persuade those in power that she was a runner to be taken seriously – despite her dainty stride and pixie steps – popped a national record of 2:23:43, to win by half a mile at Boston. Of her hopes for Olympic selection, despite missing the trial race, Markova said: "They have changed rules before, now maybe they will change them for me." However, Tom Derderian writes: "Markova felt that after this Boston performance she would not have to ask for a place on the Russian Olympic team. As the year wore on, no woman in the world ran a faster marathon, but the Russian selectors, like frowning politbureacrats, ignored Markova's Boston victory and chose three other runners."

For Japan there were more tales of dismay. Although Yumi Kokamo returned a national record at Osaka on January 26th with 2:26:26 and was selected for the Olympics, another debutante, Ademi Matsuno was not selected, even though she ran 2:27:02. Yoshiko Yamamoto ran a terrific 2:26:46 in Los Angeles but she too was ignored. The final two spots were awarded to Sachiko Yamashita who had so nearly won in the World Championships the year before, and Yuko Arimori, who had placed fourth. Although both the CIS and Japanese selectors were being

309

ruthless and following completely different philosophies in selecting their teams, it would turn out they would be vindicated in Barcelona. As ever the Japanese would be extremely well prepared, and would most likely work together to try and ensure a medal.

There was sadly no Joan Benoit Samuelson to fly the flag for America, and their team of Janis Klecker, Cathy O'Brien and Francie Larrieu-Smith carried little hope of making an impression on the favoured runners in Spain. The agonies of American Lisa Weidenbach can't be ignored: she placed fourth in the American trial for the third consecutive time.[1] Ouch.

Germany sent a real heavyweight in the form of Katrin Dörre, who had won London, and had captured the bronze in Seoul in '88; but ignored the very reasonable claims of Uta Pippig (2:27 at Boston) and Kerstin Pressler (2:29 at Los Angeles). Poland boasted the class of Wanda Panfil, the world champion from the year before in Tokyo. Panfil hadn't been up to much since then (just sixth in Boston); perhaps she had been saving herself for the big one.

Portugal had great pedigree in the form of Manuela Machado (2:27 at Boston), and perhaps Rosa Mota, who had raced for her country so brilliantly for a full decade. Could the diminutive legend rouse herself for one final hurrah? *Athletics Weekly* tipped her as a favourite to defend her crown: "The queen of marathon running, Rosa Mota, who once held the World, Olympic and European titles at the same time, has failed to finish her last two runs over the distance and has stomach problems. Even so, she will be the one every else wants to beat and is likely to dictate the pattern of the race if she makes the start line." Sadly however, Mota just couldn't make it to the start line healthy, and her wonderful top-flight career was over with back-to-back DNFs in Tokyo at the World Championships the year before and London in April. Her career statistics may be viewed in more detail in Chapter 22, but the one that tells the starkest picture is out of 21 marathons, she won 14. And when she finished a marathon, she never did place out of the top four.

Like America, Britain's women marathoning was in a fairly dire state. Veronique Marot, the London winner from 1989, was on the verge of turning 37, and plucky as the two Sallys – Eastall and Ellis – may have been, they were rank outsiders for medals. Age was, however, of no concern for New Zealand's main entrant. Lorraine Moller may have been born in June 1955, but she was all set and raring to go for her third Olympics. Of the big players from Los Angeles '84, just she and another Antipodean Lisa Martin (now Ondieki) survived. Ondieki came into the Games in great shape, having run an Australian record of 31:11 the June before the Olympics. She was the double Commonwealth champion ['86 and '90] – on the latter occasion demolishing the field by nearly *eight* minutes. Ondieki had pushed Rosa Mota so hard at Seoul four years earlier for the silver; now she was ready to go one better.

* * *

---

1. In fact Weidenbach could lay claim to being the unluckiest non-Olympian of all time: not only did she place fourth in '84, '88 and '92 in the marathon trial, but in 1980 she attempted to qualify for the Olympics in swimming. She placed fourth – where else? – in the trials.

Lengthy descriptions, critique and miscellany from Barcelona 1992 may be found in Chapter 40, but one important recap here is that for both heat and difficulty of the course, the race was to be one of the fiercest tests in Olympic history. Certainly the toughest since Mexico '68. Frank Horwill wrote in *Athletics Weekly*: "With the awesome hill to the stadium (some 7 kilometres in length), this was going to be one Olympics to search for runners with supreme strength, pedigree and ability to keep cool, both mentally and physically." The race began with the mercury hitting great heights: a stifling 29 °C to be exact, 5 degrees higher than in the cauldron of the Tokyo World Championships the year before, where a meagre 63 per cent of the runners finished. To indicate, perhaps, the greater lengths people are willing to go to in an Olympic race, an acceptable 81 per cent would finish here.

Lisa Ondieki feistily took the lead, albeit at the conservative pace of 17:58, for the first 5 kilometres. Twelve runners tucked in behind her. As the next 15 kilometres unfolded, a highly cautious, tactical race developed. Granted, the oppressive conditions meant the runners couldn't run particularly fast, but their subsequent splits of 18:29, 19:01 and 18:41 indicated that *whatever* the weather, somebody somewhere was going to have fresh legs for the second half of the race. By 20 kilometres the pack was still keying off the experience of Ondieki. Anyone with three major championship medals was better value than a highly paid pace-maker as one gets in a big-city marathon.

However, pace-making is not what Ondieki had come to Barcelona to do, and when Valentina Yegorova took over at the halfway stage, Ondieki was all too happy to do some coasting. Until, that is, Yegorova started dangerously shifting through the gears. The split for the next 5 kilometres indeed showed a devastating acceleration: 17:29. Ondieki, distraught, stepped off the course, following the role of pace-maker to the letter. First she blamed her DNF on taking on too *much* water, but then she changed her story to a far more sinister theory that her water bottles had been tampered with.

So who was this that many thought shouldn't have been in the race at all (because she was keeping Olga Markova out), suddenly bossing the Olympic marathon? Just two years earlier, Yegorova had placed a humble 21st in London. Although Yegorova was by no means new to the marathon – it was her 14th – she had hardly marked her card as a proven winner. Just one win had been scored, exactly four years earlier in the Russian city of Ufa (600 miles east of Moscow). A win is a win, but it didn't exactly have the hacks in the media tent going, "Watch her, she won Ufa in '88." However, there was one deadly sign of huge promise in her history, and it had come two years earlier, at Split in the European championships. Rosa Mota had come to Split as hot favourite to win a third European crown, to add to her two from 1982 and '86, but in her eagerness to win, had run one of her tactically poorer races and began to fade in the lead, deep into the race. The more circumspect Yegorova caught Mota at 35 kilometres and a marvellous duel developed. After exchanging a few words, Mota attempted to pull away, but Yegorova hung doggedly to her and even over the last 500 metres in the stadium, Mota was still glancing over her shoulder at her would-be assassin.

But Yegorova had not been able to defeat Mota that day, falling short by a mere five seconds; and since her win at Ufa, Yegorova had also placed second in

Leipzig (in a slow 2:48), and, more impressively, at Tokyo in December 1991. This partly atoned for her DNF in the same city at the 1991 World Championships. Bizarrely, Yegorova ran another marathon just 27 days after her Olympic qualifying run in Los Angeles, at Paris, where she ran poorly to place twelfth in 2:43. The author suggests that she merely used the run as a training spin. But the Barcelona Olympic marathon was no training spin. Yegorova was tired of placing second in marathons; let alone the collection of thirds and fourth's she had totted up as well. She had the experience of top-level racing, and the heat was unlikely to present too grave a problem as she had coped so well with it in Split.

After Biktagirova[2] had her turn in the lead for a short while, Yegorova took over again and at 25 kilometres decided to hit her rivals with a devastating surge. Her next 5 kilometres took her just 16:41, and by 30 kilometres, Yegorova had an enormous lead of 54 seconds. Observers were divided about what such a development meant. A tiresome, formulaic runaway victory by someone who took a gamble that paid off? Or a gripping struggle as the impatient one, as if by magnet, got sucked back to the pack.

The answer soon came. The tiny Yegorova (she was just 1.56 metres and 52 kilograms) had indeed overcooked it. A figure could soon be spotted behind behind her and was travelling significantly quicker. It was the 26-year-old Yuko Arimori, her presence in Barcelona based on the grounds of her fourth place in the World Championships the year before. At Split, Yegorova had been the hunter and terrified Mota into near submission; now the tables had turned. Martin and Gynn write: "Between 30 and 35 kilometres, on the downhill section through the heart of Barcelona, spectators six deep were cheering from both sides of the street. Yegorova was clocked at 35 kilometres in 2:06:36, and Arimori moved into second, 12 seconds behind." The runners arrived at the impressive statue of Columbus on the waterfront, and what lay in store was the gruelling 7-kilometre climb to the stadium. By 36 kilometres Arimori had already caught her depleted prey. Surely she would now slowly draw away to a famous win. She was born in Okayama City and was a graduate of the Nippon College of Physical Education (Martin & Gynn). Although fairly inexperienced in the marathon, Arimori was improving with every race. At the prestigious Osaka Marathon she placed sixth in 2:32, and the following year jumped to second in 2:28. This led to selection for the World Championships, where she ran to her honourable fourth. And now here she was shooting to be the best marathoner in the world. She had prepared for the race with devastating focus, having run 200 miles a week on a training camp in Spain at altitude, with a regular long run of 32 miles at 6:15 pace (Mackay).

Meanwhile, behind Arimori, a very old hand was bringing all her considerable experience to the fore. Lorraine Moller, 37-years-young, moved into third. Moller had placed 5th in Los Angeles '84, 34th in Seoul, and was now vying for an Olympic bronze medal, which it was looking increasingly likely she would earn.

With the final kilometres of the race being ticked off, Yegorova continued to

---

2. Although Biktagirova went on to finish fourth, she was later disqualified after she tested positive for the stimulant norephedrine.

hang on for all she was worth, alongside the supremely fit Arimori. Every time Arimori surged, the Russian was somehow able to respond. Back home the people from her village gathered round glued to the town's only television set. David Wallechinsky reports:

When Valentina Yegorova qualified for the Olympics, all her neighbours in the small farming village of Iziderkino were thrilled. They couldn't wait to see her on television. There was just one problem: no one in the village owned a television set. So all 1,500 villagers chipped in and bought a single, 30-year-old black-and-white set that was placed at the entrance of the home of Yegorova's parents and faced out toward the street.

There is an old saying in the marathon: once you're caught, there's no coming back. The bad news for Yegorova was that she had been caught. But wait – hadn't she, albeit unwillingly, disproved this theory when she had caught Rosa Mota in the Europeans, only for the Portuguese to go on to win? Maybe she could do a Mota. So she hung in there and hoped. "I didn't have any great urge to break away from her," she explained later, "I just wanted to keep up."

A grim struggle for acceptance is nearly at an end for Valentina Yegorova – an inspired, if controversial, choice from her national selectors. *Mark Shearman*

The packed stadium waited in expectation. They were being kept well informed of the valiant battle that was approaching. Martin and Gynn write: "Coming around the gymnastics arena with the stadium in sight, Yegorova took advantage of the brief levelling of the hilly path just before the tunnel entrance into the stadium. She found another gear, and Arimori did not respond." The athletes scampered in to the Olympic Stadium to gasps of excitement from the crowd. Just a handful of seconds separated the two runners. If 1988's Olympic marathon had been a thrilling affair with Mota prevailing by just 13 seconds, this was closer still. Yegorova powered on, and Arimori battling to the last, finally fell short by just 40 yards and 8 seconds.

* * *

It had been a hugely unpredictable and marvellous race. Beforehand *Athletics Weekly* made their traditional predictions of how the marathon result would go. Not for the first time, they almost couldn't have been wider of the mark:

313

"*AW*s women's predictions: 1 Ondieki [DNF], 2 Panfil [22nd] and 3 Kokamo [29th; only just inside 3 hours]."

After recalling how she herself had failed to win in Split, when seemingly a late favourite, Yegorova expressed delight that she had bounced back when it looked as though she had got it all wrong. The conditions simply hadn't affected the Russian like it had most of the other runners. Did she think the result might have been different had Mota been present? "It would have been the same," she declared, "the conditions were perfect for me."

After Lorraine Moller had earned her bronze medal, an Italian official got down on his knees, bowed his head to the floor, and kissed her feet. The Italian was not alone in his surprise. Michael Sandrock writes: "Some of those shocked individuals worked in promotions at the shoe company which had dropped its sponsorship of Moller just before the Olympics, telling her she was too old to continue as a world-class runner." Incredibly, Moller was still competing for the Kiwis at Atlanta '96, where she placed 46th. Her huge grin as she crossed the finish line that day was well deserved. Moller had been racing at a high level for a quarter of a century. She broke the world masters records for the 5K and the 4-mile, and secured 16 major marathon wins. Her training partner, Kim Hartman, once said: "Few exude such joy in the act, the process of running. The exemplary liver and lover of life in the classical Greek sense is Lorraine" (Sandrock).

For the Japanese, the evidence mounted that their women were following hot on the heels of their men in superb marathoning tradition. It was another silver, to go with Yamashita's near miss at the Tokyo World Championships. Surely it was only a matter of time before this running-obsessed nation would start striking gold. They didn't have long to wait. At the 1993 Stuttgart World Championships Junko Asari comfortably won the gold by 51 seconds (with colleague Tomoe Abe earning bronze). At the 1996 Olympics, Arimori was back after an uncomfortable four-year period in which she had to deal with suffocating media interest and a spree of injury problems, as she desperately fought to stay at the top of her game. Finally, four months before the Atlanta Olympics her injuries cleared up sufficiently to allow her to train full on for Olympic gold. Fatuma Roba proved too strong on this occasion; as again did Yegorova, who defeated her by 34 seconds to secure a silver, to go with her gold.

Arimori went on to miss the 2000 Sydney Olympics through injury as her legendary coach Yoshio Koide went on to inspire Naoko Takahashi to victory. Instead Arimori used her phenomenal levels of fame to launch a high profile charity Hearts of Gold, raising funds for landmine victims in Cambodia. Her agent Brendan Reilly explains: "Arimori's fame reached almost unbelievable levels in 1996, with non-stop features in magazines, and 10–15 campaigns for advertising companies. The nice thing about Japan is they have longer-term memories than most countries. Everybody in Japan knows who she is. The Emperor knows who she is." Arimori's only regret is that her coach never told her she could win the Olympics: "I focused on working hard, but my coach never said that I would win a gold medal. That I remember very well. Not many people thought I would win a medal. A gold medal was beyond my imagination and I couldn't even say as a joke that I was aiming for one."

In 1997 the Japanese women were quickly back on the golden trail, with Hiromi

The pain of victory, the joy of defeat: A deceptive image as an exhausted Yegorova leaves the celebrating to Japan's Yuko Arimori. *Mark Shearman*

Suzuki, defeating Manuela Machado[3] at the Worlds. The onslaught continued two years later at Seville, although on this occasion, the ice cool Ari Ichihoshi had to bow to the frantic efforts of Song-Ok Jong of Korea who prevailed by 3 seconds. In the short space of eight years Japanese women had secured a stunning seven major marathon medals: two golds, three silvers and two bronze. There was only one particular type of gong missing from the collection: *Olympic* gold. What price for it to happen at Sydney? A low one. The nation had been homing in on it with deadly precision for all of the 1990s, and step forward the legend that is Naoko Takahashi, to win in Sydney, by just 8 seconds over Lidia Simon, before then going on to become the first lady to break the magical 2:20 barrier at Berlin in 2001.

Still the domination continued as yet another World silver came at Paris in 2003 with Catherine Ndereba having to be at her best to see off Mizuki Noguchi by 19 seconds. But for Noguchi, this race was just a dress rehearsal for the big one: the Athens Olympic marathon, which she went on to win in magnificent style. The Japanese had done it again.

It didn't take Yegorova long to prove that she fully deserved her Olympic title. But there was one tricky pitfall to come first. She came to Boston in 1993 to race against the hapless Olga Markova who so many thought should be Olympic champion instead of Yegorova. But Markova had refused to follow her nation's

---

3. Machado had the extraordinary record in the last three World Championships of second, first, and second.

selection rules, had chased the lucrative dollar, had become the world's fastest marathoner, but stayed at home during the Barcelona Games. Markova and Yegorova, to understate it, had a score to settle. "They trained together in Florida but rarely spoke. They were not friends" (Derderian). If you don't have the gold, then the least you can do is beat the woman who has the gold. That's what Markova came to Boston to do. The two launched a tremendous duel, before Yegorova, on just six weeks of training threw in the towel and quit at 22 miles. Markova went on to win by nearly five minutes.

Yegorova showed admirable grace when she said after the race: "I am very pleased with Olga Markova's result because, as myself, she trained hard for this race. It is a good result and I am happy for her." Nice words after a bitter battle. Yegorova then won Tokyo – her favourite marathon – the following November, in a solid 2:26, before playing her part to the full in the extraordinary Boston of 1994 where strong tailwinds blew the runners to terrific times. There was no stopping Uta Pippig who roared to a 2:21, but Yegorova was in the best shape of her life too and returned a 2:23. Into the bargain, Yegorova beat Markova's Russian record by 10 seconds. This time it was Markova's turn to fail to finish.

The taint of illegitimacy over Yegorova's Olympic crown was almost extinguished. The final conclusive evidence to Yegorova's terrific class and fighting spirit came, as noted, at the 1996 Atlanta Olympics. It was a stacked field but she again had the beating of all the great names like Dörre, Simon, Machado, Pippig and McColgan. It was just Fatuma Roba who proved too good for them all. Rarely has an Olympic champion had to prove their pedigree, and defy their critics, more than Yegorova. But defy them she did, and only the very few can claim to have achieved so much, for so long.

Race result:

Valentina Yegorova	RUS	2:32:41
Yuko Arimori	JPN	2:32:49
Lorraine Moller	NZL	2:33:59
Sachiko Yamashita	JPN	2:36:26
Katrin Dörre-Heinig	GER	2:36:48
Mun Gyong-Ae	PRK	2:37:03
Manuela Machado	POR	2:38:22
Ramilya Burangulova	RUS	2:38:46
Colleen de Reuck	RSA	2:39:03
Cathy O'Brien	USA	2:39:42

Note: Madina Biktagirova (BLR; 2:35:39) was disqualified.

316

Sources:

Athletics Weekly, race preview and report, July 22nd & August 5th, 1992.
Derderian, Tom, *Boston Marathon*. Human Kinetics, 1996.
Hauman, Riël, *Century of the Marathon*. Human & Rousseau, 1996.
Horwill, Frank, in *Athletics Weekly*, August 12th, 1992.
Mackay, Duncan, in *British Runner*, March 2002.
Martin, David and Roger Gynn, *The Olympic Marathon*. Human Kinetics, 2000.
Sandrock, Michael, *Running with the Legends*. Human Kinetics, 1996.
Wallechinsky, David, *The Complete Book of the Olympics*. Aurum Press, 2000.

XXXV

No. 16 – 1984 Olympic Marathon [Women]

Sunday, August 5th

As "the little grey mouse" skittered from its hole,
running changed for ever.

In some ways this is one of the least dramatic, most one-sided marathons in the book. But it is also one of the most memorable, most important and, well, most magical. In the *Los Angeles Times'* review of the 1984 Olympics, a piece by Marlene Cimons appears, which neatly sums up what the race meant for female athletes. Cimons describes how a guy she knew once made the observation that "when women run, they always look like they're apologizing." Cimons explained: "It wasn't meant as a putdown. He simply meant that women ran as if they were still a little apprehensive and unsure of themselves. Unlike men, he said, when women approach a finish line, they never look like they are pushing. They always look like they are holding back."

In the press box on the day of the Olympic marathon Cimons sat with her friend Amby Burfoot (winner – when still in college – of the 1968 Boston Marathon, and now editor of US *Runner's World*), as they waited for the first woman to enter the stadium. Nobody loves running more than Burfoot or displays more passion for it. When the leader appeared on the track, Burfoot jumped to his feet and started screaming his lungs out. Cimons tried to remain detached and unemotional. This was easy for her she explained. Back in Washington it was hard to get worked up when you had heard the same speech 200 times. But here, she needed a prop to help her with her ruse: binoculars. Cimons writes:

I am watching the leader through my binoculars, pretending to be objective.
Behind the binoculars, I am crying.
The next morning I go out to run and it is different. How can I explain it? Somehow, after seeing a performance like that; I feel *faster.*
So I begin to push as hard as I can. No holding back.
And no apologies.

* * *

319

The idea of having a women's marathon in the Olympic Games was nothing more than a dream for many decades – nearly a century in fact. The women who ran in the 800-metres final at the Amsterdam Olympics helped matters not one bit, as after the race several of them collapsed in exhaustion, and some had to be given aid. Anti-feminists in the media and the International Amateur Athletic Federation began campaigning that women should race no further than 200-metres. The London *Daily Mail*, a paper as sensationalist in 1928, it seems, as it is today, published articles about women who partake in such "feats of endurance" would "become old too soon" (Wallechinsky).

Even the president of the International Olympic Committee, Comte de Baillet-Latour, spoke out in favour of banning women from the Olympics and returning to the ancient Greek custom of all-male competition. Those who supported female participation pointed out that the men fainted just as much as the women and that in some sports like rowing participants "were *expected* to be nearly comatose at the finish of important races" (Wallechinsky). All very farcical and comedic except for one awful fact. The IAAF then *did* go and ban women from competing in any race longer than 200-metres at the Olympics for *32 years*. And it wasn't until another twelve years after that that the 1500-metres was introduced to the Olympic programme, and another twelve after that until this famous inaugural women's Olympic marathon was finally upon us.

Before the LA Olympic marathon of '84, Joan Benoit had run eleven marathons, winning six. She had never finished outside the top four. Hailing from Cape Elizabeth, Maine, meant Benoit was automatically as tough a cookie as anyone with an interest in the sporty life, and used to long, gruelling winters would need to be. She grew up with three, not necessarily sympathetic, older brothers and immediately became something of a tomboy figure as she would try to keep up with whatever activities her siblings had in mind. "No matter what the Maine weather – snow, rain, cold, heat and humidity – Joanie was outside, following her brothers around" (Sandrock). Winters meant skiing, and lots of it. Just as appalling conditions up on the Maine slopes wouldn't stop Benoit from skiing, so too would she never sacrifice a run through inclement weather.

Before her 14th birthday, Benoit was trying out for track as a high-school freshman knowing that the competitiveness of the track was greatly appealing to her. She had already proved herself to be a fine hockey player and had won five first-place ribbons at a field day at a local country club when she was just eight. Starting out in track, Benoit's drive to train was clear for all to see. Whereas "running laps" was a torture to be dreaded for most, Benoit found it a great pleasure. She was already a trail-blazer and was, reports Sandrock, "the only girl in her high school – in fact, in the entire town – running". In 1972, the Cape Elizabeth boys' cross-country team held a meet against another school who also just had the one girl in their team. Benoit, going from hockey practice, to the race, and then back to hockey, felt "loose and terrific" in the race, which gave her the first real inkling that she had potential.

The negative effects of her competitive instinct, which was to haunt so much of her training over the next thirty years, first reared its head in February 1973 on the ski slopes. Benoit was striving for "the perfect run" towards the end of the day when conventional wisdom would have dictated that she should have been packing up for the day. She got the perfection she was after – but not in the way she wanted – a perfect leg break was her reward for crashing into a slalom gate and kept her out of track the following season.

When Benoit enrolled at Bowdoin College in Maine she just tried to fit in every-thing: study, classes, social life, hockey practice, hockey matches, oh, and running. It proved too much, and she was dropped from the hockey squad for playing with obvious fatigue. She was determined to prove her coach wrong and sprinted up and down the field like a maniac for the reserves, injuring her knee in the process. The doctor who tended to her pointed out how many commented on her running skills and why not concentrate on that and let the hockey go. That was just the incentive Benoit needed. She would never quit something on her own accord, quitting was something she just didn't do, but once ordered to by the doc, she was willing to commit to just one sport. Joan Benoit was now solely a runner.

Running with the men's team improved her form greatly and she soon trans-ferred to North Carolina State for her junior year, thinking that a bigger school would be better for her running. It helped in some ways, but for such a small-town girl, Benoit never felt completely comfortable in such a big environment. Her collegiate practices with stars Julie and Mary Shea often turned into races. Returning to Maine for the summer, Benoit didn't want to return to North Carolina but her coach convinced her to return for the cross-country season. She returned refreshed and with a better attitude, and in the fall of 1978 broke the world road 10,000-metres record in the Bonne Bell 10K. Her commitment to North Carolina finished, Benoit transferred back to Bowdoin for her final semester, now a world-class runner.

Which brings us to her first, albeit unplanned marathon. As she'd started travel-ling to races, Benoit went to the Bermuda 10K and beat her great rival, Julie Shea, for the first time. The next morning she woke up and out of the blue decided to enter the Bermuda Marathon. Running on pure adrenalin she never got tired and came second in 2:50:54. She had, however, run her body to its limits and the next day her heel hurt. Thinking it was just one of her many niggles, she ignored it and fulfilled a racing commitment for Bowdoin the next day. Then she was in real trouble and had to go and see a doctor in Boston who warned her she'd always have severe injury problems if she didn't start taking better care of herself. But Benoit's problem was that nothing could get in the way of her training, and her heel would hurt on and off for the rest of her career.

Surgery on the heel followed, and Benoit decided to focus on the 1979 Boston Marathon. Regular training weeks of 100 miles prepared her better than she'd ever imagined and she defeated the top US marathoner Patti Lyons by setting a new American record of 2:35:15. This great moment in her life was followed by four hard years of slog and graft as Benoit tried to make it as a professional runner. Her sponsors Nike sent her to New Zealand to train and race, and although not at her happiest there, she did manage to win the Auckland Marathon in a new American record of 2:31:23.

Because of her terrific powers of concentration, Benoit was able to push her body in training far further than it could cope with, and consequently it would frequently tend to break down. She was also perpetually fatigued. Benoit had two shocking marathons in a row, the first at Boston in 1981 where she had an inexplicably poor race, coming third, despite showing some of her best form ever in training.[1] Another awful race came later in the year at Columbus where she ran 2:39. Her heels still hurt and, it turns out, she was anaemic. More operations came: on her troublesome heels and her Achilles tendon. It seemed that a once-promising career could be at an end. But Benoit's surgery was successful, and she found the marathon to prove her new motivation in the Nike Eugene Marathon of September 1982. Feeling good the whole race, with heels that stood up to the challenge, Benoit ran 2:26:11, just 80 seconds off Grete Waitz's world record. It was four years now since Benoit had run well at the Boston Marathon, but after an excellent performance at the World Cross-Country Championships in Gateshead, England (where she came fourth), she approached the race with a "detached grimness".

The woman who had defeated Benoit in her 1981 damp squib, Allison Roe of New Zealand, [see Chapter 21] had come back to race, but Benoit wanted to have absolutely nothing to do with the hype that surrounded "the renaissance woman of running" and decided to go out fast. Quite how fast is hard to describe – suffice it to say she covered her first mile in 4:47! As she passed halfway in a mind-boggling 1:08:22, Roe was becoming more and more alarmed that her prey was nowhere in sight, and by the time the hills were upon her by mile 17, she dropped out in disillusion. A man running close to Benoit told her to "watch it, lady", indicating she was going to trash herself with such a fast pace. Whether his busybody antics led her to slow down and record a time less than what she was capable of, or whether he saved her race is unclear, but her 2:22:43 final clocking, despite her calmer second half was still a world record by nearly three minutes.

US Olympic marathoner Benji Durden recalls having bad blisters during the race – a fact about which he publicly complained – but Benoit, whose feet on inspection were in a far worse condition than his, refused to acknowledge this handicap to the press. "And I was annoyed she went out dancing that night," Durden recalls (Sandrock).

Benoit was quickly developing a reputation for being the most tenacious athlete around, indeed her long-time coach, Bob Sevene, found her to be the toughest athlete he ever knew, with only Lasse Viren in the same class. And Viren, of course, was only tough at Olympics.

Speaking of the Olympics, they were fast approaching; Benoit would require all her renowned stubbornness and resilience to encounter the hurdles she'd have to face.

* * *

"The sharp, searing pain in Joan Benoit's right knee came all at once at the 17-mile mark of her regular 20-mile run on the quiet roads along the outskirts of Freeport, Maine," author Michael Sandrock writes. "...This was the kind of pain that told her immediately something was seriously wrong. She hobbled through two more miles before the knee locked up completely, forcing her to walk home."

---

1. Author Tom Derderian was one of her training partners and a 2:19 marathoner. Yet before the Boston of '81 Benoit was leaving him behind in training. Yet then she went and blew up in the marathon. "Head case," thought Derderian, who decided then and there that she'd never make it at the highest level.

It was March 17th, 1984, just eight weeks before the Olympic trials to select the American women's team for the inaugural women's marathon. "I thought my heart would break," Benoit writes. A cortisone injection in Boston provided only short-term relief and soon she couldn't even lift her leg over a twig.

As a last resort, Dr Stan James in Eugene, Oregon, performed an arthroscopy, finding and removing a "fibrous mass called a plica, which had become inflamed and was interfering with the joint". There were now seventeen days before the trials of which compulsory rest was prescribed for seven. Ten days before the trials and Benoit began training with a maniacal drive and determination, putting in 15 hours a day of exercise, which included swimming, running, physio, lifting and taking a whirlpool. Favouring her right knee, she tweaked her left hamstring in sympathy. This required six to ten hours of treatment for five days in a row.

With her Olympic dream hanging by a thread Benoit drove with her fiancé, Scott Samuelson, to Olympia, Washington, to the trials knowing she needed a miracle. She got one. Although she still experienced pain in her knee, Benoit recorded a 37-second victory over Julie Brown in an excellent 2:31:04, in what she calls "the race of my life". Her coach Sevene called it one of the greatest runs by an American athlete ever, saying, "she worked her butt off on an exercise machine, and she wins the whole damn thing" (Sandrock).

Defeating the best runners in America was one thing, defeating the best in the world was quite another and Benoit still had a whole lot of work ahead of her. Returning to Maine to keep up the work on strengthening her suspect body she knew her comeback was complete when she won an exhibition 10,000 race at the Los Angeles Coliseum in 32:07. Training on her own at Cliff Island, off the coast of Maine, Benoit totally immersed herself in her fitness, running several 20–22 milers at 6:10 pace.

* * *

To the media, the big story of the women's Olympic marathon was of a showdown between the World champion and five-time winner of the New York City Marathon, Grete Waitz, and Benoit. When Benoit flew to Los Angeles she found Nike had made things just that little bit tougher by painting a huge mural of Benoit winning Boston on a wall near the Coliseum. One morning, while running with New Zealand's Lorraine Moller, the two passed by the mural just as a tourist was taking a photo. "Hey, get out the way!" the tourist yelled, not realizing that it was Benoit herself running past (Sandrock).

Pretty much everyone else in the city recognized Benoit though, and she became more and more psyched up: "I've been talking about getting a medal for three years," she said to Sevene. "And you know something? There's only one medal: the gold medal. The rest is just a cop-out." The *New York Times'* preview of the inaugural women's Olympic marathon said:

A handful of runners are given good chances to win. One scenario is right out of Hollywood: runner breaks world record, injures knee, undergoes arthroscopic surgery 17 days before United States Olympic trials, almost gives up on Olympics, changes mind, wins trials and wins gold medal.

Except for the final scene, all that has happened to 27-year-old Joan Benoit of Freeport, Maine, one of the favourites here.

Speaking of Grete Waitz as Benoit's main competitor, the *New York Times* continued: "Mrs Waitz is a fierce and smart competitor. If the race comes down to a sprint at the finish, she may have more speed than Miss Benoit. Thus, Miss Benoit will probably attempt to build a solid lead so she will not be outrun at the end." One would say what a superb piece of foresight by the *Times*, but as it was the paper couldn't quit while ahead, continuing: "Because the field is so balanced, it seems unlikely that someone will break away early and pull away. A tactical race seems probable, which means the leaders may not make their moves until at least 20 miles into the 26.2 mile race."

For Americans obviously, Benoit was the natural choice to root for. But Waitz certainly had her fans: "I'm going to cheer for Joan because I'm an American," said another observer, "But let's put it this way; I won't be disappointed if Grete wins. In fact, I'll be delighted" (Sandrock).

Where some athletes thrive under pressure others buckle. It would be pushing the point to say Waitz buckled, but she certainly didn't come into the race in the best frame of mind. In the best shape of her life, Waitz stuck in a "superb" track workout the Wednesday before the marathon, but then made what turned out to be a fatal error. Intent on getting as much rest as possible, she switched bedrooms with her brother and found that his bed was far softer than hers, which irritated her back. On Saturday morning (before the Sunday race) her back hurt a little, but instead of going to see a doctor, Waitz insisted all would be fine. By lunchtime she could hardly walk. "Everything collapsed like a house of cards," she told journalist Stefan Bakke. "I usually have trouble sleeping the night before a big race, but I was so exhausted mentally by night time that I went out like a light the minute my head touched the pillow."

Although Waitz felt better on race morning, her focus was completely gone. Instead of focusing on tactics and on psyching herself up, she was just wondering on whether she'd be able to stay the course. Waitz says she had "no aggression – my head wasn't tuned in" (Sandrock).

Race day at the Santa Monica City College was a fairly comfortable 68 °F on Sunday, August 5th, 8 a.m. Forty-nine runners representing 28 nations included eleven of the fastest fourteen runners in the short history of women's marathoning.[2] As well as Waitz, there was the rising star Ingrid Kristiansen and Rosa Mota, winner of the Chicago and Rotterdam marathons, plus the European champion, who was also improving every time out and had been fourth in the World Championships the previous year. Then there were the redoubtable Antipodeans of Lisa Martin and Lorraine Moller, with the super-vet from Great Britain, Priscilla Welch, also right in the mix.

Starting out extremely slowly (the first mile took all of 6:28) in front of packed grandstands at the Santa Monica City College track, Benoit's plan had originally been to stay with the leaders and keep the pace honest until around 18 miles

---

2. In 1970 there were just 20 female marathoners in the world (Hauman).

Joan Benoit, or 'the little grey mouse', as her mother put it, has skittered away from her foe, much to the delight of the partisan crowd. *Mark Shearman*

before making her move. But after the pedestrian beginning (5 kilometres passed in 18:15), Benoit just thought, "Damn, let me out", and threw in a couple of 5:11 miles. This strung the field out and, far from consolidating her lead, Benoit continued to push. From a 4-second lead over Ingrid Kristiansen at 10 kilometres, it became a devastating 51-second lead after 15 kilometres, over a pack of five: Waitz, Moller, Sylvie Ruegger, Julie Brown and New Zealand's Anne Audain. One second off this group came another group which contained 14 of the other main contenders (Martin & Gynn). Although Benoit's pace slowed over the next 5 kilometres, her lead grew to 72 seconds by 20 kilometres, reached in 1:08:32. "It was like a dream," Benoit wrote later. "Here I was, running comfortably and in control of the Olympic Marathon with no visible opposition" (Sandrock).

The lead grew dramatically between 18 and 21 miles because that was when Benoit had automatically programmed herself to hit the hammer. Suddenly she found herself on world-record pace, and reports Beb Sevene, she said to herself: "Wait a minute, I'd better slow down and get the win." Just when it seemed that Benoit had buried her pursuers once and for all at 30 kilometres (reached in 1:42:23 with a 110-second lead), Grete Waitz began chasing hard. She told *Athletics Weekly*: "Suddenly things started functioning, and I felt the brakes were off; there was nothing holding me back." But by then Benoit had a 2-minute lead: "I closed to within a minute of her, and when I caught sight of her back with about 5km to go I just for a moment thought I might yet win. But I soon realized it was asking a bit much to haul back a minute over 5km when somebody's travelling at 2:25 pace! So I just ran for the silver, and I was really delighted when I got it."

As Benoit approached the stadium, she said she tried to avoid looking at her image mural close to the Coliseum. "That was my first thought when my knee started to bother me," Benoit remembers. "What about the wall mural? They put it up for no reason at all. I'm not going to be there," she told the *New York Times*.

Four fairly banal qualifying track and field events had been taking place that morning in the stadium, but it was still packed to the rafters with 85,000 hopeful souls. They had been kept abreast of developments from the large video screen, and when the tiny figure of Benoit came through the tunnel "the spectator roar of adulation was so intense that conversation was impossible" (Sandrock). Her mother said later that Joan looked like a little grey mouse skittering out of a hole.

As Benoit entered the tunnel into the stadium she thought, "Once you leave this tunnel your life will be changed forever" (Sandrock). She had certainly come a long way from the days when she'd stop as cars passed her on a training run and pretend to look at the flowers. Completing the finish line straight (and feeling at the end that she could have run another marathon), Benoit was 94 seconds up on Waitz by the end and promptly took a victory lap, waving the American flag. Mary Crawford, a professor at West Chester University, wrote: "When I grew up in the 1950s, girls and women weren't allowed to test themselves in sports...The absence of images of physically competent women had real effects that women of my generation are still working to overcome. Perhaps this was the reason I watched the first women's Olympic Marathon with tears of joy at the accomplishments of the runners."

A moment of sublime joy for an athlete and a nation: her knee, tactics and self-belief have all held up to the pressure, and Joan Benoit becomes the inaugural women's Olympic Marathon champion. *Mark Shearman*

The race for the final medal was a hard-fought affair, with Kristiansen ahead of Mota at 39 kilometres but with a seven second deficit to make up by 40. The momentum was with Mota, and she went on to add a further 30-second cushion. Mota's marathon career is described in detail in Chapter 22, but it may be noted that her third place here was the second-equal *worst* finish[3] of her ten-year international marathon career!

_____

3. There are three DNFs in her record.

High-profile non-finishers included Jacqueline Gareau and Anne Audain, while in the unofficial team race Britain won with 31 points (6th, 11th and 14th), followed by Norway 32 (2nd, 4th and 26th) with Italy third on 41 (9th, 12th and 20th). Somewhat bizarrely, the ages of the British runners had a range of *a quarter of a century*. Welch was born in 1944, the incredible Joyce Smith in 1937 (running a world best for her age group) and Sarah Rowell in 1962. Who says it's a young (wo)man's game!

A long while after Benoit's triumph, the Coliseum were treated to the somewhat macabre sight of a Swiss lady named Gabriëla Andersen-Schiess feeling all of her 39 years, doing a "Dorando". The *New York Times* reports: "She listed to her left as she appeared in the tunnel, then staggered and weaved back and forth across the track as the crowd cheered in an effort to help push her through her last lap." More than $2\frac{1}{2}$ minutes passed before she completed her final 200 metres, accompanied by two members of the medical unit. She appeared to acknowledge the crowd with her right hand, not long before falling into the arms of three workers. "As she was coming up the tunnel," said Dr Richard Greenspun, the chief medical officer for athletes of the LAOOC, "my thought was this was one of the most courageous things I'd ever seen, and we shouldn't interfere." Recalls Schiess: "I missed the last water stop at 40 kilometres – I didn't see it. That was probably critical. I think the real problem was when I got to the stadium. It's so close to the end. The closer you get to the end, the more strength you lose." At first, as she navigated the home-straight, she thought she'd made it before realizing to her horror there was one lap to go. Then, echoing the sentiments of marathoners the world over, she explained: "I remember really struggling. I thought that it wasn't that far. I thought it was the finish line, right there. Then it was a little further, and a little further. When I was almost at the end, seeing the finish line, I thought, 'I'm so close now, see if I can stay on my feet.'"[4]

Malcolm Moran of the *New York Times* wrote of Benoit's win: "With a daring that successfully challenged the finest female distance runners in the world and an ease that surprised even herself, Joan Benoit took a calculated risk, ran away from the field after passing the three-mile mark, and won the first Olympic marathon for women this morning. She beat Waitz who had never before lost a marathon that she'd finished." The view of 1972 Olympic marathon gold-medal winner Frank Shorter was that: "In essence, it was one of the best tactical races ever tried in an Olympic race. When you do that, you deserve to win. Sometimes, you reach a point as an athlete where you have to say, 'Look, let's go out and see who is the best runner.' Joanie did that. She took a risk and no one went with her. It was amazing that Grete, Ingrid, and the others let her go" (Sandrock). "The way I lost today, I can't be anything but pleased," Waitz explained. "Joanie today was just too good for me."[5]

Waitz would win friends all around for her sporting manner towards defeat, and in a Games which featured the tantrum throwing Mary Decker, such an

---

4. Andersen eventually finished 37th in 2:48:42.

5. Ingrid Kristiansen was less amused, however, as she indicated to the author some 20 years later: "I wanted to cover Benoit's move, but all the Norwegian team management had instructed me to stay with Grete – and she opted to hold back..."

attitude was refreshing. In a strongly worded article for the *Los Angeles Times*, Julie Cart wrote:

> What can be said about these Olympics is that the athletes have demonstrated ways to lose with class, and ways to lose with ugliness and without grace.
>
> Grete Waitz of Norway, who won the silver medal in the women's marathon, is an example of the former. Mary Decker is an example of the latter. We love athletes for winning, but sometimes we love athletes for the way they lost. Waitz is a winner.
>
> After crossing the finish line, Waitz embraced Benoit, then waited as her team-mate, Ingrid Kristiansen, finished. Waitz applauded Kristiansen and brought her water.
>
> Decker could take a lesson from Waitz. Decker knows how to win. She needs to learn how to lose with grace and class.

When quizzed by the media about where her competitiveness came from, Benoit replied that she didn't know: "I often ask myself that, and I haven't found the answers yet. I guess it's just one challenge after another." Her aims after the Olympics were to have another crack at her own world record, and aside from that, marriage, and a far more peaceful existence. "The blueberries are behind in Maine. If you want to find me, look for a blueberry patch in Maine next week."[6]

Benoit celebrates on the victory podium while a deflated Grete Waitz forces a grin in the background. *Tony Duffy/Getty Images*

The Los Angeles Olympics still had a week of spectacular sporting action to go, but nothing was going to top this. Here are some of the memories of the *New York Times*' Scott Ostler shortly after the closing ceremony of the Los Angeles Games:

> Two hours ago it was skyrockets, blaring pop music and cheers from 94,000. Now it's helicopters and crickets.
>
> If you close your eyes, you can hear a lot more.
>
> From the Coliseum tunnel you can hear the echo of running footsteps as Joan Benoit heads home at the end of her long journey from the shores of the Pacific Ocean.
>
> You close your eyes and you can

---

6. Here was a passion that was to remain with her. Benoit was not found to be competing at the 1988 Boston Marathon due to a sore knee, but she could be seen at a stall selling her special blueberry jam.

hear the spectators gasp as Gabriëla Andersen-Schiess staggers out of that same tunnel; you can hear them boo as Carl Lewis is announced as the long-jump gold medallist after sitting out the last four dances; you can hear them yell out in warning to Mary Decker and hear them gasp in shock as she loses her balance and crash-dives off the track.

61 years ago critics called the building of the Coliseum "sheer civic folly," but the new stadium was the perfect host for the '32 Olympics, and wore its age well 52 years later.

* * *

So what became of Benoit after her brilliant Olympic triumph? Did she prove to be something of one-trick pony who never really hit the same heights again? Absolutely not is the quick answer, although things never *quite* went her way again. After winning eight of the twelve marathons she ran between 1979 to 1985, she only won twice more, and that she never graced another Olympics is a real shame but testimony to the fact that the harder you train, the harder you hurt – and few have had to fight injury quite as much as Benoit. Her undoubted highlight after Los Angeles came 14 months later when she stormed around the Chicago Marathon course in a magnificent 2:21:21 to win a wonderful duel with Ingrid Kristiansen and miss the world record by just 16 seconds (to read more about this great race, consult Chapter 17).

Unfortunately Benoit wouldn't then run another marathon for over three years (New York 1988: third in 2:32), but three years after that Benoit was an integral part of the absorbing Boston of 1991 (which almost made the author's 50-greatest list). After Wanda Panfil's relatively comfortable win in 2:24, places two through five read: Kim Jones 2:26:40, Uta Pippig 2:26:52, Joan (Benoit) Samuelson 2:26:54 and Kamila Gradus 2:26:55. What a race! After over five years of frustrating injury problems "Joanie" was seemingly back among the world's elite. This coming two years after she had tearfully hobbled round Boston in ninth place on a bad hip, and to all intents and purposes seemed to be out of the game. It was tears of delight on this day in 1991 though, as she even spoke about trying out for the Olympic 10,000-metre team: "I think it would be more of an achievement to go to another Olympics in a different event," she told *Track and Field News*, "The top priority now is the family. I'll be honest with you...I'll do what's best for them. What's best for all of us."

Her final win came at Columbus, Ohio in October 1992, in 2:32, but she was still duking it out four years later, placing 13th in the US Olympic trials, and astonishingly, eight years thereafter was even talking about trying out again for the trials for the 2004 Games. Aged 47, she was still running sub 36 minutes for 10K. Although there would be no '04 Olympic trials, it seems the Joan Benoit Samuelson story is not quite over yet.

Race result:

Joan Benoit	USA	2:24:52
Grete Waitz	NOR	2:26:18
Rosa Mota	POR	2:26:57
Ingrid Kristiansen	NOR	2:27:34
Lorraine Moller	NZL	2:28:34
Priscilla Welch	GBR	2:28:54
Lisa Martin	AUS	2:29:04
Sylvie Ruegger	CAN	2:29:09
Laura Fogli	ITA	2:29:28
Tuija Toivonen	FIN	2:32:07

Sources:

Conversations with Ingrid Kristiansen.
Athletics Weekly, August 8th, 1984.
Cart, Julie, in the *Los Angeles Times*, August 13th, 1984.
Cimons, Marlene, in the *Los Angeles Times*, August 13th, 1984.
Derderian, Tom, *Boston Marathon*. Human Kinetics, 1996.
Hauman, Riël, *Century of the Marathon*. Human & Rousseau, 1996.
Martin, David and Roger Gynn, *The Olympic Marathon*. Human Kinetics, 2000.
Moran, Malcolm, in the *New York Times*, August 6th, 1984.
New York Times, race preview, August 5th, 1984.
Ostler, Scott, in the *New York Times*, August 6th, 1984.
Sandrock, Michael, *Running with the Legends*. Human Kinetics, 1996.
Track and Field News, May 1991.
Wallechinsky, David, *The Complete Book of the Olympics*. Aurum Press, 2000.

XXXVI

No. 15 – 2004 New York City Marathon [Women]

Sunday, November 7th

Tarnished legend seeks redemption.

December 2002. At the BBC Sports Personality of the Year show, all eyes were on one woman who would surely win the evening's top award. Charlie Potter, a production assistant in the studio, recalls how 10 seconds before going on air, the powerfully built, imposing, black Arsenal football captain, Patrick Vieira, had yet to arrive, and thus the fair-skinned and boyish Potter was told to go and sit in his empty seat in the front row. The lady to Potter's right looked at him quizzically: "I'm sorry, should I know who you are?" Potter nodded sombrely: "I'm Patrick Vieira." The lady chewed her lip and told him how nervous she was. A few minutes into the show, the real Vieira arrived and Potter was hauled off the set. "I *knew* you weren't Patrick Vieira!" said the lady with a delighted giggle. Potter recalls of his neighbour: "She was sweet as an angel, so friendly and beautiful. Even if her feet did look a bit mashed."

Mashed feet or not, Potter had got up close and personal with one of the great champions of world sport, who, during 2002, had set a magnificent world record in her event. Even greater achievement would come four months hence. An icon of distance running had truly arrived in 2002, and that icon was Paula Radcliffe.

* * *

Radlciffe was born in the village of Barnton, Cheshire, on December 17th, 1973, and "can't remember" a time when she didn't run. Her family background was most certainly sporty. Radcliffe's grandfather used to be a sprinter when he was in the army, and her father's great-aunt Charlotte won a silver medal at the 1920 Paris Olympics in the 4 × 100-metre freestyle relay. And Radcliffe's grandmother, Olivia, is most certainly what could be called "game". She was recently asked to "start" a race at the Kingsley Carnival, but having initially said yes, later declined on the grounds that at age 86 maybe she shouldn't be running in races!

The running bug bit Radcliffe when she was nine and a friend encouraged her to join the local club Frodsham Harriers. Radcliffe also began running with her father, Peter, on his long Sunday runs for as long as she could keep up, before returning to play with her brother Martin in the forest. Soon she won her first inter-schools race and upon moving with the family to Oakley, just outside

331

Bedford, Radcliffe quickly joined up with the thriving club Bedford and County where her coaches to this day, Alex and Rosemary Stanton, worked with the youngsters. Radcliffe ran in her first National cross-country championships as an eleven-year-old and scraped into the top 300 out of 607 runners. Paula, her family and the Stantons were all encouraged by this juicy top-half finish. But the blood-thirsty Stanton wanted *even more* from his new charge, and indicated that Paula should up her training to two sessions a week. The young puck readily agreed.

Fast forward to the following year's National and suddenly the lean and hungry twelve-year-old Paula was eyeing up nothing less than a top-15 finish. However, the tree was growing at an alarming rate: fourth in the country she came, Bedford won the team title, and Radcliffe was more hooked on running than ever. Her progress over the next few seasons took her into the national junior team, and in the 1991 World Cross-Country Championships Radcliffe placed a promising 15th; but both Paula and Stanton believed that the following year much more could be achieved. Her training now became laced with a real edge as she dedicated herself to preparing for running at the pace that Lydia Cheromei from Kenya had run in 1991.

Although pre-race nerves overwhelmed Radcliffe the evening before the 1992 junior World Cross-Country Championships at a very snowy Boston, she also had a great desire to perform well. With temperatures stooping to as low as minus ten, Radcliffe writes: "But the conditions didn't bother me. What mattered was that my preparation had gone as well as it could have. I knew I was as ready as I could be, and I was excited about it."

After battling it out with four runners for most of the race, Radcliffe finally got a break, coming off a hill around half a mile from home where she made a desperate charge for the finish line, finally prevailing by 5 seconds over China's Wang Junxia. Radcliffe didn't lose her cool as she crossed the finish line, perhaps subconsciously realizing that this was just the beginning of a very long road. There was no punching of the air or raised arms: "I walked through the chute and calmly pulled my briefs out of my bum..." – as is expected of any self-respecting world champion.

The next few years of Radcliffe's life were an exhausting mesh of tireless, dedicated training and focused study. A grade junky, she aced her A levels and insisted on nothing less than a first in her degree in modern languages at Loughborough University. She made her senior championship track and field debut at the 1993 Stuttgart World Championships where she placed a solid seventh. At the '95 Worlds this was improved to fifth, which Radcliffe felt "mildly disappointing". After a year of disruptions in 1996 with exams and injury, Radcliffe placed fifth again at the Atlanta Olympics, which this time felt *very* disappointing. She might not necessarily have expected a medal, but she certainly had hoped for one; her lack of a polished finish in her races was starting to count against her.

This questionable finish was cruelly exposed at the 1997 "World Cross" when Derartu Tulu inflicted the first of several painful defeats on Radcliffe, as on this occasion Radcliffe appeared to have the gold medal in hand, only to have it nicked away in the last 50 metres. It was a first major championship medal, but one on the track remained elusive. Athens 1997 produced only tears, as with remarkable consistency Radcliffe placed fourth. Better than Atlanta, of course, but Radcliffe could only wail to Stanton: "What do I have to do to get a medal in these championships?"

The year 1998 proved to be something of a nadir. A frustrating second consecutive silver in the World "Cross" was followed by desperate returns on the track. In the European Championships a weak and depleted Radcliffe could only manage...fifth. "My body felt totally empty and drained. What had happened to me? Why such overwhelming exhaustion?" A blood test soon showed up a virus depleting her red cells. Her body was in no shape to prepare for the Commonwealth Games in Kuala Lumpur the following month, and she dejectedly had to sit them out as Australian Kate Anderson won in a slow 15:52.

Radcliffe felt much more confident going into the 10,000-metres final at the 1999 Seville World Championships, feeling that the distance would suit her more than the "five". It was here that Radcliffe displayed herself as a world-class runner on the track, as well as on the road and over the country. In hot, oppressive 30-degree heat, Radcliffe ran a personal best by 13 seconds, and ran a 67-second last lap, only for Gete Wami to run a 64. Still, a silver medal showed encouraging progress, and her splits of 15:25 and 15:02 showed that she was becoming exceptionally strong.

Radcliffe and her entourage believed that Paula would certainly nail a medal at the 2000 Sydney Olympics – the only question was which colour. However, in Olympic year the stakes were raised and the Ethiopians were fitter than ever. Radcliffe's arch nemesis – her questionable final lap – preyed on her mind throughout the race as she pinged through halfway in a dazzling 15:06, but she worried terribly about the wall of bodies at her heels. Sure as shooting, one by one they streaked past during that heartbreaking last lap; Tulu, Wami and then Fernanda Ribeiro. Radcliffe collapsed, exhausted and dismayed, on the track at the finish, yet another medal narrowly missed. Her new British record was scant consolation.

March 2001 finally brought Radcliffe the senior world title she had craved for so long as in a majestic finish at the "World Cross", her finishing kick startled Gete Wami, who had friskily made her dash for the finish line too soon. Radcliffe roared past with 40 metres to go: "I was pretty emotional and extremely satisfied; it had been a long hard road."

Perhaps now a track gold would follow, but instead yet more dismay followed in Edmonton at the World Championships as just four seconds divided the first four finishers. Radcliffe came fourth. The disappointment was even more acute than at Sydney because she had been less sound tactically in Edmonton, a point which husband Gary was particularly keen to pick up on with his infamous "why the fuck did you do that?" comment immediately after Paula finished. Their public fracas was beamed into millions of homes around the world and only added salt to a very painful wound.

Radlciffe's relationship with Lough is bewildering to many outsiders, and even a touch macabre. How can this woman be with someone so apparently unfeeling and hostile? Of course, if Lough really was like that they wouldn't be together – but that is his public image. Simon Barnes of *The Times* wrote of Lough in April 2002 that he was "the man every red-blooded male in Britain would most like to bop on the nose." *Eurosport* commentator Tim Hutchings described Lough during this chapter's featured race as follows:

> He's a Celt, a man with a very short temper for suffering fools, completely
> opposite temperament to Radcliffe, who's serene and peaceful and shies away
> from confrontation.

Neither Radcliffe nor Lough deny the fact that he's fiery and lacks tact and
diplomacy. But what's most unsettling to those outside their close knit circle is
that i) he appears cruel to her at times when she most craves affection and
sympathy, and ii) that she fears him. Amazingly, none of this is hidden in
Radcliffe's book!

Her public fracas with Lough at the 2001 World Championships is well
documented. What is less known is that he was equally unfeeling the year before
in Sydney after arguably Radcliffe's bravest race. When her mission failed, she
spoke to Lough via cell phone in the stands. Radcliffe writes: "Gary made no
effort to hide his frustration. He couldn't understand and kept asking why I had
not run faster through the second 5 kilometres. Being physically exhausted and
mentally wiped out, it felt like he was accusing me of not trying hard enough."

Lough's criticism could be compared to asking golfer Seve Ballesteros why he
doesn't drive the ball straighter, or asking Tim Henman why he doesn't add some
zip to his second serve. But Lough defends himself: "If I said to her 'you did
really well, you were great...' If I had come out with all that bullshit, she would
know I was telling her something I didn't believe. I don't fill her head with
crap..."

Does Radcliffe fear Lough? That's the message she conveys in her book. Before
one long run before Athens, she didn't tell Lough of a niggle she was feeling
because she was "scared" of his reaction. "Why should she have been scared?"
Lough asks. "Maybe if she'd thought I would react more calmly, she would have
mentioned it."

When Radcliffe dropped out of the Athens Olympic marathon and two old club
mates asked her if they should call Gary, she replied: "No, Gary might be mad
with me for not being able to run better." One thing that is beyond doubt though
is that Radcliffe's partnership with Lough is devastatingly effective and her
husband appears the perfect antidote to the more outwardly compassionate
personalities of her parents and the Stantons. You'll never hear any criticism of
Paula's running from them – at least not in public.

* * *

To ease the pain of all her dismay on the track, Radcliffe had one shimmering
treat on the horizon. In April 2002 she was due to run her first marathon on the
streets of London.

Before that came a tricky defence of her "World Cross" crown where she saw
off the challenge of the excellent American Deena Drossin. However, she was in
mental – and physical – turmoil, due to a painful knee problem: "I have looked at
the pictures of my crossing the finish line that afternoon and you can see the big
bags under my eyes, the drained look on my face. There is joy but it is laced with
anxiety and exhaustion." After a week of the most excruciating treatment she had

suffered under the hands of her physio, Gerard Hartmann, Radcliffe arrived in London "back to my old self and greatly looking forward to the challenge."

The tactic for Radcliffe's debut marathon was clear: hold back for the first half. But sometimes the best-laid plans are forgotten if the adrenalin's pumping. Radcliffe writes: "As we got to the *Cutty Sark*, about six miles into the race, the crowd cheered so loud and so passionately, we instinctively and unwittingly increased our speed. At least I did. I went into the *Cutty Sark* in a group and came out of it alone in the lead." And alone is how she would be for the next 20 miles. Glorious, spellbinding isolation. But, the isolation was anything but glorious for her legion of fans who knew what happened when she front ran like this. It all tended to go rather wrong. Simon Barnes summed up the feeling in *The Times*:

> Look behind you, Paula! But Paula runs and turns no more her head because she knows a fearful fiend doth close behind her tread. And they always catch her. That has been the pattern of watching Paula Radcliffe: a sort of doomed good-heartedness, a sort of courageous vulnerability, a sort of noble stupidity. She runs races as moths fly around candles and you cannot bear to watch because you know it can only end one way.

And yet the twist never came. The comeback never arrived from the more experienced marathoners and Radcliffe won by nearly 4 glorious minutes. Her time of 2:18:56 missed Catherine Ndereba's world record by just nine seconds, but no one seemed to care about that; surely it was just a matter of time before Paula would rewrite the record books.

That time came six months later on the streets of Chicago as Radcliffe was on even more devastating form. The wrinkle this time came in the form of a wickedly timed period, that arrived at 3:30 of the morning of the race. Radcliffe knew this may well lead to stomach trouble (as Uta Pippig so publicly found in Chapter 44), but such was her focus that she immediately banished the thought from her mind. As she set off along Chicago's freezing streets in a comical "Smurf-blue" hat, the world record was under threat right from the off, and halfway was reached in a terrific 69:05 – just 5 seconds off target pace, and with all credit due to Catherine Ndereba, a lead of just four seconds. Could Radcliffe possibly run negative splits off such a pace? Could she ever. Angry stomach cramps in the last few miles couldn't stop her as she flashed through the line in 2:17:18, for a huge world record. Ndereba finished over two minutes back.

The year 2002 had been one of pure glory: two major marathon wins, elusive track gold in the Commonwealths and the Europeans, plus the "World Cross", and all were in agreement with the words of Carey Pinkowski the Chicago race director: "I think she can still go a lot faster. She was so fresh at the end and recovered remarkably quickly." And to soothe any qualms from cynics that she was operating honestly, Radcliffe insisted on blood tests before and after the race: "I didn't want any questions, any issues. This was down to all my hard work."

The next marathon feat was the most jaw-dropping of all. London 2003. Yet again, however, the build-up was anything but simple. On March 8th, Radcliffe was involved in a dramatic collision with a child on her bike when coming to the end of a 2:15 tempo run in Albuquerque. "Oh my God, your face is a complete mess," observed the ever plain-speaking Gary. Fortunately, aside from the agony of recovering from a dislocated jaw, Radcliffe managed to arrive in London five weeks later, 100-per-cent ready. Her performance that day pretty much defined perfection. Without question it was one of the greatest pieces of distance running of all time – even if a great *race* it was not! But Radcliffe's performance almost defied belief. A "sluggish" first mile passed by in a mere 5:10, and the slightly downhill third one took just 4:57. It was already shaping up to be some day.

Controversially for this race Radcliffe was given two male pace-makers, Kenyans Samson Loywapet and Christopher Kandie, who were asked to run at 2:16 pace. At just five past nine after the 9 a.m. start, Radcliffe was already 25 metres ahead of the field. By 9:15 she had "run the first sub-5-minute mile by a woman in a marathon" (Powell).[1] Not to disappoint, they passed through the half in 68:02 – faster than any woman had run for that distance in 2002, and Radcliffe was resolutely sticking to the pace-makers. It wasn't long before one of them began to suffer and was duly dropped, but Radcliffe surged on telling herself she had run her second half quicker in Chicago and would do the same again here. Stomach cramps came to haunt her again, but such was her focus that she simply blanked them from her mind. She writes: "It was a joyful last mile. I checked the clock – if it took me seven minutes to run the last mile, I would still break the world record. I knew there was no way it was going to take me anything like that and I wanted to beat the record by as much as possible. People always wonder why I don't save a little for the next day but that is something I could never do. Who can guarantee there will be another day?"

Not only did Radcliffe break seven minutes for the last mile, she broke *five* minutes as well. Time: 2:15:25 – with an almost unreal 1:07:23 for the second half. Inspirational to her fans and admirers, but devastating to her opponents who must have wondered what they were doing wrong to be going down by such vast margins. On this occasion Catherine Ndereba found herself 4:30 – nearly a mile – back. And the fastest British man, Chris Cariss, finished a half-mile back. Simon Barnes wrote in *The Times*: "Britain's greatest living national treasure doubled in value yesterday, as she smashed her own world record out of sight. It was a performance of astonishing power and certainty. Radcliffe is inviting a new mythology of distance running."

There was, however, an obvious flaw to this performance, which is the aid Radcliffe received from the pace-makers. Andy Milroy wrote in the publication *Distance Running*:

> The use of male pacemakers is opportunistic and short-sighted, driven by the financial demands of race directors and runners' agents...the inclusion of male pacemakers will work against the development of women's distance running.
>
> It is much cheaper for a race director to pay for one or two elite women and a couple of male pacemakers than it is for them to attract a strong elite

---

1. Surely not!, squeals the author, diving for the record books; and indeed my scepticism of this sloppy piece of reporting from David Powell shows it to be inaccurate: Joan Benoit blasted the first mile of Boston '83 in 4:47, thus ensuring Kiwi Allison Roe's race got off to the most demoralizing of starts.

women's field. They get a good winning women's time with resultant favourable press coverage, without the cost of inviting a major women's field.

London Marathon race director Dave Bedford defended his decision to the author:

All of that controversy with Paula's pace-making was us simply saying: you have to recognize two marks for women's marathons. The average person is between 3 and 5 per cent faster when they run in a mixed race – now we know why that is! And it's only a matter of time before the IAAF will agree with that. I've got to play the politics a bit longer but that will happen.

At the end of the day with very odd exceptions, runners will look to come to London first of all, and only go elsewhere because they can't get a deal with us. We recognize that marathon running is not up there with the profiles of some other sports. But we deliver people with titles after their names. Olympic champions, world champions, world record holders...and those titles give people status to those who haven't heard of them before. That certainly helps our profile.

I asked Bedford which he preferred: having a great race or have someone with the profile of Radcliffe blasting everyone out of sight. He responded: "For a promoter having a great race is incredibly important. Paula has done a massive amount to raise the profile of the race; however, when she runs it is barely a race, because she is so significantly head and shoulders above everybody else. What do I prefer? I prefer a race. And we've had a lot in the years that I've been involved." "What was your prediction for Paula?" I then asked Bedford. "Did you think she could run that fast?"

No. I thought she could run that fast in her lifetime; and the weather conditions were perfect, and I think with the marathon you get a set of circumstances that don't happen in any other athletic event – that is the number of marathons anyone will run in their lifetime is limited – maybe to a couple a year. The training you put in has to be 100 per cent.

And I think for the marathon generally – if they turn up to the start line and the conditions are great, they'll go for it. And I think that's the exciting thing about the marathon; if the conditions are good they'll go for it – every time.

* * *

Radcliffe suffered great disappointment in the summer of 2003 when she was forced to pull out of the Paris World Championships: that elusive World crown on the track continued to elude. She was fairly quiet in the early part of 2004 before running some fast track times in the summer. The blinkers were on and the Athens Olympic marathon was her focus. She was the overwhelming favourite and yet there were three large unanswered question marks: Radcliffe had never run a Championship marathon (which demands different tactics to a big-city marathon), and she had never run a marathon in heat or over an undulating course: her three stupendous efforts all being over pancake-flat courses in cool or even cold conditions.

As we now know, Radcliffe then came to Athens suffering from a debilitating injury and zapped by an inability to process her food and build up energy. Chapter 30 describes this dramatic race as Radcliffe recorded a devastating DNF. Her first failure at the marathon had come in the most humiliating and traumatic of circumstances. Surely she would now take four to six months off to recover from such a terrible blow.

This brings us to this chapter's featured race, the 2004 New York City Marathon, where Radcliffe submitted a startling late entry form, just eleven weeks after her Athens debacle. One could find very few people who felt Radcliffe had anything to gain, and most indeed thought she had everything to lose. In fact they were positively queuing up to have a crack.

Take *Athletics Weekly*, for instance. Delighted to put Radcliffe on their cover far more frequently than any other runner, usually with a superlative attached, their editor, Jason Henderson, this time went on the attack: "Paula Radcliffe faces a no-win situation on Sunday and her decision to race so soon after the Olympics reeks of the same kind of thinking that led her to run the ill-fated 10,000m in Athens. If she wins, people will say 'so what'. If she loses, they will say she is finished." Henderson went on to point to a poll on the notorious LetsRun.com web site, where the views are often outlandish in their extremity. A poll asking if Radcliffe would win came up with a shocking, somewhat moronic, result: 83 per cent said she would lose. The human being most certainly is a fickle beast. How quickly we discard and ignore recent history when *very* recent history will do. Henderson went on to stick out his neck even further by writing:

Unless she shatters her world record in New York, which is highly unlikely given the tough nature of the course, she is unlikely to find redemption.

What about one wonders, if she prevailed in a fast time, in a close exciting race? Surely that would be redemption of sorts? Not the ultimate redemption obviously; that would have to wait for Beijing 2008, but was Radcliffe therefore to be seen to be foolhardy every time she toed the line until then?

Radcliffe describes her reasons for having a go at New York:

I was taking it day by day and enjoying my running. I came back from a run and I said to Gary, "You know what, I would quite like to run the race." It was that spontaneous when I mentioned it to Gary. It had been forming in my mind. But I would not put myself in this position if I were not confident that I could do myself justice.

I do not see New York as any different from a normal race: I am going into it wanting to win it.

The *Daily Telegraph* opted for a little fence-sitting: "Her decision to make such a high-profile return can be seen as either an extraordinary show of bravery or foolishness." The *Guardian* oozed pessimism: "If she fails to complete the course...it may deal her career a fatal blow and forever brand her as a quitter." There were others, too, who suggested the age of Radcliffe's invincibility in the marathon was over following on from her 2:15 at London. "She went to the well there and drunk pretty deep," noted television commentator Kathrine Switzer. Others pointed to the succession of injury and illness Radcliffe had suffered since that day.

With this remarkable lack of belief in her enormous ability to ponder, what competition awaited Radliffe on the Verrazano Narrows bridge? It seemed Radcliffe faced a stern test from over half a dozen athletes. Deena Kastor flew the home flag. She had won a bronze at the Olympics with a superbly tactical approach, and at the end had cast doubt on almost every part of the Radcliffe approach. Kastor's 2:21 at London 2003 showed she could run fast too. The Australian Benita Johnson was fast becoming the finest female distance runner in the world and had enjoyed great success in 2004. She thrilled Australia by unexpectedly winning the World Cross-Country Championships in March, and then won the Great North Run (a half-marathon) in October in 67 minutes; following that up a week later with a win in the Great South 10-miles.[2]

Several other fine marathoners came to race. There was Margaret Okayo, the defending champion who had impressively defeated Catherine Ndereba the previous year, and who was the reigning London champion as well. Okayo had also had to drop out of the Olympic marathon with an injury, so like Radcliffe had something to prove. The dangerous Kenyan Lorna Kiplagat could not be ignored, third the year before, fifth in the Olympic 10,000-metres final, and a winner over Radcliffe in Puerto Rico over 10K earlier in the year. Double champion from a decade earlier (1994–95), Tegla Loroupe made a nostalgic return to one of her favourite courses. Another Kenyan who could cause Radcliffe problems was the second fastest half-marathoner in history, Susan Chepkemei.

Chepkemei, who ran a world-record half of 65:40 in Lisbon in 2001, is perhaps best remembered, though, for a thrilling duel she had with Joyce Chepchumba at the Great North Run in 2001 where she eventually prevailed by just 5 seconds. She was a big city marathon winner (Rotterdam 2001) as well as being twice a runner-up (Berlin 1998 and New York 2001), and had run 8:44 on the track for 3K. Like many Kenyans, she sent a great deal of her prize money home to her family in Kenya in order to pay for her seven siblings to go to school. Because of the abundance of fine athletes in Kenya, Chepkemei was lesser known than many of her more illustrious counterparts, but she came to New York 2004 determined to enhance her standing in the world of marathoning after injury had dashed her Olympic hopes.

The first mile took an ultra-modest 5:43, but soon the pace upped until 5 miles was passed in a more buoyant 26:48 (inside course record pace). Along with pace-maker Leah Malot, Radcliffe took on what was a fairly stiff headwind. Surprisingly, the first two casualties of the race came early and from unexpected quarters. The contender Benita Johnson eased back at just 4 miles and would eventually record a disappointing 2:38, while Deena Kastor fell back at eight miles. Cramp

---

2. The author can vouch first-hand for Johnson's intense and passionate approach to the sport. Not long before her World "Cross" triumph I had one of my regular Tuesday-night track sessions with her: 5 × 1200 metres. Johnson was untouchable on the first two, faded a little on the third (we tied) and faded quite badly on the fourth, which I won comfortably. Johnson burst into tears at this humilation, and her coach promptly hauled her out of the session...This is either one fragile beast, I said to myself, or else a perfectionist who has her sights set on reaching the top. A few weeks later she was crowned champion of the world.

Making a nostalgic return to her triumph ten years before, Tegla Loroupe F7 tries to keep in touch with the new hard, fast world of women's marathoning. Paula Radcliffe slugs it out with Susan Chepkemei F6 and Lornah Kiplagat F3. *Mark Shearman*

and knee pain would eventually force her out two-thirds through. However, Radcliffe had plenty of company, most notably from Lornah Kiplagat, Tegla Loroupe and Susan Chepkemei.

Jason Henderson reports: "Halfway was passed in 70:51 as the lead group was reduced to four going over the Pulaski Bridge. Radcliffe and her rivals were 25 seconds up on course record schedule but over the Queesboro Bridge, crossing the East River and Roosevelt Island, the athletes now faced the hardest part of the course." Finally, it appeared that Radcliffe was at a big-city marathon where she would have to race, and race hard, upon entering the final 10 miles – she had usually gained herself an enormous cushion by now. The nostalgic, heart-warming return to the limelight of Loroupe was halted at mile 17 when Kiplagat injected a surge. Although only in her early 30s, Loroupe seemed to belong to a different era. The remaining trio then crossed the Harlem River into the Bronx, reaching 20 miles in 1:48:26 (Henderson).

Lornah Kiplagat paid dearly for her Loroupe-dusting surge and herself found the going too hot as the crowds thinned out through Harlem as the angry hills of Central Park lay in wait. Radcliffe's arch nemesis, stomach cramps, reared up again. The previous evening she had had to send her spaghetti bolognese back to the kitchen twice for reheating. She awoke in the night with bad indigestion and at 23 miles she was in real pain: on top of everything else she now had to hope that her stomach would hold together.

And so it came down to a mighty race-long duel between Chepkemei and Radcliffe, the like of which is rarely seen. The race has since been hailed by many as the greatest women's marathon race in history (this book only marginally disagrees), and the race's final 20 minutes were truly Hitchcockian in their suspense. The master director would have loved Radcliffe; she ticked every box on his leading-lady checklist – aloof, mysterious, ice-cool, impassive...and blonde. She was the heroine who had the audience rooting for her, but often got herself into the most fiendish of scrapes, à la Eva Marie Saint dangling off Mount Rushmore, or Grace Kelly battling a deranged murderer, or Tippi Hedren getting her flesh pecked to pieces. Would Radcliffe, like these women, escape just in the nick of time? Or would she go the way of so many other pretty blondes that Hitchcock took such glee in killing off – the way of Janet Leigh in *Psycho*...

Televison viewers the world over sat glued to their screens as Chepkemei tossed in surge after surge in the closing few miles. A metre's gap ominously appeared at the 24.5 mile mark...then 2 metres. Radcliffe quickly closed it. The same happened half a mile later, and again the Bedford street-fighter was able to match her rival's turn of speed. Into the last mile it was Radcliffe who continuously surged, but Chepkemei refused to break. The *Eurosport* commentator Tim Hutchings mused on one reason why Radcliffe was being so sternly challenged: "Radcliffe has massively raised the bar in this event, and she's bringing the other girls up with her. This is one of the greatest women's marathons races seen in many a year – it's sport at its absolute best, and whatever happens Radcliffe has run fabulously."

Into the final 500 metres and there was still no clue as to who would finally prevail. Radcliffe hadn't been able to edge herself into any sort of lead up till now. And then, oh so slowly – and surely one was just imagining this – it was Radcliffe who inched into the lead. It stayed at 2 metres for 100 yards, and then stretched to 4. Chepkemei hung on grimly but with just 200 metres to go Radcliffe finally broke her rival and began to stretch away, until she finally flashed through the line with a 4-second cushion. Redemption had come at the last possible moment. Chepkemei burst through the line, too, and the women indulged in a long victory embrace. They had been racing each other for a dozen years now, but they had never had a duel like this.

Just 77 days after her Olympic marathon ended on a kerbstone in Athens with not "a calorie of energy left in her sick and injured body, Radcliffe

Having finally made her decisive break some 300-metres from home, Paula Radcliffe goes some way to atoning for her Athens Olympic nadir three months earlier. *Mike Segar/Reuters/Corbis*

Radcliffe embraces Chepkemei after their ultimate duel. *Mike Segar/Reuters/Corbis*

gave a stunning ripost to those who wrote her off as a choker who succeeds only when running against the clock with the help of pacemakers" (Neil Wilson, *Daily Mail*). Any journalist who dared point out the fact her time was eight minutes off her world record was quickly shot down by Radcliffe: "The time didn't matter at all. What mattered was enjoying the atmosphere and enjoying the race. I don't know about redemption but it was important for me to come here and win. Athens was certainly the biggest disappointment of my career so it was important to come back and run well. It's just great to be back, feeling happy and feeling like myself again." Regarding the awful déjà vu of having a Kenyan on her shoulder in the final stages of a major race, Radcliffe explained: In a lot of races I've been in that position. I think it was a different position than on the track, because I am confident with my finishing speed. I could have gone sooner but it was about winning the race, not times. I was pretty determined.

* * *

Jason Henderson had to eat a large dose of humble pie after his previous week's outburst: "Last week I said Paula Radcliffe faced a no-win situation in New York, would struggle to find fulfilment and should save her legs for future marathons. How wrong I was. Running like a true champion, the world-record-holder earned a substantial slice of redemption by grinding out a hard-fought victory over a rival who refused to give her an inch."

George Gandy, the chief athletics coach at Loughborough University, said: "It was a tremendous performance. Not only did she come back effectively from Athens and win the race, she won it in a war of attrition over the last 10 kilometres. She gritted it out metre by metre. She answered her critics in spades. I hope the whole silly nonsense in some sections of the media is now over." Paul Hayward in the *Daily Telegraph* also agreed that any notion of Radcliffe being a quitter could be laid to rest: "We have the answer now to that question about whether she is a quitter. It took courage for Radcliffe to run in the first place, courage overcome doubt on the starting line and courage for her to win a colossal struggle with Chepkemei as the two women battered each other's spirits on the streets of Manhattan."

So redemption or not? Not surprisingly different "hacks" had different views. Matthew Norman in the *Evening Standard* wrote a piece titled: "Shame on all those Radcliffe doubters": "The glibness with which this magnificent woman was dismissed during the Olympics by chunks of the Press and the armchair athletes of

Great Britain was depressing as it was predictable. That she cracked in Athens made her no less special an athlete. But the strength she showed yesterday in renewing herself made her an even more impressive human being." Jeff Powell, however, writing for the *Daily Mail*, remained a confirmed Radcliffe-basher:

> Her apologists proclaimed that by earning a small fortune in a public race she had exorcized her demons, routed her critics and achieved vindication. Poppy-cock.
>
> It was for cash, and to test her psychological recovery, not for the British public. If there is to be redemption for her betrayal of the Olympic spirit, it can only come with a marathon win in Beijing, a fact she recognizes.

And so as of this writing, the only thing everyone agrees about with Radcliffe's career is that they disagree. For half, the Athens ghost has been exorcized, for half it hasn't. The next few years will no doubt be full of yet more thrilling races, great triumphs and heart-breaking despair.[3] But Beijing 2008 will, it seems, be the ultimate litmus test. Unless of course she crashes out there too and then London 2012 will suddenly come sharply into focus. That would be twenty years since she was first crowned champion of the world; what nice symmetry it would be to finish off as she began.

Race result:

Paula Radcliffe	GBR	2:23:10
Susan Chepkemei	KEN	2:23:14
Lyubov Denisova	RUS	2:25:18
Margaret Okayo	KEN	2:26:31
Jelena Prokopcuka	LAT	2:26:51
Luminita Zaituc	GER	2:28:15
Lornah Kiplagat	KEN	2:28:21
Larisa Zousko	RUS	2:29:32
Madai Perez	MEX	2:29:57
Kerryn McCann	AUS	2:32:06

Sources:

Conversations with Dave Bedford.
Barnes, Simon, in the *The Times*, April 15th, 2002 & April 14th, 2003.
Hayward, Paul, in the *Daily Telegraph*, November 8th, 2004.
Henderson, Jason, in *Athletics Weekly*, November 3rd & 10th, 2004.
Milroy, Andy, in *Distance Running*, May 2003.
Norman, Matthew, in the *Evening Standard*, November 8th, 2004.

---

3. Her winning streak continued at a rush in 2005 with conclusive wins at London and the World Championships.

Powell, David, in the *The Times*, April 14th, 2003.
Powell, Jeff, in the *Daily Mail*, November 10th, 2004.
Radcliffe, Paula, *Paula – My Story So Far*. Simon & Schuster, 2004.
Wilson, Neil, in the *Daily Mail*, November 8th, 2004.

XXXVII

No. 14 – 1995 World Championships [Men]

Saturday, August 12th

World's top two slug it out on a baking world stage.

The way top-level sport tends to go is this: the best player/athlete in the world usually features in the final shake-up, but the second favourite doesn't. He bit the dust a little earlier in proceedings. Or, it is the second favourite who is in there fighting at the death, while the favourite has bowed out earlier on. It is a rare sight to see the two hottest shots, right on their game at precisely the same time. This is why the Borg–McEnroe Wimbledon finals are held in such high regard as the pinnacle of that tournament's history. How many Wimbledon finals since 1981 have had the top two players gracing the final? Maybe Edberg v Becker in 1990, perhaps Sampras–Agassi in '99. Little else though. Or take golf: Tom Watson and Jack Nicklaus' "duel in the sun" at Turnberry in 1977 is seen as one of the greatest ever showdowns: the world's two leading players eyeball-to-eyeball refusing to blink. But more often than not, major golf tournaments are decided by one of the world's leading players doing battle with a significantly lesser force.

Athletics fares better – there is less luck involved; but the cases of two top contenders wearing each other down to the verge of collapse are still rare, and therefore boast iconic status in the sport. Coe v Ovett at Moscow in 1980: there was a battle and, in fact, as luck would have it, there were two. Viren v Prefontaine – Munich '72.[1] Lewis v Powell – Tokyo '91. Gebrselassie versus Tergat – Sydney 2000. All tremendous duels fought out by the top two contenders at the pinnacle of their profession. However, when we go all the way up in distance to the marathon, lady luck starts to play a part again. Over such a long race there is so much that can go wrong. Take the 1984 Olympic marathon, for instance. Most had a winner picked from one of the "big four": de Castella, Seko, Ikangaa and Salazar. And yet, the best any of those placed was fifth, leaving the medal ceremony to far lesser-known quantities.

Such is the captivating mystique of the marathon. Put your money on the hot favourite...but don't hold your breath. Occasionally, however, it is nice to have a little predictability. If you have a great stage – like the World Championships –

---

1. With apologies to Mohammed Ghammoudi and Ian Stewart – who placed second and third!

and two runners who are seen as the finest marathoners in the world – how intriguing it would be to watch them duke it out in a no-holds-barred slugfest. At the 1995 Göteborg World Championships that is precisely what happened.

* * *

The Spanish team at the European Championships in Helsinki a year earlier did a remarkable thing. For just the third time in major championship marathon racing, their athletes, Martin Fiz, Diego García and Alberto Juzdado, performed a clean sweep of the medals.[2] A year later at Göteborg, the three musketeers returned looking for a repeat. Their fearless leader was Martin Fiz, a brilliant steeplechaser who had taken naturally to marathoning, and had begun devouring fields.

Born in Vitoria on March 3rd, 1963, Fiz had made his debut in 1993 at the Helsinki Marathon where he had run a promising 2:12:47. Then, in April of 1994, he cranked the accelerator up a notch to record 2:10:21 and set the Spanish national record at the lightning-fast Boston of '94. Conditions back at Helsinki for the European Championships later on that year suited Fiz as humidity stood at around 84 per cent. Aside from Antonio Rodriguez and Antonio Pinto of Portugal, and an extremely dogged return from Britain's Richard Nerurkar, this was a race that the Spanish dominated in spectacular style, with Fiz triumphing over Diego García by 15 seconds. His 2:10:31 was certainly worth better, due to the oppressive conditions, and Fiz had undoubtedly stamped himself as a force to be recognized on the world stage.

Fiz was to get the chance to prove he was there as arguably the best marathoner in the world at the World Championships in Göteborg – this chapter's featured marathon – but first came Rotterdam Marathon in the spring of 1995. Defending champion, Vincent Rousseau, came to defend his crown, but as was his highly bizarre habit, he refused to toe the starting line since the thermometer had reached too high. He had it written into his contract that if the temperature was 16 °C or above at the start of a race then he wouldn't have to start. Rousseau had won in Rotterdam the previous year in a brilliant 2:07:51, which meant he had become just the second runner to record three sub-2.09s in a row. (The following autumn in Berlin he ran to an astounding 2:07:20, behind Samuel Lelei's 2:07:20, to become the first man in history to break 2:08 twice.)

So Fiz had Rotterdam pretty much all to himself, and he did not disappoint as he cruised to an impressive victory over Bert van Vlaanderen in 2:08:57 in a new Spanish record. In far more oppressive conditions Fiz had lopped 1½ minutes off his Boston personal best – and had stamped his mark even more emphatically on the world scene. He happily declared: "I had dreamt of winning one of the best marathons in the world. In August I hope to win a medal again at the World Championships in Göteborg." The Spaniard logged 250 kilometres a week at 2000-metres altitude, all under the steady eye of his coach (who also guided five-times Tour de France champion, Miguel Indurain.)

Aside from his countrymen, it seemed that the main competition that Fiz was to

---

2. The other countries who have won a clean sweep of medals in a major marathon championship are the USA at the St Louis Olympics of 1904, and Ethiopia at the African Games of 1987.

face in Göteborg would come from two lightning-quick Mexicans; a highly experienced Brazilian; a couple of redoubtable Englishmen; and an Australian competitor renowned for his love of championship marathons. The Mexicans came in the form of Dionicio Cerón and Andrés Espinosa, both of whom had shown great form in recent big-city marathons. Espinosa had won the New York Marathon in 1993 after coming runner-up in two dramatic Big Apple races in 1991 and 1992. In Boston 1994 he pushed Cosmas Ndeti all the way before placing second – by just two ticks of the clock – in 2:07:19. As for Cerón, he came to Göteborg to prove that he was the best marathon runner in the world. He had won London for the last two years, showing not only a capability for great pace late on in the race, but also as an astute tactician with a very calm temperament. Indeed Cerón had actually won five of his last six marathons: even Fiz's hot streak couldn't match those numbers.

Australian Steve Moneghetti's championship record was a beauty: fifth at the 1988 Seoul Olympics, fourth at the 1987 World Championships, third at the 1986 Commonwealth Games, second at the 1990 Commonwealths and a comfortable winner at the 1994 edition. A year later he would place seventh at the Atlanta Olympic Marathon. And at the 2000 Sydney Olympics he recorded yet *another* top ten finish, in a time just 5 seconds off four years earlier! He had recently placed second in London by just 3 seconds, as he had in 1989. Moneghetti may not win much, but no one it seems hung out at the sharp end more when it mattered most.

Also in the field was the Brazilian star Luiz dos Santos who had won the Chicago Marathon twice and placed third in Boston earlier in the year. He also boasted a victory in the São Paulo Marathon. One of the most experienced runners in the field, he would go on to win Fukuoka later on in the year.

Britain's Richard Nerurkar had won the first two marathons that he'd entered: Hamburg and the World Cup, both in 1993. Formerly a top cross-country and 10,000-metres runner, he had moved up in distance, and this appeared to be where his speciality now lay. In the Spanish "knockout" the year before at Helsinki, Nerurkar placed an excellent fourth. But he admits his Spanish rivals in Helsinki had tactically outmanoeuvred him, as they never gave him the chance to utilize his dangerous finishing speed, and he came to the World Championships determined to atone for that aberration.

Nerurkar brought with him a teammate who trained with maniacal dedication: Peter Whitehead. Taking the drastic action of "upping sticks", Whitehead had moved away from his home and family to Mexico, to train at altitude. "Whitehead's commitment was total," wrote David Powell in *The Times*. "He gave up his job, remortgaged his house and left his wife working in a bank in Leeds, while, for nine months he lived in Albuquerque at perfect heat and altitude environment." Such was Whitehead's extreme dedication, he commented: "If someone said to me, 'you can be Olympic champ but the price you have to pay is you will be dead the next day', I would say, 'I will take it'. That is how much being Olympic champion means to me." Whitehead committed himself to running on the strength of a 2:17, aged 29. At first he telephoned his wife regularly but after a first phone bill of £2,000, he switched to faxing. "We fax each other on a regular basis and it works out cheaper," Whitehead explained, unfortunately ignorant, it appears, of a newfangled gimmick called e-mail. "We do not see each other often but I want to be the best. She cannot come out to stay because I am making only enough to survive." One of Whitehead's heroes and inspirations was the great British triple jumper, Jonathan Edwards, who left home in Devon with no job, to go to Newcastle to try to make it as an athlete, jumping only 15 to 16 metres at the time.

* * *

In his book *Marathon Running*, Richard Nerurkar writes about the lead up to the 1995 World Championship marathon: "As I walked the short distance to the stadium, I glanced back towards the Information Tower that stood in the centre of the Athletes' Village. The temperature gauge read 32 °C. Today, Saturday 12th August, was the hottest day yet of the week's competition at the 1995 World Championships – and within a couple of hours, I would be lining up for the start of the marathon." Nerurkar didn't lack the confidence to run well in hot conditions. At previous major championships – Split in 1990, Tokyo in '91 and Barcelona '92 – he had survived well in the oppressive heat. And the previous year's Europeans hadn't been exactly cool. But this was different. This was sapping heat of the cruellest kind, and to add to Nerurkar's woes, a foot injury had meant that his background endurance training had been severely compromised.

The race, understandably, got off to a slow start. Halfway was reached in a leisurely 66:52, with Britain's Peter Whitehead relishing the conditions and the suffering that they were causing his rivals. Britain's third competitor, Mark Hudspith, had already retired through heat exhaustion and blisters. The leading pack hung together until 27 kilometres when the dangerous dos Santos put in a surge which split up the leading group. Nerurkar was dropped, but over the next 3 kilometres he slowly clawed back the lost ground. But then there was another surge, by the feisty Whitehead, and Nerurkar got dropped again. "Yes, I really felt tired there," Nerurkar said later. "The last 12 kilometres was very tough."

The question was, who would be able to deal with the fatigue and heat best? Up front, Whitehead bravely pushed on, all part of his pre-race plan. "For once I was going to run my own race. I didn't mind leading," he explained. "I ran tactically badly in London [he was twelfth] so I didn't want to make the same mistake again." Soon Whitehead found himself under attack as the big wind-up to the finish began. The world's two finest marathoners – Fiz and Cerón – had

The unlikely figure of Peter Whitehead of Britain duels with Spain's Martin Fiz. Richard Nerurkar may be spotted in the background with water bottle. *Mark Shearman*

348

started to make their push for victory. Their duel was enough to shake off the attentions of Whitehead, and then dos Santos, who finally started to fade after 37 kilometres.

Whitehead ran an isolated fourth, while dos Santos was safe in the knowledge that the bronze was his. Up front, the gold was anything but clear. Suddenly, dramatically, boldly, Cerón accelerated away from Fiz. This was his speciality when the 38-kilometre mark was reached. Cerón was the master of the lung-busting 4-kilometre burn-up. It seemed unlikely that Fiz would be able to match strides now that Cerón had seemingly pieced together another tactical master-piece.

For a kilometre Cerón slowly but surely stretched the gap. First to 5 metres, then to 10 and soon to over 20. It wasn't an unsurmountable deficit for Fiz to make up, but he certainly couldn't allow much more. Cerón continued to press on, but the gap remained constant; both men on the edge of the proverbial preci-pice, knowing that something *had* to give, someone *had* to tire. The question was: would Cerón's tactics from relatively cool marathons, like London, transfer readily to far hotter conditions – or was a more conservative approach required?

With around 3 kilometres to go, the race took yet another dramatic swing. Riël Hauman writes: "Fiz looked at his watch a couple of times, then pulled up his shorts – and set out after Cerón." Fiz would later explain: "When Cerón raced by me, I was confident I could hold my pace to the end. I thought it might be a quick move and if I could just hold on to Cerón I had a chance." It turns out Cerón had taken a huge gamble by trying to break Fiz with over 12 minutes still remaining. On his break for glory, Cerón revealed: "I was feeling really tired. I felt awful at 35 kilometres, but what did I do?" he queried. "I made the pace faster when I should have gone somewhere and died!"

Fiz surged into the lead, and this dramatic duel between the world's two top marathoners finally had no more swings to come. Fiz ran kilometres 35–40 in an astounding 14:48, and the second half of the course well over 2 minutes quicker than the first. He finally prevailed over a spent Cerón by 32 seconds. "I looked at my watch and saw that we had been running really fast," Fiz explained, "so I knew Dionicio would be tired and I felt I could take advantage of that, and it's exactly what happened."

Martin Fiz confirms his reputation as the best marathoner around at the 1995 Göteberg World Championships. *Mark Shearman*

Paul Larkins wrote in *Athletics Weekly*: "Demonstrating a combination of supreme confidence and strength, European champion Martin Fiz waited until the last 3 kilometres before closing in on Dionicio Cerón. Behind him the long time leader, Peter Whitehead, moved into the world's elite with a fourth place that only he would have

349

predicted beforehand." "Despite not getting a medal, I'm pleased with that," concluded Whitehead. "As far as I'm concerned I'll get a medal in the future. And look at the first five. They all train at altitude," he said.

*   *   *

Whitehead's terrific front running raised many eyebrows in Britain. "Who was the stocky figure in the British vest and wearing a peaked cap running in the men's marathon at the World Athletics Championships on Saturday?" asked David Powell in *The Times*:

> The one with the solid thighs, more like a sprinter's than the archetypal distance runner's. The one you never see on the road-racing circuit in Great Britain? Who was that athlete with no significant marathon record forcing the pace at 19 miles, causing Richard Nerurkar, Britain's World Cup champion, to drop away from the leading group? The one grabbing four sponges at a time at the water stations. The one relishing the lead in the final push for medals in a field containing all but two of today's leading marathoners.
>
> Who was that runner who crossed the finish line in fourth place, the best finish by a British athlete in a global marathon championship since Charlie Spedding won an Olympic bronze medal in 1984? The nearest African was more than four minutes behind.

Whitehead happily stated: "After my run here, I feel I have as good a chance as anybody, if not in Atlanta, then in Australia." But although he felt his best was yet to come; that was as good as Whitehead ever got. He finished outside the top 25 in Atlanta and did not qualify for the British team travelling to Sydney.

The arduous conditions were reflected by the slow finishing times. Just 18 runners broke 2:20, compared to 37 at the steamy – and hilly – 1992 Barcelona Olympics, and 39 at the following year's Atlanta Games. Two big names from the 1980s, Ahmed Salah and Juma Ikangaa, finished 25th and 43rd respectively.

Fiz and Cerón would remain at the forefront of world marathoning for the next couple of years. Cerón scoring a hugely impressive "threepeat" at London in '96, while Fiz came to the Athens World Championships of 1997 hot favourite to defend his crown. The race came down to a kick finish, but this time Fiz' strength let him down as he bowed to the superior speed of Abel Anton – who would go on to defend his world crown at Seville in 1999.

Race result:

Martin Fiz	ESP	2.11.41
Dionicio Cerón	MEX	2.12.13
Luíz dos Santos	BRA	2.12.49
Peter Whitehead	GBR	2.14.08
Alberto Juzdado	ESP	2.15.29
Diego García	ESP	2.15.34
Richard Nerurkar	GBR	2.15.47

350

| Steve Moneghetti | AUS | 2.16.13 |
| Andrés Espinosa | MEX | 2.16.44 |

Sources:

Hauman, Riël, *Century of the Marathon*. Human & Rousseau, 1996.
Nerurkar, Richard, *Marathon Running*. A & C Black, 2000.
Larkins, Paul, in *Athletics Weekly*, August 16th, 1995.
Powell, David, in the *The Times*, August 14th, 1995.

XXXVIII

No. 13 – 1932 Olympic Marathon [Men]

Sunday, August 7th

"I couldn't be licked. I had to win or die in the attempt."

People either tend to love sport or hate it. How then to convince a sceptic of the magnificent power of sport? There would be little better example of sport's ability to captivate, enthral and deliver happiness to huge swathes of people than the 1932 Los Angeles Olympics. The reason being that their success was such a surprise – which had a whole multitude of cynical, sneering, pessimistic newspaper hacks eating a double serving of humble pie. The newsmen had predicted the Games would be a shambles and a failure. And some wrote they shouldn't have gone ahead at all. Look around you, they said, to the Olympic organizers. People were broke. They had no money. They had few hopes, dreams, happiness, diversions or pleasure. And for the people of southern California in the late 1920s, early 1930s, there was an added frustration. A huge swathe of public money was being poured into a project that would surely only satisfy the rich playboys of the world, those who enjoyed such frivolous activities, while all those around them struggled and starved.

And yet...and yet. If ever a sporting occasion defied the sceptics, the doubters and the wise old heads, this was it. The Games of 1932 were a magnificent success, which brought untold happiness and satisfaction not just to those taking part but also to those who came to watch. After all, just for a day, people were able to forget their problems, and live in a world of fantasy and dream of better days. Six million people attended the Los Angeles Games of 1932, and most left with increased hope, energy and optimism in their hearts; and the belief that with a bit of guts, imagination and hard work, a better life could be just beyond the horizon.

It is obvious that the athletes were happy. After all, you perform best when you're happy. Aided by the fantastic facilities laid on by the IOC, Olympic records were smashed in nearly all athletic events. So good were the performances that the commentators were getting just a little carried away on occasion, not least at the London *Times*, where the scribe in question can be applauded for his enthusiasm, but ridiculed for his naivety:

With the exception of the performances in the long jump, the high jump, and

353

throwing the hammer, the previous records have not only been eclipsed but in many cases made to look almost ridiculous. Indeed, it may be said that a number of the records set up at Los Angeles will remain intact for many a generation, possibly until the Games are held once more in the United States, and moreover in the extreme west of that vast continent.[1]

The performances in Los Angeles have been so astounding that a new standard has been set up, and in future Olympic Games it may well be that keen followers of athletics will recognize in their own minds at any rate two standards for the Olympic Games: "Olympic records" and "Los Angeles Olympic records".

* * *

The 1932 Olympic marathon, will always be overshadowed by one unhappy flaw: the absence, due to the decision of the "men in suits" at the Olympic council, of one of the greatest sportsmen of all time, Finland's Paavo Nurmi. He of the twelve Olympic medals, including nine golds, who had made the exciting decision that he would compete in the '32 Games at the marathon. Finland held its trial for the 1932 Olympic marathon on June 26th in Viipuri, and Nurmi turned up – in spikes! The first 10 kilometres took place on the track, the next 20 kilometres on the roads and the final 10 kilometres on the track again. Nurmi ran for 40.2 kilometres in a swift 2:22:03 and then decided to stop; having proved to the selectors they should include him in the team, which of course they did. Athletics' greatest star was to shine on the world stage one final time, and the crowds would witness the legend who a Finnish journalist once described as follows: "There was something inhumanly stern and cruel about him, but he conquered the world by pure means: with a will that had supernatural power."

But alas, it was not to be. Riël Hauman writes in *Century of the Marathon*: "Two days before the start of the Games, on 28 July 1932, the council of the International Amateur Athletic Federation decided to suspend Nurmi on the grounds that he had received money in excess of his expenses when he ran five exhibition races in Germany the previous year. No appeal was allowed. Thus ending the greatest Olympic career of all." Nurmi attended the Olympics and sat in the stands as a frustrated spectator during the marathon. The event had indeed been deprived of its greatest potential star. If one assumes the final 2 kilometres of Nurmi's trial race would have taken 7 minutes, then he was comfortably a sub-2:30 marathoner, which would have won him the Olympics by a healthy margin.[2]

But all this brouhaha did mean that instead of a predictable, comfortable winner, the race would have just the opposite. Nurmi's absence meant that the pre-race favourite was most probably British entrant Samuel Ferris, who was one of the finest distance runners of the 1920s and early '30s. Born in Dromore, Northern Ireland, on August 29th, 1900, Ferris served in the Royal Air Force from 1918 to 1950. Martin and Gynn write: "In his early days as an airman he served in India, and here his interest in distance running blossomed as a means of

---

1. Suffice it to say that records such as 3:51 for the 1500, 14:30 for the 5K and 30:11 for the 10K no longer stood in 1984!
2. Nurmi commented later that the Olympic course was the easiest in the history of the Games and that he was confident he could have run 2:20 – thus winning by 10 minutes.

Nine-time Olympic winner Paavo Nurmi displays wonderful technique at a deserted Olympic Stadium the day before the 1932 Games begin. Nurmi had predicted a marathon win by 5 minutes, but 48 hours before this photo, he was banned from the Olympics due to accusations of professionalism. *IOC Olympic Museum/Getty Images*

keeping fit...Ferris was one of those highly gifted athletes who knew how to prepare for top-level competition and arrive in perfect form physically and mentally on the day – and he did it at three Olympic Games." At the stifling 1924 Paris Olympic marathon Ferris placed a commendable fifth, and at the Amsterdam Games four years later he sliced nearly a quarter of an hour off his Paris time to run 2:37:41, just 2½ minutes off the medals, albeit stepping down to eighth place. He ran conservatively that day, wary of leg twinges that never materialized into anything more. Surely the master tactician would throw caution to the wind in his final stab at Olympic glory at Los Angeles.

Unfortunately, Ferris travelled as part of an incomplete British team, which would surely have been a world-beater had all been able to travel. Two Scots – Donald Robertson and Duncan Wright, fought out a great duel at the AAA Championships – the former prevailing by just one tick of the clock. Sadly for Robertson the Glasgow Corporation for whom he painted coaches, refused to give him the time off to follow his Olympic dream.[3]

---

3. Another Scot, living in America, Jock Semple, begged the British selectors to take him. He had placed seventh in the 1930 Boston and had a 2:43 clocking making him an Olympic top-ten contender. It wouldn't cost the selectors a penny to send him he said, he'd just hitch. No thanks, came the reply, we'll just send an incomplete team.

355

Other nations sending leading contenders appeared to be Japan who seemed to have caught the marathon bug in a big way. "By the fall of 1931, Japan could have fielded several teams of three Olympic-calibre athletes" (Martin & Gynn). Instead of using a subjective criteria for selecting their team, the selectors opted for one Olympic trial race. The experienced Seiichiro Tsuda placed third (he nabbed sixth in the Amsterdam Olympics of '28), but the winning and second-placed men were completely unheralded Taika Gon and Onbai Kin – just 18 years old! Poor Tanji Yahagi who boasted the year's best time of 2:31:31 had to stay at home. The debate, which carries on to this day, of the wisdom of having just one trial race for an event as important as the Olympics had begun in earnest.

America sent an interesting-looking team. Jimmy Henigan had tried and failed for ten years to win the Boston Marathon, before eventually succeeding in 1931 – the year that the Boston papers reported that for the first time *a million* people lined the famous course. In 1932, Henigan secured selection for the Games by placing second at Boston, while Albert Michelsen was fourth. Michelsen held the world-best time of 2:29:01, set at Port Chester in 1925, and thus became the first man to break the 2:30 barrier. The mark would stand for nearly ten years. However, Michelsen worried terribly that the selectors would not deem him worthy. So he ran at Maryland, where he placed second to Hans Oldag. So now Henigan and Oldag were dead certs. Michelsen, meanwhile, travelled to the *Los Angeles Times* Marathon (in the city of the same name but *not* over the Olympic course) and comfortably won, overjoyed, in 2:44. But a dangerous man for the future had been spotted that day. And it came in the form of a young Argentinian scamp with the chiselled looks of the man who had made more movies than anyone else in the world that year, Clark Gable.

The scamp's name was Juan Carlos Zabala and he had shown his pedigree by almost breaking the world record for 15 miles on the track the previous month. At the *Los Angeles Times* Marathon, Zabala ran his first mile in 4:45, went through 5 in 24:30 and then 10 in 51:30! At one stage he was 9 minutes ahead of the pack (Martin & Gynn). Who was this man?

Zabala was born September 21st, 1911, in Buenos Aires. His father, a Frenchman, was killed in action in the First World War. Juan's mother died of grief, leaving baby Juan alone in the world – to become an inmate of an orphans' home in Buenos Aires. It was there, in 1925, that Alexander Sterling, an Austrian athletic instructor, spotted Juan. The Austrian saw in the shy, frail lad the potential and fighting heart of a great runner. He trained him and learned to love the boy as his own son and adopted him legally. It didn't take long for Zabala to mature into a top-level runner, and by 1931 had become the South American 10,000-metres champion. Sterling had him travelling further and further in training and at the famous Kosice Marathon in 1931, Zabala ran a stunning 2:33:19 which stood as the course record at Kosice for a full 19 years (Martin & Gynn).

Zabala's brilliance however couldn't save him in *Los Angeles Times* race, and he ran into major problems with his footwear at 19 miles. "Neither he nor his shoes were accustomed to the pounding on the macadam, with unpaved surfaces being the rule in Argentina" (Martin & Gynn). Stirling hauled his hobbling prodigy out of the race, leaving a very relieved Michelson to stroll on to victory. But Zabala had proved he was a man to be feared. But would he be able to curb his temperament and naive tactics at the Olympics? And a non-disintegrating pair of shoes would be helpful too.

*   *   *

Owing to the worldwide depression, just 29 toed the start line of the 1932 Olympic Marathon, but Nurmi aside, the best in the world had made it. Fifteen nations had sent runners, and the temperatures were a pleasant and not-too-uncomfortable 72 °F at the start. The athletes faced a fairly banal course without too many taxing climbs in a route that travelled 15 kilometres due south of the stadium, hooked abruptly west for 8 kilometres and then due north, snaking their way back up towards the Coliseum. The runners had to negotiate 2.75 laps of the track before they departed for the "mean" streets, and 80,000 fascinated fans were on hand to cheer them off.

It did not take long for Zabala to stamp his authority on the race. Braven Dyer wrote in the *Los Angeles Times*: "Zabala started out on the marathon like a young colt let out to pasture. He led the pack coming out of the stadium tunnel, and before the race was five minutes along, had established a lead over the main herd of 200 yards."

Perhaps of most interest in the immediate chasing pack was Paul deBruyn of Germany, the reigning Boston Marathon champion. He prepared for races with "Teutonic" thoroughness when his job as a coal shoveller in the cellar of the Wellington Hotel in New York City allowed. His training could be very imaginative. Tom Derderian reports in *Boston Marathon*: "When he was called on to make emergency repairs in the upper floors of the building, he would impress his superiors and the tenants by running full speed up as many as 26 flights of stairs. To him it was training, but to them it was obedience and loyalty to the job." DeBruyn had run with reckless abandon when winning Boston because he knew his German selectors back home would select him for the Olympics since he had won the German championships. A *Boston Post* reporter Ruth Bodwell described what a fine specimen he was: "A golden red-head with tiny freckles specking his smooth fair skin and blue eyes twinkling with fun and energy." All of deBruyn's preparation would count for little at the Olympics though, as his early showing on the leaderboard would be as much as he'd achieve. He'd eventually place a moderate 15th, and appeared again at the 1936 Olympics where he would fail to finish. Interestingly deBruyn then applied for and won US citizenship, and fought against his old country in the Second World War. He was still alive well into the 1990s where he could be found living in Holly Hill, Florida, and acted as the official starter at the annual Paul deBruyn 30 Kilometre Race in Ormand Beach, Florida (Derderian).

The runners cruised along, keying off Zabala and "the throngs of cheering spectators continued outside the stadium and all along the entire course, in a mammoth outpouring of interest in watching this competition unfold" (Martin & Gynn). A little before 10 miles, Zabala appeared to falter and Margarito Pomposo of Mexico assumed the lead. Zabala's brutal pacing meant that one should only try to keep up – or even take over – if one really meant it. Any

357

other action was tactical suicide. Pomposo didn't *really* mean it and would go on to finish stone-bonkers last. The halfway mark came in almost exactly 72 minutes, which meant that the runners were 2½ minutes ahead of world-record schedule.

The next man to try and usurp the South American came from Finland. The Finns were determined to run well and atone for the absence of their great leader, Paavo Nurmi. At 16 miles Lauri Virtanen arrived at Zabala's side, having taken nearly a minute out of him over the last couple of miles. The question was, had Virtanen overcooked or was Zabala fading? The answers would all come – as would many more – over the absorbing next three-quarters of an hour. Whilst Virtanen grimly hung on to his lead over the next 3 miles, the British boys Ferris and Wright were working their way through the field with detached and ruthless competence. With 10 kilometres to go they had both forged their way into the top five. They both had explicit plans. Wright wanted to take the lead and then hang on for dear life at the 20-mile mark. Ferris was more conservative but still ultimately as ambitious. Nearly 40 years after this race he described how on a training run before the big day he had spotted a hoarding bearing an advertisement for milk. When Ferris arrived at that landmark, he told himself, he would kick for the finish line, having kept the leader well in sight...

Wright carried out his plan almost to the letter; forging into a brave lead a little after 20 miles. By 22 miles he had a slim lead over Virtanen and up to a minute on Zabala, another Finn Armas Toivonen and the Japanese Seiichiro Tsuda. And then came the up-and-coming Ferris. Up until this point, Virtanen had astounded observers by running so freshly, especially considering he had also completed 15,000 metres of track competition in recent days. But finally mother nature awoke and cast her spell: Virtonen hit the wall at 23 miles and was sadly forced to retire from the fray. The Finn wasn't the only one with problems; Zabala was tiring dramatically and Wright was on his last, desperate legs. "As the runners reached control station seven (24 miles) and now started retracing their steps to the stadium, the final drama unfolded" (Martin & Gynn).

The brave Zabala once again, for the third time, claimed the precious lead, as Wright descended into second...then third...then fourth. The stadium hove into view and the final 2 miles of the race proved to be a "wild fight". A vast majority of the packed stadium had remained to witness the conclusion of this thrilling race. Zabala was clad in a white singlet and pale blue running trunks edged in white, and was still wearing a green handkerchief over his head to prevent sunburn. Sam Ferris, meanwhile, had gathered up his terrific reserves of strength and searched for the milk advertisement signalling his final big push. Disaster! A viewing stand had obscured it! Ferris suddenly realized he had less than half a mile to go and launched a ferocious assault on the white human speck in the distance. Maybe it was dying, Ferris hoped, and would reduce to survival shuffle.

The speck was certainly wilting. Zabala came into the stadium terribly exhausted, but crucially boasting a lead of around a minute – and he only had three-quarters of a lap to cover. Braven Dyer wrote in the *Los Angeles Times*:

More than 75,000 spectators stood on their toes and cheered the midget Argentine youth all the way around the oval. They knew the torture of this twenty-

358

A young and soon to be wilting Juan Carlos Zabala leads the marathon. More experienced runners lie in wait to pounce on the young pretender. *Bettmann/CORBIS*

six-mile grind and they were acknowledging the gameness of the 20-year-old schoolboy from Buenos Aires.

While the plaudits of the multitude grew into a deafening roar, three other runners appeared as if by magic. They were Samuel Ferris, of Great Britain, Armas Toivonen of Finland and Duncan McLeod Wright, another Englishman [*sic*]. No more spectacular finish has ever been recorded in the Olympic Games.

It was significantly the most keenly contested Olympic Marathon of all time. Ferris, much to his dismay, had pulled the ultimate tactical clanger and had finished the race full of running and in far better fettle than the leader. But the race belonged to Zabala, as he crossed the finish line completely spent…but victorious. Nineteen seconds later, Ferris tore across the line, aghast that the race just didn't have another five or six hundred yards to enable to him to catch up.

While Zabala stood dazed and confused in the midfield, Japan's athletes turned in a magnificent performance, returning their men home in fifth, sixth and ninth positions. They were seemingly the world's leading marathon nation – but if only Britain had sent that elusive third runner, then we'd have known for sure. The American Michelsen finally trotted in seventh – and was the first of the runners to leave the track unassisted.

A victorious Zabala is helped by teammates, while just a few seconds behind a fresh but frustrated Sam Ferris has stormed through the finish line. *Bettmann/CORBIS*

* * *

Zabala was overcome with emotion at the medal ceremony; as John Ness of the *Los Angeles Times* observed:

> With the first note of his National hymn, Juan squared his tired, drooping shoulders. A fiery light flashed from his eyes. His chin squared and his upturned features etched a painting against the sky...it was a Spanish warrior standing in the prow of a great galleon...conqueror of all the seas.
>
> Then something happened inside Zabala; the setting sun discovered sparkling rivulets streaming down his face...his chin still held high...he tried to wipe the tears away...his shoulders began to shake in rhythm with the sobs that shook his body.
>
> The band swung into the last bar. Waiting friends swept Zabala into their arms and carried their hero from the stadium. The last glimpse we had of him was an arm feebly waving the small flag of Argentina. This was the little boy going home from his birthday party.

Jean Bosquet of the same paper wrote about "the most thrilling of the Olympiads events as far as tradition is concerned":

360

A Greek had won the marathon when the Games of the Olympiad were revived more than thirty years ago at Athens. His victory had caused a nation to go wild with joy. There couldn't have been greater pandemonium at Athens though, than was seen at the Olympic stadium as the heroes of the marathon trotted – staggered – in yesterday, with cool shade chilling the throng in there.

Runner after runner, some bravely smiling, others with wide unseeing eyes. Here is drama, the drama of man's unconquerable spirit living on even when mind and muscles and organs falter.

Braven Dyer's investigative journalism even went as far as Zabala's dietary requirements, and they make for colourful reading:

They say Juan consumes two pounds of meat, three times a day. Yesterday at noon he didn't like the steak they gave him at the village. Chefs went in search of more appetizing fodder. They returned with two pounds of the finest tenderloin. Juan stowed it away in a hurry, apparently only about half satisfied, but his trainers would let him eat no more then. "After you've won the race this afternoon you can eat a whole cow if you feel like it," said Sterling.

The following morning, Zabala reflected on the race (after he had consumed a thick steak and a fruit salad for breakfast):

I thought of nothing but my position during the contest. The marathon is like a checker game. You must weigh every move carefully. Each man runs his own race. I knew what I could do, how much strength I had. 'I must not let that Finn try to break me in the first two miles. But I cannot let him get too far ahead. I wear no watch. I know by the swing of my stride how fast I am going – how fast I should go. 'I couldn't be licked. I had to win or die in the attempt. It would never have done to be beaten. I could not have gone back to the Argentine.

* * *

Zabala continued his marathon career in crazy fashion, by attempting another marathon, just *20 days* after the Olympics, on a running track! Of course he failed to finish. He then sadly (for the housewives at least) disappeared from the running scene; only to reappear on the world scene by setting a world best for 20 kilometres on the track a few months before the 1936 Berlin Olympics (Martin & Gynn). He thus earned selection for those Games but in that exciting Olympic marathon he returned yet another DNF – although he did bravely lead out the field, and at one stage led by 100 seconds. But his stamina was found wanting on this occasion, and after a fall at 28 kilometres, he retired at 32 kilometres.

Sam Ferris will be remembered as a master tactician and superb judge of pace, but critically somewhat bashful when it came to risking all when the biggest prize was at stake. In 1933 he won his eighth and final "Polytechnic" Marathon (Windsor to Chiswick), and subsequently became a director of that famous race. In all, Ferris ran 21 marathons and won 12 – a magnificent ratio that compares favourably with any other great runner in these pages. F.A.M. Webster indicates this is doubly amazing when noted that he rarely travelled further than 40 miles per week in training.

After the closing ceremony of these marvellous Olympics, Braven Dyer penned his appreciation:

> The present generation will never see another Olympic Games such as we have just witnessed. For perfection of setting, excellence of management and brilliance of presentation it is unlikely that the tenth Olympiad of Los Angeles will ever be equalled.
>
> This is not blatant boasting by a native son. As a matter of fact we southern Californians had very little to do with the success of this gigantic sports program. A benevolent God above gave us the climate. That helped. But the cast made the show and we supplied very few of the performers.
>
> Next in importance to the actors was the audience. And the whole world came to our aid in such amazing numbers that wise men with their fingers on the public pulse are still trying to figure this out. It simmers down to this – the public will still pay to see a first-class performance…the money is there, it's up to the cast to provide a real show, which is being done in the Olympics.

This was a clear and relevant message to all the sceptics, pessimists, whingers, moaners and cynical newspapermen who said the Games would be a disaster. Seventy-two years later, nothing has changed. The Olympics almost always provide a sumptuous feast of entertainment that has the media purring: and yet in the four years leading up to the festival, they always do their utmost to rain on the parade. Inexplicable.

Race result:

Juan Carlos Zabala	ARG	2:31:36
Samuel Ferris	GBR	2:31:55
Armas Toivonen	FIN	2:32:12
Duncan McLeod Wright	GBR	2:32:41
Seiichiro Tsuda	JPN	2:35:42
Onbai Kin	JPN	2:37:28
Albert Michelsen	USA	2:39:38
Oskar Heks	TCH	2:41:35
Taika Gon	JPN	2:42:52
Anders Andersen	DEN	2:44:38

Sources:

Anonymous, in *The Times*, August 8th, 1932.
Bodwell, Ruth, in the *Boston Post*, April 20th, 1932.
Bousquet, Jean, in the *Los Angeles Times*, August 8th, 1932.
Derderian, Tom, *Boston Marathon*. Human Kinetics, 1996.

Dyer, Braven, in the *Los Angeles Times*, August 8th, 1932.

Martin, David and Roger Gynn, *The Olympic Marathon*. Human Kinetics, 2000.

Ness, John, in the *Los Angeles Times*, August 8th, 1932.

Semple, Jock, John J. Kelley and Tom Murphy, *Just Call Me Jock*. Waterford Publishing Company, 1981.

Wallechinsky, David, *The Complete Book of the Olympics*. Aurum Press, 2000.

XXXIX

No. 12 – 2003 Berlin Marathon [Men]

Sunday, September 28th

The glorious sylph scythes out his past.

In the late summer of 2003, one Kenyan runner needed only two things to enable him to disregard all the nonsense that was being said about him: patience and belief. The nonsense centred on the theory that this giant of the sport was not a "winner", and yet there is a case to be made that this charming, erudite man is the greatest "all-round" distance runner of all time. Few have managed to display their credentials quite so readily on the road, the track and the country with such success. Carlos Lopes springs to mind as a contender, as he was *almost* a world beater on all surfaces, while Ron Hill displayed a more than useful range of surface prowess as well; but few others spring to mind. One feels that Kenenise Bekele will be devastating over the roads in time. But Paul Tergat, to this author at least, is the most complete distance runner the world has ever seen. Here's a list of his major achievements before the 2003 Berlin Marathon:

Cross-Country World champion 1995
10,000-metres bronze medal – World Championships 1995
Cross-Country World champion 1996
10,000m silver medal – Olympics 1996
Cross-Country World champion 1997
World-record 10,000-metres (26:27.85) 1997
10,000-metres silver medal – World Championships 1997
Cross-Country World champion 1998
Cross-Country World champion 1999
10,000-metres silver medal – World Championships 1999
10,000-metres silver medal – Olympics 2000

The glaring omission here is a World track gold medal, and one can only wonder what degree of success Tergat would have found if his arch nemesis – Haile Gebrselassie – hadn't always been there to see him off with that lethal kick. It seemed for sure that Tergat had finally got his man at Sydney in 2000 as with 300 metres he appeared to have the edge on the "master". But Gebrselassie clawed back the deficit only for Tergat to kick again. David Coleman's hapless

Born loser? Hardly, but if you put Paul Tergat in a track race against his rival Haile Gebrselassie there was only one winner, as happened at the 2000 Sydney Olympic 10,000-metre final. *Reuters/CORBIS*

commentary for the BBC shows not just the broadcaster's advancing years, but also how close and heartbreaking the race must have been for Tergat: "And it's Tergat now! Tergat's away – Tergat running for the line!...Gebrselassie wins it." It was a stunning finish to arguably the race of the Games, and one of the all-time great Olympic battles. Asked how he recovered from such disappointment, Tergat's response is "typical of his sunny, uncynical nature" (Jackson):

> One thing, my friend, you must understand is that I lost when I did the best I could. I didn't have anything, force or energy, left. So I didn't feel bad. I took it as a challenge. It was encouraging for the next competition.
>
> We have to agree that since I'm a sportsman, there will always be a winner and a loser. And so we have to accept that for me I don't feel that I lost. That day was his day, so I don't have anything to complain about.

* * *

Paul Tergat was born into a poor upbringing in the isolated Kenyan countryside as one of 17 children in a polygamous family. The journalist Jamie Jackson speaks of Tergat's inner calm and wrote in the *Observer*: "He speaks as if it is me who is in need of reassurance about some deep disappointment, rather than him. He speaks, too, as someone who is deeply interested in his country, one of a broad arc of topics that concern him." Tergat himself notes:

366

Kenya is cosmopolitan. We have so many cultures and different ethnic groups, and it is very interesting for me how we are living. We have around 42 languages. We live in a country with people who are from different countries, but we do not speak the same language. This fascinates me. And that's why when I look at the history of my country and where we have come from, it gives me a positive attitude. To understand the fight for independence [Kenya was granted independence from Britain in December 1963] and to know why we are fighting.

Tergat came from Riwo, in the Baringo district of the Rift Valley. In his youth his mother would sing him to sleep to ease his hunger pangs, and was only guaranteed food – much to his delight and excitement – by a UN-funded scheme at his school. He explains his upbringing to journalist Neil Wilson: "Life was very difficult. Poverty was rampant. Clean water was a problem. There were no health centres. It was difficult for us to go to school. Those who did were lucky, and I remember how when I went to school in 1976 how excited I was to get a free hot meal. It was a motivating factor that pushed up class attendance and enrolment." As Tergat jogged the few miles to and from school each day, Wilson notes: "he merely accepted that it was the only way to get to school, never realizing that it was the perfect training for a successful career." Indeed, at first Tergat did not like to run, and for his first 18 years he tried to avoid it: "It hurt. And I come from an area where there had never been an international runner, and so I had no idol. When I joined the military at 18 this changed. I met people that I admired a lot and that was an exciting moment for me."

Tergat is extraordinary-looking, with an appearance that Jamie Jackson observes as "almost impossibly sylph-like". What does Jackson mean by this? Certainly Tergat is blessed with the good looks of a billboard model, but does he belong to "any of a class of fairy-like beings without souls that were believed to inhabit the air" or is he more akin to a "slim, graceful woman or girl", both definitions drawn from *Reader's Digest Universal Dictionary*. A little bit of both perhaps. There is a certain feminine beauty to him with those incredible cut-glass cheek-bones; and the elegance and grace with which he moves does indeed appear somewhat otherworldly. Jackson goes on to say: "In addition to his bony face, he has long, stick-thin legs and broad, yet slim shoulders. It is a build that adds up to a lean running machine..."

It is ironic therefore that such a positive, sensible man has been thought of by many as someone who has suffered so many disappointments and must be emotionally battered by all his defeats, and that he did not possess the "heart" to win at the marathon. Not a bit of it. The marathon humbles even the greatest athletes though, and Tergat must have been wondering what it was he needed to do to "crack" the race and end up first. He seemed to have all the tools: terrific leg speed, a lifetime of race experience and the credential of the greatest half-marathoner in history. He was unbeaten at the distance between 1994 and 1999.[1]

---

1. Tergat boasts an incredible five half-marathons under the one-hour mark, plus two unofficial ones: his 59:06 in Lisbon on a course that drops too much for record purposes, and 58:51 in Milan, only to be told that the course was found to be 49 metres short and thus his time couldn't be credited.

After all of Tergat's near-misses at 10,000-metres, he made his marathon debut at London in April 2001. He was right up with master tactician Abdelkader El Mouaziz until 20 miles, when the Moroccan suddenly broke away, leaving Tergat to take second in a solid 2:08:15 debut. Real frustration followed at Chicago six months later when pace-maker Ben Kimondiu refused to drop out as expected and carried on till the end, outsprinting Tergat to win by 4 seconds. Tergat later complained that all pace-makers should advise pre-race whether they plan to finish the race (Frank).

Tergat and Gebrselassie swapped the track for the streets of London in 2002 to duel in the greatest marathon race of all time. However, although most observers thought the winner would come from one of them, they reckoned without the devastating finishing speed of Khalid Khannouchi. Second yet again for Tergat. He had the second fastest time in history – 2:05:48 – and yet was still only the "nearly man". Chicago 2002 was another phenomenal race and Tergat returned the immaculate time of 2:06:18, but he was now going backwards! Fourth. London 2003 may be investigated in Chapter 5, as Tergat found himself just three ticks of the clock behind the winner, Gezahegne Abera, in *fourth* place. It was all becoming some sort of joke – and not a very funny one at that.

In the autumn of 2003, Tergat decided to switch tack from Chicago and go for a city with rather more benign weather conditions, but a similar reputation for speed: the fast, flat, wide roads of Berlin. Brazilian Ronaldo da Costa found fame there when he finally bettered Belayneh Dinsamo's ten-year-old world mark in 1998, by running 2:06:05. Two other world records had also fallen there in recent times: Tegla Loroupe of Kenya clocked 2:20:43 in 1999, and in 2001 Naoko Takahashi ran 2:19:46.

Tergat came to Berlin with one goal in mind. Never mind the win – that would come with his superior objective. The world record for the 42.2K distance. Time to beat: Khannouchi's 2:05:38. Tergat had worried about his lack of strength in late stages of his first few marathons and so had increased his longest runs to more than 40 kilometres instead of his normal 38 kilometres and put in a four-month sustained build-up. Race day dawned and presented the runners with perfect conditions for marathoning: 7 degrees, bright and clear. The runners who toed the line were set on their way by the Mayor of Berlin, Klaus Wowereit.

The pace-makers were requested to go through halfway in around 63:30–64.00 – hardly world-record pace – but this was because the course was known to be quicker over the second half; and Tergat, ever the astute tactician, knew that the best way to run a fast marathon was to speed up in the latter stages. Tergat had two top-class pace-makers from his training group, Sammy Korir and Titus Munji, to help him in his quest. Although a very experienced marathon runner, Korir, was seen generally as one who struggled in the latter stages. His agent Federico Rosa (who also managed Tergat and Titus Munji in third), said: "He used to run well to 35 or 36 kilometres but then start to struggle. He's not one of the strongest in our training group."[2] Some 35,000 people set off behind Tergat

---

2. Before Berlin, Korir had run seven marathons between 2:08:02 and 2:09:01 and had won at Amsterdam in 1997 and 1998, Turin in 1999 and San Diego in 2002.

but none could equal his first kilometre of 2:58. He had started as he meant to go on. One down, 41 to go.

Tergat, who had discussed in detail the tactics he should use with his friend Tegla Loroupe, settled in behind his training partners and clocked 15:00 for 5 kilometres. "Only" 2:06:35 pace but the day was young. The group of ten that passed through 10 kilometres was primarily a Kenyan party, although two Japanese, Satoshi Osaki and Kurao Umeki, could be spotted invading the group. The split was a fast, but still calm, 29:57.

The pace increased just a fraction over the next 10 kilometres and by halfway a group of six passed in a suddenly very threatening 63:03. No seasoned observer could have failed to notice the world record could now be under threat. Tergat was looking fresh, his momentum was gaining, and he was still surrounded by a phalanx of pace-makers. Dramatic developments began to occur apace between kilometres 25–30. The lead group trimmed itself from six to three, as the distance and speed of the operation began to claim victims in quick succession. The three remaining runners were Tergat, tucked in behind Korir, and Munji. The defending champion Raymond Kipkoech had dropped back by 10 metres and appeared to be drifting out of contention. A few kilometres later and he was nearly a minute back. Although both Korir and Munji were both supposed to be *only* pace-makers, Tergat had the added worry of not letting them get too far ahead of him, lest they decide to make a race of it after all. He most certainly didn't want a repeat of his 2001 saga.

The split for 35 kilometres of 1:43:59 indicated that Khannouchi's world record was indeed in dire threat of taking a tumble, with the pace car flashing up a projected time of 2:05:15. But seven kilometres is a very long way when one is running on a near-empty tank. Remarkably, neither Tergat nor Korir appeared to be suffering too gravely, although the time finally came for Munji to lose his grip on the leading pair. But there was little doubt about Korir's intentions. He wanted the Berlin title and the world record, and he was going to fight his friend to the bitter end. Time-to-run.com reports:

38 kilometres: men in 1:52:38. The front two are now venturing close to the 2:05 barrier! This is absolutely incredible running and surely history in the making, where two athletes will hopefully crack the barrier together.

40 kilometres in 1:58:36, the sub 2:05 is undoubtedly under threat, however, can Tergat break his duck at the distance and win this one? Korir is running as freely as Tergat and the pacemaker duties do not seem to have blunted his desire to win. They're running side by side now, and Tergat must be feeling the enormous pressure as well as a case of *déjà-vu*.

The thrilling last 2 kilometres saw the crowds straining to spot even the slightest clue as to who would break first. Wait. Was that a half-metre gap that Tergat had possibly prised open? A full 50 centimetres? No – more like 40. With a kilometre to go Tergat was able to lengthen his stride just a shade and pull away. It seemed as though he had finally broken his long, unfortunate sequence; but what a heart-stopping last-gasp twist lay in store.

Turning left before the Brandenburg Gate and then a lesser right, Tergat's lead

369

of 20 metres seemed to assure him of victory: "The crowds watching began to respond in rapturous arm waving and applause as they witnessed the Kenyan Great going towards the making of history," reported Time-to-run.com. But then, just when it seemed all was over, Korir launched a furious assault on his rival, just like Gebrselassie had in the Sydney 10,000-metres. The gap quickly came down to just 10 metres – and then continued to shrink. Tergat, terrified now, looking over his shoulder once, twice, three times, "fearing the worst".

The finish line was just a few seconds away though now, and the great man gritted his teeth into an angry snarl and threw himself towards it, and arrived one tick of the clock ahead of the pesky pace-maker. Tergat's expression was one of relief and jubilation as he shot both arms to the heavens in celebration. Finally the man who had promised so much, and who had proven himself a winner so many times over grass – and half-marathon – had the victory he craved. The first person to joyously hug the new fastest marathoner on the planet was, quite rightly, his wife. The time was a phenomenal 2:04:55 which sliced a huge 43 seconds off the great Khannouchi's mark. It was a truly surreal day, not just for the record to fall by such a healthy margin, but for *two* runners to be in shape enough to do it at exactly the same time.

Tergat breaks the tape with Sammy Korir just behind. *Michael Kappeler/Getty Images*

Another astonishing world record then fell a few minutes later, as the Mexican runner Andrés Espinosa smashed the world mark in the M40 category by running 2:08:46, bettering the mark of Frenchman Mohamed Ezzher by nearly 2 minutes. However long Tergat's mark stands for, this correspondent submits that Espinosa's mark will stand even longer. That Espinosa had great quality was of no doubt. He was the New York City Marathon champion back in 1993 (in 2:10:04), and then had run himself into the ground in the thrilling Boston of 1994 by chasing Cosmas Ndeti to his course record of 2:07:15; Espinosa ran just 4 seconds slower.[3]

Tergat later told Neil Wilson:

When I finished I was not able even to bend down to undo my shoes. The next day I was not able to walk. The marathon is never how fast you are. Complete experience is the number one thing. That is how you win at it.

I knew deep in my head that one day I would get this world record, and today everything fell into place. It was a relief after training for so long.

---

3. His split for miles 22–25 that day was 13:48!

New York, November 2005: With city mayor Michael Bloomberg and Olympic champion Mizuki Noguchi as interested spectators, Paul Tergat wins his second major marathon, as South African Hendrik Ramaala's sprawling dive for the line is in vain. Tergat said: "The weather was incredibly hot and the last thing I expected was a sprint finish. It was really, really painful." *Mike Segar/Reuters/Corbis*

But I couldn't believe the time, I thought I could maybe do low 2:05, but 2:04 was fantastic.

I realized during the race that we were on course for a great time and I was careful not to force the pace too much. That tactic paid off.

I hope this record stands a while.

Tergat then went on to ponder what Britain's golden girl could achieve on this lightning-quick course. He wasn't shy: "If conditions were perfect, like they were for us, then I think Paula could do 2:12 on this course, certainly between 2:13 and 2:14."

John Goodbody in the London *Times* compared Tergat's run to a couple of his illustrious predecessors: "Emil Zátopek in Helsinki in 1952, would have finished more than 18 minutes – or nearly four miles – back, while Abebe Bikila, the 1960 and 1964 Olympic champion and the first of the great Ethiopian runners, would have been more than seven minutes behind the Kenyan even at his best. "Was it really such a great run?" asks *Athletics Weekly*'s statistician Ian Hodge about Tergat (who received $120,000 for his gallop):

While Tergat covered the fourth 10 kilometre segment in Berlin in 29:15, which is fast in anyone's book, I cannot call it "Beamonesque" and here are my reasons:

371

Bob Beamon, Michael Johnson and Paula Radcliffe won by the proverbial street in their greatest performances, while Tergat only just held off Sammy Korir – a pacemaker! Furthermore, Beamon and the others comprehensively beat the best in the world on the way to their records. Apart from Raymond Kipkoech, Tergat defeated no one who could previously claim a place in the world's top 10.

It is small nuances such as these which have prevented this truly magnificent effort from Tergat from making this book's top ten list, but let nothing take away from the fact that this run will deservedly be remembered for many generations to come.

In order for Tergat's record to fall it will take in the eyes of Federico Rosa, his agent, "the perfect combination of the best runners, the right pace, a fast course and good conditions. 2:04 – you don't expect anyone to run that quick." On Munji in third (who slashed 10 minutes off his personal best to clock the eighth-best time in history) Rosa noted: "he was the biggest surprise." (A look at Munji's CV, however, shows that the potential was there, since he had clocked a 60:27 for half the distance.)

Tergat's amazing run begs another question. Will the 2-hour mark ever be broken – and if so, when?

Richard Lewis wrote in *British Runner*: "It is 19 years since Britain's Steve Jones ran 2:08:05 in Chicago to hold a title that has changed hands on just five occasions since. But of all those performances, few were as significant as this run: the barrier of 2:05 had been broken and suddenly the prospect of going below two hours can be talked about realistically." David Bedford, race director of the London Marathon, mused:

I would like to think I might see it in my lifetime. It can be achieved in the next 20 years because the event is moving on all the time and this was an important step.

When it happens, when two hours is broken, it will be viewed by that generation with the same wonder that people showed when the four-minute mile barrier was broken, 50 years ago. It will be an incredible landmark. We have a different kind of athlete out there with a different approach: he is fitter and healthier and there is a whole group of people of a high standard. It is a golden time for marathon running.

And does Tergat think the great mark can ever be beaten? "Never. Forget it. It is very difficult to run 61 minutes for half a marathon so 60 minutes or just below, back-to-back, will never happen."[4]

* * *

Tergat came into the Athens Olympics lacking a little background after a

---

4. Interestingly however, Tergat was mellower in this view a few months earlier in another interview, stating: "I'd say running a marathon in under two hours is impossible, but maybe time will chide me for saying so."

frustrating calf injury had upset his plans. It was his last race in the colours of his country. He raced bravely with the leaders for as long as he could, before fading badly in the intense humidity and jogging into the stadium tenth. So bad was his state that some may have worried about him dropping out – but that would have defied the spirit of the man.

There is so much more to Tergat than merely a divinely gifted distance runner. He is also a family man (he's married with three children), and a crusader for many good causes. He is a goodwill ambassador for the World Food Programme, a UNICEF spokesman and funds education for Nairobi street children. He also owns a PR company and publishes an athletics magazine, *The Athlete* (Jackson). "I do this because of my love of athletics. I created it with Moses Kip Kiptanui [triple world steeplechase champion] and now I run it alone. It is something I would love to continue for many years."

Tergat comments about how much he has seen his country develop in the last 20 years:

My country has developed so much since I was young. If we are talking about television, for example, then 12 years ago they were countable. Now nearly every household has one, which is good because it is a way of teaching information to the public in so many areas. And now we have tremendous new universities when before it was only two. Now, if I cannot send my children out of the country for higher learning they can learn at home.

For me the sport is not all my life. I have so many things that make my life interesting and not boring. It's only that the passion that I have for the sport, you'll never take that from me. I love it, I *love* it!"

Race result:

Paul Tergat	KEN	2:04:55 (world best)
Sammy Korir	KEN	2:04:56
Titus Munji	KEN	2:06:15
Andrés Espinosa	MEX	2:08:46 (world M40 best)
Raymund Kipkoech	KEN	2:09:22
Kazuhiro Matsuda	JPN	2:09:52
Kurno Umeki	JPN	2:09:52
Andre Ramos	BRA	2:09:59

Sources:

Duncan, E, in *Agence France Press*, July 5th, 2004.
Frank, Bob, in *Athletics Weekly*, October 8th, 2003.
Goodbody, John, in *The Times*, September 29th, 2003.
Hodge, Ian, in *Athletics Weekly*, October 8th, 2003.
Jackson, Jamie, in the *Observer*, August 1st, 2004.
Ladbroke, Ian, Pat Butcher and Bob Frank, in *Athletics Weekly*, October 1st, 2003.

Landells, Steve, in *Athletics Weekly*, November 9th, 2005
Lewis, Richard, in *British Runner*, October 2003.
Time-to-run.com, race report.
Wilson, Neil, in *London Marathon Official New Programme*, 2004.

XL

No. 11 – 1992 Olympic Marathon [Men]

Sunday, August 9th

Sohn's second serving of salvation as protégé holds his nerve.

The Barcelona Olympics of 1992 were memorable and spectacular in equal measure. It was the perfect stage for Nike to dominate the Games with their superb athletes. They hand-picked four to front their lavish advertising campaign. Four sure-fire winners. Four soon-to-be household names. Four unbeatable human machines. T'was a shame then when three came up empty. "Congratulations for passing Johnson, few athletes will," said a large poster adorned by the image of Michael Johnson, clad in Nike gear. As it turned out, four athletes passed him in his disastrous 200-metres semi-final as he suffered from a viral complaint. Pole vaulter Serhei Bubka's slogan was "Spanish air traffic control has been notified", but he then failed to score a single vault in the final, blaming his "unbelievably bad" biorhythms. Then there was Nourredine Morceli, the Algerian world champion, hotly tipped for the 1500-metres: "Ever heard the Algerian national anthem? You will." Well, an Algerian did win the 1500 final, but it was Hassiba Boulmerka in the women's event who listened to her anthem, clad top-to-toe in...Diadora. Morceli meanwhile dawdled to 3:41 and 7th place in the men's final.[1] Ah – the sweet mystery of sport.

These were also the Games of 100-metres man Linford Christie – although his success seemed completely lost on the United States. When the Americans went out to collect their medals for the 100-metres relay draped in stars and stripes flags, coach Chuck Daly explained: "That Canadian guy who won the 100-yard dash and then draped himself in the Canadian flag and went round the track. He was the inspiration." Uh-huh.

* * *

The men's Olympic marathon was a nail-biting affair. Although it wasn't, however, to be a battle of the big names. This was a race where the established stars would have to take a back seat. A list of starters indicates a terrific "who's

---

1. Nike's fourth featured sportsman, Michael Jordan, did, of course, come good: as part of the United States' basketball "Dream Team".

who" of top 1980s marathoners, but we were well into the 1990s now and careers
were on the wane. For a detailed look at the star-spangled exploits of de Castella,
Salah, Ikangaa, Wakiihuri, Hussein, Moneghetti, Treacy, Pinto, Cerón and
Bordin, please refer elsewhere. Three of these great names simply failed to finish
at Barcelona '92, and the others averaged an alarming final position of 38th.
Extraordinarily, none would grace the top 25. What odds on that at the outset?
Astronomical.

Athletics Weekly's preview of the race by Paul Richardson and Dave Martin
was a somewhat hapless affair as these reporters were duped by the glorious
uncertainties of marathoning:

> Given top billing, as the only event on the last day, the 26.2m event, the most
> gruelling on the Olympic calendar, is likely to be full of surprises, as usual. The
> formidable Gelindo Bordin will be defending the title and the Japanese-based
> Kenyan, Douglas Wakiihuri, who has had a four-year plan since taking silver in
> Seoul to go one better, will again be challenging.
>
> Australian Steve Moneghetti, fifth last time, has improved considerably in the
> last two years, as have the Japanese, who were delighted when Hiromi
> Taniguchi won the world title on home soil last year.
>
> Steve Spence, of the USA, third in Tokyo, looks a danger as a time around
> 2.15 should be good enough. The Mexicans have scored some spectacular
> successes on the American circuit and a sub-2.9.30 was required to make their
> team, the toughest standard of any nation.

Athletics Weekly's prediction: 1st Spence, 2nd Wakiihuri and 3rd Moneghetti.
They came 12th, 36th and 48th – so they got their chronology right at least...
Ignore Asian runners at your peril.

* * *

The Olympic organizers knew full well that their race was going to exact a cruel
toll on the athletes, what with the brutal final 5-kilometre climb up Montjuic.
They therefore started the race at the latest possible hour – 6.30 p.m. However, it
was still – for the fourth Olympics in a row – extremely uncomfortable to say the
least. The weather at the outset, and pretty much the duration of the race, was
80 °F. The field of 112 runners was not an Olympic record (that was set in Seoul
with 118), but a record was set for the amount of nations participating – a wholly
impressive 72 – over double what it had been just 30 years earlier.[2] But wherever
it was from whence you came, this was a race where *no one* was in a hurry.

Nothing but the space it took them to fill could separate the top-50 runners at
the first 10 kilometre checkpoint, "sharing water-soaked sponges, their rivalries
forgotten, before the common enemy: the course" (Wallechinsky). Indeed the
group at this stage would have been 4 seconds down on Jim Peters at the
Olympics 40 years earlier! Jan Huruk of Poland and rising star Antonio Pinto of
Portugal (who won the London Marathon four months previously) tried to burst

---

2. In Atlanta the figure would rise to 79.

376

into the lead at 18K, but such folly was quickly dealt with. These two athletes, it seems, were playing with a contrasting set of cards, since one would place in the top seven and one would fail to finish.

Eleven kilometres further down the road found 20 runners falling foul of the heat and humidity; but the leading group of 30 was still a large amount to still be in contention with just half the race to run. The halfway split was an understandably slow and tactical 67:12. Martin and Gynn then report: "At the 22.5 kilometres feeding station, tragedy struck. Hiromi Taniguchi tangled legs with someone as he picked up his drink. Falling hard, he lost a shoe in the process. Gelindo Bordin was just behind him and had to leap into the air to avoid trampling him. Bordin strained a groin muscle, and he was out of the race." How cruel sport can be. Bordin may have endured a pretty dire 1991 by his standards, but there's little question that he came to the Olympics hoping to retain his crown. Nobody was more tactically astute or mentally tough than the Italian and the way the course was set up could well have suited his strength in the latter stages of a marathon. Japan's Taniguchi, the world champion, was pretty much out of the race from that unfortunate incident as well. However much he tried, a position amongst the leaders was always going to be just out of reach. He eventually finished a valiant eighth.

The race started to come nicely to the boil between kilometres 25–30. In front of hordes of cheering spectators, lining the streets several deep, a significant break finally came during the 27th kilometre in the form of three runners. They were 24-year-old Koichi Morishita of Japan (who had recorded the world's fastest time of 1991 with a tangy 2:08:53 at Beppu), 22-year-old Hwang Young-cho of Korea, and his teammate Kim Wan-ki. One of these athletes was bluffing, however. Seven

The 1992 Olympic Marathon saw a major breakthrough by Asian runners. Here Hwang Young-cho (1147) and Koichi Morishita (1087) attempt to keep pace with Kim Wan-Ki of Korea. *Mark Shearman*

kilometres later Wan-ki would fall back, haemorrhage 5 minutes in the last 8 kilometres, and finish 28th.

During these 7 kilometres of Asian dominance, two athletes remained within striking distance. One of whom was yet another youngster, Stephan Freigang of Germany, aged just 24. On a course, and a day, where experience seemed a necessity, it didn't seem to be turning out that way. Perhaps the wise were too fearful, while the young were rewarded by their risky antics. Freigang had first attempted the marathon in 1987, winning the Budapest event in 2:14:34; although such a feat was not enough to persuade the German Olympic Committee that he was able enough to be taken to Seoul in 1988. But he came to Barcelona as an athlete of note, since he had placed fourth in the Berlin Marathon in 1990 with a competitive 2:09:45. Now, in the Barcelona

Olympic marathon he fought a lonely vigil to rope in the two Asian leaders. Close behind, however, were the far more experienced Takeyuki Nakayama of Japan and Salvatore Bettiol of Italy, keeping a close watch for even the slightest falter.

The battle between Hwang and Morishita made for absorbing viewing for sports fans around the world. Just when it seemed that the athletes must be at their limit, then the mountain came into play. David Wallechinsky writes: "For four kilometres, Hwang and Morishita ran side by side. Whenever one sped up, the other matched him. Then they reached the bottom of the awful Monjuïc hill. Still they pressed on, one surging, the other catching up." One person wasn't watching the developments, however. Hwang's mother. Although back in Korea she was doing her bit, since she spent her entire day praying for him in a temple. The atmosphere on the race course was made eerie and hypnotic by the growing dusk, with the glorious Avenue of Fountains – now illuminated – and Plaça Espanya as a backdrop. Finally, just after 40 kilometres, a possibly decisive break was made. The runners entered into a tunnel carved through a cliff, and Hwang surged. Upon leaving the tunnel, he had built up a 20-metre gap, which was all the more valuable since the rest of the way to the stadium was all uphill. Remarkably, behind the two leaders, a nigh-on identical game of cat-and-mouse, surge and counter-surge was occurring; this battle fought between Freigang and Nakayama, with a bronze medal at stake.

Into a slowly filling stadium,[3] the athletes finally appeared. With generous cheers the crowd welcomed two athletes separated by just a little over 100 metres. They seemed both to be running strongly, and indeed as fast as at any time in the race. An investigation into the winner's "out-and-back" splits, shows that not only had negative splits occurred (where the second half of the race is covered more quickly than the first half), but that this had been done by a full 81 seconds. Hwang burst through the line with a look of sheer ecstasy on his face, and immediately collapsed – almost violently – to the ground.

A remarkable coincidence occurred after the battle for gold and silver was over. Stephan Freigang appeared hotly pursued by Japan's Nakayama. Four years earlier Nakayama had finished an unfortunate fourth at Seoul – a mere 6 seconds off Ahmed Salah. Here, he had reduced that gap, but not by enough, as it only led to more heartbreak. He now finished just 2 seconds off a medal. One of the unluckiest Olympians of all time? He has a case.

If Hwang's mother was otherwise engaged during the race, his mentor and idol was giving the race his full attention. The mentor was none other than the great Sohn Kee-chung, who had won the Olympic marathon 56 years ago *to the day*. But, of course, that was a day scarred more by bitterness and infamy than the sweet smell of success. Sohn Kee-chung's remarkable tale of redemption is explored in detail in Chapter 11, but here was a lovely case of the icing on the cake. In short, Kee-chung won the Olympic gold, but in the colours of an adopted country – Japan – that had invaded his homeland. In 1988, when the Games finally came to Seoul, Sohn was a surprise guest of honour and brought tears to

---

3. The stadium, through poor pre-planning or otherwise, had been closed to the spectators until just 30 minutes before the end of the marathon (in order to prepare it for the closing ceremonies), which is why the marathoners had a less than full house to field them.

Hwang Young-cho atones for painful memories of the 1936 Olympic Marathon as he gives Korea the title that was denied them 56 years earlier. *Mark Shearman*

the eyes of many of 100,000 spectators at the opening ceremony when he was passed the Olympic flame. And now, four years later, the final satisfying flourish on the whole episode. Sohn was there to witness one of his protégés finally win a maiden Olympic marathon gold for Korea. Upon returning to Seoul, Hwang met Sohn Kee-chung and placed his gold medal around the older man's neck. According to Wallenchinsky, Sohn told Hwang, "Now I can die without any regrets."

There is of course a further relevant factor to be considered here. That the man Hwang vanquished was a Japanese. This would have brought extra meaning to the occasion for millions, but Hwang, sportingly, dismissed the detail had any political significance. After all, Hwang pointed out, the shoes he had worn to victory were Japanese made – Asics.[4] In the press conference that followed, an emotional Hwang stated:

I was certain of having a medal, but only the gold interested me. It was important for me to win this for Sohn Kee-chung...It was also for my mother who during the entire race was at the temple praying that I would win the gold for Korea.

The idea was to run as fast as possible until 35 kilometres and then push it on from there, when I reached 35 kilometres, I was sure I could get a medal, but not necessarily the gold. I was a little scared of the Japanese. He made me very nervous.

Hwang's one regret was that he was unable to carry the Korean flag on a lap of honour because he was suffering from leg cramps. "I wanted to run another lap with the Korean flag, so it was a great shame that should happen to me."

There are three small footnotes to the race that deserve attention. In 86th place – and next to bottom – placed Haleem Hussain of the Maldive Islands. Hussain gained the distinction of being the first athlete of that nation to defeat another athlete at an Olympics. The man he beat was equally notable: Tuul Pyambuu of Mongolia, who ran 4:00:44. His time may have been a tad sluggish (indeed the slowest at an Olympics for 84 years), but his handicap was significant. Having been blinded in an explosion during his time as a construction worker in 1978, he

---

4. Some, however, would contend that this adds yet more significance to the matter!

had a cornea transplant twelve years later that restored sight in his right eye. Eighteen months later he competed in the Olympic marathon in order "to show that a man has many possibilities" (Wallenchinsky).

Finally, there's the comical tale of Salvador García, who won New York the previous year. This so impressed his superiors that he was promoted from a sergeant to a lieutenant in Mexico's presidential guard. García, however, failed to finish in Barcelona and was demoted back to sergeant.[5]

Hwang raced sparingly after the Olympics, although he did compete in the lightning-fast Boston of 1994 – where he placed fourth in 2:08:09. Injury prevented him from making the Korean team to defend his crown at Atlanta, and he subsequently retired thereafter. Indeed, none of the three medallists here would appear as a finisher at the Atlanta Games, which shows how fickle the form of top-class marathoner can be: they are so highly trained that they are forever balancing on the knife edge between world-class and also-ran.

*   *   *

David Miller of the London *Times* wrote his traditional piece summarizing what he liked and disliked about the Olympic Games. Barcelona, it seems, met with his wholehearted approval.

> The problem at the Olympic village has been that nobody wants to leave. It used to be the Commonwealth Games that carried the accolade of the friendly games. That title must be awarded unreservedly to the festival just concluded in Barcelona.
>
> It would be facile to suggest, at a time in history tormented by political and financial strife, famine and wars, that the world was a better place on account of 16 days of sport. Yet the sporting world, gathered in unique harmony, has presented a face of tranquillity mid intense competition that must surely carry some legacy of hope for mankind.

Race result:[6]

Young-cho Hwang	KOR	2:13:23
Koichi Morishita	JPN	2:13:45
Stephan Freigang	GER	2:14:00
Takeyuki Nakayama	JPN	2:14:02
Salvatore Bettiol	ITA	2:14:15
Salah Qoqaiche	MAR	2:14:25
Jan Huruk	POL	2:14:32
Hiromi Taniguchi	JPN	2:14:42

---

5. Wallechinsky refers to García finishing ninth at Barcelona. This is an error: ninth place went to García's namesake, Diego, of Spain.

6. Britain's first finisher was Stephen Brace in 27th place. "It's the toughest marathon I've ever run in," he said. "It was maximum effort all the way. I was always running at my hardest. But I didn't want to be an Olympic marathoner with a 'DNF' by my name."

| Diego Garcia | ESP | 2:14:56 |
| Jae-ryong Kim | KOR | 2:15:01 |

Sources:

Archive race footage, *The Olympic Series, Golden Moments, 1920–2002*. Paramount Pictures

Athletics Weekly, race report, August 6th, 1992.

Hauman, Riël, *Century of the Marathon*. Human & Rousseau, 1996.

Martin, David, in *Athletics Weekly* preview, July 29th, 1992.

Martin, David and Roger Gynn, *The Olympic Marathon*. Human Kinetics, 2000.

Miller, David, in *The Times*, August 11th, 1992.

Richardson, Paul, in *Athletics Weekly* preview, July 29th, 1992.

Wallechinsky, David, *The Complete Book of the Olympics*. Aurum Press, 2000.

XLI

No. 10 – 1988 Olympic Marathon [Men]

Sunday, October 2nd

The ghastly grin that said it all.

The German city of Baden-Baden (just west of Stuttgart) was the setting for the IOC to convene for their 84th Congress, on September 30th, 1981, to determine the winner of the bid to host the 1988 Olympics. The hot favourites to win the bid were Nagoya, Japan, since Tokyo had staged such a successful Olympics some 27 years earlier; but a surprise package stepped up to the plate and won the final vote 52 to 27. It was the city of Seoul, South Korea. Norman Fox, sports correspondent for the London *Times* was there:

> As South Korea is a developing country without diplomatic relations with China and the Soviet Union, their victory in today's International Olympic Committee election was an astonishing credit to their campaigning here, and a gamble by the IOC.
>
> No doubt Seoul can provide the necessary fixtures and fittings, but they will also require some years of political stability before the IOC can sleep easily on their decision.

Martin and Gynn back up Fox's scepticism by commenting: "Korea was a mystery in the minds of many. Although South Korea was a developing economic power among Pacific Rim countries, it was better known as (1) a military dictatorship struggling to move toward democracy, (2) a land that had been devastated by war 25 years before, and (3) the site of the planet's most fortified borders – a single culture divided by political differences."

The main threat to the Games would be that on the back of the diminished spectacle of the 1980 and 1984 Olympics – that there would be another raft of boycotts in Seoul. In the end, thanks to superb public relations from Juan Anotonio Samaranch, just three "hardliners" from the Communist world stayed away: North Korea, Cuba and Ethiopia. The first and the last of these did unfortunately deprive the marathon of some serious talent; in particular, that of the world record holder, Belayneh Densimo, who had run his 2:06:50 in Rotterdam in the spring of 1988.

But on the whole, the Seoul Games are remembered as an enormous success in almost every department: they were billed as the Games of "Harmony and Progress" – and even if "it sometimes appeared that there were more police than spectators, it was a friendly security, and there were no incidents" (Martin & Gynn). The leading British sports presenter, Desmond Lynam, said at the closing of the Games: "Despite the Ben Johnson affair, and one or two other minor incidents, these Games have been the best ever." When Johnson massacred Carl Lewis in their much-hyped 100-metres final, in a world best 9.79, many almost couldn't believe their eyes. But just a few hours later Johnson's urine tested positive for stanazolol – "a rapidly metabolizable steroid that stayed around a little too long" (Martin & Gynn). Carl Lewis was handed his fifth Olympic gold medal. A further four would follow over the next eight years. The Johnson saga made huge news headlines all over the world, and it appeared that just when the Olympics appeared to have done everything right, they still became mired in controversy and scandal. It only takes one to spoil a party.

Another runner who didn't exactly spoil the party but is remembered for all the wrong reasons was D. Florence Griffith Joyner. A quirky, offbeat personality (she was once escorted from a shopping mall for using her pet boa constrictor as a muffler), Griffith went through the early years of her career collecting a variety of awards for placing second, third and fourth in high profile sprint races. By 1986 she had all but retired (she had won a silver at the Los Angeles Olympics in the 200-metres), and was working in a bank and as a beautician. But in 1987 she not only returned to serious training but also became obsessed about becoming the greatest female sprinter in the world. Who to help her in this quest? None other than her idol, Ben Johnson. "Flojo" not only consulted with Johnson about his methods but also studied endless videotapes about his races, and in particular his explosive starts. She returned to the limelight on June 25th, 1988 when she ran 10.89 in San Diego, and then, three weeks later at the US Olympic trials, scored a jaw-dropping 10.49, destroying the previous world best of 10.76 belonging to Evelyn Ashford. The record was not without controversy. David Wallechinsky writes: "Although the wind gauge next to the triple jump runway 30 feet away registered an unacceptable 4.3 metres per second, the gauge at the track registered exactly 0.0."

It was assumed the gauge was faulty, but Omega insisted on defending their equipment; thus the record still stands today. Subsequent analysis by Australian physicist Nicholas Linthorne has shown that the true wind reading was probably 5.5 metres per second (Wallechinsky). Flojo went on, of course, to win the Olympics in 10.54, with a reaction time that was quicker than that of Johnson himself. But with her hero's disqualification, suspicion quickly rested on Griffith Joyner as well. Her sudden improvement and bulging muscles led many to believe she was on steroids. Mandatory random drug testing was introduced on February 25th, 1989, but Griffith Joyner had retired from athletics just the day before. She experienced an epileptic seizure in her sleep on September 21st, 1998, and died of suffocation.

* * *

A preview by Pat Butcher in the London *Times* gave due warning that the marathon race for the runners in Seoul would be a battle against the heat as much as the course: "The last test of these Games of the XXIVth Olympiad is arguably the hardest. A marathon is a trial at the best of times but for reasons best known to the National Broadcasting Corporation and the Seoul Olympic Organizing Committee, the men's race begins at 14.35 local time. And that is when the sun is at its highest and hottest." The Los Angeles silver medallist John Treacy of Ireland was back and stated before the race: "It's wide open, ten guys could win it. I'm not the favourite, but I've had a good year. I'll run as well as I can, and if I feel I've run myself to a standstill, I'll be happy." (Careful what you wish for you might get it: he did run himself to a standstill, quite literally, and subsequently dropped out.) Interestingly, Butcher notes, Carlos Lopes was among the entries, but since he looked "more like a candidate for weight watchers than world record marathons, his participation was unlikely." The favourites were Douglas Wakiihuri – the world champion; Takeyuki Nakayama, the Asian Games winner on this same course two years ago; Ahmed Salah, World silver medallist and owner of the fastest time in the race of 2:07:07 set at Rotterdam earlier in the year; Steve Moneghetti, the Commonwealth bronze medallist and fourth-place finisher at the Rome World Championships; and the Italian trio, Gelindo Bordin, Orlando Pizzolato and Gianni Poli – three superb runners with a host of major victories between them. For just a brief spell towards the end of the 1980s, Italy was arguably the strongest marathoning nation in the world.

Rob de Castella, Toshihiko Seko and Juma Ikangaa will "probably find that their reputations are insufficient for victory", observed Butcher. Seko had been relatively quiet since his disastrous run at Los Angeles '84, but his confident win at Boston in 1987 showed he was still a force to be feared. The writer and statistician Mel Watman said of Seko upon his selection for the race:

In no other country are marathon runners treated with such reverence and media attention as Japan. The accent there is not on mass participation but on elite races, sometimes with only a few dozen runners, which are televised live in full.

Not surprisingly there was a huge sigh of relief in Japan last week when Seko was chosen for the Olympics. His selection had previously been hanging in the balance, because injury had forced him to miss the Fukuoka race last December.[1]

Charlie Spedding, bronze medallist in Los Angeles, was back at the ripe old age of 36, leading the British challenge, which looked a little shaky since the withdrawal of another luminary, Hugh Jones. Spedding, it was felt, was over the hill and wouldn't be seen duking it out with the leaders. So much for popular opinion...

* * *

---

1. Seko was given one last chance to prove his worth and he didn't disappoint, winning the Lake Biwa Marathon at Otsu in March by nearly three minutes in 2.12.41. Although it was one of the slowest times of his career, he blamed the warm weather.

THE 50 GREATEST MARATHON RACES OF ALL TIME

As the runners set off, they were humbled by the knowledge that the temperatures would soar into the 80s during the race's latter stages, but comforted that their route was secure: it was lined by 36,000 policemen. The Olympic field had never been larger: 118 athletes representing 66 nations (Martin & Gynn). Juma Ikangaa's tiny frame could be seen predictably to the fore as the runners encircled the 2.9 laps at the start of the race. He had been forcing the pace in the leading marathons for six years now, and while this had resulted in far more heartbreak than it had victory, no one could question his courage or passion. After a modest 15:29 opening for 5 kilometres, the pace accelerated to 30:32 for 10 kilometres, but little inroads had been made into the large lead pack of 19. And the next 5 kilometres saw the pack not shrink but *grow*, to 33 runners, with another 11 in close attendance (15 seconds back). All the big players could be spotted hunkering in the lead pack, except one. Martin and Gynn write: "The only notable absentee from this group was Gelindo Bordin, who had drifted back into the next group, but by 20 kilometres near the entrance to the first long Han River bridge, this lead pack had split into two groups, 14 in front, and 10 more 1 second behind. Bordin advanced to the second group, along with Ikangaa [who had briefly fallen off the pace]." A pack of 20 or so runners recorded a halfway split of 64:49 – a fine time, given the oppressive conditions. The race had ensnared its first high-profile casualty by now, in the form of John Treacy. Ibrahim Hussein, the Boston champion, would be another to bow out, and during the race's duration 20 in all would fall short of completion.[2] Ikangaa continued to dictate the pace over the early stages of the race's second half, thus ensuring that anyone not prepared to run to the very edge of their limit would be found wanting.

A harsh trimming of the medal contenders occurred between 25 and 30 kilometres, as 13 tired bodies became 7. And what an exclusive club it presented. Just like in Los Angeles four years earlier, only the greatest distance runners in the world were to be found in contention with 12 kilometres to go. The list here read: Bordin, Wakiihuri, Salah, Nakayama, Spedding, Ikangaa and Seko. Two seconds off this magnificent pack was probably the biggest name of all – with the second fastest time (2:07:51) – Rob de Castella. The Australian's countryman Steve Moneghetti gasped for air – and hope – another 3 seconds behind.

The question was, how long could this wonderful who's who of 80s runners stay together? Sadly, it was Seko who lost grip first, as he began to fade alarmingly. His subsequent ninth-place finish still presented a great personal triumph for him after all his injury problems in the past year, but his displays of exultation upon finishing (in an improved position from Los Angeles) were greeted with confusion by the unforgiving Japanese media. He hadn't won – why was he celebrating? Martin and Gynn describe kilometres 35–40: "...the steady uphill, combined with dehydration, a warm day, and developing fatigue, began to relegate this talented field to a single line, each tottering on the edge of breakdown."

It was Ahmed Salah, the World Championship silver medallist and easily the fastest man in the field, who made the first significant break for glory, and as the

---

2. Although this was still a high figure, it was obvious that the tenacious spirit of marathon runners had improved plenty in the four years since Los Angeles. There 27 per cent failed to finish, compared to 17 per cent in Seoul.

The race's three eventual medallists show perfect form in the latter stages. Ahmed Salah, centre, is gearing himself up to make a break for glory. *Mike Powell/Getty Images*

race entered its final 2 kilometres he could be seen boasting a lead of some 25 yards over the world champion, Wakiihuri. Bordin "exhausted and suffering leg cramps, resigned himself to third place" (Wallechinsky). However, Bordin decided to rely on one last trick to at least secure the bronze, since he had every right to be concerned about Takeyuki Nakayama in fourth. The Italian focused all his diminishing energy on the back of the Kenyan in front of him, and commanded himself to get towed along and not to allow Wakiihuri to stretch away. The gap remained constant, and then to Bordin's great amazement it start to shrink metre by metre until the two men were level. Renewed vigour pumped into the Italian's muscles.

Gelindo Bordin was born in the small town of Longare, near Venice, in Northern Italy, the youngest of four brothers in April 1959. Tom Derderian describes Gelindo's merry and chaotic upbringing: "These sons of a farmer lived in a big house in the country with four other families. The children all lived in one big room set up like a barracks; 22 of them slept and played like crazy cousins. Gelindo worked hard on the farm in the summer. Until age 14 he defended his team's goal against soccer balls." Bordin was introduced to the weird and wonderful world of running by his older brother Nerino who was a runner of some ability, with a 2:22 marathon under his belt. When Nerino took Gelindo to a race (which Nerino won), Gelindo was immediately transfixed, and it wasn't long before he had swapped the team games that he had indulged in for so long for far more individual pursuits. At age 18 Gelindo went into the military and was able to run a great deal – this on the back of winning his regional cross-country championship, which he had won after just two months in the sport. Derderian continues:

> He grew to be tall, strong, and gregarious. He usually wore a short beard, giving his strong-featured face a biblical force, yet he could play the clown. During a training run with Bill Rodgers and Greg Meyer, Bordin dropped a step behind as they passed a stop sign. Bordin reached up and whacked the sign with his palm and fell to the ground, holding his head. The loud sound horrified Rodgers, sure that Bordin was seriously injured. As Rodgers bent over Bordin to attend to his injuries or administer last rites, Bordin burst into crazy laughter.

Bordin's career in running was almost all over before it had barely begun. After showing his promise by running 19th in the World Junior Cross-Country Championships Bordin was then almost killed by a car when out training. After being struck his mangled body was found abandoned by the roadside and Bordin was in a coma for six hours. He didn't know where he was or how he had gotten there. His skull was broken, shards of glass imbedded in the bone. Seven vertebrae were broken, and ligaments were torn in his left knee. For the next four months Bordin saw double. The doctors told him not to run for six months, but that was 23 weeks longer than he desired; and after just 21 days he was back doing what he loved – albeit in a bent-over, creaking, gasping, painful survival shuffle. Fortunately, the accident didn't mentally scar him since his first recollection of it was waking up in that hospital bed.

Tom Derderian paints a colourful character portrait of the sort of man Bordin was: "Gelindo Bordin liked a lot of things. He like to eat. He liked to cook. With glee, gusto, and garlic he cooked big meals for his friends. Bordin liked clothing; he even designed athletic clothes. His designs courageously combined colours and shapes not ordinarily found in nature. They pressed against the fine edge of fashion violation." Bordin, who had a degree in design, worked hard at his job at the Bottacini construction company from 1979 to 1986 while also pursuing a terrifying training schedule. This involved executing a tricky 13 miles in the morning before work, work until noon, and then *another* 13-miler, before working again until late. "He had no time to clown, party, or relax. He got a skin rash. It itched. He could not sleep. No medicine helped. He could not work full-time and train his best for racing" (Derderian).

So Gelindo – by this time one of the world's leading, but not great, marathoners – had a stark choice to make. Continue in this horrendous cycle of work and then more work, or cut himself some slack. Mercifully for his health and sanity he opted for the latter, deciding to take this promising body of his and attempt to extract from it every ounce of fitness and productivity he could *without* the burden of a demanding 50-hour-a-week job. Bordin, as so many before and after know, was taking a huge gamble. "All runners are just a hamstring injury away from oblivion," remarks Steve Jones, and he's not wrong.

Together with his coach, Luciano Gigliotti, and a masseur, Bordin now poured all of his considerable engineering, design and analytical skills into creating the perfect body. One of his favourite training camps was at the Pico de Teide, 3718-

metres up in the mountains of Tenerife. This is unquestionably one of the world's great places to train. No distractions, wonderful crisp, clean air, hugely undulating terrain, and countless soft, dirt trails. It is curiously undiscovered by runners as the author has witnessed in his own training there, but the world's leading cyclists (especially the T-Mobile team) swarm busily all over the region.[3]

One thing for sure, it didn't take long for Bordin's experiment to start paying off. On August 30th, 1986, Bordin came to Stuttgart, West Germany, to represent Italy in the European Championships. Former world-record holder Steve Jones was a hot favourite to win the race and he let the situation get to him, setting off on Stuttgart's hot roads like he was trying to dip under the 2-hour mark; running his first 5K in an absurd 14:27. Such exuberance served only for a massive blow-up, and it was left to a more sensible, tactically cultured runner to pace himself to the winner's line. With around 10 kilometres to go, Bordin led the chasing pack past Jones, and he then went on to sprint away from countryman Orlando Pizzolato, the double New York champion no less, to win by 13 seconds. Bordin's 2:10:54 was nearly a 40-second personal best. And so began a magnificent four-year spree, right at the top of the world marathon scene, in which Bordin's lithe frame became pretty much the hardest to beat in the world.

Bordin comfortably qualified to represent Italy at the following year's World Championships in Rome, and an adoring public got behind the "new boy" and roared him to a forward placing. The swift duo of Douglas Wakiihuri and Ahmed Salah proved too strong on this occasion, as Bordin secured the World bronze but he was obviously comfortable duking it out with the very best in the sport. Quite a few of those best were present at Boston in 1988, where the Italians descended en masse. Bordin placed fourth in 2:09:27, but he used the race as more of a training run, than a hunt for victory. Derderian comments: "Bordin ran in the pack, but he did not plan to win. He came to Boston to run in the year's most competitive marathon as part of his plan to win the Olympic gold medal in Seoul at the end of the summer. Now he felt quite pleased that his partial preparation enabled him to stay up with the leaders with such ease."

* * *

Back to this chapter's featured marathon. After Bordin had surprised and inspired himself by overtaking Wakiihuri in Seoul to move into the silver medal position, his priorities completely changed. Here was a race to be won. He gambled on Salah feeling the heat…the pressure…the fatigue – and he gambled right. Salah was overwhelmingly tired and he glanced over his left shoulder, as an athlete running scared is apt to do, to see if his executor was approaching. Great news! There was no one to be seen. If only he could just keep going for one more mile the gold medal was his. And then Salah looked over his *right* shoulder and the

---

3. The British marathoner Huw Lobb spent six weeks at El Teide in the spring of 2004 and once back in Britain promptly broke a barrier that was standing as one of the last great bastions of running: victory in the annual Man-vs-Horse Marathon in mid-Wales. In a race of some 400 "bipeds" competing against around 40 of our four-legged friends, the race sponsors William Hill offered £1000 in 1980 to the man (or woman) who could beat every single horse in the race. No one did that year and every year William Hill added £1,000 to the jackpot. Leading Kenyan runners came to have a crack. No luck. So did leading fell runners – since the race takes place over mountains and valleys. Still no luck. Then Lobb turned up – fresh from his Tenerife travails – defeated the leading horse by 2 minutes, and scooped a cool £25,000 for his gallop.

The ghastly grin: a completely spent Salah has just turned to see the grinning figure of Gelindo Bordin arriving to relieve him of the lead. *Mike Powell/Getty Images*

situation in all its ghastliness was smiling at him. Gelindo Bordin was a mere 3 metres down. For 50 metres Bordin allowed the hopelessly demoralized Salah to keep his lead before he lethally flicked up a gear and drove on by. Some 250 metres later Wakiihuri did the same and Salah suddenly was in grave danger of finishing out of the medals.

In the closest Olympic marathon for 68 years, Gelindo Bordin entered the Olympic Stadium still grinning broadly, ran 300 metres around the track and won by 15 seconds over Wakiihuri. Briefly, all four of the first athletes were on the track together. Immediately upon finishing, Bordin crossed himself, knelt down and kissed the track. Nakayama valiantly attempted to run down Salah, but the brave Djiboutian managed to hold him off by 6 seconds. The top nine in Seoul was truly a collection of the greatest marathon talent in the world, even if time's winged chariot was catching up with many. Still, what a glorious swansong for players six to nine – Spedding, Ikangaa, de Castella and Seko – even if, remarkably, they could boast one only Olympic bronze between them.

* * *

After 80 years of hurt, Italy finally had another of their men cross the line first in the Olympic Marathon, except this time in rather less macabre conditions. Pat Butcher wrote in *The Times*:

> Gelindo Bordin assuaged a little bit of Olympic misfortune for the Italians 80 years on, when he won the marathon yesterday, coming from behind in the last three kilometres.

Douglas Wakiihuri has 90 yards to travel while Gelindo Bordin has put together a tactical masterpiece to win the 1988 Olympic Marathon. *Mark Shearman*

It was in London in 1908 that Dorando Pietri – suffering from a potent mixture of red wine and strychnine collapsed when well in the lead, was helped across the line and then disqualified.

In contrast Bordin was some way behind Salah and Wakiihuri with five kilometres to run. His surge looked like a repeat of last year's world champs in Rome, where he came through to third place. But he discounted that immediately.

"I intended to stay with the leaders, and then use my good finish," Bordin said. "But I felt so bad at 30 kilometres, I had to let them go. I noticed that they didn't go away as I expected, so when I started to feel better, I went after them."

* * *

"After a week of African domination in the distance events, few people would have given a European any chance of success in the marathon, but Italian Gelindo Bordin had other ideas," wrote *Athletics Weekly*. "It was one of the most thrilling ever conclusions to an Olympic Marathon, with Bordin's margin of victory being the smallest since Finland's Hannes Kolehmainen won by 13 seconds at Antwerp in 1920" (see Chapter 19). Bronze medallist Salah was bitterly disappointed at losing and put the blame on his footwear: "When Bordin came past I could not accelerate because of a problem with my shoes. I kicked when I should have done and but for the problem with my shoes I would have won."[4]

---

4. Salah later explained the trouble was that he'd laced them on too tight. A somewhat basic error, one feels.

Britain's Charlie Spedding who only finished tenth in the London Marathon trial, justified his controversial selection with sixth place. "Spedding went from inspiration to revelation," wrote Pat Butcher. "The first was the selectors' – he was only tenth in the London Marathon. The rest was all down to him. While other, greater favourites fell away in the heat of the afternoon, Spedding hung on until 35 kilometres, and, expecting nothing (or so he said beforehand) was rewarded with sixth in 2:12:19, a marvellous feat after two years of injury and indifferent results."

A delighted Spedding noted, "As I passed 40K, I promised myself I'd never run another marathon, but I'm not sure what I'll do now. It was so hot out there that everybody slowed down. I ended up completely dehydrated. I got back to the leaders once, but when they made a second move, my legs just tied up. All I could do was hang on as long as I could. I'm very pleased."

* * *

Bordin continued to compete brilliantly but he had to give his countrymen a scare first. Six months after he won the Olympic gold medal, he announced with a sad face his retirement from the sport. The next day's headlines read *"Bordin Annuncia Il Suo Retiro."* By noon he revealed his joke to the world. The day before had been April 1st.

In the 1990 Boston, a mad pack of Africans bolted off at a pace that had Rob de Castella wondering if either they had very short memories or didn't respect the race. Gelindo Bordin ran alone, well behind the lead pack, but still at 2:05 pace. "He ran *pazzo*, but they ran *pazzissimo*. The Africans seemed spooked, like a herd of gemsbok leaping and bounding away from a hungry lion. Bordin saw panic on the Serengeti Plain," reports Derderian. Keeping his cool and refusing to accelerate, Bordin watched as one by one the Africans bit the dust. Only two would finish the race in the top ten, as Juma Ikangaa recorded yet another second place finish – his third in a row at Boston. Bordin cruised through to win by 1:33 in 2:08:19. He had broken the jinx. He had become the first Olympic gold medallist to win the Boston Marathon.

On September 1st of the same year in what *Track and Field News* called "a travesty of scheduling for the unfortunate athletes", Bordin defended his European crown in the searing heat of Split in 2:14:02, a comfortable 53 seconds up on Gianni Poli. And so thus, Bordin, although he raced sparingly in his career, is the creator of three unique achievements in marathoning. He is the only man to have ever won both the Olympic and Boston marathons, and the only man to have won the Olympic and European championships marathons. He is also the only man to have ever retained his European title. He won a stunning 8 out of 15 completed marathons (8 out of 18 overall).

Bordin's final marathon triumph came just 36 days after Split when he prevailed at Venice in 2:13:42, but that, sadly, was to be his last hurrah. A DNF at London in 1991 was followed by a moderate eighth at the World Championships. He did his best to arrive in Barcelona to defend his Olympic crown in some sort of shape, but tragedy struck at a feeding station at 22.5 kilometres. A collision saw Bordin strain a groin muscle and he subsequently pulled out of the race. One of the all-time great marathoners retired – this time for real – soon after.

392

* * *

In his traditional piece giving his closing thoughts of the Games, *Times* journalist David Miller was full of praise for the South Koreans:

> As I walked away from the closing ceremony of the 1988 Olympic Games, just before the end, a haunting oriental chorale still drifting upwards into the night sky, I was more than ever in love with Korea. Confronted with the largest Games ever, they had been the perfect hosts. The debt which the Olympic movement owes them is immense.
>
> The Koreans have the organization of the Germans, the courtesy and culture of the Orient and the sense of money of the Americans. They can hardly fail. The worst had been expected. Yet what has been achieved by a nation that 30 years ago was a bomb-site, and when it was awarded the Games in 1981 was a pariah to most socialist countries, is phenomenal.

Race result:

Gelindo Bordin	ITA	2:10:32
Douglas Wakiihuri	KEN	2:10:47
Ahmed Salah Hussein	DJI	2:10:59
Takeyuki Nakayama	JPN	2:11:05
Stephen Moneghetti	AUS	2:11:49
Charles Spedding	GBR	2:12:19
Juma Ikangaa	TAN	2:13:06
Robert de Castella	AUS	2:13:07
Toshihiko Seko	JPN	2:13:41
Ravil Kashapov	URS	2:13:49

Sources:

Athletics Weekly, race report, October 5th, 1988.
Butcher, Pat, in *The Times*, October 2nd & 3rd, 1988.
Derderian, Tom, *Boston Marathon*. Human Kinetics, 1996.
Fox, Norman, in *The Times*, October 10th, 1981.
Hauman, Riël, *Century of the Marathon*. Human & Rousseau, 1996.
Martin, David and Roger Gynn, *The Olympic Marathon*. Human Kinetics, 2000.
Miller, David, in *The Times*, October 4th, 1988.
Sandrock, Michael, *Running with the Legends*. Human Kinetics, 1996.
Wallechinsky, David, *The Complete Book of the Olympics*. Aurum Press, 2000.
Watman, Mel. *Athletics Weekly* preview, September 14th, 1988.

XLII

No. 9 – 1984 Olympic Marathon [Men]

Sunday, August 12th

Hail! Hail! The gang's all here…

Talk about bucking a trend…Before the Los Angeles Olympics of 1984, the financial pattern of Olympic Games' extravaganzas was: take on the Games and take on a mountain of debt. Montreal's Games of 1976 left their city an estimated 1 billion Canadian dollars in debt, and a generation later, the city was still crippled by the cost of the festivities. Moscow fared little better. The urban redevelopment required to put on the Games relieved its economy of an estimated $9 billion US dollars (Martin & Gynn). What city would *really* want to bear the cost of presenting the world's greatest sporting occasion? Granted, amateur sports should be for "pleasure" and not for profit, but things were getting out of hand, and for the future of the Olympic movement to be secure, something was going to have to give.

The city of Los Angeles – who hosted the Games so beautifully in 1932 – with a couple of jokers hidden discreetly up her sleeve, decided to bid again. Competition from other cities was next to none, just a token bid from the unlikely source of Teheran, quickly withdrawn. On May 18th, 1978, Los Angeles won the right to host the 1984 Games and its strategy for not *losing* money, but *making* it, soon became apparent. Under the expert leadership of the newly elected president of the Los Angeles Olympic Organizing Committee (LAOOC), Peter V. Ueberroth, Los Angeles started showing its hand. And what a commercial hand it was. Ueberroth's big idea, was, putting it simply, to make this the first ever "private-sector-funded Games". Martin and Gynn write:

Ueberroth was already an eminently successful businessman, and he relished his new challenge, proving a worthy steward of his city's Olympic Games. He first asked potential bidders for television rights to deposit $750,000 each if they even wanted to be considered. While deciding which network would get the job, Ueberroth used the interest to manage early expenses. He next brought on board corporate sponsors: big in name, flush with advertising budgets, and few in number, so as to capture absolute top dollar for permitting their membership in a most exclusive club.

The American Broadcasting Corporation (ABC) finally won the contract, but not before they had handed over the cash: $225 million no less. Ueberroth then used his imagination and experience to cost-save as much as possible in a number of imaginative ways. One of his most inspired, if simplest coups, was instead of building a new Olympic village in order to house the competitors, he simply commandeered three university campuses (those of USC, UCLA and UCSB [the University of California at Santa Barbara]): a major cost-saver indeed. Another outrageous idea was to make the traditional, classical journey of the Olympic flame relay from Athens to Los Angeles into a money-spinner. The IOC baulked at the idea, but Ueberroth won them over, and the journey netted, according to Ecker, some $11 million to benefit youth sports programmes.

With all these – and many more – cash-rich schemes safely in place, the Los Angeles Games became an enormous economic triumph. As the Games ended, "the bottom line was a profit so huge it staggered the imagination: $222,700,000 was announced!" (Martin & Gynn). Obviously a mountain of cash such as this creates problems of its own, and many different organizations wanted a piece of the pie. But it mattered not; there was more than enough pieces to go round, and many worthy projects were funded including the Amateur Athletics Foundation of Los Angeles, the maintenance of the Olympic research library and outreach programmes for community athletics and coaching education.

The only major cloud in the run-up to the Games came in the form of the Soviet Union deciding to play a game of tit-for-tat. America had boycotted Moscow's Games of 1980, so thus would the Soviets boycott Los Angeles. The men in suits had got their sweet revenge: what did they care if the hearts and dreams of hundreds of sports men and women were broken in the process. The formal Soviet announcement was that it was concerned for the safety of its athletes if they competed in Los Angeles, and that they did not care for the "hot, smoggy site". One suspects the athletes would have liked to have made their own minds up whether or not their lives were in danger. Despite the boycott, two Soviet-bloc nations, Romania and Yugoslavia, did participate and made a welcome contribution to the Games.

People primarily recall these Olympics for the outstanding feats of three great cultural heroes of US sport: Mary Lou Retton,[1] by becoming the first American woman to win an individual gymnastics medal; Edwin Moses the master of the 400-metres hurdles, repeating his gold from eight-years earlier; and Carl Lewis, the brash, cocksure sprinting machine who won quadruple gold in the 100, 200, long jump and sprint-relay. Although the crowds didn't take too kindly to Lewis' arrogance – he passed on his final four jumps, refusing to attack Bob Beamon's world record – their boos were laced with ignorance. Lewis already had six races behind him at the Games, and had five more still to go, and thus needed to conserve as much energy as possible.

---

1. David Wallechinsky tells a delightful story of how Retton took up gymnastics, after being inspired by watching the great Nadia Comãneci win at Montreal in 1976. When Comãneci popped a 10.0 in one of her drills in Canada, the scoreboard was unprepared for such perfection and had to register "1.0". When an eight-year-old Lou Retton took part in her very first competition on the uneven bars, she leapt for joy when the scoreboard flashed "1.0" for her too – not a faulty display in this case but a correct reading...Retton minded not however; she was hooked, and set about changing her 1.0s into 10.0s.

Great Britain sent a dazzling array of running talent to the Games: Moorcroft, Coe, Cram, Ovett, Hutchings and, most noticeably of all, an 18-year-old, 5-foot, 82-pound South African girl named Zola Budd. Although Budd was ranked world number one in the 5000-metres for smashing Mary Decker's world record by 6 seconds, she was unable to compete at the Olympics because South Africa had been excluded from the Olympics since 1960. However, a British grandfather allowed Budd to switch citizenship, and her path to Los Angeles was clear, albeit strewn with protestors and angry jibes.

Budd would be going up against her idol, Decker, in the 3000 final, although she would have been well advised not to get in Decker's way. A year earlier, when a slower runner impeded Decker, she simply shoved her to the ground and forged ahead. With 1300 metres to go in the Olympic final, Budd got in Decker's way. Decker had all the time in the world to slow down and pass her inexperienced rival on the outside. Instead, she "charged forward like a tailgating commuter rushing home on a Friday evening" (Wallechinsky). Spiking a deep gash into Budd's heel, Decker crashed and fell, pulling her left hip stabilizer muscle in the process. Horrified, Budd continued on in tears, to the boos and jeers from the partisan crowd. Her fight gone, she faded to seventh. The press on either side of the Atlantic attributed blame to the opposite parties and the whole charade descended into a vicious slanging match. Decker spewed her wrath of Budd to anyone who'd listen, while Budd didn't promote her innocence well by repeatedly apologizing.

The truth is neither was *at fault*. True, Budd cut into the lead a mite eagerly, but this sort of thing happens all the time and is never a case for disqualification (as Budd briefly was, before common sense prevailed, and she was reinstated). And Decker should have been less aggressive in her desire to reclaim the lead. Finally, everyone apologized for the matter getting so out of hand; although the excellence of Maricica Puică, Wendy Sly and Lynn Williams – the medallists – remained largely overlooked.

The Budd–Decker collision remains the enduring image of the LA '84 Olympics, but there are other close contenders: Sebastian Coe's ecstatic gesture of defiance to the press as he defended his 1500-metre crown is one, as is Daley Thompson's prance of delight after being awarded his second successive decathlon gold. Joan Benoit's inspiring win in the women's marathon in documented in detail in Chapter 35, which brings us on to another great highlight of the Games, the men's marathon.

*   *   *

"Sometimes, the best is last," wrote Marlene Cimons, in her preview of the race for the *Los Angeles Times*. "That's how it will be, at least in the eyes of distance running junkies. At 5pm today, the swiftest and deepest field of male distance runners ever assembled will leave the starting line at Santa Monica in the final event of the 1984 Games, the marathon." Deep the field most certainly was. If Frank Shorter and Bill Rodgers were largely responsible for turning the marathon into a mass-appeal event in the 1970s, they were ably followed by four superb and charismatic runners in Toshihiko Seko (Japan), Rob de Castella (Australia), Juma Ikangaa (Tanzania) and Alberto Salazar (USA). Between around 1980 and 1986 these four fought a long and intriguing battle for world supremacy, trading world records, big-city titles, and most of all, fighting for gold in the major championships.

De Castella had run four marathons in the past $3\frac{1}{2}$ years and had won them all; the reclusive Seko hadn't lost a marathon since 1979 – which he'd followed up with five wins on the spin; and Salazar had won New York three times in a row and Boston once. Ikangaa was either winning big-city races or else terrorizing the above three with his fearsome front-running tactics.[2] He had for company countryman Gidamis Shahanga, who had featured so prominently in the 1978 and 1982 Commonwealth Games (he won in '78). The Los Angeles Games came at almost the perfect time for all four favourites, who were close to, or at, the peak of their powers. All or some of them were bound to medal, and they all had the hopes of their respective nations pinned firmly on their shoulders.

Seko and Salazar brought "back-up" of more than reasonable class. The former was accompanied by the hugely respected Soh twins who had so dominated Japanese marathons for many years, if, and when, Seko was absent. All three had been due to compete at Moscow four years earlier, but had not done so owing to the Japanese boycott of the Games. In the American Olympic trials, old favourites Greg Meyer and Bill Rodgers could manage only seventh and eighth. Salazar's two teammates were the tough Pete Pfitzinger, who actually edged Salazar out by a single second in the trial, and the lesser-known John Tuttle.

Great Britain came ready to crash the party. They had the luxury of leaving out the up-and-coming Steve Jones (who'd go on to break the world record ten weeks hence), and instead selected Hugh Jones, a 2:09 man who won London two years earlier by three minutes. Jones had, however, been "outdipped" at the Chicago Marathon the previous year (Chapter 1) by Kenya's main hope: the trail-blazing Joseph Nzau – the first Kenyan to win a big-city marathon. Britain also boasted Geoff Smith, a runner of terrific pedigree who had lost an agonizing New York of 1983 in the final 200 metres (Chapter 32); and a runner named Charlie Spedding who was a new face but boasted a useful 100 per cent winning record in marathons: played two, won two, at Houston and London in 1984. However, surely such inexperience would count against him when up against the old stagers.

The list of contenders didn't end there, but instead they just kept on coming. Two dangerous East Africans were sent from the tiny nation of Djibouti. They were Ahmed Salah Hussein winner of the Paris Marathon, and Djama Robleh, who placed third in Paris, but had also set a national record of 2:11:25 only the month before in Lyon. Salah would go on to be a ubiquitous and highly successful presence in world marathons for the rest of the decade. Master of the mile, but now a marathon man, Rod Dixon from New Zealand, fancied his chances of an upset, as did someone with even more years on him than the 34-year-old Dixon, the 37-year-old Carlos Lopes from Portugal.

Lopes had won the World Cross-Country Championships for the second time earlier in the year, had scored a silver in the 10,000-metres way back at the 1976

_____

2. Ikangaa was due to bring a sidekick with him in the form of Richard Mbewa, but he was tragically shot by a policeman as he trained on a golf course. The cop had mistaken him for a thief.

Olympics, and had bowed to de Castella in a marvellous race at Rotterdam 1983 by a mere 2 seconds. His 2:08:39 that day ranked him sixth on the all-time lists, and his 10,000-metre personal best was a devastating 27:17, second in the world only behind countryman Fernando Mamede. Just 15 days before the Olympic Marathon, Lopes was merrily out training (in Portugal) when a Mercedes-Benz struck him. As he flew over the hood and watched his elbow smash through the windshield he thought, "There goes the Olympics" (Wallechinsky). But fortunately his injuries were minor and he recovered to take his place at the start. "It's a problem in Portugal," explained Lopes. "We do not have parks, so I had to run on the highway."

Finally, mention should go to the entrants of Ireland. Their team was made up of Jeremiah Kiernan, a very strong runner who could well feature in the top ten; Richard Hooper, who would go on to execute the rare feat of three consecutive Olympic Marathons [Moscow, LA and Seoul], and *18 years* later would still be running less than three minutes slower than the great Antonio Pinto at a half-marathon in Lisbon; and finally, and most intriguingly, a debutant for the distance, 27-year-old John Treacy. Irish pubs had stayed open all night in celebration of his double win at the World Cross-Country Championships in 1978 and 1979, and biomechanical tests had indicated that Treacy would make a good marathoner, and thus the Irish selected him. Treacy didn't appear to be in the greatest of form after placing just tenth in the 10,000-metres final six days earlier, but such a run still demonstrated leg speed to be feared. Although Treacy had never run a marathon, he had trained like a marathoner for the past year. He often went on 23, 26 and 29-mile runs, around his home in Providence, Rhode Island. If Treacy could still be with the leaders deep into the race he could be a real threat.

In all, seven different starters had clocked times under 2:09. Let the shoot-out commence.

*　*　*

This will be forever known as the "killersmog" marathon, and unlike the women the previous weekend who began their marathon in the cooler morning hours, the men began their race at 5 p.m. with the idea being that they'd enter the Los Angeles Coliseum just as the closing ceremony was getting under way. In the shade, the temperature was a pleasant 72 °F, but the race took place almost entirely out of the shade in conditions significantly warmer. One person who was wary of the heat more than most was the American hope Alberto Salazar. Martin and Gynn write: "Salazar discovered through laboratory physiological testing that he fell into the minority who sweat excessively in a warm environment. He could lose as much as two to three litres of fluid per hour (Armstrong et al. 1986). That may be fine for evaporative capabilities, but one cannot absorb more than about one litre per hour while racing." Salazar certainly had a lot on his mind as he set out determined to run 5-minute miles, hoping that would be enough to win in such oppressive conditions. However, there was the real chance with a field as classy as this that Waldemar Cierpinski's Olympic record from 1976 of 2:09:55 might come under severe attack – and that was significantly under 5-minute miling.

In total, 107 athletes from 59 nations set out for 2½ laps of the Santa Monica track and the familiar front-running figure of Juma Ikangaa was quickly to the fore. This marathon wasn't just noteworthy for the magnificent Caucasian talent on offer, but for the numerous presence in the formative stages of African runners. The African marathon running scene was certainly starting to make its presence felt, leading to the dominance we see today in so many big-city marathons. The first two 5-kilometre splits took place in almost identical times of 15:35 and 15:34, but where the first split hadn't really done any damage to the huge pack, a smaller pack had formed by the time the 10 kilometres were reached. Of the dozen or so African runners who featured, only six would manage to finish (Martin & Gynn), one of them being the leader, Ahmed Ismail of Somalia, who would go on to place 47th out of 78 finishers. The Africans were still paying their dues and learning that marathon running doesn't come easily, even to those with great talent.

There was a significant acceleration injected by the Africans as the next 5 kilometres passed in a brutal 14:51. As they had done in the Commonwealth marathon of 1982, Tanzanians Ikangaa and Shahanga led, and they had the dangerous Salah and Ismail for company. Two Kenyans followed close behind in the form of Joseph Nzau and Kimurgor Ngeny. Lopes and de Castella lurked menacingly, but poor Alberto Salazar was already showing signs of distress. He had never been *quite* the same runner since his monumental win at Boston '82 where he ran himself to the most extreme levels of heat exhaustion and dehydration. And here was the heat playing havoc with his plans again.

Around a mile before halfway, Takeshi Soh, who had up till now been observing proceedings from the back of the pack, decided to test both himself and the rest of the field with a surge. He opened up a lead of 6 seconds while the "hard men" Nzau and Shahanga valiantly kept the gap to only 40 metres. For company they had none other than Carlos Lopes, who was drawing on all his experience to spar for the lead. The heat wasn't affecting his 37-year-old body as much as the experts had predicted. Yet Lopes' marathon career so far consisted of the excellent duel with de Castella at Rotterdam in '83, but bookending that, two DNFs at New York '82 and Rotterdam of '84. Soh's twin followed almost immediately behind these three, as did eight others. Charlie Spedding and John Treacy were both enjoying terrific runs and seemed to be running comfortably. Seko and de Castella, whom so many fancied, kept close order as well. With the first half of the race passing quickly (a shade over 1:05), the second half would truly be a searing examination.

"Never had so many good runners been so close together this late in a marathon," report Martin and Gynn, as by 30 kilometres there was scarcely any change from the halfway mark. There was almost no change in the leading dozen with the top four now consisting of Treacy, Spedding, Ikangaa and Nzau. The course had been mainly downhill or flat thus far, but now began a long, slight incline up to the stadium. The question on everyone's lips was who would be the first to make a bold bid for home. Rob de Castella was the focus of many. A superb judge of pace and phenomenally strong, his preferred strategy was the long tempo burn up from around 10 kilometres out. He didn't boast great natural pace or kick, but when he had a "flyer" going, there were precious few who could keep up.

What "Deek's" supporters didn't know is that he came into the race a little tired and jaded, and that for 30 kilometres he had only been barely hanging on to the "coat-tails" of his rivals. In the 1972 Olympic marathon one of the pre-race favourites, Ron Hill, had made a classic "over-training" error. He reasoned that if he was destroying the Boston and Commonwealth fields of 1970 on such-and-such training, then surely if he upped the mileage another notch, then a victory in Munich would be even more conclusive. But agonizingly for Hill, he upped it too much and came to the Games low on energy and weary. One-fifth of a century after Los Angeles, the author spoke to de Castella (aka "Deek") about what happened at a water stop at around 32 kilometres (the 20-mile mark), when he suddenly got dropped by the field. "When I looked up the leading guys had 50 metres on me. Before I knew, it was 100," Deek recalled with a sigh. But how could a mere water stop, a procedure he must be so well versed in, cause him to crash out of contention of the race? Deek then painted the picture of him hanging by a thread over a precipice. When you're "so close to the edge anyway," he explained, "it doesn't take much to tip the balance." In this case the killer catalyst of defeat was the simple action of slowing, reaching for a plastic bottle, taking a couple of sups and accelerating again. If there's one piece of training advice for runners that is as priceless as any, it is de Castella's oft repeated refrain: "TRAIN SMARTER NOT HARDER". Coming into Los Angeles, Deek had just trained too hard. His dream of holding the Commonwealth, World and Olympic crowns all at the same time had gone.

Was the 5 foot 6 inch, 126 pound Lopes heading for another of his DNFs, the pundits wondered? Not at this rate – the man was really starting to motor. At 35 kilometres the inexperienced converts from successful track careers, Lopes, Spedding and Treacy, detached themselves from not just de Castella but also the Africans and the Japanese. The US television commentators dwelt endlessly and tiresomely upon the ailing American Salazar, out of touch a minute or so behind the leading pack. No coming back for him now. Two thousand metres of grind later and the unlikely trio remained together. And then Lopes accelerated. After just 500 metres he had already secured himself a valuable lead, and over the next mile and a half (which would take him up to 40 kilometres), he would continue with this new blistering pace. "Everything was hitting just perfectly...all the cylinders were on go," he would later tell *Track and Field News*.

Lopes' famous 5-kilometre split for between 35 and 40 kilometres was a magnificent 14:33, which was enough to put 22 seconds of daylight between him and his two chasers. "After 37 kilometres, I was convinced I would win," Lopes explained, and his convictions were correct. The final 2.2 kilometres of the race saw him stretch his lead to 35 seconds, while behind him Treacy and Spedding fought a white-knuckle duel for second. Just before they entered the stadium, Treacy gained a 7-metre advantage on Spedding and he then proceeded to blast a 67-second final lap to secure the silver.[3] Spedding happily settled for bronze.

The finish of the marathon was a terrific affair as it meshed beautifully with the

---

3. This was Ireland's first medal in athletics at the Olympics since Ron Delaney's thrilling gold in the 1500-metres at Melbourne 1956.

401

Carlos Lopes wins the great Olympic Marathon of 1984. *Mark Shearman*

closing ceremonies. The idea was the brainchild of Dr Primo Nebiolo, the IAAF president "who was becoming increasingly respected for his keen sense of effective sports promotion" (Martin & Gynn). The *New York Times*' Frank Litsky wrote:

There was singing and dancing. There were fireworks and a laser show and a 23,000-square-foot stage. There was a simulated flying saucer, suspended from a helicopter, with flashing lights that hovered overhead for a few minutes and then flew off. Tonight's colourful closing ceremony had a little of everything and a lot of show business. It even had something no previous closing ceremony had had – a live sports event. The plan was for the first finishers in the men's marathon to enter the Coliseum about 25 minutes after the start of the ceremony. And that was just what happened.

As the runners came in, the shock sunk in that none of the "big four" had medalled. "He ran well," said coach Pat Clohessy of de Castella, who battled through to fifth. "He beat Ikangaa. He beat Salazar. He beat Seko, and he beat Dixon. He fought it out – that's to his credit."

Outside the Coliseum there was a billboard with large green and gold letters that read "DEEK", with the letters streaked to denote speed. The Australian advertising bureau paid for the billboard to promote its favourite son. De Castella won a poll in 1983 as the most popular Australian. Although this was his first marathon defeat for four years, Deek didn't think Australia would be too disappointed: "I received thousands of telegrams from people back home before the race. They didn't tell me to win, just to do the best I can. I hope they realized I did try my best. I just didn't have it. It's a tough race. You can't explain what happened in one or two reasons. You just can't count on anything in a marathon."

As for poor Toshihiko Seko (14th), he simply died in the last 5 miles and was easily beaten by his countryman Takeshi Soh, something that had never happened before. If de Castella was possibly over-trained, then Seko definitely was. He explained: "On July 30th, I ran a hard 20K and August 1st I ran a 40K. I was not prepared for this race today but I tried my best to win." His regime, set up by his legendary coach 72-year-old Kiyoshi Nakamura, obviously took too much out of Seko, who complained of stomach cramps and dehydration in the final 5 miles. But outwardly at least, Seko harboured no ill feelings toward

Nakamura. Upon greeting him outside a press tent, Seko smiled and bowed respectfully.

As for Salazar, the stunt of shredding his racing singlet for increased ventilation, so that just "USA" remained, couldn't save him: "I thought a 2:10 would win the race. I felt that to go any faster than that pace was suicidal. If I was able to, I'd pick up a little at the end." But when the time came he could not:

> I've never really run a good race in the heat. Maybe even with the heat training I can't run a good race in the heat.
>
> It was about at the 15-mile point that I knew it was all over. I feel bad because the crowds were great and I didn't feel that I represented my country as well as I could have. People went crazy when they saw the USA jersey go by. It showed an Olympic spirit because they weren't just cheering for the top three. I gave it my best; I just don't know why I'm not running well.
>
> The medallists are encouragement for me. They had bad years and came back. It showed that if you keep heart, you'll be back sooner or later. I'll be back.

But he never did run a world-class marathon again. He did, however, run a world-class *ultra-marathon*, when he burst back into the limelight to win the famous South African Comrades race in 1994.

* * *

Lopes celebrates. *Mark Shearman*

Pat Butcher wrote in the London *Times*: "But for injuries [Carlos Lopes] would probably have dominated world distance running in the last decade, and this was fitting achievement for a modest man whose competitiveness is evident, and much appreciated, in every race he runs." Malcolm Moran quizzed in the *New York Times*: "How did a 37-year-old loan officer from a Lisbon bank run away from the best-known and most successful marathoners in the world to win his nation's first gold medal in track and field?" "There is no explanation," replied Lopes. "That's how it is. I came prepared for this; prepared for any climate. I came prepared to win. The keys are endurance and happiness. I bet on my youthfulness." Alan Greenberg of the *Los Angeles Times* wrote a portrait of Lopes. He wrote:

> Three weeks ago Carlos Lopes was hit by a car. In Sunday's Olympic final, he hit back at the greatest marathon field ever assembled – and blew their doors off.
>
> And unlike the car accident which caused him to miss three days training, this was no glancing blow. This was Lopes, the 1976 Olympic silver medallist at 10K hammering the lead pack with a burst at 23-miles that made the last three miles seem academic.
>
> And nobody knew it better than Lopes, the former goatherder-turned-balding-middle-aged-crazy – he's 37. He started waving to the Coliseum crowd almost as soon as he exited the tunnel more than a quarter mile *before* the finish line.
>
> That other CL – Carl Lewis – gets some rivals ticked off when he does that. Not Lopes. When you've already run 26 hard miles, and you're the oldest competitor ever to win a major international marathon, you celebrate any way you please.

Lopes, noted Greenberg, had a history of being overshadowed. At 10K it was Lopes who set the pace for countryman Fernando Memede when Mamede ran his world record. "At the Montreal Olympics, Lopes was right with Finland's Lasse Viren, until Viren outkicked him to win the gold medal, his second of the Games. In the marathon he's always been overshadowed. First by Salazar, then by Seko. Then by Deek. Until now."

Lopes had taken guidance from the same coach, Mario Pereira, for 18 years. Progress was slow. At 25, Lopes failed to qualify for the final at the 1972 Munich Games in his speciality, the 10K. The turning point came in 1975 when the government changed and Pereira persuaded it to provide "jobs" for athletes. At Los Angeles he was listed as a loan officer in a bank. "But don't expect him to talk interest rates over split times," wrote Greenberg. Lopes suffered severe Achilles tendonitis after the 1976 Olympics, but after six long years in the doldrums, eventually returned to his peak in 1982, when he set the then European record for the 10,000. At the 1983 World Championships at Helsinki, Lopes was second going into the final lap of the 10,000 but faded to finish sixth. "If a runner wants to remain tough at an old age, he can," Lopes told the *Runner* magazine. "It's only a matter of making up his mind to do it." The following year Lopes proved he was a worthy Olympic champion by ending his marathon career with a magnificent flourish by running to a 2:07:12 world record in Rotterdam.

*　　*　　*

"When I got to 20 miles I said, 'I'm feeling great – where's the wall?'" reported Irish hero John Treacy. Although, he also concedes, the gold was never quite an option: "At 35 kilometres, Lopes just took off," he said. "Charlie and I tried to go with him, but we just didn't have it. At that point I knew I was just going for the silver." Reigning New York champion Rod Dixon summed up the general reaction to Treacy's feat: "I was surprised at the outcome, especially John Treacy finishing second." Treacy also competed in the 1980 Moscow Games – fifth in the 5000 and a collapsed DNF in the 10,000 final because of dehydration. "I learned my lesson after that. I was well hydrated before today's race."

Treacy, who lived in Providence, Rhode Island with his wife and baby daughter, was reared in the tiny Irish village of Villierstown (population: 150) in Waterford County. His father was postmaster of the village and owned a general store. Treacy began running in high school, and when he finished third in the junior World Cross-Country Championship, he was recruited by Providence College, at age 17. After graduating in 1978, he took a job with the Irish Industrial Export Board. But too much work and not enough training hampered his running. "I knew I had to go back to my college coaches, where I ran well. I had to get back to Providence if I was going to make it." Make it, he most certainly did, and would go on to be a much feared marathoner for the next several years, particularly at Boston where he place third in both 1988 and 1989, giving the Africans Ibrahim Hussein and Abebe Mekonnen real scares. He was selected again for the Seoul Olympics, but failed to finish there.

*　　*　　*

A delighted Charlie Spedding noted how, late on in the race, "It was strange to look back and see somebody like de Castella struggling. When you see that it does you a world of good, believe me. My plan was to make a jump right at the tunnel, but John went earlier. He got a 6-yard lead on me and I know it was not much but it just seemed to make the difference. I couldn't make it up." Seven-time national sportswriter of the year Rick Reilly wrote in the *Los Angeles Times*:

Between Carlos Lopes, 37, and Charlie Spedding, 32, more was done for the middle-age craze of the running world on Sunday, than a month of backrubs.

Lopes you might have heard of. But Charlie Spedding? Yes, Spedding. It was Spedding, a small, wiry Brit, who left the Coliseum wearing a medal, not Deek, or Salazar, or Seko or any of the others who make more money wearing certain brands of shoes than Spedding has made in a lifetime.

And you want to hear something stranger still? Charlie Spedding knew it would happen. . .

"I didn't say it to anybody, but I believed that if I ran the race of my life, I could win a medal here," he said. "And I did. For me to win the bronze medal here had to be the race of my life."

The boys back in Durham city, England will never believe it.

"I have a feeling one of two people back home will want to buy me a beer or two," Spedding said with a lucky grin. "And it's not in my nature to refuse."

The following year, Spedding fought out a famous duel with Steve Jones on the streets of London before finally missing out by just 17 seconds. There then followed two years of indifferent form and injuries, before rebounding to make the British team for Seoul. Here the author must take the rarest of issue with Martin and Gynn who state that Spedding ran "quite well" in Korea. His sixth place was a whole lot better than that. British endurance coach Alan Storey states the case more accurately: "It was an unbelievable run by Charlie [at Seoul] after all the problems he's had. No one could forecast that sort of performance, he ran himself into the deck."

*   *   *

The medal ceremony where Lopes is flanked by two fine talents in Ireland's John Treacy (left), and Charlie Spedding (right). *Mark Shearman*

As has been his way for several decades, David Miller of the London *Times* wrote a reflective piece about how he thought the Games had gone. Somewhat against the odds, the Angelinos had impressed him:

It has been a memorable Games: unexpectedly friendly and hospitable in the land of the fast buck, predominantly efficient in its organization, and pleasingly relaxed and comfortable for the athletes in the villages. It has been a triumph for Peter Ueberroth and the LAOOC in the face of five years of almost unbroken criticism, and a generous gift to the sporting people of 140 nations by the 50,000 tirelessly courteous volunteers.

The traffic flowed and air was reasonably clean, though some competitors suffered. There were no terrorists or the armed fanatics which the Soviet block professed to fear. The Romanians and Chinese came, finished second and fourth respectively in the medals table and contributed artistically and handsomely to the quality of performances.

The US dominance of the Olympics was extreme.
Final medal table:

	Gold	*Silver*	*Bronze*
USA	83	61	30
Romania	20	16	17
W. Germany	17	19	23
China	15	8	9
Italy	14	6	12

The USSR's medal tally four years earlier had been nearly identical to America's here. Going back over the previous seven Olympics, the gold count between the USSR and the USA stood at: USSR 240 – USA 224. What a battle.

The last word goes to the inspirational – and indefatigable – Julia Wark, who worked at the Coliseum's information booth. Wark, it turns out was well qualified for her position: this was the *second* Los Angeles Olympics at which she'd worked! She explained: "I was the last employee to leave the Olympic office in 1933. I was the one that turned the key in the door for the final time. Now here I am again. Isn't this fantastic? Isn't this wonderful?"

Race result:

Carlos Lopes	POR	2:09:21
John Treacy	IRL	2:09:56
Charlie Spedding	GBR	2:09:58
Tekeshi Soh	JPN	2:10:55
Robert de Castella	AUS	2:11:09
Juma Ikangaa	TAN	2:11:10
Joseph Nzau	KEN	2:11:28
Djama Robleh	DJI	2:11:39
Jeremiah Kiernan	IRL	2:12:20
Rod Dixon	NZL	2:12:57

Sources:

Conversations with Alberto Salazar.
Conversations with Rob de Castella.
Butcher, Pat, in *The Times*, August 13th, 1984.
Cimons, Marlene, in the *Los Angeles Times*, August 12th, 1984.
Greenberg, Alan, in the *Los Angeles Times*, August 13th, 1984.
Hauman, Riël, *Century of the Marathon*. Human & Rousseau, 1996.
Litsky, Frank, in the *New York Times*, August 13th, 1984.
Martin, David and Roger Gynn, *The Olympic Marathon*. Human Kinetics, 2000.
Miller, David, in *The Times*, August 14th, 1984.
Moran, Malcolm, in the *New York Times*, August 13th, 1983
Reilly, Rick, in the *Los Angeles Times*, August 12th, 1984.
Wallechinsky, David, *The Complete Book of the Olympics*. Aurum Press, 2000.

XLIII

No. 8 – 1984 Chicago Marathon [Men]

Sunday, October 21st

The "Runner's runner" hits rivals with "eyeballs-out, gut-wrenching, lung-buster."

For whatever reason, and Steve Jones maintains it is because he is Welsh, the British selectors gave him a consistently hard time throughout his athletics career. They even decided to leave him out of the British marathon team for the 1988 Olympics, when he was still one of the world's finest marathoners. Eventually they realized their error and gave Jones the call-up, but he felt the request had come too late to prepare properly and so declined. Britain's representatives in the 1988 Olympics placed a banal 6th, 21st and 33rd, with the latter two running 2:16 and 2:20. Jones's time at the New York the following month was 2:08:20. Jones wasn't the only great British runner the selectors left out for Seoul. A fellow named Sebastian Coe, who'd won the blue-ribbon event of the previous two Olympics – the 1500-metres – was deemed not worthy because he had a cold during the trials. The Olympics were duly won in a time $3\frac{1}{2}$ seconds slower than 1984, and many believe Coe was denied his "threepeat". But that is another story.

The story here is of a man nicknamed the "runner's runner" – who ran purely for the love of the sport and was constantly battling the prejudices against him. A humble RAF mechanic who tuned fighter planes, Jones ran like a man possessed, while also nursing a healthy thirst for the "amber nectar". Jones started out his career as a 17-minute 5K man, and his breakthrough only came after several years of 70-mile weeks, when he placed seventh in the 1976 Welsh Cross-Country Championships. He would go on to win the event nine times. Jones has been known to say: "I don't think I have too much talent particularly. I just work hard." But his greatest talent is that in both training and racing he was able to stretch the pain barrier – both mental and physical – a little further than the next man. Running to his limit, to the extent that he would sometimes vomit during workouts, was the Jones trademark.

It wasn't just British selectors who seemed to have it in for Jones. In the early days it was the Welsh ones too. Despite his seventh-place finish in the Welsh championships, Jones wasn't selected for the World Cross-Country Championships that year to be held in Wales – even though the Welsh board submitted a team of nine, including four reserves. Some club runners become very melodra-

Steve Jones: A hard worker, a hard drinker, and a very hard runner. *Simon Bruty/Getty Images*

matic at such snubs, but Jones used it as motivation instead: "Not getting picked really upset me," he said. "That was really the kick up the backside I needed. I said, 'Next year, I'll make sure you'll *have* to pick me" (Sandrock).

Pick him they did and Jones began in 1977 a spree that would include 11 outings in the World Cross-Country Championships. From 103rd that year Jones pulled a shocker the next by placing eleventh. He would then place solidly for the next several years before rebounding from a disappointment at the 1983 Chicago Marathon by overtaking American Pat Porter in the 1984 World Cross-Country Championships in the final 30 metres to grab the bronze medal. Nine years earlier a fairly unknown Bill Rodgers had made his great marathon breakthrough after a surprising bronze medal at the "World Cross", and now Jones prepared to follow even more spectacularly in those footsteps.

First, however, came the 1984 Olympics which were somewhat disappointing for Jones as, slightly over-raced, he placed just eighth in the 10,000-metres final, and was then rocked when his coach Bob Wallis retired shortly thereafter. But Jones was not to stay down for long and vowed that at Chicago, two months after the Olympics, he'd redeem himself for choking in the LA smog.

The 1984 edition of Chicago falls between a great high and low of Jones's career. In 1983 he came to compete, but pulled a tendon in his foot the night before the race on an innocuous 20-minute jog with fellow Brit Hugh Jones. He sailed to 16 miles in 79 minutes in the '83 affair, but then his foot seized up and he had to pull out. That being the low, the high was 1985, of which more later.

But 1984 is my selection to the *50 Greatest Marathons* list because it was a more dramatic race, with a deeper field, and had that crucial element of surprise. Everyone knew all about "Jonesy" by the fall of '85, but a year earlier his extraordinary feat in the Windy City would startle the world of athletics and sport in general. Also, 1984 saw a stunning battle for second place between two of the greatest marathoners of all time.

Chicago Marathon race director Bob Bright described the elite runners at the 1984 race as "the most glittering array of distance talent outside the Olympics". All the media talk and hype before the race was of the showdown between the Commonwealth and World champion Rob de Castella and the Olympic champion Carlos Lopes of Portugal. Jones remembers: "Carlos and Rob were the stars, and the whole race was built up around them." Michael Sandrock writes in *Running with the Legends*: "Keen observers would have recognized Jones's pedigree. But to

410

most, Jones was a track and cross-country runner, viewed as someone who would run with the leaders until 20 miles, then drop back."

The race proceeded fairly uneventfully – if very quickly – to 10 miles in 48:40. On the race commentary, Alberto Salazar cried, "They have to start slowing down." But they did the opposite. Upon hearing the 10-mile split there was a conversation eerily reminiscent of that between Emil Zátopek and Jim Peters at the Helsinki Olympics of 1952. On this occasion when Jones heard "48:40" he turned to Rob de Castella and asked, "Is that right?" "What's the matter? Too slow for you?" de Castella replied.

In truth the pace did feel somewhat sluggish to Jones, and it soon became obvious that he was feeling the searing pace less than the others. He recalls to the author: "It felt so easy, I remember looking around and enjoying the atmosphere, and looking above trying to see all the helicopters." In a pack which included Kenyans Simeon Kigen, Gabriel Kamau and Joseph Nzau, Englishman Geoff Smith, as well as Lopes and de Castella, it was Kigen who was the first to drop back. Sandrock writes: "Jones ran smoothly behind de Castella, occasionally coming to the front of the pack. He ran with his head cocked to the side, as if he were listening to the others' footsteps, trying to determine if they were feeling as good as he was." Jones then recollects: "Just before 16 miles, de Castella looked across at me and surged. Every time he surged, I surged with him, and covered. That's when I knew Rob was thinking about me." Lopes gave Jones less concerns as he states: "He was up and down. I knew on a given day, Carlos was the best in the world, but he was not always at his best. He wasn't always consistent."

After a fall at a water stop at 19 miles the Kenyan Kamau surged to the front and Jones quickly covered the move – and then went straight past. Not only was Jones now running further than he ever had in his life, he was about to do it on his own. De Castella observed and wondered whether the new man was serious: whether he really intended to run for the tape. To Deek's credit, he decided Jones *was* serious and urgently required chasing. Carlos Lopes joined rank, and together these two put their heads down and started gunning for the Welshman.

Seasoned campaigners watched and wondered. Could a man who had never before run more than 20 miles really drop the world's two finest marathoners? Lopes and de Castella had different reasons for not having covered Jones's move the *moment* it happened. Lopes simply hadn't felt strong enough, while de Castella's experience told him that Jones would come back to the pack. But astonishingly, Jones just kept extending his lead. He recalls: "My legs were sore more than heavy, mostly at the top of my quads. I wasn't in a panic, and I never looked behind me. I felt good up to 20 miles but it was tough after that. I did have an edge. Everyone was telling me I'd collapse and hit the wall, but I didn't experience any of that" (Sandrock).

Miles 20 and 21 passed by in a slick 4:47 and a blinding 4:42, and the split for 24 miles was an incredible 1:57:24. Jones heard the split being called, but it meant nothing to him. And when someone from the press truck yelled that 5-minute miling would give him the record, Jones thought this meant the course one. But it was the world time that was seriously under threat. Jones admits: "In the last two miles anything could still have happened. I was first aware of the exact time only right near the end, when I saw the finish clock reading 2:07:32, and I had to watch

411

it ticking away over the last 200 metres. I thought, "the clock's going too fast", not that I was running too slow.

Jones's last 10 kilometres took an astounding 29:38, and a reporter was quickly sticking a microphone in his face: "Do you realize you broke the record?" Jones had no idea what he meant. While Jones was dealing with the press, the World and Olympic champions played out a fascinating duel. De Castella boldly made his bid for home 2 miles from the end but he'd gone too early and Lopes passed him in the final 200 metres, finishing in 2:09:06, 61 seconds behind Jones.

While the press were swamping Jones that evening with his phone going off throughout the night, newspapers the world over picked up on the theme: "World-beater from Nowhere." Charlie Spedding wrote in *Athletics Weekly*: "His opponents were the best in the world. The course was fast, the weather was cool. He let the pack take him to 19 miles at perfect pace and he then found himself in the right place at the right time to move into the history books with an eyeballs-out, lung-busting, gut-wrenching six-mile surge to the finish. But there is nothing sensational about that for Steve Jones...that is the way he always runs." Jones returned to England – back to tuning his fighter planes – with a check for $35,000, far more than he earned in a whole year with the RAF, to a raucous welcome. "They are great company," Steve said of his work mates, "I'm just Steve to them, not someone like Sebastian Coe or Steve Cram, whom they just see on TV." Jones ran in, not one, but two races the following weekend: a cross-country for the RAF, which he won; and the Swindon Half-Marathon.

* * *

Six months later Jones became embroiled in a classic duel with fellow Brit Charlie Spedding at the 1985 London Marathon. Jones explains how in the pre-race publicity Spedding was portrayed as the purist marathoner, a classic amateur, and a brave Olympian (after his bronze the previous year in Los Angeles). Jones was given less favourable press: a bounty hunter who chased records and money off in the States. He recalled to the author at a press conference at the 2004 London Marathon:

> Brendan Foster, the race commentator, made no secret who he was rooting for. Charlie was a northerner like him, and he kept saying over and over this was a race between a man who ran for medals and another who ran for the money. Yet here I was holding down a full-time job in the RAF, while Charlie was employed by Nike! Despite my world record, everyone made him the favourite. Of course all such talk just made me more determined.

With nothing separating Spedding and Jones deep into the race, many recall Jones toiling in the face of nature's call. The Welshman turned to Spedding and asked what he'd do in a similar situation. "I'd stop," deadpanned Spedding.

The reporting of the incident was somewhat erratic by the press. Here are two professional journalists' accounts of what happened next, appearing in the *same* paper (*The Times*). Michael Horsnell: "The tunnel of the Tower Hotel allowed Jones the privacy necessary to relieve himself." Pat Butcher: "Jones succeeded in winning, despite a bout of stomach cramp, which forced him into the gutter

Six months after his Chicago world record, Jones breaks the tape in another superb win. This time at London by 17 seconds over Charlie Spedding. *Mike Powell/Getty Images*

in front of the Tower, where he relieved himself." (Horsnell, incidentally, reported matters as they happened; Butcher opted to use his "journalistic licence" to the extreme. Butcher was right about one thing though. Despite his problems Jones went on to win by 17 seconds in 2:08:16.)

Jones was by no means finished for the year though. In August he set a new world best of 61:14 for the half-marathon and arrived at the 1985 Chicago Marathon well known and enormously respected by the running fraternity. His world record had fallen to Carlos Lopes' mighty run at Rotterdam the previous April, but many were predicting that Jones would have a go at retrieving it. Jones was up for the challenge. What followed was the most awesome front-running that had ever been seen. And the author is hard-pressed to name a time it has been seen since either. "Jones killed the rabbit at three miles!" crowed the race announcer[1] as the Welshman flew through the first 3 miles in 4:46, 4:42 and 4:48. But he was just getting warmed up as miles 4 and 5 passed in 4:39 and 4:34. His 10K split was 29:30 with his second 5 kilometres taking an astounding 13:43 (Hauman). Yes, that's 1 hour 55 minute pace for the marathon.

After Jones had dropped his last challenger, the somewhat irritating Simeon Kigen (who kept stepping on the back of Jones's shoe) halfway passed just 29 seconds slower than his world best in 61:43, and it now became a question of what damage this astonishingly brave runner had done to his legs and lungs. The answer came as he kept clicking off sub-5-minute miles up to number 21, but noticeably started to slow after that. But the record was still in sight. Riël Hauman writes: "Jones found it increasingly hard to maintain his rhythm, yet succeeded in picking up the pace when he came into the finishing straight and saw how close he was to the record. "I realized that I still had a chance at the record. So I sprinted." It was not to be, however, and he missed Lopes' time by a scant one second. Robleh set a new Africa record in third. Jones was typically insouciant about his near-miss: "I didn't get the bonus for the record, but I picked up a

---

1. The "rabbit" was Englishman Carl Thackery.

413

bit of money for winning the race. The money and the fame are irrelevant, really. The last 5 miles hurt, really hurt. I just lost my concentration. But there will be other races – I'm just a hamstring injury away from oblivion; you've got to look at it like that." De Castella was "stunned" afterwards, writes Michael Sandrock, and walked into the media tent, came up and shook hands with Jones. "Steve surprised me a great deal," says de Castella, "first of all because he was able to go out so fast, but mainly because he was able to continue on and only slow down a little bit."

Two disappointing years followed, in which Jones struggled to recapture his best form, although he did run two memorable marathons. He "did a Chicago" and went out incredibly fast in his first championship marathon (the European) at Stuttgart, in very humid conditions and this time fell victim to his exuberance. He finished a very painful 20th. On another humid day at Boston '87, he and countryman Geoff Smith fought Toshihiko Seko with all their might, but the Japanese was just too strong. Smith and Jones kicked for the finish line for the honours of second. Jones won.

As noted at the start of this chapter, 1988 was also a painful year after the British selectors decided to leave Jones out of their squad for the Seoul Olympics. He made mockery of their judgement however, by winning New York in a new course record of 2:08:20. "I just put my head down...and I never looked back," he said later, after a jaw-dropping 4:28 for mile 17 that dropped Ireland's John Treacy.

Over twenty years on from the bright Chicago day where Jones made his name, he is still passionate about his sport – albeit if he is described on internet message boards now as just "a grandfather with reading glasses". And he also had plenty of advice to offer those wishing to follow in his footsteps of greatness. At the 2004 London Marathon, Jones commented on what is currently wrong with British distance running. I asked what he thought of today's runners' work ethic. Jones replied that he thought the current crop could perhaps push a little harder:

> It may be my Alzheimer's kicking in, but I remember running the hardest I could every time out. Between 1981 and 1985 I barely ever got tired in training, but to reach such a level took twelve long years of flogging myself. Today's runners say it's hard to run and work, but I know how hard it is – I worked 60 to 70 hours a week.
>
> I well remember those 11:30-at-night workouts! Worried if when I got home whether my wife would still be living there – hoping she would be – but I wouldn't know for sure...That was the dedication I needed.
>
> Today's runners don't seem to race a great deal – we were prolific racers. They are too professional now, seemingly concerned with stuff like appearance fees. We all just got out and raced each other as much as possible. I became a professional athlete because I could, not because I had to.

When quizzed by Michael Sandrock where his speciality lay: cross-country, the track, or the road, Jones replied: "I'm just a runner – and I will always be a runner because I just love the sport."

414

Race result:

Steve Jones	WAL	2:08:05
Carlos Lopes	POR	2:09:06
Robert de Castella	AUS	2:09:09
Gabriel Kamau	KEN	2:10:05
Geoff Smith	ENG	2:10:08

Sources:

Conversations with Steve Jones.
Butcher, Pat, in *The Times*, April 23rd, 1985.
Chicago Marathon web site.
Hauman, Riël, *Century of the Marathon*. Human & Rousseau, 1996.
Horsnell, Michael, in *The Times*, April 23rd, 1985.
Sandrock, Michael, in *Running with the Legends*. Human Kinetics, 1996.
Spedding, Charlie, in *Athletics Weekly*, October 24th, 1984.

XLIV

No. 7 – 1996 Boston Marathon [Women]

Monday, April 15th

"Why is the sky blue? Why do people run marathons at all?"

Before the race commentary for this chapter begins, it is necessary to discuss the subject of doping – the dark cloud of which hangs over a protagonist of the upcoming pages. The author, however, asks those readers who feel that she therefore doesn't warrant inclusion in the book to be patient and examine the evidence that I have closely investigated. The results of my findings tell me that this chapter should very much be a part of the book, and submit that its contents is one of the richest and varied of all the races included. Everything is here: history, politics, scandal, suffering, joy, drama and, yes, the seventh greatest marathon race of all time.

* * *

The doping controversy that hit German marathoner Uta Pippig in the late 1990s shocked her thousands of devoted fans in Europe and America. Not Uta, they said. Anyone but this sunny personality, with the cover-girl looks, the megawatt grin and the fierce drive to become the finest marathon runner of her era. Pippig had watched the big four – Waitz, Kristiansen, Mota and Benoit Samuelson – dominate women's marathoning in the 1980s. Then, as the new decade began, she pounced and became *the* woman to beat. There is a belief – not among Pippig's detractors, but among her friends and family – that Pippig falling foul of the DLV (the German athletics association) was one drugs bust just waiting to happen. For to them, for nearly ten years, the DLV had been after her blood (quite literally). Because to the DLV, Uta Pippig was a deserter.

Pippig was born in Leipzig, East Germany on September 7th, 1965, to parents who both worked as doctors. When Pippig was four, her parents changed their job locations and moved to the countryside just outside Berlin. From an early age Uta had it preached to her that real life was all about hard word and, as she herself writes, one should "approach all challenging tasks with confidence and determination". Uta was naturally gifted at sports and at one school sports day won eight gold medals and a silver. Running home to proudly show her parents, her perfectionist father, predictably, asked her about the silver. Tough love maybe, but it instilled in Uta an even greater drive to excel.

417

Low-key running began at the age of 13 when Pippig accompanied a girlfriend to the local athletics club SC BlauWeib Petershagen. She immediately took to the camaraderie and competition and the feeling of joy of being at one with nature. By the age of 18 Uta's athletic ability was starting to flourish, and she was quickly outgrowing what her small, happy-go-lucky club could offer her. If she wanted her running to progress, it was time to join one of the major East German sports federations. Pippig went to pretty much the swankiest of the lot – ASK (the Army Sports Club) in Potsdam. "Look," she said, "I can run really good." So they saw. Under the tutelage of Dieter Hogen – one of the world's most famous marathon coaches, who would also become her partner for many years – Pippig quickly developed into one of East Germany's leading distance runners.

However, when Pippig wanted to compete against the rest of the world and to travel to races outside of East Germany, she and Hogen ran slap bang into the most obtuse of bureaucratic walls. "They were afraid if we left the country, we wouldn't come back," Hogen relates. "They were right." Feeling she was in a "kind of prison", Pippig became more and more desperate. And then the Berlin Wall came down. Here was her chance. Pippig writes: "After much discussion and reflection Dieter and I came to the same conclusion. Desperate to seek challenges outside of the walls of East Germany, we decided to risk the consequences of violating my responsibilities as a member of the Army Sports Club, and flee the shackles of my country. If caught, I would be considered a deserter. But to us, the potential rewards were worth the perils of failure." On January 5th, 1990, without a dollar in their pocket, Pippig and Hogen drove a small car loaded with three suitcases across the border. Three months after their escape, the harsh political situation in East Germany eased after the Communist Party were voted out and the Christian Democratic Party (CDU) came to power. "As a result," says Pippig, "a general amnesty was declared thus liberating my state of mind to match my being. Finally my vision had come true."

* * *

In April 1990, Pippig began a seven-year love affair with the Boston Marathon. In seven races she went 2nd, 3rd, 3rd, 1st, 1st, 1st, 4th. She also won the Berlin Marathon in 1990, 1992 and 1995. And the New York crown fell to her in 1993. What a career, and what an impact she had made on so many tens of thousands of fans. They were under her spell and for every trademark kiss that Uta blew to a fan towards the end of a race, another heart melted.

Following the Boston Marathon of 1996, this chapter's featured marathon, Pippig writes, with some understatement, that, "my life and running deviated from its intended course". For the next three years, from 1997 to 1999 Pippig battled illness and injury, and to cap it all, on April 29th, 1998, a urine sample of Pippig's was found to have an "unnatural testosterone of epitestosterone ratio". The DLV – based in Leipzig – was responsible for Pippig's subsequent suspension from competition. The DLV's vice president, Theo Rous, noted that Pippig was suspended, not banned, and that her guilt "has not been proven". Twenty-seven months later and still Pippig had not been proven guilty as her case was finally settled.

An investigation into the facts of her case indicates, overwhelmingly, that the

Uta Pippig tells reporters how she won Boston '95. *Pierre Lussatto*

whole affair was a botched job, with major inconsistencies. Pippig was not informed that she was under suspicion until *four months* after her test. Compare this with former Olympic 5000-metres gold-medal winner Dieter Baumann, who was informed immediately that he, too, had failed a doping test, for the steroid nandrolone. The impression conveyed to the public was that Bauman – not only a winner in Barcelona, but a top five finisher in the Seoul and Atlanta – was a model athlete who should retain his present status, while all along receiving unprecedented support from several members of the official doping laboratory at the Cologne Sporthochschule (Sports College). Pippig, by contrast, received not a shred of comparable support.

The attorney-at-law and notary public Jens-Peter Ketels wrote in an open letter to the DLV on December 15th, 1999:

In view of the fact that effective anti-doping measures require the absolute guarantee of a neutral and hence fair investigation, the behaviour exhibited by the Association's chairman and Wilhelm Schänzer, head of the laboratory, and his staff appears totally inappropriate.

Although the athlete Uta Pippig has had to face an investigation which has now lasted more than 20 months, no reasons have yet been given for the July 16th, 1999 decision of the legal committee of the DLV to impose a two-year

419

ban on her. Although evidence of a forbidden substance in Ms Pippig's body has yet to be submitted, and although nothing has been done until now to identify the substance allegedly involved in a concrete manner, Ms. Pippig was not given nearly as much support – particularly as far as exonerating circumstances are concerned – as has now been the case for Mr Baumann.

Ms Pippig was not informed of the suspicion against her until four months after the samples were evaluated. She was robbed of the possibility of immediately undergoing examinations that would have been necessary to make a counter case. The factor is particularly important in Ms Pippig's case because the unanimous opinion of all the experts consulted that the increase in testosterone/epitestosterone quotient observed in her case had pathological causes, failed to convince either the anti-doping commission or the legal committee of the DLV.

Neither the Association's investigation nor the DLV's legal committee cleared up the many contradictions in Ms Pippig's case. The only decisive criterion for the guilty verdict against her was the alleged result of the urine samples, which had been swapped and had leaked; the decision was taken without clearing up the details of the case, without considering the experts' opinions to the contrary submitted in the case, without consulting the doctors treating the athlete, without taking into account the athlete's physical condition when the samples were taken, without comparing the alleged finding with earlier samples and without offering Ms Pippig nearly the kind of support now being given to Mr Baumann.

Pippig herself points to two key factors in her case: she had been on a lot of medication at the time of the test because of lengthy illness, and yet none of these drugs showed up in the test samples. Why was this? Surely this irregularity casts doubt on the accuracy of the tests straight away. Also in an interview with the German newspaper *Frankfurter Allgemeine Zeitung*, the athlete said her hormones were "crazy" because she had recently stopped taking birth-control pills after 15 years.

Pippig of all people is one to shun stimulants since they had been forced on her growing up in the East German system. She has since admitted she took the pills given to her for a short while (since you'd get slung out of the club if you disobeyed), before she spoke to her mother about them. Her mother told her that they were bad for her and to stop immediately. So, although Pippig continued to accept the pills, she stopped taking them. Because she continued to run so well, the officials didn't suspect anything. Finally, it is also important to note that Uta Pippig has taken and successfully passed several other drug tests. Each of her drug tests following her wins in the Boston Marathon from 1994 to 1996, for example, came up clean.

On August 7th, 2000, 27 months into the whole sorry mess, a line was drawn under the matter and a settlement made. The board of arbitration asserted that Pippig's case "wasn't a case of banned drug use." At a Berlin Press Conference, Pippig commented: "I am happy that this case has come to an end." Dieter Hogen commented that the verdict had gone their way: "This means for us that Uta never used illegal substances." Although an all-out acquittal was not forthcoming, the board of arbitration stated that the verdict didn't go in Pippig's favour, nor did it go against her. Pippig decided not to issue a countermove against the DLV. She had been locking horns with Clemens Prokop, the DLV's representative, for the past eight years and explained: "From now on, I can't spend my life talking about the judgement with the team. The training should again be my primary focus."

The whole issue, therefore, ended as a stalemate. Helmut Digel, the president of the DLV defended the judgment in Berlin's *Tagesspiegel* newspaper, stating that: "the article reflects neither an acquittal nor a condemnation." Digel then had to field questions about why the Baumann and Pippig cases were handled so differently. "We have treated all the cases of the past eight years equally," said Digel to the paper. Pippig disagrees: "These cases were handled completely disproportionately. For everything I am being cleared of, I am being totally ignored by the Track and Field Association and its legal commission." Dieter Hogen was even blunter: "Despite all the proof that we have gathered for Uta's innocence, it is an outrage to see what the committee has decided to do in Baumann's case. It is a shame to see such a thing happen in Germany."

All this evidence points to Pippig being an innocent in the war against doping in sport. The 1976 Olympian and *Sports Illustrated* feature writer Don Kardong wrote at the time an article entitled: "All Drug Scandals Are Not Created Equal." Kardong points to the Ben Johnson scandal and acknowledges it *was* a scandal; as was the police discovering a van filled with a cornucopia of pharmaceuticals meant to boost the hemoglobin and speed the recovery of endurance cyclists in the Tour de France. "If cycling takes a lifetime to recover from exposing its squalid underside to the public eye, so be it. They earned that punishment." But, Kardong asks, is the drug bust of Kathy Jager, a 56-year-old masters competitor from Phoenix a scandal? Jager followed doctor's orders and took medication to regulate her hormone levels after the menopause. She wrote down all her medication on her declaration forms. Stupidly, Jager failed to notice that her prescription for methyltestosterone was on the banned list. Naive on Jager's part, yes, but hardly a scandal.

It is a murky and complex issue, and people should be willing to seek out the facts before condemning. We are all guilty of it, from the club runner to the most decorated of sports' writers. They don't come much more decorated than Ian Wooldridge of the British tabloid the *Daily Mail*. He has happily travelled to every Olympics for the last 40 years, but now only writes about athletics to spew venomous scorn over everyone who takes part in it because every one of us, Wooldridge implies may be crooked.

Finally, consider the quagmire that the Association of Tennis Professionals (ATP) are currently in. At the end of 2003, British player Greg Rusedski was accused of taking nandrolone, only to get let off a few months later because, like seven of his predecessors, he had only been taking supplements given out by the ATP in the form of salt tablets. For some reason, these had traces of the banned drug. But is Greg Rusedski, one of the most powerful servers in history, guilty of doping? It seems not. He campaigned vehemently for a fair hearing and he got it. Uta Pippig can only look at a case like this – an athlete, like her, who switched nationalities (from Canadian to British), but had his case heard in his hometown (Montreal) – and wish that she'd been treated in kind.

421

So now – with the sceptics hopefully appeased, or at least enlightened, let us turn to happier times: the seventh greatest marathon race of all time...

* * *

Boston. April 13th, 1996, two days before the 100th running of the granddaddy of marathons. The author went for a final training run with a colleague who had flown over from London for the race. Conditions for the easy six-miler? Poor, bordering on dire. Around minus 6 °C, a vicious blizzard had descended on Beantown and dumped four to six inches of snow on the marathon course. The great British marathoner Ron Hill chose this race to be his 114th and last marathon. He maintains to this day that had the race taken place on April 13th, people would have died; the conditions were that severe.

Sunday before "Super Monday" dawned bright and breezy. The snow started to melt away under the sun's glare. On Tuesday, April 16th, 1996, the day after the marathon, cold, hard, unforgiving, horizontal rain started to fall at first light, and did not let up for twelve hours. If the race had been run on this horrendous day, the medical staff would have been dealing with a massive influx of hypothermia sufferers as well. But on Monday, April 15th, when a world-record 38,706 people turned up for the greatest running festival of all time, there was not a cloud in the brilliant blue sky. Temperatures were mid-50s rising to early 60s. It was a perfect early summer's day. Incredible.

The Boston Marathon had come a long way since Monday, April 18th, 1897, when Tom Burke, the sprinter and double gold-medallist from the Athens Olympics the year before, acted as race starter for the new marathon race. He did a roll call, expecting to hear 18 "ayes!" He got 15 – not bad. Burke was missing a couple of useful tools for his job of setting the runners off: a starting line and a gun. But not to be dissuaded, Burke scuffed a line across the dirt road with the heel of his boot. And then he said, "Go!" The 15 game fellows set off for the city of Boston 25 miles away, and 10 would finish. They were competing not in America's first ever marathon race – as many assume – but its second.

The Knickerbocker AC had sponsored the first American marathon from Stamford, Connecticut, to New York City in 1896 (Derderian). A man named John J. McDermott had won that day, and he was the favourite for the Boston event too. Despite suffering from serious cramps with a couple of miles to go, which required a vicious massage, McDermott did prevail in the inaugural Boston Marathon, in a time of 2:55:10, over 3½ minutes quicker than Spiridon Louis had managed in Athens. McDermott suffered in other ways apart from cramp though. After the race he said: "This will probably be my last long race. I hate to be called a quitter and a coward, but look at my feet." The long hard road had turned them into a bloody pulp. But not only did McDermott return the following year; there was a race to greet him, too. And the amount of starters had rocketed: from 15 to 25. All impressive enough, but who'd have guessed what lay 98 years down the road...

Uta Pippig and Cosmas N'deti came to Boston in 1996 to defend their crowns. N'deti, he of the superb pace-judgement, was looking for an unprecedented four Boston wins in a row. He was boastful and cocky in the lead up to the race. "Take a look at my race number!" N'deti crowed (it was number 1); "this is where I shall finish – number 1!" It seems his Lord Jesus wanted it that way, or so his powerful Christian beliefs persuaded him. But N'deti's confidence was his undoing. Instead of hanging back and patiently waiting to pounce late on in the race, as in previous years, this year he did his pouncing from the gun. As early as two miles, race analyst Frank Shorter pointed out that N'deti was running too fast. He eventually finished third, as countryman Moses Tanui led Kenya to a one–two–three finish.

Would Kenya take the women's race as well? It seemed quite likely. Unlike N'deti, Uta Pippig had been virtually invisible over race weekend. Joan Benoit Samuelson said this was because she was not confident, that she didn't think she could defeat Tegla Loroupe, the double New York champion. Loroupe, who had covered over 33,000 miles of running by the time she was 20 years old, had indeed had a meteoric rise to the top of world marathoning. Now 22, she came to Boston looking to atone for a real disappointment the year before when she had contested for the lead until deep into the race before fading to an agonizing ninth, complaining of a stomach virus. Just days before her defence of the New York crown the following autumn (of '95), Loroupe lost her beloved 33-year-old sister, Albina, from a mysterious malady. "She was an inspiration to me, she gave me a lot of advice," Loroupe said of her sister.

But despite all her troubles, Loroupe boasted impressive form coming into Boston, having won thee half-marathons in Tokyo, Egmond and Lisbon; plus triumphing in the Gasparilla 15K Distance Classic. Loroupe trained in Germany, and the snowy Boston weather didn't faze her. Looking forward to the race, Loroupe said: "I just have to run my own race. I cannot follow somebody else because I cannot depend on someone else's steps when I do not know how much they have put in their training. When I got to halfway last year, I was completely exhausted, I was almost completely out. But now I hope for the best. Physically, I am fine."

This all spelt bad news for Pippig who was feeling the pressure of going for three Boston wins in a row. But in 1994, with a heavy cold the week before, she had still blasted to a magnificent 2:21:45 course record. The following year, she had seen off the attentions of Elana Meyer and Loroupe and won by 100 seconds; comfortable enough in the end. Little could Pippig have ever foreseen just how uncomfortable the 1996 Boston would be.

* * *

Race director Guy Morse had planned this 100th Boston race for three years, and the village of Hopkinton was a seething mass of excited, happy humanity in the hours before the noon start. "This was a day when the backyard of Hopkinton High School was transformed into a road runners' Woodstock," wrote Dan Shaughnessy in the *Boston Globe*. "It was a day when almost 40,000 people attempted to run a marathon – and most of them finished." People wondered how long it would take all 38,000 starters to pass through the narrow start. Half an hour? An hour perhaps? It took just 11 minutes as this dreamy day, with its dreamy weather, just got better and better.

The excitement of the occasion overtook both the front-runners who took off like hares – covering the first mile in a shade over 4:30, and the more leisurely runners like the author – then hoping for a 3-hour clocking – surging through the early miles at around 6-minute pace. If there was one day that people believed they could run fast, then this was it. All of us middle-of-the-pack runners were paying dearly for our exuberance 10 miles on down the road, but we couldn't help ourselves. The Boston Marathon was the place to be if you were a runner, and we were there – and we felt on top of the world. Unlike Uta Pippig.

From very early on in the race, Pippig began suffering from female issues at the worst possible time. She was in agony. This day sent straight from the angels certainly wasn't sprinkling any magic dust on her. "I had some problems with my period," Pippig would later explain. "I didn't expect it would become this bad. After 4 miles I was thinking several times to drop out because it hurt so much." By 6 miles, Pippig was barely hanging on to the lead group of Kim Jones of the United States, Alla Jiliaeva of Russia and Nobuko Funjimara of Japan. Through Framingham and Natick they travelled. "Pippig was in pain," Dan Shaughnessy wrote, "She was a mess. And she thought about dropping out of the race."

The menstruation cramps were followed by torrid diarrhoea, which, as we know, quickly dehydrates the body. With Pippig's body in meltdown, she somehow trotted on. Why she didn't do the *sensible* thing and pull out, only she can answer. Michael Gee in the *Boston Herald* hazarded a guess:

Why is the sky blue? Why do people run marathons at all? Pippig looked inside herself, looked at the letters DNF, and thought – or, more likely, felt – "not me." Confronted with the unthinkable, failure, she chose pain instead.

Pippig was stopping at water stations not to drink, but to freshen up. Distance running, like childbirth, isn't exactly a dainty process. If the champion was going to be beaten, she wanted to keep her dignity.

By halfway, Pippig was not just hanging on, but somehow forcing her wrecked body into the lead. Tegla Loroupe had been watching the German's suffering from some 50 metres back. Now it was time for her to go to work. Loroupe drew up level with Pippig and then slowly eased past. Pippig was unable to respond. Over the next several miles Loroupe built up a lead, metre by metre. By 30 kilometres, Loroupe was 10 metres in front, which became 15 as Heartbreak Hill approached (20 miles). Pippig liked hills, she trained on ones far steeper in Boulder. She charged up Heartbreak, but just as it seemed she'd draw level with Loroupe, Pippig faded – just a little at first, then more dramatically. With 5 miles remaining Loroupe boasted a 100-yard lead. With 3 miles remaining it had more than doubled. Television race commentators started calling the race as hers.

Eight years to the day after the race, the author chatted to Loroupe in a London hotel where she was promoting her charity, The Tegla Loroupe Peace Foundation. I told her of this book, and of her inclusion in it. She beamed. Then I told her the race she featured in and her eyes clouded over: the smiling features replaced by ones of sorrow and confusion.

"You remember the race, of course," I asked.

"Oh, I remember the race; I'll never forget it. It was terrible for me, a terrible race."

"You have a 30-second lead over Uta Pippig with 2 miles to go, and what happened? Your legs cramped up? You were just too exhausted?"

"No!" Loroupe replied, her eyes wide with indignation, "I could have run and run, I was not tired! What happened was I just missed my bottle at the water stop and had to turn and reach for it. As I did so I pulled all these muscles here," – she pointed to her left thigh and midriff – "Suddenly it was very difficult to run fast. There was nothing I could do."

"You heard the crowds yelling? You knew Pippig was drawing near?"

"Yes, I knew she was coming. But the more I would try to speed up, the slower I would run."

None of the press reports the author has consulted refer to this: Loroupe's cramping, yes, but not the reason for it. The reports just indicate that the toughness of Boston's hills had been her undoing, and she had cramped up because she could take no more.

Whatever the case, it wasn't long before Pippig realized there was hope. Her adoring fans roared her on, telling her she could catch the Kenyan. "I thought I could not catch Tegla, she was too far away," said Pippig. "Come on, guys, listen to yourselves, it is such a big gap," she said to the imploring crowd. But spurred on by this electric connection she had with her supporters, Pippig gave chase. "I just kept saying, 'Hey, you can do it, just go. Push, push and try to win the race.'"

The 25-mile marker came and Pippig burst past the faltering Loroupe; the German suddenly looking fresh and full of energy. Dan Shaughnessy wrote:

The images are vivid. Running down Beacon Street, Pippig was gaining on Loroupe as the two ran toward Kenmore. Without breaking stride, Pippig grabbed a water bottle, ripped the plastic yellow top with her teeth, tossed the cap to the pavement, then took a sip. She kept running and gulped again. She raised the bottle to her lips for one final drink, gaining ground with each step.

Her thirst quenched, Pippig spiked the bottle to the ground, then sped past Loroupe like a Miata passing an 18-wheeler on an uphill grade of Route 495. The folks near Kenmore roared.

Pippig knew she had it. She made a crazy "can-you-believe-it?" mug-face at the TV cameras, and then blew her kisses to the crowd. "I could never imagine that I could fly, but all of a sudden, I was flying. It's the nicest win of my life, it's amazing."

Winning her third Boston Marathon in a row, in the most dramatic and breathtaking of circumstances, Uta Pippig cemented her name in sporting Boston folklore. "The marathon is a thing where you never now what's going to happen the nexst moment. It's 26.2 miles and even the last 2 kilometres can change everything," Pippig explained.

Pippig checked into the Boston University Medical Centre for recuperation and tests following the race, and to escape from the inquisitive media and her hoards of supporters. Three days later she attended a press conference and made reporters laugh when she kicked off the questioning herself, asking the reporters, "How do you guys feel?" That was what they wanted to ask her. "Of course I was

The moment that thrilled Beantown: a rejuvenated Uta Pippig catches up long-time leader Tegla Loroupe at 25 miles. *Victah Sailer, Photo Run*

surprised that I won," Pippig explained. "I prepared so hard for this race, so I said, 'you can't stop here.' I slowed down, and looked at the road, and I said, 'you can't drop out.' " Where had Pippig found that incredible inner strength from? someone asked. In response, Pippig gave a snapshot into her past: "When you had to deal with the Stassi [secret police]. That's very difficult – but it made me strong."

Bob Hanna wrote in the Massachusetts paper the *Standard-Times*:

Ten or 20 or 30 years down the road, when people talk about the 100th Boston Marathon, they will talk about Uta Pippig. The two became irrevocably entwined when Pippig burst past Kenyan Tegla Loroupe near the 25-mile mark to win her third straight Boston.

To say she stole the show would be an understatement. This was one of the most courageous performances not only in the history of marathon running, but in the history of sports. This, boys and girls, is one tough lady.

What greater tribute to the millions of runners who have labored over the 26 miles from Hopkinton to Boston for 100 years than the grit and determination exhibited by this 30-year-old refugee from East Germany?

* * *

If Alberto Salazar never quite fully recovered from forcing himself to the very limit at the 1982 Boston, Pippig, it seems, was never quite the same runner either. At the Atlanta Olympics she suffered a bitterly disappointing DNF when her

426

Pippig with the author at the 1997 Boston Marathon prize-giving, where she had been hunting for her fourth win in a row. She got her fourth – fourth place that is. *Pierre Lussatto*

sodden feet in the pouring rain caused her feet to slip in her shoes, and thus her legs to seize up and go into spasm. "I hope you have a tissue," Pippig said, when addressing a crowd of runners in Boulder, Colorado after the Games, wanting to know what had happened. Pippig handled the disappointment better than her parents, who couldn't stop crying when she visited them after the race she was favoured by many to win. "I can run at least," she told them. "There are people out there who would like to run and can't."

Soon it would be Pippig herself who wouldn't be able to run because of her run-in with the DLV. But not until after she had returned to Boston to shoot for a fourth crown in a row. She only managed fourth, as a stress-fracture of her metatarsis over the winter months had held back her progress.

Pippig's drugs ban robbed her of quite possibly the best years of her career, but she has bounced back well over the past few years. She has become a US citizen, run some reasonable races and concentrated on three of her great loves: motivational speaking, charity work – in particular with the Boston-based Dana-Farber Cancer Institute – and nutritional studies, a subject in which she is an expert and gives constant advice. She still loves to run, and there is time for her yet to run some more classy marathons in the masters division; just ask Lorraine Moller and Priscilla Welch. Meanwhile Pippig will continue to bring joy to running fans the world over with her charm, kindness and that "contagious condition: the genuine, gleaming white smile that spreads to everyone around her" (Green).

Race result:

Uta Pippig	GER	2:27:12
Tegla Loroupe	KEN	2:28:37
Nobuko Fujimura	JPN	2:29:24
Sonja Krolik	GER	2:29:24
Larisa Zouzko	RUS	2:31:06
Franziska Rochat-Moser	SUI	2:31:06
Madina Biktagirova	BUL	2:31:38
Alla Jiliaeva	RUS	2:32:32
Valentina Enaki	MOL	2:33:58
Marcia Narloch	USA	2:34:27

Note: A strong headwind kept times slow.

Sources:

Conversations with Tegla Loroupe.
Baker, Jim, in the *Boston Herald*, April 16th, 1996.
Derderian, Tom, *Boston Marathon*. Human Kinetics, 1996.
Green, Woody, essay: Destiny Earned: The Running Life, May 1996.
Gee, Michael, in the *Boston Herald*, April 16th, 1996.
Hanna, Bob, in the *Standard Times* (Massachusetts), April 16th, 1996.
Kardong, Don, in *Sports Illustrated*, November 1999.
Sandrock, Michael, *Running with the Legends*. Human Kinetics, 1996.
Shaughnessy, Dan, in the *Boston Globe*, April 16th, 1996.
Pippig, Uta, quoted in *Frankfurter Allgemeine Zeitung*.
www.uta-pippig.com Uta Pippig web site.

XLV

No. 6 – 1908 Olympic Marathon [Men]

Friday, July 24th

"No Roman of prime ever bore himself better; the great breed is not yet extinct."

Old habits die hard. If present day athletics' officials – deservedly or otherwise – often get short shrift for being stubborn, inflexible individuals, then one should at least be relieved that things have progressed since the 1908 London Olympics. Here, relations between American and British hierarchies descended to a bitter, back-stabbing, name-calling, cringing, moaning, whining nadir. And the track and field officials could certainly be blamed for a fair share of the disputes. Things were most certainly not helped by the startling marathon race that closed the Games – but the wheels had actually come off well before then...

The thoughts of the trainer of the United States' team at the end of the Games seemed to sum up the bitter mood. When asked what message he had for the American people, he muttered: "Just tell them I am glad it is all over." The problems seemed to stem from the fact that everything the Americans did, and everywhere they turned, there appeared to be bias against them, or so they squealed anyway.

H.F. Porter of the Irish-American athletic club, the winner of the high jump, spoke for the American competitors when he said in the *New York Times*:

> In nearly every event the boys had to compete not only against their competitors but against prejudiced judges. The judges may not have been intentionally unfair, but they could not control their feelings, which were antagonistic to the Americans. This was especially true in the field events, where the boys came in closer contact with the judges. The Americans were continually nagged and made uncomfortable. The officials were discourteous to our men, and, further, by their encouragement of the other men, tried to beat us.

Boiling point came on the penultimate day of the Games, with the 400-metre final. David Wallechinsky writes: "Few events in Olympic history have caused as much controversy as the final of the 1908 400 metres in London." The facts of the case are straightforward. There were four finalists for the one-lap final. The hot

429

favourite was Lieutenant Wyndham Halswelle, veteran of the Boer War who, although London-born, was actually a Scot. In his semi-final he ran a scintillating 48.4 for the Olympic record. Twelve years later at the Antwerp Games, the winner there (Bevil Rudd) would be over a second off that time. The Lieutenant's three competitors in the final were to be three Americans: John Taylor, William Robbins and John Carpenter. Alarm bells rang in the minds of the British officials. They panicked. What if the Americans used sharp practice to stop Halswelle winning? What if they somehow ganged up on him? What if they got in his way and stopped him overtaking them?

With this paranoia circling freely, officials were placed at every 20 metres around the track, keeping a beedy eye out for anything remotely suspicious. The race began, and an American, Robbins, zoomed into a 12-yard lead by halfway. This folly was punished as, coming into the home-stretch, he was passed by his teammate, Carpenter, with Halswelle keeping close order. Eighty metres out and the British favourite made his bid for victory. Neatly moving wide of Carpenter, Halswelle began his kick to take himself into the lead. Carpenter, however, had other ideas as he swerved wide to block Halswelle's path.[1] This was just the type of infraction the ubiquitous officials were on the look out for. "Foul!" they yelled. "No race!" and the tape was broken before Carpenter arrived. Taylor, reports Wallechinsky, who seems to have played little part in proceedings, "was physically pulled off the track by officials".

Mayhem followed as adults from opposing nations yelled at each other like spoilt children. The track wasn't cleared for half an hour. Officials disqualified Carpenter, ordered a rerun two days later, and decided to lay down strings on the track to divide the runners.[2] They need not have bothered. There was no way the two remaining Americans were going to have a part in such a circus. So it was that the hapless Halswelle had to tour the lap in embarrassed solitude in 50 seconds flat. Far from his victory bringing him pleasure, it instead brought him such dissatisfaction that he quit all sports and returned to his regiment. Lieutenant Halswelle duly served in the First World War, where he was massacred on the fields of France on March 31st, 1915.

H.F. Porter continued his personal diatribe by writing in *The New York Times*:

Thoughtful men in England have serious doubts, and these doubts are being expressed in some of the most influential newspapers, as to whether the Olympian games serve any good purpose, while theoretically they are supposed to foster international friendship. The result of the meeting just finished has been to create international dissensions and kindle animosities.

All the American officials and athletes now here are convinced that the US was robbed of the 400m run, while the English public at any rate, is equally certain that the American runners had a prearranged plan to keep Halswelle out of first place in that event by fair means or foul.

Despite the conservatism of the press, the English public is imbibed with a

---

1. There were no lane markings in those days.
2. To see how this looks one should consult the movie *Chariots of Fire*.

fierce prejudice against American athletics, which it probably will cherish for years to come.

The Olympiad leaves minor heart-burnings with the representatives of other nations, and altogether, while an athletic success, as a means of promoting international friendship it has been a deplorable failure.

Strong words indeed, but Porter wasn't the only one airing his fury. The American commissioner to the Games, James E. Sullivan, took his vehemence right to the very top with a cablegram to President Roosevelt:

The Olympic Games have not improved the friendly relations of America and England from an athletic standpoint. The governing bodies will be apart in the future. It is a pity that the Amateur Athletic Association [AAA] had control of the Games. It should not have been necessary for America to have to be protesting and protesting, and put in a position where letters were necessary every day. It looked as though the officials of the AAA wanted to control every-thing themselves, and would not take other countries into their confidence. They were working under the old customs, and thought those the best.

I shall never forget as long as I live the scene during the 400m race. The public had been inflamed against the Americans, and the judges, taking a signal from some man on the field, threw up their hands, broke the tape, and called the race off before they knew what had happened. It is ridiculous for them to say that they could see what happened 100 yards away. If Carpenter had fouled Halswelle the judges should have allowed him to finish, and then, if the man at the corner declared a foul, Carpenter could have been disqualified, and the race should have been given to the second man, who was Robbins. Mind you, I am not admitting any foul.

* * *

With all this bad feeling in the air, the marathon race arrived on July 24th. The *New York Times* gave an enthusiastic, if wildly speculative, preview of the race:

The great feature of the Olympiad, at present occupying the attention of the athletic loving public, is to take place today. It is the marathon run, a contest of endurance, covering a stretch of twenty-six and one-third miles, and beside it all other events, which momentarily interest, pale into insignificance. It will attract to the lawn of Windsor castle, the scene of the start, the most superb group of distance runners that the world can offer.

With delicious lack of accuracy the paper went on to predict the main contenders:

The choice of the Americans is Joseph Forshaw, Missouri athletic club, and T.P. Morrisey, Mercury athletic club, Yonkers; Longboat, the great Canadian Indian, who will run under protest, is the choice of the Canadians, and A. Duncan of the Salford Harriers, who won the marathon trial over practically the same course, and Price of the Birchfield Harriers are thought to be sure of finishing first by the British. America will be represented by Weldon Lawrence

431

(YMCA), Sidney H. Hatch (First Regiment AA Chicago); N.J. Ryan, John F. Hayes (Irish American AC); T.P. Morrisey, Joseph Forshaw and Lewis Tewinina (Carlisle Indian School).

Seven runners bold and true – but would they be able to topple the might of the British, or for that matter, the rest of the world?

Before we analyse the actual race itself, it is worth pausing for a moment to inspect how far the runners were to actually travel, because this particular marathon is famous for being the first ever to cover the recognized distance of 26 miles 385 yards. How did this come to be? If anyone would know it is the esteemed British statistician Stan Greenberg, who revealed his research in a spirited letter to *Athletics Weekly* in February 1988. Greenberg, the author of *Olympic Games Records*, wrote:

> Once and for all can we put an end to the fanciful fiction about how the final distance of the 1908 marathon was arrived at? It is a purely media aberration that the so-called extra 385 yards were added so that the race would end in front of the royal box at the old White City stadium.
>
> My researches indicate that the race was always going to finish in front of the King, and that virtually all the changes went on at the other end of the race, in Windsor.
>
> Originally it was due to be a 25 mile race. It was then changed slightly by altering the start point near the bridge. Then the start was changed again to the gates of Windsor Castle.
>
> At the request of the Princess Royal (later Queen Mary) the start was moved a final time to the grounds of the castle, under the windows of the royal nursery. I have spent many hours checking this account and I am certain that it is correct.

"A glorious hot July afternoon" is how the London *Times* described the day of the marathon, although it was quick to point out that the "glorious" part most probably applied to pursuits other than distance running: "...with hardly a breath of wind, [it was] ideal for a bathe or a game of cricket perhaps, but terrible for a feat of endurance of 'wind,' stamina, muscle, and feet, and the task of the men – 26 odd miles over roads in many places hard and dusty, and with the sun blazing down for long times together – seemed to the writer perfectly appalling." So, perhaps not so glorious after all.

The Official Report of the Games indicates that the Oxo Company was in charge of catering to the athletes and in their wisdom put on a lavish spread for the runners during the race: hot and cold Oxo, Oxo and soda, rice pudding, raisins, bananas, soda and milk. Their representatives also provided 'eau de Cologne' and sponges en route. Little wonder then that the *Official Centenary History of the AAA* states these runners were: "The best fed and most fragrant marathon runners in history"!

At just after half-past two the Princess of Wales started the race – and the 55 men, grouped in four rows – headed for their first appointment, the boys of Eton College. "Eton turned out in force to see the men go by," *The Times* reports, "the famous wall where so many historic football games have been fought out was crowded – and the boys seemed most interested, if not wildly enthusiastic." Thomas Jack of Britain led at 2 miles in the absurdly fast time of 10:11 – needless to say he doesn't appear in the list of finishers. Slowing to 15:42 for 3 miles, Jack was followed by more Brits Price and Lord.[3] Either the home nation was displaying a stellar bunch of highly trained human running machines, or else these three – and other British competitors following close behind – were about to perform the ultimate display of en masse crash and burn...

Another Brit, Alex Duncan, could be seen in the leading bunch at 5 miles, but after about 7 miles he was walking. "It was disappointing to find one of Great Britain's champions in trouble so early in the race; but there was a long way to go and anything might happen" (*The Times*). Who knew? Maybe the walk would do Duncan good, perhaps his energy would return and he'd make up the lost ground, and would again feature on the leaderboard. Or maybe not.

The roads to London were lined with people:

In some cases there were a single row perhaps, in others three or four rows; in the towns which one passed through, Windsor, Slough, Uxbridge, and Harrow, and, indeed over all the last part of the course, the spectators were packed as tightly as possible, and then only leaving a part of the road open, but enough to ensure no discomfort to the competitors. And every one excited to see the runners go by.

It was a memorable day, and there seemed to be a feeling that this, after all, was a thing to be seen in one's own country probably once only in a lifetime; for it will be many years before the revived Olympic games are again held in England.[4] As one went past, too, one noticed, of course, all kinds of nationalities and colour; a "turbaned" Turk near Ruislip was watching with intense interest; Japanese, Indians, and Negroes were scattered here and there.

One thing is for sure, *The Times* couldn't get away with descriptions like that today. Nor, one feels, would it want to try.

As the runners trooped along it is reported that the "whole countryside" had turned out to watch, and that the school children, many of whom were waving flags, were the most vociferous with their support. News came of Jack Price arriving at 12 miles in a preposterous 63 minutes. Yet another DNF for the Brits coming right up – indeed a disastrous seven of their eleven starters would fail to finish. The South African Charles Hefferon had watched this comedy of errors by the home nation with interest, but soon it was time to stop being a passive participant and start making an active strike for glory. Hefferon had actually been born in England – in Newbury, Berkshire – but had since moved to South Africa and become a citizen there. From 1904 to 1908 he won the South African 4-mile championship five times in a row. In the trial for the Olympic marathon, Hefferon

---

3. Lord faltered during the 16th mile, got going again, quickly collapsed, got going a mile later and came a creditable 15th, albeit taking a whopping 3 hours and 4 minutes for the final 23 miles.

4. The scribe is forgiven for failing to predict two world wars and the havoc that they would play with the Olympic calendar.

dropped out at 11 miles in a race Kennedy McArthur went on to win. To McArthur's horror, his achievement was ignored by the selectors and it was Hefferon who was sent to England. McArthur, of course, got his just deserts four years later when he went on to win in Stockholm.

Soon after the halfway mark of the race *The Times* reports: "At this time Hefferon was running beautifully and seemed quite fresh, and before Harrow was reached he had established a long lead, with Longboat [1907 Boston champion but who would fail to finish here at the 17 miles], Appleby [yet another UK drop-out] and the Italian Dorando Pietri who had been going most gamely, behind him.

As at Eton, the boys of Harrow school were out in large numbers, and a little further down the road, just before Sudbury Hill, it was time for Longboat to hand in his chips. He refused to go quietly though and his tactics in his moment of doom resemble those of a seven-year-old tackling his first cross-country run: "round the famous hill there was one rather nasty bit to climb – Longboat was walking. He was second, in front of Pietri, and twice as the latter got near to him, he went away at a run; but Pietri eventually got past."

By mile 18, Hefferon had taken a healthy lead, and by the 19th he was a full minute ahead; but a mile or so later, even he was heard to be struggling. Between Sudbury and Harlesden (miles 21–23) Hefferon kept his lead, with Pietri forever creeping up to him, and Hefferon looking a "sorry plight". At 24 miles Hefferon dropped into a dejected walk and Pietri shimmied past. Pietri was a confectioner who resided in the city of Carpi. He had trained himself for the race without any supervision. He was the Italian long-distance champion and had won the Paris Marathon the previous year.

Meanwhile the stadium waited patiently for the runners while being entertained by the sight of "pole jumpers flinging themselves over the bar the height of two tall men, the high diver shooting gracefully through the air in the centre, and the wrestlers struggling on the mat at the other end." Carriages of the westbound trains were filled to overflowing, and by 3 p.m. practically every seat all around the ground was filled. The mighty concourse of men and women, packed in dense masses from the edge of the bicycle track up to the top row of seats high up against the sky, was "a wonderful and inspiring sight". "Clear the course for the Marathon race," came the announcement through the megaphone. *The Times* reports:

> There is a continual clamour of tens of thousands of people talking and shouting. There is an indescribable thrill of excitement in the air. Five o'clock comes and goes – they ought really to be here. Suddenly at the top of the far-off stand they begin to clap; but it is a false alarm. It is a wonderful moment. All these thousands of people waiting to see one man drag his tired legs over the 200 yards of the track at the end of a 26-mile run – the crowning moment of these great Olympic Games.

At last Dorando Pietri arrived. But the 2 miles since he'd taken out Hefferon had not translated into a carefree victory march. Instead, they had hurt badly. He appeared, tired, dazed, bewildered and hardly conscious, in red shorts and white vest, his hair turned white from the dust, he staggered on to the track. He looked

Dorando Pietri claimed after the race that he could have finished unaided. Not if this telling image is anything to go by, in which the Italian appears to be out for the count. *Bettmann/CORBIS*

about him, hardly knowing where he was. The tape lay shimmering 200 yards in the distance. Pietri covered 50 yards, then 100, then 150, surely he'll make it now. But no:

> Fifty yards. And he cannot even do that. He falls on the track, gets up, staggers on a few yards and falls again and yet again; and then he reaches the last turn. The goal is in sight, though his closed eyes cannot see it. He is surrounded by officials almost, if not quite, supporting him, urging and cheering him on. If they were not there he would fall. He cannot run straight. And yet 50 yards from the end he suddenly bursts into a pathetic, almost a horrible, parody of a spurt, drops again ten yards from the tape, rises, staggers forward over those last terrible few yards, and has reached the goal (*The Times*).

Inevitably, the American supporters and officials had been following this grisly little cameo with intense interest; and their interest was only heightened when the next man to trot into the stadium was one of theirs. It was Johnny Hayes, and compared to Pietri he seemed fresh, strong and was obviously performing an action known as running, not some strange vaudeville act like his predecessor. Indeed, Hayes had run a magnificently judged race and positively bounded through the finish line. So had several of the Americans – no fewer than four

Pietri staggers through the line aided by a steadying arm. *Hulton Archive/Getty Images*

John Hayes arrived half a minute down on Pietri, full of running. *Hulton Archive/Getty Images*

found their way to a top-ten finish, some more comfortably than others: "They come in, one after the other, Americans, Indians, Canadians, none of them, happily, in the same dreadful state as Pietri, but with a bewildered look on their faces, drawn and pale with exhaustion, as though wondering what they are doing. It seems as if the first Englishman will never come." Indeed one had to wait until William Clarke finally appeared in twelfth place, 21 minutes after Hayes. The pitiful list of accomplishment for the home nation reads: 12th, 13th, 15th, 17th, DNF, DNF, DNF, DNF, DNF, DNF, DNF.

The Americans immediately appealed about Pietri receiving aid to finish, but disgracefully it was decided to postpone the enquiry until after the medal ceremony. Therefore, instead of Hayes having the satisfaction of seeing his flag

436

raised, the Italian flag went up instead. Thereafter the American appeal was heard and Pietri was quickly disqualified. *The Times* reports:

> The unfortunate man had his agonized struggle to no purpose. Altogether the finish of the race was far from satisfactory. The rule about attendants not being allowed on the course was flagrantly broken. The position of those in authority was undoubtedly difficult. It seemed inhuman to leave Pietri to struggle on unaided, and inhuman to urge him to continue.
>
> It did not seem right that thousands of people should witness a man suffering as he did. It seemed hard that he should lose the victory after having reached the stadium so long before any one else. And yet, after all, the race was not to the stadium entrance, but to the finish in front of the royal box, and it is extremely doubtful whether, by his own unaided exertions, Pietri could ever have got so far.

The next day, Pietri returned to the stadium to receive a special trophy in recognition of his efforts. From the "pitiable, tottering, agonized wreck" of 24 hours earlier, the little Italian confectioner now appeared as a quiet, self-possessed, sturdy young man, and became an instant hero to the masses. A mighty roar went up from the whole assembly as he made his way to the tail end of the procession of prize-winners, and the shouts and cheers and cries of applause and sympathy were renewed again and again when it came to his turn to climb up the broad red-carpeted steps, placed almost exactly where he had fallen for the last time at the end of his struggle, and received from the hands of England's Queen a beautiful cup, her own personal gift, with which "her woman's heart had prompted her to mark the sympathy which, in common with all who saw the tragic finish of the race, she felt for his pluck and his disappointment" (*The Times*).

To this day the Brits love the plucky loser, and they certainly did nearly 100 years ago. Not even the cheers for Hayes as his teammates paraded him on their shoulders around the stadium could compete with the noise made for Pietri. "And now – the bathos of it," *The Times* reported, "– the man who has been so signally honoured is to supply a music-hall turn.[5] Verily we are a strange nation."

So what of the runners who competed – how did they "read" it all? Bronze-medal winner, Joseph Forshaw, the second American to finish, and who was but 64 seconds behind Hefferon, was freshest of all after the race. He intriguingly told the *Associated Press*:

> I was next to the last man to leave Windsor. My instructions were to keep Tewanina [USA] with me, and if I weakened to send Tewanina along to win the race if he could do so. I held back until about eleven miles from the finish, nursing Tewanina along, who was suffering from bad knees. We passed men time after time. Duncan, the Englishman who was expected to win the race was left behind at Uxbridge. Tewanina, when he saw Duncan ahead, went up to tire

---

5. Was Pietri abandoning his amateur values and getting sucked into the world of commercialism right before our very eyes? No, he claimed. Although he *had* signed the contract (under stress of his first emotion) and could not withdraw from it, he would only appear for a single week and would devote the entire proceeds to charity.

him out, which from what I have heard since, he succeeded in doing.

Not until I reached the Scrubs did I know that I was well up with the leaders. I fact, I did not know how many men were in front of me until then. The people who lined the course treated us finely, and they were of great assistance in cheering us up and giving a man heart to run through lines of sportsmen such as turned out to give us a cheer as we passed. Of course I am tired, but there is no stiffness.

Forshaw, who spent his life in the Midwestern United States, went on to appear in three Olympics, finishing twelfth at the Intercalated Games of Athens in 1906 in a time of around 3:30, and also competing at Stockholm in 1912, where he squeezed into the top ten with a 2:49 clocking.

Hayes' description of his adventure is equally thoughtful and enlightening, as he described what food and drink he took on:

I took nothing to eat or drink on the journey; I think to do so is a great mistake. Before starting I partook of a light luncheon consisting of two ounces of beef, two slices of toast, and a cup of tea. During the race I merely bathed my face with Florida water and gargled my throat with brandy.

I ran my own race throughout, covering in almost mechanical fashion the first five or six miles at a rate of six minutes per mile. After that I went as hard as I could to the finish. Ten miles from home I was ten minutes behind the leader, and then I began to go through the field. I passed Hefferon on nearing the stadium, but saw nothing of Pietri until I entered the arena. I smoke and drink only in moderation.

Hayes' teammates hoist him up aloft a table and parade him around the stadium. *IOC Olympic Museum/Getty Images*

John J. Hayes was born in New York City of Irish parents on April 10th, 1886. He was formerly a member of St Bartholomew's Club, where he developed into a good long-distance runner. He later joined the Irish-American Athletic Club, under whose colours he competed. He took part in many long-distance events, but did not figure in any race of national importance until the previous May when he finished second to Thomas Morrissey in the Boston Marathon. Hayes prepared for the 1908 Olympic marathon on the cinder path on the roof of the Bloomingdale building, Fifty-ninth Street and Third Avenue, where his employer installed a cinder-path track, so as to enable Hayes to train during the night without interfering with his work in the store, where he was employed. In addition to being one of the youngest competitors at the Olympiad he was also one of the smallest – 5 foot 3 inches in height and just 125 pounds. He was described as quiet and very mild mannered, and "popular with his business associates and the members of the Irish-American AC" (*New York Times*).

And what about Pietri? How did he feel when it became obvious he was going to win? How did it feel when it suddenly became less obvious? And how did he feel when he had it all taken away?: "I felt all right until I entered the stadium. When I heard the people cheering and knew I had nearly won, a thrill passed through me and I felt my strength going. I fell down, but tried to struggle to the tape but fell again. I never lost consciousness of what was going on, and if the doctor had not ordered the attendants to pick me up I believe I could have finished unaided." On the morning of the race he had a meal of beefsteak and a cup of coffee with a view to building up his strength for the strain. It was a larger breakfast than he had been accustomed to and Pietri indicated that this breach of the ordinary rule may have had something to do with his collapse.

*   *   *

If there was a shred of doubt as to the identity of the winner, the *New York Times* made sure it wasn't going to come from them. Their straight-talking, no-frills headline told it how it was:

> The Italian, Dorando, assisted over the line in lead,
> collapses and is disqualified.

And then, in block letters, *screaming* at the reader:

HAYES FRESH AT THE FINISH

The report began: "Americans are joyful, having taken first, third, fourth and ninth in the long race." And continued:

It would be no exaggeration in the minds of any of the 100,000 spectators who witnessed the finishing struggle of the marathon race, won by John J Hayes of New York, at the Olympian arena today to say that it was the most thrilling athletic event that has occurred since that marathon race in ancient Greece, where the victor fell at the goal and, with a wave of triumph, died.

The veteran athletes of Europe, America, Africa, and Australia, who have seen the greatest struggle of every sort on land and water for athletic supremacy, declared that there was nothing comparable to the great race today with their memories or in the other Olympiads since the modern cycle of these began.

Since the beginning of the Olympic Games, the great rivalry has been between England and America, and Englishmen consoled themselves for all the American successes by the thought that in the domain of long-distance running they always had been supreme, and whatever prizes they failed to grasp, in this [the marathon] the colonials would pick up.

439

The *NY Times* then calmed down a little from this elated state to pay tribute to Pietri. Although Hayes, they noted, ran and won a good race, the real hero of the day was Pietri:

> The admiration and sympathy of every person in the stadium went out to the gallant Italian, who, although he did not win, deserved to win and did more within the limit of his powers than any other man who ran.
>
> It is a question whether public opinion will ever support another marathon race here. Pietri's condition when he finished, and the condition of many of the contestants in todays event, lead people to think it is worse than prizefighting or bullfighting.

Sir Arthur Conan Doyle, the great writer and creator and Sherlock Holmes, was present at the finish line and was even one of those to help tend to the ailing Pietri.[6] Sir Arthur wrote:

> I think in that great assembly not any man would have wished to see victory torn at the last instant from the plucky little Italian. Thank God he is on his feet again, the little red legs going incoherently, but drumming, hard driven by the supreme will within. There is a groan as he falls again, a cheer as he restaggers to his feet. It is horrible, yet fascinating, this struggle between a set purpose and an utterly exhausted frame. Surely he is done now; he cannot rise again.
>
> From under the archway has darted a second runner, Hayes, the stars and stripes on his breast, going gallantly and well with his strength. There are only twenty yards – if the Italian can do it. He staggers up, no trace of intelligence upon his set face, and again the red legs break into their strange automatic amble. Will he fall again? No, he says and balances; then he is through the tape into a score of friendly arms. He has gone to the extreme of human endurance. No Roman of prime ever bore himself better; the great breed is not yet extinct.
>
> I confess I cannot see how the judges could come to any other decision, and yet the tragedy remains. It was, as matters stood, a fair and square win for the American, since without help Pietri must have lain senseless on the track.

On the subject of the Americans, Sir Arthur laces his words with so much sugary topping to have even the sweetest of pallets flinching: "These Americans specialize, and yet they retain the remarkable appearance of all-around excellence. There is no hypertrophy of special muscle; all is symmetry and balance, beauty and grace."

Concluding this review of how the media interpreted Dorando's adventure, let us end with the thoughts of the squeamish views of the New York *Daily News'* editorial:

> Nothing more painful or deplorable was ever seen at a public spectacle. It was painful in the exhibition of human exhaustion; deplorable in the exhibition of official folly. It may be questioned whether so great a trial of human endurance

---

6. Doyle originally trained as a doctor, but gave up medicine in 1890, after his first Sherlock Holmes book, *A Study in Scarlet*, was published.

should be sanctioned. We hope the stadium authorities will severely repudiate the action of the officials who helped the Italian. We congratulate America on her compete and conclusive victory. It left England entirely out of the reckoning.

Simmering under all the excitement, a large question remained. What had the marathon done to affect the rocky relationship between Britain and America? After the race, rumours abounded that the British officials had been so attentive in their efforts to get Pietri round the track by fair means or foul because they were aware that Hayes was closing fast...and anything had to be done to prevent an American winning the big race. One person who certainly had his suspicions was James E. Sullivan, the American commissioner to the Games whose thoughts in a cablegram to President Roosevelt we have already seen this chapter. Sullivan went on to compare how the officials behaved in the 400-metre final and the marathon:

Look how differently they acted yesterday. Although the officials themselves had broken the most important rule governing the marathon race by helping Pietri, the tape was not broken, and the Italian was allowed to finish. Pietri should have been taken from the track and the tape left for Hayes, the actual winner, to break. Plucky man as Pietri is, Hayes was the winner under all the rules of racing. It was inhuman to drive that man around the track in the condition he was in, and it was unfair to Hayes, who was robbed of the honor of breasting the tape.[7]

* * *

By the Monday after the Games had closed, emotions were cooling and the *New York Times* was sanguine enough to quote a blurb from the London *Daily Mail* which philosophised that perhaps all and sundry had become a little too worked up in the heat of the battle. The *Mail*'s editorial said: "After all, the number of unpleasant incidents is surprisingly small, and the initial feeling may be removed by second thoughts and fuller information. Perhaps with Olympic Games, as with peace conferences, they may not realize the highest hopes of their projectors, yet they help the world forward." Hear, hear.

So what became of Hayes and Pietri after the Games? Hayes turned professional, along with Pietri. They began colliding at flashy venues like New York's Madison Square Garden. Riël Hauman reports on the first match-up between the two: "The two contestants tossed a coin for the starting position; Hayes won and took the inside position. Pietri pulled away after 25 miles. After the 26th mile spectators, thinking the race was over, streamed onto the track and blows had to be resorted to in order to clear a path for the runners. After the race Pietri indicated that he had shown that he was indeed the better runner." Just one month later, Pietri took on Tom Longboat at the same venue, and remarkably,

7. When one studies the medals table for the 1908, it appears that the Americans were indeed unbeatable in athletics, whatever barriers came in their way. Interestingly, although the UK won 38 gold medals to America's 22 in all other sports, the medal count in track and field read US 33, UK 17.

collapsed again during the 26th mile, and was carried to the dressing room uncon-
scious. But this time he received $3750 for his efforts! On November 25th, 1908,
he again defeated Hayes at the Garden, running 2:44:20. He and the American
had to negotiate an absurd 260 laps of the track.

Back in Italy, Pietri was celebrated with poems and festivals. He ended up
defeating Hayes four times, and his best time over the marathon ended up being
2:38:48 in Buenos Aires in May 1909 – on a course 205 metres long. When he
retired he had won 88 out of the 128 races in his career (both amateur and pro),
and 8 out of 17 marathons (Hauman). Pietri retired in 1911, but his considerable
wealth soon evaporated, due mainly to a light-fingered brother. The rest of his
days were spent resting his fleet feet – behind the wheel of a taxi. He died in San
Remo on February 7th, 1942.

Johnny Hayes outlived Pietri by 23 years and popped up after his racing days
were over as the marathon coach for the US team at the 1912 Olympics.
However, it appears his man-management skills weren't as adroit as his running.
The great Clarence DeMar who was on that team writes furiously about the
henpecking interference of the coaches at the Stockholm Games, which, DeMar
says, led to many of the team running lame and being "hopelessly outclassed".
DeMar returned to the Olympics twelve years later, but he wasn't going to have
Johnny Hayes – or anyone else – interfering with his training. DeMar wrote to the
new marathon coach and ordered that "he must not bother me on the trip".
Finally, the coach replied that there would be no trouble.

The highly impressive amateur marathon record of Hayes reads:

1906	Boston	5th	2:55 (circa 24.5 miles)
1907	Boston	3rd	2:30 ,,
1907	Yonkers	1st	2:44 ,,
1908	Boston	2nd	2:26 ,,
1908	Olympics	1st	2:55 (26.2 miles)

Race result:

John Hayes	USA	2:55:18
Charles Hefferon	SOA	2:56:06
Joseph Forshaw	USA	2:57:10
Alton Welton	USA	2:59:44
William Wood	CAN	3:01:44
Frederick Simpson	CAN	3:04:28
Harry Lawson	CAN	3:06:47
Johan Swanberg	SWE	3:07:50
Lewis Tewanima	USA	3:09:15
Kaarlo Nieminen	FIN	3:09:50

Note: Dorando Pietri (ITA); 2:54:46 was disqualified.

Sources:

Daily Mail, July 25th, 1908.

DeMar, Clarence, *The Clarence DeMar Story*. Cedarwinds Publishing Co., 1937.

Doyle, Sir Arthur Conan, letter to the *New York Times*, July 25th, 1908.

Greenberg, Stan, letter to *Athletics Weekly*, February 1988.

Hauman, Riël, *Century of the Marathon*. Human & Rousseau, 1996.

Martin, David and Roger Gynn, *The Olympic Marathon*. Human Kinetics, 2000.

New York Daily News, July 25th, 1908.

New York Times, July 21st–27th, 1908.

The Times, July 21st–27th, 1908.

Wallechinsky, David, *The Complete Book of the Olympics*. Aurum Press, 2000.

XLVI

No. 5 – 1982 Commonwealth Games Marathon [Men]

Friday, October 8th

Down-and-out Deek delves deep.

Aussies love a sporting hero. Multi-Olympic swimming champion Ian "Flipper" Thorpe is currently the most revered sportsman in the nation and has reached a degree of popularity tasted only by the rare few. National cricket captain Mark Taylor was an astoundingly popular character, while Pat Rafter was the darling of the Australian tennis scene for several years, annually bringing agony to Melbourne's Flinders Park when he'd capitulate, or cramp up, or both, at the Australian Open. And of course there's the inimitable Cathy Freeman and *that* night at the Sydney Olympics. Super Monday. The pressure on Freeman's shoulders must have been unbearable; for it may be nice to be an Australian when you win, but it's doubly nasty when you lose.

A similar pressure to Freeman's rested upon the shoulders of François Robert de Castella – known to the running fraternity as "Deek" – on the evening of October 7th, 1982, the night before the Commonwealth Games marathon, to be held in Brisbane. The world-record holder at the time after his brilliant win at the Fukuoka Marathon the previous December (2:08:18), most Australians expected the 25-year-old biophysicist to end the successful Games with a golden flourish.

It seemed wherever one looked in the Australian sporting media of 1982 that one image beamed back: de Castella's. Born on February 27th, 1957, to Rolet and Anne de Castella, Rob was just eleven when he started accompanying Rolet on his early morning jogs. At 14 he began attending the acclaimed Xavier College in Melbourne where he was taught history by Pat Clohessy, a former top Australian middle-distance runner and coach of the cross-country team. Author Michael Sandrock writes: "He knew how to coach; Deek had the motivation to run; and beginning in 1971, they formed one of the most productive, rewarding coach/ athlete relationships ever." Deek, or "Tree" as his other nickname goes, due to his thick, muscular legs which have been likened to Australian gum trees, didn't run his first marathon for eight years after Clohessy had first met him. But then he ran three marathons in a year, steadily progressing with each one: the Victoria Marathon, 2:14:44; the Australian Champs, 2:13:23; and the Olympic trials, 2:12:24. After a wobble at the Moscow Olympics, Deek ran to another big PB in the 1980 Fukuoka race, a 2:10:44, and then dedicated 1981 to a return trip to the

Fukuoka race. His patience and focus paid off. With many 120-mile weeks under his belt, and a 13:34 5000-metres clocking, Deek came to Japan ready. Tough American front-runner Gary Bjorklund ran 15-minute 5Ks to 30K, assuming there wouldn't be anyone around by then, but he was wrong, as Deek suddenly surged by. "BJ" recalls: "When you're in the company of a de Castella and he has a flyer going, and he puts the hammer down and runs away from you when you're running as fast as we were, you can only shake your head." This was indeed the race that made de Castella an international force, as his 2:08:18 became the new world record. "Nearly every top marathoner in history has run that course, and to take 1:19 off Clayton's record is pretty awesome," Deek crowed.

*   *   *

However, the public were ignorant of de Castella's conditioning upon coming into the 1982 Commonwealth Games, as author Mike Jenkinson explains:

> Deek felt rundown and tired, with an irritated spinal disc. The couple [Deek and wife, Gayelene] had moved house in Canberra about four weeks earlier and the back trouble had begun, apparently, as a strain from shifting furniture. It had worsened after an otherwise encouraging 48km run and he was in such discomfort he had to stop training for two days and endure the mental stress of a further two days on sharply reduced mileage.

Up until Brisbane, one of the first major races of Deek's career was the 1980 Moscow Olympics, which he went into with heavy legs and rather unwell. He'd fallen into the trap of over-training and placed an underachieving tenth. On the eve of the Commonwealth Marathon, Deek was greatly concerned that he'd committed the same error again.

The day before the marathon, Brisbane's *Daily Sun* gave a potted form of the race:

Rob de Castella (no. 28) Australia
With a time of 2:08:18 and a great competitive record, he is the man to beat. Under great pressure though.
Juma Ikangaa (623) Tanzania
The 20-year-old African champion is claimed by his countrymen to be better than defending Games champion Gidamis Shahanga.
Michael Gratton (233) England
From a country where 20,000 people start in a single marathon. His selectors have judged him one of their best.
John Graham (577) Scotland
De Castella rates him among his strongest rivals, but he has been ill recently.
Kevin Ryan (505) New Zealand
A classy international performer slipping into the veteran class, but ran a career best last time out. Dangerous.
Gidamis Shahanga (629) Tanzania
The defending champion and superb winner in the 10,000m on the track last weekend. Will take some beating.

Making a dash for it: With just a few minutes on the clock, Tanzanian tearaways Juma Ikangaa (left) and defending champion Gidamis Shahanga have opened up a gap on the main pack. *Mark Shearman*

Of these runners, I asked Deek over 20 years later whom he personally feared the most: "John Graham was definitely someone to look out for and I had a whole lot of respect for the Tanzanians. Shahanga was defending champion and I'd seen what Ikangaa was capable of, although this was his major break-through."

De Castella's timetable the night before the race was delightfully quirky. Bed at 8.45 p.m. for a fitful sleep. Rise at 1.30 a.m. to make a few slices of toast and chat with room-mate. Back to bed at 2 a.m., and doze till 3.45 a.m. when he awakes and begins to dress for the day ahead. At the spartan hour of 0445, the marathon competitors boarded the bus for the ride to the start/finish in Stanley Street, on the banks of the Brisbane River.

The start was set for 6 a.m. and 3000 spectators were on hand to see the gun go off. Although the morning was cool, the humidity was a menacing 94 per cent. A fast time was, theoretically, not on. Three Africans (Ikangaa, Shahanga and Kenyan Sammy Mogare) set off as though they were contesting the 1500-metres final and de Castella breathed a sigh of relief that pace-making duties would not fall to him.

After 10 kilometres the Africans had settled and their lead was whittled down to just 5 seconds, but upon noting this, instead of settling back into the pack, as de Castella expected, the Tanzanian pair "shot off like a pair of startled rabbits", running kilometers 10–15 in 15:13 to Deek's 15:23. They were now out of sight and this psychological burden of not being able to see the leaders then remained with the Australian for the next 23 kilometres. But he didn't panic.

At around the half-marathon mark the leaders dashed past the Crest Hotel and an anxious Gayelene de Castella. After they passed she waited nearly a full minute for even a glimpse of her husband. "I thought he had lost it at that stage," Gaylene recalls. "They had such a lead...all that training. I felt sad for him. No one could pick up so much time and win." Deek's coach Pat Clohessy was more clinical in his judgement: "I just thought the Africans were running too fast and were sure to slow up. On the other hand Rob was running fast enough and he looked really good."

447

The grim chase: Kevin Ryan 505, Graham Laing 579, Rob de Castella 28 and John Graham 577 get their heads down and try to keep the leaders in sight. *Mark Shearman*

De Castella ran kilometres 20–25 in a pacy 15:13, which surely would have brought him some way back into the race. But instead he'd leaked two more precious seconds. It was at this stage he decided he'd have to leave the comfort of the chasing pack and go rabbit-hunting alone. "From here on I really started to compete," Deek said, "I attacked the hills much more aggressively."

As the string of runners passed along Coronation Drive in front of a noisy crowd of 6000, Jenkinson writes: "Some of them had been up drinking all night in anticipation of the big race and clapped and shouted encouragement but Rob detected disappointment amongst the clamour." Deek thought: "I could sense they were resigned to me coming third, but I thought I could catch them. I didn't know if I would, but I thought I could."

Kilometres 30–35 brought some of the course's hills into play, which suited Deek who has said in the past that hill training is the best sort of preparation one can do. And he'd come prepared. However, although he attacked the topography around St Lucia near the university boldly, he was still a daunting 58 seconds in

448

arrears with less than 10 kilometres to go. Jenkinson writes: "This was the stage when the cold fingers of doubt took hold of Clohessy." For his part, Clohessy recalls:

When Rob didn't appear to be making up any ground and Tanzanians were still going well, I began to get really worried. The day before, when we had planned the race, Rob said he wanted to make a big effort at about 25 kilometres and I had said, "No, wait. The last 10 kilometres will be the time to pour it on." Now I began to wonder I hadn't given the wrong advice. For about ten minutes I couldn't get any information on how far he was behind and I was worried all right.

Deek tells the author: "I remember being startled at Pat's look of concern when I passed. When I saw that look I began to run in a completely different way." How did your concern about the deficit and of letting your country down haunt you? I asked. His reply is revealing to the thinking of a champion: "It didn't. You must have 100 per cent positive conviction in the marathon. The moment you let a negative thought creep into your mind it immediately becomes magnified and the task becomes difficult to bear."

Kilometres 33–35 arrived and finally the strain was beginning to tell on the leaders. Shahanga was losing ground on his countryman on every hill, while Ikangaa ran the University loop 20 seconds slower than the Australian. Things started to happen very quickly to Deek now, alternating between the good and bad. A good thing was that he finally caught sight of the leaders, but the bad was that they looked so far ahead Deek remembers it seeming as though they were in a different race. Then the mild nausea he had been feeling turned into knifing pain in the stomach. This lasted around half a mile as Deek recalls: "I had felt some stomach discomfort from the early stages but it became worse when I ran up a very sharp hill along Sir Fred Schonell Drive. I couldn't run easily but I didn't dare slow too much. I had to let go of my bowels and there was some diarrhoea, but it was mostly wind. I ran through the pain which lasted about 700 metres."

With the sight of a tiny figure in green shorts appearing on TV monitors behind the leaders, Clohessy leapt to his feet shouting. "He's closing! He's closing!" It was a television image that thrilled Australia, and a thousand kilometres away on Sydney's Harbour Bridge "distracted commuters brought traffic to a halt" (Jenkinson). With 5 kilometres to go, de Castella finally caught the valiant Shahanga who didn't even have the puff left for a token resistance; but the real drama had only just begun. Ikangaa was now only 80 metres ahead, his stride remained fluid, but the grimace on his face betrayed the fact that he'd tried to run one of the greatest marathons in history, and he wasn't quite ready to throw in the towel yet.

As de Castella came upon Ikangaa's shoulder the fans cheered and surged towards the street – this is what they'd stayed up all night to see. Ikangaa recalls: "I heard the shouts 'Castella, Castella' and I knew the moment had arrived for him to overcome me." But Ikangaa refused to just lie down and instead injected a sharp and immediate surge. De Castella was unfazed by such a brazen tactic: "Either he's got a lot left or else he's not being very sensible," he thought. He suspected it was the latter but was hesitant to stay back lest Ikangaa find the momentum and hope to gather his resources. Deek drove back and then stormed on into the lead. But Ikangaa put in yet another spurt of his own and recaptured the lead. Mike Jenkinson writes: "So they slugged it out for a kilometre, a desperate, riveting duel between two depleted but utterly determined men. Rob took the lead for a third time and was able to pry a little gap." Deek's time for the 35 to 40-kilometre stretch was an astounding 15:03. "I was amazed at my time for this 5 kilometre, especially as I had so much pain and couldn't run easily because of the cramp for most of it," he explains.

Over the final 2195 metres Deek worked at widening the gap over the brilliant little Tanzanian. Was he feeling strong or exhausted during this time? A bit of both: "Although my legs felt weary, I still had my strength left. When we were side by side I knew it was all looking better for me." Deek suggests to the author that Ikangaa panicked when he turned and saw Deek running him down: "He just need to tuck in behind me – that would have given him a better chance. His change of pace was a sign of panic."

Ecstasy and relief for Rob de Castella as he meets the demands of a nation. *Mark Shearman*

Turning onto Stanley Street, crammed with thousands of chanting fans, de Castella only felt certain of victory in the final 50–100 metres. He allowed himself to wave to the crowd as he crossed the line, finishing in 2:09:18, just 60 seconds off his world best. With humidity at a crucifying 100 per cent that morning, it was arguably the greatest marathon ever run. The brave Ikangaa followed on just 12 seconds behind. In the euphoric scenes that followed with Clohessy and Gayelene, Deek told the adoring press: "I thought I was going to blow it, but Pat had told me the race would be decided in the last 10 kilometres. We judged it well...it was spot on. I had a stitch and was a little worried with 9 kilometres to go, but I felt strong and knew I could keep going till the finish." As for the Africans, they were clearly landing on the world scene but some of their naivety had Deek perplexed. He asked their coaches why the runners never stopped at water stations, and was told that it was to retain rhythm. Madness. Ikangaa also stated: "If I had known de Castella's finishing power, I wouldn't have run so slow for the first half of the race." Deek was quick to pour scorn on such a fancy: "If he had gone any faster he would just have died earlier. I would have caught him at an earlier stage of the race, that's all."

Many of the press wrote about how fresh and pain-free Deek appeared at the race's end, but looks can be deceiving he assures the author: "You have to remember that most of my opponents weighed around 55 kilos, and I was near 70! I'm sure I was doing significant damage to my body and ultimately I was hurting. But I guess I just didn't show it." Deek remarks on how important this race was in the history of the marathon: "It was a race that opened people's eyes to the mystique and unpredictable nature of the marathon. Before people didn't understand how dramatic it was and how fortunes could change so quickly. The spectators probably did think I'd had it. One minute is a long time to wait when you're standing by the side of the road." Deek acknowledges that the race was *the* turning point in his career: "Before then I was well known as a sportsman – suddenly I was a bit of a hero."

$$* \quad * \quad *$$

The hard and fast running Ikangaa never did manage to truly control his enthusiasm in the big marathons. Three times he was a runner-up in Boston, and for someone with so much talent he should have won more than he did. He does, however, frequently crop up throughout the pages of this book since his brave, fearless front-running was the catalyst for many superb marathons, and a nod must go to his terrific 2:08:00 to take the New York crown of 1989. He had been "learning from my mistakes", he said afterwards.

As for Deek, 1983 would prove to be another exceptional year. He warmed up for the inaugural World Championships at Helsinki with a quite stunning performance at Rotterdam in April. In what was ultimately a staged race billed by IMG as the battle between the two great heavyweights of world marathoning, Deek and Alberto Salazar, one man was overlooked: track star and future Olympic marathon champion Carlos Lopes. Although Salazar could place just fifth here, the race was anything but an anti-climax.

Top British marathoner Hugh Jones remembers watching the race on television. "I just can't believe that de Castella won that race," says Jones. "Here was Lopes with far superior speed [and a track 10K PB nearly a minute quicker], dead level with de Castella with a kilometre to go. He was surely hot favourite. But unbelievably, de Castella was still able to burn him off." Indeed, Deek had ensured that the brutal 5 kilometres between 35 and 40 run in 14:39 would mean that the sting from Lopes' kick would have been dulled. "With 500 metres to go, I just put my head down and ran as hard as I could," Deek explains. "Almost a sprint." Amazingly, it was enough, and Lopes trailed in two ticks adrift.[1]

De Castella would go on to win the inaugural World crown in 1983 with another gut-wrenching sustained burst from 34K, leaving the brave Kebede Balcha of Ethiopia 24 seconds adrift. But in the big one, the 1984 Los Angeles Olympic marathon, he placed a disappointed fifth [for detailed comment of this race, see Chapter 42]. He easily defended his Commonwealth crown in 1986, the same year in which he flew down Boston's hills in a 2:07:51 course record. "I'm pleased...it might just be my best run ever," he declared.

---

1. Deek recalls to the author that he and Lopes began kicking for the tape in this race a full 3 kilometres from home.

I asked him what it felt like on that to be running better than anyone else in the world: "It was very, very satisfying. I ended up just racing against myself – trying to beat the pace car. It's like the tap analogy: you know that if ever you want a little more energy, or a little more speed, all you've got to do is go and turn the tap." Deek went on to run in two more Olympic marathons – four in all – to give him a finishing tally of 10th, 5th, 8th and 26th. Reflecting on his lack of an Olympic medal to Michael Sandrock, Deek explained: "I don't have any regrets about the way I did things; just that I didn't win an Olympic medal. But nothing goes exactly the way you want it to. There is never a perfect life, and there is never a perfect career." Deek retired from marathoning in 1993 after London, intending to return to it, but never getting the chance, since by then he was working full time.

* * *

The author caught up with Deek in the spring of 2004 and found him as busy and sanguine as ever. One of the questions I asked is if he had any regrets about the ferocity with which he trained. To an extent, he did: "My feeling was that if I did regular 50K'ers, then 42K should be a walk in the park. It's partly psychological and part physiological. But it's a dangerous thing to do. So risky. I came to the '84 Olympics a little over-trained – having dug myself into a hole. I naively thought: the more I train, the better I'll be.[2] I wouldn't necessarily recommend the training that I did to an athlete today." Deek only runs a little these days (20–30 minutes a day), preferring instead karate for his kicks (apologies for the pun): He derives satisfaction, he says, from the flexibility, strength and mental discipline the sport requires. He is making a success of the company he founded in 1997, Smart-Start, tackling obesity and lifestyle issues amongst young Australians. Remarkably, Australia is the second most obese nation in the world. "We tend to be a nation of sports watchers now, and not sports doers," Deek explains.

When he lost his house in a forest fire a few years ago he represented many of his neighbours who also became homeless and became a spokesman for them as they fought the insurance companies. He'll never be able to replace all the medals and books he lost and the incident was a "financial disaster" (with the insurance company covering only half his loss). But none of his loved ones were hurt, which, he points out, is of sole importance.

I asked him what his ultimate lesson for the marathon was, and his answer is as thoughtful and no nonsense as the man himself: "You MUST respect it! I learnt that quickly, but I'm always annoyed at the lack of respect so many runners of all levels give it." The respect Deek gave his sport repaid him handsomely. He will always be remembered as one of the all-time greats of marathoning. A brutally tough competitor, but laid-back, friendly and approachable as well. A true one-of-a-kind.

---

2. Deek's words have an almost identical ring to those of Ron Hill regarding his quest to win the 1972 Olympics.

Race Result:

Rob de Castella	AUS	2:09:18
Juma Ikangaa	TAN	2:09:30
Mike Gratton	ENG	2:12:06
John Graham	SCO	2:13:04
Kevin Ryan	NZL	2:13:42
Gidamis Shahanga	TAN	2:14:25

Sources:

Conversations with Rob de Castella.

Conversations with Hugh Jones.

Brisbane Daily Sun, October 7th, 1982.

de Castella, Rob and Mike Jenkinson, *Deek: The Making of Australia's World Marathon Champion*. William Collins Pty Ltd, Sydney, 1984.

Derderian, Tom, *Boston Marathon*. Human Kinetics, 1996.

Hauman, Riël, *Century of the Marathon, 1896-1996*. Human & Rousseau, 1996.

Sandrock, Michael, *Running with the Legends*. Human Kinetics, 1996.

XLVII

No. 4 – 1952 Olympic Marathon [Men]

Sunday, July 27th

I run until I can't run anymore. And then I run some more.

On any informed list that judged Olympic Games for all-round excellence, the Helsinki Olympics of 1952 would earn the highest marks. That is, for organization, harmony and competitive excellence. This author's top five Olympics, in chronological order, are: Helsinki 1952, Rome 1960, Seoul 1988, Barcelona 1992 and Sydney 2000. What is striking about this list is how long it took for the Olympic movement to really get going. If my list was a top six, then Los Angeles 1932 would sneak into the mix, for there was the first real evidence that the imagination of the world had been captured. But it was Helsinki '52 where the sporting public truly became hooked on the global spectacle that the Olympic movement was becoming.

Interestingly, of course, it is no coincidence that Helsinki benefited from the advent of television, from which the Olympics have never looked back. After 1960, there is something of a stutter. The Tokyo Games of 1964 were superb in many ways and would definitely make any top-ten list; but thereafter greed, politics, corruption, boycotts, terrorism, death and near-bankruptcy sullied the movement greatly. It was left to Seoul in 1988 to restore some much sought after peace and goodwill, and allowing for a wrinkle at Atlanta 1996, the Olympic movement seems in ruder health than ever before. Indeed, the passionate battle between several of the world's most dynamic cities for the 2012 Games – narrowly won by London over Paris – indicates the Olympics are in safe hands for at least the next fifty years.

The London *Times* of Monday, July 21st, 1952, carried a piece about the opening of Helsinki '52 with the byline: "Memorable start to Olympic Games." The report went on to say of the opening ceremony:

At any rate the rain in no way lessened the ardour of the 70,000 spectators, most of whom followed the proceedings, without any head cover from stands which reached up so high that the spectacle was almost that of a crowd perched on the slopes of a steep mountain.

The climax of the ceremony was announced from the great notice board at one end of the stadium that no less a person then Paavo Nurmi had been chosen as the last bearer of the torch kindled in far-off Greece. What a cheer arose, and what a thrill for many others besides the Finns themselves, when that immortal figure appeared through the marathon gate, and still fleet of foot ran round the track to kindle the sacred flame in the huge bowl at the southern end of the arena.

After the wonderful Nurmi moment, there came the 1952 edition of a streaker...or was she a ghost? Or perhaps an angel?:

It was then that anti-climax suddenly entered on the scene in the person of a young, fair-headed girl in white diaphanous robes flowing in the wind. Tripping round the track in a half-silence which betokened amazement, she reached the rostrum from which not long since the president of the organized communications had asked the president of the Finnish Republic to declare the Games open.

She not only reached the rostrum but mounted it and seized the microphone. "Dear friends" she declared before some officials realized what was happening and forcibly removed the intruder.

The 17-year-old student Barbara Player was temporarily held in custody. The whole affair was "over so quickly that it left little impression beyond astonishment that such an intrusion by a girl so oddly and scantily clothed had been possible."

The always-entertaining parade of nations then followed as the teams marched with their flags, bearing the nation's name – in Finnish – underneath. English speakers either had to know their flags well or have deductible powers of translation. Iso-Britannia was simple enough, but Yadysvallat (USA) and Nevvostoliitto (USSR) were trickier.

* * *

The eagerly awaited 1952 Olympic marathon promised a rare treat indeed, a duel between two dominant and superb runners. An Englishman named Jim Peters – who dominates Chapter 4 of this book – and, in the words of the American runner Johnny Kelley, Jnr, "the Czechoslovakian Choo-Choo, the unbelievable 145-pound human piston, the thrashing, churning, agonizing, grimacing, running automaton."

Emil Zátopek was born on September 22nd, 1922. His birthplace in Moravia lies halfway between Budapest and Prague and around 100 kilometres north-east of Vienna. He was one of eight children and his parents were of humble means – his father a carpenter in a local factory. Despite the economic depression in many parts of the world while Emil was growing up, he had a happy childhood. He and his siblings lived, according to Bob Phillips, "...in a tranquil rural setting" and spent their time "hiking through the neighbouring meadows and fields, building wood cabins in the forests, swimming in the nearby river, tending their father's beehives." The problem was what to do after finishing school. In the mid-1990s, the writer and runner Michael Sandrock made the pilgrimage to Zátopek's home, as runners from all over the world have done, to meet the legend face to face. Theirs is a superb interview that reveals the very essence of the man.

Zátopek came across as intelligent, humorous, compassionate and, well into his seventies, as vital as ever. Zátopek explained that despite the scores of thousands who applied, he was one of the lucky 100 chosen for an apprenticeship at the famous Buta shoe factory, headquartered in Toronto, with the main employer in Zlín. After working in the factory for a short while, a bad day came for Zátopek. The company had organized a footrace across the city and he was obliged to run. Ugh. This wasn't his idea of fun. Zátopek feigned a knee injury, but the doctor who examined him could find nothing wrong and Emil was signed up. He recalls: "But then, ahh, once I was entered, I tried to win. I came in second." Zátopek's talent was immediately recognized and he was invited to join the local running club up the hill from the factory.

Czechoslovakia was invaded by Germany in 1939, and Zátopek had discovered the joy of running during the darkest days of the Second World War. He explained to Sandrock: "It was during the war, and for me, being in the club was a great pleasure. Because it was a sad time, not a favourable time. It was not allowed to dance, maybe. It was not possible to buy chocolate, maybe. It was very *triste*, very sad. But in the stadium, oh, it was very nice. We young boys had not only training but pleasure, too. To run. To jump. To have fun." For the next five years Zátopek trained and competed only in Czechoslovakia. After seeing how other people trained for a year or so, Zátopek decided to blaze his own trail. Calling his unique methods "very simple and very primitive", he then went on to smash himself in his workouts by taking on a workload that was the most brutal that had ever been seen before. One of his original sessions he describes as: "Speed and stamina. Speed, by running short distance, maybe 100 metres, and stamina, not to have rest during the training. 100 metres fast [his voice rises]; 100 metres easy [lowering his voice]. This way I was able to run faster than by using the former training methods. Why should I practice running slow? I already know how to run slow. I must learn how to run fast." Zátopek's methods were ridiculed and dismissed by his colleagues, but he felt that as long as they brought improvement to his running – which they seemed to be – then he would persevere with them.

After the end of the war, Zátopek was accepted into the Czech military academy in Prague for officer training. This was an ideal situation because he found out that far from his training being restricted, his superiors actually wanted him to run. He knew that his basic speed was poor, but that his determination and stamina were valuable assets. Zátopek was entered into his first international race in 1946, the 5000-metres at the European Championships in Oslo. The legendary British miler Sydney Wooderson, moving up in distance, won the race, and Zátopek placed an encouraging third (in 14:25).

One of Zátopek's great quirks, when training through the winter cold and snow, was to run in heavy army boots. This put less stress on his ankles, and when the boots wore out Emil merely had to ask his superiors for a replacement. And then, when he wore a lightweight pair of shoes for racing – whoosh! – could he travel! Sandrock writes: "Aided by the unbearable lightness of his competition shoes, Zátopek pulled a shocker in his first 5000-metre race of 1947, clocking 14:08.2, the second-fastest 5000 of all time. Zátopek ended 1947 undefeated and was ranked first in the world in the 5000." After a second consecutive winter of brutal "boot-

457

training", Zátopek began thinking of his first Olympics, set for London, July 1948. Deciding to do both the "five" and the "ten", Zátopek was not considered favourite for the latter. His problem was that the Finnish world-record holder, Viljo Heino, would be opposing him. News travelled less quickly in those days, and although Zátopek's best time for the 10,000-metres (29:37) was under two seconds slower than Heino, Zátopek was seen by only the best informed as a threat.

But Zátopek had a very dangerous plan, and so ferocious was his determination to carry out this plan that Heino was in for the battle of his life if he was going to strike gold. Zátopek wanted to keep his pace at 71 seconds a lap. If this ever slipped, he positioned a friend in the crowd who would hold up a red shirt, which signalled the falter. For eight laps Zátopek sat in the comfort of the pack, and then, suddenly, at the beginning of lap nine the red shirt appeared. The Czech locomotive put in a burst of acceleration that carried him to the front of the field. Heino responded and surged back past Zátopek. A lap later and the red shirt appeared again, and again Zátopek surged, this time dropping the valiant Finn once and for all. Zátopek continued to worry that he might be challenged, and it was only near the end when he asked an official where Heino was (who replied that he had dropped out) that he knew he had secured the gold. He broke the 30-minute barrier by 0.4 of a second and won by 47 seconds over Alain Mimoun of France, who would go on to be a great rival and friend to Zátopek.

A legend is born: Zátopek rocketed to world-wide athletic fame when he won the 10,000-metres at the 1948 London Olympics. Here, his delighted teammates come to the aid of their friend. *Bettmann/CORBIS*

Zátopek was on a high and the intoxication of his own exuberance cost him dear the following day in the heats of the 5000-metres. Instead of just coasting through to qualify for the final, Emil naively chased Eric Ahlden of Sweden all the way. Bill Lucas, the British representative in that heat, recalled the event to the author 57 years later: "Zátopek was in my heat of the 5K and fought out an unnecessary battle down the straight to win only the day after winning the 10K, in a quick time for those days. He was then deprived of victory in the final by Gaston Reiff because he misjudged the race completely by letting Reiff get away and then deciding at 300 metres to go that he could win, but failed by inches." That final Lucas speaks of has gone down as one of the all-time greats of track and field. Metre by metre the gap came down over that legendary final lap – but with just 200 metres left to run it was still over 30 metres. Zátopek dug even deeper and the crowd gasped and then started to roar their haunting chant: " Zá-to-pek! Zá-to-pek! Zá-to-pek!" Had Reiff not reacted to their shouts that alerted him to the danger, he may well have been caught by the sprinting maniac in the red vest. As it was, with a final desperate shimmy of his own, the Belgian forced himself over the line a metre-and-a-half up.[1]

Although it was obviously a disappointment for Zátopek not to secure the double, he had announced himself as the world's premier distance runner, and the Olympic crowds – in monsoon conditions – had loved what they'd seen. Word spread all over the world: there was a new star in athletics, and if he may not have had the speed of a deer, he did have the strength of a bull. And there was something about him, too. What was it? Was he merry, or was he sad? Did he love running, or did he hate it? ("He runs like he has just been stabbed in the heart," said one coach). Was he a superb tactician, or a bit loopy? If people didn't know quite what to make of Zátopek, they were fairly sure they wanted to see more of him, and they were equally certain that they probably would.

The next few years saw the Zátopek name blossom, into one linked with pure quality. It also became linked with world records. He got his first on June 11th, 1949 when he ran 29:28 in Ostrava. This brought him great respect from his military superiors, until to their shock, he quickly lost the record to Heino. "Emil, you must run again," said Zátopek's boss. "Allow me three weeks without military duty," Zátopek replied. "Free time for me to practice more. Two weeks very intensive training, and one week easier, easier, easier until I try for the record" (Sandrock). The training paid off as he knocked 6 seconds off Heino's mark when he had another crack. In 1950 Zátopek went to Turku, the city of Paavo Nurmi's birth, and lopped an incredible 18 seconds off his world mark. The Finnish fans adopted Zátopek as one of their own that night and gave him a long standing ovation.

Despite falling sick from eating a spoiled goose, Zátopek won the double at the 1950 European Championships, getting revenge over Reiff in the "five". And then, on September 15th, 1951, came what Australian legend Ron Clarke calls "probably the best performance ever". Zátopek had been dreaming of another world record – the hour run – and lined up at his favourite track at Houstka

---

1. Reiff would go on to break the world record for 3000 metres the following year, running 7:58.8.

Stadium, not far from Prague, situated in the woods, sheltered with high trees and no dust. The conditions were perfect, writes Michael Sandrock, "and so was Zátopek". At the time only five other people had broken 30 minutes for the 10,000, and here Zátopek did it back to back. His first 10K taking 29:53, and then leaking just 5 seconds over the next 10K to reach 20,000 metres in 59:51. He covered another 52 metres in the final 9 seconds. "This I think was my best race; it was the best distance for me. It suited me."

*   *   *

Zátopek fell ill in the spring of 1952 – perhaps a somewhat fortuitous event since it meant that he fell into no over-training traps and arrived for the Helsinki Olympics loose and ready. In the *Four-Minute Mile*, Roger Bannister tells a stunning tale about what a remarkably relaxed and amiable fellow Zátopek was. An Autralian reporter burst into his room the night before the 10,000-metres final. But instead of angrily throwing the man out, Zátopek granted him a 20-minute interview, and then offered him half his bed when he found the scribe didn't have one of his own!

The weather gods at Helsinki certainly seemed to be smiling on Zátopek. He recalls: "It was very interesting. Opening ceremony. Heavy rain. Representatives were marching. But the next day, for the 10,000 metres, fine weather. Next day after, rain. Then 5000 final, sunny weather. But, then it was nice weather till marathon. Raining days, but never in long-distance races," he laughs. Emil, of course, came to Helsinki as world-record holder and Olympic champion in the "dime"[2]. Because his name began some way into the alphabet, Zátopek was the last of the 32 runners to be called at the start of the 10,000, and officials placed him in row three of the starters. Some way to treat a legend. But Zátopek recalls: "And my adversaries said, 'Oh, oh, Zátopek, please oh, oh, please come on in front.' They let me come in the first place in the start position. It was good sporting. After this, Ready, boom, I went into leading, and they line behind me. Everybody knew me then, and nobody tried to disturb me" (Sandrock).

After the fancied Englishman Gordon Pirie had sparred with Zátopek in the first half of the race, halfway arrived in a fast 14:43, and it came down to a straight battle between Zátopek and his close friend Alain Mimoun. Although Zátopek tired, he certainly didn't fade, and he just had too much strength for the Frenchman. "Zatu"'s heavy panting meant that lapped runners were alerted to an impending Czech locomotive well in advance and would always move wide to allow him to pass on the inside. Time: a new Olympic record of 29:17; 15 seconds up on Mimoun. Mission one – possibly the most straightforward – was complete. The London *Times* reported the event: "The race in the end merely showed that Zátopek, for all his rolling eyes, protruding tongue, and flogging of himself with his right arm – which any ordinary mortal might be pardoned for thinking indicated complete exhaustion, even the close approach of apoplexy – has reserves of strength and speed denied to all his contemporaries over the distances."

---

2. American parlance for the 10,000.

Zátopek's questionable leg speed, however, would be put fully to the test in the 5000 metres. He took a good lesson from his eager tactics in the heats from London 1948, and ensured he left himself with energy for the final. There, some terrific milers, moving up in distance – and of course Mimoun – were waiting. "OK, 5000," Zátopek tells Sandrock, "it was very different. Basically, I was not the favourite. Chris Chataway, oh, very fast runner. Gaston Reiff, Olympic champion from London, also faster me. Schade, who had the best timing from 5000 metres in 1952." After halfway, Zátopek was still in contention and decided to push on, saying to a surprised Schade: "Come on, Herbert, run a few laps with me." Pirie, Mimoun, Reiff and Chataway lay in wait with their deadly kicks. The *Times* wrote: "At 4000m even he may have been feeling his own pace – but his face carries so many expressions at the same time that there was no immediate chance of discovering what was happening to him inside."

Inside, Zátopek was gearing everything up for his plan of kicking for home at the bell. Things unexpectedly took a turn for the better when Reiff dropped out with half a mile to go. Four hundred metres was by now easy for Zátopek to sprint, of course. His regular daily diet was 40×400 metres in training. It all looked good, but Zátopek was up against supremely gifted runners of whom only Pirie wouldn't be up for the challenge. In one of running's great quotes Zátopek explains: "Boom! And I started to sprint...And they were *twice* as fast as me! Until 300 metres to go, Chataway, Schade, Mimoun, all three in front, ohh oh. And you see, gold medal, silver medal, bronze medal; for me, potato. What to do? What to do? But to give up? Never! Nah, no, no! I must run, *argghhhh!*"

Forty years after the great event and Zátopek's words came "tumbling out in a nearly inarticulate cry, like that of some trapped wild animal," Sandrock writes. "He speaks ferociously, his round face expanding. Zátopek growls and viciously bares his teeth, rising from his chair, bursting with energy; he is powerful, strong, and in his prime again, ready to battle all comers."

Rounding the final turn, Zátopek poured on yet more pressure and Chataway in his inexperience bumped the track kerb and came tumbling down.[3] It was just Mimoun and Schade left but they simply couldn't match Zátopek's enormous strength; and he prevailed by 1.1 seconds in 14:06.6. The 70,000 crowd who were there to see this marvellous race knew they had witnessed something special. And with the angels seemingly looking on, one of athletics' neatest stories quickly followed.

Zátopek's wife, Dana, was originally not going to be able to watch Emil in the "five" because it clashed with her checking-in for her javelin competition, but then she *could* watch because the hammer competition overran, but then she *couldn't* watch because her nerves couldn't stand it. "Dana! Emil wins 5000 metres in a new record!" yelled a Soviet coach to her. As Dana emerged to partake in the javelin, she spotted her spouse and yelled: "Oh you won *prima*, where is your gold medal? Give it to me. I'll bring it for good luck." Dana promptly went and tossed

---

3. Two years after this race, Chataway not only paced Sir Roger Bannister to the 4-minute mile, but six months later broke the 5000-metre world record after a magnificent duel with Vladimir Kuts. Fifty years after that, the "Red Fox" was still going strong! A superb 1:39 clocking in the Great North Run (half-marathon) was followed by a 5000 track race to celebrate the 50th anniversary of his Kuts duel. He ran 22:19.

On the same day that Zátopek won his gut-wrenching 5000-metres final in Helsinki, his inspired wife Dana tossed the javelin 50.82 metres, to strike gold for herself. Zátopek shows her what he thinks. *Hulton-Deutsch Collection/CORBIS*

the spear 2 metres further than she ever had before, turned a cartwheel of delight on the infield grass, and won her own gold. Sweet dreams are made of this.[4]

* * *

Three days later Zátopek went hunting for the family's fourth gold of the Games. The lofty achievements of Englishman Jim Peters are described in detail in Chapter 4, but a reminder here should point out that he was the world-record holder in the event (2:20:42 at the Polytechnic Chiswick race just six weeks earlier) and was the overwhelming favourite. Think Paula Radcliffe, Athens 2004, and you have some idea. Peters was the man Zátopek feared, and thus he constructed a simple plan. Zátopek recalled:

In the end I dropped all tactical considerations and decided to keep my eye on the best competitor. The papers wrote that the favourite was Jim Peters and that his number was 187. When we took our places in front of the grandstand, I caught sight of a runner with his number, and I immediately went and asked if he really was Peters. After all, there is nothing like making sure. If the newspapers had got it wrong and I had "tailed" somebody else by mistake, who knows what the outcome would have been? [Abrahams].

Aside from Peters, the obvious contenders were the Koreans and the Japanese – both nations sent full teams. And the key contenders from London 1948 had returned. Choi Yoon-chil of Korea, who had led so deep into the London race before finally collapsing, came to race, as did the defending champion Delfo Cabrera, who looked fit and ready. Korea, indeed, had filled all three of the podium positions at Boston in 1950, leaving many Americans incredulous as to what was suddenly wrong with their runners. Old Clarence DeMar thought he had the answer: "The Koreans' performance tells what you can do by hard work. We have too many machines in this country." One wonders to what horror DeMar would greet today's world.

To give back-up to Peters – if any were needed – Britain sent two excellent runners in Stanley Cox and Geoff Iden. Cox placed second to the world-record holder at the "Poly" in a magnificent 2:21:42. Surely the course must be inaccu-

4. Zátopek later spoke of how he inspired Dana to gold; but Dana was having none of it: Ok, she said, go and inspire another girl and see if she can throw 50 metres!

rate? said the ubiquitous sceptics. Upon remeasurement, they were proved to be right. It was found to be a little long! So if Peters, who had smashed the world record by almost 5 minutes, could be viewed as the "King" there was no question that Cox deserved the title of "Crown Prince". In third place at the "Poly" came the more circumspect but still dangerous Iden (2:26:53). Another nation to look out for came from the unlikely source of Belgium, who, in Jean Leblond and Charles DeWachtere, had a couple of 2:23 men. The home nation, Finland, made sure they had a strong team, led by the hotly tipped Veikko Karvonen.

* * *

Under temperatures that were a little warm for marathoning (64 °F), in front of a packed stadium, 66 starters were sent on their way – 40 of whom were Europeans from 20 nations. (Martin & Gynn). None of Zátopek's competitors knew quite what to make of his presence. *Surely* 20,000 metres of hard track racing would have taken their toll on his body in the previous days; and besides, he was a novice at the marathon. But Zátopek eagerly anticipated the grind of the marathon. He did frequent 10 to 20-mile runs in army boots for fun. Would the marathon, he wondered, really cause him any more problems than his overwhelmingly hard training?

The London *Times* describes the route:

The route was two and half laps round the stadium and then the main highway leading from Helsinki to the north, with a turn round approximately 13 miles at the Ructinkla fork and back over the same route to the stadium, where about three-quarters of a lap remained to be run.

The road surface was supposed to be good enough, but the ups and downs were rather more severe than the Windsor to Chiswick course, and the return journey was into whatever wind there was – generally pronounced in Helsinki during the last week or so.

Any question of whether Jim Peters would run conservatively or a fast, hard race were answered on the 'b' of 'bang'. The clearly apprehensive Englishman bolted off like a startled pony and, after a brief and unruly lead by Aslam of Pakistan, Peters led the runners out of the stadium. He got to work on building his lead. Peters was determined not to let Zátopek have it easy. But, of course, there's setting out fast and setting out madly, and Peters' tactical concoction included far more of the latter ingredient.

All the great marathon tacticians point to the first 10 kilometres as a time where the race is never won but often lost. After Peters' split for just the first 5 kilometres alarm bells were being triggered: 15:43. Unless he was planning on a sweet 2:11:06 marathon, this was not an advisable cadence. Three runners followed behind, around 100 metres down the road. Cox, Zátopek and Gustaf Jansson, the double Swedish champion from 1951 and '52 [and looking ahead, 1953]. Jansson had also placed second at the famous Košice Marathon in 1950, and had thus proved himself no mug. But this was the first time he had appeared on a truly international stage.

Peters slowed a little over the next section to reach 10 kilometres in a more advisable 31:55 – but this was still 2:15 pace. But then, just as it appeared that he would continue to ease off and let the field come back to him, another acceleration – with a 5-kilometre split of 16:03, even though the stretch was the hardest of the course with plenty of hills. When one is forcing the pace like this in a major race, dancing with death and defying nature, the one thing that adds to the mental torture is company – and this, remarkably, is what Peters got. Over the next few kilometres Jansson hauled back the lead and arrived to join him, and Zátopek followed very close behind. A minute further back came the Englishman Cox and the unlikely figure of Reinaldo Gorno. This Argentinian was the next best that nation had to offer after the reigning Olympic champion Delfo Cabrera. After finishing second to Cabrera in several South American championships, this race here appeared to be a changing of the Argentinian guard.

By 20 kilometres, Zátopek was up to join Peters and Jansson. There are many versions of what happened next as one of running's most famous conversations followed. Zátopek had been careful in training to run his intervals for as long as 2 hours and 20 minutes to prepare him for the marathon, but he had no experience of judging the necessary pace. This worried him, so a little before halfway Zátopek turned to Peters and asked something *along the lines of*: "I know virtually nothing about marathon running, but don't you think we ought to go a little faster?"

The eminent historian Roberto Quercetani submits that Peters could find no suitable reply to this harrowing question – since Peters was, of course, running at his limit. But most other reporters relate that Peters fatally agreed with Zátopek: "The pace, Emil, it is too slow." The calculating Zátopek mind thoughtfully considered this scrap of new intelligence – for about 5 seconds – and concluded it commanded him to hit the hammer. So he did – urging the depleted Peters to join him. But he could not. At least Peters was able to continue to run though; unlike his poor British teammate, Stan Cox, who collapsed and required an ambulance.[5] Peters later told *Athletics Weekly*: "I was the favourite and I was confident. Emil had already won the 5000 and 10,000 metres, and people said there was no way he could beat me after four hard races. When he came up to me and asked if the pace was right, I said it was too slow just to kid him, but he got away from me. Then I got a cramp for the first time ever at 13 miles."

Forty years later, on a visit to America, Zátopek revealed how even the great have doubts: "I could not decide to let him alone," he explained. "If he's not able to run more, who can help me? Then he fell more and more behind. It was new for me" (Hauman). "So far so good," gasped *The Times*:

It was not even too alarming – though one really ought to have felt alarmed – when at 20 kilometres, Zátopek raced into a lead. One could almost see him doing it. Running behind anyone has never been to his liking and a little thing like a marathon was clearly not going to alter his mood and method. Peters was now 10 seconds behind the leader, but, with Jansson, was still keeping up what

---

5. For some reason before the start of the race Cox's pulse was raging at 120, and a Finnish doctor advised him not to run (Hauman). However, as discussed later in the chapter, Cox and Peters' journey to Helsinki may have been at the root of their problems.

obviously was a stiff pace. Corno and Cabrera were there, but Cox was over two minutes behind the leaders. One learned soon afterwards that he had fallen out.

Zátopek and Jansson reached the halfway mark together, at a specially constructed monument that still stands today. They were around 15 seconds up on Peters. Zátopek tells Michael Sandrock about his charming naivety and how his inexperience in the marathon scared him: "At 21 kilometres I had this, oh, this vision; 21 kilometres more, whhooh, what will it be like? Of course, the organizers tried to make it more easy. They organized this refreshing station that had everything: chocolate, mineral water, and oh, everything possible. And coming to the 26th kilometre, at this refreshment station, they gave a half lemon to Jansson. He took it, and they gave another half lemon to me." Zátopek shakes his head, waving his hands in front of him, writes Sandrock. "Oh, I said, no, no, no. I don't take it, because I had no experience. I was not used during the training to eat or drink some thing. Training, training, training, and I did not ever take refreshments. But...," he laughs, smacking his lips, "we ran together, but then," patting his stomach:

I thought, I'm idiot; there was lemon, and I don't take. But oh, to run back for half a lemon, it would also be stupid. No, I said, I have to go ahead. And I will see. I will be better than Jansson; at the next refreshment station, I will take two or three lemons! But, I don't know, 500 or 600 metres more later, Jansson was tired. What to do? I decide, no, no, no lemon, nothing. It was also stupid. I was afraid to take something.

Zátopek ploughed on. He began to overheat, so somewhat amusingly he rolled up his red running vest up to his armpits to allow the breeze to cool his body. He concentrated on relaxing, on not panicking, of pattering along – to hell with his pace. He later told the *Los Angeles Times*: "I looked ahead, and I can see nothing of the city. I want to quit, yes, but how to get back to town? I am 20 kilometres away, so I say I must run back. So I run. The only thing I can see ahead is a very high tower with a flame on top, the Olympic flame. So I decide I must run to the flame." By 28 kilometres Jansson was indeed desperately feeling the pressure and Zátopek finally started to ease into a 5-second advantage. It began to grow, second by second, until by the 30K mark Zátopek passed in 1:38:42 and Jansson in 1:39:08 (Martin & Gynn). Peters clung on in third and behind him came a remarkable procession of *three* brave Argentinians: Gorno, Cabrera and Corsino Fernandez. A few minutes later, as the 20-mile mark was passed, Peters' leg cramps became intolerable, and right in front of former British marathon great Sam Ferris, Peters hobbled to a standstill. How remarkable that 52 years after this event, another overwhelming British favourite in the Olympic marathon would pull out at almost the same stage, in almost the same position.

What had happened to Cox and Peters? Why had their races followed such a disastrous course? Obviously, Peters' pacing folly had a major part to play, but Martin and Gynn offer another interesting explanation: "Both Peters and Cox flew to Helsinki in a partly converted military bomber, and they endured an icy windblast on their left from a poorly fitting door during the nine-hour flight. Cox and Peters both had problems during the race with left-side muscle cramping, and the question remains whether that was related to the bone-chilling cold they had experienced on their flight."

Zátopek, meanwhile, just kept on stretching his lead. He told himself to relax and chatted amiably with spectators and cyclists. The *Times* reported:

> Zátopek clearly was in terrific form and fettle, challenging and almost gay. As he ran he half stopped at the ice-cream vendors and professed his ignorance of how to time his effort in a marathon. None the less, he succeeded in getting Peters and Jansson to fall into the trap of "racing" with or after him instead of setting their own schedule and keeping to it – Zátopek or no Zátopek.

Zátopek's 5-kilometre stretches were taking over 18 minutes now, but that made no difference to his challengers: none were making an impression on him. His lead soon approached half a mile in length. George Gretton nails the reason why Zátopek found himself in such an enviable position: "The pattern for victory had been set in the earlier stages while Zátopek was still able to pit his judgment against his adversaries, and, as he had calculated, it was then only a question of holding out. This was quintessential Zátopek."

The Olympic flame to which he ran finally loomed large. The crowds grew ever thicker and although the last 5 kilometres took Zátopek 18:08 to cover, they took the chasing pack even longer. Soon the great master was upon the stadium and the capacity crowd rose to salute him. In a speech in Montreal in the late 1960s, Zátopek recalled the end of the race:

A refreshed looking Zátopek displays none of the pain and worry that had bothered him in the previous 143 minutes, as he wins the 1952 Olympic Marathon. *Bettmann/CORBIS*

> Alone, my mouth parched and more and more tired out with every kilometre I staggered along, peering out over the heads of the spectators to see whether the Olympic Stadium wasn't in view yet.
>
> I was only brought out of my trance by the ceremonial fanfares as I ran through the Marathon Gateway. People were standing up from their seats, waving to me and calling out greetings with joy. And I was so very grateful to them, though I didn't manage to do more than to take great care not to stumble and make a fool of myself. In the goal I was overjoyed with the sudden, wonderful feeling of being able to stand on my own feet and having to run no more.

466

Derrick Young writes in *Ten Greatest Races*: "And, as he ran into the stadium after 26 faultless, fluent, fabulous miles, the capacity 68,000 spectators rose as one man to him. And they cried just one word. 'Zat-o-pek. Zat-o-pek. Zat-o-pek.' They were lucky. They saw him at his best."

Terrific battles were waged behind Zátopek for the minor positions, indeed five men would finish in a calvalcade – just 66 seconds between them. The unheralded Gorno passed Jansson for the silver, while the Swede bravely hung on for the bronze. The Korean Choi proved his exceptional effort in London four years earlier was no fluke by taking fourth, a few steps ahead of the Finn Karvonen and the worthy defending champion Cabrera.

* * *

At the closing ceremonies the crowd continued with their famous refrain, now with an added word: "Zátopek, Zátopek, Bye-bye, Zátopek!" Emil recalled the moment wistfully to Michael Sandrock: "It was a little sad...that it belonged to history. And I knew there could be no repetition. It is possible only once. Then, on the fifth of August, we return home. All the team." Zátopek goes on to pay tribute to the Finns for putting on such a magnificent Games. Wherever he went in Finland he was saluted – even though he had crushed the best they had to offer, and taken Heino's world records. The Finns indeed took to calling him "satu pekka", which translates as "fairy-tale guy". Zatu notes: "The Helsinki Olympics were for us the best. At that time, there were no problems with a boycott of the Games, or doping, or commercial difficulties. At Helsinki it was very sportive and fair. It was perfect. A perfect Olympics."

The *Times* concurred that it had been a hugely successful Games, as it reported the closing ceremony:

> So many extraordinary things had happened in that time that the spectators on this occasion, and especially the Finns, might have been pardoned if their minds wandered a little to the immediate past rather than to the future four years ahead for which the ceremonial called upon the youth of every country to prepare. Helsinki had had her finest sporting hour. Melbourne, on the other side of the world, is to have hers in due course and the very distance and difference between the two cities seemed to underline the expanding influence of the Games.

* * *

Although Zátopek had to fulfil a huge raft of celebratory engagements on his return home, his magical season of 1952 was by no means over. Just a few months after Helsinki, he went after the world 30K track record and got it – by 3½ minutes in 1:35:23. The following year he lowered his 10,000 record to 29:01.6, and in 1954 he outdid himself in sensational style. His military superiors called on him one day and said sternly: "Emil, you have world record 10,000, 15,000, 20,000, 30,000, but no 5000. 5000 is Olympic event. Can you get it?" (Sandrock). Zátopek submitted that it was possible, but that he would require three weeks to train. He then embarked on the most strenuous training arguably ever undertaken.

Zátopek tells Sandrock: "I ran every day 100 × 400 metres. In the woods, 400 metres, Arrhh! 50 times in the morning, 50 times in the afternoon. Every day for two weeks. Oh, it was a lot of work." A simple breakdown of the distances Zátopek was running goes: 3-kilometres warm-up; 50 × 400 metres = 20 kilometres; 50 × 150-metres recovery = 7.5 kilometres, 2-kilometres warm-down; 3 + 20 + 7.5 + 2 = 32.5 kilometres, *multiplied* by two = 65 kilometres, or over 40 miles, of running, day in, day out for two weeks. Gunder Hägg's record of 13:58 was surely in Zátopek's sights.

He flew to Paris after a week of recovery, attacked the record, but with 4 kilometres run Emil was 3 seconds off the required pace. However, a final 2:43 kilometre brought him home in 13:57.2 – one second under the record. He had done it. *Then* the very next day, he became the first person to break the 29-minute barrier for 10,000 metres, when he ran 28:54.2 at Brussels' Heysel Stadium. Zátopek still insisted on proving his championship credentials though, and in the summer of 1954 he comfortably defended his European 10,000 title while stepping down to the bronze in the 5000. Between May 1948 and July 1954 Zátopek won an astounding 38 consecutive 10,000s on the trot.

By the time the Melbourne 1956 Olympics came along, Zátopek was slowing down but was still favourite in the eyes of many to retain his marathon title. Always innovative, Zátopek searched for new ways in which to strengthen his legs, even carrying his wife Dana on his back and running with her as one experiment. This, of course, led to problems and Zátopek was diagnosed with a hernia. "Do not run for two months," doctors warned him. "You are funny," Zátopek replied. "Because in two months, the Olympics will be over" (Sandrock).

Zátopek sadly came to Melbourne far short of the conditioning he was used to and the world missed out on seeing what could have been one of the great battles: Zátopek v Kuts. Commentators still picked Zátopek to win the marathon, but on this occasion he could manage *only* sixth – still a remarkable return considering his lack of fitness. He arrived at the finish, for want of a better word, totally gaga and, dropping to his knees, did not notice his great friend Alain Mimoun waiting for him. "Emil, why don't you congratulate me? I am an Olympic champion. It was I who won." Zátopek snapped out of his trance, took off his cap, saluted Mimoun and then embraced him (Wallechinsky). "Alain, you are really a hero. Always second, and in your last competition, you are Olympic champion. Congratulations." Mimoun, later said how this moment meant more to him than the medal itself.

Zátopek's last outing came after winning a race he was by no means tipped for, at the annual cross-country race in San Sebastián, Spain, in January 1958. Zátopek defeated George Knight by a full 70 metres, even though Knight had run the fastest 10,000 just the year before. But there's no way the master was going to retire on a downbeat note. And the same can be said for Dana who won a silver medal at the Rome Olympics, to cement her place as one of the greatest javelin throwers of all time.

* * *

After his retirement, Zátopek rose fast through the ranks of the army – to the lofty heights of lieutenant-colonel. He was a hero and fêted wherever he went. The

Australian Ron Clarke (the first man to break 28 minutes for the 10,000) visited Zátopek on a tour of Europe in 1966 and witnessed the adulation first-hand. At peak hour Zátopek would just leave his car wherever he pleased on Prague's busy shopping streets, and furious policemen, upon seeing the owner, would beam, gush and flip their tickets book over for Emil to autograph.

But in April 1968 his life spiralled out of control. Bob Phillips writes: "The newly appointed First Secretary of the Czech Communist Party, Alexander Dubcek, introduced liberalising reforms under the title of "socialism with a human face." Among the signatories of Dubcek's "Manifesto of 2000 Words" were Emil and Dana Zátopek. Then the "Prague Spring" was brought to a brutal end on 20 August 1968, when 200,000 Soviet and Warsaw Pact troops entered the country." Zátopek explains to Michael Sandrock what he would find when he returned home after travelling for his running: "We were back in a country where time was stopped. No progress; nothing. Then we tried to fight for more progress, more democracy, for the country not to be so closed, and *retard*. And I was very keen for it. With new leaders, it could be useful to move this stagnation." The uprising was crushed, however, as Soviet tanks rolled in, and Zátopek was expelled from the army and the Communist Party. He was given lowly jobs such as with the Prague sanitation department, and then sent out into the countryside to do geological research. Typically, Zátopek made the best of his new, almost surreal life of boring for minerals and uranium: "I liked it and found it very interesting. Because the earth is nice not only from above, but from inside" (Sandrock).

To the rest of the world it appeared as if Zátopek had fallen off the face of the earth. But not to the Czech Sports Ministry, who in 1975 hired him to read, translate and explain foreign publications, as they searched for tips in training and techniques. In short he became a spy! – albeit one even more recognizable than James Bond. He served in this capacity until his retirement in 1982. Emil lived out his days happily with Dana, although a pinched nerve prevented him from running. Michael Sandrock wrote of his 1995 visit: "But he is still a vital, strong man. Evening comes, and we walk out of the house into the lush garden, where he grabs a handful of berries growing on the plentiful bushes, munching on them like a hungry animal. 'Ah, how sweet these are,' he says." When Sandrock and Zátopek conversed with a runner on one of the forest trails where Emil did so much of his training, Sandrock mentioned the famous Zátopek grimace that he always wore when racing. "Don't let those photos of Emil fool you," said the runner. "I think he is the only happy man in Czechoslovakia."

In late 2000, an increasingly frail Emil was struck by a heart attack and died in a Prague hospital aged 78, on November 21st. He and Dana had been married for 52 years. Zátopek, of course, commanded large obituaries in national papers all over the world. The same theme persisted throughout that this was one of the best-loved sportsmen the world had ever seen. Such is the great dedication required by top-level athletes – in whatever sport – that they often fall short in the personality stakes. Paavo Nurmi was not loved by his fellow competitors, such was his blinkered, aloof approach. A modern-day example in a different sport could apply to the golfer Nick Faldo. Tennis great John McEnroe suffered through his outrageous temper; Carl Lewis through his arrogance. But everyone loved Emil.

After Ron Clarke's shopping trip with him, Zátopek pressed a small package into his hand: it was Zátopek's gold medal from the Helsinki 10,000. Zátopek told Clarke he deserved it. Clarke comments in his book *The Lonely Breed*:

No-one cherishes any gift more than I do this: my only Olympic gold medal; and not because of what it is...but because of the man whose spirit it represents. His enthusiasm, his friendliness, his love of life, shone through every moment.
There is not and never was, a greater man that Emil Zátopek.

Race result:

Emil Zátopek	CZE	2:23:03
Reinaldo Gorno	ARG	2:25:35
Gustaf Jansson	SWE	2:26:07
Yoon-chil Choi	KOR	2:26:36
Veikko Karvonen	FIN	2:26:41
Delfo Cabrera	ARG	2:26:42
Jozsef Dobronyi	HUN	2:28:04
Erkki Puolakka	FIN	2:29:35
Geoffrey Iden	GBR	2:30:42
Wallace Hayward	SOA	2:31:50

Sources:

Conversations with Bill Lucas.
Derderian, Tom, *Boston Marathon*. Human Kinetics, 1996.
Gretton, George, *Out in Front*. Pelham Books, 1968.
Hauman, Riël, *Century of the Marathon*. Human & Rousseau, 1996.
Martin, David and Roger Gynn, *The Olympic Marathon*. Human Kinetics, 2000.
Phillips, Bob, *Zátopek! Zátopek! Zátopek!* The Parrs Wood Press, 2002.
Sandrock, Michael, *Running with the Legends*. Human Kinetics, 1996.
The Times, July 21st-29th, 1952.
Wallechinsky, David, *The Complete Book of the Olympics*. Aurum Press, 2000.
Young, Derrick, *The Ten Greatest Races*. A.C.M. Webb Publishing, 1972.

XLVIII

No. 3 – 1960 Olympic Marathon [Men]

Saturday, September 10th

"There can never have been such a dramatic moment in Olympic history..."

Film critic John Walker describes the 1953 Oscar-nominated motion picture *Roman Holiday* as a "wispy, charming, old-fashioned romantic comedy shot in Rome and a little obsessed by the locations." William Wyler, the director of the movie, may have caught flak from the critics for being "too ponderously inflexible" with his work, but he will surely make no apology for his "obsession" with the city of Rome. Gregory Peck and Audrey Hepburn were memorable enough in a sugary kind of way, but the real scene-stealer of this movie was its setting. And if it was the historic and haunting set piece of Rome that transfixed moviegoers in 1953, then seven years later sports lovers were equally captivated by the city's wonder and grace.

All Olympics tend to have three outstanding heroes. True, they have several hundred gold-medal winners, but there always seem to be three athletes who set such perfect standards that their names are forever associated with those Games. Recent years, for instance, have boasted Spitz, Viren and Korbut at Munich; Lewis, Thompson and Coe at Los Angeles; and Freeman, Redgrave and Thorpe at Sydney. The Rome Games of 1960 were no different. Not only was there the small matter of a brash, friendly 18-year-old boxer named Cassius Marcellus Clay[1] (aka Muhammed Ali), who confidently destroyed the hopes of anyone who dared step into the ring with him; but there was also the sublimely gifted winner of the men's marathon to whom this chapter is dedicated; and perhaps most movingly of all, the electrifying antics of Wilma Rudolph of St Bethleham, Tennessee.

Born on June 23rd, 1940, Wilma Rudolph was the original, real-life version of

---

1. This was the Olympics in which Clay famously rebuked a Soviet journalist for daring to ask how he felt about not being able to eat at certain restaurants back home. Clay furiously responded: "Russian, we got qualified men working on that problem. We got the biggest and the prettiest cars. We get all the food we can eat. America is the greatest country in the world, and as far as places I can't eat goes, I got lots of places I can eat – more places I can than I can't" (Wallechinsky). Clay promptly visited a "can't" restaurant on his return home, where he was duly refused service. His illusions of being an all-American boy extinguished, Clay threw his Olympic gold medal into the Ohio River – an action which Muhammed Ali later said gave him a "new, secret strength".

the movie character, Forrest Gump. She was born prematurely and weighed in at just 4½ pounds. David Wallechinsky writes: "She suffered through polio, double pneumonia, and scarlet fever, which caused her to lose the use of her left leg. From the age of 6 she wore a brace." She had 22 siblings. After years of pains-taking, somewhat unscientific physiotherapy, Wilma was able to graduate from her brace into an orthopaedic shoe, and even took the tentative steps of joining her brothers on the basketball court. One day, to her mother's horror, she found her daughter playing basketball barefoot, having thrown away the shoe she hated so much. But, just like Forrest Gump, the feeling of moving about how nature originally intended, inspired Wilma not just to move, but to do so with great haste, and by the age of 16 she was a star runner. The US Olympic selectors were sufficiently impressed to take her to Melbourne Games of 1956 where Wilma captured a bronze medal in the 4×100 metre relay. Four years later, the 5-foot 11-inch Rudolph, now a mother and a member of Tennessee State University, returned to Olympic action in Rome.

There, Rudolph dominated the sprints, succeeding where the great Betty Cuthbert had before her, by winning the triple crown of 100-metres, 200-metres and 4×100-metres (where she ran the glory leg). Her time in the final was a world record by a third of a second, but unfortunately was not sanctioned due to an illegal wind reading. Images of Rudolph in full flow are spellbinding indeed, and it's hard to imagine that such a magnificent specimen could ever have been so lame.

* * *

The Romans only had five years to prepare their city for the Games but they did not disappoint, as it would comfortably rank high on any listing of the most successful and harmonious Olympics. Martin and Gynn write:

> The setting could not have been more historic. Dating back to the fifth century BC, Rome was nearly as old as the ancient Greek Games themselves, and even some of its aged sports venues were used for competition. Wrestling, for example, was contested in the 1,650-years-old Basilica of Maxentius in the Roman Forum. Ironically, however, it had been the Roman emperor Theodosius who issued the edict in AD 393 to abolish the ancient Greek Olympic Games. How times change!

For the first time ever more than 5000 athletes competed at the Games (4738 men and 610 women; Martin, Gynn), and 84 'geopolitical entities' had marchers in the opening ceremony, an impressive rise of 17 from harder to reach Melbourne (which had around 3200 competitors).[2] These Games were the last in which South Africa would participate until 1992.

To escape Rome's intense high-summer heat, the marathon race's start was delayed until 5.30 p.m., and oddly enough, neither the start nor finish occurred in

---

2. Although the lure of Australia becomes clear when one sees that just two fewer nations sent athletes "down under" in 1956 than they did to Helsinki in 1952.

the Olympic Stadium. The course was a triangular route, taking in such historical sites as the old Roman Forum, going under the Arch of Constantine, and past the ancient Circus Maximus, the scene of the city's chariot racing some 2000 years before. The final 11 kilometres of the journey consisted of the ancient Via Appia Antica, or the Roman Appian Way. This stretch, of enormous historical significance, was a fairly narrow route "lined with large cypress trees and pines, monuments and statues, with ancient cobblestones still existent in many places" (Martin & Gynn). Since the arrival of the athletes along Appian Way would coincide with dusk setting in, Italian soldiers lined the route holding aloft hundreds of spectacular fire torches, while they also valiantly tried to keep the eager spectators from infringing on to the course.

The favourites for the Rome Olympic marathon came from two clear sources. First, there was the Soviet world-record holder Sergey Popov. After the Englishman Jim Peters had dominated the world marathon record books for 6½ years, Popov tore into Peters' outstanding 2:17:39 mark set in the Windsor–Chiswick Polytechnic race, with a 2:15:17 clocking at the Stockholm European Championships of 1958. No one else came within 5 minutes of him, and no Soviet runner would beat Popov's time until 1970 (Hauman). Popov proved that he was no one-trick pony with another outstanding run in Koice in October 1959 (2:17:45). By the time the 1950s had closed no other athlete aside from Peters and Popov had ever broken 2:18.

Popov, however, was expected to be pushed all the way in Rome by Rhadi ben Abdesselem, a whippet-thin Moroccan, who had displayed his class earlier in the year by cutting a swathe through the Anglo-French domination of the International Cross-Country Championships and becoming the first non-European to win the race in its 58-year history.

Then there were the Brits, who had been showing some fancy footwork in their trial races. At the Polytechnic trial race the old and the new were on show: Arthur Keily, aged 39, won in 2:19:06, and he was followed by a debutant, *17 years* his junior, Brian Kilby. There was just one place to be decided, and this was grabbed by another new British star, Dennis O'Gorman, who returned an excellent 2:18:15 in Liverpool. To illustrate the depth of the British, they had to leave Fred Norris, who ran 2:19:08 in Liverpool, at home.

The United States sent an unusually weak team, although they did boast one wonderfully charismatic star in Johnny J. Kelley, jnr. Kelley had been to the Melbourne Olympics where he'd loved meeting and jogging with his hero: the "Czechoslovakian Choo-Choo", as he and other young American runners liked to call Emil Zátopek. But Kelley had a poor race in Melbourne, plodding to the finish in 21st. Kelley won Boston in 1957 and placed second for the following two years. In the 1960 Boston, Kelley returned hoping to win, but DNF'd in a black haze of blisters, despair and exhaustion. He quit the sport he loved so much. He was no longer a young man, of course, but an "ancient" 30. He was sick of all the demeaning jobs he'd taken which allowed him to run. He now had the job teaching English, the house with the white picket fence, the garden, the family, the dog. Why not lead a normal life? So he took to the thrilling adrenalin rush of mowing his lawn on a Saturday morning, to replace his "fartlek". A neighbour came and commended him for doing the right thing. The neighbour told Kelley he was "past it" after all. And Kelley saw red. "I'm not that old! Not as old as you, you old bastard!" thought Kelley. "Maybe you've given up, but not me!" (Derderian). And with that Kelley abandoned his mower and headed off for a race he knew of – if he hurried he might just make the start. Kelley made the start and won the race. Three weeks later he won the famous Yonkers Marathon that earned him selection for Rome. Once there, although he didn't trouble the leaders, Kelley ran respectably for 19th. Over 30 years later, he was *still* running Boston. So he never did kick the running bug after all.

America's other two runners for Rome were the somewhat more obscure names of Alexander Breckenridge and Gordon McKenzie.[3] Neither would threaten the top 25.

Author Derrick Young writes of the pre-race contenders: "The knowledgeable predicted Rhadi, the Moroccan who liked to run from the front, whose power in the tough, relentless churn of winter cross-country made him almost a natural favourite.

Or the powerful Britons? Keily and Kilby. The Russian Popov? Or the New Zealander Magee, running on the wings of seeing two countrymen already sweep to golds."

And so, this seemingly fairly open race got under way with athletes from an unprecedented 35 nations digging for gold (at Melbourne just 23 nations had entered runners). Although the sting from the sun's rays were losing their venom, the temperature at the outset was still an uncomfortable 72°F. The marathon course was fascinatingly laid out with the organizers determined to squeeze in as many historical classics as possible. Martin and Gynn write:

> The start was at the Campidoglio, the most sacred of Rome's seven hills. It is known for its beautiful piazza, designed by Michelangelo, that contains the equestrian statue of Marcus Aurelius. The finish was at the Arch of Constantine, built in A.D. 315, adjacent to the Colosseum.
>
> During the first few kilometres, the usual confusion of athletes jockeying to identify their optimal race pace was even more complicated because of the need to dash around monuments and across plazas.

The obvious problem for both the athletes and television producers with the start of the race so late, was that darkness would fall during the latter stages. This problem was solved by hundreds of torchbearers holding up spectacular flares to illuminate the night sky. It made for a haunting and unforgettable scene.

A leading group of four soon formed. The veteran Briton Arthur Keily was in the mix, as was Aurele Vandendriessche of Belgium, who had won five Belgian titles and would go on to score impressive back-to-back wins at Boston in 1963–4. To complete the group was Morocco's Rhadi, and a completely unknown runner,

3. McKenzie was married to Christine McKenzie, a feisty and attractive English woman who was a keen athlete herself. She astounded reporters by running alongside her husband at the 1960 Boston in barefeet, yelling encouragement for around a quarter of a mile. Some years later she applied to run in a 4-mile road race but was disallowed because of the theory that such a vast distance would make a shapely woman such as McKenzie unfeminine and muscular. She appealed and attended a hearing. At a crucial moment McKenzie threw off her fur coat to reveal just a bikini. She asked the panel how unfeminine and muscular they found her. None of the above, they replied, and allowed her to race.

surely soon to disappear from the sharp end of the race, number 11, Ethiopian Abebe Bikila, a member of Emperor Haile Selassie's Imperial Palace guards. Journalists and seasoned observers looked at each other knowingly. These unknown rabbits – will they ever learn?

A large group settled in behind these four pace-setters and 10 kilometres passed in a decidedly nippy 31:07. The other Briton Brian Kilby floated up to join the pack – looking about half the age of his teammate, which of course he was. Ireland's Albert Messitt forged into the lead for a while, with another Moroccan Allal Saoudi, wearing an enormous headband – which could have passed for a bandage – tucking into his left. All the while the unknown, barefoot Ethiopian kept up.

Over the next 5 kilometres the sequence of runners continually changed, but Messitt, who had won the Irish Olympic trial in only 2:28, soon gave way and indeed failed to finish. The suicidal pace of the first 10 kilometres certainly sorted out those who were fit and those who were merely game. The next 5 kilometres took a lengthier 16:55, although Martin and Gynn then give a 20-kilometres split of 62:39, indicating a spectacular acceleration. There was an acceleration, but not that extreme, and obviously the checkpoints had been inaccurately placed. But the crunch moment had still arrived, and it had done so because Rhadi had disliked being in such crowded company: "Rhadi took stock of the condition of the three around him, realized that now was the moment, still not yet halfway through the 26 miles, to put in the killer thrust. He surged away in the cruellest burst any of the four had yet suffered. And he went on, and on, and...until the others were almost lost in the murk of 200 yards of space separating them from the leader (Young).

All were dropped except one man. Bikila. This new, unknown athlete, also lagged, but only by around 60 yards. The Ethiopian worked his arms a little harder. And then he lengthened his stride. And metre by metre he began to reel in a startled Rhadi. By 25 kilometres the race had become the ultimate two-horse battle, between the favourite and the unknown. Vandendriessche and Keily "destroyed by the crippling war they had just been demobbed from" (Young) got swallowed up by the pack, and Vandendriessche made a sorry departure from the action soon after. But his was a marathon career that had many triumphs to come.

The brave New Zealander Magee and world-record holder Popov took up the chase. Magee was coached by one of the finest running coaches ever, Arthur Lydiard, who had already enjoyed a terrific Games, since his two other protégés, Peter Snell and Murray Halberg, had struck gold in the 800 and 5000-metres respectively. Magee's conservative astute pacing had allowed him to command of the best of the rest, and he soon became a strong favourite to take the bronze, since Popov was looking ever more a spent force with each passing kilometre. But however well Magee ran, he was never going to make an impact on the two flying leaders, who were over a quarter of a mile down the road. They were coming back to no one.

Finally, after three consecutive sets of 10 kilometres in 31:07, 31:32 and 31:50 (Gretton), which put Rhadi and Bikila around 30 seconds up on Popov's world record pace, they *finally* began to slow over kilometres 30–40, which they would

THE 50 GREATEST MARATHON RACES OF ALL TIME

cover in a more circumspect 34:04. It was during this time that an acutely worrying development occurred for Rhadi. Instead of leading Bikila by a stride, which was how he preferred to race – no one *ever* led him, it was suddenly the new man, Bikila, who led by a stride. Rhadi's supporters and friends knew something was wrong. Although their man trailed by just a fraction of a second, the fact that he was not controlling the race, had his supporters gulping.

On to the Appian Way the crowds thickened, and the word passed around that a terrific battle was fast approaching. The crowd buzzed in anticipation. The media just panicked. In this day and age Bikila's anonymity would not cause too much distress amongst the sportswriters covering the race. Mobile phones would be whipped out and picture messages accompanied by a question mark zapped to headquarters. Fax machines would spew out desperate SOS messages. E-mail inboxes would fill up fast. But here, with no such gadgets at their disposal, befuddled scribes turned to each other for help. "Tell me what you know, and I'll tell you what I know." "Well, Rhadi is the best cross-country runner in the world, and Bikila is used to being on his feet because he's a bodyguard in a country beginning with the letter 'E', or maybe 'U'. It's in Africa. OK, what do you know?" "I know he must be very forgetful because he left his shoes back at the athlete's village." "That's *all* you know?!" "Uh huh." A correspondent from *L'Equipe* newspaper later admitted he had written off Bikila before the race. He recalled looking through the list of entries on Friday and had spotted that Abebe

Calmly scratching his chin, Abebe Bikila debates what action to take regarding the company of the Moroccan Rhadi Ben Abdesselem. *AFP/Getty Images*

had done 2:21:33 before coming to Rome. "But I say to myself, it is not possible in the desert, and I look down for other winner."

Suddenly the two warriors had arrived, cutting into Popov's world-record mark with every stride. They were not quite side by side, Bikila that threatening yard in front. And then he began to steel himself for a plan he had hatched in his mind a few days before the big race. Bikila had noticed that along the ancient Via Appia stood the ancient Obelisco di Azum (Obelisk of Axum), which Italian soldiers had plundered from Ethiopia and brought to Rome after their invasion in 1936. Just as the runners would pass the obelisk, there was a slight incline, and it was here that Bikila decided he would start his kick for home, provided he was in contention, which he knew he would be. The obelisk was just half a kilometre from the finish, and when Bikila and Rhadi came down the Via Appia for real, Bikila set his plan in motion – and kicked.

The small gap Bikila had protected suddenly started to visibly grow. The African was getting away as Rhadi's smooth stride lost its glide, faltering with every hesitant step. Bikila surged down the route where his ancestors had been humiliated and driven as slaves. No discomfort featured on the Ethiopian's thin, high-browed face. In the wonderful race footage of him running toward the finish line, Bikila appears to be trotting along a beach at dusk, perhaps towards the sea for an evening dip before dinner. While his white teeth flashed in the darkness, his bare feet remained unblistered. "Extending his arms in victory and as if to embrace the entire Arch of Constantine, he was bathed for only a brief moment in the television illumination. The gold medal was his" (Martin &Gynn). In becoming the first black African to win the Olympic marathon, Bikila had also broken Popov's world record by a mere 0.8 of a second. The exhausted Rhadi arrived 25 seconds later. As far as is known his silver medal came in his only ever marathon. Barry Magee brought yet more glory on Arthur Lydiard's methods and hung on to bronze. Magee would go on to win the prestigious Fukuoka Marathon in December, smashing the old course record by nearly 3 minutes as he ran 2:19:04.

Upon Bikila's victory, while he proceeded to carry out faintly comical hamstring stretches, the facts and figures came in a torrent. Zátopek's Olympic record hadn't just fallen; it had been demolished, by 7:47. Alain Mimoun of Melbourne's triumph would have been 2 whole miles down on the leader on this occasion. And here he was in Rome, as the defending champion, nearly 3 miles down as a placed 34th in 2:31. But let no one question the pedigree of Mimoun. He was recently ranked the 43rd greatest Olympic athlete of all time in a huge study by Calvin Shulman of the London *Times*, justified by three Olympic silvers and one gold over four successive Olympics of 1948–60.

Bikila's first words to the waiting throngs became famous and are still remembered today. *That was nothing!* People recall him saying. *I could do it again...now!* His actual words were: "We are a poor people, and not used to mechanized transport. So we run everywhere. Twenty-six miles is nothing to me. Of course, I could have kept going for a long time. I could have gone round again without difficulty. Bare feet? Oh, we always take our shoes off for competition. So much more comfortable (Young).

477

* * *

The London *Times* reported the closing of the Games, and Bikila's triumph, in moving fashion:

> We came to smile, we stayed to cheer in the *Stadio Olimpic* here this evening as the 1960 Olympic Games were brought to a close. There can never have been such a dramatic moment in Olympic history as that this evening when all the lights in this great bowl went out and round the massed tiers the Roman newspaper torches burst into flame, thousands upon thousands of them until the whole stadium seemed a shimmering flame.
>
> The bare-footed Abebe finished as if at the end of a training spin, legs driving well, arms moving effortlessly. He waved aside those who offered him blankets, limbered down gently, raised his hands in pleasure in the darkness – and danced about in search of relaxation. There was never any hint to the casual onlooker that this colourful character, a member of the household guard of Emperor Haile Selassie, had just run 26 miles 385 yards in the world's fastest time of 2hr 15 min 16.2 secs.

An editor by the name of David Talbot proudly put his name is large block letters at the top of the *Ethiopian Herald* at the time of Bikila's triumph. But Talbot, therefore, is the one the buck stops at, for making the huge gaffe of not flagging a single Ethiopian runner as a contender for the 1960 Olympic marathon in the *Herald*'s lengthy preview piece. After Bikila won however, Talbot et al. woke up in a big way. The *Herald* editorial of September 11th, 1960 read (with erratic spelling and made-up words unaltered):

> Our attention is called to the spectacular achievement of Abebe Bikila who won the much-coveted 1960 Olympics marathon gold medal, finishing by 100 yards ahead of the silver medallist Rhadi of Morocco. We hail Abebe for his great feat of endurance, athlety and sportsmanship. We are proud of him for having won for his country its first gold medal in the famous arena of International Games – the Olympics. We wish him many more winnings.
>
> Nineteen-sixty is the second entry of Ethiopia into the Olympics. This makes Abebe's laurels all the more appreciated. It should be noticed that many of the countries that have repeatedly participated in these International Games did not have the good fortune to win a gold medal. This is a challenge to all interested in sports and athletics in Ethiopia, government and private, to prepare for the 1964 meet in Tokyo.

The *Herald*'s huge banner headline on Friday 16th September read:

HIS IMPERIAL MAJESTY DECORATES ABEBE BIKILA
1960 OLYMPICS MARATHON GOLD MEDALIST.

TENS THOUSANDS GIVE HERO WARM, TUMULTUOUS WELCOME.

His majesty recognizes Olympiad's efforts

The Emperor spoke the following words to Bikila:

> We are very much pleased, for you have ably shown to the world that sport is neither new nor foreign to Ethiopia.
>
> We have been closely following the other Ethiopian Olympic athletes who have also done their best.
>
> We see before us your friend who got a fracture on his arm during the cycle race, and it testifies that all of you have done you best at the Olympics.
>
> To win the laurel of world victory in a race, which demands spiritual and physical strength, is a significant event that brings global reputation to Our country.
>
> The precedent laid down by you opens the road for the future generation for better hope and greater honours.

Bikila replied to the Emperor's words:

> Truthfully I am pleasantly surprised at Addis Ababa's enormous ovation, and feel that my countrymen are great lovers of sports. I had the occasion to see the way that other nations welcomed their Olympic stars; but felt, when the plane landed at the airport that Ethiopia, my country, has lived up remarkably to this sporting and athletic tradition.

Maurice F. Edwards, a British AAA coach at the time, wrote an interesting letter to the *Herald*, rightly pouring scorn on the claim that Bikila was an untrained athlete:

> Of the six runners chosen to represent Ethiopia at the Games, it is unfair to say that they were "practically untrained and unsupervised".
>
> Success in Olympic competition does not come to an untrained athlete. It would be misleading to the youth of the nation, who may be inspired to follow Abebe's example, to suggest that such success was gained with little preparation or effort.
>
> It was my privilege to be of some assistance to the athletics teams of the Imperial bodyguard during their Olympic preparations and I know the extent of the rigorous training that was undertaken by the athletes under the supervision of their sports officers. Without this lengthy period of preliminary training, no performance of merit would have been possible.

* * *

Upon returning home Bikila enjoyed three happy months of acclaim and happiness. Aged 28 his greatness had only just begun, but then real life kicked in. And real life in the poorest of countries often means revolution. Bikila kept well from the fighting and the carnage, sensibly taking refuge on the basketball court. But it mattered not. He was still thrown into jail. He explains: "I was playing basketball when the revolution broke out. I had absolutely nothing to do with it. But everybody suspected everybody and I was thrown into jail." Good sense prevailed and Bikila was almost immediately released. But gone was his job as the Emperor sacked his entire bodyguard. Gone, too, was Abebe's precious plot of land and a life of poverty followed for him, his wife and young son. Not that Bikila wanted for much. His coach at the time, Onni Niskanen, remarked: "He doesn't smoke or drink. He lives a Spartan life" (Young).

A year after Rome, Bikila had faced his challenges head on and he appeared at the International Marathon in Athens seeking to conquer all again. The Belgian Vandendriessche was there who had provided such a stern challenge at the Olympics, but again Bikila was a comfortable winner. Bikila's military duties meant that he raced sparingly outside Ethiopia, but in 1963 he did make a high-profile appearance at Boston where he became the seventh Olympic champion to attempt to win at Boston. He became the seventh to fail, too, as Vandendriessche caught sight of Bikila through the mist deep in to the race and took off "like a rocket to the moon". It was a painful defeat for Bikila who had succumbed to Boston's hills, and was his only marathon defeat in 13 completed races.[4] Still, there could be no doubt that coming into the Tokyo Olympics, he had to be viewed as the leading threat.

Just 36 days before his marathon defence, however, Bikila was diagnosed with appendicitis and had to surrender to hospital to have his appendix removed. Such an infirmity usually takes a long, slow, frustrating several months to heal; give it half a year, the docs said, just to be safe. But Bikila had no such luxury. He felt he had no option but to defy the doctors' orders – his nation was counting on him. Eleven days' rest was all he took, before returning to strenuous, lung-busting training.

The multiple world-record breaking Australian Ron Clarke came to Tokyo to win the marathon. Other competitors saw Clarke as a machine, someone who could run for ever if need be. The English and the Japanese sent very strong teams, the latter of course on their home soil. Silver or bronze wouldn't be enough for them: they had to go for broke. And then there was the Irishman, Jim Hogan, who would "sell his last gasp for gold out there".

A partisan and passionate 80,000 roared the 68 lean, fit, sinewy machines on their way. The first 5 kilometres were suicidally fast (15:06), with Ron Clarke leading from Hogan. Bikila had to work his way through the field to regain contact. Peter Wilson of the *Daily Mirror* wrote: "He is like a metronome on legs. The black vest might have been sprayed on his dark form; his shorts are the colour of dried blood. There isn't an ounce of spare flesh on his frame, and his legs could belong to some sinewy old rooster." After Bikila had made contact, he set about Hogan and Clarke as a ravenous stray dog might an old chicken carcass. He thrust and parried and turned up the heat. Clarke and Hogan hung on for dear life. If it were a boxing match, the trainers would have had blood-stained towels at the ready in order to stop the bout. Quite simply, Clarke and Hogan were as brave as the African, but not as able. Before halfway Bikila's challengers were gone. Clarke clung on to a place just inside the top ten, albeit over 8 minutes off the pace, while Hogan stumbled along the side of the road, to the point of collapse, before finally carding a DNF.

---

4. He failed to finish his final two.

Four years later, Bikila is resplendent in pristine footwear, scorching to another world record at the Tokyo Olympic stadium. *IOC/Getty Images*

The marathon runners of Japan are well-known for their inscrutable demeanour on the race course. The good news for Tokyo's packed Olympic Stadium was that a runner with the most inscrutable demeanour of them all entered the stadium first, but it was not one of theirs. As Bikila shimmied along the cinders alone in the race with more than a 4-minute cushion, the crowd could take solace that they were witnessing before them the most perfect marathoner ever. Bikila celebrated with another of his famous flashing grins as he broke the world record yet again in the Olympic marathon, but this time not by a mere 0.8 of a second. Basil Heatley's 2:13:55 set earlier in the year in Chiswick had now been replaced by a magnificent 2:12:11.

As Bikila slowed to a walk after the winning line, his muscles found they needed to celebrate too. Now that they were no longer working, they needed to dance, be merry and keep loose. For nearly 5 minutes, therefore, Bikila indulged in an elaborate display of callisthenics and stretches. The crowd oooh'd and aaah'd. What was this? they asked. Was he not tired? Did he not crave rest? Finally, Bikila was able to welcome the second man into the stadium. To the ecstatic delight of the crowd it *was* one of theirs: Kokichi Tsuburaya. He entered the stadium in a reasonably fresh state, but not sadly, as fresh as the man who followed, the now former world-record holder, Heatley (of Britain). Heatley put his head down and unleashed a cruel kick on Tsuburaya to defeat him by 3 seconds. It was the fourth time a British man had earned silver in the Olympic marathon. Following in the footsteps of Ferris ('32), Harper ('36) and Richards ('48), Heatly had done more than was asked of him. He would have seen off "Emil the Great" by more than a mile, but he was unlucky: Heatley was up against a man a decade ahead of his time.

Tsuburaya was an instant hero in Japan, but the pressure was now placed on him to perform even better in Mexico four years hence. He was allowed to give up his job and dedicate himself to his running. Injuries inevitably followed this bout of over-training, and every time the poor soul attempted to make a comeback the realization dawned that he was not half the runner he was. David Wallechinsky reports him taking his own life by slashing his right carotid artery with a razor blade, leaving the suicide note that said it all: "Cannot run any more."

* * *

Despite all the copy that exists about Bikila in books about running and the Olympics, the intricacies of the great one's training and character still remain clouded in mystery. The author mentioned to a colleague one day about striving

481

THE 50 GREATEST MARATHON RACES OF ALL TIME

to unearth more about the inner secrets of Bikila. "I think my dad interviewed him once," my friend replied. My excitement at this piece of serendipity was tempered by the fact that my friend's father, the writer George Gretton, was long gone. Where was this interview? No one seemed to know. Finally, after around a year of waiting, the interview found its way to me. It had appeared in Gretton's 1968 book, *Out in Front*, and wasn't actually carried out by Gretton himself, but a colleague of his: Berhanu Tibebu of the *Ethiopian Herald*. The interview is distressing because Tibebu caught Bikila – a year before the Mexico Olympics – at his most optimistic. Bikila was relishing the chance of shooting for a third consecutive success in the marathon, and was even eyeing up the Munich Olympics of 1972. He'd be 40 by then. Not a problem, Bikila said: "If you keep yourself in good shape, you can never be too old for the Olympics."
Tibebu wrote:

Bikila believes that a marathon runner need not be lacking strength to compete at top level after the age of 35. Constant practice makes the athlete's body grow stronger and stronger. He may not be in a better position to break records than at an earlier age, but Bikila believes that the body well strengthened through constant practice, greatly contributes to the athlete's chance of winning the Olympics.

He is a self-composed man full of energy and tenacity. His face expresses determination and confidence. Pleasant to talk with, he is well versed in giving illustrations of what he discussed by using witticisms and proverbs. He is neither aggressive not shy. He says he loves running and that he is very much interested in it. He aims at beating his opponents first, as he says, to keep up the name of his country, and then at breaking his own record to see by how much he can improve over his previous achievement.

Bikila told me that he relies purely on methods he himself has evolved in the various competitions in which he has participated during the past 7 years, and that he does not owe anything to any athlete. As for the advice of a coach, he seriously pays attention to it, but adds that he greatly depends on his own methods and judgment.

To prove that Bikila was an astute observer as well as a supreme competitor, Tibebu writes: "Among the runners Bikila most admires he mentions the Moroccan Abdesselem Rhadi. He also mentioned the name of his own countyman, Mamo Wolde. Bikila believes that, with greater effort and encouragement, Mamo Wolde will show a remarkable result in Olympic competition."
Interestingly, Bikila was a passionate horseman, a sport which he pursued not in any way to aid his athletics but simply because he loved riding as a pastime. As well as riding a lot in his youth, Bikila frequently played a game known as Gena, a hockey-type game played between villages. It is played without goals, with the aim being to dribble with the ball to a point regarded as the farthest end of the opponent's position, as agreed by the two parties. One therefore imagines that it involves a tremendous amount of fast running. The young Abebe was a master of Gena. Commenting on Bikila's exercises after his Tokyo run, Tibebu notes: "What he regards as most essential for the marathon race is physical exercise.

Before he starts any training session, he does gymnastics. Physical exercises after a marathon race, when several competitors fall by the way fainting is indeed a great feat to accomplish. But for Bikila, whether at the beginning or the end, physical exercise is a 'must'."

The Mexico Olympics arrived, and Bikila was there. But sadly he really wasn't fit this time, running in agony with a fractured fibula of the left leg. Realizing he would have to pull out at 17 kilometres, he turned to his countryman who he admired so much, Mamo Wolde, and urged him to go forth and conquer. "Sir! Yes, Sir!" Wolde replied, and shot off down the road to give chase and won by over 3 minutes. It was the highlight of a long and terrific Olympic career for Wolde that began way back in 1956 where he ran in the 4 × 400 relay, the 800 and the 1500. He would go on to secure bronze in the marathon at Munich in 1972, aged 40.

* * *

Bikila didn't know it but he had run his last marathon. Five months after Mexico City, on March 22nd, 1969, Bikila was driving his Volkswagen Beetle, a gift of the government, 130 kilometres south of Addis Ababa, when he swerved to avoid a speeding Land-Rover. He overturned in a ditch and fractured his sixth and seventh vertebra rendering him almost paralyzed. He never recovered use of his legs and only minimal use of his arms. This was enough for him to participate and promote wheelchair sports though, and he competed at the Paraplegic Games in summer 1970 at Stoke Mandeville Hospital in Britain. No medal this time, but that smile was still there.

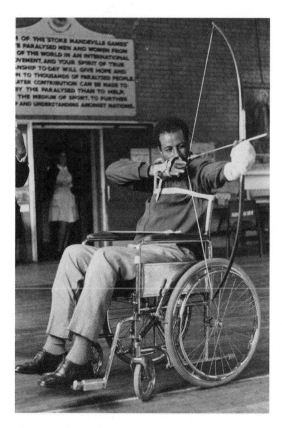

Shooting for gold – quite literally: Bikila participated in the Paraplegic Games at England's Stoke Mandeville hospital in the archery competition, July 1970. *Hulton-Deutsch Collection/CORBIS*

Bikila was the guest of honour at the Munich Olympics where he was hugely welcomed. He died on October 22nd, 1973 of a brain haemorrhage. He was 41. In the year of his death, Bikila stated: "It was the will of God that I won the Olympics, and it was the will of God that I met with my accident. I accepted those victories as I accept this tragedy. I have to accept both circumstances as facts of life and live happily (Hauman). Bikila's early death raised him to near-deified status with young Ethiopian runners. Abebe Mekonnen who won Boston in 1989 and several other major marathon summed up Bikila's legacy: "I feel so deeply about him that I sometimes even cry when I see his picture. I always pray for him. It is his great inspiration that has made us as good as we are. It is because of him that we are known worldwide. To me Abebe is almost a God – he sacrificed for Ethiopia, his country and his flag. He is an unforgettable memory. It is my dream to be like him" (Derderian).

Race result:

Abebe Bikila	ETH	2:15:16
Rhadi ben Abdesselem	MAR	2:15:41
Barrington Magee	NZL	2:17:18
Konstantin Vorobiev	URS	2:19:09
Sergey Popov	URS	2:19:18
Thyge Togersen	DEN	2:21:03
Abebe Wakgira	ETH	2:21:09
Benaissa Bakir	MAR	2:21:21
Osvaldo Suarez	ARG	2:21:26
Franjo Skrinjar	YUG	2:21:40

Sources:

Derderian, Tom, *Boston Marathon*. Human Kinetics, 1996.
Edwards, Maurice, letter to the *Ethiopian Herald*, September 1960.
Ethiopian *Herald*, September 9th–16th, 1960.
Gretton, George, *Out In Front*. Pelham Books, 1968.
Hauman, Riël, *Century of the Marathon*. Human & Rousseau, 1996.
Martin, David and Roger Gynn, *The Olympic Marathon*. Human Kinetics, 2000.
The Times, September 12th, 1960.
Wilson, Peter, in the *Daily Mirror*, October 22nd, 1968.
Young, Derrick, *The Ten Greatest Races*. A.C.M. Webb Publishing, 1972.
Wallechinsky, David, *The Complete Book of the Olympics*. Aurum Press, 2000.

IL

No. 2 – 1982 Boston Marathon [Men]

Monday, April 19th

"The winner was a dried-out, dehydrated, unsalted potato chip."

It happens, they say, to great sportsmen. They are happily executing their magnificent careers, when something seems to happen. They plateau. Suddenly, instead of making what they do seem simple, they start making mistakes, and, putting it bluntly, they start losing. One of the greatest of all golfers, Seve Ballesteros, could put it down to one shot: an horrendous shank to the 15th at the US Masters in 1986. Before that he was marching imperiously to a third green jacket, instead his ball found a deal-breaking watery grave. "He was never the same after that, you know," the all-knowing golf fans will tell you.

The same for tennis star John McEnroe. He was imperiously crushing Ivan Lendl in the final of the 1984 French Open, before he inexplicably collapsed and something inside him died. True, Mac went on to win Wimbledon the following month – almost out of sheer anger – but he would never win another Grand Slam after that, and eventually retired, eight frustrated, expletive-strewn years later. These turning points often happen far sooner than one would expect. The broiling Boston Marathon of 1982 was one of these occasions. Except its brutal punishment didn't spell the beginning of the end for one fine runner's career, but two.

* * *

For those who didn't believe in a little romance and the odd fairy tale, the 1982 Boston had all the makings of a damp squib. The newspaper commentators were in almost unanimous agreement as to the winners of both the chaps and the dames. Alberto Salazar and Grete Waitz, said Steve Harris. I concur, said George Kimball. Ditto, said Toni Reavis. And me, said Sonny Reizner. Only Bill Squires and Tommy Leonard rejected the herd and bizarrely nominated Lorraine Moller for the women's race – who never set foot on the course. Waitz was the multiple former world-record holder and triple New York champion. She came to Boston ready to do serious damage to her best of 2:25:41, set in 1980 at New York, and for that matter Alison Roe's new world best of 2:25:28, set at New York '81.[1]

---

1. Roe's world best at New York the previous fall was later erased from the record books because the course came up 148m short on a remeasurement.

Boston's generous downhills were there for Waitz to attack and conquer. But instead they conquered her.

With just three miles to go, Waitz, leading without another woman in sight, dropped out. "You can slow down and still win!", the spectators told her. "Just jog it in!" they pleaded. "Power-walk and the laurel wreath is all yours." But the pain in Waitz's quadriceps had become unbearable. The unheralded West German Charlotte Teske came to the finish thinking she was second in a moderate 2:29. Cheer up, a cop said, you're the winner. "I didn't really beat her," said Teske later. Waitz lost to the brute that the Boston course can be.

The overwhelming men's favourite, Alberto Salazar, came to Boston as arguably the best marathoner in the world. Now that "Boston Billy's" (Rodgers') time as number one had passed, and the Japanese Toshihiko Seko was yet to fully mature, the only man to lay claim to Salazar's title of world's best was the Australian Rob de Castella (aka "Deek"). Between them they'd barely lost a single marathon, and their management company, IMG, would subsequently organize for them to go head-to-head in a showdown at Rotterdam in 1983 to reveal the best runner and Deek would win, although Salazar wasn't quite himself that day. Still recovering from Boston '82 most probably.

"Running on the edge" is how author Riël Hauman describes Salazar's training and racing. He was born in Havana on August 7th, 1958 and began fairly serious running at the age of 13. By this time Alberto's father, José, had fled with his family from Castro's revolution, and relocated in Wayland, Massachusetts: "José was a man who would go back to his native Cuba at the drop of a beret to drag Fidel Castro kicking and screaming into the sea, but instead of launching a solo Bay of Pigs invasion, José Salazar worked as a civil engineer on high-rise buildings and fathered a large family: Christine, Ricardo, Alberto, and Fernando" (Derderian). When the almighty creator was handing out athletic ability, it was Ricardo who was blessed with talent aplenty, while Alberto was in another queue having a stubborn streak installed. Ricardo popped a tasty 4:24 mile in high school and also broke the record for running the half-mile round the block at home from another kid. He told Alberto to give the record a go, but time and again Alberto just "wound up walking and looking at the ground" (Derderian). Alberto would never make it as a distance runner, Ricardo concluded: not only did he have an awkward, lanky style, but crucially, he had a low pain threshold.

Against the odds though, Alberto finally started to run for Wayland High School, and as a "bag-of-bones" 15-year-old began tagging along with the star runners at the Greater Boston Track Club. Salazar, like any young puck, was looking for something to excel at in life. He greatly admired Bill Rodgers (over ten years his senior) at the *GBTC*, and was delighted when Rodgers pulled a shocker by placing third in the World Cross of 1975. With his father and Ricardo, Salazar watched in thrilled amazement as Rodgers then roared to his great Boston win of '75. That was it, thought Alberto. He would become a marathoner too.

*   *   *

To fulfil this dream, Salazar began to train with a feverish intensity. Far too feverish and intense for a lad so young. When he left for college in Oregon in 1976, he was strictly instructed by his coach Bill Squires to limit himself to 70 miles a week. But soon he was doing a hundred. Not for the first time in his career his heart was ruling his head. But with strength and determination like this, Salazar couldn't help but rapidly develop into one of the finest runners in the land. The famous Falmouth road race of 1978 was nearly his undoing, however. Chasing Bill Rodgers hard in the fierce heat, Salazar faded from second to tenth and collapsed at the finish, suffering from hyperthermia. His temperature was taken at a not-so-cool 105.6 degrees. He was placed in a rubber raft filled with 100 pounds of ice, whereupon his temperature plummeted to below 90, and the last rites of the Roman Catholic Church were given. But he recovered. Later on, the physiotherapist Bill Bates fell back on all his medical training to diagnose Salazar as "heat sensitive" – something the man in the street could already tell you. Bill Dellinger, his coach in Eugene, commented: "We've never had anyone at Oregon handle the load Alberto has shown he can handle, not even Steve Prefontaine."

Salazar bounced back from this torrid experience at Falmouth, and his results kept on improving. In 1980 he came to New York for his first marathon as the most promising young rookie anyone could remember, and, proudly wearing the green and yellow colours of the University of Oregon, defeated the Mexican Rodolpho Gomez in the first of their two superb New York duels, by 32 seconds in 2:09:41. The following year after another twelve-month stint of gut-wrenching training, Salazar returned to the Big Apple and promptly declared that he would run 2:08. Few people doubted him. In the World Cup 10,000-metres he had run 27:40, and shortly before the marathon he had completed a training session in which he ran three repeat miles in 4:12 with less than 3-minute recoveries (Hauman).

The 1981 New York marathon was televised nationally for the first time, and Salazar soared to halfway in 64:10 with John Graham and José Gomez for company. Not for much longer though. A 17th-mile surge of 4:33 saw Salazar out on his own "the determination etched on his face." He flashed through the line in 2:08:13 and Derek Clayton's world record that had stood for twelve years had fallen. "It's like Roger Bannister's first 4-minute!" exulted Allan Steinfeld, the marathon's technical director, in a good old-fashioned piece of hyperbole. There was disappointment later when the course was found to be 148 metres short on a remeasurement, and Salazar's record was voided. But there was one indisputable fact that couldn't be queried, Salazar was one of the great forces of distance running: "There are three things that you don't bet against. They are taxes, death – and Alberto," mused Bill Squires.

* * *

Weren't the wise old hacks just being a little hasty though? Surely there'd be someone at Boston '82 to keep Salazar busy. And of course there were, although not it must be said from a noticeably bare foreign field. But the home challenge was strong. Bill Rodgers was aging but he was definitely the finest 34-year-old marathoner in the world; and the lure of winning Boston number five kept him training fantastically hard. His confrontation with Salazar was heavily promoted: "Wonder Boy" versus "Old Smoothy". There was also a farmboy called Dickie Beardsley, 26, from Rush City, Minnesota, who contrary to Salazar's unnatural gait, had a running style sent straight from the angels. Tom Derderian wrote: "Beardsely ran with fluid motion in his free-floating, relaxed stride and that to watch him was like watching a natural dancer take the floor with God-given talent. Bill Squires thought God had made Dick Beardsley for long-distance running."

Beardsley had won the popular Grandma's Marathon in Duluth, Minnesota the previous summer in 2:09:37, but this only caused the cynics to nod their heads and say: "Uh huh, how short was it?" But recall, that it wasn't the first time that Beardsley had shown his class – he was certainly at least a 2:11 man, since he had famously tied the inaugural London Marathon in March of 1981 with Inge Simonsen of Norway. Beardsley was improving in a hurry and came to Boston intent on running in the lead, however fast that meant he'd have to go. Derderian gives more insight into Beardsley's upbringing and mental outlook: "As a boy Beardsley often walked his dog through a nearby swamp. As the going got deeper and muckier he liked it more and more. He spent his free time trapping and hunting. He liked the excuse it gave him to wander alone over the countryside." Beardsley went to train in the spring of '82 to Georgia, with a friend Dean Matthews, who was expected to force a fast early pace in the marathon. Ed Mendoza, Ron Tabb, John Lodwick (fourth the year before in 2:11) were others whom the scribes picked to be up there.

* * *

April 19th, 1982 dawned bright, sunny...and hot. The thermometer would threaten to touch 70 Fahrenheit all day. The plot thickened. What was that expert diagnosis Bill Bates had come up with? Ah yes, heat sensitive. Maybe Alberto had something to think about after all.

Things started out quietly – and somewhat slowly – and as the runners passed through the first few miles it seemed they were travelling with an impending sense of doom. The spectators were quiet – almost a little dozy – as they bathed under the sun's rays. But sooner or later the beer would kick in, and Patriot's Day in Boston is almost the biggest excuse of the year to party. And there was another thing: no one was going to beat Salazar running off a slow pace. The attack had to be taken to him. Spars and jabs had to be landed. Did he have a weak spot? Yes: Falmouth fours years earlier. The heat had nearly killed him. Would he suffer again? Only one way to find out. But the attacks took a while to materialize, and little had developed by 10 kilometres. Tom Derderian writes: "It did not look like a record day. Salazar, Beardsley, and Rodgers ran patiently in a big pack. Salazar thought that Tabb and Matthews were constantly pushing the pace with lots of stupid surges, acting like a couple of jerks to accomplish nothing but destroying their own rhythm. Salazar sat back laughing at the two fools. Burn baby, burn yourself up."

A little before halfway Bill Rodgers led the marathon with Matthews (who would eventually be forced out of the race with foot problems). But they were way down on the checkpoint record set as far back as 1970 by the "flying doc", Ron Hill. And then, quite suddenly, everything changed. The fireworks started. Here was the best marathoner in the world at the world's most prestigious race on a beautiful day. There were over a million spectators on the course. The time had come to get this thing going. The whole pack moved up a gear as they sensed halfway approaching. The girls of Wellesley College let their lungs rev up, and then they let rip. Halfway was surprisingly reached in silky smooth 1:04:04. But Boston's first half is, of course, the only kind thing about her, and only a small portion of the lead pack would survive the race running at anything close to this speed – and indeed several wouldn't survive at all.

With grim determination, Rodgers hung onto his lead. Funny to think it was only seven years earlier that he had sprung on to the world scene with such merry fire and brilliance. He seemed to have been around for longer, and it also seemed that he should be slowing down a little by now. But instead, there he was leading the Boston Marathon with the comfortable-looking Ed Mendoza. Salazar and Beardsley lurked patiently, like two piranhas under a sailboat, waiting for the sailors to dip their toes in the water.

When the runners turned the corner at the fire station at a little before 17.5 miles, Dick Beardsley decided it was time to take the initiative, and tossed in a surge. He looked stylish and relaxed in his dark New Balance vest and white painter's cap with the visor flipped up. Meanwhile, Salazar was a little worried about what Bill Rodger's had once told him. "Someday, the marathon will humble you," Bill darkly remarked. Would this be the day? thought Salazar. In the flurry of attack from Beardsley's surge, "Salazar squinted and held on" (Derderian).

Perhaps predictably it was the grand old man Rodgers who slipped first. Never again would he challenge for the very top honours at Boston, although, incredibly,

Four-time champion Bill Rodgers (1) dukes it out with Dick Beardsley (3), Alberto Salazar (2) and Ed Mendoza in the race's first half. *Steve Sutton/Duomo/Corbis*

four years hence, aged 38, he would electrify the crowds and storm through the late stages to finish fourth behind Rob de Castella. But on this day, on the very hills where he had done so much damage in his previous four wins, he would have to let the new batch get away. Ed Mendoza was next to bite the dust. And unlike Rodgers, his grip on the race had loosened so dramatically that he would not make it to the finish. Rodgers would go on to score a very game fourth. Up ahead, a fierce duel had unfolded of already grim and epic proportion. Before the race Salazar had irritated Beardsley by claiming that he didn't view anyone in the field as a threat. "Beardsley thought that as long as somebody is human, he's beatable" (Derderian).

One of the four taxing hills sped by, and then another, and still another, but Beardsley and Salazar could not be separated. The spectators roared their approval. It was Beardsley who led, with Salazar tucked in behind. Well, it's a kicker's world, he thought. He also thought it was far too risky to try and break this overwhelmingly tough runner yet. There was still 6 miles to go. At countless points along the way, the locals loaded up their loudspeakers with the harmonious sound of Vangelis, or, more specifically, the theme tune to the previous summer's hit movie *Chariots of Fire*. "The glorious music mixed with the cheers made Mendoza's slipping and Rodgers's breaking seem surreal" (Derderian).

Beardsley kept his lead at a yard or so through Cleveland Circle. Less than 4 miles to go now. Salazar recalls to the author: "With 4 or 5 miles to go I was pretty confident I could soften him up by introducing the occasional surge..." But 15 minutes later the gladiators arrived at Kenmore Square seemingly tied together by invisible string. One horrendous mile to go. Beardsley recalled later: "I was actually getting more and more confident. Alberto would try to make a move but I would see his shadow come up on me and see that he was trying to pass me and then I surged."

What Beardsley needed most in the last mile was a smooth, clear road to run down with no interruptions from the crowd, police or road surface. But interruptions are just what he got. In triplicate. First, a fan grabbed at him just before Kenmore Square, "then a bus ran into me," and finally a tightening of his right, hamstring muscle. "I was going to make a late surge but all of a sudden my right hamstring tightened up on me and I was limping. Alberto saw that and, as good a runner as Alberto is, he knew that was a time to surge."

Salazar surged and quickly opened up a lead of 30 yards. But then, just as it appeared it would continue to stretch, the lead settled and Beardsley collected himself for one final spectacular rally. Ironically the pothole into which Beardsley stepped stretched out the knot in his "hammy". Beardsley bore down again, and yard by yard the gap shrunk. But still his problems with outside forces weren't over. Michael Madden reported in the *Boston Globe*:

Beardsley was being harassed, impeded and even struck by a phalanx of 10 Boston, State and Metropolitan District Police motorcycles accompanying the runners. A Boston motorcycle zigzagged just behind Beardsley's heels as he made the turn from Commonwealth Avenue onto Hereford street and a State Police motorcycle positioned itself directly behind Salazar and in front of Beardsley on the run along Hereford street, impeding Beardsley's path.

Salazar reaches the finish line with Beardsley in tow. *Steve Sutton/Duomo/Corbis*

But with just 300 yards to go Beardsley stopped worrying about being struck from behind by a tonne of metal, and focused on Salazar's back. Incredibly he drew level yet again, only for yet another mindless and incompetent State trooper to sideswipe him. Beardsley pushed the bike from his path with his arm and was impeded as he made the turn. Salazar drew away for the final time less than 150 yards from the finish. He looked over his shoulder twice with the look of a man running for his life, before finally the promised land engulfed him. Salazar explains to the author how he'd made the schoolboy error of not knowing exactly where the finish line was: "When I turned the final corner I thought there was still half a mile to go. Big mistake! There were less than 200 yards. I didn't want to leave it that late." It was the closest Boston Marathon in its 86-year history, and the first time in any marathon anywhere that two broke 2:09 in the same race. Jerry Nason wrote in the *Globe*: "If there never was another Boston Marathon, this super struggle would be the one by which to remember them all."

As the two embraced at the finish, Beardsley told Salazar: "You ran a hell of a race." "You had me hurting," replied Salazar. "We had each other hurting," noted Beardsley later.

* * *

"I took him to the finish line..." gasped a tearful Beardsley straight after. "I took him to the finish line. Oh, I wanted to win so bad...I wanted it so bad." There were no well-formed, coherent sentences from Beardsley, just breathless utterances of pain and anguish:

The two warriors celebrate on the podium. *Bettmann/CORBIS*

491

I wanted it so much...my right leg tightened up on at the Eliot Lounge [¾ of a mile from the finish]...Oh, my, I wanted to win so bad...The police motorcycle ran right into me; it actually hit me...I can't believe it...What do you have to do to win here?...I stepped into a pothole...I wanted it so bad. I didn't want the race to come down to what it did. I don't know what I can do on a track, but I know what Alberto can do.

As for Salazar: if only he could summon up anything like the energy of Beardsley's hyper-babble. Instead, the winner was once again in real trouble at a race finish line. Leigh Montville in the *Globe* wrote: "Alberto Salazar was a potato chip. That was what the doctor [Tom O'Donnell] said. The winner of the 86th Boston Marathon was a dried-out, dehydrated, unsalted, flat and crisp potato chip. A cold potato chip." The 68-degree temperature and the monumental effort to see off Beardsley had drawn every extra bit of fluid from Salazar's slender, 141-pound body. The trailing wind had evaporated the sweat as soon as it appeared; and then the absence of sweat once he stopped running left him dry and vulnerable and cold.

The champion lay on an army cot in the grim half-light of the medical area in the Prudential Centre basement garage, unable to talk, surrounded by eight different medical people. Author Mike Jenkinson once described him as having a "boyish vulnerablility", and he was spot on here. "I don't feel so good," Salazar whispered to a nurse. She strapped a flat band of black rubber around his right arm and began to take his temperature. "What's his temperature?" asked his wife

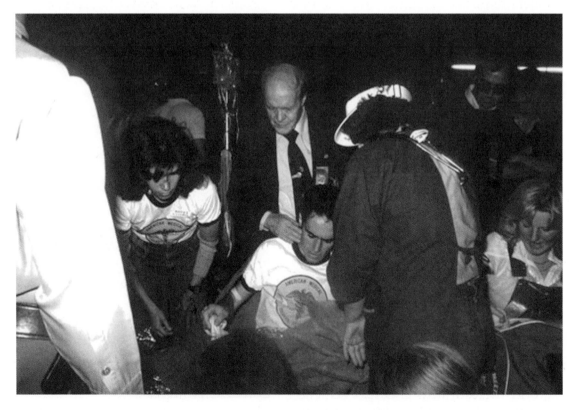

I don't feel so good: Race director Jock Semple overlooks Alberto Salazar who is starting to suffer from hypothermia. *Steve Sutton/Duomo/Corbis*

Molly as she softly stroked his forehead. "Eighty-eight." Eighty-eight measly little pips on the mercury. Count 'em. Normal is 98.6. Whichever way you slice it, Salazar was seriously unwell. Dr William Castelli of Framingham ordered an intravenous solution of dextrose and saline to be prepared. A needle was jabbed into his right arm, and another was prepared for his left. The medical term for his problem was hypothermia (as opposed to hyperthermia in Falmouth). Fluids and then more fluids were pumped in.

"Oooooh," Salazar said. "Now my hamstrings are cramping." Leigh Montville writes: "Jock Semple, the venerable marathon organizer and trainer moved closer to the cot. The IVs were pumping into each arm. Four NASA chrome mylar wraps were spread across Salazar's body. Semple started working the legs, trying to work the knotted muscles loose. Molly Salazar still was stroking her husband's forehead. He was shivering." "What happens if his temperature goes even lower?" José Salazar wanted to know. "We've seen 85 in here," the doc replied. "He's OK." Just. A reporter asked José if he had ever told Alberto to drop out if he felt unwell. José shook his head: "Nobody tells anything to any of my sons. This is the third time I've seen something like this. Alberto's brother did the same thing in a race in Marlborough. He fell down and got up. He didn't know where he was. He kept banging into trees, just banging into trees. He kept going."

An hour or so later, the "potato chip" had had six bags of fluids pumped into it and its temperature had risen to a respectable 97. It was sitting on the cot, dressing, and getting ready to leave. The potato chip was becoming human again. The subterranean aid station soon resembled a disaster zone as over a thousand runners required assistance after the race. "This is the worst by far I've seen in the last few years," said Dr Castelli. "It was the weather. It was dry, warm, low humidity and windy, and that dehydrates. The runners weren't stopping enough; instead they landed up here." One aide was heard saying: "It's amazing what people will do to their bodies just for fun."

*　　*　　*

Later, as Salazar sipped on a Coke and munched a chicken sandwich he recounted the race from when Mendoza slipped:

I knew he [Beardsley] would be tough. I could see his face. He looked really fresh. I was just concentrating on looking at Beardsley's back. Whenever I'd pull up even, he'd always accelerate and pull away. It was a very fast pace for the weather.

He was never more than five yards in front. We sprinted down those hills. I could feel my hamstring going down.

It was really difficult to stay with him. I'd been getting side stitches since halfway, and I was just hanging on by the skin of my teeth. It would have been easy to slack off. But I started thinking about a promise I once made to myself never to lose a marathon. Anybody can run a great race when everything's going perfectly; a true champion will win even when things aren't so great.

I could see him tightening up and, with a half-mile to go, I had 20 to 30 yards. But I was just waiting for him. I looked back – I knew he was there.

493

Nearly 23 years later I asked which race he'd suffered in more: the "last rites" race of Falmouth '78 or Boston '82. Salazar opts for the latter: "The amount of pain was about the same. But remember that at Boston we were running for four times as long – so, yes, that was tougher. The toughest of my life."

When Beardsley had calmed down a little he displayed a great attitude: "What else can I say? Alberto is the best, no doubt about it. But there'll be another time, maybe in New York City, maybe here next year."

* * *

But Beardsley's hope and dreams of a rematch would never materialize, and neither would return to the course that took such a toll as they ran their famous "duel in the sun". Salazar beat Rodolpho Gomez in New York six months later by just 4 seconds in another magnificent duel, but unbeknown to anyone, least of all him, he'd never win another marathon. "I did whatever I had to do to be the best," Salazar later said of his running career. "It really was an obsession."

He was in good spirits as his much-publicized IMG battle against Rob de Castella came along in the spring of 1983. As they rode a bus touring the course before the race, Salazar suddenly leapt out of his seat at the finish line, and dipped his body in front of Deek's shouting "Gotcha!" Wishful thinking as his knackered body could manage just fifth. Instead it was Carlos Lopes' turn to shine and he pushed Deek to the very limit before falling shy by two seconds. Lopes would of course earn his revenge at the famous Olympic marathon of 1984, where a run-down Salazar could manage just 15th.

Knee and hamstring problems hit him – and then an even worse malady: his body started suffering from an endocrine imbalance and New York in 1982 was to be his last major win for twelve years. He would later tell *Runner's World*: "My immune system was totally shot. I caught everything. I was always sick, always run down. In hindsight, I started running poorly after the Boston Marathon in 1982...it was the beginning of my long, gradual decline. Training for the Olympics in '83 and '84, I was sick constantly. I had 12 colds in 12 months."

But there was one incredible fairy-tale comeback for Salazar. In 1993, on the advice of a friend, he started taking the antidepressant drug Prozac, which boosts levels of the neurotransmitter serotonin (Hauman). Two days later he was suddenly running six by a mile in 4:42. "I thought my watch was broken," but it wasn't; it was just Salazar – aged 35 – showing that he still had the class. The following year he entered the famous Comrades ultra-marathon in South Africa, and won by 4 minutes, having at one stage led by 10 minutes. He still suffered though: "At one point, I even walked a little. I've never done that in a race. I just asked the Lord to help me through. I prayed more during this race than I've prayed in a year." Does one hit the wall in an ultra? I ask. "They say it comes at about 40 miles. But for me it was halfway!"

When *Track and Field News* asked road-racing writer Jack Welch to choose the two best marathoners of the 1980s, he named Alberto Salazar and Joan Benoit. On Salazar, he wrote: "The Finns call it *sisu*. In Japanese its *konjo*. Guts. A defiance of defeat as much as a determination to win. Surely there have been fast runners, athletes with golden prizes. But there is only one Salazar." American great Bill Rodgers tells the author: "What was amazing about Alberto Salazar

494

was the way he kept his focus and never let money deter him: he was gonna do this, this, and this, and would not be moved. Those are the best runners today – now that money is in the sport."

As for Dickie Beardsley, injuries and woeful misfortune hit him too. He started a dairy farm in Minnesota that he named "Marathon Dairy Farm". Tom Derderian bluntly reports his chapter of accidents: "In 1989 he suffered a mangling accident when caught in a piece of farm machinery. He recovered from that, but a few years later a car hit him during a training run." Two months after this, he lost control of his car in a blizzard and flipped it over. After 19 operations he became addicted to painkillers. Beardsley was finally, fortunately, caught forging prescriptions in order to help with the pain of his withdrawal symptoms: "My bones ached so much that, if I'd had a saw, I would have sawn off my arms and legs," he said. He was fined $1000 for his forgeries and ordered to do 240 hours community service: "I was out of control and thank goodness I got caught. If I had not got caught when I did, I would have died within a day or two."

Grateful still to be among us, Beardsley lives life to the full now. He presents and produces a fishing programme in America's Midwest, and had recovered well enough to run again to a high standard. He has completed nearly 60 marathons, and in February 2005 ran an excellent 2:43 for the Napa Valley Marathon to win the Masters division, aged 49. Beardsley was a popular guest at the 2005 London Marathon – its 25th anniversary – where it honoured all its champions. In the two major marathons where he made his name, Beardsley tied one and lost one, but in all other respects he is just that – a champion.

* * *

These days Salazar is extremely busy working in the Nike marketing department (it only took the author around 75 phone calls before he finally cornered him at his desk), but is spending more and more time on the Oregon Project, the programme he founded three years ago to identify and nurture the best young talent in the US.

When I made contact, he and his wife, Molly, were in the process of clearing out their children's bedrooms in order to make room for top young American runners to come and live in the Salazars' West Hills home and pursue their dreams. One such runner was an 18-year-old elite runner from Roseville, California, named Caitlin Chock. Doug Binder writes on Oregonlive.com: "Chock placed fifth in the 5,000 meters at the World Junior Championships in July in Italy – shaving 18 seconds off her own U.S. record. She was a Foot Locker Cross Country Championships finalist as a high school junior, and she twice has set the U.S. junior record in the 5,000. She has the kind of talent that Alberto Salazar is looking for." "We need to go further down the pipeline," Salazar said. "The younger we get them, the better."

Salazar said Dathan Ritzenhein, considered by many the nation's best young long-distance runner, has told him he will continue to work out with his coach in Boulder, Colorado, but will make frequent trips to Portland to make use of the Oregon Project's training resources. "We're refocusing in terms of the marathon," Salazar said. "We've got to get faster guys coming into the programme from the get-go...We need guys who are already fast at the five [thousand] and ten [thousand] before we get there." After all running has given Salazar, he is now pouring back all his energy into the sport he loves. The boom years of running of the seventies and eighties may be in the past, but the world's love for the race is greater than ever; it's just talent at the sharp end that needs nourishing, and Salazar is taking on the challenge in the States.

The author received this e-mail from Salazar after their interview:

Hi William! It was nice talking to you. It's people like you with a passion for our sport that are keeping it alive during these tough times. Keep it up and good luck! – Alberto

It was humbling to receive, since the message came from a man who's doing more to keep the sport thriving than almost any other.

Race result:

A. Salazar, Eugene	OR	2:08:52
D. Beardsley	MN	2:08:54
J. Lodwick	TX	2:12:01
B. Rodgers	MA	2:12:38
K. Stahl	SWE	2:12:46
D. Rinde	CA	2:15:04
T. Baker	MD	2:16:32
R. Callison	OH	2:16:35.

Sources:

Conversations with Bill Rodgers.
Conversations with Alberto Salazar.
Binder, Doug, in Oregonlive.com. November 4th, 2004.
Carey, Joseph, in the *Boston Herald American*. April 20th, 1982.
Concannon, Joe, in the *Boston Globe*. April 20th, 1982.
Derderian, Tom, *Boston Marathon*. Human Kinetics, 1996.
Hauman, Riël, *Century of the Marathon*. Human & Rousseau, 1996.
Horgan, Tim, in the *Boston Herald American*. April 20th, 1982.
Madden, Michael, in the *Boston Globe*. April 20th, 1982.
Montville, Leigh, in the *Boston Globe*. April 20th, 1982.
Nason, Jerry, in the *Boston Globe*. April 20th, 1982.
Powell, David, in *The Times*, April 11th, 2005.

L

No. 1 – 2002 London Marathon [Men]

Sunday, April 14th

Mighty Geb makes his debut.

As this book has attempted to convey, the marathon is certainly a race to keep its fans guessing. The day after the London Marathon 2002, Simon Barnes, chief sports correspondent for *The Times*, wrote: "Marathon is another country, they do things differently there. So it was that the race over the longest distance made new people of those we thought we understood. It made a winner of a professional loser and it made a loser out of a man who has made victory his trade." I have striven to allow as few anomalies as possible to qualify for the top-50 list, but if there *are* any, I am at least sure that the most important decision – the greatest marathon race of all time – has been made correctly. The only field I can think of that rivals this London 2002 men's field for sheer depth of class is the 1984 Olympic marathon; but in that case running greats such as de Castella, Salazar, Seko and Ikangaa were all just off their "A" games. Not so here.[1]

Apart from the Olympic champion Gezahegne Abera who had to pull out of the race through injury (but would capitalize in a much weaker field a year later, see Chapter 45), the cast of characters here is a spine-tingling "who's who" of early 21st-century distance running talent, with their William Hill betting odds in parentheses:

Haile Gebrselassie (ETH) – arguably the greatest runner of all time (2–1)
Abdelkhedar El Mouaziz (MOR) – London winner in 1999 and 2001; New York winner, 2000 (2–1)
Khalid Khannouchi (USA) – world record holder and three-time winner of Chicago Marathon (6–1)
Paul Tergat (KEN) – five-times World Cross-Country champ, double Olympic silver-medallist (7–1)
Tesfaye Jifar (ETH) – Geb's training partner; New York City champion; 2:06:49 PB (10–1)

---

1. In all, there are four other marathons in the book that have scored 9½ out of 10 for *quality of field*. They are: the Los Angeles 1984 Olympics (both men and women), the men's 1988 Olympic marathon; and the men's 1984 edition of Chicago.

Antonio Pinto (POR) – London winner 1992, 1997, 2000; course record holder (14–1)
Tesfaye Tola (ETH) – 2:06:57 at Amsterdam; 4th in 2001 World Champs (16–1)
Stefano Baldini (ITA) – London runner-up 1997; European Champion 1998; World bronze medallist 2001 (20–1)

Gebrselassie (often referred to in this chapter by his nickname "Geb" for simplicity) was the most fascinating entrant of the above. When his presence in the race – for his debut marathon – became known in December 2001, the world-record holder at 5000 and 10,000-metres plus the double Olympic and four-time World champion at 10,000-metres revealed some interesting clues as to where he gets his stamina. His father, Bekele, then 75, had an 18-month-old son and still worked on his farm near Addis Ababa. Bekele's partner was 38 and together they had three children. He told the *Daily Express*:

If I have ever wondered where my strength came from, then now I know," said Geb. "After my mother died he was on his own for a long while. Then he met this lady and he is now a father again. It's funny, because my dad never wanted me to be an athlete and then when I won my first Mercedes car he realized I am doing what I am good at.

Geb came to London in December to reveal the reasons behind his decision to compete:

The marathon is so important to me and it has such a tradition in Ethiopia after what Abebe Bikila achieved when he won the 1960 Olympics. I cannot wait to race here, I thrive on new challenges and at the moment there is no greater one than a marathon.

I am going to spend the next four months training for it. I have already started doing more work on the roads and though it will be a different pace to what I am used to, I am sure I will cope.

In the autumn of 2001 journalist Richard Lewis went to visit Geb at his home in Ethiopia the day after the Great Ethiopian Run. The race itself had not passed by without incident as the tens of thousands of runners had become overexcited before the race began and people were pushing and shoving to an extent that a situation of general mayhem existed. Nobody was listening to any of the officials. Only one man could solve this. Call for Geb. Lewis writes: "As the crowd heard his voice, a hush befell the area. Haile was talking and order was restored."

The following day, upon meeting with Lewis, Geb explained what all his considerable riches and accolades meant: "Money is important to me. Look around. You see I have a comfortable home; I have a good standard of living. But what is more important to me is that my money can be used by me to make as many people happy as I can." Together with his wife Alem, with whom he has three children, and brother Assefa, Geb runs a construction company that constructs buildings across four parts of Ethiopia.

Imagine how I feel when it is pay day at my company where I employ 200

498

people in a country where standards are not high and many people do not have jobs.

No one believes how fantastic I feel. They are my workers, I go down and hand the money over to the people. Just to see their faces is wonderful. I know their family can eat, can live properly. It is a special feeling.

And while Alem and Assefa are doing the hands-on part of running the show, it all frees up Geb to run for his country – and his company. Other career highlights include the setting of 16 world records, being unbeaten at 10,000-metres between June 1993 and August 2001. He is, according to *British Runner*, the first man to run both sub-13 minutes for the 5000-metres and sub-27 for 10,000, and the first to hold the world records at both since Henry Rono in 1978.

*   *   *

But the enticing question on the lips of athletics fans all over the world was: would Geb be able to transfer his track brilliance over to the brutal demands of the marathon? Especially against the stellar field that race director Dave Bedford had assembled. Upon Geb's confirmed entry, he was installed as the 2–1 joint favourite – along with Morocco's defending champion, Abdelkader El Mouaziz, the champion from 1999 and 2001. The fact that neither of these two would finish in the top two would show how strong the race would prove to be.

In an interview with *Athletics Weekly*, the 1993 London Marathon champion, Eamonn Martin, pinned his money firmly on Paul Tergat: "If I was to back one athlete I would go for Tergat. He has the experience of running two marathons and although people have said he has not made a big impact, he has still recorded two very good times." Martin found that Gebrselassie's "bouncy" style would not stand him in good stead for marathoning – if his legs got sore as they did in a 10-kilometre track race, they'd positively scream here. Martin completely dismissed Khannouchi's claims with the somewhat odd theory that he was only a big-city specialist in America. Sounds to this author that being a "big city specialist" is a useful claim to have whatever the "big city" may be. Antonio Pinto was another of Martin's ones to watch as he noted that his "timing and preparation is often perfect and he won't be far away."

Khalid Khannouchi was indeed a big-city specialist, his city of choice being Chicago. However, despite being the world-record holder from his blitz at Chicago in 1999, Khannouchi remained something of a misunderstood figure by many, helped in no small matter by the media's portrayal of him around the turn of the millennium. The worst "hatchet job" of all came from where he least expected – Chicago. If there was one place that Khannouchi felt loved and admired, it was in Chicago, but here suddenly, on May 7th, 2000, the *Chicago Tribune* was tearing him to pieces, in an article by the prolific sportswriter Rick Morrissey.[2]

2. As is often the case with "hatchet jobs", they tend to be written by those who don't actually *specialize* in what they're referring to. Morrissey may well be a prolific writer, but he is not primarily an athletics writer. He often has at least two pieces a day in the *Tribune*, and on this particular day his other article (on the cover page of the sports section) was entitled "The ten (unwritten) commandments of Baseball".

Khannouchi, wrote Morrissey, had chosen to "run the wrong course" when he competed in the London Marathon of 2000, and to put it even more bluntly, had "taken the money and run".

The root of the story goes back to 1993 when Khannouchi arrived in the US, penniless, but with the dream of becoming a professional runner. To supplement his income he became a dishwasher, a waiter, a postboy and eventually a clerk in an athletic association that organized races. "I had a rough time, but I found time to train, running through Brooklyn and Manhattan at midnight," he told the *Daily Telegraph*. He then married an American woman named Sandra and began to pursue the dream of becoming a US citizen that involved a seven-year battle with the Department of Immigration and Naturalization Services (INS).

The ultimate dream for Khannouchi was to represent America in the Sydney 2000 Olympic Marathon, but since he was hearing so little from the INS, Khannouchi agreed to an invitation to run in the 2000 London Marathon. Perversely, after so many years of waiting, Khannouchi finally received positive news that his citizenship could well be approved just a week before London. But with the good news came the bad: the Moroccan Athletic Federation indicated that they would bar Khannouchi running in the Olympic marathon for America because he had once represented Morocco in some world competitions. Khannouchi writes:

I had to think about this: What if I got citizenship (there was still a 20 to 25 percent chance it would not happen), did not run London and then the Moroccan federation succeeded in preventing me from running in the US trials? Then I would have wasted months of training for a spring marathon and once again failed to run London [he had pulled out the year before through injury]. I also wanted to prove myself on a course other than Chicago because some people think it's the only place I can win. I did not feel I had any choice but to go ahead and run.

So Khannouchi ran in the famous 2000 London Marathon in which Antonio Pinto scorched to a European record. But ankle and hamstring problems meant that not only did Khannouchi place third in 2:08:36, but he also put himself out of the US trials. Khannouchi responded to Morrissey's accusations that he was a "greedy athlete" by indicating that his contract stipulated that he only need to toe the starting line to pick up his $175,000 appearance money ($75,000 less than the figure that Morrissey gave), and not then run through 26 miles of pain. But, Khannouchi writes: "I did the honourable thing and lived up to my contract." The strangest aspect of the Morrissey article is that in some ways it seemed to want to support Khannouchi, admitting that he sounded "a sweetheart of a guy". Morrissey writes: "He didn't put enough faith in either the merits of his case or the hard work of his legal team, and he certainly didn't trust the system. That's understandable, given the INS' notorious record of inertia." But after Morrissey's line about Khannouchi taking the money and running he writes: "That would seem to make him just like any other greedy professional athlete in this country. Welcome, Khalid. It shouldn't be long before you're demanding to renegotiate your shoe contract and telling everyone that you don't get enough

500

respect." Although Morrissey's article is typical of a scribe with a grudge to bear who cares more about whether he writes a feisty piece than a fair one, journalists such as these are still enormously influential. Articles like these are noticed and spun over different papers all over the world and, as the cliché goes, mud sticks.

Redemption for Khannouchi missing the 2000 Olympics, partly came in Chicago the following autumn when he returned to the Windy City to win for the third time in 2:07:01. This meant his marathon record coming into the 2002 London was an [almost] immaculate:

October 12th, 1997	Chicago	2:07:10	1st
October 11th, 1998	Chicago	2:07:19	2nd
October 24th, 1999	Chicago	2:05:42	1st (world record)
April 18th, 2000	London	2:08:36	3rd
August 3rd, 2001	Edmonton	–	DNF
October 22nd, 2001	Chicago	2:07:01	1st (American record)

The two flaws in the list are his slowish London debut from 2000, and the ugly blob at Edmonton in 2001 – his "annus horribilis" – where he competed just seven times, winning a solitary once (a slow 29:36 for the Abraham Rosa 10K) and DNF-ing thrice.

So by the time the London Marathon of 2002 came along, Khalid Khannouchi's reputation with the man in the street was somewhat murky. Misunderstood, misrepresented and, it seems, already labelled yesterday's man; Khalid Khannouchi was without doubt a man with a mission. He writes on his web site:

Leading up to the London Marathon I felt like I was the underdog. The last year and a half consisted of injuries and disappointments and even though I was the marathon world record holder, I was no longer the object of attention that I was in the past.

I must admit that at times my feelings were hurt by the lack of attention. I was the most consistent marathoner in the race and I was feeling as if I wasn't getting the kind of respect that my record deserved. I felt I needed to show the world that I was still a great marathon runner.

However, ominously for his opponents, Khannouchi goes on to explain that the lack of attention could well be a bonus since the pressure was now off. For the first time ever before a big race Khalid's sleep was not disturbed by nightmares about turning up at the start without his shoes. In what he describes as the most painful race of his career, Khannouchi came to the Chicago Marathon of 1998 feeling all sorts of pressure, and when Ondoro Osorro came past him late on in the race it felt as though, "he was running a 1500 and I was running a 10,000." Khannouchi cramped up in that race and even considered dropping out, before finishing second in a still excellent 2:07:18. But none of that horrid expectation rested with Khannouchi any longer, it seemed.

Was he really yesterday's hero? His wife and coach, Sandra, knew for sure that he wasn't, that he was approaching the form of his life. Sandra, thus, was terribly nervous. But while Sandra Khannouchi couldn't sleep at night, her husband – who had to do the actual racing – was out like a light.

* * *

The day before the race had seen a whiff of controversy with Gebrselassie asking the pace-makers to go through midway in 62:30, which all of his competitors felt was too fast, and prompted top British marathon coach Alan Storey to predict mayhem. Khannouchi writes: "Geb asked for the fastest pace, 62:30. His coach talked him out of 62 flat. The others wanted to go at 63 or 63:15. So two sets of pacers were set up. Geb would be in the fast group with anyone that dared to go at that pace. Most of the elite group would go out with the slower group. I was in the middle, not sure what would happen. If Geb went out at 62:30, would I run alone behind him or try to go his pace?" As it turned out, as the race got underway, Geb realized that his eyes were too big even for his stomach and set off at a more reasonable canter, with one large group forming behind the pace-setters. Khannouchi recalls it being comfortable in the pack, and although there was regular surging, there was always the slow down as well; but the American always tried to stay at the same pace. "For some runners," Khanouchi writes, "it was a brave decision to stay at that pace. Two rabbits from Portugal stayed in front for about 17 miles. Then the race began."

After the 17-mile mark, Gebrselassie commenced something of a ding-dong with El Mouaziz, who alternated the lead a few times. At the 20-mile mark Gebrselassie put in the biggest pack-splitting surge of the race so far. Tergat, Khannouchi and Jifar managed to stay in touch with Geb, but it wasn't too long before Jifar had to drop back too. "To run with these two runners was very special," Khannouchi writes. "When I came to the US, in the early years when I worked in Brooklyn, they were an inspiration to me. I watched them and admired them. Now I was running alongside them in what would turn out to be the greatest marathon ever. To beat them would be something unbelievable."

Legends only need apply: an icon of the track meets an icon of the 'country', meets an icon of the road. The 2002 London Marathon, with this stellar cast, had it all. *Mark Shearman*

The next few miles were top-level distance running at its harshest, with Geb and Khannouchi trading surges, and Tergat maintaining a watching brief a few paces behind. Suddenly though during the 25th mile, yet another surge proved too much for Geb and his calf locked up. "That was the face of Gebrselassie as we have never see it before," wrote Simon Barnes of *The Times* the next day. "With the hubris of the great he had asked the

502

Khalid Khannouchi flashes across the line in a new world record with Paul Tergat visible in the background. *Mark Shearman*

pacemaker to set off at world record pace. But the race took him into what the commentators always love to call 'unknown territory' and in those badlands of the mind he got lost and left himself for dead."

So it was now down to just Khannouchi – the forgotten man – and Tergat, who had yet to prove himself as the complete marathoner. During mile 26 Tergat started to slip inch by inch away from Khannouchi's slipstream. They'd raced each other four times previously. Tergat had won them all. Khannouchi joked it was time the Kenyan let him win. "I looked back several times and he was falling further back. You don't know if you will win until you cross the finish line, but I was growing more confident every step of that last mile."

Although Khannouchi likes to "milk it up" with the crowds during the final moments of his marathon victories, this time there would be no time for that, even though it looked as though he was safe from Tergat. Suddenly the clock became a factor again. We'd all forgotten about the clock, so riveting had the "street battles" been. Khannouchi gritted his teeth and flew through the line to break his own world record by a mere 4 seconds. "The marathon is about yourself," says Khannouchi. "You go out there to prove yourself. There are many great marathons and many great marathoners, but on any given day, the best man wins. Paula Radcliffe was amazing. It was a great day for all of marathoning."

David Powell in *The Times* agreed:

On this greatest single day in commercial marathon history – there has never been one of such fast times – neither winner looked exhausted. Like Paula Radcliffe, who had completed a women's race victory half an hour earlier, Khannouchi had energy to celebrate.

Since all factors came together – great athletes who had prepared well, excellent pacing for the men, and fine weather, a magnificent mass field producing the greatest number of finishers, almost 33,000 – it is hard to imagine how the London Marathon is going to improve on this. Since 1997, each race has been better than the one before.

"Every year we ask ourselves 'how are we going to beat it'," Nick Bitel, the chief executive said. "But this year we mean it."

Behind the big guns there was still magnificent quality to behold with Stefano Baldini, a star at the Londons of 1997 and 2003, setting an Italian record with 2:07:29, the great Antonio Pinto finishing a lowly seventh for him in 2:09:10, and Britain's Mark Steinle, improving each time out with 2:09:17 to creep up to eighth on the all-time British list. Simon Barnes wrote:

> Yesterday saw two track stars run their first marathons and we saw them both as never before. We saw the invulnerablility of the ever-vulnerable Paula Radcliffe and we saw the vulnerability of the never-vulnerable Haile Gebrselassie. The women's race was a one-woman show, with Radcliffe steaming away from the rest.
>
> The men's race was the exact opposite: a rapidly moving crowd of elite runners going shoulder-to-shoulder at world record pace. You kept waiting for the field in the men's race to stretch: under that kind of pressure, the field normally pulls out like chewing gum. But they stayed tightly grouped for mile after mile at the same killing pace.

When asked in the press conferences to follow if he was now the "greatest", Khannouchi answered: "My win here does not make me the greatest. It is very difficult to call someone the greatest, there is not just one." This was Tergat's third second-place in marathons to go with four track 10K silvers behind Gebrselassi between 1996 and 2000 at two Olympics and two World Championships; but he was not down at all: "It was a great performance from me," Tergat said, "2:05 is a personal best. It was an incredible race. I thought 62:30 was too fast for halfway but I was strong. The most important thing is I've transferred my speed to the marathon, I've learned a lot." Gebrselassie amused the media with his wit: "I'm very happy, I knocked 42 minutes from my personal best [at age 15 in Addis Ababa]. The weather was fantastic, the pace-making wonderful. I enjoyed the whole race except the last 2 kilometres when I had muscle cramp." His manager, Jos Hermens, admitted he pulled his calf muscle six weeks before the race.

Journalist Roger Robinson recalls to the author asking the three athletes the penetrating question: "How did each of you feel at 24 miles?" The answers are revealing as to their state of minds:

> Gebrselassie: *I wanted to go faster, but I couldn't.*
> Tergat: *I'm in the company of two fantastic runners, something's going to happen.*
> Khannouchi: *If I can beat these guys, it would be something special.*

What's illuminating about these answers is the mindset the runners were in; with both Gebrselassie and Tergat having negative feelings about how the race was was going – something of an impending sense of doom – whereas Khannouchi sized up the situation in all its intensity and thought, "Right! Let's get stuck in!"

To the less informed, Khannouchi's win was something of a shock: even those with privileged inside information had not backed him. A member of the organizing committee, the late John Jeffery, recalled the confidence Khannouchi's wife Sandra had when she spoke of her husband's impending triumph before the race: "My Khalid will win," she confided to Jeffery. "Well, Sandra," Jeffery replied, "it's interesting to hear you say that, because in this country it has been known for us to place the odd penny or two on the outcome of a race." "Well, you don't need to look any further for your winner," assured Sandra. Jeffrey scuttled back to his friends on the committee and shared his scoop, to which they all gave knowing nods and an occasional scoff. As Khannouchi stampeded his way down The Mall a few days later, Sandra turned to Jeffery and squealed: "I told you! Didn't I tell you! I told you my Khalid would win!" "Oh, yes, Sandra, you certainly did, you most certainly did!" beamed Jeffery – who had put all his loot on Pinto.

It had certainly been a pricey day for the marathon organizers. Both world records set them back £178,000, and chief executive Nick Bitel admitted: "We could not take out insurance at a reasonable premium against world records being broken, not when we put out these sorts of fields. We could not even get a quote from any insurance company to cover the men's race."

Race organizer Dave Bedford grimaced: "This is the most we have ever paid out. But we are delighted." Bedford conceded to the author that it had already been an expensive race, way before the gun had fired:

I believe that just about every year our fields are stronger than an Olympic field. I want the race to be de facto, the Olympic Games or World Championship. We spend a lot of money in order to achieve that – more than two million pounds – so it's not a coincidence.

When I think about marathon day, I will get excited by three things. I'll get excited by a British win, I'll get excited by a close race, and I'll get excited by a record. A record *and* a great race – is absolutely stunning.

And commenting on the winner, Bedford directly contrasted opinion with Rick Morrissey, declaring: "Khalid is a worthy person. He is a real gentleman with high moral standards, and he will yet run faster than he has here."

Race director Dave Bedford beams with satisfaction as his two leading ponies have produced a dream day for London. *Mark Shearman*

*   *   *

As alluded to, Paula Radcliffe also made her spectacular marathon debut on this day, and her adventures here and elsewhere may be properly enjoyed in Chapter 36. But it is worth here just revisiting the words of Simon Barnes, who wrote on the front page of *The Times*: "It is spring: there are butterflies to be seen again. Yesterday Paula Radcliffe shed the chrysalis of the Plucky British Loser and emerged as a gorgeous, fully formed victor. A new species of butterfly, hitherto unknown to science: scientific name Paula Gloriosa. I wonder if it is one of those species that goes on and on, or whether it fades and dies as soon as it appears." We were of course to find out the answer six months – and one year – later.

Astonishingly, Khannouchi too had another great marathon in him for the year – partaking in a race of breathtaking quality at Chicago in October. For a while it looked like he might have met his match as the fabulous running style of Toshinari Takaoka of Japan (the national record holder at 3000, 5000 and 10,000-metres) opened up a 17-second lead at 35 kilometres. But not to be outdone, Khannouchi hit the hammer and took 37 seconds out of Takaoka in the final 7 kilometres to win in his third, and the world's fourth sub-2:06 clocking (2:05:56). Takaoka's valiant efforts for victory meant he was beaten on the line for third by the fast-finishing, little-known Kenyan, Daniel Njenga. Paul Tergat found himself a couple of seconds further back, still struggling to find the winning recipe in marathons. But as Chapter 39 has shown, when the winning recipe *was* found, it was spectacular.

Race result:

Khalid Khannouchi	USA	2:05:38
Paul Tergat	KEN	2:05:48
Haile Gebrselassie	ETH	2:06:35
Abdelkader El Mouaziz	MAR	2:06:52
Ian Syster	RSA	2:07:06
Stefano Baldini	ITA	2:07:29
Antonio Pinto	POR	2:09:10
Mark Steinle	GBR	2:09:17
Tesfaye Jifar	ETH	2:09:50
Mohammed El Hattab	MAR	2:11:50

Sources:

Conversations with David Bedford.
Conversations with John Jeffery.
Conversations with Roger Robinson.
Barnes, Simon, in *The Times*, April 15th, 2002.
www.khannouchi.com, Khalid Khannouchi web site.

Landells, Steve, in *Athletics Weekly*, April 17th, 2002.
Lewis, Richard, in the *Daily Express,* December 4th, 2001.
Lewis, Richard, in the *British Runner*, January 2002.
Morrissey, Rick, in the *Chicago Tribune,* May 7th, 2000.
Powell, David, in *The Times*, April 15th, 2002.

Bubbling Under

Here is a brief description of some great marathons that narrowly missed the cut (and which are not discussed in the text):

1897, Boston. The road to Boston starts here with a 7-minute win for John J. McDermott in 2:55:10.

1928, Amsterdam. Boughera El Ouafi of France wins exciting Olympic Marathon by less than 30 seconds over Manuel Plaza of Chile.

1935, Tokyo. The tiny Fusashige Suzuki of Japan breaks the 2:30 barrier for the first time by running 2:27:49

1941, Boston. Great rivals Les Pawson (three-time champion) and Johnny A. Kelley (twice champion, seven-time runner-up) fight out their finest battle. Pawson wins by 44 seconds.

1946, Boston. Stylianos Kyriakides, the ultimate Greek messenger. "Win, or die," said his countrymen as they paid his way to Boston to act as a spokesman for his starving, destitute country. Upon winning Stylianos spoke to reporters. His message was clear: he wanted a boatload of food, milk and medicine for his country. He got it.

1967, Toronto. Aged just 13, Canadian Maureen Wilton breaks the women's world record by 4 minutes with her 3:15:22 run.

1968, Boston. Unknown 21-year collegiate runner, Ambrose Burfoot, stuns reporters by winning the big race by over a minute. He now edits US *Runner's World*.

1969, Athens. First reserve for the top-50 list. Bill Adcocks' extraordinary 2:11:07 run at the Athens Classic Marathon, which comfortably withstood all comers until the 2004 Olympics, despite a barrage of attention from some decorated Kenyan runners. Adcocks writes in *The Road to Athens* of his feelings late into the race: "What exhilaration! Who could fail to be inspred? I was certainly feeling in fine form. The back was behaving impeccably. The legs were in good shape. The feet were flying. There was no feeling of distress at all. Only a desire to power on."

1970, Oregon. Caroline Walker, aged a mere 16, lowers the world record by nearly 5 minutes with a 3:02:53.

1971, Boston. Alvaro Majia and Pat McMahon battle through the heat with the former prevailing by just 5 seconds

1971, Werribee. Australia's Adrienne Beames gives a glimpse of what the women can really do, by running 2:46:30, a world record by over a quarter of an hour, in the cold, wind and rain.

1974, Christchurch. England's Ian Thompson roars to the Commonwealth title in 2:09:12, over 2 minutes on his nearest rival.

1995, Berlin. Samuel Lelei and Vincent Rousseau duel spectacularly to record astounding times of 2:07:02 and 2:07:20. Lelei beat his previous best by a massive

4:09, and Rousseau became the first man to break 2:08 twice. Antonio Pinto was third.

1998, Berlin. Brazil's Ronaldo da Costa finally snaps Densimo's world mark of some ten-years standing by running 2:06:05. "I wanted to run under 2:08, but when I saw how good the conditions were I just went for it," said da Costa.

2004, Athens Olympic marathon. Italy's Stefano Baldini becomes a deserved Olympic champion after a nearly a decade of running marathons at the very highest level. He defeats America's Meb Keflezighi by 34 seconds, by running the fastest ever time over the Athens course of 2:10:55. The heroic Vanderlei de Lima placed third, having been attacked by a fanatic when leading with less than 10 kilometres to go.

Glossary

Here is a description of how the categories have been marked. As noted in the introduction, breaking down the categories like this places emphasis on objectivity rather than subjectivity, as the following highlights:

1) *Quality of race winner* **[30]**

This mark is grading the pedigree of the actual race winner. Although the book is not looking to highlight great runners – rather great races – a crucial component of a great race is to have top quality runners at the sharp end. Therefore the marks in this category are generally high with many race winners receiving at least an eight out of 10. Grete Waitz and Paula Radcliffe both boast a 9.5 in this category, as does Khalid Khannouchi. Rod Dixon however only returns a 7.5, since he was not a purist marathoner but just happened to be involved in one of the most dramatic races of all.

This mark also takes into account how long the protagonist was around at the top of the sport, how consistent he/she was and how many major honours he/she won. Three other examples of grades are Carlos Lopes with 9, Martin Fiz 8.5, and Joseph McGhee with just 6 (a marathon famed for reasons other than quality of winner).

2) *Quality of race field* **[20]**

Here I have carefully analysed the fields of the races; taking into account not just the winner but the next half a dozen runners, and, importantly, any big names who dropped out who often had a significant bearing on the outcome, but a small injury or just sheer exhaustion at having the pace for so long meant that they could no longer continue.

3) *Quality of winner's time* **[20]**

Obviously many factors come into play here, although generally speaking great races tend to breed fast times. But the most important consideration is what generation the race took place in. A time of 2:14 nowadays would field an extremely low mark, but back in the 1950s and early '60s it was laudable. A 2:30 now would be awarded a 1/10; but back in the 1920s a 9. Also, times are not penalized for being slow if the weather conditions were severe or the course particularly testing. The Olympics of '92 for instance were won in the slowest Olympic time since 1968, but the mark isn't too low because of the severity of the course and conditions. All world records have received a 10/10.

4) *Profile of event* **[25]**

This is one of the easiest grades to award with a simple sliding scale. The Olympics, as the world's most prestigious marathon, is awarded top marks, and then a selection of marathons are awarded 9: London, Boston, the World

Championships, etc. New York fields an 8.5, Rotterdam an 8, the Commonwealth Games an 8, etc.

5) *Drama of event* [25]

This category ignores the quality of field, winner or time and focuses on how dramatic the key moments of the race were. Was there a thrilling sprint finish? Did the long time leader lose his grip on the title in the final stages? Were there any memorable incidents like the leaders going off course or tripping over at vital times, or visibly descending into extreme physical and mental difficulty?

6) *Sacrifice of winner* [15]

Closely related to the previous category. Although the displays of Paula Radcliffe are dazzling, she doesn't appear to suffer too much, which drains them of some of their human spectacle. What makes sporting confrontations particularly memorable is when the protagonists are clearly toiling over their craft. Whether it be an attack of nerves and panic, like Goran Ivanisevic serving three double faults in the game that finally made him Wimbledon champion, or Jean Van der Velde taking a 7 at the 72nd hole at the Open when a six would have given him victory. Or, more often in marathon races, just physical exhaustion and toil, like the depths Alberto Salazar had to visit to win Boston in 1982, or Uta Pippig the same race in 1996. The greater the sacrifice the higher the mark.

7) *Course difficulty* [10]

The topography and undulations of the course are the most obvious considerations here. But other factors, such as how many twists and turns a course has, are included too. London, for instance, would be an even quicker course if it followed a straighter path, and wasn't run on a cobbled surface for half a mile. The more difficult a course, the higher the mark. The course difficulty mark for the straight and flat Fukuoka course is a 5, whereas the gruelling examination that was the Barcelona Olympics gets a 9.

8) *Weather conditions* [5]

A straightforward category to mark. Wind, rain, heat, cold and humidity are the five categories considered, and these are well documented in the reportage of the race. Weather conditions of around 65–75° get a 7; 75–85° an 8; 85–95° a 9, and above 95 – which has been known – a 10. It is difficult to run fast in high winds or the pouring rain, and some runners – Frank Shorter being a notable case – struggle in such conditions. It is rare that marathons are run in bitterly cold weather, but occasionally they occur, indeed Paula Radcliffe's world record at Chicago was all the more remarkable for the icy weather that the Windy City served up.

9) *Memorability of race* [20]

An important category with a subtle difference from the one that follows. This mark concentrates on how spectacular one facet, or all facets of the race were as a whole, and disregards the profile of the race or whether anything particularly newsworthy happened like a world record, or a big name winning after years in the wilderness, or the breakthrough of a new star. Examples of "memorability" include Liz McColgan losing the London Marathon in almost the last step; two runners duelling to the line in baking temperatures; or stories of real suffering and sacrifice, like Pietri and Peters' horrifying collapses.

10) *Overall news headline worthiness worldwide* [20]

All big city marathons tend to get significant media coverage from the city of the race in which it is held. Boston, for instance, gets acres of press both before and after the race in local Boston television, newspapers and radio, but fairly little coverage elsewhere. The Olympics and World Championships receive healthy coverage the world over, as does the breaking of a world record. This mark thus disregards how spectacular or exciting a race was and focuses purely on how significant a bearing it had on the world stage.

Appendix

An analysis of how the grades were awarded.

1   London 2002 (men)

	Weighting (x by)	Mark	Weighted Mark
Quality of Winner [Khannouchi]	3	9.5	28.5
Quality of Field	2	9.5	19
Quality of Time	2	10	20
Profile of Event	2.5	9	22.5
Drama of Race	2.5	9	22.5
Sacrifice of Winner	1.5	7	10.5
Course difficulty	1	7	7
Weather conditions	0.5	6	3
Memorability of race	2	8.5	17
World/local news worthiness	2	9	18
		168/190	88.4%

2   Boston 1982 (men)

	Weighting (x by)	Mark	Weighted Mark
Quality of Winner [Salazar]	3	9	27
Quality of Field	2	7	14
Quality of Time	2	9	18
Profile of Event	2.5	9	22.5
Drama of Race	2.5	9.5	23.75
Sacrifice of Winner	1.5	9.5	14.25
Course difficulty	1	8	8
Weather conditions	0.5	9	4.5
Memorability of race	2	8.5	17
World/local news worthiness	2	8.5	17
		166/190	87.4%

3   Olympic 1960 (men)

	Weighting (x by)	Mark	Weighted Mark
Quality of Winner [Bikila]	3	9.5	28.5
Quality of Field	2	7.5	15
Quality of Time	2	9.5	19

515

Profile of Event	2.5	10	25
Drama of Race	2.5	8.5	21.25
Sacrifice of Winner	1.5	6.5	9.75
Course difficulty	1	7.5	7.5
Weather conditions	0.5	7.5	3.75
Memorability of race	2	9	18
World/local news worthiness	2	9	18
		165.75/190	87.2%

4   Olympic 1952 (men)

	Weighting (x by)	Mark	Weighted Mark
Quality of Winner [Zátopek]	3	9	27
Quality of Field	2	9	18
Quality of Time	2	9	18
Profile of Event	2.5	10	25
Drama of Race	2.5	7.5	18.75
Sacrifice of Winner	1.5	7	10.5
Course difficulty	1	6.5	6.5
Weather conditions	0.5	6.5	3.75
Memorability of race	2	9	18
World/local news worthiness	2	9.5	19
		164.5/190	86.6%

5   Commonwealth 1982 (men)

	Weighting (x by)	Mark	Weighted Mark
Quality of Winner [de Castella]	3	9	27
Quality of Field	2	7.5	15
Quality of Time	2	8.5	17
Profile of Event	2.5	8	20
Drama of Race	2.5	9.5	23.75
Sacrifice of Winner	1.5	9	13.5
Course difficulty	1	9	9
Weather conditions	0.5	8	4
Memorability of race	2	9.5	19
World/local news worthiness	2	8	16
		164.25/190	86.4%

6 *Olympic 1908 (men)*

	Weighting (x by)	Mark	Weighted Mark
Quality of Winner [*Hayes*]	3	8	24
Quality of Field	2	7.5	15
Quality of Time	2	7	14
Profile of Event	2.5	10	25
Drama of Race	2.5	9.5	23.75
Sacrifice of Winner	1.5	8	12
Course difficulty	1	8	8
Weather conditions	0.5	8.5	4.25
Memorability of race	2	9.5	19
World/local news worthiness	2	9.5	19
		164/190	86.3%

7 *Boston 1996 (women)*

	Weighting (x by)	Mark	Weighted Mark
Quality of Winner [*Pippig*]	3	9	27
Quality of Field	2	7.5	15
Quality of Time	2	7	14
Profile of Event	2.5	9	22.5
Drama of Race	2.5	9.5	23.75
Sacrifice of Winner	1.5	9.5	14.25
Course difficulty	1	8	8
Weather conditions	0.5	8	4
Memorability of race	2	9	18
World/local news worthiness	2	8.5	17
		163.5/190	86.1%

8 *Chicago 1984 (men)*

	Weighting (x by)	Mark	Weighted Mark
Quality of Winner [*Jones*]	3	8.5	25.5
Quality of Field	2	9.5	19
Quality of Time	2	10	20
Profile of Event	2.5	9	22.5
Drama of Race	2.5	8	20
Sacrifice of Winner	1.5	8	12
Course difficulty	1	6	6
Weather conditions	0.5	6	3
Memorability of race	2	8.5	17
World/local news worthiness	2	9	18
		163/190	85.8%

9   Olympic 1984 (men)

	Weighting (x by)	Mark	Weighted Mark
Quality of Winner [Lopes]	3	9	27
Quality of Field	2	8.5	15
Quality of Time	2	8.5	15
Profile of Event	2.5	10	25
Drama of Race	2.5	8.5	21.25
Sacrifice of Winner	1.5	6.5	9.75
Course difficulty	1	7	8
Weather conditions	0.5	8	4
Memorability of race	2	8	16
World/local news worthiness	2	8	16
		162/190	85.3%

10   Olympic 1988 (men)

	Weighting (x by)	Mark	Weighted Mark
Quality of Winner [Bordin]	3	9	27
Quality of Field	2	9.5	19
Quality of Time	2	8	16
Profile of Event	2.5	10	25
Drama of Race	2.5	9	22.5
Sacrifice of Winner	1.5	7	10.5
Course difficulty	1	7.5	7.5
Weather conditions	0.5	8	4
Memorability of race	2	7.5	15
World/local news worthiness	2	7.5	15
		161.5/190	85.0%

11   Olympic 1992 (men)

	Weighting (x by)	Mark	Weighted Mark
Quality of Winner [Young-cho]	3	8	24
Quality of Field	2	9	18
Quality of Time	2	6.5	13
Profile of Event	2.5	10	25
Drama of Race	2.5	9	22.5
Sacrifice of Winner	1.5	8	12
Course difficulty	1	9	9
Weather conditions	0.5	9	4.5
Memorability of race	2	8	16
World/local news worthiness	2	8.5	17
		161/190	84.7%

12   Berlin 2003 (men)

	Weighting (x by)	Mark	Weighted Mark
Quality of Winner [Tergat]	3	9	27
Quality of Field	2	7.5	15
Quality of Time	2	10	20
Profile of Event	2.5	8	20
Drama of Race	2.5	9	22.5
Sacrifice of Winner	1.5	7.5	11.25
Course difficulty	1	6	6
Weather conditions	0.5	6	3
Memorability of race	2	9	18
World/local news worthiness	2	9	18
		160.75/190	84.6%

13   Olympic 1932 (men)

	Weighting (x by)	Mark	Weighted Mark
Quality of Winner [Zabala]	3	8	27
Quality of Field	2	9	15
Quality of Time	2	9	14
Profile of Event	2.5	10	22.5
Drama of Race	2.5	8	23.75
Sacrifice of Winner	1.5	9	14.25
Course difficulty	1	7.5	8
Weather conditions	0.5	7	4
Memorability of race	2	7.5	18
World/local news worthiness	2	8	17
		160.5/190	84.5%

14   World Championships 1995 (men)

	Weighting (x by)	Mark	Weighted Mark
Quality of Winner [Fiz]	3	8.5	25.5
Quality of Field	2	8.5	17
Quality of Time	2	8	16
Profile of Event	2.5	9	22.5
Drama of Race	2.5	8.5	21.25
Sacrifice of Winner	1.5	8.5	12.75
Course difficulty	1	7.5	7.5
Weather conditions	0.5	9.5	4.75
Memorability of race	2	8.5	17
World/local news worthiness	2	8	16
		160.25/190	84.3%

15 *New York 2004 (women)*

	Weighting (x by)	*Mark*	*Weighted Mark*
Quality of Winner [*Radcliffe*]	3	9.5	28.5
Quality of Field	2	7.5	15
Quality of Time	2	7.5	15
Profile of Event	2.5	8.5	21.25
Drama of Race	2.5	9	22.5
Sacrifice of Winner	1.5	8	12
Course difficulty	1	7.5	7.5
Weather conditions	0.5	6.5	3.25
Memorability of race	2	9	18
World/local news worthiness	2	8.5	17
		160/190	84.2%

16 *Olympic 1984 (women)*

	Weighting (x by)	*Mark*	*Weighted Mark*
Quality of Winner [*Benoit*]	3	9	27
Quality of Field	2	9.5	19
Quality of Time	2	8	16
Profile of Event	2.5	10	25
Drama of Race	2.5	6.5	16.25
Sacrifice of Winner	1.5	6.5	9.75
Course difficulty	1	7	7
Weather conditions	0.5	7.5	3.75
Memorability of race	2	9	18
World/local news worthiness	2	9	18
		159.75/190	84.1%

17 *Olympic 1992 (women)*

	Weighting (x by)	*Mark*	*Weighted Mark*
Quality of Winner [*Yegorova*]	3	8.5	25.5
Quality of Field	2	8.5	17
Quality of Time	2	6.5	13
Profile of Event	2.5	10	25
Drama of Race	2.5	9	22.5
Sacrifice of Winner	1.5	7.5	11.25
Course difficulty	1	9	9
Weather conditions	0.5	8.5	4.25
Memorability of race	2	8	16
World/local news worthiness	2	8	16
		159.5/190	84.0%

520

18   Boston 1988 (men)

	Weighting (x by)	Mark	Weighted Mark
Quality of Winner [Hussein]	3	8.5	25.5
Quality of Field	2	9	18
Quality of Time	2	8.5	17
Profile of Event	2.5	9	22.5
Drama of Race	2.5	9	22.5
Sacrifice of Winner	1.5	7.5	11.25
Course difficulty	1	8	8
Weather conditions	0.5	7	3.5
Memorability of race	2	8	16
World/local news worthiness	2	7.5	15
		159.25/190	83.8%

19   New York 1983 (men)

	Weighting (x by)	Mark	Weighted Mark
Quality of Winner [Dixon]	3	7.5	22.5
Quality of Field	2	7	14
Quality of Time	2	8	16
Profile of Event	2.5	8.5	21.25
Drama of Race	2.5	9.5	23.75
Sacrifice of Winner	1.5	9	13.5
Course difficulty	1	8	8
Weather conditions	0.5	8	4
Memorability of race	2	9	18
World/local news worthiness	2	9	18
		159/190	83.7%

20   Boston 2000 (men)

	Weighting (x by)	Mark	Weighted Mark
Quality of Winner [Lagat]	3	8	24
Quality of Field	2	8.5	17
Quality of Time	2	7.5	15
Profile of Event	2.5	9	22.5
Drama of Race	2.5	9.5	23.75
Sacrifice of Winner	1.5	8	12
Course difficulty	1	8	8
Weather conditions	0.5	7	3.5
Memorability of race	2	9	18
World/local news worthiness	2	7.5	15
		158.75/190	83.6%

21   Olympic 2004 (women)

	Weighting (x by)	Mark	Weighted Mark
Quality of Winner [Noguchi]	3	7.5	22.5
Quality of Field	2	7.5	15
Quality of Time	2	7	14
Profile of Event	2.5	10	25
Drama of Race	2.5	9	22.5
Sacrifice of Winner	1.5	6.5	9.75
Course difficulty	1	9	9
Weather conditions	0.5	9	4.5
Memorability of race	2	9	18
World/local news worthiness	2	9	18
		158.25/190	83.3%

22   Fukuoka 1983 (men)

	Weighting (x by)	Mark	Weighted Mark
Quality of Winner [Seko]	3	9	27
Quality of Field	2	9	18
Quality of Time	2	8.5	17
Profile of Event	2.5	9	22.5
Drama of Race	2.5	9	22.5
Sacrifice of Winner	1.5	8	12
Course difficulty	1	5	5
Weather conditions	0.5	6	3
Memorability of race	2	8.5	17
World/local news worthiness	2	7	14
		158/190	83.2%

23   Boston 1978 (men)

	Weighting (x by)	Mark	Weighted Mark
Quality of Winner [Rodgers]	3	9	27
Quality of Field	2	8	16
Quality of Time	2	8	16
Profile of Event	2.5	9	22.5
Drama of Race	2.5	9	22.5
Sacrifice of Winner	1.5	7.5	11.25
Course difficulty	1	8	8
Weather conditions	0.5	5	2.5
Memorability of race	2	8.5	17
World/local news worthiness	2	7.5	15
		157.75/190	83.0%

24   Boston 1980 (women)

	Weighting (x by)	Mark	Weighted Mark
Quality of Winner [Gareau]	3	8	24
Quality of Field	2	7.5	15
Quality of Time	2	8	16
Profile of Event	2.5	9	22.5
Drama of Race	2.5	9.5	23.75
Sacrifice of Winner	1.5	6	9
Course difficulty	1	8	8
Weather conditions	0.5	8.5	4.25
Memorability of race	2	8	16
World/local news worthiness	2	9.5	19
		157.5/190	82.9%

25   Olympic 1976 (men)

	Weighting (x by)	Mark	Weighted Mark
Quality of Winner [Cierpinski]	3	8	24
Quality of Field	2	9.5	19
Quality of Time	2	8.5	17
Profile of Event	2.5	10	25
Drama of Race	2.5	8.5	21.25
Sacrifice of Winner	1.5	6.5	9.75
Course difficulty	1	6.5	6.5
Weather conditions	0.5	7.5	3.75
Memorability of race	2	7.5	15
World/local news worthiness	2	8	16
		157.25/190	82.8%

26   Fukuoka 1967 (men)

	Weighting (x by)	Mark	Weighted Mark
Quality of Winner [Clayton]	3	8.5	25.5
Quality of Field	2	8	16
Quality of Time	2	10	20
Profile of Event	2.5	9	22.5
Drama of Race	2.5	8	20
Sacrifice of Winner	1.5	8	12
Course difficulty	1	5	5
Weather conditions	0.5	6	3
Memorability of race	2	8	16
World/local news worthiness	2	8.5	17
		157/190	82.6%

27   Olympic 1996 (men)

	Weighting (x by)	Mark	Weighted Mark
Quality of Winner [*Thugwane*]	3	8	24
Quality of Field	2	9	18
Quality of Time	2	6.5	13
Profile of Event	2.5	10	25
Drama of Race	2.5	9	22.5
Sacrifice of Winner	1.5	7	10.5
Course difficulty	1	8	8
Weather conditions	0.5	7.5	3.75
Memorability of race	2	8	16
World/local news worthiness	2	8	16
		156.75/190	82.5%

28   Olympic 1948 (men)

	Weighting (x by)	Mark	Weighted Mark
Quality of Winner [*Cabrera*]	3	8	24
Quality of Field	2	8	16
Quality of Time	2	6	112
Profile of Event	2.5	10	25
Drama of Race	2.5	9	22.5
Sacrifice of Winner	1.5	7	10.5
Course difficulty	1	8.5	8.5
Weather conditions	0.5	8	4
Memorability of race	2	8.5	17
World/local news worthiness	2	8.5	17
		156.5/190	82.4%

29   Olympic 1988 (women)

	Weighting (x by)	Mark	Weighted Mark
Quality of Winner [*Mota*]	3	9	27
Quality of Field	2	9	18
Quality of Time	2	7.5	15
Profile of Event	2.5	10	25
Drama of Race	2.5	8	20
Sacrifice of Winner	1.5	7	10.5
Course difficulty	1	8	8
Weather conditions	0.5	8	4
Memorability of race	2	7	14
World/local news worthiness	2	7.5	15
		156.5/190	82.3%

30 Boston 1981 (women)

	Weighting (x by)	Mark	Weighted Mark
Quality of Winner [Roe]	3	8.5	25.5
Quality of Field	2	8.5	17
Quality of Time	2	9	18
Profile of Event	2.5	9	22.5
Drama of Race	2.5	9	22.5
Sacrifice of Winner	1.5	6	9
Course difficulty	1	8	8
Weather conditions	0.5	5.5	2.75
Memorability of race	2	8	16
World/local news worthiness	2	7.5	16
		156.25/190	82.2%

31 London 1997 (men)

	Weighting (x by)	Mark	Weighted Mark
Quality of Winner [Pinto]	3	9	27
Quality of Field	2	9	18
Quality of Time	2	8.5	17
Profile of Event	2.5	9	22.5
Drama of Race	2.5	8.5	21.25
Sacrifice of Winner	1.5	7	10.5
Course difficulty	1	7	7
Weather conditions	0.5	5.5	2.75
Memorability of race	2	8	16
World/local news worthiness	2	7	14
		156/190	82.1%

32 Olympic 1920 (men)

	Weighting (x by)	Mark	Weighted Mark
Quality of Winner [Kolehmainen]	3	9	27
Quality of Field	2	6.5	13
Quality of Time	2	10	20
Profile of Event	2.5	10	25
Drama of Race	2.5	8.5	21.25
Sacrifice of Winner	1.5	7	10.5
Course difficulty	1	6	6
Weather conditions	0.5	5	2.5
Memorability of race	2	7.5	15
World/local news worthiness	2	7.5	15
		155.25/190	81.7%

525

33   London 1989 (men)

	Weighting (x by)	Mark	Weighted Mark
Quality of Winner [*Wakiihuri*]	3	8.5	25.5
Quality of Field	2	8.5	17
Quality of Time	2	7.5	15
Profile of Event	2.5	9	22.5
Drama of Race	2.5	9	22.5
Sacrifice of Winner	1.5	7	10.5
Course difficulty	1	7	7
Weather conditions	0.5	5.5	2.75
Memorability of race	2	8.5	17
World/local news worthiness	2	7.5	15
		154.75/190	81.5%

34   London 1985 (women)

	Weighting (x by)	Mark	Weighted Mark
Quality of Winner [*Kristiansen*]	3	9.5	28.5
Quality of Field	2	6	12
Quality of Time	2	10	20
Profile of Event	2.5	9	22.5
Drama of Race	2.5	7.5	18.75
Sacrifice of Winner	1.5	7.5	11.25
Course difficulty	1	7	7
Weather conditions	0.5	5	2.5
Memorability of race	2	8	16
World/local news worthiness	2	8	16
		154.5/190	81.3%

35   Boston 1922 (men)

	Weighting (x by)	Mark	Weighted Mark
Quality of Winner [*DeMar*]	3	9	27
Quality of Field	2	8	16
Quality of Time	2	9	18
Profile of Event	2.5	9	22.5
Drama of Race	2.5	7	17.5
Sacrifice of Winner	1.5	6.5	9.75
Course difficulty	1	8	8
Weather conditions	0.5	5	2.5
Memorability of race	2	7.5	15
World/local news worthiness	2	9	18
		154.25/190	81.2%

36   London 1995 (men)

	Weighting (x by)	Mark	Weighted Mark
Quality of Winner [Ceron]	3	8.5	25.5
Quality of Field	2	8.5	17
Quality of Time	2	7.5	15
Profile of Event	2.5	9	22.5
Drama of Race	2.5	9	22.5
Sacrifice of Winner	1.5	7.5	11.25
Course difficulty	1	7	7
Weather conditions	0.5	6.5	3.25
Memorability of race	2	8	16
World/local news worthiness	2	7	14
		154/190	81.1%

37   Olympic 1972 (men)

	Weighting (x by)	Mark	Weighted Mark
Quality of Winner [Shorter]	3	9	27
Quality of Field	2	9	18
Quality of Time	2	7	14
Profile of Event	2.5	10	25
Drama of Race	2.5	6.5	16.25
Sacrifice of Winner	1.5	6.5	9.75
Course difficulty	1	6.5	6.5
Weather conditions	0.5	6.5	3.25
Memorability of race	2	8.5	17
World/local news worthiness	2	8.5	17
		153.75/190	81.0%

38   World Championships 1991 (women)

	Weighting (x by)	Mark	Weighted Mark
Quality of Winner [Panfil]	3	8.5	25.5
Quality of Field	2	8	16
Quality of Time	2	7	14
Profile of Event	2.5	9	22.5
Drama of Race	2.5	9	22.5
Sacrifice of Winner	1.5	8	12
Course difficulty	1	7	7
Weather conditions	0.5	8.5	4.25
Memorability of race	2	7.5	15
World/local news worthiness	2	7.5	15
		153.75/190	80.9%

39   New York 1979 (women)

	Weighting (x by)	Mark	Weighted Mark
Quality of Winner [Waitz]	3	9.5	28.5
Quality of Field	2	7	14
Quality of Time	2	10	20
Profile of Event	2.5	8.5	21.25
Drama of Race	2.5	7.5	18.75
Sacrifice of Winner	1.5	7	10.5
Course difficulty	1	7.5	7.5
Weather conditions	0.5	6	3
Memorability of race	2	7.5	15
World/local news worthiness	2	7.5	15
		153.5/190	80.8%

40   Olympic 1936 (men)

	Weighting (x by)	Mark	Weighted Mark
Quality of Winner [Kee-Chung]	3	8.5	25.5
Quality of Field	2	7.5	15
Quality of Time	2	8	16
Profile of Event	2.5	10	25
Drama of Race	2.5	7	17.5
Sacrifice of Winner	1.5	7	10.5
Course difficulty	1	7	7
Weather conditions	0.5	7	3.5
Memorability of race	2	8.5	17
World/local news worthiness	2	8	16
		153/190	80.5%

41   Fukuoka 1975 (men)

	Weighting (x by)	Mark	Weighted Mark
Quality of Winner [Drayton]	3	8	24
Quality of Field	2	9	18
Quality of Time	2	8	16
Profile of Event	2.5	9	22.5
Drama of Race	2.5	8.5	21.25
Sacrifice of Winner	1.5	8.5	12.75
Course difficulty	1	5	5
Weather conditions	0.5	5.5	2.75
Memorability of race	2	8	16
World/local news worthiness	2	7	14
		152.75/190	80.4%

42   Berlin 2001 (women)

	Weighting (x by)	Mark	Weighted Mark
Quality of Winner [*Takahashi*]	3	9	27
Quality of Field	2	7	14
Quality of Time	2	10	20
Profile of Event	2.5	8	20
Drama of Race	2.5	8	20
Sacrifice of Winner	1.5	8	12
Course difficulty	1	8	6
Weather conditions	0.5	6	3
Memorability of race	2	7	14
World/local news worthiness	2	8	16
		152/190	80.0%

43   London 1997 (women)

	Weighting (x by)	Mark	Weighted Mark
Quality of Winner [*Chepchumba*]	3	8.5	25.5
Quality of Field	2	7.5	15
Quality of Time	2	6.5	13
Profile of Event	2.5	9	22.5
Drama of Race	2.5	9.5	23.75
Sacrifice of Winner	1.5	7.5	11.25
Course difficulty	1	7	7
Weather conditions	0.5	5.5	2.75
Memorability of race	2	8.5	17
World/local news worthiness	2	7	14
		151.75/190	79.9%

44   Commonwealth 1970 (men)

	Weighting (x by)	Mark	Weighted Mark
Quality of Winner [*Hill*]	3	9	27
Quality of Field	2	8	16
Quality of Time	2	9	18
Profile of Event	2.5	7.5	18.75
Drama of Race	2.5	7.5	18.75
Sacrifice of Winner	1.5	8.5	5.5
Course difficulty	1	7	7
Weather conditions	0.5	6	3
Memorability of race	2	8.5	17
World/local news worthiness	2	6.5	13
		151.25/190	79.6%

45   Boston 2000 (women)

	Weighting (x by)	Mark	Weighted Mark
Quality of Winner [Ndereba]	3	9	27
Quality of Field	2	7	14
Quality of Time	2	6.5	13
Profile of Event	2.5	9	22.5
Drama of Race	2.5	8.5	20
Sacrifice of Winner	1.5	7.5	11.25
Course difficulty	1	8	8
Weather conditions	0.5	8	4
Memorability of race	2	8.5	17
World/local news worthiness	2	7	14
		150.75/190	79.3%

46   London 2003 (men)

	Weighting (x by)	Mark	Weighted Mark
Quality of Winner [Abera]	3	8.5	25.5
Quality of Field	2	8	16
Quality of Time	2	6.5	13
Profile of Event	2.5	9	22.5
Drama of Race	2.5	9	22.5
Sacrifice of Winner	1.5	6	9
Course difficulty	1	7	7
Weather conditions	0.5	5	2.5
Memorability of race	2	9	18
World/local news worthiness	2	7	14
		150/190	78.9%

47   Commonwealth 1954 (men)

	Weighting (x by)	Mark	Weighted Mark
Quality of Winner [McGhee]	3	6	18
Quality of Field	2	6	12
Quality of Time	2	5	10
Profile of Event	2.5	8	20
Drama of Race	2.5	9.5	22.5
Sacrifice of Winner	1.5	9	13.5
Course difficulty	1	9	9
Weather conditions	0.5	9.5	4.75
Memorability of race	2	9.5	19
World/local news worthiness	2	9.5	19
		147.75/190	77.8%

48   Olympic 1896 (men)

	Weighting (x by)	Mark	Weighted Mark
Quality of Winner [Louis]	3	5	15
Quality of Field	2	4	8
Quality of Time	2	7	14
Profile of Event	2.5	10	25
Drama of Race	2.5	9.5	22.5
Sacrifice of Winner	1.5	8.5	12.75
Course difficulty	1	9	9
Weather conditions	0.5	8.5	4.25
Memorability of race	2	9	18
World/local news worthiness	2	9	18
		146.5/190	77.1%

49   Chicago 1983 (men)

	Weighting (x by)	Mark	Weighted Mark
Quality of Winner [Nzau]	3	7.5	22.5
Quality of Field	2	7	14
Quality of Time	2	7	14
Profile of Event	2.5	8	20
Drama of Race	2.5	9.5	23.75
Sacrifice of Winner	1.5	8	12
Course difficulty	1	6	6
Weather conditions	0.5	7	3.5
Memorability of race	2	8	16
World/local news worthiness	2	6.5	13
		144.75/190	76.2%

50   Boston 1967 (women)

	Weighting (x by)	Mark	Weighted Mark
Quality of Winner [Gibb]	3	6	18
Quality of Field	2	3	6
Quality of Time	2	7	14
Profile of Event	2.5	9	22.5
Drama of Race	2.5	9	22.5
Sacrifice of Winner	1.5	7	10.5
Course difficulty	1	8	8
Weather conditions	0.5	7.5	3.75
Memorability of race	2	9.5	19
World/local news worthiness	2	9.5	19
		143.25/190	75.4%

531

Snapshot Analysis

Marathons featured:

Olympic	18
Boston	10
London	7
Fukuoka	3
New York	3
Commonwealth	3
World	2
Chicago	2
Berlin	2

Decade Breakdown:

1890s	1
1900s	1
1910s	0
1920s	2
1930s	2
1940s	1
1950s	2
1960s	3
1970s	6
1980s	15
1990s	9
2000s	8

Genders:

Men	35
Women	15

Winning Nations featured:

USA	9
Kenya	8
Japan	3
Portugal	3
Argentina	2
Australia	2
Canada	2
England	2
Ethiopia	2
Germany	2
Korea	2
New Zealand	2
Norway	2
Czechoslovakia	1
Finland	1
Greece	1
Italy	1
Mexico	1
Poland	1
Russia	1
Scotland	1
Spain	1
South Africa	1
Wales	1

Index

Page references in *italics* refer to illustrations
Page references as 123n4 refer to footnotes

Abdesselem, Rhadi ben 473–9, *476*, 482–4
Abera, Gezahegne 44–8, *45, 47*, 45–8, 288–92, *289, 290*
Abe, Tomoe 314
Adams, Gillian 110, 112
Adcocks, Bill *62*, 65–6, 509
Alder, James 221–2, 223n6
Alder, Jim 62–3, 65–6
Alemu, Elfenesh 48n4, 277, 279
Amdur, Neil 110, 124, 295, 297
Andersen–Schiess, Gabriëla 327
Anninos, Charalambos 26
Anton, Abel 350
Arimori, Yuko *118*, 309–17, *315*
Arri, Valerio 170–2
Arsenault, Serge 242
Asari, Junko 314
Athens Marathon 1969: 509

Balcha, Kebede 451
Baldini, Stefano *45, 46, 47*, 45–8, 65, 176–8, *177*, 180, 503, 510
Barbados Marathon 19, 19n5
Barnes, Simon 283, 336, 504
Barron, Gayle 243
basketball 123–4
Beames, Adrienne 80, 509
Beardsley, Dick 488–96, *489, 491*
Bedford, David 43–4, 47, 76, 140, 163, 178–9, 337, 372, 505, *505*
Beirut Marathon 19
Benoit, Joan *see* Samuelson, Joan, née Benoit\
Berlin Marathon
    1995 men 509–10
    1998 men 510
    2001 women 83–6, 529
    2003 men 368–74, 519
Bikila, Abebe 232, 302, 475–84, *476, 481, 483*
Bitel, Nick 503, 505
Biwott, Simon 44
Bjorklund, Gary 262
Blaikie, David 241
Bloomberg, Michael *371*
Bogacheva, Irina 53–4
Bong-ju, Lee 45, 209–12, *211*, 215
Bonner, Elizabeth 80
Bordin, Gelindo 161, 197, 259, 303, 385–93, *387, 390, 391*
Bosquet, Jean 360–1
Boston Athletic Association 2
Boston Celtics 2–3
Boston Marathon
    1897 men 422, 509
    1898 men 422

1900 men 146
1901 men 146, 181
1907 men 181
1910 men 143
1911 men 141, 144, 147
1912 men 181
1913 men 181
1917 men 145
1920 men 145
1921 men 145
1922 men 141, 145–8, 150, 526
1923 men 141, 148
1924 men 141, 148
1925 men 145, *147*
1927 men 141
1928 men 141
1930 men 141, 149
1931 men 146–7
1935 men 99, 144
1936 men 99, 181
1939 men 99, 181
1941 men 509
1945 men 99, 144, 199
1946 men 199n1, 509
1950 men 462
1954 men 148
1963 men 474, 480
1964 men 474
1967 women 1–15, 531
1968 men 319, 509
1971 men 509
1974 men 90
1975 men 181n1, 257
1975 women 13
1976 men 93
1977 men 93, 172
1977 women *94*
1978 men 258–63, 522
1979 men 267
1979 women 181, 321
1980 women 181, 237–53, 523
1981 women 181–7, 525
1982 men 485–96
1982 women 485–6, 515
1983 women 186–7
1984 men 299
1985 men 299
1986 men 261
1987 men 272, 414
1988 men 301–8, 521
1988 women 192
1989 men 483
1989 women 157
1990 men 392

1990 women 418
1991 men 307
1991 women 117, 329, 418
1992 women 120, 418
1993 women 315–16, 418
1994 men 370
1994 women 316, 418, 423
1995 women 418, 423
1996 men 288
1996 women 418, 422–8, 517
1997 women *427*
1998 men 288
2000 men 287–92, 521
2000 women 49–55, 530
2001 men 45
2002 women 55
criticism of organisation 93
women runners 11–12
Brasher, Chris 135, 154
Briggs, Arnold 6, 8
British Empire and Commonwealth Games
    Marathons
    1954 Vancouver men 36–42, 530
    1970 Edinburgh men 64–71, 529
    1974 Christchurch men 509
    1982 Brisbane men 446–51, 453, 516
    1986 women 192
    1990 Auckland men 164
    1994 men 164
Broos, Auguste 170
Brown, Ellison 'Tarzan' 98–9, 101, 181
Brown, Walter 2–3
Brundage, Avery 124
Budd, Zola 397
Buniak, Peter 87–8
Burfoot, Amby 3, 256, 319
Burke, Tom 422
Butcher, Pat 83, 84, 390–1, 392

Cabrera, Delfo 171, 201–5, *202, 204*
Caffery, Jack 146
Cart, Julie 328
Castelli, William 493
Catalano, Patti, née Lyons 181–7, *182*
Cerón, Dionicio 136–40, *138*, 208, 347–51
Chataway, Chris 461, 461n3
cheating and/or disqualification
    Belokas, Spiridon 29
    Biktagirova 312n2
    Lorz, F 29n7, 131
    Miranda, Oscar 240n1
    Pietri, Dorando 434–43
    Ruiz, Rosie 238–53, *239, 244*
    Südhaus, Norbert 130–1
Chebet, Joseph 288
Chepchumba, Joyce 74, *75*, 75–8, *76*, 81
Chepkemei, Susan 339–44, *340, 342*
Chettle, David 90–5
Chicago Marathon
    1983 men 15–19, 531
    1984 men 409–12, 415, 517
    1985 men 413
    1996 men 175
    1998 men 501
    2001 women 54
    2002 men 506

2002 women 335
Chun-ae, Lim 105
Cierpinski, Waldemar 230–5, *231, 232, 234*
Cimons, Marlene 319, 397
Cindolo, Giuseppe 90–5
Clarke, Ron 480–1
Clayton, Derek 63, 67, *128*, 217–24, *218*
Clay, Cassius 471n1
Clohessy, Pat 445, 449
Cloney, William 7–8, 8, 240–3, 244–5, 247
close finishes
    Antwerp 1920 men 171
    Atlanta 1996 men 212
    Barcelona 1992 women 313
    Boston 1982 men 491
    Boston 1988 men 305
    Boston 1991 women 117
    Boston 2000 men 289–91
    Fukuoka 1966 218
    London 1989 men 162–3
    London 1995 men 137
    London 1997 men 177
    London 1997 women 75–6
    London 2003 men 45
    New York 1994 men 210, 210n4
    New York City 1983 men 296–7
    New York City 2004 women 341
    Seoul 1988 men 391
Coca-Cola 130
Cockerell, William 179n3, 223, 261–2, 282, 422, 424,
    427, 495–6
Coello, Gina 119
Collins, Patrick 283
Conan Doyle, Sir Arthur 440
Concannon, Joe 289n3, 301, 305–6
Cote, George 49
course distances 34, 168, 171, 432
course length 90, 222–3, 222n5
course planning 18
Cox, Stan 36
Crombie-Hicks, Shona 24n3
crowd control 258–9
Crump, Jack 40

Davis, Bill 181
de Baillet–Latour, Comte 320
deBruyn, Paul 357
de Castella, François Robert 'Deek' 16, 129, 397–8,
    400–2, 410–15, 414, 445–53, *448, 450*
de Coubertin, Pierre 167
de Reuck, Colleen *209*
Decker, Mary 397
DeMar, Clarence 49, 65, 141–50, *147, 149*, 442, 462
Densimo, Belayneh 383
Derderian, Tom 8, 58, 88, 99, 117, 120, 145, 146,
    182, 183–4, *185*, 191, 256, 257, 272, 302, 307,
    322n1, 387–8. 389, 422
Detroit Marathon 1969 men 89
Dias, Manuel 101
Diem, Carl 98
Dinsamo, Belayneh 210
Dixon, Rod 293–9, *297, 298*
DNF rates 116, 116n3
Dörre, Katrin *118*, 118–19, 193–7, *193*, 310
dos Santos, Luiz 347–51
Downes, Steven 135

Drayton, Jerome 64, 88–95, *94*, 172, 229
Drew, Julian 213
drop out rates 116, 116n3
Dyer, Braven 358–9, 361, 362
Dzhumanazarov, Satymkul *234*

Edwards, Maurice F 479
El Mouaziz, Abdelkader *45*, 45–6
El Ouafi, Boughèra 171
Emptage, John 247–8
Enschede Marathon 1953 34–5
Espinosa, Andrés 370
European Championships Marathon
　1969 Athens men 63
　1971 men 160
　1982 Athens women 190
　1990 Stuttgart men 389
　1990 Stuttgart women 196
Evans, Paul 175–8, 180, 209, 209n3

Farm School, Thompson's Island 142, 142n2
fartlek training 212n6
Faulkner, Jack 246
Ferris, Sam 33, 100
Ferris, Samuel 354–5, 358–63
Fixx, Jim 256
Fiz, Martin 209–12, 215, 346–51, 348*, *349*
Flack, 'Teddy' 26–27
Fleming, Tom 181n1
Forshaw, Joseph 437–8
Forster, Kevin 159
Foster, Brendan 412
Foster, Jack 230
Freigang, Stephan 377–81
Fukuoka Marathon
　1960 men 477
　1966 men 218
　1967 men 217–21, 224, 523
　1968 men 65
　1969 men 63–4
　1971 men 127
　1975 men 90–2, 95, 528
　1976 men 92
　1978 men 267
　1979 men 268
　1980 men 269
　1983 men 163, 268–71, 274, 522
Fultz, Jack 93, 258–9, 282

Gailly, Etienne 200–5, *202*
Galloway, Jeff 257
Garcia, Salvador 380
Gareau, Jacqueline 237–42, 244–5, 249–50, 251–2, *251*
Gebrselassie, Haile 47, 365, *366*, 368, 497–9, 502–7, *502*
Gee, Michael 287–8, 424
Gibb, Roberta 1, 4–6, *5*, 10, 12, 13
Gitsham, Chris 170
'glossary' 511–13
Gold, Arthur 68–9, 160
Gorman, Michiko *94*
Gorno, Reinaldo 464–7, 470
Graham, John 446, *448*
Gratton, Michael 446
Greenberg, Alan 404

Greenberg, Stan 432
Greig, Dale 80
Gynn, Roger *see* Martin, David

Haile Selassie, Emperor 478–80
Halswelle, Wyndham 430
Hanna, Bob 426
Harper, Ernie 99, 101–4, *102*
Hauman, Riël 24, 151, 161, 162, 413
Havana Marathon 19
Hayes, Johnny 144, 435, *436*, 438–43
Heatley, Basil 60–1
Hefferon, Charles 433–4, 437
Heino, Viljo 458
Henderson, Jason 340, 342
Henigan, Jimmy 'Smilin' 145, 146–7, *149*
Henigan, Tommy 146
Herodotus 21, 21n1, 22
Hill, Ron 57–71, *62, 67, 70*, 89, 127–9, *128*, 132, 160, 228–9, 422
Hitler, Adolf *31*, 97, 104n4
Hoag, Steve 181n1
Holden, Jack 200
Homer 23
Honolulu Marathon *209*
Hussain, Haleem 379
Hussein, Ibrahim 302–8, *304, 305*

Ichihoshi, Ari 315
Ikangaa, Juma 270–1, 301–8, *304, 305*, 385, 397–8, 446, 447–50, *447*, 451
Ivanova, Zoya 191

Jansson, Gustaf 463–7, 470
Jenkinson, Mike 446
Jones, Hugh 16–19, *17*, 196, 398
Jones, Melanie 163
Jones, Steve 16, *155*, 389, 398, 406, 409–15, *410, 413*
Jong, Song-Ok 52, 315
Joyner, D Florence Griffith 384

Kardong, Donald 232
Kastor, Deena, née Drossin 277, 285–6
Kee-chung, Sohn (at one time Kitei Son) 100–3, *102, 103*, 104, 105, *105*, 171, *204*, 378–9
Kelley, Johnny 'the elder' 98–9, 144, 199, 287
Kelley, Johnny 'the younger' 3, 473
Ketels, Jens-Peter 419–20
Khannouchi, Khalid 43, 44, 499–507, *502, 503, 505*
Kigen, Simeon 16–17
Kimaiyo, Eric 176–8, 180
Kimihara, Kenji 5
Kin, Onbai 99
Kiplagat, Lornah *340*
Kokowska, Renata 75
Kolehmainen, Johannes Petter 'Hannes' 145, 168–72, *169, 171*
Kolehmainen, Tatu 170
Korir, Sammy 368–74, *370*
Kristiansen, Ingrid 81, 81n2, 151–8, 153*, 155*, 186, 191, 282–3, 283n2, 324–30
Krolik, Sonja 75, *75*
Kyriakides, Stylianos 199, 199n1, 509

Lagat, Elijah 288–90, *289, 290*
Laing, Graham *448*

Landells, Steve 45, 47
Lazaro, Francisco 190, 190n1
Lebow, Fred 108, 111, 152n1, 247, 301, 307
Lemke, Gary 208–9
Lepper, Merry 80
Lismont, Karel 130, 131–2, 160, 229–30, 232
Lobb, Huw 389n3
London Marathon
    1981 488
    1984 women 152
    1985 men 406, 412
    1985 women 152–5, 158, 526
    1986 men 272
    1989 men 162–5, 526
    1995 men 135–40, 527
    1995 women 139
    1996 men 139–40, 215
    1997 men 173–80, 525
    1997 women 73–8, 529
    1998 women 77
    2000 men 500
    2002 men 497–506, 515
    2002 women 334–5, 503
    2003 men 43–8, 530
    2003 women 335–6
    2004 men 223
Longboat, Tom 181
Lopes, Carlos 398–407, *402, 403*, 410–15, 451
Loroupe, Tegla 81, 83, *340*, 423–8, *426*
Lorz, Frank 131
Lossman, Jüri 169–72
Lough, Gary 333–4
Louis, Spiridon 25–32, *28, 30, 31*, 98, 422
Lucas, Bill 203
Lyons, Patti 237–8, 242

Machado, Manuela 74, 75
Macleod, Ian 136, 137, 174, 175
Magee, Barry 477
Maina, Anthony 50–1
Major, John 136
Man-vs-Horse Marathon 389n3
Marathon, battle of 21n1, 21–3
Marek, Steve 248–9
Markova, Olga 315–16
Marot, Veronique 73, 158, 159, 163, 192
Martin, Dave 376
Martin, David and Roger Gynn 25, 26, 97, 98, 131,
    169–70, 227, 230, 313, 354–5, 377, 383, 384,
    395–6, 399, 402, 472, 474
Martin, Eamonn 499
Martin, Lisa 192–5, *193*, 197, 311
Matsumoto, Rick 90, 91, 92
McArthur, Kennedy 434
McColgan, Elizabeth 73–8, *75, 76*, 139
McDermott, John J 422
McGhee, Joseph 36–7, 38–9, *41*
McKenzie, Christine 474n3
McKenzie, Gordon 474
McKiernan, Catherina 77
Mekonnen, Abebe 483
Mellor, Chuck 145, *147*
Melpomene 79
Mendoza, Ed *489*
Meyer, Elana 51, 54
Michelson, Albert 171–2

Miles, Johnny *149*
Miller, David 105, 380, 406
Miller, Tommy 8–10, *9*
Mimoun, Alain 460–1, 477
Miranda, Oscar 240n1
Moller, Lorraine 186–7, 310–17
Moneghetti, Steve 46n3, *137*, 137–40, 162–4, *162,
    163*, 347
Moore, Kenny 130
Morishita, Koichi 105, 377–81, *377*
Morrissey, Rick 499–501, 499n2
Morris, Tracey 277
Morrow, Susan 246–7
Morse, Guy 423
Mota, Rosa 81, *118*, 118, 119–20, 156, 189–97, *193,
    195*, 310–11, 324–30
Mott, Sue 173, 214, 282
Munji, Titus 368–74

Nakamura, Ken 279
Nakamura, Kiyoshi 161, 266–7, 269, 271, 272, 402–3
Nakayama, Takeyuki 378, 387
name changes
    Buniak – Drayton 88
    Kee-chung – Son – Kee-chung 100, 105, 106
    Ruiz – Vivas 252
    Sung-yong – Nan – Sung-yong 100, 106
Nason, Jerry 289n3
Ndereba, Catherine 50–5, *52, 53*, 85, 276, 280, 284,
    315
N'deti, Cosmas 49, 422–3
Ndoo, Philip 226
Nebiolo, Primo 402
Nerurkar, Richard 174–8, 180, 209–12, 215, 347–8,
    348
Ness, John 360
New York City Marathon
    1970 women 109
    1978 women 108–9
    1979 women 109–10, 112–13, 245, 528
    1981 men 487
    1982 men 494
    1983 men 293–9, 521
    1987 women 192
    1988 men 414
    1988 women 194n4
    1989 men 451
    1989 women 157
    1991 men 380
    1993 men 370
    1993 women 418
    1994 men 210, 210n4
    2003 women 55
    2004 women 338–44, 520
    2005 men *371*
Ngolepus, Joseph *45*
Nijboer, Gerard *234*
Noguchi, Mizuki 278, 281, *281*, 284–6, 315, *371*
Nordic walking 157
Nurmi, Paavo 2n1, 354, *355*, 455–6, 469
Nzau, Joseph 16–19, 398

Okayo, Margaret 55
Olympic Games
    1896 Athens 25
    1896 Athens Marathon men 25–32, *28*, 531

1908 London 429–31, 441
1908 London Marathon men 390, 431–43, 517
1912 Stockholm 442
1912 Stockholm Marathon men 144–5, 168, 170, 190n1, 438
1920 Antwerp Marathon men 167–72, 525
1924 Paris Marathon men 148–9, 355
1928 Amsterdam 4, 79
1928 Amsterdam Marathon men 149, 171, 355, 509
1932 Los Angeles 353–4, 362
1932 Los Angeles Marathon men 100, 171, 354–63, 519
1936 Berlin 31, 97–8, 99–104, 106, 171, 528
1948 London Marathon men 171, 199–204, 524
1952 Helsinki 455–6, 460–2, 467
1952 Helsinki Marathon men 462–7, 470, 516
1952 Melbourne Marathon men 468
1960 Rome 471–2, 478
1960 Rome Marathon men 472–9, 484, 515–16
1964 Tokyo Marathon men 480–1
1968 Mexico Marathon men 221, 483
1972 Munich 123–5, 127
1972 Munich Marathon men 69, 127–33, 527
1976 Montreal 225–7, 233–4
1976 Montreal Marathon men 92, 227–35, 523
1980 Moscow 268
1984 Los Angeles 328–9, 395–7, 406–7
1984 Los Angeles Marathon men 18, 272, 397–407, 518
1984 Los Angeles Marathon women 79, 152, 186, 190, 191, 323–30, 520
1988 Seoul 383–4, 393
1988 Seoul Marathon men 161, 272–3, 384–93, 518
1988 Seoul Marathon women 189, 192–7, *193*, 524
1992 Barcelona Marathon men 105, 164, 375–81, 518
1992 Barcelona Marathon women 186, 309–17, 520
1996 Atlanta 207–8
1996 Atlanta Marathon men 173, 208–15, 524
1996 Atlanta Marathon women 73–4, 314
2000 Sydney Marathon women 81–2
2004 Athens 275
2004 Athens Marathon men 372–3, 510
2004 Athens Marathon women 275–86, 337–8, 522
Olympic Games in general
  boycotts 226, 226n1, 255, 268
  emblem 167, 167n2
  marathon finish coinciding with closing ceremony 401–2
  oath 167
  Olympiads 167
  origins 23–4
  torch 98, 456
Ondieki, Lisa 311
Ondieki, Yobes 195
Oregon Marathon women 1970 509
Ostler, Scott 328
O'Sullivan, Sonia 50–1n2

pace-makers 175, 176, 336–7, 368, 369, 502
pacing, art of 143
Panfil, Wanda 117–21, *118, 119, 193*, 310

Pan-American Games Marathon 1951 203
Pan-American Games Marathon 1971 126
Parades, Benjamin 210
Pede-Erdkamp, Anni 80, 109
Pedrosa, José 189–90, 191–2, 194
Peters, James 'Jim' 33–42, *38, 39, 41*, 462–5
Phidippides 21–2, 190, 252
Philip, Robert 282
Piercy, Violet 79
Pietri, Dorando 131, 390, 434–43, *435, 436, 438*, 439–43
Pinto, Antonio 43, 43n1, 136–8, 140, 173–80, *177, 178*, 503
Pippig, Uta 81, 316, 417–22, *419, 426, 427*
Pizzolato, Orlando 389
Player, Barbara 456
Polovinskaya, Tatyana 194
Polytechnic Marathons 33–5, 220, 361
Popov, Sergey 473, 475, 477
Port Chester Marathon 171–2
Porter Payne, 'Billy' 207
Porter, H F 429, 430–1
Powell, David 74, 76, 138, 139, 350, 503
Powell, Jeff 282
power walking 157
Powers, John 241–2, 289, 289n3, 290
Pyambuu, Tuul 379–80

race distances 24–5, 147
race 'categories' description 511–13
race 'marks' analysis 515–31
races featured analysis 533
Radcliffe, Paula 276–86, *278, 280*, 331–44, *340, 341, 342*, 503, *505*
Ramaala, Hendrik *371*
Ramadhani, Samson 46–8
Reavis, Toni 243
records
  countries winning all three top places 346, 346n2
  DNF 91n1
  five brothers 155
  large winning margins 109
  men 154n2, 171, 222, 370–3
  most low times 261
  most times competed in Boston Marathon 99
  most wins in New York City Marathon 110, 111
  multiple marathon wins 192
  never finishing below 4th 310
  Olympic and Boston marathon winners 392
  Olympic and European marathon winners 392
  only one defeat in completed races 480
  percentage of races won 197
  three events 155
  winning six consecutive major marathons 85
  winning three consecutive marathons 267
  women 80, 154, 154n2, 156
Reilly, Rick 405
Richardson, Paul 376
Richards, Tom 200–2, 205
Ritola, Willie 146–7, 146n6, 147n7
Roba, Fatuma 49–55, *52*, 74
Robertson, Donald 355
Robinson, Malcolm 243
Robleh, Djama 398
Rodgers, Bill 'Boston Billy' 15–16, 49, 90–5, 93, 125, 239, 250–1, 252, 255–63, *260, 261, 262*, 267, 272,

487–90, *489*
Rodgers, Charles 240, 257, *262*, 272
Roelants, Gaston 63
Roe, Allison, née Deed 182–7, *185, 186,* 322
roller skating 183n2
Rostron, Frank 36, 40
Rotterdam Marathon 1995: 346
Rousseau, Vincent 139–40, 346
route mistakes 210n4, 222, 232
Ruiz, Rosie 238–53, *239, 244*
Ryan, Kevin 258, *448*
Ryan, Mike 218–19

Salah, Ahmed 161–4, *162, 163,* 386–7, *387,* 389–93,
   390, 398
Salazar, Alberto 163, 222n5, 270–1, 397–8, 399, 400,
   403, 485–96, *489, 491, 492*
Samaranch, Juan Antonio 208
Sampson, Mildred 80
Samuelson, Joan, née Benoit 80–1, 155–6, 156n3,
   182–4, 186, 187, 197, 320–30, *325, 326, 328*
Samuelson, Scott 323
Samuel, Martin 282
Sandrock, Michael 194, 265, 266, 267, 273, 322, 324,
   326, 456–7, 460, 461, 469
Sasaki, Seiichiro 218–21, 224
Schlesinger, Dan 269
Seko, Toshihiko 265–74, 272, 273, 385–6, 397–8,
   402–3
selectors
   C I S 309–10
   Canada 90
   Great Britain 68–9, 99, 159–60, 175, 192, 355,
      355n3, 409
   Japan 85, 309–10, 356
   United States of America 124–5
   Wales 409–10
Semple, Jock 1–4, 7, 8–10, *9, 12,* 12–13, 94, 241,
   241–3, *492*
Shahanga, Gidamis 294–6, 297, 447–9, *447*
Shaughnessy, Dan 287, 425
Shea, Julie 183, 187
Shiaku, Tamao 100
Shorter, Frank 125–33, *128,* 219, 227–35, 258, 271
Siegel, Erich 11
Silva, German 210, 210n4
'silver medal is defeat' 108
Simonsen, Inge 488
Simon, Lidia 74, *75,* 75, 77, 81
Sly, Phil 223–4
Smith, Geoff 293–9, *294, 297,* 398
Smith, Red 225
Smoke, Albert 146
Sobanska, Malgorzata *138*
Sockalexis, Andrew 181
Soh, Shigeru 267, 270, 398, 400
Soh, Takeshi 90, 270, 398, 400, 402
Spedding, Charlie 159, 385, 392, 398, 400–1, 405–6,
   412–13
Stanton, Alex 332, 334
Stanton, Rosemary 332, 334
Steinle, Mark 503–4
Stenroos, Albin 149
Stephens, Helen 104n4
Strug, Kerri 208n1
Südhaus, Norbert 130–1

Sullivan, James E 431, 441
Sung–yong, Nam (at one time Shoryu Nan) 100,
   101–4
Suzuki, Fusashige 100
Switzer, Kathrine 1, 6–13, *9, 12,* 240, 243

Takahashi, Naoko 54, *82, 84,* 82–6, 276
Tanui, Moses 49, 288–92, *289, 290*
television influence 276
Tergat, Paul 44–5, *45,* 223, 365–74, *366, 370, 371,*
   499–507
Teske, Charlotte 486
Tewanima, Lewis *169*
Thugwane, Josiah 171, 173, *174,* 178, 208–15, *209,*
   211
Tibebu, Berhanu 482
Tikkanen, Esa 258
Tokyo Marathon 1935 509
Tokyo Marathon 1983 269
Toronto Marathon women 1967 509
training advice 35
training intensity 59–60, 61, 218
Treacy, John 303–8, 399, 400–1, 405
treadmill 158
Trivoulidas, Peter 145
Tsuburaya, Kokichi 481
Tsudo, Seiichiro 99

Ueberroth, Peter V 395–6
ultra marathon 403

Vandendriessche, Aurele 474–5, 480
Vasilakos, Kharilaos 25–32
Viren, Lasse 227–8, 233

Wainaina, Eric 211, 291
Waitz, Grete, née Andersen 77, 80–1, 107–12, *111,*
   112, 151, 192, *193,* 194, 194n4, *273, 298,* 323–30,
   328, 485–6
Wakiihuri, Douglas 160–5, *162, 163,* 387, *387,*
   389–93, *391*
Walker, Caroline 80
Wallechinsky, David 30, 103, 105, 214, 227–8, 233,
   396n1, 429
Wange, Willy B 33–4, 36
Wan-Ki, Kim *377*
Wark, Julia 407
Watman, Mel 294
Weidenbach, Lisa 310, 310n1
Welch, Priscilla 192
Wells, Jeff 255, 258, 259–63, *260*
Werribee Marathon women 509
Whitehead, Peter 347–50, *348*
Wilton, Maureen 80
Winter, Liane 13
Wolde, Mamo 89, 130, 302, 482–3
Wolde, Mamo 302
women racing distances 4, 79, 320
World Championships Marathon
   1983 men 451
   1987 Rome men 161
   1987 Rome women 191
   1991 Tokyo women 117–21, 527
   1993 Stuttgart women 314
   1995 Göteberg men 346–51, 519
   1997 Athens men 350

1999 Seville men 350
Wright, Duncan 355, 358–63
Wright, Duncan McLeod 39n3

Yamada, Kanematsu 99
Yamaguchi, Eri 220n4
Yamashita, Sachiko *118*, 118–20
Yegorova, Velentina 117, 309–17, *313, 315*
Yelling, Liz 277

Yoon-chil, Choi 462, 470
Young-cho, Hwang 105, 377–81, *377, 379*
Young, Andrew 207

Zabala, Juan Carlos 2n1, 98, 100–1, 171, 356–63, *359, 360*
Zátopekova, Dana 461–2, *462*, 468–9
Zátopek, Emil 171, 199, 228, 456–70, *458, 462, 466*
Zuna, Fred 145, 146, 148, 148n8